My book ~

in recognition and

celebration of

Our Lives for Africa

Heather

Mt Kenya notelet designed for Granny Heather
by Debbie Rooken-Smith

Daisy's Daughter
Our Lives for Africa
This is a true story, self-published by Heather, a pensioner.

Daisy's Daughter
Our Lives for Africa

Autobiography
Heather Rooken-Smith
www.daisysdaughterbook.com

Cover original watercolour 'Wally warthog & Tootsie-Wootsie porcupine' by Kenya world-renowned wildlife artist Karen Laurence-Rowe www.karenlaurence-rowe.com

Cover design and typography by Diane van der Westhuizen & Lindsay Rooken-Smith Jenions

Book layout and photograph formatting by author Diane van der Westhuizen (dianevanwestauthor@gmail.com)
For authors who require assistance with self-publishing, Diane is available to help with editing, book cover design, layout, photo formatting and eBooks.

Second Edition, first printing 2017
ISBN 978-0-620-68543-6 (RSA)
ISBN 0620685433 (USA)

Daisy's Daughter
Our Lives for Africa

Dedication

As I've wandered down the corridors of time in writing 'Daisy's Daughter, Our Lives for Africa', my heart and mind have come alive, often in melancholy mood with tears at the amazing memories my late husband, Ian, and I shared in our extraordinary life. We've traversed half of the southern part of this continent together from the equator in East Africa, Kenya, down to Rhodesia (Zimbabwe), war-torn Angola, South West Africa (Namibia), and what is now known as Nelson Mandela's Rainbow Nation of South Africa.

These pages reiterate for me the extent to which I value and hold so dear my life with Ian, an honourable, brave man who walked beside me in faith and unending spirit of hope no matter what we faced, always putting his family first, whilst dedicating his talents and abilities towards helping develop segments of this continent he loved so much and in which he believed.

To my family, friends and animals that have gone before me, and to those who still share their lives with me, your many gifts of unending kindness, love and support through the years remain with me always. In sincerity and gratitude, from my heart, thank you.

Africa
N
W
E
S
Atlantic Ocean
Indian Ocean
2
6
8
4
5
7
3
1
1 South Africa
2 Kenya
3 Botswana
4 Mozambique
5 Zimbabwe
6 Angola
7 Namibia
8 Zambia
by Kathryn van der Mescht

Foreword

Throughout these pages, one realises just how much Daisy 'shaped' Heather's life. Whenever faced with a tough decision, be it planning ahead, contemplating the layout of a home, veggie patch, orchard or garden, one can imagine Heather, as a wife and mother, asking herself, "I wonder what my mother, Daisy, would do?"

Heather's journey through life epitomises the true East African pioneer spirit. She has endured all manner of hardship, lived off the land, brought up a family and created a number of lovely homes. She never lost her love for Africa and nature and along the way, found time to rear orphan animals and birds which, wherever she lived, became part of her extended family.

Born in 1933 and educated in Kenya, she started training at the Nakuru War Memorial Hospital where, starting in the early 1930s, many family members were born. Her nursing training, which was to hold her in good stead throughout her life, ended just before she married Ian to become a farmer's wife; a tough but idyllic life, interrupted by the Kenya Emergency. To be alone whilst one's husband is chasing terrorists in the forests is one thing, to be on one's own on a farm bordering Mau Mau territory, must have been terrifying.

'Daisy's Daughter' is an informative and entertaining read, and throughout, Heather comes across as a caring person, one who empathised with all living things. She respected her staff, their customs and beliefs; their problems became hers and she was quite prepared to take on any professional who she felt was not providing the correct care.

The move from Laikipia to Hoey's Bridge saw Heather blossom from a young girl into a mother, supportive partner and true friend. Subsequent relocations from Westlands to Malindi in Kenya were followed by moving to Angola. Less than 18 months after their arrival, the Portuguese Government, with little warning decided to cede control of their African colonies, and Ian, Heather and family, and many others, with the breakdown of the local administration, looting of banks and shops, were left to fend for themselves.

After a tortuous journey they reached South West Africa (Namibia) with few possessions and almost penniless. Ian stated that he 'would never again own land in Africa', and accepted an offer to manage a 45,000 acre Ranch at Omitara, some 180 kilometres inland from Windhoek. Heather created yet another home, this time in an area where German and Herero were the main languages and these 19 years were to be the longest they lived in one place and perhaps their best.

To have lost so much, including her beloved father for reasons she only recently became aware of, her youngest son, and then her eldest daughter followed by her husband, both to cancer, and to still 'pen' her trip through life at the age of 82, with such depth, passion and clarity, is a lesson to all of us who have yet to write or complete our memoirs. By the end of her story, Heather is once again residing in Namibia, this time in the far north Caprivi, a Province of this country she dearly loves.

Heather covers the good, the bad and the ugly that one finds in Africa. In my opinion, by virtue of its diversity, it is the best 'book of life' to be written by a Kenya-born; a pioneer in the true spirit of her grandparents who provided a solid foundation for others to follow.

Bruce Rooken-Smith
Merrivale
Kwa-Zulu Natal
South Africa

A special thank you to all Readers of 'Daisy's Daughter, Our Lives for Africa' – your interest and support is greatly appreciated. At the back of my book is a Family Index. On my website, www.daisysdaughterbook.com, there are about 118 colour and black and white pics. Through 'Daisy's Daughter', I've made new friends from all around the world and thoroughly enjoyed corresponding with them. Many folk have generously shared with me interesting and remarkable snippets of their lives – without doubt, intriguing stories waiting to be recorded.

Our family history is a real life African Saga.

It began in Britain in July 1819 when the Government needed settlers to emigrate to the Cape of Good Hope, South Africa, which at that time was British territory. As an incentive to members of the general public to take up this challenge, the then Chancellor of the Exchequer, the Right Honourable Nicholas Vansittart, submitted to the House of Commons a vote of £50,000 hoping to attract those of a pioneering spirit and the many unemployed people in the country to leave their familiar lives for a future in southern Africa.

After the Napoleonic wars against France, about 300,000 British sailors and soldiers needed employment. Due to factories using children as labourers, unemployment grew. Lord Charles Somerset, the Governor of the Cape, planned an agricultural settlement as a 'buffer' between the *Xhosas* (African tribe) and the Cape Colony to reduce the need for military to maintain the frontier. The scheme was first tried on a small scale and due to its success the Government wished to try the experiment with a larger number of Britons as it seemed to offer a solution to the problems both in the Cape and Britain.

Settlers were promised their own farm in Africa, and the idea of starting afresh in a new land held a romantic appeal for many struggling to make a living in Britain. It has been speculated that, had the real reason behind the Government's plan been made known, possibly far fewer settlers would have undertaken the arduous and perilous sea voyages to the Cape. Word was that southern Africa was like an English park while other accounts painted a far less exciting or favourable impression. This great opportunity and enormous challenge was taken up by a large number of Britons, amongst whom were many skilled tradesmen and professional men who would bring with them knowledge, expertise, the relevant tools, equipment and goods to help build this faraway country. Some Settlers were wealthy people, bringing their indentured servants with them.

The *first* British Government sponsored emigration scheme to South Africa was in 1820. Some 4,000 people were landed in the Cape and Eastern Cape. From 1857 to 1867, the *second* major wave of British Government aided immigration took place, this time also to Natal.

Our Cape Settler founding fathers, *Thomas Griffin* from Finsbury, Islington (*on my father, Lionel Carol's, side*); *William Alexander Smith* from Kintore, Aberdeen, Scotland (*on my husband, Ian's, side*); and *Thomas Aggett* from Torquay (*on my mother, Daisy's, side*) left their familiar homes and embarked with their families, amongst the many different parties, on Government Settler Scheme sailing ships bound for Algoa Bay (now the modern city and harbour, Port Elizabeth) on the Indian Ocean shores of the Eastern Cape of South Africa.

Some of these large families (common in those times) met for the first time on board ship or later in South Africa, and came to marry one another, creating vastly complicated family trees. Others became acquainted and wed later when their families moved once more from South Africa to Kenya as Settlers.

We have no records of what our Settler founding fathers and their families took with them or of the provisions provided for the sea journey; how drinking and washing water was stored or ablutions took place. Living conditions on board these ships were cramped and extremely traumatic. Outbreaks of whooping cough, smallpox and measles beset the voyagers resulting in many recorded deaths of children. These hazardous journeys often lasted for as long as 4 months.

I have often marvelled at the courage of the Settlers in the many adversities they faced. These settler ships were wooden and cumbersome cockleshells with caulk between the timbers, deep in the bowels, heavy, carried ballast and were extremely claustrophobic. I saw two of this type of vessel when I visited the Maritime Museum in Fremantle near Perth, Western Australia, in the 1980s. One ship was in its original form; the other had been a shipwreck off the Australian coast and was in half, giving an excellent idea of how and what Settler families had to contend with during extended time at sea, all at the mercy of the elements. How anyone survived these settler voyages, I find difficult to comprehend. It was thought provoking to see these ships. Top deck and three floors below, living space was at a premium. Due to a lack of fresh air in the accommodation sections, one imagines an extremely unhealthy and unpleasant environment. With small children aboard to care for as well, parents must have struggled considerably.

It is recorded that many folk took helmets with flaps reaching to the shoulders, probably for the fierce African sun. Perhaps the women chose a few precious heirlooms or valued sentimental items packed into wooden chests and old-fashioned travelling trunks. Definitely the great Family Bible – one has been found in the *Jenkins* part of our family with beautiful interesting inscriptions; our *Aggett* Family Bible would later go to my sister, Marge.

I imagine the personal possessions women would have taken were some cooking utensils, cutlery and crockery, recipes, sewing and knitting items, possibly a few treasured pieces of crocheted cloths, collars and beautifully hand-sewn quilts and, of course, clothing and shoes for the adults, children and babies. Add to this, some amount of stationery and ink, candles or lanterns and a supply of medicines. The men, more likely (apart from the tools of their trade), would have chosen supplies of tobacco, perhaps some stocks of Scottish whisky or the like, builder's tools, hunter's gear, sturdy boots, saddles and bridles, agricultural implements, crop and vegetable seeds, perhaps even flower seeds for proposed gardens. The packing lists must have been very precise.

Apart from their admirable bravery, my mind has boggled at the enormity of the challenges the British Settlers faced and what they decided to take with them. Considerations would have been the long sea voyage in severely cramped accommodations, then the unfamiliar landscape and weather they faced in foreign Africa. Add to this, disease, distances and availability of provisions for everyday use and possibly even thoughts of wild animals or wary inhabitants they might encounter. There was simply no turning back once they'd set sail. Maize, rye, wheat, barley and vegetables were grown and later wool farming became successful. The weather, seasons, drought, crop disease and hostilities would prove difficult.

Our founding families of *Griffin, Smith* and *Aggett*, with their many children and subsequent marriages – creating a complex lineage – would vastly extend our family to include the surnames Rooken-Smith, Ulyate, Foster, Case, Jenkins, Roberts, Chart, Nye-Chart, Bedward-Williams, Bastard (de Batard), Hurt, Rand Overy, Corfield and Eeles, to mention some. The *Charts* of our extended family were gifted and artistic; the *Eeles* family had previously been umbrella manufacturers.

Did our Settler families have some wealth; were they poor or middle-class Britons; what was the level of their education? We have few clues, mostly records of marriages, births and deaths and farm names on which the emigrants settled, some of these names long gone now.

Thomas Griffin (my great great-grandfather of Irish descent on my father's side) was the first of our founding fathers to sail to the Cape. Registered as a gunsmith, and with his heavily pregnant wife, Sarah, a midwife, they sailed with their 7 children on the first 1820 British settler ship, the *Chapman*. Ship's records, under the 'List of Bailie's Party' reflect the names of both parents and their children. Baby Margaret was born at sea on 9th December 1819, the day the *Chapman* finally set sail. They reached their destination, Algoa Bay, on 10th April 1820.

John Bailie's Party, in 96 wagons, was the first to leave for their location near the mouth of the Fish River, and arrived at Cuylerville on 28th April, 7 miles from Kaffir's Drift. The route taken was via Jagers Drift on the Bushman's River instead of through Uitenhage, as it was feared the Settlers might infect the townspeople with whooping cough and measles.

Thomas Griffin had been required to deposit £20 with the Government before he left England as security for certain expenses, and, like others, was to have received 100 acres of land, provided he remained 3 years on the location and built a house. John Bailie's grant of land at the Fish River mouth was 10,000 acres to be divided amongst the Settlers of his party. For about 2 years, Thomas remained at this location and built 3 houses which were all destroyed by the natives. After these great losses he moved to Algoa Bay (renamed Port Elizabeth in 1820), where he is listed as one of the residents in 1822, as a cobbler. Many Settlers had left their locations by this time and taken up varied occupations in the surrounding areas. Thomas and Sarah had another 4 children in the Cape, totalling 11. In 1825, Thomas moved with other Settlers to Uitenhage, but returned to Port Elizabeth as Messenger of the Court in 1826. He later prospered in Port Elizabeth as a businessman, and Griffin's Green and Griffin Street were named after him. He served with 3 of his sons in the Kaffir War of 1834-35 and subsequent wars. Thomas, born in 1784, died at Port Elizabeth in 1843 and was buried there.

Henry Griffin (Thomas' youngest child) later relocated to Pietermaritzburg in Natal. There the family grew even larger. On her death, Thomas' wife, Sarah, was buried in Pietermaritzburg. It was here my great-grandfather, Stephen William (Bill), died in 1903; and where my grandfather, Charles Oliver Griffin, was a Magistrate. The Griffin name is well documented and recorded in Port Elizabeth and Natal, and many times during my travels in Australia, as well as in California in 2004, I've noticed the name Griffin.

William Alexander Smith (Ian's father) was our 2nd Cape founding father to make the crossing from Britain to South Africa. At the time, William was about 5.

He sailed in 1859 with his parents and younger siblings – a brother, James, and his sister, Marjorie Weir Smith. James Smith (William's father), was a sawyer (one who saws timber into planks) from Kintore, Aberdeen, Scotland. He married Margaret Tivendale in 1854, the year before compulsory registration in Scotland (1st January 1855). We think the Smith family made the voyage on either the ship *Aurifera* or the *New Great Britain*. James and Margaret had another 8 children in South Africa, totalling 11. William taught himself to read and write. As a young shepherd boy, he'd watched from the lofty anthills many of the tribal wars of the Eastern Cape and recorded these and other stories in journals. He became a farmer, and would buy several properties in the area over the years, two being the farms *Bloomfield* and *Rooken*.

There would be many Settlers with the common surname *Smith* in the Eastern Cape, a number of them in the Cathcart area. William farmed *Rooken* from 1885 to 1907 (which was sold to Calvin Evens whose family still owns it in 2017 with the same farm name) and did exceedingly well, "...the first to grow 800 bags of wheat in a season; 1,000 bags of potatoes in one crop; and when Rinderpest came along, was the biggest individual cattle owner in the Cathcart District." **(Rinderpest, a German word for 'cattle plague', an infectious viral disease was eventually eradicated in 2011).*

To differentiate one family from another the name of their farm followed the surname *Smith*. William became *Smith* of *Rooken*. He called himself *William Alexander Smith*, otherwise known as *W. Rooken Smith* (per his Will and other documents) and is known to the family as WAS for short, though he never actually changed his surname to *Rooken-Smith*. When exactly or how the hyphen came into the *Rooken-Smith* surname I don't know. Perhaps it originated with the natural flick of a clerk's pen.

Thomas Aggett (my grandfather on my mother's side) was the last of our founding fathers to brave the dangerous settler sea voyage. Together with his sisters, Emma Jane, and Elizabeth Ann, they sailed as adults from Devon to South Africa's shores, possibly a little later than 1867, and settled in the Cape Victoria East District. Apparently, the family had originally been potato farmers in England.

<u>Daisy's parents and siblings</u>

Thomas Aggett married Marjorie Weir Smith (William Alexander Smith's sister). They had 9 children, all born in the Cape. *Daisy Alice* (my mother) was the second youngest. The name of their farm was *Gwato* near the little town of Alice, hence Daisy's second Christian name.

William Alexander Smith married 3 times and fathered 17 children.

Emma Jane Aggett (Thomas Aggett's sister) was <u>William's 1st wife</u>. This union produced 8 children born *Smith* (referred to by the family as the *first litter*). William also brought up 2 other children.

Emma Jane died of natural causes. William's journal records her death as follows: 'In October 1897, I lost my wife, Emma Jane, and my mother, Margaret (Tivendale) in one week. My mother died on a

Sunday morning and while I was on my way to see my mother I met a boy with a note saying that my wife was very ill and I must come back at once. I knew my mother was not expected to live but she had her children and my Dad (James) with her and my wife was alone. So I returned at once without seeing mother; neither did I attend her funeral. The next Sunday morning my wife passed away leaving me with eight of our own children and two adopted ones.'

Janet Peebles, a governess, was William's 2nd wife. They had 5 children (the *second litter*). These children were also born *Smith.* Janet died in 1918.

Ian's mother:

Caroline Hedwig Augusta Spangenberg (born 07.08.1893) was William's 3rd wife. Both her parents came from Berlin, Germany. She was in charge of a nursing home in Quigney, East London, in the Eastern Cape and had been nursing William's daughter, Gertrude (3rd born from the *first litter*) – this being how they met, and then found that they both enjoyed playing tennis. Caroline was 28 when she married William, an enormous age difference as he was 67. Their wedding ceremony was in March 1921, part of their honeymoon being spent at Hogsback in the Eastern Cape. William and Caroline had 4 children, all born with the surname *Rooken-Smith* (the *third litter*). The first 2 children, Janet and Gordon Cameron, died. Ron was born in 1926. Ian (my husband), the youngest, was born in 1930 when William was 76.

Caroline was known as *Mater* to her children, grandchildren and most people in our family. Our 4 offspring Keith, Beryl, Lindsay and Stuart only spoke to or referred to her as *Mater*, this being a term of endearment much the same way as being called 'Granny'.

William became grandfather, great-grandfather, and great great-grandfather to so many of us.

Brief outline of Kenya's early history

Kenya (47th largest country in the world) straddles the equator in East Africa with a land mass of approximately 586,600 square kilometres, has a beautiful, diverse landscape and an interesting, at times, turbulent history. One of the most successful farming production areas in Africa are the Kenya Highlands. The capital was, and remains, Nairobi.

The country is bordered on the south-east by the Indian Ocean; north-east by Somalia; north by Ethiopia; north-west by South Sudan; west by Uganda and south by Tanzania. The word *Kenya* is derived from the languages of the indigenous Kikuyu, Embu and Kamba peoples meaning *mountain of whiteness* referring to the snow-capped peaks of Mount Kenya. The country was renamed in 1920 when the East Africa Protectorate was officially known as the Kenya Colony. Situated in the highlands, Mount Kenya at 17,058 ft is the highest point, 2nd only in majesty on the continent to Mount Kilimanjaro standing at 19,341 ft that can be seen from Kenya to the south of the neighbouring Tanzania border.

On 7th April 1498, Portuguese explorer, Vasco da Gama, first set eyes on the Kenya coast of green lush land where he found much wealth. "Sheiks and their retinues wearing robes of velvet and silk and gold-thread, with turbans of silk and gold, and swords and daggers mounted in silver."

There were fine towns and settlements along the coastline such as Mombasa, Malindi and Lamu (founded in 1370, Kenya's oldest continually inhabited town, with Lamu Old Town designated UNESCO world heritage status in 2001), mainly built by Arabs, and settled along with Egyptians, Phoenicians, Persians, Chinese and Indians, all of whom had traded. The Kenya coast was host to many explorers and merchants throughout the centuries, Malindi remaining an important Swahili settlement since the 14th century, once rivalling Mombasa for dominance. Through the Arab Sultan of Malindi, contact was made with the Chinese Ming Dynasty in 1414 and the fleet of the Chinese Explorer, Zheng He, visited Malindi the same year. The evils of slavery are well documented having been practiced during Biblical times in most civilisations, and the Kenya coast formed part of the East African region trading with the Arabs and Indians particularly for ivory and slaves. At one time, almost 90% of the Kenyan coastal population was enslaved.

War was then waged for years between the Portuguese and Arabs. The Portuguese, finally defeated, departed in 1729, leaving great buildings, amongst them historic Fort Jesus at Mombasa, and some other shrines along the coast. Then the Court of Muscat, ruled by Said bin Sultan, Sultan of Muscat, Oman, reannexed the old African Empire. He would later move his capital to Zanzibar, and after his death, his 6th son became the Sultan of Zanzibar.

Deep within the continent, tribal wars were raging, with customs, taboos, superstitions and witchcraft dominating the life of the inhabitants.

The British first entered Kenya in 1823, at the request of the reigning Chief. Britain continued her task of policing the seas for the suppression and eventual end to slavery. The Abolition of Slavery Act passed in 1807 called for forfeiture of ships engaged in slavery and a fine of £100 for each slave discovered on board. This took 80 years to accomplish and was done, unaided by any other Western Power, and which remains a credit to the country and her Royal Navy. Other European nations were eventually encouraged to pass anti-slavery laws due to the constant action of the Royal Navy. Britain now took control, and East Africa came into being.

Kenya, the most attractive of the East African countries – the other two being Uganda and Tanganyika – became a British Protectorate in 1895. Uganda, a Protectorate was established in 1894-96. Tanganyika, a state in East Africa, became part of German East Africa in 1884; was ceded to Britain as a League of Nations mandate in 1919; gained *Uhuru* Independence in 1961, and united with Zanzibar in 1964 as the United Republic of Tanzania.

Kenya Settlers

Much the same as the British Government had needed Settlers for South Africa, having now acquired the East Africa Protectorate, again the Government required Settlers to move this new land forward. The response was slow. Initially, British folk found the Government's offer to lease land unpopular and the Europeans were more interested in a way to get to the fertile land around Lake Victoria.

Attitudes would change when construction of the railway commenced at Mombasa in December 1895. The majority of the skilled and unskilled manpower was provided by the significant inflow of peoples from India, who would later form the nucleus of the Indian communities in Kenya and Uganda.

Two maneless lions dragged Indian railway workers and African labourers from their tents at night from March to December 1898 while the railroad was being built through Tsavo. The terrifying stealth and grisly accounts of the lions later became famous in Lt. Col. John Henry Patterson's 1907 published book, 'The Maneaters of Tsavo'. The number put forward of people killed reached 135 though an exact count of the dead was never known. Both lions were hunted down and shot by Patterson. In 1924, after the lion skins had been used as floor rugs by Patterson for many years and were in very poor condition, they were sold to the Chicago Field Museum, Illinois, USA, where they were reconstructed and put on display together with the original skulls.

In 1901, the first locomotive reached Kisumu on Lake Victoria. It was imperative the railway be profitable. Export of cash crops seemed the answer, and in the same year the Commissioner extended invitation to South Africans to settle, but they too responded with disinterest. The railway line was completed by 1903. European settlers were first to be allocated small areas of land in Kiambu district, which had formerly been occupied by Africans and which the Kikuyu regarded as part of their legitimate area of expansion.

An agreement was made between the Governor and the Maasai in 1904 to move the Maasai into two Reserves, one being south of the railway line (where they remain to this day – the Maasai Mara), and the other in the north, in Laikipia. By doing so, it left the Rift Valley from Naivasha to Nakuru and the plains east of Nairobi, empty of people.

By 1906, more than 1,550 square miles of land (4,000 square kilometres) had been leased or sold. Now interested, a considerable number of South African farmers settled in the country bringing with them everything they owned, including livestock and machinery.

Chapter One
1952 Daisy's 'Marmalade'

"Marriage is like marmalade, you take the bitter with the sweet."

These were the words my remarkable mother, Daisy Alice Griffin, born Aggett, and previously Eeles from her first marriage, said to me on my wedding day in Ol'Kalou, Kenya. I was 18. It was a Saturday with clear sunny skies in March 1952.

My half-sister, Marge, almost 19 years older than me, who I've always loved so dearly and only ever thought of as my full-sister, was dressing me for the 'going away' part of my nuptials when my mother came in to say her private goodbye to me. I'd be leaving on honeymoon with my 21 year old husband, *Ian Rooken-Smith.* Then we'd start our lives together on his farm *Uruku* in the Laikipia district.

First, I would like to share with you my resolute, courageous and caring mother's background. Without it my story might not convey with sufficient clarity the huge impact Daisy's life had on my own ability to cope with the tough lessons I would face. Looking at Daisy's life, and later my own, it became apparent to me that her 'marmalade' wisdom wasn't confined to marriage. The 'sweet' would aptly apply to the many happy, positive times in both our lives; the 'bitter' would be tart blows and pitfalls which would prove, for both of us, not to be in short supply.

It was my mother's will and unending bravery through all kinds of adversity, mostly as a single parent, running the two farms she'd lived on in Kenya, getting up and on with life regardless of circumstances, that remain etched in my memory. She never quit on anything. Throughout the remainder of my life, as if she were silently prodding me forward, it was Daisy's strength of spirit that had me put one foot in front of the other. My amazing, kind mother was loved, adored and remembered by so many.

In 1908, when Daisy was 15, her parents, Thomas and Marjorie, having been British Settlers to the Cape in the 1800s, decided to emigrate again. This time they'd be going to British East Africa, Kenya, after William Alexander Smith (Marjorie's brother) had taken his first trip there in 1906. William was shown the country – a long safari by rail and porter – by Arthur Cecil Hoey, who'd been a pupil on William's

Cathcart farm in the Eastern Cape directly after the Anglo/Boer War. They ended up in the Masendera Valley paralleling the Southern Guaso Nyiro River. This area was later to become part of the (now renowned) Maasai Mara. William stood and looked over that marvellous country in 1906, seemingly empty of human habitation, and proclaimed that he had found the land of 'milk and honey'. Kenya had William so entranced with its beauty and potential that he applied for land in the Masendera. The Guaso Nyiro River is also known as the Uaso Nyiro Ewaso Nyiro / Ewaso Ng'iro (meaning brown or muddy water) – rising on the west side of Mount Kenya it flows north; rising on the Mau Escarpment, it flows south through the Rift Valley, hence the name Southern Guaso Nyiro.

Hoey went to Kenya from South Africa in 1904. A farm market town in Western Kenya, Hoey's Bridge (now Moi's Bridge) near Kitale, would be named after Arthur Hoey, as he settled in the area and built the bridge across the Nzoia River. He would also become a member of the Legislative Council.

Having undertaken to bring back sufficient settlers to occupy some 10 farms, William sailed with his family and two Webb family members to Mombasa, Kenya. Included in the voyage were all sorts of agricultural tools and equipment, wagons, horses and sheep. Others of the group sailed separately. Unfortunately, they landed at the old Mombasa harbour where the animals had to be thrown overboard and made to swim for shore. They had a frustrating time collecting livestock all over Mombasa town. William was known to have remarked next day that his pedigree sheep looked quite unlike sheep after swimming through the surf! Their big Cape wagons had to be partially dismantled in order to make passage through the narrow Mombasa streets to the railway station, and on the way a lot of the trek chains, yokes, sledges etc. were stolen. From Mombasa, they travelled inland by train with all their possessions and animals to Nakuru where they set about acquiring and training work oxen. It was here that William met Winston Churchill who apparently 'spoke up for the settlers' at a Nakuru meeting with the Commissioner of Lands. Eventually, they were able to leave by ox-wagon over the Mau to the Southern Guaso Nyiro Plains, choosing a very much more difficult route because of abundant water.

William writes in his notes: 'Our group now consisted of 6 wagons and a scotch cart with 6 spans of oxen. There were horses, cattle and sheep, of which 50 were purebred Merino. Our manpower was myself and my wife, 4 sons, 2 grown daughters and my brother-in-law, Bill Peebles, plus 3 Browns, 4 Ulyates, 2 Webbs and 2 little girls. Our African staff consisted of 12 men, 2 of whom were Cape Coloured wagon drivers from the South African farm. The Aggetts, Hurts and Bowkers also took up land there.'

Having journeyed for 90 days, William's group finally arrived at the Southern Guaso Nyiro Plains to take up land in April 1908. The time the settlers spent there was a matter of survival. Frank Smith (William's 2nd child from the *first litter*) was very badly mauled by a wounded lioness. His younger brother, Donald (7th child from the *first litter*), took him by ox-wagon to Kijabe and from there by train to hospital in Nairobi, a trip that took several weeks. Over the years, Frank's wounds would flare up again. He was very crippled in one arm and one leg. Thomas Aggett, returning on foot from digging a furrow one day, was horrified to see a lion devouring his favourite mare which still had his rifle attached to her saddle. Only with great difficulty was he able to catch his second horse. Willie Smith (4th child from the *first litter*), Norman Webb and Robert Ulyate were probably the first to have opened the track from Narok through the Kedong to the settlement of Kijabe, in search of supplies for the Masendera settlers.

In 1911, when the Laikipia Maasai were moved south by the British Government to join the majority of their tribe (relocated there in 1904), the settlers were moved out – a huge upheaval for both the Maasai and settlers. William, no doubt, felt some sense of deep disappointment at the settlers' removal from his 'beloved Masendera'. The Smiths then made their homes on the Pesi River/Laikipia; the Aggetts around Naivasha/Nanyuki; the Charts/Jenkins around Gilgil; others settled all around Kenya. Daisy's elder brother, Boyce Aggett (5th born of 9 children) for years traded goods by wagon into Maasailand, lived and died at Kijabe. George Aggett (7th born of the 9 Aggett children) learnt the Maasai language (Maa) fluently and was initiated as a blood brother whilst assisting at these trading posts. (George Edward Aggett, grandson of George Aggett, is still farming on *Kifuku* in Laikipia in

2016. **George Edward Aggett, born 12.4.1966, died 14.9.2016 due to injuries sustained in a plane crash near Lake Naivasha on 8.9.2016. R.I.P.).*

Daisy's parents moved to *Karati,* the Aggett farm at Naivasha in the Rift Valley Province. This became the central point for the Aggett and Smith families. The farmhouse was set up in the hills in lion country, way behind the present day township of Naivasha, overlooking the great lake of that name. In those days, the waters of Lake Naivasha reached right up to the railway line.

Having had no schooling since leaving their farm *Gwato* in the Eastern Cape, Daisy was sent to the Kenya Rift Valley Academy at Kijabe, run by the Protestant Africa Inland Mission which had been in existence since 1903. There she took a course in shorthand, typing and journalism which enabled her to find employment as a journalist with the East African Standard, Nairobi's leading newspaper. It was during this time in Nairobi when she was about 20 that Daisy met and married her first husband, Frederick Harry Eeles (known as Harry), in 1913. A while later and for reasons unknown Harry Eeles decided to return to England. At the time, Daisy was pregnant with her first child and didn't want to leave her family. Harry departed for England alone and Daisy went to live with her mother on *Karati*. During the remainder of Daisy's pregnancy and following my sister, Marge's, birth in September 1915, Harry made no attempt to contact Daisy. The marriage ended some years later with news via a letter from his brother, George, advising of Harry's death in England.

My Granny Marjorie Aggett (called Gran Aggett by many) died at Naivasha aged 64 on 22nd December 1922, before I was born.

My father, Lionel Carol Griffin, was born on 11th November 1896 in Pietermaritzburg, Natal. Given founding father Thomas Griffin's Royal Navy background, it's not surprising then that my father followed in the footsteps of his great-grandfather and chose a military career. Thomas had served 15 years in the Royal Navy. He fought in the battle of Trafalgar under Lord Nelson aboard *HMS Mars*. After this, he was an Armourer at the Tower of London.

Lionel Carol fought for his King and Country at the outbreak of WWI. He'd returned to England from South Africa and enlisted in the Black Watch Regiment, rising to rank of Sergeant. He then left the army and joined the Royal Navy aged 19, first aboard *HMS Pembroke II* (a shore-based ship, we assume used for training), followed by *HMS Royal Oak* (serving as a stoker) from July 11th 1916 to September 4th 1916. Lionel Carol's Royal Navy Record No. K32568 notes, amongst other details, his 'Occupation farmer, born in Maritzburg, Natal; height five-foot seven-and-three-quarter inches, chest forty-two-and-a-half inches, hair brown, eyes blue, complexion fresh, scar on left shin.' Ashore once more, Lionel Carol immediately re-enlisted in the Army, this time with the Royal Irish Rifles where he was commissioned and rose to rank of Captain.

Sent to Amiens in Northern France, he was at the Battle of the Somme (1st July 1916 to 18th November 1916), one of the most famous battles of WWI where the devastating loss of life epitomised the horrors of war. Casualties suffered by British forces neared 420,000 – almost 60,000 the first day alone; nearly 200,000 French and 500,000 Germans.

The forgotten tragedy of WWI (also known as the Great War) is the incredible contribution made by the horses, where as many went into the line of fire as humans, carrying cavalry, hauling and ferrying ammunition and millions of tons of rations, and brought back on carriages the wounded on stretchers. The horses suffered immensely getting stuck in barbed wire, caught in mustard gas attacks, mired and drowning in mud, falling in shell holes, left injured in no-man's land and sent into battle against howitzers and tanks. Of British horses alone, an estimated 100,000 were killed and the Royal Veterinary Corps treated two-and-a-quarter million cases on battlefields. Another toll on the horses was exhaustion, damage to their eyesight, utter terror from the constant smell of blood which they never forgot, and shell-shock. Horses on the German side were fed sawdust mixed with their food to ease their hunger when fodder was often in short supply. The Germans also cruelly scattered metal spikes (named Caltrops) on battlefields that went into the horses' hooves resulting in them having to be shot.

When WWI was over, Lionel Carol decided to go to the large military training camp at Aldershot in Hampshire, England and became a Physical Training Officer. An extremely strong man, he was able to lift himself on the bar using one arm only. After such a full military life, my father chose to return again to Africa, opting to make Kenya his new home this time. Here he served briefly in the East African Mounted Rifles before discharge.

It was at this time that my parents, Daisy and Lionel Carol met. In order to be able to put some money together to marry my mother, my father hunted a big bull elephant along the Tana River and was paid £1 per pound weight for its ivory. We became a family of 5 children. My elder half-sister, Marge, and half-brother, Neville, who was born in 1918 after Daisy's marriage to Harry had ended. Neville's father was a hunter. He was later killed by an elephant. My father accepted Marge and Neville as his own children and never differentiated in any way whatsoever between us 5.

Daisy took a fair amount of heat from her family for her out-of-wedlock baby, Neville. My stern Aunt May, my mother's elder sister, in particular seemed to find some sort of satisfaction at constantly rubbing this 'scandalous behaviour of an illegitimate child' in Daisy's face. Despite Aunt May's authoritarian and rigid manner, the family held her nursing abilities in high regard. She'd been Matron of Addington Hospital in Durban at one time, and had also saved several family members' lives who'd been involved in awful accidents.

Then there were my own two full-blood older brothers, Terence (Terry) and Kenneth (Ken). I was what is generally, in South African Afrikaans, termed a 'laat-lammetjie' (a late child), my birth being 8 years after Ken. Daisy was 40 at the time.

Marge was blue eyed, blondish, clever and good at everything including exquisite needlework. She was training to be a teacher.

Neville (15 years older than me) was brainy, tall and had curly brown hair and bright blue eyes. Very handsome, the women were always chasing him. He had excellent manners and could whistle beautifully, was a good horseman, a precise shot and had a superb sharp wit. All his life, so Neville told me, he suffered the stigma of being an illegitimate child.

My brother, Terry, hated school and was rebellious. He attended Nakuru School and Prince of Wales in Nairobi, and absconded from both on several occasions. He had an exuberant character. Six-foot four-inches tall, black curly hair and brown eyes, he was also a 'looker'. I loved Terry dearly.

Ken. A quiet character, he was a gifted musician, and was also an excellent horseman. He was a surrogate father to me. Physically strong, five-foot ten-inches tall, with hazel eyes and auburn, slightly curly hair, Ken had all the mannerisms of my father.

My parents initially lived on the farm *Bella Vista* at Oleolondo, Kenya – hilly, dry, arid country, but with the lovely Melawa River, famous for its rainbow trout, running through the area. During these hard times, my father took various jobs: being a professional hunter when needed, felling timber at Elburgon, gold prospecting in the Kakamega district, then long-distance transport by ox-wagon and eventually by lorry. My mother did the farming and helped out with the catering of the hunting safaris. Eventually, my parents left Bella Vista and moved to Ol'Kalou, where they bought a farm named *Anchorage*, made their first real home and began serious farming. My childhood and many of my marriage memories are of this particular farm, Anchorage.

Of Thomas and Marjorie Aggett's 5 daughters – Nellie, Jane, May, Daisy and Ethel – vivacious Daisy was said to have been the best looking with hazel eyes, thick lustrous black hair and neat hands. She excelled at music, dancing and singing, and took part in Nairobi theatrical performances. Daisy was a wonderful home-maker, gardener and expert at cooking, baking, pickling and bottling. She also spoke Kikuyu, was an excellent shot and huntress, and was respected by all communities. We all took my mother for granted. Only when I started writing 'Daisy's Daughter' in 2006, did I recognise and value her many sacrifices, and realise how passionate she'd been about Kenya.

After my birth, my father was always away fighting the enemy for his King and Country, or off at a moment's notice on safari, employed by Ker and Downey as a professional hunter. One of his many clients was King Ferdinand of Bulgaria.

Maybe my earliest memory of my father when I was 4 years old (1937) is of our first house at Anchorage. It was a crudely built mud and wattle house with a thatch roof, and a curtain instead of a door to my room. I still remember clearly that night so long ago, my mother bending over me saying, "Don't be afraid, Daddy's going to shoot it," while a rampaging buffalo bull was encircling the house bellowing madly in the darkness. A thunderous shot rang out, so close it was terrifying. Then all became still again. Presumably, I no longer had any fear because I felt safe with my brave father being there for us. The silence of the forest, familiar and soothing to me, had returned. In hindsight, I think the buffalo might have been wounded to have behaved in this manner during the night. I do not recall my parents speaking of it later.

I remember the day, at the outbreak of WWII in 1939 when my father joined the East African Forces. By this time, we'd moved into the permanent Anchorage house made of timber, the cedar having been cut on the farm. The mauve wisteria was in full bloom making a beautiful show over one of the pergolas on the driveway. Lionel Carol was posted to Army Service Corps attaining the rank of Captain, and served in Abyssinia (now Ethiopia). Daisy was left to make all the plans, run the property, take decisions and face the risks on her own. Soon after my father left, my three brothers enlisted, all young, Ken only sixteen; and were gone to battle.

In the early war years, several people asked Daisy to store trunks of personal items for them. Anchorage had a loft which was under the entire roof area, containing our superfluous items, furniture and old books etc. but with sufficient space, so it was no trouble. I used to play up there quite often. The lighter weight cabin trunks (the enormous plywood trunks that were taken on sea voyages in those days) were lifted up into the loft with relative ease.

I have few memories of my father during the war years. One was of our first car, a 'Rugby', which had a canvas retractable roof on a pram-like metal structure, with half-doors. There were many scary times as we crossed the Simba Bridge at Gilgil. The bridge had been built by felling a number of huge, long cedar trees which were laid across the very deep and extremely narrow gorge, then mud was packed tightly between the giant tree trunks. My father would drive the Rugby to the start of the bridge where my mother would then get out, take me by the hand and lead me across. This really was a terrifying experience. I could envisage falling into the depths from which I knew there was no coming back. Then, standing outside the car, my father would engage the gear and operate the handheld accelerator and very slowly walk and steer the car at the same time across the bridge. Always, I thought it a miracle we survived this part of the journey and heaved a sigh of relief once we were safely across. During the WWII years, a concrete structure was built alongside the old cedar log bridge.

Another recollection of the Rugby is that of my father coming to a halt one day, due to a noise he'd heard, which he thought was perhaps something amiss with the car. Getting out, he walked around the vehicle examining the tyres and generally checking all was well. Finding nothing wrong, we were on our way once more, but within moments the sound was back. Again, my father stopped and did a thorough exterior check of the car. The sound turned out to be coming from Carlisle, a 40 year old mentally handicapped fellow sitting in the back seat with me who'd been humming as we drove. Carlisle imagined he was an Army major and always dressed in military fashion, even wearing some kind of medals. Daisy often had Carlisle to stay as his mother was elderly and ailing. We called her Granny Atheston. They lived at *Ol Joro Orok* about 15 miles from us.

I recall being fixated on my father's every movement as he knocked down his raw egg and Worcestershire Sauce 'quick breakfast drink'. Since I was fascinated with all that he did, his shaving ritual in particular always filled me with pride and wonder as I stood at my Daddy's side. On our safari trips, I'd watch the camp-boy bring hot water to the tarpaulin basin and pay great attention as my father sharpened his razor (the old cut-throat blade type the barbers used) on the leather strop. I was enthralled at how he covered his face in shaving soap, which was on a stick, and at how he used the brush to make the frothy suds. Then, my eyes never leaving his face and the motion of his hands, I'd watch the precision of the entire shaving procedure of face and neck with the dangerously sharp blade, rinsed in an enamel mug at regular intervals. I always felt an acute sense of disappointment when this procedure was over. He'd pat his face dry and smile at me. I could have watched this part of his manly cleansing quite easily for hours on end, so great was my admiration of my father and joy in the time spent with him. In reality, our occasions of being together were few and precious to me. He always smelled so nice and clean.

Lionel Carol was educated at Hilton College, Hilton, near Pietermaritzburg and played rugby for the first team in 1912. He refused to change the day of my birth, being a Friday the 13th, as he was one of 13 survivors during a skirmish against the Germans in South West Africa and considered 13 to be a lucky number. He was handsome with short cropped hair tending to be curly, was a meticulous, neat and tidy person and a stickler for duty. Always loving, he spoilt me and I felt safe from all scary things when I was with him. My father had a way about him; his strength and power instilled in me a sense of security.

During the years of war my father had given his patriotic military service to his country. Here was a man who'd immediately down tools no matter what he was busy doing to take up the call to arms whenever his country needed him, which turned out to be on more than a couple of occasions. Without the slightest utterance of complaint or question, he'd collect his military gear, say goodbye and be off. My mother calmly accepted (outwardly anyway), the situation for she knew it was the duty of every able-bodied man to join up and support his country and freedom. Consequently, my young years are mostly memories of a family of women, small nephews and nieces, and various cousins at Anchorage farm.

I remember my father well, though very sadly and with deep regret, I hardly knew him. The last time I saw him, I was going on 9 in 1942.

On occasion, I'd heard the adults at Anchorage having hushed discussions about divorce, though it meant nothing to me as I didn't understand what the word meant. Later, my mother explained to me that she and my father would be getting divorced and he wouldn't be living with us anymore, which I still couldn't properly comprehend because it didn't seem to imply that I'd no longer be seeing him at all. It was way over my head and young mind.

I never asked questions regarding my mother's actions on anything. I'd never had reason to. In the era in which I was brought up, children didn't question their parents. At the time of this divorce news being revealed to me, I clearly remember looking through the World Wide Magazine for Men by candlelight – stories of great, brave and scary adventures. I'd slept in Daisy's bed, having eaten several pieces of Brooklax which tasted like chocolate, a real luxury. My mother kept it in a little red and white flat tin box on her bedside table. She never said anything when I had to get up and go with a torch to the newly built toilet. The resultant upset stomach taught me a lesson about the laxative Brooklax.

The last time I saw my father, I wasn't aware that I'd never again see him. I was overjoyed to know my Daddy had arrived home as I waited for these rare occasions with great anticipation and excitement. Everything about him for me was a wonderment of happiness as I was his 'special' girl. But, on that day the sense of joy seemed to fade.

I can't remember my parents sitting and chatting. I think I may have been told to go and play because I don't recall being with them in the sitting room with its lovely vases of flowers, pictures and fireplace, or at the big table in the spacious pantry, the two places where we usually had our togetherness. There was a sombre kind of silence in the house which starkly overshadowed our familiar gaiety at my parents seeing one another. My father silently hugged me because shortly after his arrival, he was about to leave again and it was still only morning time. That was unusual too as he'd hardly been with us at all. Had I known he was going away forever, I think I would have cried or clung to him. Everything in those last few moments, it now seems to me in hindsight, was done hurriedly.

My mother wasn't there at the goodbye. Again, that was odd. I don't know where she was. My father led me to the side verandah where I sat on his lap a short while, then he hugged me again and said goodbye quietly. His car was already under the wisteria pergola with the engine ticking over. I said nothing as I watched him get in. As he drove off I went to stand under the wisteria a few moments, quite mystified, then I ran a short way after the car, but he didn't stop.

Standing still, etched in my mind is the picture of him as he drove down the long road, passing on the right the tall green hedge and the pink roses in bloom, then under the last pergola of brilliant orange and green Golden Shower. Finally, the car turned slightly left on the mile long farm road banked on both sides by my mother's profusely flowering blue agapanthus. Within half a minute, he was gone; a very painful memory for me. I cannot remember uttering a single word. Probably I felt numb as neither did I cry.

My father had a cat named 'Walker' that disappeared when he left and then just as suddenly would return on the occasions he came home on short leaves. Once my father was gone for good, Walker tabby cat never returned. Later on at Nakuru School, I really felt the stigma of being the only child of divorced parents. In those days, it was considered a disgrace.

When I was going on 11 my brother Terry died. At the outbreak of World War II, he'd immediately joined the Kenya Regiment being drafted to the Armoured Car 11th Division then sent to Burma with the British 14th Army. He contracted typhoid fever and died at the age of 21 on 7th September 1944, and is buried in the Military Cemetery in Imphal, grave #2.D.13. Just a few days before Terry died my mother received a letter from the young man in the bed next to him, saying Terry had asked him to write. Then Neville arrived on short compassionate leave from his post in Tanganyika (now Tanzania), to tell Daisy of Terry's death.

The shock and sorrow was so great my mother locked herself in her bedroom for three days to grieve privately. Through the door, I never heard her cry, sob or emit any moans of heartache. Mwangi, our loyal and trusted Kikuyu staff member, didn't take Daisy even a cup of coffee during that time. There was always a bottle of water and a glass next to her bed and she had piped water in her bedroom. Mwangi was the much-respected *major domo* of the household, my mother's right-hand, as he'd been with our family for so long. A small-framed, sensitive and intelligent man, Mwangi, without words, sensed that Daisy would let him know when she could face food or something other to drink. He let her fight her death demons over the loss of Terry in peace, in her own way.

In 1979, whilst cattle ranching near Omitara, South West Africa (now Namibia), I would feel a new bitter dimension to Daisy's 'marmalade' and come to understand her silent pain at losing one of her children when our youngest son, Stuart, died. In time, I learnt to exclude the sad thoughts from my mind. Then out of the blue they'd hit me again with a vengeance, seemingly for no apparent reason, and I'd feel lost in longing for my precious child until I could quietly pull myself together.

At Nakuru boarding school with me were two Chandler children, a brother and younger sister. Daisy, one day, explained to me that my father had married their mother. I remained silent, extremely heart-sore and utterly perplexed as to why my father never visited me. I loved him so dearly and he loved me, and I couldn't understand why he'd had to go away. I spoke, once, briefly at junior school to the Chandler son, he was friendly. The daughter and I never conversed. In January 1945, I remember my mother and other members of the family again speaking in hushed tones, and wondered what it was all about. Back at Nakuru boarding school, I was told that my, "Daddy had died." He'd been very sick with pneumonia. The way I understood and remembered it, he'd become sick while fighting in the war. Lionel Carol died on 20th January 1945, four months after my brother, Terry's death. I would turn 12 in November that year.

With the end of WWII in September 1945, Neville came home having done military duty in Abyssinia and Burma. Ken returned from Burma a very sick man. He had an abscess on the liver from which he took almost a year to recover.

I always remember my father with loving pride, his fearlessness and his ability to do so many and varied things. 'Necessity' certainly was 'the mother of invention' in those days. Lionel Carol, to me, lived a life that mattered, just as Daisy did.

Life and history sometimes have a harsh way of repeating themselves. Daisy's bitter 'marmalade' would surface again in 1991, bringing back a rush of heartache and memories at losing my father when I was approaching the sensitive years of adolescence. This time though, in Windhoek, Namibia, I would be the comforter of our 12 year old grandson, Stuart, and hear myself saying, "Your mother has died."

Our beautiful daughter, Beryl, died of cancer. My solace after Beryl's death would be to gaze skywards each evening. For somewhere in the huge, mostly unfathomable expanse of cosmos, is a twinkle of light regardless of a clear night or passing clouds – a star, registered by the International Star Registry and named for all eternity after our beloved elder daughter, Beryl Marjorie.

Chapter Two
Nugu No More

As a young child, *Nugu* (pronounced 'Noogoo'), a Kenya Swahili African word meaning 'monkey' was my nickname though my father and mother called me Heather. My brothers, Terry and Ken gave me the nickname, probably because I was so much younger and always climbing up trees and fences or being fidgety, never a minute still. Swahili (Kiswahili) is spoken in about 12 African countries. Depending on where one lives there are variations to Swahili. Even in the same country, Swahili can vary though many words are the same. We spoke Settler Swahili (Settla/Kisetla). In Kikuyu, 'monkey' is *Nūgū* and the pronounciation is 'Nogo'.

Since the age of six I'd been compared with my second cousin, Mary. She had golden curls, big blue eyes and the family referred to her as 'our Angel'. In comparison, I was just very ordinary with dark hair and brown eyes, even called the ugly duckling at times and was quite used to this. I didn't mind at all being spoken to as Nugu and actually found the name endearing, apart from which I could outrun all my little cousins which gave me immense, quiet and gleeful pleasure!

My high school years were spent at boarding school in Nairobi at the Kenya High School (affectionately referred to as 'the Heifer Boma'). I was in Huxley House and turned 17 shortly before my final exams.

The first job I had, for about 6 weeks, was assisting Dr Anne Spoerry who lived in a rented farmhouse very close to Anchorage. Her small surgery and clinic were situated at the back of her home where on a daily basis she tended to the many waiting Kikuyu who called her 'Mama Daktari' (Mother Doctor), needing attention for anything from headaches to cuts, infections, broken bones, many with boils or sores on their legs, adults and children with worms and various other medical conditions.

I worked half-days with Dr Spoerry. Neville would drive me there for 8 in the morning and fetch me again at lunchtime. Dr Spoerry was our family doctor and close friend, often spending time with us for tea, meals or drinks and joining in at the popular Ol'Kalou Club just down the road from our house. Daisy had sectioned off a corner of Anchorage farm for the establishment of this much-needed social gathering place.

Anne Spoerry was the most caring doctor and down to earth person with no airs or graces and was known to us by her first name. We didn't call her 'doctor'. Our family respected, trusted and regarded her as a dear person and had great faith in her medical expertise and abilities. She later took flying lessons and bought her own aeroplane becoming famous as 'The Flying Doctor'.

Seeing as I was interested in a nursing career, Daisy thought it an excellent idea that I work for Dr Spoerry for a short while to see if she considered me suitable nurse material. I personally assisted her, cleaning wounds, sterilising medical and surgical equipment, taking temperatures and blood pressure, packing the medicine cupboard and suchlike. Never did I give out medicine. She also taught me to give intra-muscular and subcutaneous injections, how to choose the site accordingly on the anatomy, pinch or hold the flesh and be quick with the needle. I felt very nervous giving my first injection, but soon became quite adept at it and my initial anxiousness passed.

Originally from France, Anne was, however, fluent in English (though she retained the French nasal intonation), but she didn't speak Swahili. To counteract this she employed a young Kikuyu assistant, Francis, who spoke and wrote a bit of English. He'd first talk to the patient in Kikuyu to ascertain the medical needs then write on a slip of paper the English translation. I remember two occasions of Francis' handwritten notes that gave me a smile. 'This man is suffering from a sore on the end of the leg' (foot); and 'This man has snakes in his belly' (meaning tapeworm).

Dr Spoerry was very kind, patient and tolerant with me during my learning experience with her. In all that she did medically in our hours together she constantly taught me, and would test my knowledge the following day by asking me questions. Her dress code was always a pair of close fitting, stove-pipe type trousers with a loose open-neck golf shirt and short ankle boots, making it easy for her to 'doctor' at any time, or ride a horse should she choose to do so at short notice, without having to change her attire. Dr Spoerry was a tough, 'no ditherer' woman quite at ease in the presence of men and oftentimes preferred masculine company. She had a shock of thick, light coloured hair flecked with grey that she'd run her fingers through to push back her fringe from her face, and didn't wear makeup.

A job as probationer came up at Nakuru War Memorial Hospital. Dr Spoerry urged Daisy that I try for the post. With many good luck wishes, I was interviewed by Matron McDougal and given the position. From then on, no-one called me Nugu anymore. I was known as 'Nurse Griffin', but the Nugu term of endearment has remained in my heart. I will always remain grateful for Dr Anne Spoerry's medical tutorship. It would stand me in good stead. I feel privileged to have spent this time, albeit relatively short, under her excellent guidance.

My mother gave me permission to wear lipstick, and Marge kindly let me have one of her own, an American make in dark red by the trade name 'Tangee'. It was absolutely lovely and very flattering, the only make-up I owned.

On my 18th birthday in 1951, six years after my father's death, I received £750 left to me in his Will. Daisy outfitted me with three new dresses and two pairs of white sandals, all so feminine. I can't remember ever having had swanky shop-bought clothes before, such a luxury for me. The Standard Bank of Nakuru issued me with a cheque book (in 2016, I still bank with the Standard). The first item I bought was a little Philips radio costing 50 shillings (the equivalent of South African Rand 5) which I put in my room in the Nurses' Hostel. I botched the writing of the first cheque and felt very sheepish having to make out another! The next thing I purchased was a beautiful little round china brooch, made and hand-painted in England, of pink roses and forget-me-nots surrounded by green rose leaves costing me 15 shillings (Rand 1.50). The remainder of the money I kept in my banking account as savings.

About six weeks later, during the Christmas holidays, Ian had taken a few days off from farming and joined our family for the festivities. Having previously put a dampener on his earlier male advances, I now responded to his renewed interest in me. The two of us just clicked. We became 'an item' and shortly thereafter announced our engagement. Daisy and the entire family were absolutely delighted. Without further ado, wedding arrangements were planned, the date set, the ceremony to be held at St. Peter's Church, Ol'Kalou. Soon after the wedding invitations had been sent out, gifts started to arrive. My mother made sure I noted in a detailed list all the items and names of the generous, caring people who'd sent them.

St. Peter's had a particular significance for my family, the funds for the building of the Church having been raised, almost entirely, in several ways by my mother, Daisy.

Uncle Alick Roberts (married to Aunt May, Daisy's elder sister), reckoned that the Laikipia area, per past records and memories, experienced a severe drought about every 11 years or so. Everything suffered then. The earth became quite bare, the masses of game moved elsewhere, and fodder had to be bought for livestock, but even that wasn't sufficient, so cattle were grazed along the verges of the roads and farmers had to sell at any price, while others had to mill prickly pear as feed. Some farmers even cut down foliage of trees to feed the cattle, many becoming so weak they lay down in the rivers while drinking and died. It was heartbreaking to see the effects these severely dry times had on animals, wildlife, the countryside and people.

The drought spread even further to other districts (including to our Anchorage farm in the Central Province), lasting a number of years. One of these times coincided with our wedding in 1952. Even Ian cut tree foliage to feed his cattle. I saw many die from weakness, lying down whilst drinking in the dwindling Pesi River on Ian's farm, Uruku.

The wetlands surrounding Lake Ol'Bolossat, as well as the freshwater lake itself also suffered (the level once told to me to be below a man's knees). During an earlier drought, two of the Lake hippopotami decided to take up residence in our Anchorage dam, which was quite large, deep, and not so far away. Though Anchorage felt the effects of the dry conditions, because the dam was man-made there was usually sufficient water for irrigation on that part of the farm, and certainly enough left over for a pair of hippos to wallow around in. We had other dams as well, and piped water from boreholes to livestock troughs, though the house relied entirely on rainwater run-off from the roof into the enormous underground well and three water tanks situated at the corners of the homestead.

Running the farm with Daisy to assist her, Neville was empathetic towards the African staff and perceptive in that he put into place shorter working hours for them and an increase in their pay. They all loved and respected him. He also brought with him from Ethiopia some Eragrostis seed that produced a fine-stemmed, very leafy grass that grew well in high altitudes and could be used for grazing or cut fodder. When the hippo started becoming quite aggressive, using the tractor, agricultural mower and the one-ton-load capacity trailer, Neville literally fed the pair a ton of the grass daily. Very soon they were docile enough to allow visitors to watch them at leisure. The fee charged to view the hippo was a shilling a person. All the money collected went into the Church Fund. This was the first way money was raised for the building of St. Peter's.

Daisy also started a second-hand clothing swap or sell shop at our farm home. Again, all the money was put into an account for the building of the Church. As accommodation was difficult to get, my mother boarded two mechanics from the nearby town of Ol'Kalou. One man was affectionately known as Tukie (pronounced 'Tookie'). Almost every word he spoke was unacceptable 'bad language'. Daisy had a tin with a slot made in the top. Every time Tukie swore he had to put ten cents into the tin. This small change also went to the church fund. Construction of St. Peter's would cost £2,000. Once sufficient funds had been raised and the hippo were tame enough, a Mr Carr Hartley, the Game Catcher from Rumuruti, came to Anchorage in 1947 and enticed the two large animals into huge crates, hoisted them onto lorries and transported them to Mombasa where they were then shipped to the London Zoo. The hippopotami were, appropriately, named Daisy and Neville.

St. Peter's was built of Ol'Kalou quarry-cut grey blocks of stone. The builders were from the community, and the lectern was cut from Anchorage farm cedar and dedicated to the memory of my brother, Terence Oliver Griffin. We were honoured to have the first wedding ceremony in the new church, blessed by our Reverend Wilfred Walton.

Bride Heather May Isobel Griffin (born 13th November 1933, Nakuru War Memorial Hospital, Nakuru) married groom Ian Rooken-

Smith (born at Uruku Farm, Laikipia, 5th June 1930) at St. Peter's Church, Ol'Kalou, on 22nd March 1952.

To choose my bridal attire, my mother, Marge, and I, having been up before daylight, drove to Nairobi where we spent a long day looking in several boutiques. The trip from Anchorage and return was about 2 hours either way, over some poor dirt roads though once we got to Gilgil the main Nairobi road was tarmac. En route there, we always had a pit stop for tea at the Bell Inn in Naivasha, and lunch was at the Nairobi Stanley Hotel in Delamere Avenue. We had an old grey Ford pick-up that just chugged along with a homemade cedar-wood box-body cover over the back.

I settled on Rita's Boutique. The wedding gown I chose was a copy of the one worn by ballet dancer, Moira Shearer. A simple but exquisite gown, made of oyster-coloured embossed satin, figure-hugging with a very long row of tiny buttons down the front, a gathered bodice, cap sleeves ringed with fringe, and above-the-elbow matching gloves.

Marge, my Matron of Honour, favoured an elegant powder-blue creation with matching hat. For the 3 bridesmaids, my delightful nieces, Janet, Shirley and Jennifer, my heart was set on lemon-coloured organdie long frocks, designed and made by a seamstress. Daisy's dress would be mushroom-pink with a tiny floral black motif, her outfit completed all in black with matching shoes, handbag, gloves and a small hat. My stunning going-away ensemble was dark green, had a heavily white-embroidered bodice, and a full circular skirt.

Three days before the wedding, the hairdresser at Yvonne's Salon in Nakuru did a perm on my hair and overcooked it, burning a small round area on my scalp that was quite painful. When I complained, the lady explained that the perm lotion was applied to the hair around the heavy metal curlers (clamped close to the scalp) and the lotion had to stay on till it stopped sizzling. For me, it was altogether a hateful experience. My fine brown hair would be a short-style perm of curls beneath my veil. In reality, it was a miracle no worse damage was done. My mother was furious.

Daisy and many members of both our families gave us a big, beautiful and traditional wedding with easily 300 guests attending from our own and several other districts travelling from Nanyuki, Nairobi and various distant areas. Some of my dear Nakuru Primary boarding school friends were there too – Jean and Mary Chart, Henry Hauschild's family, Louisa de Bruin, the Van Dyk boys Dawie and Piet and their sister Beatie, Janet Forrester, Sarah and her sister, Margaret Rowlandson, and Peter White.

My brother, Ken, gave me away and Neville was Ian's best man. It had been planned that as Ian and I came out of the Church, Marge's youngest son, Rob, would come forward with a white satin covered horse-shoe with a sprig of real white heather for luck.

The reception was held at Anchorage with a full view of the majestic Aberdare Mountains from Daisy's garden. The house, from early morning, was a hive of activity. Mwangi, fanatically tidy, quick and extremely efficient, cleaned and put each room in absolute order; beautifully and correctly set long tables with crockery and silverware on spotless white damask cloths, made sure sufficient ice was made, and saw to the flowers to be cut by the gardeners. He would later quietly, and with great pride, carry the tall drinks of imported South African sparkling wine to all the guests, nary a drop spilt or a glass broken from his steady tray. There was a law in Daisy's home which no-one dared cross – all our staff were spoken to and treated with respect.

Rho (also Kikuyu), our cook – a naturally big man, but more than a little overweight, I think from all the food tasting over the years in Daisy's kitchen – was nearly run off his feet assisting various members of the family who were still baking or making every item of tea party edibles imaginable. Kariuki, the kitchen *toto* (general run-around helper), a young, tall and slender lad, rushed frantically backwards and forwards bringing vegetables from the garden or fetching eggs, kept the *kuni* (wood) stove burning, did the washing-up, and without question, obeyed every instruction from both Mwangi and Rho. Even the cars were polished.

Our magnificent wedding cake was on a separate small table atop an exquisite hand-embroidered cloth, so as to be on show for everyone to admire. My cousin, Iva Roberts, produced the handmade masterpiece, a three-tier fruit cake covered in delicate icing with doves, floral creations and net, all in white.

The masses of Church flower arrangements were from Daisy's garden, all arranged by Marge. The mile-long driveway to the house from the main road was bordered on both sides by ribbons of full-bloom blue Agapanthus. Then came the first pergola covered in orange Golden Shower creeper; the last 100 yards of garden-fence draped with abundant trusses of deep pink Dorothy Perkins roses reaching the second pergola, covered in mauve Wisteria. The tall hedges were trimmed; the newly mown lawn a carpet of green.

I think I could best describe my 18 year old bridal feelings as mystified numbness. I was aware the whole procedure had cost my single-parent farming mother a small fortune, especially in the hard times Kenyans experienced after the war, not forgetting the difficult period of serious drought that had followed. Daisy had her heart set on my marrying Ian. She spared no expense or labour of love to ensure our wedding day was the ultimate success and would remain a wonderful memory for both of us. She accepted Ian as her son and he adored her, calling her 'Mum'. Everyone took care of me, and did all the necessary to make me feel spoilt and special ensuring the whole experience went without a hitch. I just did as I was told, was bathed and dressed by loving relatives, my face powdered and Marge's Tangee lipstick applied.

My groom, Ian, was handsome and slim, brown-eyed with a long, straight nose, a lovely smile and good straight teeth, with a shock of black hair which he slicked back and down with Brylcream. He had very good manners and was extremely shy. Ian had started smoking at age 14. At six-foot two-inches tall, he seemed to tower above my five-foot-one frame, the top of my head reaching Ian's shoulder.

Ian was my one and only real boyfriend, though I grew up and was friends with other boys. I met him one afternoon when I was 14, and he 17. Coming around the side of the house, I found a strange grey car parked near the back door. Ian was getting his things out of the boot. He looked up and saw me. I had no idea who he was and we didn't introduce ourselves.

The young man followed me inside and I hovered around listening to the conversation as he told Daisy that Uncle Will had given him the farm Uruku at Thomson's Falls, and sent him to Kenya from South Africa to start on his own. Though he'd been a bright pupil, he said he didn't finish his schooling at Selborne College, East London, in the Eastern Cape. Apparently, his family was unhappy that at the age of 17 Ian had wanted to begin his adult life and gone off to farm in Kenya.

'Maisie' was the name Ian had painted on his American second-hand grey saloon car, which rather impressed me since none of our family owned such a swanky looking vehicle. I knew where South Africa was, geography being my favourite school subject. So between the faraway country and Ian's smart car, my teenage mind was intrigued. He seemed a brave young fellow to travel so far and start farming on his own. Nice too and, of course, I'd noticed his good looks.

Daisy seemed to know immediately who Uncle Will was. I got the impression he was quite an important man. After Ian left, I asked about his father, William, being my mother's Uncle, as my curious mind had some trouble getting around that fact. Daisy explained our family tree slowly, and in some instances a couple of times over.

Thomas Aggett marrying William's sister explained the part of Uncle Will being Daisy's uncle. Then William marrying Thomas' sister followed by another two marriages and an abundance of children certainly made for an intriguing, but complex family tree. I was quite in awe of my mother's rendition of Uncle Will. He certainly appeared to have been a 'busy' man. A further small twist to the family tree was my (half-) sister, Marge, marrying Harold Rooken-Smith in 1934, half-brother to Ian who became my husband in 1952. Basically, we two half-sisters married our two second-cousin half-brothers.

Daisy got up from her chair. "It's time to check the garden for fresh flowers in the vases," she said, a daily ritual of hers, our home always filled with the floral scents of copious blooms. Then she stood still a few minutes to relate to me a hunting story she'd suddenly remembered when she'd accompanied Uncle Will.

One of the African men had waded into Lake Naivasha and suddenly been taken by what Uncle Will felt certain was a huge python as the attack happened so fast and remained below water. Without the characteristic evidence of a crocodile's lunge and roll, a croc was ruled out as the culprit. As the man was pulled under the water he held his arm up, clutching in his hand a packet of cigarettes, presumably to keep them from getting wet.

Finished telling her tale, Daisy went outside into her much-loved garden paradise. I knew I'd have some nightmares about that snake story. Uncle George Aggett (Daisy's elder brother whom she was very fond of and close to), had two python skins on his dining room wall, 24 and 28 foot long! Pythons that size could easily swallow a buck so I didn't think they'd have too much difficulty expanding their jaws around a human.

There were plenty of snakes on Anchorage, especially puff adders. African rock pythons were common in the country, usually found near water. Gave me the creeps! I couldn't boast about being big and brave when it came to these reptiles even though I knew they had a purpose in the animal world. The Lake Naivasha python and cigarette packet incident reminded me of another short snake story Daisy had told me that gave me quite a few sleepless nights.

A man had come out from the UK to Kenya with his wife. She was afraid of snakes and everything, even the flies. So he decided that to try and help cure her fear of snakes he'd catch one, put it in their bedroom and then lock his wife in the room with the reptile. All of which he did. There followed a lot of furniture-scraping sounds and screaming -- then an ominous silence. The man opened the bedroom door to find his wife dead. The story ended there, with one not knowing if the snake had been poisonous or not and/or bitten the wife, or if she'd just died of fright. Now and then, I'd have troubled sleep thinking how cruel this had been, both for the man's wife and the snake. I imagined she'd desperately pulled furniture around to get away from the snake, probably jumping onto a cupboard, chest of drawers or suchlike. The snake in turn, already traumatised from being captured and now confined in a small unfamiliar space with all this sudden movement, and sensing fear, would naturally have tried to slither under the furniture to hide, or terrified perhaps tried to strike the woman.

To try to get my thoughts off the snake stuff, I deliberately cast my mind to Uncle Will and all his offspring. When I finished school, I'd hoped to follow a nursing career and envisaged William's 17 newborn children booking out an entire hospital nursery. That gave me a smile!

Personally, I would sadly never have the pleasure or opportunity of meeting William as by the time Ian and I married, his amazing father had passed on. Ian's mother, Mater, unfortunately, was unable to travel from the Cape to attend our Kenya wedding though she sent us a very generous gift of £100 (a lot of money in those days) and her best wishes.

William tells us his personal experience of a part of Kenya's history. I find his writing charming and captivating, and greatly admire his self-taught way with words:

'A Short Sketch of my first trip to East Africa

On 14th August 1906, after three days crawling through dense bush, we came out on the Southern Guaso Nyiro Plains at a place called the Masendera – a 'No-Man's land' teeming with game. I had the Kipsigis/Lumbwa Chief Kiplangat with me as gun bearer and guide. On arriving at the camping place on the edge of what seemed to be endless forest towards the north and equally endless plains to the south, the first thing I noticed was what looked like part of a broken-down sod wall about a mile to the south across a shallow valley.

After telling the cook where to have the tents pitched and a good supply of firewood collected, I took Kiplangat with me and started to go towards the sod wall. We hadn't gone more than 50 yards when I saw a milk-white Antelope standing about 100 yards in front of us. She was intently listening to the noise our boys were making. Kiplangat urged me to pikapika (*piga piga/hit-hit*) but I tried to tell him that I wanted to see the male. We stood still and admired the beautiful creature for a minute or two when at last she saw us. She seemed to drop into the earth. We went to see what had become of her when we got to the place we found that she had been standing on the very brink of a donga about 5 feet deep which was covered with a sort of long grass, so she stepped into this unseen donga and made her escape down it. I made diligent inquiries from Kiplangat and others but they had never heard of such an animal, so she was probably an Albino, but of what sort I don't know to this day. Her general appearance and the way she moved her ears was that of a young Kudu (*antelope species*) cow.

As we had left Hoey shooting pigeons a good way back, I sent Kiplangat back to camp and I went on to see the sod wall but I had gone only about half a mile when I walked into a lot of small game. I shot 2 Tomies (*Thomson's Gazelle*), 2 Grants (*Grant's Gazelle*) and 2 Robertsi (*all three being antelope species/subspecies*). They were all so close together that I dragged them into a heap and as it was getting dusk I tied my handkerchief to the big horn of a Grant thinking that the white handkerchief would keep night prowlers off. Next morning the sod wall had disappeared and so had all my bucks. All that was left of them was the forehead and horns. My hankie was tramped into the blood and stomach refuse.

When I got back to camp Hoey had bestirred himself and gone off with a few boys. I got Molo a Kaffir and one of Hoey's personal boys and also went to see what had become of the sod wall. *(Word 'kaffir' originating from Arabic for 'non-believer' – William was a staunch Presbyterian Christian – though more likely, Molo was of the Kavirondo tribe which later William spells incorrectly as 'Kaffirondo'. In 1976, South African Law would ban this word as offensive and actionable).*

On the way we heard several shots and met one of Hoey's boys coming back. He told us that Hoey had wounded 3 Wildebeeste *(antelope)*. There they were in that patch of long grass and it looked in the distance as if 2 or 3 Wildebeeste were huddled together, so I started to stalk them, but had great difficulty in keeping low down owing to having a severe cut below my left knee. Trying to cut a way for the porters I had slashed at an overhanging bough of tough underbrush which refused to yield. I made a second cut and then a desperate slash at it. The slash went through, the panga jerked out of my hand and went spinning up in the air like a boomerang, came back and stuck in my knee and from there I had to drag my left leg for about 10 days. I could not bend the knee at all without going down head first so that running was impossible.

When I got to the edge of the patch of grass I looked over and behold the Wildebeeste turned out to be a big Rhino cow with a new born calf and she had already become aware of us and was circling around her calf at a good speed and always widening the circle. I dropped on my right knee and held out my hand behind me to get my 450 express. As nothing came to hand I glanced around and saw Molo legging it as hard as he could with my gun about 300 yards away. I felt like shooting the cowardly wretch for leaving me in such a fix. I had no intention of shooting a cow with a young calf or shooting her at all unless in self-defence.

I was forced to crawl away downward dragging my left leg till I got a safe distance away then got up and followed Molo for half a mile but failed to find him. Instead I found a sort of mound in long grass and a fierce looking old Wildebeeste bull being shepherded by a young Hartebeeste cow (*antelope*) who did her best to lead the old beast away from me but always kept between him and me so that I could not get a shot at him. They kept circling around me. Whenever they were partly out of sight she started to run and tried to entice him away but he would not follow her. Then she would run back to him and place herself between us. At last I got a chance and put a 303 through him. He danced around more vigorously than ever. After a while I got another chance and gave him another 303 which seemed to have no effect. He whisked his tail and danced around faster than before.

Just then something gave me a dig behind the shoulder. The Rhino Cow's long curved horn flashed through my mind and I jumped sideways as far as my stiff leg would let me. I nearly let out a yell. On looking around I found Molo handing me my 450. I had got a terrible fright and let the animals continue their game of dancing around while I cursed Molo in the best language I knew – Dutch and English of which he didn't understand a single word. He only grinned while I told him what I thought of him. I took the gun from him and tried to kick him but failed on account of my lame leg. I then succeeded in putting a 450 bullet through the Bull's shoulders. He gave an extra flourish of his tail and dropped down dead. His guardian stood beside him till I came quite close then walked quietly away frequently looking around and stood at 100 yards.

I left Molo skinning while I went to camp and sent porters to bring the meat. The Hartebeeste cow stayed and was still there when the boys left. Now what struck me as being strange is that these animals do not inter-breed and they are seldom seen together. By what strange coincidence of nature did this devoted alliance take place? Moreover by what strange instinct did this young Hartebeeste cow sense the danger to her grisly old companion, for no mother would have been more diligently devoted to her grown-up son than she was to that surly old bull.

I have read quite a lot of hunting books by British, French and German hunters and have heard many Dutch tales of adventure but I don't remember ever reading or hearing of/any such happening as I have here related. I should like to hear of anyone having a similar experience.

On reaching camp late in the afternoon I found that Holz had also returned and complained of bad shooting. "I have fired over 20 shots and got nothing," said he. "I must be clean off shooting today".

"At what distance have you been shooting?" said I.

"At anything from 50 to 300, but it made no difference."

"Let me see your gun." He handed it to me. I remarked, "You have 500 yards sight up."

"Well I'll be hanged, I never noticed it," he said. "That accounts for my bad shooting!"

Later on our return I saw some more of my Rhino cow. I call her my Rhino cow because she was the first that I had seen at close quarters. She had an exceptionally long horn of a flattish shape and curved like a Turkish sword. A very formidable looking weapon. Again I had to try and run as best I could and got stuck in long dense grass, so I turned to shoot in self-defence and was more than glad to see her and her calf going off in the other direction.

I have skipped several notable and laughable incidents such as being lost; having to bridge the Guaso Nyiro; lions in our camp at the salt Marsh; the porters rushing our tent at midnight and getting stuck in the tent door. They fought each other at the tent entrance and squealed like a herd of pigs so that I could not get out, till a long Kaffirondo *(Kavirondo – Bantu tribe of western Kenya)* got in-between my legs and rose up suddenly which sent me slithering down his slippery back and I landed outside the tent on my hands and knees – an undignified position in which to meet lions. A laughable incident indeed!

We had plenty of game meat which I could not face and for two days we had only an ostrich egg between two of us and two more days to go. After finishing the egg we returned to the Masendera.

Homeward Bound

Next morning we were up and off by dawn. The porters' loads were light and we legged it to Kiplangat's kraal (*Dutch/Afrikaans for encircled homestead of many huts*) which we reached at dusk the second evening. I had been two full days without a mouthful of food. On reaching Kiplangat's hut, Hoey dipped into a mess of real *watu* (*indigenous peoples*) potage (*thick soup*). Hungry as I was I could not tackle it. Kiplangat, however, gave me plenty of native sterilised milk. Here I paid off Kiplangat giving him 10 Rupees instead of 5 and the game skins with which he was delighted and before we settled down for the night I gave him a big tot of pure Brandy which loosened his tongue. He told us his people were all good people, no bad talk amongst them. The grog had gone to his head and he talked on nearly all night. I had a good sleep; he was still sitting by the fire talking.

We reached Sotik Post on the evening of the second day. We were off again at dawn and crossed the floating bridge before sunrise and covered the 40 miles from Sotik Post to Kericho in a day and a half. We crossed 18 rivers in flood; 6 were native bridged and we had to strip more or less at the other 12.

Next day, we were off again early to catch the train at Lumbwa and were there in good time only having done 16 miles from Kericho to Lumbwa where I paid off the porters.

Hoey and I took the train and parted at Londiani, he going to his home and I came on to Naivasha. When I arrived at the rest-house some 5 or 6 men were enjoying their meal at a table. I called a waiter and told him I wanted a room and something to eat, but they took no notice of me. I approached the waiter twice. The third time I used pretty strong language which made them sit up and take notice. The diners also took notice.

After they had finished their meal the eldest of them, and apparently the principal man came over to my table and said, "Excuse me, my name is Bailey."

I replied, "My name is Smith."

He: "You are apparently a stranger out from England."

"I am a stranger but from the Cape Colony."

He: "What part?"

"Cathcart."

"Oh, then you will know Queenstown which is my home," and so we became acquainted.

Later he told me his mother was a Campbell from Argyle, near Alice. At present time Argyle belonged to my Dad. He turned out to be John Bailey and no relation of Tom Bailey's.

It being Saturday evening he invited me to stay over Sunday with him at his camp nearby which I did and during our talk I happened to know many people in Queenstown and Alice that he also knew. I bade Mr John Bailey of Queenstown Good-bye next day and left for Naivasha still feeling tired and decided to stay for a day or two at Naivasha.

When I got to Naivasha there was a sale or something of that sort on at the station. I enquired about the Hotel and if the Hotel-keeper was anywhere about and was told he was at the Hotel. So I strolled up to the Hotel and found nobody in attendance but an old gardener looking chap told me that the Honourable Seymour was at the station. I asked him to describe the Honourable Seymour. He did and I at once said, "That is the little fellow I saw chasing pigs and popping them into a box."

"That's him," said the old fellow, "he went to the station to send away some young pigs."

I waited and when he at last turned up I greeted him and said, "I saw you chasing pigs at the station."

"Yes," said he, "one must do something for a living." Later on he said, "There is no train tomorrow, I'll drive you out to the Government Farm about 5 miles from here."

So we decided to go out after breakfast. He had 2 mules in-spanned in a light sort of Scotch-cart and a horse in front and a leader with a long rein as lead. It was mostly downhill with big round boulders on either side of the track.

We started at a good speed being down hill without brakes. We zigzagged from one side to the other. I thought every minute we would crash on one of the big stones. I heartily wished to be elsewhere, what with missing rocks by a hair's breadth and Seymour keeping up a running fire of curses and abuse of the leader, it was the most detestable ride I ever had.

I was still tired and stayed over Tuesday. And Wednesday morning I took train for Nairobi. Next day I went to the Governor's Office intending to thank him for letting me go south and to tell him what I had seen of the Southern Guaso Nyiro Plains. I had also made a rough sketch of mountains, kopjes (*hills)* and rivers which I intended handing to the Governor but unfortunately he had gone to Uganda and his clerk did not know when he would return. As the Boat train left the next day I went straight to the Land Office and handed in my report and sketch.

They made a copy of my report and the sketch which must have been a very crude specimen as I never had even a lesson at sketching and had never tried it before. I also handed in an application for 3 farms on the Southern Guaso Nyiro Plains at a cost of £35 per farm, which pretty nearly cleared me out of cash.

Next day I boarded the Boat train for Mombasa and caught the 'Kerber' a 5,000 ton Austrian-Lloyd Boat.

There were only 8 or 10 passengers on board all from Nairobi. D.P. England Kerr a fine big handsome man with black curly hair and violet blue eyes was the most outstanding man on board. He had also been on a hunting trip. We very soon became friends. His name England Kerr struck me as unusual. He told me his Mother was English and her maiden name was England. Said he, "Kerr is a very common Scottish name, but I don't think there are many England Kerr's about."

We moved along very smoothly till we got out to the open sea then we ran into the Indian monsoon. The sea became very boisterous and lashed over the after part of the ship day and night. I was the only one on deck for 3 or 4 days. While passing Quelimane (*a port on the Mozambique coast*) I was leaning over the rail looking at the land and beach which looked above us and wondering why it seemed to be above us, when a well-known voice called me by name as plainly and distinctly as if he was standing beside me. From that minute I could not get the voice out of my head. I at once knew something unusual had happened to my old brother-in-law, Mr. W. Terwin, for he had called my name.

The reader may call it telepathy, presentiment or anything els am convinced there is more in these matters than some care to admi I have had experience of it twice before and found it quite correct.

By the time we reached Durban I was the only passenger, all the others having left at Beira and Delagoa. I had to trans-ship at Durban from the 'Kerber' to the 'Armadale'.

There were quite a lot of passengers on the 'Armadale' and more coming on. Among those coming on was one whom I noticed by his manner and speech and knew him to be a Scot of the right sort. I don't remember how we became acquainted, but it wasn't long till we became quite friendly. We seemed to take to each other like ducks take to water. He was interested in my East African experiences and we seemed to have much in common.

I happened to say late in the evening, "Well, we will be in East London tomorrow morning. I wonder if my wife will be there to meet me."

He: "If she knows you are coming she will be there to meet you all right, I know my wife would if it were me."

He then told me his own love romance which I reproduce here.

He said: "I came straight out to a General Dealer's business in Ladysmith. There was an English girl from London in the Ladies department who was there 2 years before me. She was a nice girl and I liked her from the start but being poor I was shy to make any advances so kept my feelings to myself."

After being there about 2 years the girl said to me, "Do you know the old Boss wants to sell out and retire?"

I replied, "I have heard something of it and that would probably mean a shift for one or both of us."

She replied, "You know this is a good business and one could do well here. I know you must have some money, so have I. Don't you think we could buy the business between us and carry it on? We could pay what we have got and get terms for the remainder."

I was taken aback for I had never thought of such a thing. After some hesitation I said, "I'll think it over and let you know in the morning."

When we opened the shop the next morning we met and I told her I had considered the matter and could only join her on one condition,

ue partners in every sense for first you agree to be

with my own words, "I'll think the matter over and
morning." And so we entered into partnership
than getting married.

"But first and foremost we had to approach the old Boss who was quite pleased with our suggestion and gave us his blessing by wishing us the best of luck and hoped we would never regret our bargain."

So they took over the business and got married.

Said he, "It is the best thing I ever did was to marry that girl. We have been married for 8 years. We have four children we are both exceedingly happy, and I don't think there is a finer woman in the world than my wife. We have done exceedingly well in every way. For the last 3 years I have been Mayor of Ladysmith."

We sat and talked perhaps like two kids well into the small hours of the morning, so that I slept late. When I stepped out of my Deck Cabin I saw my wife and some others going away. They had been through the under deck Cabins but failed to find me. I ran after them and brought them back.

Almost the first thing they told me was that my old brother-in-law, Mr. W. Terwin, had passed away. He was hale and hearty when I left but I was not surprised as I had a premonition when passing Quelimane. I could give several instances of these happenings.

W.R.S.

But why a final note extend
A lengthening out – a closing end
Unless it be to wish you well
Who long have listened to my tale.'

William's story describing the stealth of the lion had me realise how terrifying it must have been during the time the 'Maneaters of Tsavo' reigned terror on the railway line construction workers. The date of William's narrative below coincides with their 90-day ox-wagon journey to the Southern Guaso Nyiro Plains to take up land when they first moved to Kenya.

'Lions and their Occult Powers

It was not till February 1908 that I had any personal experience of the occult power of the lion and then I had many but shall only mention one. We had been having a strenuous time climbing the northern slope of the snow and making the road, and the day we got up the last steep pinch of the snow and went over the crest to the southern slope had been very strenuous getting up 6 wagons, 230 loose cattle and 1,200 sheep. The oxen being raw and for stocking and yoking, by the time we got all up it was already late and we were forced to camp in thick brush wood.

To protect our stock we were forced to adopt a sort of military sentry-go, at night. Our method of camping was to form a hollow square with wagons and oxen, make a skeleton kraal in the centre for the sheep and the loose cattle to lie between the tied-up oxen and wagons and the sheep, and a white man with his gun and a native with a lantern. The sentries went on in 2 hourly shifts, the first at 6 in the evening and the last at 4 in the morning.

We had got everything fixed up satisfactorily with fires around the camp and it was the sentry's duty to walk around the camp for 2 hours to keep the fires going. We had supper and it was already dark. My wife climbed up into our big tent wagon and lay down. I got up a little later and was in the act of taking off my boots when the sentry came up to the back of the wagon and spoke to me. I at once asked where his gun was.

He replied, "The native has not yet come to take the lantern."

I replied, "It is your duty to have your gun and it is also your duty to have the native with the lantern; with your slackness we will have lions in the camp."

At the same moment a cow made a strange sort of bellow. I said, "See what is wrong with that cow."

He turned around, caught the cow by the horn and said, "Her neck is broken, there he goes, there he goes."

I said, "What goes?"

"A lion!"

That lion had threaded and zigzagged his way out without disturbing a single animal. Not a beast moved. The cow had her neck broken with a single snap only 6 yards from where I was sitting and 4 yards from the sentry with the lantern. That lion zigzagged his way out among loose cattle and through the tied-up oxen.

It is a well-known fact to all who have lived in lion infested parts that game and cattle will mix freely with lions without fear and at another time cattle will go mad with fear when lions are still a long way off.

All the instances I have related point to some strange abnormal power of which we know but little.

I had a very big ox taken from under our noses, we also had dogs but nothing was known only when the ox was missing the next day; but this belongs to another story.'

W. ROOKEN-SMITH.

In 1909, Theodore Roosevelt (age 50), 26th President of the United States, headed an epic hunting safari to British East Africa shortly after completing his 2nd term in Office. He arrived by steamer at Mombasa in April that year with his 19 year old son, Kermit, the official photographer.

The nearly year-long expedition (ending 14th March 1910) led by R.J. Cunninghame (legendary hunter-tracker), was joined now and then by Frederick Selous (famous big game hunter-explorer) and included scientists and taxidermists from the Smithsonian Institute. There were 250 porters and guides who called Roosevelt, *Bwana Tumbo* (Mr Stomach). Partly funded by the Smithsonian Institute, the purpose of the hunting trip through Kenya, Uganda, Belgian Congo (now Democratic Republic of Congo) and the Nile to Khartoum was to collect specimens for the Smithsonian's new Natural History Museum (now known as the National Museum of Natural History).

This East African Smithsonian expedition amassed a total of 23,151 natural history specimens (taking Smithsonian naturalists 8 years to catalogue), more than half of which were botanical plants, as well as carnivores, ungulates, rodents, insectivores and bats. Specimens of mammals alone numbered 5,013. There was extensive coverage in the press of the expedition (plus political cartoons), and for a year a magazine (paying Roosevelt, which helped fund his portion of the trip) published monthly articles which were later put together and became Roosevelt's book, 'African Game Trails' (1910).

Roosevelt and his son, between the two of them, shot and killed 512 animals of which there were 43 birds, 17 lion, 3 leopard, 7 cheetah, 9 hyena, 10 buffalo, 37 antelope, 11 black rhino, 9 white rhino and 11 elephant (on the slopes of Mount Kenya).

In 1909 when Roosevelt made his trip to Kenya, Daisy's Aggett family ran a trading store on the Southern Guaso Nyiro Plains. Daisy's elder sister, Jane (4th born of the 9 children), used to enjoy telling the following story: Roosevelt had sent his standard-bearer ahead with the 'Stars and Stripes' banner. Having crossed the Southern Guaso Nyiro River, Roosevelt came upon the Aggett Store where he was greeted by Daisy halfway up a flag-pole unfurling the 'Union Jack'. Daisy was about 16 at the time. (Contributed by Jane's grandson, Robin Hurt).

On Page 180 of Roosevelt's book, 'African Game Trails', he refers to 'Ulyate's brother-in-law, Smith' being mauled by a lioness – this is Frank Smith (William's son).

Roosevelt gave Daisy her first lipstick. I regret now not having asked my mother more about this. During WWII, the women made lipsticks by melting down and cooling lots of old lipsticks. I only remember the gist of this as I was too young to actually understand how important this was for women. They made their own soaps as well as face creams from fresh ingredients. After WWII, all sorts of happy stuff happened like new cars, dress shops etc. I remember that Daisy had been to Nairobi and seen the Max Factor beauty salon lady who told her that her correct lipstick colour was Max Factor 'Redwood' – it was an occasion and the women flocked to Nairobi for this luxury.

Nugu's transition to young womanhood pleased me when at age 14, for my Confirmation at the Nairobi Cathedral, my white crepe dress of classic lines and veil was made by an English seamstress, Kay Beddingfield living in Ol'Kalou, who told me that I had all the curves in the right places. This was the first real compliment I ever was given about my looks and figure. I had some teenage pimples, but not badly, and thank heavens, gone was the hateful plate I'd had to wear to straighten my bottom teeth. Visiting the dentist was a nightmare for me. Apart from good straight legs, my elders said what nice eyebrows I had!

Never did my mother mention sex in any form to me. I was a farm child and had seen bulls and stallions covering cows and mares, the cat having kittens, dogs mating and the Muscovy drakes endlessly chasing their submitting wives – all this was perfectly natural to me. So, I did know to good extent the reproduction of the animal kingdom, but certainly not the human world.

I learnt about menstruation at school – the secret society of girls already menstruating. There was the 'sacred book' in which girls who'd already started their periods would write their names. If you were 'in the book' you were somebody and sort of superior. I borrowed a pad, stained it with red ink and showed it to my friend, Pansy Adams. She was dubious. When I actually did start menstruating at just over 11 years of age, it was at school. I had to see the Matron, a Mrs Smithyman, a lady we all loved, to get the necessary sanitary towels. Thereafter, my mother bought packets for me to take to school. When unable to swim, we just said to the teacher on duty, "My name is in the book." I soon learnt to call this 'the curse'. From this time on, Daisy instructed me to wash all my panties by hand (I still do, and taught my daughters the same).

In High School, our dull and drab, pale complexioned Quaker-like (because of her blunt-cut hairstyle), but good biology teacher nicknamed 'Big Hornet', Miss Joan Harnett, made a technical drawing for us of a male sperm which would eventually join up with an ovum. This we had to copy into our exercise books. Some girls thought it hilarious and heckled poor Hornet saying, "But, how does the sperm get into the ovum?" She went all red in the face and somehow managed to move on to the next subject. I felt embarrassed at the heckling, not knowing exactly why I felt so.

Shortly after first meeting Ian, he started visiting me. He'd take the weekend off from farming at Uruku (leisure time was Saturday afternoon and all of Sunday), and either ride his horse to Thomson's Falls or get a lift to the town Station. From there, he'd catch the Nairobi bound train which had to pass through our farm. When the train slowed at a certain spot on Anchorage, not far from the hippo dam, Ian would throw out his old leather suitcase and jump clear of the moving carriages. Most times the case would fly open, leaving his clothes strewn around, all the watu shouting and laughing at the hilarious sight. Then he'd tramp the half-mile to the bottom of our drive, followed by the up-hill mile to the house. Daisy was very worried Ian might injure himself with the train-jumps. The locals were always jumping on and off the daily train to suit themselves. Being a steam engine, the train was slow. Passenger cars were full with mostly Kikuyus either coming from or going back to their homelands, or simply moving to the next station.

There came a time when Ian bought an old motor-bike and visited on that. Then a second-hand Ford pick-up costing him £40 from Clive Aspinall of the Desert Locust Control, which he wrote off one night by driving into an enormous ditch about 15 miles from Anchorage. The ditch had been dug across the road with no warning signs posted for motorists. He could've been killed – the entire car fitted into the ditch!

At our Saturday night parties first held at my mother's home and eventually at the Ol'Kalou Clubhouse, my dancing partner was Dawie Van Dyk. I did love dancing the night away with him to the romantic music of the time. One of my favourite numbers was Dinah Shore's 'Buttons and Bows'. Lots of times the folks just watched us and, of course, there was always a member of the family staying on till the Last Waltz, when we all went home.

Ian was not a good dancer and tended to steer away from being dragged onto the floor. He liked to smoke and watch the goings-on instead! I had no interest whatsoever in attempting to dance with him. For the rest of his life he would not go onto the dance floor if he could avoid doing so. One night at Ol'Kalou Club, Ian punched Kali Welmans on the nose for being rude or something to our cousin 'Angel' Mary. I never did find out exactly what the problem was. In return, Ian was given a good thump on his 'trumpet'. There was a lot of blood on the back step of the Clubhouse. It was all such a scandal that our peers packed up the dancing and we all went home feeling confused about why we'd been done out of a happy evening. Ian, though, was the hero amongst the girls.

I did not really quite understand all the 'lovey-dovey' stuff (so-called in our school-girl jargon), and eventually wrote to Ian from school saying I didn't want to have this sort of correspondence, that I wanted my mother's love only. Ian got the pip with me and started looking at 'Angel' Mary. I knew that the romantic side of courtship was not clearly understood by me even though I'd been a bridesmaid 3 times. It didn't make much sense pursuing it either since I was still a scholar.

When I left school and felt more grown-up, wearing lipstick and a nurse's uniform and earning a salary of 100 shillings a month (Rand 10), Ian started courting me again during the Christmas holidays and I reciprocated with more enthusiasm. He was thoughtful and always brought us chocolates, tomatoes and various other vegetables he grew for market. Daisy received more in the way of chocolate than I did! Ian and I just seemed right for one another. We came from the same background, shared the same interests, both enjoyed fishing and loved horses and animals. It seemed natural that our fondness for one another grew quite fast into a wedding engagement, and Daisy was a happy, even busier mother planning the details.

One day, Ian asked me to wait at the bottom of the road, the mile from our house. I told my mother I was going to meet him and we'd spend the day over at Henry Hauschild's farm (whose mother was a dear friend of Daisy's) where Ian was reaping wheat on land he'd hired to make some extra cash. Early that morning, I walked the mile and sat waiting – and waiting. Luckily, I'd taken my fine embroidery with me as I'd started making items for my 'bottom draw', all sorts of table and tray cloths, place mats and dressing table sets. I can't remember feeling hungry or thirsty. In any case, I was surrounded by the most beautiful show of agapanthus and the flowering gum trees, so there was shade, and green kikuyu grass to sit on, making me well hidden from passing traffic on the secondary road. In the paddock opposite there were horses to watch. I don't remember any care, worry or fear at having to sit and wait. I wasn't at all fazed. Maybe I was in a dream-world. But, I never did this again. And, Ian never again made me wait alone like this. By about 4 in the afternoon, I returned home.

My mother only asked me, "Why did Ian not come in?"

I told her I'd waited all day and he'd never arrived to pick me up.

Neville, overhearing our conversation scathingly commented, "Silly girl!"

I didn't care. I knew I was in love. Later that evening, Ian arrived and said he'd had tractor problems, being unable to keep our appointment. He would always put work before pleasure.

By the time of our wedding, Ian had a new car, a shining black Ford Consul, making us feel very smart and modern. Mr Golding, a boarding friend of Daisy's, had loaned Ian the money to purchase the car, something which I didn't know about till later. The black Ford was decorated with white ribbons, had the usual tin can tied onto the back bumper, several lipstick-written 'Just Married' messages on the rear window, and unnoticed by us, on the car doors as well. I never did find out from Ian what happened to 'Maisie' the swanky, grey Studebaker saloon car. She may have become scrap since she was old and had travelled from South Africa to Kenya; then done a return trip, Kenya to South Africa, and back again, when Ian attended his father, William Alexander's, funeral in the Cape, East London in 1948.

As farmers, we knew it wasn't possible to spend too much time away from daily work, so arranged that our honeymoon would only be a 5 day period, booked at the Rainbow Trout Inn, a picturesque cosy little private hotel on the Kinangop. This wasn't too far from Anchorage and we could safely arrive before nightfall. Knowing very little about housekeeping or cooking, I never gave either a thought as I wouldn't be doing any on honeymoon. I was totally uninterested even though I saw how my mother and Mwangi produced wonderful food, jams and pickles etc. I reckoned I'd start cooking when I had to!

The only other words my mother ever said to me about marriage were to never let the sun set on our quarrels, and that I was never to come to her with our marital problems. I was going to live in my brand new house on my handsome husband, Ian's, farm Uruku. We'd have a family and lead a peaceful, happy life on our beautiful property with the spectacular waterfall in the garden, and a river full of rainbow trout. My children would be able to wander around amongst the farm animals and have their ponies and dogs. All would be a wonderful fairyland. We could visit my beloved mother often, and see our dear family and friends. All my teenage dreams had come true. My heart and mind were abuzz with the many wonders happening in my life. What more could any new bride wish for! I felt a warm 'pink glow' of happiness envelop me.

As a wedding gift, my mother's friend, Peggy Forrester, made 3 exquisite nightgowns for me. One was emerald green georgette with black lace insets and black satin ribbons. The other 2 were slinky, pale pink embossed satin, one with the whole bodice gathered; the other had a smocked bodice and embroidered roses all over. I looked at these delicately feminine, magical garments in wonder. I'd never before seen such beautiful luxury and hadn't known lingerie existed!

Marge fussed, prettying me in my going-away outfit. Without any knock of politeness, the door of the bedroom was suddenly flung open by my fierce Aunt May. With her raven-black dyed hair making her look even more senior than her years, she stood feet planted firmly together, back as straight as a ruler, and with one hand on the door knob, she glowered and hissed at me, "Never let your husband see you naked, it's like using someone else's toothbrush!"

I didn't move. Aunt May stood a few second as if to make sure I'd taken heed of her dire warning, then just as suddenly, about turned, and shut the door. I remembered harsh Aunt May's bedroom at her farm *Aggetton* very well. There was a large screen at the end of the bed and Uncle Alick's bedroom was far away down an extremely long passage. I wasn't very experienced myself, but I had an inkling of what did, or more precisely, what didn't go on in there!

Marge had averted her eyes and immediately started checking my honeymoon suitcase when Aunt May closed the bedroom door behind her. On finding my favourite pyjamas the local Indian tailor had made for me, she held them up, studied the worn items some moments in disdain, then discarded them on the bed, stating with an air of sisterly certainty, "You're not going to need those anymore!"

Nakedness would become a natural and comfortable part of our married intimacy and love between Ian and myself and would continue all our lives, so I never did figure out Aunt May's dire 'toothbrush' warning! Although Ian was not one for holding hands in front of others, throughout our years together we were always openly affectionate to one another with hugs, arms around shoulders or embracing. Ian enjoyed cuddling in bed and remained appreciative and respectful of my femininity whilst maintaining pride in his own neat and tidy physical appearance.

Little did I know what lay ahead, though I suppose the idyll I'd painted for us in my mind of pastoral married bliss on Uruku was worth the short while we lived it – from honeymoon to 7 months later, for self-protection, a gun would be almost as often in my hand as a baby's bottle.

Chapter Three
William's Uruku

Uruku ('u-rookoo') has no meaning as a name. Years before, Ian's father, William, dreamt he saw these letters on the rock face behind the Pesi River Falls on the farm and decided to give the property this name.

We'd planned that the front of our new Uruku homestead, which we started building during our engagement, faced the waterfall. Though it couldn't be seen from the house, one could hear the constant flow of water over the edge which gave a soothing background sound to daily life. To view the Pesi River Falls, you had to walk across grey stone outcrops then into forest glade. We hoped to create gardens stretching from the house to the magnificence of the cascading water with its showering misty spray, 40 feet wide with a 60 foot drop into a huge pool where there were plenty of wild rainbow trout.

Happy and excited to be starting our life together at last, we set off from our wedding reception in our shiny black Ford Consul, stopping at the impressive Simba Bridge canyon to wipe off the 'just-married' lipstick messages en route to the Brown Trout Inn for our honeymoon. Neither of us had ever stayed in any form of hotel, funds for such luxuries being beyond the financial reach of our average family living standards. So this event in itself seemed quite incredible to us, adding a further dimension of wonder to the overwhelmingly amazing wedding day our families had so generously given us. And we certainly wouldn't be disappointed.

The Brown Trout Inn was surrounded by stunning high-altitude gardens with a trout river running a hand's breadth away, and the large, chintzy en suite bedroom had a fireplace and chimney, several windows and a real eiderdown on the luxurious bed. Each evening at 6.30, a silent and efficient attendant came to light a roaring cedar-wood fire, close the drapes and prepare the bed for our retirement after a delicious dinner. There was a desk under one window where I sat in the sunny afternoons writing all our thank you letters, while Ian took time off to go trout fishing. Whatever he caught, all of which was pan-sized fish, was handed in at the kitchen and later served to us as a fried dinner course.

Ian was a good fisherman, whether freshwater or sea angling and it was always a real relaxation for him. I never was any good at trout fishing, so I spent lazy mornings feeling very spoilt, swanning around our suite in my new luxurious lingerie and kept admiring myself in the several long mirrors: this just wasn't me! I indulged in leisurely hot baths, and once dressed I spent time walking around the beautiful English country gardens, chatting to the other guests and excitedly awaiting Ian's return for lunch.

Having wiped off the just-married lipstick writings on our car we felt confident that no-one at the Inn would guess we were newly-weds. One morning, Ian went to the Ford to get some extra tackle as he'd lost several fishing flies. He discovered to his dismay that the dirt road dust had accumulated quite thickly and stuck to the oily lipstick residue left on one of the car doors, now to be seen in a distinctive grey colour against the black bodywork of the Ford. The car had been parked in a garage behind the Inn. Not noticing the give-away dusty grey writing residue till now (what we thought was our well-kept secret), our hosts had, because from the morning after our arrival they made an obvious effort to spoil us. Ian hurriedly arranged for a bucket of water and brush and thoroughly washed the car himself. We were a very shy young couple.

Ian especially, was anxious to get back to Uruku. Our 5 days of honeymoon had been idyllic, with every wonderful luxury possible and no expense spared. We'd have to call in at Anchorage as my dog, Giftie, and cats, Quizzie and Simon were coming to their new home too. I understood that we'd had our leisure and celebration time and back to the reality of farming was what really counted. As we both well knew and had been taught by our parents, 'money didn't grow on trees' and if you didn't devote yourself to working constantly for your living, quite simply you wouldn't 'eat'. As a husband now, and as was custom in those days, Ian had assumed full responsibility from Daisy for taking care of me as his wife. Gladly and freely, I gave him the balance of the £750 in my bank account to put towards the building of our lives together. Daisy had also ensured that Ian took out a life policy with me as beneficiary in case anything should happen to him so that I would be taken care of financially.

We returned enthusiastically to our incomplete house on Uruku designed to be pleasurable and spacious for children. The attractive grey stone blocks had been quarried from the stone outcrops and a Sikh, Mr Tara Singh from Ol'Kalou, both a mason and carpenter employed for the building project, would do a wonderful job, very pleasing to both of us. The old farmhouse made of wood and corrugated iron roofing where Ian had been born, was dismantled and the materials were transported across the river to be used in our new home. This meant driving down to the Pesi River bank, descending a fairly gentle slope then entering the water at its shallowest and widest part where the river bed was solid rock. One had to proceed slowly across because of the very large loose pebbles. On the other side was a really steep bank then a drive through some cedar forest before coming upon a clearing where stood our almost completed homestead. Scenically, it was an absolutely beautiful site, though we'd realise later that from a security point of view it hadn't been the best choice of location.

Ian would often climb down to the waterfall pool and catch our fish supper which I'd pan fry on a primus stove. At the back of the house was cedar forest; at the front a glade of cedar and exceptionally big Podo trees (also known in South Africa as 'yellow wood') along the river. To begin with, Ian and I lived in the garage and 2 storerooms. Eventually, we were able to make a real home and had the joy and renewed surprises of again unpacking all our wedding presents.

It was essential that we have hot water in our new home. Under Ian's supervision, Mr Singh installed a water heating system of the type common on farms and which Daisy had on Anchorage. We'd never been short of hot water for ablutions, cooking and various other purposes all the years I could remember going back to my childhood. A simple yet absolutely reliable hot-water system, it consisted of a brick and concrete structure with a bottom, two sides, and a closed back with a chimney. The front of the structure was left open specifically in which to place wood logs for a fire that was kept burning most of the time except during late night hours when the wood burnt down to embers making it easy to restart the fire in the morning. A cleaned 200 gallon steel oil drum placed horizontally above the fire was supported on metal struts with cold water piped into the drum at the base and hot water piped from the top to the kitchen and bathroom. A 15 foot high steam escape pipe was fitted as a safety measure to ensure that the drum would not burst.

Since both of us had been born to elderly parents, Ian and I decided to start a family soonest possible not wanting to repeat the enormous age differences between our parents and ourselves. By July, I was a positive pregnancy. Now my days were filled with plans for the coming new baby, exercises and reading several childbirth books. Tommy Burrows from Carlisle (on the border of Scotland and England), had been a convalescing soldier at Anchorage during the war. As a gift, he sent us a Beatrix Potter frieze for the baby's room decoration. Marge and family gave us the necessary bassinet and pram. Other family gave us second-hand quality baby clothing. Mrs Cheshire, a friend of my mother's, made a beautiful satin baby's eiderdown, blue on one side, pink on the other.

We employed a houseman who'd approached us asking for work. He was a Kikuyu named Mwangi (like Daisy's Mwangi, this being a common Kikuyu name). Mwangi was the nicest person imaginable, keen and willing to learn all he could in his new position, respectful, neat and tidy in his person. An all-round good man, but unlike Daisy's Mwangi, he hadn't learnt to cook before. This was not an issue at all as it was high time I tried. Many times in my newly married life when it came to preparing food, I thought about how I'd taken Daisy and Mwangi's cooking and baking for granted and shown no interest or made any attempt myself. Without doubt, Mwangi's pancakes were the best. I wondered if I'd ever manage to match them. And, his abilities in the kitchen to make scrumptious edibles didn't end there. He baked the lightest of sponge cakes. I couldn't remember a time Daisy's Mwangi hadn't been part of my life when I was growing up and never an occasion of anything except absolute loyalty, kindness and caring from him. I loved Daisy's Mwangi.

Ian was very critical of his two fried eggs. They had to be perfect, the white solid and the yolk runny. A broken yolk meant frying another egg in its place. Breakfast was an important meal in our home and I was on a cooking learning curve. Once, when Ian's fried eggs weren't 'just right', he picked up the wedding gift silver salt-cellar and threw it on the floor. It still has one squiffy leg! I said nothing, neither did he – I simply picked up the salt-cellar, wiped it off and put it back on the centre of the table where it would remain all our lives. Ian would not only have to see it, but also use it daily! The 'flying salt-cellar' didn't spark any argument between us. We went to bed that night as much in love as we'd been when we'd woken up in the morning!

I tried bottling fruit since we had plenty of pineapples available at the Indian *dukas* (shops) in Thomson's Falls. This was disastrous as I never made the Kilner jars hot so when I put in the boiling fruit, the jars simply shattered. In my early married days and for some years afterwards, I relied on the Kenya Cookery Book and Household Guide, compiled by members of St Andrew's Church Woman's Guild. It was a great help and recommended for every Kenyan kitchen. There were easily understood recipes with no fancy trappings, tips and hints for most situations from cleaning to coping with poisons. Any cooking disasters I simply kept to myself! But my mother's excellent, much-used and worn 'The Practical Cookery Book for South Africa', 24th Edition written by Mrs S van Tulleken of the Transvaal (now a collector's book) and prefaced by Mrs Isie K Smuts of Irene, 11th August 1923, taught me almost all I know about cooking.

We had a new wood stove that only our Mwangi, a quick and clever man, knew how to work, Ian having shown him. It seemed also that I never had the time to stay by the stove and keep feeding it fast burning cedar wood. Being perceptive, Mwangi noticed and thoughtfully kept the fire going. Mostly, he helped to clean up, sweep and polish floors, scrape the putty from window glass with a razor blade then polish the panes, chop wood and make the dog food as the house still wasn't completely finished. In my new expectant condition, and as Ian was out most of the day creating his farm, I depended on Mwangi a great deal and we became fond of him. I hoped he'd be able to stay with us as our family grew. Perhaps our children would have the pleasure of growing up with him just as I'd had with Daisy's Mwangi. Occasionally, Ian and I would go to Ol'Kalou to see Daisy or Marge and Harold.

My world had been so transformed since we'd married and I'd gone to Uruku with Ian as his wife. Sometimes, I'd quietly marvel to myself at all the amazing happenings. The growing changes within my body were a physical and visual reminder of the many new responsibilities I now had, plus the wonderful and exciting challenges that lay ahead.

Apart from Giftie and our cats and guard dogs, Uncle George Aggett (one of my favourite uncles), living on the farm *Mutara* not far from us at Uruku, gave us a hen parrot called *Kasuku* (parrot in Swahili) who'd been in the family for about 30 years. She was an African Grey, best of all parrots for talking and imitating, and certainly kept us amused. Kasuku used to sing the nursery rhyme, 'Pop goes the Weasel', and say, "*Taka nini?*" (What do you want?), every time Mwangi walked past her on the back verandah during the day. At night, she slept in her covered cage in our bedroom. Kasuku could copy the sound of the squeaky back door, the dogs barking and the meow of the cats. Quite often, she'd imitate Uncle George farting which had Ian and me in stitches with laughter!

By now, we had farm fowls for daily fresh eggs. They were kept in a chicken-run at night and I fed and collected the eggs. We also had an increasingly huge flock of geese living on the river just above the Falls.

During WWI (1914 – 1918), British statistics initially put the Kings African Rifles at 70 British Officers; 3 non-Commissioned Officers and 2, 325 Africans – by the end of the war 1,193 British Officers; 1,497 non-Commissioned Officers and over 30,000 Africans. 24,000 Kenyans lost their lives. 163,000 Africans served during the war as carriers for food and weapons also acting as ambulances and taxis in war zones, of whom 4,300 were killed by enemy fire at battle fronts in comparison to the staggering 42,318 who perished from diseases of whom approximately 76% died due to influenza.

The Germans constantly plotted to bomb the Kenya-Uganda Railway so as to defeat the British. Thankfully, this did not happen.

My Aunt Ethel (Daisy's younger sister), gave me her handwritten tribute to the WWI memory of Russell Bowker, buried on the mountain summit of Mt Margaret in the Kedong Valley. Aunt Ethel and my mother often spoke to me of Russell Bowker, a war legend in Kenya, saying he always wore a cap made of leopard skin with its real teeth in the front. (His great-grandson, Russell Bowker-Douglass lives in Australia). I don't know who authored the tribute:

WORLD WAR 1914 – 1918

Pioneers from South Africa, hardy and strong
Here at last the chance you have been wanting so long,
If you are eager and keen for a bit of a scrap
You must follow the leader of the
"Leopard Skin Cap"

So it's snatch up your rifle, and saddle your steed
We must gallop to succour brave comrades in need.
And be sure German knuckles will soon get a rap
If it comes to a tussle with
The "Leopard Skin Cap"

We can go on short rations, we'll have to I fear,
We can hardly get biscuits, much less beef and beer.
Who looks after supplies?
I must teach that young chap he's got to look after
The "Leopard Skin Cap"

We know how to take cover – can shoot just a bit,
And we don't overload with superfluous kit.
No! there isn't much chance of a snooze or a nap
When you're under the command of
"The Leopard Skin Cap"

So it's through to Tabora and on to the Lake.
There is a lot of good country it will pay us to take,
In the ranks of our foes, there'll be many a gap
If they think they can tackle
The "Leopard Skin Cap"

Here's to our leader, who's aye to the fore,
Fighters for water in peace-time, his country in war

And I've no less doubt of a large piece of the map
When it meets with the men of
The "Leopard Skin Cap"

The horrors of war leave their painful and traumatic scar, particularly on those who serve or suffer injury, and cut short the futures of so many who give their lives in wartime so that others may live in peace. I wonder how the British forces in Africa would have fared in WWI without the African carriers. It is my personal belief that all who serve should be recognised equally.

William's son, Willie (William Aggett Smith, 4th born of 8 from the *first litter*) was shot and killed by a German sniper at Longido during WWI, as were 9 others, all buried in one large grave. The sniper, rumour has it, was said to be an Afrikaner who'd fought in the Boer War then sided with the Germans in German East Africa (later to become Tanganyika then Tanzania). WWI history records a battle against the Germans at Longido in the Kilimanjaro area on 3rd November 1914. Longido is a small town in the Arusha Region of (present day) Tanzania, at the foot of Mount Longido. William shares with us in a poem his feelings of heartache at the death of Willie. The 'two at Rooken lea' refer to William's 2 other children who died at a young age, Beatrice Ellen (6th born from the *first litter*, age 7) and George Peebles (2nd born from the *second litter*, died during infancy) who were both buried on the farm *Rooken*.

'IN MEMORIAM

My people are scattered far and wide,
By mountain stream and sea;
Oh God protect them by Thy might
Wherever they might be.

Four are in cemeteries laid,
And two at Rooken lea*,
And one, who fought at Longido Hill,
Lies there beneath a tree.

The young lion will roar
When his kill is o'er;
And the zebra stampede in fear;
The hyena may howl,
And the jackal yell,
But will our Willie hear?'

**Note: 'lea' is a grassland meadow.*

Ian recalled well the story as told to him by his father (as do many other family members, and which is printed in the Family History), that whilst William and a party of men, including George Aggett, were searching for Willie's grave in the Longido area, the following incident occurred:

'Everyone had settled down for the night sleeping in the open around the camp fire. George Aggett, who always slept with his arms above his head and under the pillow, was awakened by a foul smell. On opening his eyes, he looked straight into those of a lion which was standing over him! He whipped the pillow from under his head and hit the lion which roared and leapt away. Everyone was awake instantly, and needless to say no-one slept again that night. The men kept the fire well stoked and the pride of lion kept their distance, but did not move off until daylight.'

William returned to South Africa in 1918, and farmed at Queenstown in the Eastern Cape, as well as at Umtata in the Transkei. But his great love of Kenya, aptly reflected in his words below, would draw him back to the country about 11 years later:

'LINES ON MT. KENYA
Eastward Kenya rears his shoulders high,
His frozen crest against the sky;
And at his feet the Guaso Nyiro
Winds through mimosa park and meadow.
When the western setting sun
Has cleared the snow-cloud dark and dull,
Kenya stands out bold and clear –
Veteran of many a changing year!
To me, there is something awesome in the sight,
When seen by the sun's wavering light,

Of the Great Creator's wondrous might;
He who created that mountain old
Ages and ages ere the world grew cold;
Or cold enough for snow to lie
On Kenya's hoary head so high.
And on Kenya's western face
Many deep scars there you may trace,
And many more, you may never know,
That lies between the forest and the snow.
A wild waste or solitude;
Of tall grass and scanty wood,
The home of beasts fierce and wild,
Where man seldom dares to intrude,
For the mists may gather at any time
Just above the forest line,
And rushes up the mountain side
With the speed of coming light
And enshroud all in a cloud of night.
And those scars, both deep and long,
Are rushing torrents fierce and strong:
Caused by the ever-melting snow,
That feeds the Guaso Nyiro far below –
A silent river that on-ward glides
Through rocks and foliage she seems to steal
With scarcely a murmur
And northward holds her course
Till she reaches Archer's Post,
Then turns eastward with little pomp
And loses herself in the Lorian Swamp.'
by William Alexander Rooken-Smith

After WWI there was a depression, but despite this set-back, the country once again rapidly progressed, becoming known as a Crown Colony. The entire strip of the Kenya coastline, reaching 10 miles inland including the island of Mombasa, was leased from the Sultan of Zanzibar, and remained as a Protectorate under the title of the Kenya

Protectorate. A new deepwater dock was built at Kilindini, and a further 2 were started in 1927. By the early 1930s, these new berths plus 2 more were completed, making a total of 5 of the finest on the whole coastline from Durban in South Africa to Port Said in Egypt. Then an oil pier was commenced. The railway lines had reached every centre, right through to Kampala, capital of Uganda, giving direct communication with Mombasa – so came into being the Railways and Harbours of East Africa.

A 1936 Kenya population census estimated 3,261,522 inhabitants, including 18,269 Europeans; 41,835 Asians and 12,855 Arabs (2013 = 44,611,813 with 1% being non-African – Asian, Europeans and Arabs). On the coast the Arab and Swahili races predominated; further inland were the Bantu speaking peoples, and the non-Bantu tribes such as Maasai, Somalis and the Galla. Christian mission stations representing 13 societies, namely British, French, Italian, Swedish, American and Roman Catholic had schools for elementary education and handcrafts. On the coast, Mohammedanism (Islam) was and remains the principle religion. Mombasa (Kenya's second largest city) is located on the south coast. Known as Mombasa Island, it is set on a coral island separated from the mainland by a creek on either side – Tudor Creek, and Kilindini Harbour (western side). Mombasa Old Town with its arabesque mystique, ancient port and Fort Jesus are on the eastern side of the island.

In rural areas, councils were established for roads, health, veterinary departments, hospitals and clinics. The main towns had Government hospitals, fully equipped clinics, doctors and nursing staff. Primary and secondary schools were built, as well as a number of private schools.

Malaria was a principal health hazard, but was preventable in some measure with quinine, and much later, related drugs, and was treatable if caught in time.

Another preventative method was the regular spraying of houses, huts, vegetation and gardens with DDT (years later found to have some serious negative side-effects). Daisy sprayed the air in her home every evening using a flit-pump containing a bought mixture that had a distinct paraffin and disinfectant smell as there were no aerosols in those days. The spray killed any mosquitoes and other insects. Usually done at 6 in the evening, the rooms were closed for a period before being used. At that time we didn't have mosquito nets.

Tourism flourished. *Safari* is a Swahili word, now widely used, especially when undertaking long trips. Sport fishermen could angle for Rainbow trout on the western slopes of the Aberdare Mountains or Brown trout on the eastern slopes. Black bass were found in dams and lakes. The coastal deep-sea fishing became legendary and an industry. Game Parks and a Marine Park were established and became famous in their own right, many books being written on the subject. The country became sensational, tourism being the biggest fiscal revenue earner for the Government. Nairobi's Embakasi Airport opened in 1958, and was replaced in 1978 with a new structure, Jomo Kenyatta International Airport.

Coffee, sisal, dairy products, wheat, vegetables, flowers, pyrethrum, pineapples, other fruits and many more crops, too numerous to mention, were planted and reaped, including for export. All types of livestock were imported. There were great activities in the agricultural sphere, with Royal Shows.

This was a great progressive country, which had everything from fertile land to moderate climate and good people, from all walks of life and different cultures, who contributed in some way or another to building the country and moving it forward. Farmers, from all nationalities, on the whole, had no interest in politics, and were dedicated, diligent and caring. Together with their staff and labourers, without whom the agricultural sector could not have achieved such success, they were immersed in nation-building. Real and great successful industries were created. Beef, Pork, Dairy and Cheese Boards were managed by elected committees which took in all that the country could and did produce.

Labourers had their specific jobs, jealously guarded. Normal work days started at 7 in the morning, known as 'the first hour', and ended at 3 in the afternoon, with breaks for meals. *Syces* (grooms) were employed to take care of everything to do with horses though stallions and bulls, because of their nature, had their own grooms. Dairies, operating at least twice daily, had their own milking staff. Piggeries had their workers; calves and sheep their own herdsmen. Beef and dairy cattle were never left unattended in case of problems with bloat or snakebite; the herdsmen would immediately alert the farmer who'd take the necessary action.

On the agricultural side, drivers were in charge of specific tractors. *Shambas* (fields) of maize were kept clean after harrowing by hand-workers, usually women, and later on crop-spraying was introduced against borer beetle.

In homesteads, the cooks were kings in their own domain, baking bread and cakes, roasting meat and so forth, many times assisted by an appointed youngster run-around known as a *toto jikoni.* Usually, households had one main houseman (not the cook or toto jikoni). Housemen were stylishly dressed on special occasions (like Daisy's Mwangi was for our wedding) in a plain white cotton ankle length robe known as a *kanzu* (like a kaftan), coloured *cummerbund* (red or green broad waist band), and red, black or green *fez* (small, neat and round brimless hat with one large tassel). They maintained the homes on a daily basis, set and waited on tables, and were proud of their many abilities (no mean feat with various tasks) to do with running an efficient, neat and clean homestead. Recognition of achievement was important – not only were staff proud of their accomplishments, employers were also proud of their staff. I only have to think of my mother in this regard, as with so many other family members and friends of family, who were genuinely and sincerely proud of their staffs' accomplishments and rewarded such achievements.

Ayahs (nannies) were in charge of the children, going everywhere the parents went. They too were recognised as an important support system in daily life. Most employers dressed their ayahs in various plain-coloured knee-length frocks that buttoned-up at the front, with matching aprons and headscarves (worn in the African custom), and comfortable shoes (the latter bought from Bata). Later, ayahs preferred the new imports made of durable plastic.

Drivers took care of cars. Many staff stayed years in the same employment. Farm workers (with approval of their employers), cultivated land on the farms where they were employed, enabling them to grow potatoes, sweet potatoes, spinach, peas, pumpkin and maize the year round, and were allowed to keep sheep and poultry as well. Members of extended families also resided with employees.

The Bride Price was recognised, accepted and respected as the way marriages were conducted by tribal laws. The requirements of money, property, livestock or services were given by the bridegroom to the future father-in-law or to his family, in order to establish rights over the bride-to-be. A tremendous amount of bargaining took place between elders of the respective families. It was quite customary for men to have a number of wives, and in those days a wife bore a second child usually after the first child's second birthday. It was noted that while a woman was breast-feeding, it was taboo for her husband to enter her hut. Other wives attended to his needs, hoed and planted his shambas, took care of the livestock and kept the 'home' fires burning. I never met or knew of anyone among our family, friends or associates, while I lived in Kenya, who interfered with tribal customs, apart from the missionaries who brought Christianity. They tried and succeeded in part, to indoctrinate the indigenous peoples with their ideals of western customs, cultureand religion.

Uncle George Aggett (born 29.04.1891), who'd lived with the Maasai as a blood-brother and spoke their language Maa fluently, was also fluent in Swahili, Samburu, Kipsigis and Kikuyu, as well as Afrikaans (a South African language) and English. Uncle George always dressed in khaki bush-jacket and long trousers which he changed twice a day. Aunt Preto was a stickler for cleanliness so these outfits were washed and starched by hand then ironed to perfection by the *dhobi* (laundry man). Uncle George always looked smart and smelled so nice, just like my father. While on a trip to California USA where he'd gone to visit their daughter, Yvonne, the kids followed Uncle George down the street, so I was told, calling him something like Buffalo Bill because of his outfit and bush-hat.

William returned to Kenya from South Africa in 1929 and lived at Uruku. He played doctor and midwife rolled into one when he delivered his 3rd wife, Mater, of their 4th child – being William's 17th and last child, his youngest son, my husband, Ian. Accounts of William never cease to amaze me. Prior to Ian's birth, it had been decided that when the time came, Aunt May living at Aggetton 50 miles away, would attend Mater as midwife for the confinement. The doctor would be fetched from Rumuruti, 40 miles in the other direction. Quite often in life, even the best thought-out plans go awry; babies arrive when they must, regardless of whatever else is happening.

That year 1930, Kenya, and particularly the Laikipia area, had torrential rains. The roads were practically impassable. Mater went into labour. William sent Harold (aged 18, from William's *second litter*) to fetch Aunt May in William's car (the model before the Model A Ford). It was a very slow vehicle with flimsily made bodywork, no hood and was operated by way of a peculiar set of gears, rods and suchlike to make it move. Marge described this as, "Not being a car for travelling on Kenya roads." She was 15. At the same time, but headed in the opposite direction, William sent Lex (Harold's elder brother) to fetch the doctor from Rumuruti. Lex was in his own car, a Model A Ford *chorrie* (word commonly used by us to describe the Model A and B Fords – *chorrie* originating from Afrikaans *tjor* meaning in English *crock* for a car that is old or decrepit). The roads were horrendous and everyone arrived back too late. It was 5th June 1930 – William had delivered their baby boy, Ian – a rare occasion when Aunt May's highly esteemed nursing skills hadn't been required after all.

Due to ill-health, William went back to South Africa in about 1932 with Mater and their 3 sons, Gordon, Ron and Ian, and bought the farm *Ocean View* in the Komga area, not far from East London. Their 1st child, a daughter Janet (born 03.04.1922), had died of diphtheria at the age of 4; Gordon (born 05.12.1924) would die in 1935 of peritonitis. I can only imagine the grief Mater and William felt to lose 2 of their children so young. Certainly William again suffered an immense sense of loss now having 5 of his children pass on - Beatrice Ellen, George Peebles, Willie, Janet and Gordon. With his health deteriorating, William sold Ocean View and bought *Gonubie Manor* on the Gonubie River at the coast near East London. When even this proved too much for him and with Ron and Ian away at school, Gonubie Manor was sold and they bought a house in Vincent, a suburb of East London.

WWII (1939 to 1945) the approximate total number of Colonial forces from Africa was 1,355,347 (also referred to as 'Africa's forgotten soldiers in WWII') – of whom, British forces numbered 334,000 from South Africa; 289,530 King's African Rifles (Kenya, Tanzania, Uganda and Malawi); Egypt 100,000; from Southern Africa 77,767 (being Lesotho, Botswana, Swaziland, Zambia, Rhodesia); and 6,500 from Mauritius and the Seychelles. The balance were from: France (Vichy and Free French) Colonial troops 190,000 (being Algeria, Senegal, Mali, Burkina Faso, Benin, Chad, Guinea, Ivory Coast, Niger, and Republic of Congo); Italy (Eritrean colonial troops) 60,000; Independent 30,000 (Abyssinia/Ethiopia – Patriots); and Belgium (Congo) 24,000.

98,240 Kenyans were recruited as *Askaris* into the King's African Rifles, 30% of the unit's total strength. The vast majority of Kenya soldiers, most of whom were volunteers, were African – due to British Army policy, they weren't able to rise above rank of Warrant Officer. Kenyan soldiers served in the successful East African Campaign against the Italians to the north of Kenya's border in Italian East Africa, where at the start of the war Italian forces numbered 250,000 compared to 2,900 men from the King's African Rifles. They were responsible for the defence of the whole of British East Africa together with the Somaliland Camel Corps and Sudan Defence Force. Significant numbers of captured Italian POWs (Prisoners of War) were interned in Kenya camps and used in civil infrastructure projects. Daisy would have some of them stay in our Anchorage home. The 1939/40 drought in Kenya (known as the 'famine of the Italian') encouraged peoples from the *Akamba* tribe to enlist. Kenyans also served in the Royal Navy and Royal Air Force as well as in Madagascar and Burma (against the Japanese), alongside troops from West-Africa.

In 1942, the entire British Eastern Fleet transferred to Kilindini near Mombasa. Supplying significant quantities of tea and tobacco, Kenya was a source of important agricultural products in the British Empire.

Hudson Boyce Aggett, youngest child of 2 sons born to Daisy's eldest of 3 brothers, Ted Aggett (married to Claire/Aunt Bon), died during WWII on the Troopship SS Khedive Ismail. The turbine steamship, originally built as an ocean liner in 1922 was converted into a troop carrier in 1940. Daisy often spoke of this tragic death in her Aggett family.

On 5th February 1944, with 1,511 people aboard, the Khedive Ismail left Kilindini Harbour, Mombasa as part of Convoy KR-8 to Colombo, Ceylon. Saturday, 12th February 1944, in the afternoon between 2 and 3 o'clock in the One-and-a-Half Degree Channel south-west of the Maldives, some passengers were on deck sunbathing having had lunch, though most were below watching a concert when a lookout sighted a periscope port side, the submarine positioned to attack. Khedive Ismail's DEMS gunners opened fire at the same time the Japanese sub fired 4 torpedoes, 2 hitting the Troopship. With her stern in roaring flames and smoke she broke in two, sinking in under 3 minutes. With no time to launch lifeboats, those below deck had little chance of survival. Aboard were 996 members of the East African Artillery's 301st Field Regiment, 271 Royal Navy personnel, 19 WRNS, 53 nursing sisters and their matron, 9 members of the First Aid Nursing Yeomanry and a war correspondent.

Loss of life 1,297 being 77 women and 1,220 men, was the 3rd largest from Allied shipping in WWII and the worst single loss of British servicewomen. The Japanese sub was immediately hunted by the Destroyers HMS Petard and Paladin and a two-and-a-half hour battle ensued during which Paladin lowered a motorboat and sea boat to pick up survivors from the Khedive Ismail. Tragically, some who'd survived the original sinking and were still in the water lost their lives or were wounded due to the shallow but necessary depth charges. When the sub was forced to surface, Paladin moved to ram her at high speed when Petard signalled that it was a Type B1 sub, considerably larger than the destroyer. In trying to take avoiding action, too late, Paladin suffered a glancing blow which ripped a 15 foot gash in her hull from the sub's hydroplanes. Eventually, the submarine was blown in half when a 7th torpedo from Petard made its mark. The 2 halves of the sub upended and sank with all hands.

Survivors and crew scrambled to transfer from Paladin to Petard. For 36 hours, Petard towed the destroyer to Addu Atoll to ready her for the long voyage to South Africa for repairs. Major Aggett, Hudson Boyce 322300 – United Kingdom General List (born 11.06.1913) was 30 years old – Memorial Column 7, East Africa Memorial Kenya. I shudder to think what would have become of the world and the 'free life' of humanity had Hitler attained his goals and the Allied forces not won.

The 5th February would be a significant date in our Aggett family. Not only was it the day the Khedive Ismail sailed from Mombasa in 1944, it was also the same day that Ted and Claire's eldest son, Aubrey Aggett, married Joy Norman in Johannesburg, South Africa. The newly-weds returned to Aubrey's farm at Nanyuki, Kenya, where they had 3 children – Michael, Jill and Neil Hudson.

William, in South Africa, fell off his horse at the age of 93 and did not really recover from a severely broken hip. Having kept copious journals throughout his life, he now spent most of his time lying down writing or re-writing stories, some of which were typed up, presumably, by Mater. William died on 18th October 1948, a few weeks short of his 94th birthday. Mater adored William and always referred to him as, "Daddy." She never remarried. The house in Vincent being too big for her alone, she sold it and bought a ground floor flat with a small balcony in East London.

I wish to thank William here for his marvellous writings on Kenya, and share a last poem of his on the Aberdares, the mountains we too loved so much. The Aberdares would temporarily play a huge role in our lives from 1952 with considerable traumatic impact on the daily life of many other Kenyans as well.

'THE ABERDARE
Southward the massive Aberdare
Heaves his rugged forehead bare
And often for a while
Seems to either frown or smile,
Caused by the light or wandering shade
That flits across the forest glade.
Here Buffalo or Elephants roam
Far above the settler's home
And in bamboo forest feel secure
Against the raid of their pursuer;

And the Hunter, however bold,
Will pause ere entering that stronghold,
For he already knows full well
The might of those that inward dwell;
And should he venture further in
The advantage lies with those within.
Bamboos swaying far wide
Like rollers of the ocean tide,
Or like waves of a restless sea,
With here and there a cedar tree,
Or like fields of ripening corn
Moved by the early breeze of morn.
A fairer view, it were hard to find
Than Bamboo and woolly wood combined
As round the summits they gracefully wind,
And here are many dusky bowers
Where Bongo spend the daylight hours
And venture forth with evening shades
To graze along the open glades,
Then vanish at the first dawn of morn,
As if the light they fear or scorn,
And stealth-fully hide in the thicket green,
An ample and darksome screen.
Such is the life the Bongo leads.

On Kinangop's high and misty meads,
And on Aberdare's eastern breast,
At times so peaceful and at rest,
Yet holds the Buffalo for its guest,
Fiercest of all the woodland game
That ever roamed o'er hill or plain
Crashing the Bamboo with his pace,
The African Buffalo holds first place.
The tracker and hunter by profession
Could ill resist such strong temptation –
The lure of Ivory and its possession –

Had dulled all better or wise discretion.
He there follows up his quest
Hoping they will take their noontide rest
A fierce old Buffalo senses danger from afar
And at once prepares for immediate war.
Hard by a steep and noisy rill
Rushing from its parent hill,
The Buffalo stands motionless and still.
Behind a cedar he had ta'en his stand
Hidden by many a leafy wand
And watches the hunter advance, gun in hand.
The hunter pauses near the tree
And wonders where his quest may be.
He carefully scans the scene around,
His eye and mind are on the ground
As if that fresh spoor could tell
How far they may be up the dell.

The Buffalo charges like a flash
And to the earth the hunter dashed.
His force and speed down the hill
Carries him past his mark against his will.
The hunter snatched his gun and hat
And limped some paces further back
And hid behind the very tree
And waited for what he hoped to see;
Nor had he long to wait
Ere Buffalo merged from Bamboo brake
In fiercer mood than before.
He glanced the place hast'ly o'er
A moment darted here and there,
A moment searched every where,
A moment stopped to sniff the air.
The rifle rapped out its deadly knell
And in turn the Buffalo fell.
One long bellow and deep moan

Proved his fierce life was passed and gone:
For no life has yet had power
To withstand the rifle's leaden shower
When directed by a practised eye and hand –
No living thing can its power withstand.
The hunter rises stiff and sore
And looks his fallen foeman o'er
And deep the oath he inward swore:
In Bamboo forest to hunt no more.'
by William Alexander Rooken-Smith

Kenya's Mountain Bongo antelope, also known as Eastern Bongo, is now critically endangered, hunted for its striking reddish-brown coat with white vertical stripes. Only about 100 of them remain in the wild. They are found in the Aberdares Conservation Area, the Mau Forest, and Mt. Kenya National Park, and are fully protected by the Kenya Wildlife Service.

1952 was a significant year for us, though not only because of our marriage. Ian was working so hard to build a future for us on Uruku. This particular year would coincide with the start of troubled times to come.

King George VI died on 6th February 1952 whilst young Elizabeth was on holiday in Kenya at Tree Tops with her husband Philip, Duke of Edinburgh. She was crowned Elizabeth II the same year, remains on the throne in 2016 and is the longest reigning member of the British monarchy. True to her word, she has devoted her life to serving her people.

Uruku's nearest town and railhead was Thomson's Falls about 30 miles away. During the wet weather the road on most occasions was impassable. Horses – I remember Peter a tall chestnut gelding from Uncle George's stock – were the only sure way of getting to all the most inaccessible parts where no vehicle could go.

In 1948, William gave Ian Uruku, and paid for 25 Ayrshire cows to help Ian start his dairy farming venture. Ian bought a bull from Harold White, an Australian farmer in Ol'Kalou. The cream produced was turned into butter at the Kenya Co-Operative Creameries at Naivasha. Ten and twenty gallon cans were sent weekly by train to the creameries. The little calves were kept in stables till they were old enough to go out and graze. Ian also had a growing beef herd, and now started a really large piggery for baconers and weaners which were also sent by train from Thomson's Falls to Uplands Bacon Factory at Limuru.

Uruku was ranch country, not naturally suited to agriculture – the opposite of Daisy's farm which had fertile soil for crops, orchards and dairy, but was not natural beef-stock country. Ian decided to increase our income by clearing and draining the swamp for the cultivation and irrigation of tomatoes and cucumbers, and also put in a total of 22,000 pineapple suckers which were sent by rail to us for collection at Thomson's Falls. Burning the swamp first, Ian then cut in channels for irrigation between large plots which were drained. Then he was able to plough, harrow and plant. Hard, physical farm work and the dedication and efforts involved in becoming a successful farmer Ian was used to, and had witnessed. His father having been a shepherd boy in his youth in the Cape and then diligently applying his mind and talents to success, was a tough task-master. It was required by William that Ian, as a youngster, had to milk and feed the cows twice a day and cut the lucerne. Ian had to be up very early in order to complete some of his chores before going to school.

Mater was an extremely efficient, good-looking, dark-haired, tall woman, edging on 6 foot. She was also a shrewd businesswoman. Her long hair was her pride, always worn in a bun with a substantial number of hairpins giving her long locks a crinkly appearance when she let her hair loose at night. Coming from German stock and having been a Hospital Matron, she was disciplined and didn't tolerate lackadaisical attitude or behaviour. Ian remembered more than several occasions receiving a 'thick ear' from his mother. Sundays were strictly religious. Bible reading was done at the dining room table, and playing games of any sort was forbidden. Ian was never allowed to eat at the table without wearing a jacket. The children were never given toys, sweets or pocket money. Despite, or perhaps due to, William's strict religious beliefs which formed part of their daily life, Ian completely steered away from religion once he left home to start farming in Kenya.

While William and Mater lived on Uruku (until 1932 when Ian was 2 years old), Daisy made a point of being a friend to her Uncle Will's much younger wife, Mater. Not only because the two women shared 1893 as their birth year, but also due to Mater not being popular amongst William's side of the family. More than likely, this was due to the somewhat 'frowned-upon' big age difference between William and Mater. Daisy understood as she had first hand experience of harsh attitudes from some members of her own family. Mater could seem a little stand-offish, which was not intentional, but more from her austere German upbringing. She played the piano beautifully, music being another thing she had in common with Daisy. Mater also made the most delicious scones, so baking was a further mutual interest. Another similarity the two shared was that Mater was unafraid of hard work, had little time for idleness, and was outspoken and forthright in attitude and beliefs. She was also a very good seamstress.

Ian would now and again laughingly relate to me his mother's words when he was in for a scolding. "Come here you *shenzi* chicken!" she'd shout (meaning rubbish). I have spent many hours in intriguing conversation with Mater, finding her early life with William riveting. She also told me William corresponded with British Prime Minister Winston Churchill, never forgetting to send best wishes for his birthday, and always received a reply from the Prime Minister's Office. William became a respected member of the community both in Kenya and the Eastern Cape. I think Mater was a much-misunderstood woman, and had a strong sense of loyalty. She absolutely adored her sons, Ron and Ian, and was immensely proud of them. After William died her 2 boys were her life.

Directly out of college, Ron had joined the South African Air Force and became a pilot. He then returned to Kenya with his lovely wife, Daphne, in the late 1940s and farmed on *Glenavon* near Uruku (Glenavon having been bought by Mater from Marge and Harold). They had 2 children, Dereck and Ann, and all loved to be with immediate family and play tennis. I never saw Ron ride a horse. Daphne (very religious) and Ron visited Ol'Kalou on Sundays for church meetings. She greatly impressed the congregation with her superb singing voice. At their invitation and with my mother's blessing, I went to Glenavon for a week when I was 14 soon after I'd first met Ian with his fancy car at Anchorage. One evening, Ian came over from Uruku to have supper with us. He and Ron stayed up to chat while Daphne and I went to bed. Sometime later while I was asleep, I felt a kiss on my lips. Opening my eyes, I found Ian had quietly slipped into my room then quickly left. I fell asleep again – awestruck!

It wasn't long before Ron found farming wasn't his passion in life. Wanting something more adventurous, he took up crocodile hunting, though eventually returned to flying as a senior commercial pilot for Central African Airways in Rhodesia. Ron married twice, his 2nd wife, Joan, a beautiful blonde air hostess – they had one son, Michael. When Ron retired from Central African Airways, they settled in Mossel Bay on the South African east coast and went into commercial fishing which was very successful.

Our Uruku neighbour, Ian's elderly half-brother Donald Smith (Bertha, his wife, was sometimes also called Betty) was successfully cultivating citrus, in particular oranges, along the Pesi River that bordered his farm *Ol Morijo*. All this produce was packed in wooden-slatted boxes and also sent by train from Thomson's Falls to the Nairobi markets. Donald had gone to Tanganyika (Tanzania) after WWI to work as a coffee farm manager. When the bottom fell out of coffee in about 1937, he'd returned to Ol Morijo. (Out of interest, the sap from the ol-Morijo tree, also known as the arrow-poison tree or by its botanical name, Acokanthera schimperi, is one of the most commonly used plants for poison preparations in East Africa, and was used for making poison for Maasai arrows, and maybe still is. There were a lot of these trees in the Laikipia area. Maasai names start with '*ol*').

One morning around 10 o'clock on Uruku, Ian found an ostrich mother-hen dead. She'd been caught in a fence having been chased, no doubt by some predator, leaving 19 disoriented chicks. He told me to quickly get in the car and off we raced. Reaching the chicks, Ian jumped out saying I should take over the wheel while he rounded up the young, caught and safely deposited them on the back seat of the car. We reared them in a stable till they were old enough to go out and graze in a paddock. Finally, they were freed and returned to the wild. That exercise of stopping, starting and getting the hang of the car accelerator and brake (terrifying for me), was part of my 2nd driving lesson!

For a cost of £60, Ian bought an old Model A Ford chorrie. This was the most amazing car. It was 'open' to the elements with only a roof covering over the driver and passenger seats; the half-doors had no window glass, and the back was open (known as a box-body). It was also very noisy, rough and rigid, high off the ground, and most uncomfortable, but never once let us down. Even in the remotest areas one could get spare parts. Many Indian-owned dukas stocked a great assortment of groceries, haberdashery and hardware items, including essential Ford motor parts, tyres and petrol. From an army surplus depot in Nairobi, Ian bought very cheaply the engineless shell of a Bren gun carrier and converted it into a trailer which proved very useful for transporting the tomatoes to the sheds before they were boxed then sent by rail to Nairobi vegetable markets. Our small Ford Consul car, really a town car, was simply no match for these gruelling farm conditions, so sadly but with no difficulty, we sold it. Ian then bought a second-hand Ford *bakkie* (South African slang word for pick-up truck) with a V6 engine. This car was not only powerful, but big, comfortable and a pleasure to drive, and did the required farm work with ease. Eventually, we also sold the Model A Ford and just had the lovely big, dark green Ford V6.

We did the house painting ourselves and put down the parquet floors in a week. This entailed keeping a primus stove going with just simmering tar in a pot on the burner. Each parquet block was carefully dipped into the hot tar then laid down in herring-bone patterns on the concrete floor, and kept strictly even by using a spirit-level moved to cover all angles. Once we'd moved into the new stone house, I so wanted to get started on the garden. Daisy's 'green fingers' and my many happy years spent in her beautiful Anchorage grounds made me long to try my hand at growing a pretty play environment for our children as I'd had as a child. Kinangop Nurseries had sent our order by train. We'd immediately set out the plants in various beds from the front of the house facing towards the Falls, as originally planned. That was about the last I saw of the plants because shortly after this excitement I wouldn't be home enough on Uruku to take proper care of them.

I was 4 months pregnant, looking forward to our first baby and my 19th birthday in November. We had no wireless on the farm, just Ian's old His Master's Voice wind-up gramophone and records from his bachelor days. Plenty of fun was had by us in the evenings listening to seven singles, being the music of the time which we both enjoyed. At Daisy's, I'd been so used to hearing the BBC morning and evening news that kept farmers up-to-date with daily events. I wasn't missing that contact with the outside world as I had so many other things happening to keep my mind occupied on Uruku. We seldom had visitors and were pretty much isolated. None of it mattered though. Ian and I were perfectly content with one another's company and I so looked forward to time with him in the evenings. Then it was early to bed and up with the sparrows. We were young and in love. Being cut off from society or a social life was hardly a thought that entered my head. But, my newly married life of happiness with Ian on Uruku would turn, in a flash, into an unforgettable nightmare of horror and fear.

And, it wouldn't be the first and last time we'd live the terrifying experience of an African country gripped in violent turmoil. Twenty-three years later, in West-African Angola, we'd flee the civil war with thousands of other refugees by escorted convoy into neighbouring South West Africa, thankfully an African country that would have a far more peaceful transition to Independence.

Chapter Four

Mau Mau, Baby Bottles, Revolver at My Hip

"Where is Ian? Awful things have happened. Pack some clothes, you're coming home to be safe with me," my mother said in a no-nonsense voice, when she unexpectedly arrived at our house on 20th October 1952.

It was a hot sunny day. Ian was working on his irrigation scheme not too far from the house. I was busily pregnant, practicing the exercises for expectant mothers, one of which was to sit cross-legged as often as possible. Whilst sitting on our bed doing this, I'd be knitting small garments for the new baby or reading Dr Spock which had been passed on to me. Fat lot of good that book was! Ian never took a keen interest in these womanly goings-on mother-to-be things.

The dogs began barking as soon as they heard the far off rumble of the old grey Ford pick-up truck. It was a great surprise to see Daisy, but the moment she said I was to go home with her to Anchorage to be safe, I knew there was trouble as she was in a state of urgency – so unlike her. Ian had heard the car and commotion from the dogs, seen the clouds of dust, and knew someone had come to the house. He came rushing back from the swamp where he'd been cultivating tomatoes and cucumbers.

Daisy explained there'd been growing discontent amongst the Kikuyu tribe regarding land the British Government had allocated to European settler farmers. Sir Evelyn Baring, the new Governor of Kenya, had now declared a State of Emergency on 20th October. History would record that the Colonial Office in London had been informed of this on August 17th 1952 (originally as far back as 1949 when the Mau Mau was taking shape, the then Governor was warned, but ignored the information). But, it was only with Baring's arrival that the seriousness of the situation was totally realised.

Having no wireless to hear daily news, Daisy knew we wouldn't be aware of these developments, hence her hurried arrival at Uruku to tell us and fetch me. Ian understood the implications immediately and turned to me saying, "Get ready, and I'll come on the weekend to see you."

I had little time to put my things together. Daisy was most anxious to get back home. She'd driven about 50 miles on rough dirt roads then probably waited half-an-hour for me to pack.

"There's no time for tea," she said firmly, and away we went in a whirl of dust, driving through the Pesi River to get back to the main road. There wasn't even time to speak to Ian alone. Just a quick hug and kiss goodbye.

My pets had only just settled in our new home. Now I had to leave my 2 cats, Quizzie-tabby and Siamese-Simon, and Giftie, my 13 year old female black and white Springer Spaniel. Quizzie and Giftie had been my constant, faithful companions since I was 7 years old. Simon was a new member of the family. Danny was a beige-coloured Ridgeback and Ian's special dog who went everywhere with him. Our other 3 were dark liver-coloured Ridgeback guard dogs kept outside the house.

I can't remember any details of the trip to Daisy's. Instead, my mind was on the news filtering back. Gangs in Nairobi (believed to be Mau Mau) had been setting fire to African homes; a Senior Chief had been speared to death in broad daylight; and 2 white women had been murdered, one in September 1952 and the other in early October. The British Government was going to send troops to Kenya to help, so the situation must have been dire. It was all very frightening. Nothing like this had happened before.

The sole ambition of farmers like us living 'in the moment' on remote properties was to farm livestock and crops, produce commodities which would be of benefit to the people, and bring in revenue for the country from exports. Only a handful of farmers were involved in politics. The majority were disinterested. We were dependent on 'word of mouth' news passed on one to another from those who were able to hear BBC broadcasts or who'd been informed of events via someone else. We'd no idea that during the past month hostilities had increased. Some 40 or more people in Nairobi had been murdered. The Mau Mau had officially been declared terrorists and, apart from their traditional pangas, had now acquired firearms.

Farming came first at the beginning of the Mau Mau, but soon some farming activities had to be abandoned. Good neighbour relations are essential to farmers (a perfect example being in the event of fire when all neighbours come to the rescue and give assistance). With the State of Emergency having been declared, it was clear we'd have to look out for one another even more now, take things a day at a time, and hope that whatever the issues were they'd be resolved sometime soon.

For the moment, I only knew I was safe with Daisy, though extremely worried about leaving Ian and my pets. Everything had been so unexpected and rushed. There wasn't time to pack Giftie, Quizzie and Simon to go to Anchorage as well, and I hadn't thought to ask Daisy if I could take them with me. But, I knew Ian would take good care of them. I obeyed my mother without question. She was absolutely calm.

The commonly used acronym, *Mau Mau* (Mzungu Aende Ulaya – Mwafrika Apate Uhuru) which is translated as 'White man return Abroad – Independence for the African' was the name by which the rebellion, born in 1947, became known. The well-known slogan used was 'Uhuru (Freedom) from Poverty, Hunger and Disease'. The aim of Mau Mau was to drive out the white man from Kenya. This also resulted in violent divisions within the Kikuyu community. There were hideous murders of many good and innocent Kikuyu as the Mau Mau terrorised their own people into joining their movement and mercilessly took the lives of those who showed loyalty to the Government and farmers.

Mau Mau was a secret, nationalistic and terrorist insurrection, mainly amongst the Kikuyu (there were a few members from the Meru and Embu tribes) using guerrilla tactics to spread fear and death within each section of their societies. Land had become an issue. With over-population in the Kikuyu Homelands, there was, quite simply, not enough. Those who took the Mau Mau Initiation Oath of Allegiance dared not break what they had promised to do, for certain death would follow.

We were plum centre of Mau Mau territory. The Aberdare Mountain range (160km of rain forest giving way to almost impenetrable bamboo, then moorland) provided perfect cover and was the densest Mau Mau stronghold. Soon Mau Mau oath-taking ceremonies were taking place on these farms, their labour being Kikuyu. The Naivasha area was south of the Aberdares. From Daisy's garden to the foothills of the Aberdares was approximately 14 miles as the crow flies.

On 27th October 1952, seven days after the State of Emergency had been declared Eric Bowyer was killed in North Kinangop in his bathroom. 22nd November 1952 was the brutal murder of Commander I.H. Meiklejohn. His wife, Dorothy, a medical doctor, was badly cut up and had a broken arm, but somehow managed to drive to Thomson's Falls Police Station. They were attacked in their farmhouse at dinner time not far from the town. The community was utterly shocked as Dorothy treated the local Kikuyu free of charge. She and her husband were very nice elderly folk, known as 'do-gooders'. Ian personally knew both of them well though I'd only met the couple once. They were good friends of Uncle George and Aunt Preto. What was next to come? It was a worrying situation. I've no idea what happened to Dorothy afterwards.

The Government enforced curfews from 7 in the evening to 7 in the morning. For greater and more efficient protection, the farmers had organised that the larger homesteads would become 'central points' where the elderly and infirm, wives and families, taking their own weapons, food and bedding, would spend each night.

This was a huge set-back to daily farming operations, but it was totally understood that safety came first. It meant that our menfolk were freer to take part in patrolling the dangerous mountain areas. Wives had to be particularly well-organised, prepared for any eventuality, pre-pack food for their husband's week away, lock up their homes and be on time for the curfew. Once they'd returned to their own properties after the morning 7 o'clock curfew had ended, agriculture and animal husbandry had to continue, mostly with enormous difficulty. Many times this was injurious to the farming calendar for a number of the labour, having been terrorised and in great fear, had simply disappeared.

The farming men then worked out a system whereby they'd be in groups of approximately 5, carrying their own private weapons, taking turns in doing weekly tracking duty, beginning at night, in the extensive, dense Aberdare Mountain forests. But, it wasn't till they became 'pseudo gangsters' (soon realising they'd have to infiltrate the Mau Mau) that they had much success in capturing the terrorists. This was accomplished by wearing the filthy dirty, smelly clothes (or whatever was available) from any captured guerrilla then smearing their skins with either burnt cork or a charcoal mixture and just plain dirt, and growing beards, thereby resembling one of the Mau Mau. While on duty in the mountains, going up or coming down the mountain ranges, rules were strict. Absolutely no talking, smoking, cooking or making of fires. No wearing of wrist watches. Walk in single file patrols. And only those who could converse in the language were allowed to speak.

In this way a great deal of information was gleaned and collated. All who were captured were handed over to the Government security bodies. Living, working and sleeping in the mountain forest dense underbrush was freezing cold, damp, and on most occasions wet. The mountain mists were so thick that at times while on patrol, the man behind couldn't see the man ahead. But, the system worked very well. Many Mau Mau gangs were found in their brush-covers and flushed out. Returning, our men looked distinctly like *njangiris* (meaning marauder, bandit, vagrant, outcast or fugitive from justice), a word used by loyal Kikuyu who hadn't taken the oath, to describe Mau Mau members. After these patrols, our men were physically and mentally exhausted, and sorely in need of a good bath. Daisy put disinfectant in the bathwater, and Mwangi was repulsed when he washed Ian's clothes. Next day, our men would be up early to continue their farming where they'd left off.

Changes in the style of living happened overnight. Polo-playing came to a halt and was sorely missed. The usual socialising on a Saturday night abruptly stopped. No more fun. Children were not allowed out of sight. No-one travelled alone. House staff were no longer required in the evenings. People made sure they were barricaded in by 7 at night. Newscasts from Nairobi were heard several times a day. Worst of all was that no-one could be sure of staff loyalty simply because there was no outward sign that a person had taken the Mau Mau Oath. Later on, it was noticed that the sudden growing of a beard was a clear indication. But, many thousands of Kikuyu remained loyal to their employers – they too, like us, were caught up in terror, fear and intimidation not of their making.

In Oath-taking ceremonies of the Mau Mau, the initiate was forced to consume human and animal body parts, especially the genitals and brain. The drinking of fresh blood and a number of other foul practices took place, such as drinking the fluid from a victim's eyes, intercourse with dead animals, and the use of rotting intestines for the encircling of places (being the manner in which they would be marked for attack). Having taken the Oath, there was no turning back. The Mau Mau operated in small gangs, expert at making their well-concealed hides in the dense undergrowth and bamboo thickets of the Aberdare Mountain forests. Sometimes they had disastrous results from using their homemade guns made from metal pipes, which, having crude working mechanisms, didn't always work. Most of them were regular users of *mbange* (bangi, cannabis, marijuana or bhang, dagga). Smoking of mbange had a hallucinogenic influence. The plant could be found any and everywhere, whether wild or cultivated, in Kenya. They also chewed a soft pinkish-coloured twig-like root, locally known as *miraa*. It was supposed to have the qualities of keeping one awake and curbing hunger.

The number of Mau Mau hardcore terrorists and their leaders was estimated to be 15,000. Harold predicted no easy solution or quick fix to the situation. He was right. At the closure of this violent uprising, 7 long years later in 1959, there were approximately 500 still at large. It was the Kikuyu women who were most adamant in ridding their tribe of Mau Mau.

During these early days of the Emergency, while I was pregnant and until after our baby boy, Keith, was born, I lived with my mother at Anchorage. Ian, Neville and Ken did their turn of duty in the Aberdares. Having come down from the mountains, Ian would leave the next day, worried about Uruku, about an hour and a half drive each way. The Thomson's Falls stretch of road was very rough and stony; the Uruku section red earth. Because part of the road was so stony sometimes the petrol tank would need a temporary repair en route. From past experience, Ian always carried a piece of Lux toilet soap which perfectly gummed up any holes made by flying stones until he could do the necessary repairs.

We saw little of our menfolk and worried about them constantly. It was their rule never to divulge too much to us in case it got out and about to the ears of any 'would-be' Mau Mau, or perhaps they were afraid that idle talk could be passed on to willing ears. House staff could easily pick up the slightest information.

Anchorage became one of the designated homestead central points and safe-haven to sometimes 11 people at night, though usually 7 or 8, with their food and bedding. I remember clearly the Jarolomek couple. They were Czechs, not fluent in English, who'd recently bought land in the district. The only sleeping space for them at Daisy's was under the long dining-room table. Very reticent, both were blond, she a plump little woman and he a tall, rugged-looking man. Having left their Communist country and bravely facing a new life in Kenya, they now had to try and survive Mau Mau terrorism which they simply couldn't comprehend.

Mrs Cheshire, a middle-aged, bejewelled and feisty French lady slept in a single bed in Daisy's best spare room, decorated all in blue, which was next to the small side verandah that was my favourite nook as a girl. There I'd sit quietly on my own in the mornings, next to the wisteria-covered pergola, embroidering delicate linen for what would one day be my 'bottom drawer' when I married. This was a must for girls of my era, the art of embroidery having been taught to us in junior and senior school.

I shared a central spare bedroom with widowed Marta Hauschild, a much-loved and very kind but sensitive, nervous elderly lady. She was a great friend of my mother's. Due to the State of Emergency, the Mau Mau and fear for her safety, Mrs Hauschild now started having terrible recurring nightmares from WWII owing to her family's traumatic experiences during the Nazi regime. We had single beds in our room, mine perhaps 2 feet from hers behind a wall that sectioned off an area of the bedroom. On the other side of the wall, there was another single bed.

Mrs Hauschild would suddenly sit up in bed during the night and start shouting, "Now they are coming! Now they are coming!" After waking properly, she'd fitfully sleep again. Before dawn, she was up and ready to go back to her farm. Mrs Hauschild's memories of Hitler's

Germany must have been utterly terrifying. Her husband had been taken for a few days by the Nazis. So they came to Kenya. Mrs Hauschild also suffered from a stomach ailment. Each night, she would ingest powdered charcoal to ease this condition. In the faint bedroom light, when she'd suddenly sit up terrified from her nightmares and start shouting, her black charcoal mouth against her frail face was an image that would unnerve me. On nights Ian was back from patrol in the mountains, we'd sleep together in the single bed on the other side of the wall near the window. For me, I felt safe knowing he was beside me and found comfort and much-needed relaxation in his arms. Mrs Hauschild too felt more secure with Ian in the same room – she adored him. Henry, her son and my good school friend, was not in the country at the time, hence his mother staying with Daisy. As I became more heavily pregnant, I started getting horrible and most painful cramps in my legs. The first time, I couldn't understand what was happening, neither could Ian. It never entered our heads that perhaps sleeping separately would give me more space.

My mother's bedroom had a camp-bed in it for me if there were extra people to accommodate. The bedrooms slept in by the women all adjoined one bathroom off the passage from Daisy's room. A huge and very cold room at night, the bathroom had a big window of opaque glass above the washbasin, and a separate lavatory directly outside looking onto the back garden, reached by a connecting door through the outside bathroom wall. There were potties in each bedroom for night use. The men used Mr Golding's en suite bathroom adjoining his twin bedroom, which also had an outside lavatory.

Sometime in the late 1940s, Mr Golding had entered our lives. He would live with Daisy as a boarder for many years. To begin with, the elderly and eccentric gentleman had an en suite cottage to himself in the back garden.

Major Arthur E Golding had lived in Egypt where he'd met and married a Greek timber heiress from Cairo. He'd made a fortune from a tender put out by the Egyptian Government to provide wooden stakes for an enormous project. This was done by taking an oblong standard stake and splitting it from the top across at an angle to the bottom, thereby making two stakes out of one. While waiting at a petrol station one day, Mr Golding had idly watched as a man cut his hand badly removing his car battery. In those days, the battery was fixed into place with awkward sharp metal bands onto the running board (a ledge beneath the doors of certain old cars). Mr Golding went home and designed a new method of attaching batteries, which patent brought in further funds. By now, he and his wife had become wealthy, owning a jewellery shop in Alexandria, and buildings in Cairo. Things were beginning to stir politically in Egypt. Then Mr Golding's wife died. Seeing 'the writing on the wall' with regard to Egypt's future (King Farouk would be overthrown in 1952), Mr Golding decided to leave it all behind. He quickly transferred his money and chose to come to Kenya. Initially, he'd boarded with a lady, Mrs Alcorn, living in Nairobi, who'd been at the Rift Valley Academy in Kijabe with Daisy. Mrs Alcorn found Mr Golding to be a most unhappy and extremely difficult man. So she sent a telegram to Daisy saying he'd be on the next train to Ol'Kalou, would Daisy meet him at the station and have the gentleman stay for a while? My mother was waiting for Mr Golding on the station platform. He stepped down from the train carriage, looked at Daisy and said, "Well, I won't be staying here long!"

Mr Golding was absolutely meticulous and neat, always dressed only in khaki overalls. He kept his snow-white hair as short as possible and went to the barber every 3 weeks. His handwriting was perfect italic and he used only purple ink. Mr Golding finally settled down at Anchorage and became a good and true friend to all the members of our family. Though he had some funny quirks, such as always counting stairs or paces in case he had to get out in a hurry, we were very fond of him and enjoyed having him with us. Once Mau Mau began, my mother moved Mr Golding into one of the 2 en suite bedrooms in the main house where his security awareness proved invaluable. When something extraordinary happened, the elderly gentleman would quote an Egyptian proverb, "And the smoke goes up the chimney just the same!"

Extra wire mesh security was put onto all the windows. The outside leading doors were fitted with 3 more inside wooden bars across the top, middle and bottom. On the front verandah a large gate was installed which was permanently locked and bars put across the top so there could never be entry through this area. The only entrance left to be freely opened and shut was the back verandah door, now also heightened and strengthened, that led onto the back patio which meant that area had to be secured as well. We were now living in a type of fortress, and only went outside when absolutely necessary.

Mr Golding was in charge of checking the entire house come 6 every evening, ready for the start of the 7 o'clock curfew. All doors and windows would be locked and additional securities checked and in place. With his double-barrelled shotgun that always had 2 cartridges up the spout (and 2 spare in his pocket), he'd do the rounds securing windows and doors and drawing curtains extremely carefully. No chink of light could be seen from the outside, and no peering eyes could catch the slightest movement within the house through gaps in the drapes. Once everything was to his absolute satisfaction, Mr Golding without fail would say, "Altrua, may I get you a brandy and ginger?" *Altrua* (taken from the word altruism) was the name Mr Golding gave my mother.

And, Daisy would reply in the same manner each time. "Yes, thank you, Mr Golding." This was their ritual at the end of a day. In some small way during the anxiety of Mau Mau nights, it was comforting to witness what became a perfectly normal evening routine. The 2 would then settle into their chairs, one each side of the fireplace in the sitting room, shotguns at their sides. Mr Golding would keep stoking the embers. "Shaking the fire," he'd say, and both would have another brandy and ginger.

We would usually eat off our laps. Only occasionally we would eat supper at the large table in the pantry. Mostly bread and butter, cheese and good homemade soup kept hot on the wood stove in the kitchen. Mr Golding would always say, "Altrua, this is the best soup ever. If only you could tin and sell it."

The evening news broadcast was at 7 o'clock, and again at 9. After Rosemary (Neville's wife), Jean (Ken's wife) and I had washed up the few dishes in the scullery, we'd all retire. If Neville and Ken weren't away doing duty in the Aberdares, the 4 of them would go back to their own homes on Anchorage, otherwise Rosemary and Jean slept at Daisy's.

Mr Golding always used to say, "I shall retire now, I wish you all Good Night." Then picking up his shotgun, he'd do a 'once more' round of checking the security, then go to his quarters. He would be up at 7 in the morning and appear ready-dressed for breakfast at 8. Mr Golding was a creature of habit and a master at whatever he put his hand to, even to copying paintings.

During Mau Mau, there was no music in our Anchorage home. The only merriment was when Mrs Cheshire, in her attractive French accent, would tell how she'd react if any terrorists entered the front side door near her bedroom. She said she'd grab the nearest vase off the piano and hurl it at them! That would put them off their stroke as a start!

We no longer had electric light from the petrol Petter engine which was at the back of one of the storerooms. It was too noisy and we needed to be able to hear sounds outside at night. We used Dietz paraffin lamps or candles. In the sitting room was a hissing Tilley lamp which gave off good light, but had to be regularly pumped to keep the pressure and light. All of us had torches. Anchorage was a huge rambling house. Off the back verandah was another double spare bedroom, a storeroom kept for the perpetual potato crop, the ironing room and the kitchen.

I'd always been an avid reader, but I never read a single book all the time I was at Daisy's during Mau Mau. There just wasn't enough light and I was exhausted every night. The evenings were the most dangerous times. We lived in endless caution and anxiety for there was no telling what could happen unexpectedly, no matter how careful we were even in broad daylight. Conversations all centred around the newscasts, which were mostly grim, and at times extremely shocking, reminding and reinforcing in all of us that no carelessness would be tolerated. Yes, we were all fearful, but never did this get us down. We remained determined and resolute.

My Czech-made handgun automatic revolver was a 0.25 which had 2 cartridge clips, each holding about 10 bullets for rapid firing. So, at all times there were 10 spare bullets ready to be fired one after the other. One was always up the spout and the safety catch was easy to release in a single movement to pull the trigger. The other cartridge case was kept handy in my apron pocket, or when travelling, in my handbag. This gun was slim and light, suitable for a woman to use and would keep on firing so long as the trigger was held. It had its own holster which in turn was fixed onto a belt so that the gun was carried a little lower than the waist on the hip, quick to reach. It was easy to slip out the empty cartridge, put in the new one and slot in a bullet ready for firing. I had plenty of practice from Davo Davidson, the Labour Officer, who taught me to go for the chest, that being a larger target and therefore less likely to be missed.

Marge had an even smaller handgun than mine, a 0.22, which I remember she kept in her bosom most times. I never saw her carrying it on a belt around her waist. You'd never have known she had a gun in her bra. My mother didn't have a handgun, she believed in shotguns used at close quarters, as did Mr Golding. Neville and Ken had handguns and rifles. Their wives, Rosemary and Jean (both from overseas), having small children and feeling uncomfortable with firearms, never carried any weapons. Neville, Ken and Ian were in the thick of Mau Mau territory, as were a lot of the younger and middle-aged able-bodied men and farmers in our Aberdare area. Ian always wore his cartridge belt which had slim slots for holding extra ammo for the Mauser 30.03 rifle. At night, the rifle was put down beside his bed, his revolver on the bedside table. While on horseback, the Mauser was carried in a tough rawhide gun-sling such as you see cowboys in films, with a strong attachment clip-on to the Australian saddle making it easy to draw the gun and fire, even at a gallop. Ian made the gun-sling himself. Peter, Ian's tall chestnut horse, was quite used to the Mauser and the shots fired from it. Ian's handgun was an automatic 9 mm, a much bigger calibre firearm than mine.

On 3 separate occasions, Ian and I had been shot at. Only once did a bullet hit our vehicle, penetrating the rear side-window while we were travelling up Simba Hill. The 2nd time was in the late afternoon when a bullet whizzed past us as we were returning home from visiting a hard-up neighbour who'd sold us 30 geese; the 3rd occasion being not far from Anchorage when we were returning to Uruku. We were lucky these shots were so inaccurate. Ian and I became inured to the discipline of having to be armed – in a way, as necessary and habitual as cleaning one's teeth.

Eventually, it became law to have both holster and gun tied with leather thongs to the thigh. All other weapons not in use were kept locked away in gun-safes that were bolted from the inside into the floor. Despite these precautions, there were some people who hid their firearms thinking no-one employed by them would find out, but this carelessness was the cause of many guns and ammunition being stolen. No matter where you went, your gun never left your side. This was the Golden Rule, and everyone was responsible for his or her gun. No gun was to be left in the care of someone else. It was a great trial to families who had children.

For four-and-a-half months I lived in safety at Daisy's. As my belly grew larger and I had no suitable maternity clothes, Mrs Cheshire, an excellent seamstress, sat for hours during the day in mother's room using her Singer cabinet treadle-sewing machine. She made me smart outfits – pink, blue and green linen tops, and plain grey skirts with the open space left for the expansion of the tummy was my daily wear. The material we bought at 'Damn Cheap' Shah's Indian duka in Ol'Kalou village. He was a friendly and dapper little man and everything in his shop was damn cheap – hence the name. All the farmers regularly supported him. My dear friend, Cynthia, gave me a lovely brown and green cotton patterned dress which she'd used for her 2 pregnancies. These clothes I'd later carefully put away for future use.

I saw very little of Ian since his time was spent between Uruku and doing the monthly week of duty in the Aberdare Mountains. The British Government, at the beginning of the Emergency, had immediately sent one Battalion of Lancashire Fusiliers, flown in from the Middle East, and sent to this particular area. It was decided that the central point homesteads, such as Anchorage, would each be given one Fusilier for day duty and two for night duty. This new arrangement was a great relief and help to our menfolk, knowing that their families would be better guarded while they were away in the mountains tracking the terrorists. The Fusiliers slept in Mr Golding's other twin bedroom off his own very large suite. During the course of the conflict, other British units such as the Royal Highland Regiment, Royal Marines, Gloucester Regiment, and the Buffs all did their share of duty in other areas.

The murders nearest to Anchorage, about 10 miles as the crow flies, were those of Charles Hamilton Ferguson and Richard Bingley on 1st January 1953. They lived in a remote farmhouse in an area close to Thomson's Falls, but on the lower reaches of the Aberdare Mountains and overlooking Lake Ol'Bolossat. As was usual, dinner was announced by the houseman. While Charles and Richard started to eat, the houseman led in a gang of Mau Mau who attacked and disembowelled the 2 men, then chopped them into pieces. My brother, Ken, was one of the first on the scene and his brief description was that the attack had been very savage and that the bodies 'looked like mincemeat'. At this time, Ken was working with 3 Samburu trackers, a number of Home Guards and some Forest Guards. He refused to discuss anything further about the goriness of the attack.

After this, came the particularly savage Ruck murders on January 24th 1953. A labourer came to tell Mr Ruck there was a sick animal and that he should come at once. Having got Ruck outside, the Mau Mau then hamstrung him followed by fetching a pregnant Mrs Ruck, who they proceeded to disembowel in full view of her husband. After further gory deeds, the gang then went upstairs where they butchered the son, Michael, aged 6, while he lay sleeping in his bed. Peter Steenkamp, a superb Policeman, was called out, and he managed to track and kill all 5 of the perpetrators.

Six weeks before my baby was due, Daisy sent me to Mona and Reg Haig-Thomas of the Prisons Department in Nakuru, where I was also safe. There I waited out the days. Ian came to visit me, and very luckily on that day, my 'waters' broke shortly after lunch at the Stag's Head Hotel in Nakuru. The next morning, 6th March 1953, at 9.30, I became the mother of a baby boy we named Keith. Ten days later, Ian collected me and took me to Anchorage again. The menfolk were still away, the Fusilier Guards continued their duties, and strict security had remained in place.

The Lari massacre of March 1953, meted out by Mau Mau on their own Kikuyu people who were considered to be traitors because they'd refused to take the Oath, was horrific in the extreme. 120 Kikuyu lost their lives in the Mau Mau onslaught – children murdered, pregnant women disembowelled, some slashed to death, others burned alive in their huts, many maimed for life.

Anthony Gibson, a Farm Manager, was killed 17 miles outside Nyeri on 7th February, followed on 21st April by Geoffrey Le Mesurier Lavers in Nairobi.

Then the Meloncelli family murders occurred on 25th April 1953. The father was shot dead in an ambush while sitting in his vehicle waiting for the farm gate to be opened. Mrs Meloncelli and her 2 children had only been in the country for 10 days having come to join her husband who was working at the Chehe Sawmill in the forest fringe of Mount Kenya. They'd only been on the sawmill premises 2 days when this attack took place. On hearing the commotion, Mrs Meloncelli and the 2 children hid in cupboards from where they were dragged out and slaughtered. These murders particularly upset me. I cannot begin to imagine the utter terror of those children and their mother. This area was in the Nanyuki district not so far from Uruku. James MacDougall was killed in his house 4 miles outside Nyeri on 21st July 1953.

Mau Mau gangs not only foully murdered people, but also disembowelled pet cats and dogs while alive and pinned them out on front lawns. They also cruelly hamstrung cattle, including prime dairy cows, by cutting each animal's hamstring tendons on the hind legs behind and slightly above the hock (knee). The animal would fall down in dreadful agony, totally unable to move. I don't know what farmers did when they found their cattle in this way, but usually a cow or horse with a broken leg is put down.

We now experienced the Mau Mau use of rotten entrails and our homestead being 'marked'. The second Golden Rule of security was that no-one at any time, for any reason, should leave the homestead. On this particular night, after baby Keith had been put to sleep and as I was preparing to have a bath, I noticed a shadowy image at the bottom of the outside leading bathroom door (that adjoined a small verandah and the lavatory). Between the bottom of the door and the floor was about a one inch gap. There was also a sickening stench coming through under the door. The following morning, Neville investigated and found the rotten remains of entrails that had been dragged all around the house marking the premises, with bits deposited at the bathroom door. The day following the rotten entrails incident, at 7 o'clock in the morning and as was usual now, Daisy, holding her loaded shotgun, met the house staff, Mwangi and Kariuki, at the kitchen door. She let them in to make the fire in the wood stove, boil water for early morning tea and do the normal household cleaning. Due to the circumstances of some of the gruesome murders that had taken place, we had to acknowledge that farm or household staff had possibly been terrorised enough to lead in a gang of Mau Mau. So on this particular morning, when Kariuki brought the morning tea tray to my mother's bedroom door it was a shock for him to find her standing there with the shotgun pointing at him. He never returned to work after this incident.

It then became clear to us that Mau Mau had infiltrated the Kikuyu working on the farms, and that we should take even greater care with security arrangements. Why? Because anyone who had taken the Oath simply disappeared to work for the Mau Mau, a fact proved time and again under interrogation. Obviously, Kariuki had joined their ranks. Mwangi remained faithful to my mother and never did take the Oath.

By the time baby Keith was 6 weeks old, he was crying a lot and still not doing very well on my breastfeeding. Marge realised he'd have to be bottle-fed on cow's milk and water, and took over. Harold and Marge were about to move to another farm, *Merrowdown*, at Soy in the Uashin Gishu District in safe Western Kenya. Marge, in the middle of moving from Basella Farm in Ol'Kalou was, luckily for me, visiting for a while at Anchorage. I was so grateful to get some rest and sleep. Keith took to the sterilised cow's milk with no problem whatsoever. I'd almost starved him. Mother of 4 children, Marge had plenty of experience and I knew Keith was in expert hands. He thrived. By the time Marge moved to her new home, Keith was well on his way to gaining weight. As he grew accustomed to the cow's milk, so the ratio was increased and the added water decreased.

Ian and I now decided that I should go back to our home at Uruku. I was so happy to be reunited with my beloved animals. Giftie would not leave me for a second. Quizzie was out somewhere in the bush, but when she returned she was very affectionate. Simon was lying on our bed. Kasuku danced up and down, screeched and whistled. It was good to be home again, but nothing was easy. Baby Keith and I had to go everywhere Ian and his rifle went – long hours around the farm each day. Just as at Anchorage, come 7 at night, all had to be locked up securely with staff back at their homes, and the Emergency laws strictly obeyed. No-one was afoot till 7 in the morning. On days when Ian worked in his garage mending farm machinery, I'd be able to stay at home. For security during the day, I'd chain Danny, Ian's big Ridgeback dog, to the door of the nursery. Kasuku parrot, free on her perch during daylight hours would make piercingly squeaky noises in imitation whenever a door was opened or shut, being an additional and very good form of alarm system for us. At night, she still slept in our bedroom in her covered cage, never making a sound till morning when I removed the blanket. Danny slept in our room next to Ian's side of the bed, and Giftie on the floor on my side.

One day when Keith was about a year old, we left for shopping in Thomson's Falls. I think my beloved dog, Giftie, may have tried to follow the car. We never knew what happened, but on our return home she was nowhere to be found. Ian was of the opinion she'd been taken by a leopard, there were plenty in our area along the Pesi River. Because of the security measures we all had to take during Mau Mau days, discipline and restrictions sometimes meant we'd have to leave pets behind. I wondered if that morning, for some reason, Giftie had perhaps thought I was going away again and didn't want me to leave her behind. Ian, in empathy, said that Giftie would've known little if it was a leopard. It was the only solace I had after so many wonderful years with her, my dearest childhood companion. For weeks, I carried a silent inner pain, in the beginning still hopeful of seeing her come through the door.

Davo Davidson had already taught me how to use my revolver, now he again came to visit. This time, he showed us how to make the nightly changes, in case any information had been given by our houseman, Mwangi, to would-be Mau Mau attackers. Since our bedroom had huge bay windows, Davo insisted we put nails into the pelmets on which to hang blankets making a total blackout. I was still getting up at night and lighting a candle while seeing to baby Keith. Each night, our chairs in the sitting room were moved to different positions and the bedroom furniture completely changed around. Other nights we slept in a different room. Next morning, all furniture was returned to normal positions so that Mwangi wouldn't notice. This only happened in our Uruku house. At Anchorage, nothing was moved about.

After returning with Ian to Uruku one day, Daisy's cook, Rho, who'd been with her since I was a child, was taken away by the Police. Unbeknown to her, Rho had become of some importance in the Mau Mau and had been exposed. My mother was extremely upset at having to understand that he had become a Mau Mau member right under her nose. She truly thought her staff to be loyal. With Rho and Kariuki both gone, Mwangi, a dear person who loved Daisy, was in complete charge ordering and deciding things, and so proud of all he did. Neville had an outside staff member come in and cut wood for the kitchen stove.

On a number of nights Mau Mau came to Uruku. Their modus operandi – Davo had warned us about this – would be to call one another making hooting sounds like owls, then from another quarter would be an answering call. It was eerie and somewhat frightening waiting for something to happen. The worst night ever was when they decapitated 7 little calves, and put their bloodied heads on the fence poles facing our bedroom windows so that Ian would immediately see them on going out the next morning to start the day's work at 7 o'clock. We never heard a thing during the night, probably because of the crashing water from the Pesi Falls which sounded something like the endless breaking waves on a beach. Ian wouldn't allow me to see this ghoulish horror of the calves' heads. I've been grateful to him all my life – he protected me from the visual memory of this ghastly happening. There was no sign of the calves' carcasses. Presumably they'd been taken as food. Later, a huge gang of Mau Mau was flushed by the Police from deep within the Ndaragwa Forest which came down to a few yards behind our house.

The Lancashire Fusiliers now came to Uruku in an armoured vehicle at least twice a night. When they arrived, we'd get up and I'd make tea on the primus stove for everyone then we'd lock ourselves in before the servicemen departed. Because of the remoteness of our house, we were issued with a hand-grenade and kept this with us at all times. It was a very great responsibility and I always felt nervous handling it. At night the hand-grenade was with Ian. When we had to drive through the Pesi River we had it with us in the car. During the day it was hidden in our bedroom. I don't know of any other family who was issued with a hand-grenade. It was a fearsome weapon, for me an abomination. At all times, I was conscious that we had it in our possession and was scared to death of a time when we should have to use it. Ian was more at ease though, and felt we were well enough armed.

One morning, Ian came to tell me he'd been called by our reliable houseman, Mwangi, who'd shouted, "Come at once to see to a sick bull!"

Baby Keith at the time had a seriously suppurating ear, probably caused from all the wind and dust while we waited for Ian everyday to finish farm work before we could go home. I categorically refused to allow Ian to go and attend to the sick bull, saying we should instead leave immediately for Thomson's Falls as it was imperative we get Keith to Dr Lowie. Unbeknown to us, a little higher up in the Ndaragwa Forests there was a Mau Mau gang who'd pressured Mwangi to lead Ian away from the house so they could kill him. On returning from Dr Lowie, we found the Police had been and taken Mwangi away as he was apparently in on the murder plot. A newly captured Mau Mau had given all the details. The Police had swooped immediately, and not a moment too soon, otherwise we surely would have been caught on our return trip from Thomson's Falls.

Another incident took place soon after our Mwangi was taken into custody. Ian had a 'funny' feeling (call it a premonition), that he should go at once to Uncle George and Aunt Preto on Mutara. I was left alone, with the hand-grenade in our bedroom, our dog Danny and baby Keith, while Ian hastened over to see if things were all right with the elderly couple. He was driving down Mutara farmhouse road when a gang of Mau Mau, on their murderous way to Uncle George's, saw the car dust, turned around and made off. At the same time, the Maasai working for Uncle George saw them and gave chase.

On another occasion, Ian was called out to the Ndaragwa Police Station to help with tracking a gang. We arrived there around 7 in the evening. I was left at the Police station with baby Keith who was about

5 months old. There was a stark Police dormitory with about 8 iron bedsteads, each with a filthy dirty mattress. We waited here for Ian to return, so that I could at least lie Keith down to sleep. The one and only Officer left in charge, an Englishman from the UK, was absolutely drunk, swigging from bottles of whisky whilst sitting on one of the beds in the dormitory. This night ended badly. One of the volunteers from England, Eric (I forget his surname), accidentally shot himself in the foot with a Sten-gun while stumbling back in the dark to the Police Station. The shot sliced his foot into fragments, the bones sticking out through the remains of the boot. There was no first aid equipment at the Police Station.

When Ian arrived back, he was the obvious choice to help Eric. One of the dirty mattresses was put into the back of our Peugeot LDV bakkie which had a canopy on the back (we only had this vehicle for 3 months before selling it: Ian found it to be hopeless for farm conditions). With Eric carefully set down on the mattress, and baby Keith and me also in the back, despite the curfew, Ian first drove us back to Uruku. This took about 20 minutes. At home, I quickly cut up Ian's special pyjamas (kept for if and when he ever had to go to hospital) into wide strips to bind up Eric's foot, still in the boot, to help stanch the bleeding. We hurriedly filled the thermos with boiling water for heating Keith's baby bottle, got a pillow and blanket for Eric, and put all the baby paraphernalia in the car. Before leaving the house, I grabbed the bottle of Gilbey's Gin and gave Eric small sips all the way to the Nakuru War Memorial Hospital. He was in severe shock and agony and I had no alternative pain medication for him. Dettol was all I had in the way of medicine. At the hospital, about 60 miles from our house, after Emergency staff had taken Eric inside, we filled in the necessary paperwork and then left. Eric's foot was later amputated. I did write several times to Eric once he was back in England. Perhaps someone reading this will know of him.

Several shooting accidents happened during Mau Mau days. It's amazing there weren't more.

One was Ian's elder half-brother, Donald Smith, who grew citrus on his farm, Ol Morijo, next to us. Preparing to have his bath on the night of 14th February 1953, he'd lifted his foot onto the side of the bath to undo his shoe laces. The gun slipped out of his holster, hit the bath rim and sent a bullet up his spine. He died instantly. Donald's wife, Betty, had to cope with this ghastly tragedy. I think a neighbour came over to help her. At the time, I was away waiting to have baby Keith, and only found out about this tragic turn of events on my return to Anchorage. Betty's mother, Grandma Montefiore, had been living on Ol Morijo for some time with Donald and Betty. Following Donald's accidental death, it was decided that Grandma Montefiore would move to Daisy's. Donald & Betty's youngest son, Peter, was taken out of high school to run Ol Morijo temporarily until their eldest son, Geoff, could assume responsibility. Betty later moved to Nanyuki. A grand, also dearly-loved old lady in her 80s, Grandma Montefiore's everyday attire was Victorian with crocheted detachable collars. She read any book she could get hold of (probably to get her mind off the current situation) late into the night by candlelight. She was given the room I had as a girl. When she'd fallen asleep, my mother would do nightly checks, tiptoe in and blow out the candle which had usually burnt right down in the holder.

Then, Uncle Alick Roberts, while cleaning his gun had forgotten he had a bullet up the spout and accidentally shot off the end of an index finger.

Another was a man sitting between 2 others on the front seat of a moving vehicle with his chin propped on the end of a loaded rifle. The car bumped over something on the road, the gun went off and he was instantly killed. This happened in the Ol'Kalou area not far from Daisy's home.

Yet more tragedy – near Ol Joro Orok when a small child of 4, playing around in a bedroom, found a loaded rifle behind a wardrobe and shot his elder sibling.

One of our own Ol'Kalou farmers, Erik Hovmand (a Dane), and Dr Anne Spoerry were on a night-tracking duty on a farm. Dr Spoerry heard a noise to the side of her. She called out but received no reply, so firing her shotgun she mistakenly wounded the young Danish farmer, whose lower leg had to be amputated. My brother, Neville, was on the same patrol and testified to this tragedy. Dr Spoerry had been born in

Cannes in 1918, and with her brother joined the French Resistance working with Odette and Captain Henri in WWII. Both were captured and imprisoned. We heard many tales of that truly terrible time. She came to Kenya to get away from Europe and all she'd experienced in wartime, and to find a new meaningful and fulfilling life.

A young South African man, who came especially to help guard his family and who'd never seen a Mau Mau, shot a uniformed Kikuyu Forest guard who was walking beside his bicycle on day duty on a track at the edge of the forest. This incident appalled and shocked the whole community.

In Nairobi, a man with a loaded sawn-off shotgun under his pillow accidentally shot and killed his wife lying in bed beside him. He said that one of the buttons on his pillowcase had become caught around the trigger of his gun. In trying to get the gun loose from the button, the weapon had fired.

I can't remember absolute details or the name of the woman who committed suicide, but fear of the Mau Mau terror and the horror of the atrocities they committed were just too much for her and she went 'off her head'. At night, in a flimsy nightdress, she sneaked out of the house without waking her husband and meandered into the forest (I think on a farm in Rongai) where she hanged herself, and was found next morning.

Danny, our Ridgeback, saved Ian's life. There was a repair job to be done on the rear wheel of the tractor, and Ian was squatting down to look at it. Suddenly, there was a rush of movement and a commotion behind Ian's back. An unknown man jumped out of the bush and rushed at Ian with a sharpened hacksaw blade. But Danny got to him first and held him on the ground, and just in time! Ian quite easily tied up the stranger, rolled him into the back of the bakkie and drove to Ndaragwa Police Station where it was found the man was completely under the influence of *mbange*.

Weeks later, on return from a day's shopping trip to Thomson's Falls, Ian was traumatised to find our faithful dog, Danny, dead and chopped up. The Mau Mau had been and cunningly brought with them a bitch in season knowing that her 'scent' would naturally attract Danny, making him vulnerable and easy prey to what they had in mind for our excellent guard dog. When the 2 canines mated and were temporarily inseparable, the Mau Mau proceeded to hack them both to death with *simis* (a heavy, narrow panga-like lethal weapon with both sides of the blade sharpened and the hilt covered in rawhide). Ian wouldn't allow me near the scene, so I was yet again spared the gruesome and tragic picture.

These awful happenings were beyond our control: there was nothing that could be done. It's difficult to describe the futility we felt in trying to anticipate what we might have to face on the morrow, and the helplessness we felt in these situations, as well as the feeling of total repulsion at the brutality. The sadness still hasn't gone away. Ian didn't say anything. What he thought was plain to see on his face. He buried Danny himself and I didn't even know where his grave was. Ian remained tight-lipped and never spoke of this again.

Chapter Five
Nugu's Journey

Ready with my 0.25 revolver on my hip – part of my everyday life, like putting on lipstick – Keith and I would accompany Ian when his work day began at 7 in the morning. Together with whatever labour force was available and equipment necessary, we'd load up the farm vehicle and set off with baby in his carrycot. There were a lot of necessary items to take along each time – nappies, creams and lotions, bottles of prepared cow's milk, playthings and rattles for Keith. Not forgetting the baskets containing primus stove filled with paraffin, plus the primus-pricker, a small bottle of methylated spirits, matches, cooking pot and water for heating baby's bottles. We also needed a blanket to sit on, an umbrella for shade, needlework or knitting to keep me busy, plus sandwiches, coffee and drinking water. We were out all day on Uruku cattle lands till 3 in the afternoon when manual labour stopped and Ian would fetch us. Then we'd all go home.

The hours Keith and I waited were long, seemed endless and dragged – day after day – playing with and taking care of my little son whilst keeping a sharp lookout. My revolver was ever handy, Ian's Mauser rifle propped up against the trunk of the tree we sat under – he was clearing the bush for a new fence line. The rifle was not for my use. I didn't know how to use it and hadn't been taught. I was merely guarding it for Ian as he was unable to be responsible for the firearm at the same time as putting up miles of dead-straight fencing. I'd have to move the blanket and all the paraphernalia to follow the shade.

We were out of sight as Ian first put up the long thin marker poles with white flags. Then the workers hacked their way through the trees and bush in between, one painstaking mile at a time, finally followed by the men erecting the shorter fencing poles with the five-strand wire threaded horizontally. I could hear the car move further down the line and stop then start up again as the measuring progressed. Out in the bush, the silence was deafening with only bird sounds as interruptions now and then. Every noise carried. As I could clearly hear the men's voices as they worked, I didn't feel tense or anxious and knew that if I had to fire a shot with my revolver Ian would certainly hear and immediately rush back to us. Every time I moved the blanket, I made sure I could easily reach the ammunition belt and the rifle which was always loaded with the safety catch on. I felt more nervous about guarding the Mauser than I did of being attacked.

Keith slept several times during the day giving me the opportunity to do my embroidery. Then my thoughts would turn to the harsh reality of the life we were now forced to lead due to the Mau Mau Emergency. There were no choices. I'd remember my safe, carefree days of youth – a mind-shatteringly different state compared to the present horror of terrifying murders, the ever-vigilant, armed lifestyle thrust upon us.

My childhood days were mainly spent in the carefree euphoria of glorious sunshine, animals, and a secure home life. I had lived on and off with Marge and Harold on Glenavon farm (about 50 miles from Anchorage), from the age of 9 months until I was 6 years old (at the start of World War II). My mother was very ill yet still had to cope with running her farm. She was also of the opinion that it would be good for Marge to have some practice looking after a child. Marge, almost 19 years older than me, became a second mother. I grew up with their 2 eldest children (3 and 5 years younger than me), Don and Bruce. The other 2, Rob and Janet, followed later. I saw Daisy often, as I was constantly going between the two homes, so my memories are betwixt and between. Marge used to take us for long walks on the plain behind her home. Sometimes, she'd pack us all up to go and stay with Daisy for weeks on end (Harold was away a lot in the army) then we'd return to Glenavon. I was raised in a very loving environment, mostly in female company.

From the time we were toddlers, we learned to speak Swahili and thought in the language as well. Many words crept into our mother tongue and stuck for the remainder of our lives. I love Swahili. It's pleasing to the ear and expresses both beautifully and graphically single words that have many meanings.

On Marge's play verandah was the loveliest dapple-grey wooden rocking-horse which made me long for a real pony of my own. I have memories of the salvia hedges with beautiful bluish-purple blooms either side of the garden path, the scent permeating the stillness of the air, bees buzzing in the warmth of the sun, and thought it all magical. Mingled with these scents was the sweet smell of fresh cows' milk in a back storeroom being separated into thick luscious cream – at breakfast time this was poured over our hot, sugared oatmeal porridge – absolutely delicious!

Outside, in the space between the ground and the verandah cedar flooring, lived a large puff adder that came out regularly to sunbathe then quickly disappeared on hearing footsteps in the passage. Young Bruce would tell his Mummy he'd seen a snake. There came the day when Marge, in a really terrifying moment for her, found the puff adder sunbathing, probably asleep, near the playpen and within Bruce's reach.

One night at Anchorage, we 3 children had been put to bed in my bedroom. Marge was away at the time. Aunty Vi (Harold's elder sister) and Daisy were taking care of us. The grown-ups had retired to bed as well. Suddenly, Bruce aged about 4, woke up screaming 'his head off'. In dashed Aunty Vi and my mother. Lighting a hurricane lamp they saw Bruce covered in *siafu* (safari ants). Some were really dug in. It took considerable time to pick them all off and out of his hair. Once before at Glenavon, both Don and Bruce were attacked by siafu at night – Harold and Marge put the boys in a bath of hot water making it easier to pick off the biting insects. From the time of this Anchorage incident onwards, our bedstead legs were stood in tins of paraffin. Siafu can consume live animals, right down to the bone. They're red-coloured, not that large, vicious, and march in long columns, down, over and up everything, devouring anything in their way once they're on the warpath. No small animal can escape once these ants have taken hold. Most everyone is afraid of them. Daisy remembered the night her cat and 3 kittens were completely devoured by siafu. She was 15, travelling with her parents around the Guaso Nyiro, living in a covered wagon, and the cat and kittens were in a box placed on the ground overnight. She said it was a traumatic experience to find her beloved pets simply gone in the morning.

During my childhood, wonderful and exciting Christmases were a time to look forward to for one never knew how Santa Claus would arrive or what he'd bring. At Gilgil Country Club one year, he came in a Bren gun carrier which put the boys on cloud nine, but was a little awesome for the girls. At Anchorage, the Christmas tree was always a young living cedar in the forest garden. Amongst the decorations we'd see our presents. Dressed up in our special clothes and shoes, we'd have a proper tea party with Marge's children, the grown-ups and kitchen staff. I remember vividly one particular Christmas when Don and Bruce were with me, and the presents I received – a Didi doll that wet itself when fed, and a doll's cot. My two-wheeler bicycle, received much later when I was back living permanently with my mother, was a great present, providing me with endless pleasure.

The forest garden was a fairytale place with a maze of pathways, flowerbeds of all the much-loved imported bulbs and huge trees where I spent many happy hours in wonderland. It was deep into the cedar woodland, with a stream running right through and down into a dam in a big open paddock where horses grazed. Daisy with her green fingers and the help of a few Kikuyu women – also gifted in gardening – created an Eden visited by many people. A carpenter, employed by a very handsome Asian contractor named Yassim, made my big, wide swing that comfortably seated 3 adults and at least 4 children. Daisy herself made furniture from thick green saplings into decorative tables and chairs nailed together in a circular pattern. She also made a bridge across the stream from a felled cedar tree with sides of wide trellis along its length, so we could better keep our balance. And fairies lived in the gardens. This I found out the afternoon my mother received the news of my brother, Terry's, death in Burma. I was taken on a long walk by a girl called Lydia, to keep me out of the house. She promised if I was good and didn't make a fuss the fairies would leave something for me on top of the post near the magnificent Golden Shower creeper-covered pergola. Sure enough, on our return there was a tiny celluloid doll waiting for me. Since then I know it's a good thing to believe in fairies!

My dog, Giftie, accompanied me everywhere. We'd wander across the farm checking bird nests to see if there were any eggs, go swimming in the dam, visit the horses and calves, the pigs and their squealing piglets. Through the orchards and Daisy's rambling gardens we'd continue to the forest garden and my special swing.

Anchorage farm was at an altitude of 8,000 feet. The great cedar forest came down almost to the backyard. We would sit on the front verandah, and using binoculars, gaze in wonder across to the Melawa Plains where we could clearly see the plains game – kongoni (the East African hartebeest), ostriches, zebra, Thomson's gazelle, steinbuck, and black rhino (*Diceros bicornis* – now critically endangered, these incredible animals can weigh as much as 1,364 kg, have two horns, are very short-sighted and have fiery tempers).

Across the Melawa Plains lay the spectacular Aberdare Mountains reaching an altitude of 14,000 feet. We could see the waterfalls spill down the deep valleys and gorges to the *Wanjohi* and *Happy Valleys* (the latter of some renown), both tucked away behind Whaleback Hill. Throughout the day the colours of the mountain would change from shades of blue, mauve and purple. No wonder the Kikuyu traditional belief is that they are one of the homes of *Ngai*, or God.

The densely forested Aberdare Mountains which thrust directly north were intercepted at every gorge by long pearl-like strings of silver waterfalls. This is what my home, Anchorage faced, as we'd sit on the front verandah at morning tea, late afternoon for freshly ground coffee, or simply to take in the stunning and ever-changing views. My home conjures up many images of halcyon days, golden and sunny, rains that left everything sparking fresh, plants which were willing to grow and flowered profusely. At this altitude, everything obligingly grew under my mother's careful, ceaseless nurturing.

Under the roof at Anchorage was a loft packed with a treasure trove of long forgotten items: trunks filled with old-fashioned clothes and shoes that held a particular fascination for me; masses of photograph albums, old newspapers and books. In a ply-wood box was an exciting jumble of Christmas decorations, tinsel and homemade streamers – the delicate glass baubles wrapped in tissue were kept separately. There was a lot of extra furniture, baby cot and outgrown toys, and a number of brown steamer trunks left with us for safekeeping, awaiting collection by their owners.

In those days of my young childhood, it was Daisy's habit to have two cooks. They'd take it in turns to do six-monthly duty, giving the other cook time to be with his family. Managi came to my mother as a young man. He'd been with us for years when he succumbed to cancer. His funeral was held in the forest garden. It was a big occasion with his relatives, friends and folks from neighbouring farms attending. Daisy and I used to go regularly to put flowers on Managi's grave. It was only Rho and Mwangi with us from then, Kariuki came later as Rho's helper.

Daisy was greatly loved by her Kikuyu staff and nicknamed *Memsahib Viazi* (Mrs Potato) because she grew and stored so many potatoes. The potato room (about 12 square metres) was separate to the barn. Daisy's imported Dutch seed-potatoes would be laid on the floor in alternate layers of straw and potatoes until the potatoes grew 'eyes' and were planted out. My mother always shared her garden fare with her staff. On their birthdays, Neville ensured they received a money gift.

As small children who grew up together, Don, Bruce, cousin Peter (Donald Smith's younger son), and myself always played outside in the rambling gardens where Daisy had built a large doll's house for me with 4 child-size chairs and a table. She gave me all the usual little girl's toys such as exquisite china tea sets, doll's cot, pram and furniture.

Usually we were barefoot. Shoes and sandshoes for sport came later when we started school and had to wear uniforms. Our feet were regularly checked for jiggers – *chigoe*, a tropical flea that burrows under the skin and lays its eggs. Small whitish-yellow swellings would show between the toes and under the nails. When the jiggers became intensely itchy, it was the clue that they were ready to be removed. Jiggers were a never-ending problem for the African children having no shoes, living in earthen-floored huts surrounded by bare earth. The Kikuyu well know the sort of dreadful damage a chigoe can cause (eating away the flesh of the foot and/or inflicting gangrene) and are experts at removing the parasites without breaking the sac, otherwise serious infection sets in. Mwangi always removed our jiggers. My mother would get a very fine sewing needle, clean the end with methylated spirits then burn the tip over a candle flame till the steel turned blue. Whilst Daisy stood close by telling me not to move, Mwangi would hold my foot firmly between his knees, then with the needle loosen the surrounding skin with great care and lift out the unbroken sac no bigger than a match head. He'd show it to me then almost ceremoniously burn it in the fire that heated our bath water. The first time I had a jigger dug out of my little toe I was terrified of the needle, but with Mwangi's expertise soon learnt there really was little pain.

I can remember being utterly intrigued and at the same time horrified on several occasions when my mother had to deal with members of her Kikuyu staff coming to her with a tale that a male relation had been cursed and would soon die because he'd found a dead pigeon placed in front of his closed hut door. So strong was this superstition that it was not unusual for the supposedly 'cursed' person to actually die.

One day, Don, Bruce, Peter and I were playing in Anchorage garden when suddenly there was a whining noise coming from above and behind. When it came closer, we saw it was an aeroplane with clouds of smoke trailing into the sky.

Peter, who seemed positive, screamed out, "It's a Spitfire!"

We ran around the house once watching the circling plane. Then there was a thunderous crashing noise and we knew it had hit the ground. Marge and Aunty Vi jumped into the grey Ford pick-up and sped off to find out if there were survivors. They'd estimated the plane went down somewhere at the top end of Anchorage. On the way there, they found some locals who too had witnessed the crash and were actually carrying 2 of the survivors. One man died in the crash. Marge drove the pilot, Captain Frogge, and crewman, Frank Brindley, to hospital in the big military camp at Gilgil. Later, we were told the Captain had been searching for a flat place to land. All he could see were fields of golden wheat ready for harvesting. But it was then too late – the wing of the Blenheim clipped a large cedar tree and down the plane went into a deep valley. A guard named Sergeant Griffin (no relation) was posted to keep an eye on the plane crash site until the investigation was over. Daisy packed a full Christmas dinner and together we took this to the Sergeant. While he and my mother were chatting, I idly picked up an oval object and was severely reprimanded, so gently put it down. At New Year, Daisy once again packed up a food parcel for the Sergeant. He told her 2 small Kikuyu children had unobtrusively sneaked into the investigation area and been killed instantly by the very same bomb I'd picked up. Bombs had been carried on the plane for warfare and when it crashed the bombs had been scattered.

We spent a lot of time on safaris and adventurous fishing trips along the Melawa River, parts of which were inaccessible because of cliffs or rocks, but most of the river was suitable for casting fishing lines. There were some special spots particularly popular for rainbow trout and camping. These were simply glorious years. The preparations always caused great excitement in anticipation of these three-week expeditions. In my day, we'd upgraded from a wagon with 6 or 8 oxen to a lorry. We took everything imaginable with us, including eggs coated with isinglass (a sealant preservative), ceramic demijohns in wicker-work in which were cooked sausages with liquid lard poured over them to keep out the air. Paraffin and hurricane lamps, drums of petrol, camp beds and tables, crockery, bedding and the canvas handbasins on tripods, first aid kits and the rifles. A cook and general factotum came along to clean the camp and bring plenty of firewood for the ever-burning fire to keep lions at bay. The first time I heard a hyena call right close by it was so frightening I jumped clean over the camp fire into my father's arms – a great leap which caused no end of amusement. Lions I'd often heard, usually in the distance, so was used to their roars. However, one night while I was with Marge, there was a terrible commotion immediately behind the homestead. Thorn-tree and brush *bomas* (camps) were built very close to the house where cattle were kept for safety. On this particular night, a big lion had jumped over the stacked prickly hedge, caught a fat steer and dragged it out. The bellowing cattle stampeded, breaking through the thorn protection. Harold went out with his rifle hoping to get the lion, but he was too late – the ox was dead and the lion had disappeared.

I often visited my elderly Uncle Frank Smith who'd been badly mauled by a lioness in 1908, the year William and his family first moved to Kenya as settlers from South Africa. Frank's grandson, Sid Dyer, relates the story: 'Frank was out hunting with a companion on the Southern Guaso Nyiro Plains when a lioness leaped onto his horse causing Frank to be thrown off. What saved his life was Frank casting his right arm down the lioness' throat in an effort to choke her. This caused her to try to cough him free whilst dragging Frank around and scratching at him like a rag doll until his companion could shoot her. Frank was badly mauled on his legs and right arm and the tendons in his wrist had been bitten through. Frank's companion took him back to their camp where a Colonel Ashton kept his wounds clean and open by flushing them with permanganate to prevent gangrene setting in. Frank's younger brother, Donald, then took him to Kijabe by ox wagon, a trip lasting 11 days. From there, they travelled another day by train to Nairobi where Frank received medical treatment and spent 6 months recovering. Frank suffered immensely from these injuries for the remainder of his life. Despite this, he was still an excellent horseman, and at one time ran a very successful ox wagon transport company from Londiani to Eldoret (then known as '64') before the railway branch was constructed. Frank's daughter, Patsy, took care of him until his death in 1969.'

Donald Smith also suffered a serious injury when he was out shooting with his father, William. A wounded Greater Bustard shot by William went charging off so William propped his loaded shotgun against a bush while he and young Donald gave chase. The Bustard came hurtling back around the bush, causing the shotgun to fall and go off, hitting Donald who was nearby, in the leg. The wound was so bad that the femoral artery could plainly be seen pumping. Aunt May administered her incredible first aid skills and accompanied Donald on the ox wagon and train trip to Nairobi where he was treated in hospital. She saved his life. His leg wasn't amputated, but was an awful sight. I was fond of my Uncle Donald and only ever remember him wearing long trousers. A Greater Bustard – *Otis Kori Kori* – is a very large game bird; males have a wingspan of up to 275cm.

Billy was my own first horse, a very elderly bay gelding, bequeathed to me by dear Mr Butner. I never did ride Billy. Soon after coming to me he developed lymphangitis for which there was no cure, and died.

Mr Butner, a middle-aged German Count who used to help out on the farms for his keep, travelling all over various districts, lived on and off with us and several members of our family when he was in our area. He was a tall, thin gentleman with perfect Teutonic manners. Mr Butner always wore the distinctive Australian hat (from his previous nomadic life in Australia), an army-like khaki jacket, jodhpurs, puttees and brown boots, and went everywhere with his rifle. His old bay horse, Billy, could be left unhitched while he waited patiently for Mr Butner to fetch him, then they'd go on to the next place where there was work waiting to be done. All the farming men had long gone, having joined the Forces, so the women needed Mr Butner's able help, there being many things they couldn't manage alone.

It was a world of total safety, the only sounds being those of the farm animals. The ploughing was done by oxen and driver. Every now and again you'd hear the crack of the long hippo-hide whip in the air to spur them on. Cultivating the pyrethrum shambas (fields) was done by Mr Butner and his mule pulling a small single share plough to turn the soil gently, holding the long reins and softly whistling. It was compulsory to have the oxen branded with specific letters on their hind quarters to prove they'd been inoculated against three major cattle scourges – AM was for Rinderpest; T showed immunity to East Coast Fever; and PO was for Pleuro-pneumonia.

Then one day, dreadful news reached us. Mr Butner had committed suicide by shooting himself. This was so shocking to me, especially when I learnt he had no family or contacts in Germany. I was completely mystified on being told that in Mr Butner's Will he'd left Billy to me, his rifle and scabbard to my brother, Ken, and that there were no other possessions. Everyone who knew Mr Butner respected and admired him. We never found out the real reason for him taking his own life. I shed tears realising the utter loneliness and sense of not belonging anywhere, which may have contributed to the hopelessness in Mr Butner's mind.

My second horse was 'Blackbird', a docile black mare with white flecks on her rump. Together we attended the districts Children's Pony Camps and Gymkhanas held in Naivasha. Alice Hauschild, Henry's sister, knitted my scarlet jerseys. Blackbird's matching scarlet saddle blankets were made by my mother, and my smart khaki overalls were sewn by 'Damn Cheap' of Ol'Kalou. My mother embroidered my initials on the top pockets in scarlet thread. Tents were provided sleeping 4 each, and every child brought his or her own camp bed and equipment, eating utensils and so forth. It was a fun time for all of us with our horses. At night, we'd have a barbeque and huge bonfires were kept going till we fell into our camp beds, happily exhausted.

The happiest time of my school years was the first year when I was sent to my teacher aunt, Marge Coombe (out from England), who married my uncle Fred Chart. They lived on the farm *Satima* in the Wanjohi Valley, at the foothills of the Aberdare Mountain range, home to the Ndorobo tribe and the magnificent Bongo antelope.

It was here too that the Happy Valley of scandalous events, newspaper headlines, tales, books and the movie 'White Mischief' snuggled so attractively between the Aberdare gorges, approximately 18 miles by car across the plains from Anchorage.

I believe Aunt Marge had originally come out as governess to some of the Happy Valley children. These residents came from wealthy, well-connected families in Britain. They kept to themselves and I'm told were extremely good and kind to their staff. Stories of fabulous photographic and hunting safaris for big game, affordable only by the rich and famous; the enigma of Lord Erroll's murder which never seemed to 'die' – as a small child, I clearly remember my peers endlessly chatting and discussing this intrigue. Even at that early age it fascinated me. Our lower income farming lives didn't mingle with theirs, though. Most of my clothes were hand-downs sent from family living in South Africa. Our car was the old Ford pick-up. But I lived an idyllic childhood of constant daily adventure, enjoying my various pets and a devoted family. I wouldn't have traded a day for a different life.

Driving to school at Aunt Marge's, along the dirt track crossing the plains in our old Ford we'd be chased by angry rhinos coming perilously near to the back of the car. It was so exhilarating, though we were always relieved to get out of range of the disturbed rhino which could easily tip over a vehicle since no car could travel at any great speed. So numerous were the black rhino, we knew each time we crossed the plains to get to family homes at the foot of the Aberdares that we'd encounter these great lumbering, sure-footed beasts, quietly grazing in ones or twos minding their own business. Then suddenly they'd hear the strange mechanical noises, prick up their ears, raise their heads and see the car. Without further ado, they'd charge with thunderous assault, puffing and snorting, kicking up clouds of dust. No way could anyone travelling in a car manage to sneak past a rhino! Although their eyesight is poor, their hearing is exceptional. For all we knew it's possible they may have thoroughly enjoyed the chase, which scared the daylights out of most of us, but was awesomely exciting!

My teacher, Aunt Marge's, gardens were filled with every kind of English plant. It was a great pleasure being with my cousin, Angel Mary in particular, and the older cousins. We'd go for walks along the mountain streams abundant with trout, and into the great apple orchards. The apples were picked and stored in high, long cedar cupboards in the house, the aroma permeating every room.

In the mornings after breakfast, it was time for each of us to be mounted on an old, docile bay gelding named *Mbuni* (meaning ostrich) and taught to ride by being placed in a basket saddle and strapped in securely. Then the horse was led by a syce (groom) for approximately half-an-hour. We always made for the storerooms and open garages covered by sweet-smelling yellow and white honeysuckle. This was the breeding place and home to chameleons that we children loved to catch and handle, then put back carefully. The Kikuyu syce didn't like chameleons since there are many superstitions about them, but so long as he didn't have to touch them, he was happy to while away the time leading the horse wherever we wanted to go.

Schoolwork was done in a gentle manner and we were read all the timeless and enchanting classics and poetry. I learnt to read avidly at Aunt Marge's, and thoroughly enjoyed Kipling and Dr Doolittle books, time-honoured fairytales, the Wind in the Willows and so many others. Jean (Aunt Marge's eldest child and sister to Angel Mary), older than us, found and kept hidden an old lower jawbone of a cow – suddenly with a shout she'd give chase. The rest of us with much shrieking and screaming in mock terror would make for the wooden fence. Once on top of the paling, we'd be immune to any attack. I don't think Jean particularly enjoyed this game, but she played along as the thrill of it kept the smaller children outside and occupied during leisure times.

We were taught to make cards and gifts for birthdays and Christmas, which were presented at the right time with much pride. Children were never taken shopping and they were well-behaved. My mother hadn't much time on her hands, so she instilled in me that writing to old and lonely people was our duty, a good deed, and the least one could do. One lady I knew only as Granny Medifant, who lived in South Africa. She crocheted my doll's clothes in a flamingo-pink colour. There were a number of elderly retired and eccentric people. I've no idea of how or why they came to be there. Word of anyone or anything out of the ordinary soon spread. The farming and rural folk were a small community and knew everybody.

I remember so well going on our monthly Kijabe trips to see my Uncle Boyce Aggett who owned the hotel. We'd then make sure to visit an old Scot, Mr Rennie, and take farm butter, eggs and so on for him. He fascinated Daisy with stories of the times he worked as a personal carpenter for Queen Mary. On each visit he'd take out a suede-wrapped bundle in which were kept his precious tools, all beautifully engraved with the Royal Crest. Mr Rennie lived in a one-room rondavel (a round room with a door, small window and thatched roof). He had an upright dining chair, a stool with a loose cushion under which he kept his folded spare trousers, and a single bed at the end of which bantam chickens roosted each night. Sitting on the stool and cushion creased and ironed his trousers. This method really bewildered me since in our home we had a *dhobi* man (staff member who washed, starched and ironed to perfection). Droppings from the bantams were swept daily into a little heap and used on the vegetable patch. The window was so covered in thick grey cobwebs one couldn't see through the 4 glass panes, so in a way they served as a curtain. On a small low table was an old-fashioned wind-up box gramophone (the pictures of which used to be shown on 'His Master's Voice' advertisements), and his two records were of patriotic Scottish songs.

Mr Rennie also had a 4 gallon tin with a lid on top that had a small hole in it. Near the bottom of the tin was a sticky, sickly mess of red raspberry drops that with time had melted together. I cringed when offered a sweet, but my mother's stern look made me take one out of politeness. After that, I couldn't stomach eating anything with artificial raspberry flavouring. I could tell that Mr Rennie was someone special and I also knew we seemed to be the only visitors to his humble abode. He'd frequently suddenly exclaim, "Oh! The blue bells of Scotland!" I realised he was very poor indeed. Mr Rennie was a real gentleman. I was always glad my mother took an interest in his life and treated him with kindness.

One of our neighbours was a South African, a Mr Martins, who'd come to work at the saw mills in the cedar forests on the hills behind our farm Anchorage. His eldest step-daughter, Lydia, was the girl who came on several occasions as a nanny for me. I was great friends with the younger step-daughter, Rosie, who schooled with me at both primary and secondary levels. Mr Martins was openly a strong Nazi supporter. It was his weekly habit to visit my mother to hear on her wireless the 7 o'clock evening BBC news broadcast. In Daisy's house it was a ruling that we all stand to attention at the signature tune, just before hearing, "This is the BBC calling from London." My mother encouraged Mr Martins' visits because she gained a lot of satisfaction and secret delight when he had to stand to attention. I can remember him no longer coming to hear the news when the tide turned and Britain began winning the war.

Fairly close to Anchorage lived an elderly retired English jockey known as Mr Downs. One couldn't help but notice his rolling gait and extremely bandy legs. He owned a thoroughbred racehorse, a mare named 'Spearfish'. She was for sale. Spearfish and Mr Downs lived in a very large, oblong barn-like house made of stone, in which was a very roomy inglenook. An armchair was so placed to be near the fire, while the remainder of the area was thickly spread every day with fresh golden wheat straw. Here the two of them lived very happily. Each night, Spearfish was brought into the cosy warmth of the room. I could well imagine Mr Downs with his glass of whisky as the two of them passed the evening hours in utter serenity and companionship. My brother, Neville, took me with him when he bought Spearfish in order to give her a home when Mr Downs left, presumably for England. She continued to live a gentle life, this time with our horses in the freedom of a beautiful paddock with cedar trees.

The accident to my uncle Alick Roberts – when an ox's horn pierced his temple going into his brain – always left me in awe. In those days, cattle were long-horned and had to be dipped every week for fear of them contracting East Coast Fever, a deadly parasitic disease for which there was no inoculation. Uncle Alick was working together with his

Maasai herders, tall and handsome, who smear their bodies and hair with red ochre clay. The Maasai are noted for their bravery. In those times, they survived off a mixture of milk and blood from the jugular veins of their massive cattle herds. A cattle dipping tank comprises a long, narrow and deep concrete structure filled with water into which the chemical mixture to kill ticks that carry East Coast Fever is added. The cattle plunge into the tank and swim to the other end. At angles off from the tank are several concrete paths called 'races' with strong upright poles and beams for the cattle to stand a while, giving time for the dip mixture to run off their bodies, down the channels and back into the dipping tank. Uncle Alick was standing alongside one of the races when an ox with very long horns tossed its head. One horn pierced his temple and brain, exiting with a piece hanging down his face. The Maasai herder standing nearest to him picked up a clump of fresh cattle dung and clapped it onto the side of Uncle Alick's temple, ensuring no more of his brain could exit the wound. He was then carried to the homestead and the doctor summoned. In the meantime, his wife, my fierce Aunt May, who'd been a nursing sister, took care of him.

Dr Tennant came well over 100 miles on wet, bad roads from Nakuru. He operated a couple of days later with Uncle Alick lying on the kitchen table, using hurricane lamps for illumination. Uncle Alick was eventually sent to England. The doctors attending him praised the quick action of the Maasai herdsman saying the fresh cowpat had saved his life, and that no more could possibly have been done for him. He was away for a year being taught to walk and talk again. Apparently, after not speaking for 6 months, his first word was, "Damn." Returning to Kenya by ship, Uncle Alick went back to all he'd previously done on his farm Aggetton in Nanyuki. He again drove cars and lorries, branded and dipped cattle, went on hunting safaris, and was even accurate enough to win the Bisley Shooting Competitions 3 times. His speech remained halting, erratic and in quick outbursts. He also had extremely vivid dreams. One time I remember, while he was staying with us. Uncle Alick dreamt his daughter, Iris, was drowning, so he leapt up, grabbed the electric light bulb hanging by its flex above his bed, then dived through the wooden wardrobe door – at which point he woke up and realised what had happened. I remember this vividly because Uncle

Alick was so apologetic to my mother and then went on to discuss the whole matter with her while I stood nearby listening. He was much loved. My 5 cousins told me that when they misbehaved – not bad naughty, just normal children's mischief – Uncle Alick hung them up on the hat hooks by their braces till they said, "Sorry."

Once, my mother sent me to stay with my harsh Aunt May for a few days holiday (my second Christian name, May, is after this aunt). I can only ever remember her as having a prickly character, not a bit like her sister, my mother, Daisy. I was somewhat afraid of Aunt May. One evening, she made me a cup of the most deliciously sweet cocoa. When I'd finished drinking this delight, and not wanting to leave even the tiniest drop, I rapturously licked the sides of the cup where the cocoa had dripped down. Aunt May saw me and sent me to my room immediately for poor table manners. Still, I have to admit she was an amazing nurse and saved 2 more lives.

The Roberts family took a safari somewhere in the Guaso Nyiro. In those days, lorries had only half-doors made of wood. It was necessary to hop over into the driving seat, with the children sitting on the camping gear in the back. The lorry turned over due to the lugga (a very wide and deep area of sand in a dry river bed, which accumulates each time there is flooding), and 10 year old Clive (my Uncle George's son), was trapped beneath the cab. First, he had to be dug out, then Aunt May administered the procedure to get him breathing again. His lungs were full of sand and his chest caved in. She worked wonders. I'm told it was a miracle the boy lived.

My brother, Ken, was 8 years older than me. When he was 8 years old at Nakuru Primary School, a boy in the same class, in a rough and tumble threw a sharpened ruler. It landed in Ken's eye, who at the time was minding his own business. He was found by the dormitory mistress, lying in pain on his bed. The eye was totally blind. No matter how many operations he had, the sight was never restored. Eventually, after WWII, Ken was given a glass eye which solved the problems and pain he had suffered. He remained an expert shot.

The highlight of my government Primary School boarding days in Nakuru were the Saturday morning riding lessons with our lovable

Molly Llewellyn (all her pupils adored her as we did the horses), and our Irish, Scottish and English dancing lessons.

One year, I won the Girls' Fancy Dress Competition. My mother brought the Ol'Kalou Station Master's wife with her to the school so that she could dress me completely as an Indian girl. I wore the lady's jewellery and clothes, and she put the traditional Hindi make-up on me. My prize was 10 shillings, which somehow got lost in the melee after the whole thing was over.

The school was surrounded by huge Pepper trees. Any number of enormous caterpillars lived there. My great friend, Pixie, would handle the hairless, beautifully coloured creepy-crawlies, but I refused to touch them.

Menengai Crater is behind and above Nakuru town and the school. We were taken in the school bus to see it as part of a geography lesson, and once, to watch the eclipse of the sun through broken pieces of brown or green glass from beer bottles. Menengai is an enlarged volcanic crater usually known as a caldera. We were told it was the 3rd largest crater in the world. The steep slopes were strewn with small, bright and sharp pieces of lava.

One of the school's War efforts was to take us children to nearby farms, where we were each given an army haversack. Then we had to break off the ripe wheat heads, which was an awful, tough job and hell on our fingers, but we all managed to fill our haversacks. Harvesters did the real job of harvesting the wheat, but presumably this was our war effort in saving fuel!

When I travelled in the car with Daisy, she taught then tested me on local and world geography. For example, longest river in the world, highest mountain, capital cities etc. – which is why Geography was one of my best subjects from the first year I learnt it at school.

On my mother's rare shopping trips to Nakuru, Rho, our cook, would accompany her. She'd buy a 2 pound tin of IXL Jam, usually melon and ginger, marmite, some sweets and biscuits, and put the lot into a *kikapu* (Kikuyu hand-woven reed basket). They'd drive to the back of my dormitory at 2 in the afternoon when all the children in hostels would be resting, and park under the giant Pepper trees so I wouldn't see them. Then Daisy would send Rho to find me in the dormitory.

"*Memsahib kidogo,*" (little miss) he'd call quietly.

Immediately, I knew who it was. I'd get off my bed and go to Rho at the dormitory back door where he'd give me my tuck. As it was a rare event, I was always so surprised and excited that I'd only notice too late that Rho and the emptied kikapu had disappeared. I never even saw nor heard the car leaving. All these scrumptious things I'd been left had to be taken directly to the dining room where they were marked with our names, locked in a cupboard and given out at appropriate times.

The very last thing I did at Nakuru Primary School was to copy my winning essay into the School Book of Records. The subject was 'Nakuru Lake' (surrounded by hills and ringed by green-topped fever trees with yellow blossoms), which at that time had almost dried up. When we children were taken there to observe the flamingos and their habitat, we walked some way across the Lake in about half an inch of slimy, smelly soda-encrusted mud flats – little did we know we'd have to write a long essay about this excursion. The flamingos, in their thousands, were an incredible and marvellous pink and white sight, unafraid of us, and a never to be forgotten image.

One afternoon, my very plump Aunty Vi (later to be my sister-in-law) came with her man friend, a farmer in the district, to the milking boma to see the Friesian cows and fetch me home. On the way back, they were holding hands which I thought soppy. I was very cheeky to her. She warned me that she'd give me a smacking. I retorted that she was too fat to run. Before I could say another word she caught me and gave me a good spanking. It was most embarrassing being spanked in front of a man. I felt very humble afterwards. I'd been showing off, so I deserved the hiding. I was about 7 at the time. The next time I was punished I was 14, and had lately become too big for my boots. My mother had taken all she could put up with and ordered me to my room while she fetched a leather belt and gave me a good thrashing. It all happened so suddenly. I was very surprised and most ashamed. Those were the only punishments I ever received. I deserved both.

When Aunty Vi stayed with us at Anchorage during WWII, as a further source of income during these very tough financial years, she had incubators and large numbers of various poultry, and kept the house in eggs, turkeys, chickens and ducks. One Muscovy drake was named

Stalin. The name suited him very well because he had a bunch of bushy whiskers (not feathers or quills) either side his beak and used to strut around the very large backyard with his wives, about 8 of them, following. Daisy, being so busy outside with the farm work was very glad to have Vi who was a tremendous help with the housekeeping. Breeding chickens in a big way required that straw was used for their bedding which had to be replaced regularly for hygiene of the egg-laying poultry. We always had plenty of chicken and eggs to eat. The substantial quantities of eggs for sale were kept in large wooden boxes with latches, the inside of each box stacked with trays of eggs totalling 144 eggs per wooden box. During school holidays, I helped Aunty Vi with the washing and weighing of each egg, a time-consuming and delicate task.

Aunty Vi also brought with her a knitting machine, making endless pairs of socks for the soldiers at the front. This machine was a big, heavy cast-iron contraption with a circular ring on which there were hooks for the wool stitches. As the sock progressed, a heavy weight was attached to pull it evenly downwards. It was a fascinating machine for any child to play with. One day, I rotated the handle and the hooked needles picked up the skin at the end of my left-hand fingers. I screamed blue murder. Aunty Vi came running and reverse turned the handle to undo me. Never again did I touch her knitting machine having lost all interest in it after this scary, rather painful lesson!

Until the day of my wedding, I called Marge, "Sister", and Vi, "Aunty Vi."

It gave me a smile to think that I'd never heard of Ian's existence until I was 14 when he unexpectedly arrived at Anchorage in his fancy saloon car. Considering Vi being so much in my young life and her brother, Harold marrying Marge and Harold being Ian's elder half-brother, I wondered how it was that I'd never heard of William's youngest child, Ian, before. I was in fact, per the family tree, Aunt to some related children a few years younger than myself, but as kids growing up together they called me Heather and not Aunt Heather. Perhaps it had something to do with such an extended 2 families of Smiths and Aggetts and my having so many uncles, aunts and cousins that with Ian living in South Africa and there being an 18 year age gap between Harold and himself, Ian never seemed to come up in family conversation. Or perhaps I wasn't paying enough attention. It was something of an amusing puzzle to me, but one that certainly had a happy ending in my favour.

My memories of days gone by were interrupted by the sound in the distance of the Ford continuously moving as baby Keith and I waited on the blanket under the tree. Hurriedly, I put my embroidery away and started packing everything ready for loading onto the car when Ian stopped. He preferred not to be kept waiting since it was time to take the staff home and it wasn't a good idea to be hanging around unnecessarily during Mau Mau. All I desperately wanted was to be back in my house away from this anxiety where it was just my baby and me alone in the bush.

Back at the homestead, the men would climb off, collect and put away all the tools in the shed, then go to their families. I'd take Keith inside, put him into the big cot I'd had as a baby, fetch everything from the car, bath and feed him. Next, the animals needed their food. Last of all, I'd see to our supper which meant stoking up the wood stove to get it hot again. By 7, the house was hunkered down, everything securely locked, and the blackout blankets put up across our bedroom windows. No longer did we stay up and listen to favourite records on our wind-up gramophone, nor keep the lamp going to read before going to sleep. I sorely missed not being in our recently completed homestead during the day and being able to relax with my husband in the evenings. Ian had toiled endlessly to give us the life we had planned. I'd yearned for our 'idyllic' Uruku, wanting our children to experience the security, safety, and freedom of an unhindered, happy farm upbringing.

What with the drought, Mau Mau and subsequent difficulties of farming in an area under such duress during the State of Emergency, Ian was tired out and slept heavily at night. I was the watchful one. One night, I awoke to hear crunching noises going on next to me. Putting my hand out, I felt our cat Simon, eating a mouse on Ian's chest! I had to wake Ian to tell him! Because of security restrictions, I could only light a candle, and as quickly as possible cleaned up. After a good laugh and a cup of tea from one of the thermos flasks, we finally managed to get back to sleep again.

The drought worsened. Harold and Marge were now living in Western Kenya at Soy. On Harold's advice, Ian decided the best thing to do was to sell Uruku and move to a safer, more productive, higher rainfall area. This meant a lot more changes. It was better for me and baby Keith to stay with Marge at Merrowdown while Ian and Harold went off in search of a suitable farm that we'd be able to afford. After a month of travelling around the entire Western Kenya area, a 1,802 acre property was found near Hoey's Bridge (reminding us of William's former farm-pupil, A C Hoey), with one boundary being the Little Nzoia River. Whilst staying with Marge and Harold, I became pregnant with my second baby.

Our lives on Uruku and at Anchorage had been totally controlled by security measures. We'd lived each day and night one at a time and thought ourselves lucky that nothing worse had happened to us through gruelling Mau Mau times. We well knew that many other Kenyans had to endure the constant daily fear of terrorist attacks. Thankfully and gratefully, we'd have to live in the thick of Mau Mau only until late 1953 when we moved to our new farm, *Westlands*.

Shortly before we left Uruku, Ian returned the hand-grenade to the Lancashire Fusiliers – that alone signified to me one change for the better.

Chapter Six
Westlands

Having stayed overnight with Daisy, we left next morning after breakfast and drove over the hills of the Dundori Forest Range. Reaching the main north-bound tarmac road at Nakuru, it led us directly through the town of Eldoret in Western Kenya. Twenty-one miles further on towards the town of Kitale on the left-hand side was the farm turn-off to Westlands. We arrived by lunchtime.

Westlands had been allowed to run down as the owner, Mr Barnes, was a very elderly bachelor, unable to cope much longer. The house was a minute red brick building with one bedroom, a bathroom, no indoor toilet, and a small sitting room with a fireplace and chimney. Away from the house was the long-drop lavatory. The bedroom had a crack 4 inches wide from the top of the hinge side of the door frame to the ceiling, that apparently pulled together once the rains came. An outhouse, best described as a dark, smelly and soot-filled hovel was the kitchen which had an old Dover cast-iron wood burning stove, very much the worse for wear. Only Lugusi, the cook-cum-general-house factotum we inherited (almost permanently inebriated on locally brewed beer known as *pombe)*, knew how to work this stove.

We had to start everything, from farm to home, again. The best things we knew definitely were that the rainfall records kept for years showed an average of 80 inches per year, and we no longer had to carry firearms, as we lived in a Mau Mau free area. From our tiny front porch we could see the top of Koitoboss – 4,321 metres, the highest peak on Mt Elgon, Kenya's 2nd highest mountain, on the western border with Uganda.

First thing to do was to employ labour. Mr Barnes had paid off and given his few elderly employees their bonuses and all had gone to retire in their homelands, except Lugusi, who agreed to stay on for a few months to help me. By some luck, 'Turkana' arrived on the scene. With some difficulty we understood him to say he wanted cattle work. Turkana was a tall, proud, young Turkana tribesman with a pungent smell about him and no lustre to his skin from being permanently dusty, carrying his spear and wearing only a dirty, oily loincloth. He was unfamiliar with the Swahili language. Turkana indicated to us that he had no other name and wanted to work for money to buy clothes, and then would return to the Turkana tribal homelands in Northern Kenya where all his family lived.

Ian had put everything we owned, including cattle, horses, machinery, furniture and all the packed-up boxes on the train at Thomson's Falls. They arrived all at once 3 days later at Heard's railway siding right next to the farm. The first animals to be offloaded were the particularly exhausted in-milk Ayrshire dairy cows. Turkana took them to the river then herded the cows across a main road, and very slowly guided them to the milking shed where an attempt was made to milk them by hand as usual. However, their udders were swollen and hard and the milk came out in thick rubbery threads. How Turkana managed alone to milk all the cows I never did understand. In a few days they were thankfully back to normal. He certainly was showing his abilities from the start.

Soon other men came for employment. It wasn't long before we had enough labour. Turkana stayed one year as a herdsman. During that time, he had accumulated all the clothing and possessions he deemed necessary, one item being a battery-operated radio. As Ian said, "*Kwaheri*" (goodbye), he casually mentioned to Turkana that to make clothes last longer they should be washed regularly, and then added, "You too must wash!"

Turkana replied that he'd been, "Washed at birth and that is the only time required by his people." Ian missed Turkana and his quiet, knowing ways with cattle. Some years later, we visited the Turkana people when we holidayed at Lake Rudolf (now Lake Turkana). Only then were we able to imagine the stir Turkana must have caused when, all dressed up and with some precious belongings he'd returned home, because the custom of the Turkana tribe was to be naked.

Starting from scratch a 2nd time was extremely difficult, particularly as we were very cash-strapped. As the farm had been allowed to regress for a long time, the little fencing there was would have to be replaced, the road needed to be bulldozed and built up. The cattle dipping tank had been unused for years and all the boma (paddock) poles had rotted or been eaten away by white ants. Added to this, there was no water pump for getting water to the house, and the undulating arable land was not terraced. There were a few relatives of Lugusi, all elderly, well beyond working ability. Their dog population was out of control, wandering everywhere killing the small game.

We also had to set up various farming business and co-operative facilities, as well as bank accounts and arrange our doctor and dentist, chemist and grocery store contacts in the nearest town, Eldoret. Like all Kenya small towns, Eldoret had almost every conceivable necessity. I did my monthly grocery shopping at Madatally's where just about everything was available. The owner was a very affable, good-looking young Indian. Our banking was done at Barclays. Shops were owned by various Kenya-born folk. The Mercedes Benz agency belonged to the brothers Khan who were Sikhs. Mr Pinto, a Persian, owned the homeopathic shop. The Long Bar owner (his family originally from Goa in India) looked like Sammy Davis Junior and was nicknamed 'Speedy Gonzalez' because he never stopped rushing around. We came to know all of them very well, became fond of them and they will never be forgotten.

No sooner were the majority of things organised and we'd settled into the tiny house, than the Government sent Ian his Kenya Regiment Military Training Call-up papers. He would have to go for 6 months to the Camp at Lanet, just outside Nakuru (compulsory training for all Kenya young men).

Hoey's Bridge being a sandy area meant that plough discs had to be changed for new ones about 3 times during the deep-ploughing phase. Ian had started planting maize and having only one old tractor it was imperative to fix any breakdowns immediately to avoid delays in the schedule. He was changing big plough discs one morning, trying to get a bolt securely seated using a hammer when a splinter of steel from one of the discs shot up straight into the pupil of his right eye. Ian struggled on and managed to complete changing all 6 discs. By nightfall he was in absolute agony from eye pain. Realising the seriousness of the situation regarding Ian's eyesight and knowing he needed medical attention, I insisted we go to Eldoret the following morning to see Dr Peake (a relation to the famous Moffat family of early missionary/African exploration). He took one look at Ian's eye and said go to Nakuru. We returned home to collect baby Keith's necessities then took him to Marge and drove to Nakuru. There Dr Johnson tried to pull out the splinter with no success, only to drive it deeper into Ian's pupil. He then telephoned the only eye specialist in Nairobi, Dr Heath, where a strong magnet was placed over the eye. Within minutes the splinter came out easily, and we were on our way home. After this, Ian was blind in that eye, but it didn't prevent him from being the 2nd best shot in his platoon in the Kenya Regiment. If you looked at him, you wouldn't notice anything wrong with his right eye. Although Ian was right-handed, from then on he used his left eye for sighting in weapons and shooting, and remained a good shot all the years. At the start of his training, he was given weekend leaves to come back to the farm.

I managed for a short while to keep things going. But, as my 2nd pregnancy advanced, which wasn't going well, it became impossible for me to cope with running the farm alone. I returned with baby Keith to my mother at Anchorage. Harold, cattle farming 23 or so miles from us temporarily took over Westlands. He put in a manager, a Mr James, who had to be carefully watched because he did very little, spending a lot of time locked in the house. This information was given to us by Lugusi. Then it was discovered that Mr James was a heavy drinker. He'd put us into debt by selling off tractor fuel very cheaply to certain neighbours in order to keep a plentiful supply of liquor within easy reach.

On Leave-Outs, Ian would come home to us at Anchorage and help with patrol duties as the Mau Mau were still very active in the Central Highlands. There were more dreadful murders. Tree Tops, the famous Lodge was burnt down. Crops were set afire. Farm animals were mutilated and had to be put down. Generally, things had hardly improved. Security was as tight as ever. In April, 'Operation Anvil' was put in place, and the Security Forces destroyed much of the Mau Mau passive resistance organisation in and around Nairobi. Thousands who were arrested were taken to special detainee camps where they were screened, all of which took a painstakingly long time, and ended with about 16,000 who remained as being active Mau Mau supporters.

The murder by panga of 4 year old, Andrew Stephens, on 4th April 1954, particularly affected me. The little boy was slashed to death outside his home while innocently riding his tricycle.

On 23rd June 1954, I was delivered by breech of a baby girl, named Beryl Marjorie (born on her great-grandmother's, my Granny Aggett's, birthday). Thanks to my mother, Keith, Beryl and I continued to live at Anchorage while Ian completed training camp.

Another widely known Mau Mau case was that of Arundell Gray Leakey. He was kidnapped and buried alive in October 1954. His wife was shot dead on their farm 5 miles from Nyeri, after she'd hidden her daughter in the ceiling which saved her life.

On Ian's 'Passing Out' Parade Day, Keith stayed with Daisy and I took Beryl back to the War Memorial Hospital where she'd been born, to be taken care of while I celebrated with my husband and his fellow 'new' soldiers. They were now to be sent to do duties at the detention camps. It took 4 months for Ian's case to be heard before the Agricultural Committee (as a married farmer with a family). Then he was released and we were able to return to Westlands. By this time, our farming programme had ground to a halt. Being in debt worsened the situation. We were advised to take out a Government loan as farmers had been informed by the Kenya Co-operative Dairies of a plan to supply fresh whole milk to Uganda on a daily basis. The loan was granted. Soonest possible, Ian bought in a herd of good quality Friesian cows and 2 pedigree bulls. At the same time, Ian decided to substantially increase the scale of maize production and put 1,000 of the 1,802 acres comprising Westlands under the plough. On such a massive scale of proposed productivity, he would need finance and approached the Land and Agricultural Bank of Kenya. They assisted, enabling Ian to cover the costs of relevant machinery, equipment and fertilisers etc. The milk quota and maize projects then ran simultaneously, and the months of frustration for Ian when work on the farm had stagnated to a virtual standstill were now a thing of the past. He surged forward with enthusiasm in turning Westlands around. Every day saw improvement as his plans were turned into reality.

From the Nuffield Agents in Eldoret, Ian bought 3 big new orange-coloured tractors with hydraulic ploughs and harrows, cultivators and maize-seed planters. The arrangement was that the tractors would be replaced every year with new ones, ensuring a trouble-free maintenance programme as no time could be wasted on breakdowns or unnecessary interruptions to the maize production schedule. The old tractor was kept purely for dairy work. Ian employed and trained 6 tractor drivers. They started work at 7 in the morning and brought their food and drink, had their meal breaks then went back to work. Two drivers were allocated to each new tractor, working day and night shifts. The day shift ran from 7 in the morning to 7 at night when the other shift took over. Daily tractor maintenance was done at 6 in the evening and again at 6 in the morning. The drivers never swapped tractors. With Ian's thorough guidance, these men became utterly reliable and proud of their work and machines.

On the dairy side of operations, the dairy farmers nearest the Ugandan border were given a milk quota. Early in the mornings, fresh whole milk was immediately put through the cooling machines Ian had bought, then poured into 10 gallon sterilised milk cans and sealed (sterilised by steam jets). It was then loaded onto the farm long-wheelbase Land Rover and taken to the adjoining tarred main road to await our route milk lorry; the cans were then transferred and driven non-stop to Uganda. There was a time schedule to be carefully adhered to. Never were we late. On the Uganda return trip, the milk lorry would deposit our empty cans at the same location and we'd pick them up the following morning. It all ran like clockwork. Most mornings, it was my job to deliver our 10 cans of milk to the main road. Ian built 2 enormous moveable and highly successful milking byres, which were pulled by the old tractor every day to fresh ground. This ensured that the cows never walked or stood in mud. It wasn't too long before we had a good-sized herd of young purebred milk-producing Friesians, ensuring us a doubled quota increase. We then kept the small herd of Ayrshire cattle as a hobby. To improve their quality, Ian imported a pedigree, virgin bull named 'Ben' and 2 in-calf heifers from Montague Simpson, a famous breeder from Johannesburg, South Africa. They came by ship to Mombasa. An agent sent us a telegram to say they'd been put on the train with an attendant. Three days later, they arrived at the siding close to our farm road. Ben proved to be an excellent sire though he had a fiery temperament. Anyone in his vicinity gave him a wide berth as Ben became known for his vicious nature.

The Ayrshire bull calves were castrated, and at a year old were sent to the beef herd, taken care of by Chalagut. He was an elderly Tiriki man always dressed in oily beaten skins and a *kaross* (a skin cloak which still has the fur or hair of the animal on it). Chalagut was never without his heavy *knobkerrie* (a stout wooden stick with a knob at the end and used as a club or missile by African tribesmen) and a short throwing spear. He was tough, scrawny, very wrinkled and had a shaven head. Dedicated to the cattle, he always referred to them as 'my cattle'. A good old man with very few needs, Chalagut was utterly reliable and lived his daily life with 'his cattle' from sunup till sundown. Beef animals, when ready, were sent to the Kenya Meat Commission just outside Nairobi. This was a highly successful organisation not only for beef, but hides and skins plus all the by-products of the beef industry. All Friesian bull calves were slaughtered to feed the farm staff.

One day, a down-and-out man drove to our house to ask Ian if he would lend him a tractor. Ian said, "No," because Lugusi told us this man was the person who'd bought the farm fuel cheaply from Mr James thereby enabling him to have an endless supply of liquor at our expense. Only a short time later, the district was scandalised to find out the Welfare had been called in, and had found this man's simple-witted wife had been kept chained to the bed every day while the husband was away or working on his farm. It seemed inconceivable that such a thing could have taken place and been kept so well-hidden from neighbours. It was common knowledge that staff knew everything that went on in households. The house staff member eventually reported this incident to the young English Police Officer at Soy Police Station.

Diesel in tankers was delivered by the fuel company to the farm and pumped into the storage tanks that had been installed. The diesel was then transferred into drums which were taken by trailer to wherever the tractors were working, ensuring the drivers could refuel immediately.

The 1,000 acres for maize first had to be cleared and terraced, the sandy loam ploughed to a depth of at least 12 inches, in some parts up to 18 inches, followed by disc harrowing. Tooth harrowing followed to get the soil absolutely weed-free and well broken-down to a suitable condition for dry maize seed planting and fertilising. South African Maize Wonder Planters was the newest agricultural implement. An enormous quantity of fertiliser was trucked in and stacked on each shamba. This intense preparation was well worth the effort. When the rains broke early in April, they gave the seed that extra boost so needed for exceptional harvests. If something really went wrong with the tractors during the night, such as a burst inner tube (impossible to change alone), the driver with his torch would come to the house, stand at the storm ditch perimeter of the back garden and call out to us. I would wake Ian, who'd go to the window to find out what the matter was. If necessary, he'd get dressed and go with the driver in the Land Rover to the tractor and fix whatever the mechanical or tyre problem was. Many times, Ian would tell the driver what to do or where to find something, then he'd go back to bed and have no recollection of it in the morning.

The young calves also had their own herdsman and were kept in a paddock adjoining the road to the house. While sitting on an anthill whiling away the time, one day the herdsman saw a python catch a 6 month old calf, but was able to chase the snake off with his knobkerrie. We never found that python, and from what the herdsman told us, Ian estimated it to be 12 foot long. Pythons were a problem as they were quite common along the Little Nzoia River on our western border.

Jeusi and Asha (Chalagut's wife), both Tiriki women, came asking me for work. The Tiriki is a sub-tribe of the Abaluhya of Western Kenya. Both women were wearing beaten-hide skins and karosses, were barefoot and smelt strongly of wood-smoke and rancid fat which formed at the top of their calabashes and was used as an emollient on their body skin. I put them onto clearing the brush and long grass around the house. Although there was an abundance of Jacarandas, blue gums and indigenous trees, there was no garden, just a pear-shaped sandy smooth driveway. With Jeusi's first salary, she went shopping at the Indian duka at Hoey's Bridge, and bought several lengths of bright flowered cotton material, then asked me to make dresses for her. Jeusi was absolutely fascinated with my second-hand Singer hand-operated sewing machine. A frail little woman, she found she couldn't keep up with the work so went back to looking after her grandchildren. Jeusi told me that the women of her tribe used wild basil when menstruating, and that it was also a good cleaner for their milk calabashes.

Asha, who'd started off clearing the garden around the house, now asked whether she could work inside. She was an endearing and unpolished woman, going on 50, very scrawny with some missing front top and bottom teeth (removed in case of Tetanus, a tribal custom). As I had 2 small children, 15 months apart, I thought this a good idea, so took her to the Indian tailor in Eldoret. He made some red, blue and green uniforms with matching head scarves and aprons for her. Asha was delighted and laundered these garments with great care. Small, heavy metal irons, heated on the wood-burning stove were used for pressing the clothes and linen. Now Asha learned how to make beds, knit, looked at magazines upside down, and even did some cooking on the wood-stove. She took to looking after Keith and Beryl 'like a duck to water' and was such an enthusiastic and punctual person. Arriving at 7 in the morning, she'd find the children dressed and ready to go for their early morning walk – Beryl in her pram and Keith ambling along beside them, with all the dogs in tow. They were back at 8 for breakfast. Asha measured time by checking the sun's position. Beryl had a mid-morning nap, so Asha and Keith would go off to see the horses, cows or calves, look at the machinery or go with Ian in the old Land Rover to see how work was going on the far side of the farm where the 3 tractors were continuously working.

Because we had to use milk cooling machines, Ian had bought a large generator that supplied the house with electricity. My mother now bought me a small Hoover washing machine. This was heaven to Asha, who quickly learnt how to operate it. From lunchtime till 4 in the afternoon Asha went home, returning in time for tea and another long walk on the farm roads with the children and dogs and back again for baby baths at 6. Much of Asha's time was spent entertaining Keith and Beryl on the swing and see-saw, looking at all the animals, playing with toys, just walking around or sitting on the lounge carpet looking at magazines. But, when Ian started to play polo again, the whole scene changed. Wherever we went for polo weekends, Asha came too. She was amongst a group of ayahs all looking after children so it was one big get-together for them. For polo tournaments where we had to sleep away over weekends, Asha took the bedding we'd given her. Many times she slept between the children's beds in the rooms allocated by our hosts. Asha loved her job and enjoyed being the boss in our home. She took a certain amount of pleasure in bossing the other staff around.

News from Anchorage in 1956 reached us of Mr Golding's sudden admittance to Nakuru Hospital. He'd suffered many years of stomach problems and indigestion for which he took Milk of Magnesia as well as a stomach powder mixed with water on a daily basis that he kept in his bedroom at Daisy's. During Mau Mau when I was living at Anchorage for safety's sake, Mr Golding once accidentally mixed his plaster of Paris powder and drank it down mistakenly thinking it was his stomach powder. This error in 'medication' Grandma Montefiore found highly amusing. She remarked at the time with a click of her too-loose dentures, "Perhaps he'll be passing statuettes soon!" ending her comment with a "Humph!" in her usual way, as if she'd scored a point.

The plaster of Paris incident reminded me of another 'stomach woe' Mr Golding unfortunately experienced when he was a relatively new boarder with my mother. I was at hostel at the time. On that particular day, Daisy wasn't feeling well. Mwangi made a stew for Mr Golding's evening meal and kept it hot in the oven of the *kuni* (wood) stove. Daisy just had toast for her supper. Mr Golding dished some stew for himself. Soon after, he started vomiting followed by bouts of diarrhoea. In the morning, my mother asked Mwangi about the ingredients he'd put in the brown stew. Quite innocently, he replied that he'd found some shallots in the potato store that he'd sliced up, fried and added to the cooking pot. It had been an unintentional mistake, but the 'shallots' in the potato store were actually Daisy's daffodil bulbs. I think it was lucky in this instance that due to Mr Golding's inherent sensitive stomach condition he always had a small appetite, as all parts of daffodils are toxic (including to dogs) causing abdominal pain, nausea, vomiting and diarrhoea. Mwangi mistook the daffodil bulbs for onions.

Daisy's news of Mr Golding's prognosis in hospital was serious. He'd been diagnosed with cancer of the liver, which after all the years of him suffering stomach ailments now made sense to us all. His condition deteriorated rapidly. Ian and I, with the children, hurriedly arranged a trip to see him. I didn't know what to say to the old man and just fell on his neck sobbing and hugging him. I don't recall Ian's words to him. We stayed only a short time, but long enough for Mr Golding to know we loved him and that he was part of our family. He lived another week and died on 15th April 1956. Being a Freemason, he had a solid cedar coffin with a brass plaque on the top giving his name. His service was held at our little Church of St Peter's in Ol'Kalou and he was buried in the small Church cemetery. I don't remember Mr Golding ever complaining about anything in life. He was special to us all and had been Daisy's close friend for years whilst boarding with her at Anchorage. Mr Golding had proved invaluable during the horrors of Mau Mau. Although saddened, Ian and I were also glad we'd got there in time to say our farewells. Daisy took Mr Golding's death badly and missed his companionship immensely. Every evening come sundowner time, she particularly remembered their customary drink of Brandy and Ginger to end a busy day. My mother's life was now extremely lonely.

There was an enormous and never-ending list of things to be done on Westlands, but we welcomed the challenge and were very happy in our lives. It had been a wise decision to move to Western Kenya for its security and abundant rainfall. The farm was beginning to show some profit for Ian's dedicated work.

From 1952 to 1956, colonial Government forces killed more than 11,000 Mau Mau. Official statistics of deaths at the hands of Mau Mau were 68 whites; 26 Asians; and 2,000 loyal Kikuyu foully and brutally murdered. Causes of deaths varied – by panga and/or knobkerrie, being ambushed, shot, knifed or burnt to death, buried alive, disembowelled, strangled, mutilated – whatever the manner, the Mau Mau had their methods of merciless killings.

Africa's history over the years has often documented the hideous deaths meted out by African on fellow African (which still continues in 2016). Mau Mau days would be an era of significance. As the lines became blurred of who was hardened Mau Mau and who was not, in the endless days that stretched into years, of flushing out and dealing with the perpetrators, tragically many innocent Kenyan Africans suffered unfairly, unnecessarily and unjustly. The harsh and callous nature of war, anywhere in the world, has proven that the boundaries between innocent and guilty at times of conflict become an ugly, overlapping shade of grey. Innocent lives get caught up in the turbulent cauldron, leaving humanity with the smear of shame and a bitter gall taste in the mouth and, hopefully to ponder later and face some of the grave injustices of past actions.

The Government approached the farmers asking them to help by employing Kikuyu men who'd previously been Mau Mau sympathisers but were now 'de-oathed'. Knowing the Kikuyu tribe as being conscientious and diligent workers, we had no hesitation in accepting the offer. We were sent Kamau who became our gardener and a great favourite; Mwangi, for the stabled pedigree cattle (being 4 bulls and 3 cows); and a very pleasant man, Wambugu, who became our houseman. Kamau was an old man when he came to us, this being the reason why we decided he'd work in the garden. He also took care of the chickens and ducks, made the dog food and washed the cars. It quickly became apparent that he not only loved our children and they him, but that he was genuinely fond of us as a family, as we were of him. As with Asha, Kamau and Wambugu enjoyed their jobs at the house, were punctual, absolutely reliable and completely trustworthy. I considered myself lucky they were in our employ.

Mater came to stay with us for 4 months when Keith was about 3 and Beryl 15 months old. She took over the cooking, and made some shirts for Keith on my old sewing machine. I got on well with her and she was always kind and friendly towards me, happily accepting me as her youngest son's wife. She rearranged all the sitting room furniture. Ian said not to make a fuss and rather just let her carry on in her way and we'd put things back in their place when she went back home to the Cape. So I let her take over as she pleased. This gave me a good opportunity to get into the garden at last and complete making a lawn, put in flower beds and do some planting etc. which I found most enjoyable. After her return to South Africa, Mater sent me a parcel with 3 lovely new dresses plus a 'designer' raincoat each for Marge and me.

When Beryl was about 2 years old, we took our first annual one-month holiday at Malindi on the coast. We put Asha on the passenger train at Eldoret giving her full instructions of exactly where we would find her. Ian and I then took it in turns to drive through the night with the children asleep in the back of the car, in time to meet the train at 8 the following morning at the Mombasa Railway Station. Asha had yet to see the sea, and was instructed by the farm staff to bring home a bottle of sea water – in their culture, supposed to have a medicinal value when ingested.

Malindi then became our regular yearly vacation destination. Asha thoroughly delighted in these train trips. She had her bedding, money to buy food en route, an endless assortment of travelling companions and heard masses of thrilling stories. Once, near Voi, the train had to be stopped because a bull elephant would not get off the tracks. There was great excitement amongst the passengers. When the elephant finally moved off and the train slowly inched forward, the bull stood still close by, near enough for Asha to have a really good look at him. She was so thrilled that she couldn't stop talking about this experience. How big the elephant was! It was the 1st occasion she'd seen such an enormous animal. Once, at Soy, though from a distance, she'd seen a rare and very beautiful Rothschild's giraffe – a spectacularly dark mottled giraffe with a third horn in the middle of the forehead – but she'd never seen an elephant before.

From Mombasa, we still had 80 miles of rough road through palm plantations and beautiful forest then 2 ferries to cross before reaching Malindi. Asha's experience of the 1st ferry at *Shimo-La-Tewa* (the meaning of which we understood to be 'Hole of the Rock-Cod') was terrifying for her, but thrilling for us, especially the children. The ferry carried vehicles and people on foot or bicycles from one side of the creek to the other, being hauled across the sea water by men pulling on steel cables that lay across the surface from the one bank to the other anchored in huge concrete blocks. On approaching the ferry crossing, cars had to slow down to a crawl, engage low gear and wait in the queue if the ferry was still crossing. If it had already docked, the ferry boss would signal to drive carefully down the steep embankment onto the lowered ferry ramp which was a little under sea water. Once the pedestrian passengers, cyclists and 6 cars were aboard, the ramp was raised. Then a team of muscled, bare-chested men wearing traditional *kikois* (brightly coloured plain or patterned cotton loincloths) tied around their waists, skin glistening from the humidity and sweat of exertion, would begin hauling on the cables. Intermittently, they chorused in unison, "*Harambee*" (a work chant meaning pull or work together), "*Harambee,*" to keep up their strength and momentum whilst others at the same time blew eeric hooting sounds on conch shells.

It was an enthralling experience completely captivating one's senses, giving me 'goose bumps'. Contentedly, my mind and body became captured in the charm of this unique 'picture' unfolding around me. With the waves lapping the ferry and seagulls flying overhead, the softest breeze teased my skin as the sea spray mist touched my face, the sunshine and humidity mixed to a gentle shimmering quiver dancing over the water. It's one of those times in your life when you want the world to stop turning and stand still, just for a bit, so you can linger in the moment, hesitant to break the magic.

Crossing the water, there was a lot of animated chatter and jabbering amongst ferry passengers. Vehicle occupants could leave their cars and walk around, many giving out cigarettes, biscuits and cool drinks for the teams of men. Reaching the other side, the front deck was splashed down into the water. The pedestrians and cyclists would surge onto the embankment followed by the cars driving off slowly and carefully, one at a time in low gear up the steep hill. Before embarking on the ferry, if there was time waiting in the queue of cars, we'd make a beeline to buy delicious freshly roasted cashew nuts wrapped in newspaper cones from the vendors under the trees. They kept their charcoal braziers going from 6 in the morning to 6 in the evening. The most delicious cashew nuts ever! Hot to the touch, sometimes slightly burned around the edges, with a smoky taste. After the 1st ferry crossing even Asha was fired up for the next one. When the new main tarmac Mombasa-Malindi road was completed it by-passed the narrower Shimo-La-Tewa creek crossing which was more convenient for motorists. Kilifi Ferry, the wider crossing of the 2, some time later replaced the teams of men hauling on the cables with engine-propelled tug boats guiding the ferry, so most of the excitement was lost.

We gave Asha a blue swimsuit. She spent many happy hours with the children playing in gently lapping waves or on the beach at Silversands where Vi and her farming husband, Bertie Case, with their 2 children, Tony and Hazel, owned a holiday home. Vi's children were born late in her life; Tony only about 2 years older than Keith and Hazel 2 months younger. As farm life was very busy we had little time for socialising, so it was wonderful spending time together fishing, snorkelling, boating, picnicking, sightseeing and collecting sea shells.

Shopping was interesting and exciting in the different Arab and Indian dukas jam-packed with all sorts of items and an abundance of exquisite silks and cottons in a multitude of colours and patterns. Owning a 'Malindi shirt' (not unlike those from Hawaii in bright floral prints) and a kikoi or *kitenge* (worn by women, also known as a *khanga* – brightly coloured patterned sarong with a Swahili proverb on it) all in light-weight cool cotton was fashionable. There were plenty of street vendors, many on bicycles, and African women carrying woven palm-frond baskets offering a variety of perishables – cashews, peanuts and tropical fruit such as mangoes, bananas, paw-paws and coconuts, even sugar-cane on occasions. Our lunches and suppers were relaxing and leisurely. We always ate fish as this was a luxury for us being farmers.

As with most holidays, the days passed quickly. Soon it was time to return to Westlands. The trip back was the same, but in reverse, with Asha on the train while Ian and I took it in turns to drive through the night with the sleeping children, arriving in time to collect her at Eldoret station the following day. For a few days after being home, Asha was almost a celebrity amongst the staff. She related a host of fascinating tales to keenly interested listeners, spellbound with her animated descriptions and experiences, so far removed from their mundane farm lives. We'd brought back some bottles of sea water as requested by our staff, but never found out if it lived up to their expectations medicinally as the sea water took 2nd place once Asha started the running commentaries of her holiday!

After a couple of holidays at Malindi, Ian was so keen on boats that he sent to Hartley's of New Zealand for a particular boat-plan. The 2 of us began building our own boat, a 13-footer we named 'Shrimp'. Ian had done carpentry at school and regularly used this skill in his farm work so he wasn't fazed by this 1st time boat-building challenge, including importing Teak and Meranti plywood. We could work on the boat only when Ian had several hours at a time off work. Following the pattern exactly, our 1st task was to complete the timber skeleton, being the keel that runs along the bottom with the ribs across. After that came moulding the hull of Meranti plywood onto the skeleton, and finally applying the layer of fibreglass. I was the general dogsbody fetching and carrying saws, screws and this-and-that, backwards and forwards, holding things steady exactly as Ian needed them. Then I plunged sacks into half-drums of boiling water to be able to put them onto the wide plywood side-strips so Ian could bend and mould them for attaching to the ribs. The last really messy, awful job was to affix the fibreglass skin over the hull, during which my special sewing scissors saw their end. Ian then found an old car chassis in the farm scrap yard and modified it to make a trailer into which Shrimp fitted. The final touch was a 60 horsepower Mercury petrol outboard motor. Very proud of our efforts we both were, as was Asha. On our next Malindi trip, she helped launch Shrimp. Whenever we returned to Westlands, Shrimp was kept undercover on Vi and Bertie's Malindi property.

During the many leisure hours with Asha, she told me some of the customs of her people. She said that when a Tiriki died, the head was severed from the body and buried far apart under a tree – this had something to do with their strong beliefs about the spirits. Asha also told me that their women were not circumcised, only the men. None of the men working for us had more than one wife, and none had been converted to Christianity. Their beliefs were in natural objects, certain animals and the forefathers. For example, they believed that in many trees lived spirits, so when the Kenya Government started major tar-road projects – like the Mombasa/Malindi tarmac road – certain trees literally could not be removed because of the spirit living there. Asha never had children of her own. She felt quite at ease telling me stories, and seemed perfectly happy to fall in with our ways and customs in the enjoyment of Christmas with a tree, Easter with chocolate eggs, birthdays and fancy dress parties. At all times we respected her tribal beliefs (as with all our staff) and refrained entirely from any mention of religion.

Since Marge and Harold had moved to Merrowdown and we'd followed to the same area of Western Kenya, there was an arrangement between us that we'd take it in turns doing the lunchtime Christmas festive fare. This particular 25th of December 1956, it was Marge's duty. Keith's fourth birthday would be two months later. Marge bought the most splendid big red and green Christmas crackers made in England, advertised as having the usual paper hats, small printed witty sayings and jokes, plus an assortment of toy animals inside. With some help from us adults, Keith pulled one of his crackers out of which he got a metal rhino about an inch long. Very pleased with it he was, remembering the rhino that had chased our car when we'd visited the game park en route to Malindi for our holiday earlier that year. We arrived home around 6 in the evening, all of us tired after a wonderful Christmas day of fun, presents, happy times with family and scrumptious food. A couple of days later, Keith came to me and said he'd swallowed the rhino. I'd initially been a little worried when I first saw the cracker-toy as it was heavy and I felt sure it was made of lead, as were so many toys of the time, such as little tin soldiers and farm animals. Deliberately, I had Keith use the potty so I could check his stools for an appearance of the lead rhino, but it didn't arrive.

Worried, I took Keith to Dr Peake in Eldoret in the morning who, although he considered the matter of some concern, found it also to be a little amusing. Examining Keith, Dr Peake couldn't feel any presence of the rhino in Keith's gut. He said we should return the following day and that I should continue checking the potty. Next morning, we returned to Dr Peake who this time felt the rhino. He gave me a laxative for Keith saying more than likely it would soon be expelled easily into the potty which would put my mind at rest. Off we went home. I administered the dose of opening medicine to Keith before he went to bed that evening. All I could think about before I fell asleep was how relieved I'd be to see the lead rhino. I woke several times during the night to monitor him, but his sleep was normal and peaceful. Ian, as usual, was up early to start farm work. He came back to tell me he'd take Keith in to Dr Peake as he had to go urgently into O'Shea's Hardware in the main street for plough bolts. I told Ian that Keith had not yet been on the potty and perhaps it wasn't such a good idea, but he said not to worry and to get Keith ready as he had to leave. My advice to Ian was to first take Keith to Dr Peake then go to O'Shea's.

The 2 arrived back home around 11.30 that morning. When they drove up to the house, I wondered why Ian was laughing so much. Then the story came out. Thinking he'd only be a few minutes, Ian had first gone into O'Shea's, parking directly in front of the shop entrance. Unable to find the spares he needed, he'd faffed around overlooking the time, quite forgetting Keith's laxative. Coming out of the hardware store, Ian was confronted with his young son's naked bottom, shorts down round his ankles, relieving himself in the gutter in front of the car while shoppers hurriedly passed by trying to avert their eyes. Terribly embarrassed, Ian hurriedly cleaned Keith's bottom and legs with his handkerchief, put him back in the car then walked across the street to Fairworths, a new Indian-owned swanky clothing shop, and bought Keith a pair of underpants and shorts. That was the 1st flush of the laxative. By the afternoon, the rhino had made its long-awaited appearance with a clunk into the potty.

There was never enough labour at maize harvest time. For 2 years, Ian sent one man from the farm to recruit labour from the Kerio Valley then he would fetch them in the farm lorry, making several trips over rough and treacherously narrow, winding roads down into the homelands. Once harvesting was over, this contract labour force would be returned by the same route. All this was such a hassle that Ian decided the answer was to buy a maize harvester. Reaping the harvest became much quicker, though there always had to be some follow-up with hand labour as quite a lot of cobs were dropped by the machine.

Each member of staff was given 2 acres of cultivated maize (being a section of our own shambas), that had been harrowed, fertilised, dosed for borer beetle, crop sprayed from the air and then harvested for them. The tractor drivers also knew that part of their efforts was for their own 2 acre maize bloc. All were allowed fowls, a few goats, and their own small shambas for vegetables near an underground spring which naturally kept the soil moist. The staff could channel the water wherever and whenever it was needed for their potatoes, peas, pumpkins and spinach. They all received a gallon of separated milk each evening plus 2 pounds of maize meal daily, and had plenty of meat from the slaughtered Friesian bull calves. Their uniforms were provided. Apart from their monthly wages, they received one month's paid leave enabling them to return to their homelands to visit and help their families.

While I was away for 3 weeks in Nakuru War Memorial Hospital (due to complications), waiting to have my 3rd child, a girl named Lindsay born on 26th January 1958, Asha took care of Ian's polo sticks. Keith and Beryl stayed with Marge. Between the syce and Asha, she knew exactly which polo stick Ian needed when he raced off the playing field with a broken stick. She had an enjoyable life, but one thing puzzled her a lot. "Why did white people have an obsession, day after day, about making beds?" In her opinion, it was a waste of time!

Jock, our black Alsatian, had been given to us as a pup. As an adult, he'd set the parameters around the house. No-one dared cross those lines without being invited by one of us. Jock fully understood the rules. He never attacked anyone working with Ian. Very late at night, he'd end his vigil with a perfected leap through the widely spaced bars on the bedroom window and fall asleep by Ian's bedside. Whenever we were away from the house, he was always overjoyed to see us return. He mated with a wild bitch and she had a nest of puppies under the dense bougainvillea hedge at the back of the house. The pups were abandoned just as they began walking around, so I fed them and eventually found homes for them. They were spectacularly coloured, all dappled with black and brown blotches. It was evident their mother had been a wild dog. We never saw her nor even knew she'd had the puppies. I kept one I named Dingo – another faithful canine.

Normally, Jock went everywhere with Ian. The weekend I was delivered with Lindsay, Ian and Jock stayed at Anchorage with Daisy. The day of Lindsay's birth, Jock had been left on the front seat of the car, but found his way around the hospital to us just as we were coming out of the delivery room. The doctor missed the baby's birth, and the 2 nursing sisters who attended me instead could hardly believe their eyes when Jock appeared. They simply smiled about the incident, making no fuss at all.

The renovations we'd done to our little house were extensive. We now had 2 big bedrooms, 3 smaller children's bedrooms, a large lounge and separate dining room. The house had been repainted and now had 2 entrances, front and back. Ian had installed a new hot-water system (using the same plan and structure as at Uruku), as well as a bathroom and an indoor toilet. Also built on was a pantry and passage leading to the old kitchen in which we'd put in a good second-hand wood-burning stove. The electric generator could be switched on and off from a set of press-buttons just above our bed that proved to be most sensible and worth the cost

Marge and Harold moved to Ellegerini, a small-holding at Kaptagat, in 1958. Their eldest child, Don, took over running Merrowdown and married Mary Foster in 1959. We would stay with Marge and Harold at Ellegerini when there were polo tournaments at Kaptagat and Kipkabus.

Keith disappeared one morning. I went into a state of shock and panicked, thinking he may have fallen down the outside long-drop toilet, and had to lie down being rendered incapable of even moving, whilst Ian, Asha and Kamau went looking in different directions. Ian took the torch to shine light down the outside toilet. I managed to join the search when Ian told me with certainty Keith hadn't fallen down the long-drop. Kamau found Keith picking and eating loganberries which grew wild (a hybrid between a blackberry and raspberry) in Ben's paddock. It was by some miracle that vicious bull Ben didn't attack or charge Keith as he could clearly see the lad. At the time, Mwangi (Ben's syce and the only person able to handle him) was off-duty at home. I had to draw Keith away from the loganberries by patiently and quietly talking to him. Often, I picked loganberries for pudding so Keith knew what they were, though never from the bushes in Ben's camp. Luckily, Keith was very obedient and listened to me, climbing through the wire fence, the way he'd got in!

The theft of green maize (on-the-cob) snapped off the stalks became a serious problem. Once again, Ian sent a man to the Elgeyo Reserve in the Kerio Valley to recruit men who would be guards employed to watch over the shambas. Ian made 2 trips with the farm lorry, and again traversed the hair-raising escarpment. He brought back 90 men who were willing to take day and night duties guarding the maize fields. This effectively put an end to the theft which had become uncontrollable owing to the enormous acreage under cultivation. Guards also had to be used once the maize had been harvested, bagged and then stacked. Each bag held 200 pounds of shelled maize; every stack totalled 1,000 bags that were raised off the ground on horizontal eucalyptus poles, standing on the open shambas. Fuel consumption was cut since less transport was done. This also solved the rodent, moth and weevil problem in that vast quantities of maize cobs no longer needed to be stored in the old thatch-roofed shed. When the bagged maize reached a required dryness (measured with a special instrument inserted into the shelled maize in the bag), it was then transported to the railway siding for onward transmission to the Kenya Farmers Association which distributed the grain to the millers.

Ian now bought 'Royal Cob', a dark bay polo pony from another farmer and polo-playing friend, Micky Buswell (married to Myrtle), living at Lugari in the same area as us. This was to be the highest price paid up to that time in Kenya for a polo pony. Ian really deserved to have an excellent mount as he was a spectacular polo player and could now better afford the price. He also bought a new Mercedes 220, and Asha, particularly, felt smart, as did we. A couple of years later, whilst on loan to and in the care of someone else per their particular request, Royal Cob died of Biliary (tick-bite fever). Ian was devastated. But, as was his way and the manner in which I would learn Ian dealt with personal heartache, he said little and didn't speak of this again.

One day, Kamau, who'd been mowing the lawn, came running to the kitchen. "Quickly come and look!" he shouted to me, highly agitated in a fretful state, quite unlike Kamau. I knew immediately something serious was wrong. When I reached the summer house, there was Keith holding his throat and coughing, hardly able to speak. He was about 6 at the time, and had climbed onto the surrounding low wall, wrapped a coir string (made from coconut fibre) that was holding a creeper, around his neck and jumped. Kamau, always mindful of the children's whereabouts in the garden, had seen this happen and hurriedly cut the cord with his panga, saving Keith, who had the marks around his neck for months. The old man was shaken up by this incident, as were we, and sincerely grateful Kamau had noticed Keith in time.

My 4th pregnancy had been erratic and difficult. We weren't sure whether we'd lose the baby during the early stages. The onset and continuation of Daisy's poor state of health was of great concern to the family. Various medical opinions were sought though no definite diagnosis could be made. Everyone was baffled. No medication seemed to help. It was Daisy, herself, who decided to stay in her own home.

Between Marge and me, and Neville & Ken's wives, Rosemary and Jean, we took it in turns to nurse Daisy day and night as her condition progressed to the stage where she needed constant care. I alternated with Marge in making several one-month trips to Anchorage. Ian bought me a second-hand Ford Zephyr from Harold. I piled the 3 children in together with our necessities for the month's stay which was a day's drive either way. Daisy delighted in Lindsay who sat on her bed and brought some baby gaiety into her pain-filled days and nights.

Dr Anne Spoerry, still living in her rented farmhouse near Anchorage, saw Daisy 3 or 4 times a day – a sensitive caring friend and an empathetic thorough doctor. It was a great relief to us all to know that Anne regularly monitored Daisy's condition. Some of my mother's treatment was a dreaded and harrowing experience. Not only for her, but for us as well witnessing it, particularly when trying to find veins that had not collapsed. Marge and Neville were unable to cope with this procedure and left the room. Daisy had no appetite for food regardless of what we offered her, but was forced on doctor's orders to eat raw minced liver and white bread spread with a considerable amount of raw chopped garlic which made her exceedingly nauseous. The days were long and trying as Daisy battled her debilitating and exhausting illness.

The little Philips battery-operated radio I'd bought with some of the money my father left me when I was a probationer at Nakuru War Memorial Hospital I gave to my mother when she became bedridden. Neville fixed up a proper aerial for good reception. While Daisy lay in bed day after day and night after night for almost 6 months, she listened to David Dunlop who was a radio announcer on the Nairobi Broadcasting station.

One afternoon, when I thought my mother was asleep I switched off the radio. She was alert in an instant and wanted it turned on again. I realised immediately that the chatting was taking her mind off her serious condition and pain. Then she said to me that she wondered what David looked like? I wrote a quick note to David asking him to please send a photograph of himself.

By return post, we received a studio photo which Daisy propped up alongside the radio. It made a world of difference to our mother to have the photograph and be able to put David's face to his name and voice that brought her so much interest and comfort during the few months left to her.

Bless the Kenya people.

Chapter Seven
Altrua Daisy

About 5 days after my return home from night duty looking after Daisy, Harold arrived to say he'd received a telephone message with the sad news that my mother had died that day. Marge was at Anchorage. Harold was staying with Don and Mary at Merrowdown. Daisy had become unconscious shortly after I'd left Anchorage. Neville had taken her to the Nakuru War Memorial Hospital where after a few days she'd died. It was 8th July 1960, 4 days before Daisy's 67th birthday.

My mother had stipulated in her Will that an autopsy should be performed. Dr Craddock (our Nakuru family physician), in a letter to all of us, wrote that the reason for our beloved mother's death was 'Emphysema, caused by heavy chain-smoking for so many years'. He said that no-one should wish she live any longer under conditions of such terrible suffering. Her heart was found to be enlarged to the size of that of an ox, being tightly compressed by her lungs which were one mass of froth-like substance. She'd spent a year extremely sick, then 6 months in her bed. The last 2 weeks of her life she was kept on oxygen day and night which had to be sent by train from Nairobi. The nightmare was over, but in the months and years since, I've experienced this loss more severely than at the actual time.

My Granny Marjorie Aggett taught my mother that heaven or hell was on planet Earth. This I, too, firmly believe. My mother and I would have long chats about 'after-death'. As she'd done throughout her life, Daisy faced her illness with courage and no self-pity. She'd promised, if it were possible, to communicate with us after she'd gone. I've had many vivid dreams since the deaths of my beloved ones, but never yet a visitation. Daisy's funeral service was on a morning at St Peter's, Ol'Kalou. She was buried in the tiny cemetery, a fitting place of rest as she'd worked so faithfully towards having the Church built. Ian and I had driven through with the children. People came from miles to pay my mother their last respects. It was fitting to see again Mr Golding's handwritten testament to Daisy's character and her contribution to the community that he'd placed 7 years before inside the lectern (dedicated to my brother, Terence Oliver Griffin):

"Mrs D.A. Griffin is a real altruist and I call her ALTRUA, which name I coined from the word 'altruist'. Altrua is a name she both likes and richly deserves, for her generosity, kindness and thought for others knows no bounds. This Church at Ol'Kalou was built almost entirely from the work, influence, energy and organising ability of Altrua. She is loved and respected by all who know her. This record has been made on 7 April 1953 by Arthur E Golding. Ol'Kalou," and was signed by Mr Golding.

Looking back on my mother's life, what strikes me most is how progressive a thinker she was, how she put into practice her ideas – and carried people through their difficulties. Daisy had also struggled financially as a single parent when Marge and Neville were young, sewing newspapers together to make blankets, and using bicarbonate of soda for cleaning their teeth.

It was my mother who initiated the plan to collect funds for and build the memorial stone in Nairobi bearing the wording: 'IN PROUD MEMORY OF PIONEER MARY WALSH died 20.6.1922 – Erected by Pioneer Admirers (in the year 1956)'. A fiery-tempered woman, Mary left Ireland at 17 after marrying and went to Australia where her 2 children and husband died, then went to Rhodesia where she married John Walsh. By 1896 they'd moved to Kenya. Mary was one of the earliest Nakuru inhabitants. Here she baked bread for the railway labour force. Mary set up and ran various business ventures – tearooms, dairies and bakeries and built trading stores. She was also known as *Memsahib Kiboko* (Mrs or Madam Whip) for her rhino-hide whip which she was not shy in using to keep order amongst her customers. Mary also raised and traded cattle, and travelled with donkeys for trading with Africans. Daisy spoke about 'Pioneer Mary' and told me that Mary walked from Mombasa to Nairobi, in those days an incredible feat of endurance and against all odds crossing through lion-infested, waterless and hostile country. Originally named by the Maasai, *Nakuru's* proper spelling is *Nakurro* meaning *bald place* which translates as *a flat, dry place that collects rainwater.*

Daisy was a gifted pianist, and taught herself to play the piano accordion. It seemed to me that music helped her through her own difficulties and tragedies. Apart from these 2 musical instruments, she also had a wind-up box gramophone and stacks of records, particularly of Victor Sylvester's music.

During the WWII years, many women were running their farms most of the time and deserve credit for coping alone. The Legislative Council governing Kenya had several agents chosen by the Kenya Farmer's Association who regularly visited the farms. These men were unsuitable for war duty – either they were too elderly or infirm though some were land owners and able to produce food. They played a valuable part in helping farming women with sound advice and sorted out labour problems. Progress for anyone was slow. Just to keep going was most times good enough. First thing Daisy did, was to get a dairy herd going by buying in a few good Friesian cows, and imported a ferocious bull named Belvedere Minn from Holland who would improve the milk production in his female offspring, also siring top quality bull calves. Within a few years, my mother's Friesian herd had become well-known. Each cow was given a name and number, and twice daily her milk was weighed and recorded. Generally speaking, a bull was kept to cover 25 cows and would have to be replaced after some years, depending on certain health factors and other criteria. Excess bull calves were sold or slaughtered and the meat given to the farm staff as part of their rations. Next on Daisy's list was to set up a piggery of Large Whites. Part of their food ration was thick sour milk since there was plenty available. The Government sent 2 German Jews, newly arrived in Kenya, to help on the farm. They ran the piggery expertly. Baconers were regularly sent from Ol'Kalou by train to the Uplands Bacon Factory. Daisy had a smoke-house built in which the hams and bacon were hung and cured. Pieces of beef being preserved lay in large enamel basins and had to be turned daily.

Once a year, my mother had a big soap-making operation with interesting and varied recipes for toilet soap. Some of the ingredients were ostrich eggs, glycerine or prickly pears, pumpkins, milk, raw bacon and potatoes, to which scent could be added. She also produced the most splendid kitchen and laundry soap with maize meal to give an abrasive texture, which became very hard and lathered beautifully. When the soap mixture had cooked then cooled sufficiently, it was poured into wooden boxes lined with damp Americani cotton-cloth which was then folded up and over the top completely covering the soap. Using a panga, the soap was cut into bars or cakes the following day. The kitchen and laundry soap could take up to a month to dry out.

As far as my childhood memory goes, Americani cotton-cloth was available countrywide. This wonderfully durable, natural-coloured tough and cheap cotton from America was used for a multitude of purposes, including wrapping for parcels instead of paper. The cloth was meticulously folded and carefully hand-sewn to make a secure package, then the address was written in ink or indelible pencil. My mother also used Americani material for bandaging wounds, as was the case the morning Terry accidentally minced off the tips of his fingers on his left hand. Ken and I were watching Terry working the big steel mincing machine mounted on a sawn-off cedar tree trunk in the backyard. Mwangi was cutting venison into chunks while Terry turned the mincing handle with his right hand whilst simultaneously feeding the meat into the wide mouth of the machine with his left hand and pushing it down. When Terry suddenly started screaming, Daisy rushed to help him. Vi, running outside from the kitchen, immediately ushered me inside the house away from the scene. For many days, Terry nursed his extremely painful hand swathed in Americani bandages (about the size of a large ball) made from a torn-up bed-sheet liberally soaked in smelly cod liver oil. We always had a plentiful supply of cod liver oil (in one gallon tins) as this was fed daily to the calves and also used for veterinary purposes. These are the last memories I have of my brother, Terry. Shortly after this, my father and 3 brothers all enlisted in the East African Forces and went off to fight in WWII.

As Daisy's home was always 'open house', we were rarely without visitors. Most days someone popped in for tea or coffee. Many people in predicaments or needing all sorts of help or comfort began relying on my mother. She was an expert at baking bread in the Dutch oven built in the backyard, and usually took 1st prize at any show. Daisy imported fruit trees from South Africa which arrived in hessian-wrapped bundles, the roots of the plants bound with moss and kept damp. Very soon, her gifted 'green fingers' returned an abundance of peaches and plums and there was much bottling and crystallising of the fruit. Violets grew in abundance in the Ol'Kalou climate. My mother even took to crystallising them (much the same as one does with ginger) though it took her a few trials to turn out perfectly crystallised violets which were then used as decorations on birthday or 'special occasion' cakes.

Cotton-seed cake was imported from Uganda and given as a supplement to the grain and bran mixture fed to cows. Horses and dogs loved the flat pieces of cake, as did I. When the seed had been removed from the soft, white downy cotton fibre used for the manufacture of textiles, rich reddish-colour oil was first extracted. Then the remaining solids were compressed and put through rollers making the small irregular-sized flat cotton-seed cakes or cubes. Rich in food value these were added to the feeds for in-milk dairy cows mainly, and given as titbits for horses. The pieces were very hard, khaki in colour with a nutty flavour. Kenya dairy farmers ordered it in great quantities from the Kenya Farmer's Co-op. In the afternoons, I'd often accompany my mother walking to the milking shed. Together with Giftie, we'd sit on top of the now loose seed cake in the storeroom, me nibbling at small pieces and Giftie crunching up her titbits. Daisy said I should search for pieces of shiny silver metal parts which had broken off the Ugandan machinery and carelessly become mixed in with the cakes when bagged. One of the farm worker's jobs was to fill a shovel with seed cake and carefully check there were no metal pieces as he fed a small quantity to each in-milk cow. The long feeding trough was directly in front of this store, giving me a view of all the comings and goings. The cows, all knowing their names, eagerly awaited being called, ambling in to be yoked into each compartment where their weighed food ration (per the amount of milk each produced) was placed as soon as the already-milked cow left to enter another holding-pen. The vast quantities of seed cake and the oil residue gave the cedar timber floor in the storeroom and the feeding troughs an exceptionally smooth, buffed surface with a lovely deep burgundy gleam and particularly pleasing aroma.

Sometimes at the end of milking, while the milk was being separated, my mother would give me half a cup of cream with a sweet smell and taste – occasions which I relished. Washing-up of milk buckets and the many parts of the cream separator had to be done with boiling water, the milking staff putting every effort into doing their jobs thoroughly but quickly under Daisy's watchful scrutiny. Everything to do with milk and cream had to be scrupulously cleaned. Most evenings, Giftie and I walked home alone in the twilight. My mother attended the twice-daily milking of the cows at 7 in the morning and 4 in the afternoon, and in between saw to other farm routines, running Anchorage very efficiently. In the evenings, only after the cows had been put out to pasture, the calves and pigs fed, all dairy equipment safely stored and sheds closed for the night, the milking and other staff gone home till 7 the following morning, would Daisy walk back to the house. She was usually in time to hear the BBC London news broadcast at 7 by which time it was already dark; the next newscast was at 9.

Milk was separated into cream and skim milk, the latter being fed in abundance to the farm staff, calves and pigs. The cream was sent twice weekly by train from Ol'Kalou Station to the Kenya Co-operative Creamery in Naivasha where butter and cheeses were made. A voluptuous, vivacious single Italian woman, Liduska Hornik, and her 2 cheese-makers settled in the Wanjohi Valley and produced excellent Gorgonzola cheeses which were much sought after in the country. My mother always had Duska's Gorgonzola in her pantry.

The British East African Command over the war years sent to Daisy a total of over 2,000 Armed Forces men from different countries of the British Empire including Australia and South Africa. There was one from Malta named Horace who I remember well. All needed recuperation in one way or another. Some were sent to help them with facing the tragedy of their families perishing in the London Blitz, others for a little leave to take their minds off war, servicemen convalescing, or those suffering emotional stress. Horace was a Major who spoke English, a perfect gentleman. He remained at Anchorage as a guest, just being companionable to everyone, driving Daisy to Nakuru or Nairobi when necessary. Once hostilities were over he returned to Malta. To all these men my mother was known as 'Mum Griffin of Ol'Kalou'. Before the war ended, she was rewarded with an official letter of thanks saying, "You are doing as valuable war work as anyone in the forces or munitions factories."

Early every Saturday morning, Mary Patten organised women from Ol'Kalou to leave for Gilgil Military Camp where there was a NAAFI

(Navy Army Air Force Institute) tent. They returned home after the mess closed at midday. NAAFI was an organisation providing canteens, etc., for British Military personnel at home or overseas. Eventually, a larger area was built with roofing providing shade, under which were trestle tables. Here the women gave out tea, coffee, milk, sandwiches and home baked goodies such as bread, scones, cakes, pastries, jam tarts and the like to Servicemen. All the baking and making butter, plus other farm produce was made ready the day before. Vi and Marge endlessly knitted socks on Vi's circular knitting machine to take to NAAFI.

Many Italian prisoners of war captured by the East African Campaign in the Italian East African countries of Abyssinia (Ethiopia) and Eritrea were also sent to Kenya farms. I remember four who happily worked at Anchorage. One was Micheli, a short fat elderly man who spent his time doing mainly what he wanted to or thought should be done to the garden. Wherever he went he sang, simply grateful to be away from the war zone. Two others were a carpenter and a stone mason who renovated and extended the old homestead. They turned Anchorage house into a really big, comfortable and pleasant home with a huge front verandah and many spacious rooms. Great cedar beams were installed in both the sitting and dining rooms which shared a large back-to-back fireplace. Floors and doors were of cedar. The large grey stone building blocks came from a nearby quarry arranged through Yassim, the same Asian contractor whose carpenter had made my big swing in the forest garden. There was one man who was so intolerable and disrespectful in his behaviour towards my mother that she returned him to the Prisoner of War Camp. Italian Prisoners of War built permanent roads, including the wonderfully engineered Escarpment which runs up the side of the Great Rift Valley leading to Nairobi. Halfway up, tucked into the niche of the wall-face, is the beautiful little Italian chapel, a reminder of all they did for Kenya's infrastructure.

The end of the war in May 1945 signified a new beginning. To lift the spirits of people in the district and bring some much-needed socialising into their lives, my mother started hosting very popular Saturday night dance parties at Anchorage. These were gay and happy occasions, a true and perfect reflection of the sincere optimism and faith our farming community had in the beautiful land of Kenya. Daisy would send off to Nairobi for the latest in musical hits, and had all the 'golden oldies'. The ladies would arrive in their prettiest long frocks, the men in their best casual wear. All brought something in the way of delicious eats and Alice Hauschild, her famous Jewish coffee and cashew nut cake, everyone's favourite. Mr Hauschild partnered my mother, both of them expert dancers, for the Viennese Waltz. Everyone would stand back and watch, as at the same time, my mother could perfectly balance a beer bottle on her head till the dance ended. Mrs Hauschild never participated in the dancing.

After WWII, Uganda produced cotton on a massive scale (cotton gins being fairly simple machines separated the seed from the raw cotton) and Americani cloth was no longer imported. Kenya's pork and dairy industries were thriving – all pork products were as good as any obtainable in England. Danish and New Zealand cheese-makers were brought to the country. Buyers came from as far away as the Belgian Congo to buy Friesian breeding stock from Daisy. Many of the Italians sent to help out on the Kenya farms opted to stay on after the war and with their many and varied skills made the country their home, running businesses, buying property etc. After my brothers, Neville and Ken, returned from active duty, they took over running Anchorage. Daisy no longer needed to go to the milking shed or be on farm duty. I was relieved to see my mother have time for herself and be able to pursue her own interests after so many years of stoic dedication and commitment.

Daisy gave an unused corner of her farm to the community to form a Country Club. A Clubhouse with a hall for weddings and various functions, a manager's house, a tennis court and polo ground were built. The Saturday night dance parties now took place at the Ol'Kalou Country Club Hall and became a weekly get-together. Sunday morning Church services were held in the reception area of the Clubhouse. Those not religiously inclined were able to have a quiet chat and pink gins at the bar with friends, or enjoy a game of tennis or polo. Conduct was genteel and civilised. Everyone had something to look forward to over weekends. The generosity of life that the country had returned for the great efforts and investment of finances, time and plain hard work would be ploughed back into the land. Great ideas and plans were discussed or exchanged in the Club hall for progress and building, importing of new cars, farm machinery and livestock.

Another arrangement the community thoroughly enjoyed at the Club was with a Mr Preston who came monthly from Nakuru with his pretty daughter and all his equipment for a film night with trailers, newsreels, Disney cartoons and a main film. Margaret and Alec Scade were the Club's managers. The only other dance party I remember attending not being at Daisy's or Ol'Kalou Country Club was when I left high school. A grand party was held for matriculants of our district at the Gilgil Country Club. In no way, did I consider this as having any comparison with my mother's parties. Firstly, I was amongst strangers and although we'd all been to the Nairobi High Schools, we'd never before come in contact and I felt very out of it. Secondly, I didn't have my usual dancing partner, Dawie, and few of the boys present knew how to dance. To make matters worse, the occasion ended at midnight. Cousin Mary and I attended together. For me, it was a disappointing affair.

Now that Ol'Kalou had a Country Club, Reverend Wilfred Walton, his wife, Stella, and their 2 little boys came from England to start a parish. This was when thoughts and ideas turned to collecting money to build St Peter's Church. Apart from the income generated from Daisy's 2 hippo being viewed by members of the public for a shilling each and her second-hand clothing swap or sell shop, there were fêtes and bazaars held at the Club with all sorts of things to do, games to be played and generally fun times for all. Davo Davidson, the Labour Officer, was there too and did his shooting trick by flicking a playing card into the air and splitting it in half with one shot. He was Australian by birth, and had at some time prior been one of Al Capone's bodyguards – needless to say, he was a whiz crack shot. At this time, two children, Claude and Francine from the Congo, came to spend holidays with me in order to learn English. Their parents owned a copper mine. I still have the beautiful gift of 3 large beaten copper spoons they brought for my mother.

Daisy grew beautiful yellow arums in her forest garden that were sent by train to a Nairobi florist. Anything sent by train always arrived at its destination. The Indian Stationmaster and Postmaster in Ol'Kalou were absolutely dependable. My mother and I were regularly invited for tea which was made with lavender-infused milk and accompanied by very sweet, flat cakes. Here, while I can, I wish to pay special tribute to the many Indian men (and by association their families) for their excellent, reliable, meticulous and efficient service over the years in Kenyan commerce and Government Departments. The farmers in Ol'Kalou (and other districts) were extended tremendous trust by the Indian duka-owners and given credit facilities until the harvests were brought in and paid for by the Kenya Legislative Government. Without this privilege the farmers, generally, would not have survived.

General shopping was done locally in the village, though special items were bought in Nakuru, or as a last resort, Nairobi. As both these towns were distant, all manner of important items were ordered by mail from large companies, and the goods despatched by the reliable daily train to Ol'Kalou. Somebody once sent a heavily pregnant bitch by train. She was put into the dog-box located in the caboose. On arrival, there were also 7 puppies. The Indian Stationmaster sent a telegram to the owner saying, "Bitch and 7 sons of bitch have arrived." In those days, telegrams in tan-coloured envelopes were delivered by a man on a bicycle within a 3 mile radius of the Post Office. Anchorage fell into that category.

Daisy was the first in the district to buy a refrigerator. After she died, everything in the kitchen, scullery and pantry was given to Mwangi – pots, pans, cake tins, mincing machine, crockery and cutlery, scales, other varied equipment, groceries, a large table and chairs, and her Electrolux fridge. Starting as a toto jikoni for my mother when she was 20, Mwangi had given her almost 47 years of loyal and excellent service. He'd been part of our family for so long we were only too pleased that he should have these items. The time had come for him to fulfil his own dreams. Mwangi was an excellent, experienced cook and baker. With his organisational skills from working alongside Daisy, he rented what used to be the Indian shoemaker's duka next to the Post Office in Ol'Kalou and opened his own little café. Neville arranged transport and remunerated him generously as Daisy had wished. He even took over Post Office Box Number One, Daisy's postal address all the years.

Dr Anne Spoerry, I later heard, moved from her rented farmhouse near Anchorage to a farm, Lolokwe, she'd bought in the Subukia district.

Five months after my mother's death, our 4th child was born by emergency caesarean section on 3rd December 1960 in Kitale Hospital. A son, we named him Alexander Stuart after Ian's father, William Alexander. Stuart grew into a fine, blond haired, grey-eyed young child – very different to the other 3 all with dark hair and brown eyes. He was spoilt by Asha.

My godson, our nephew, Terry Griffin (youngest of my brother, Ken, and his wife, Jean's, 2 children) came to stay. He was about 10, Beryl 7 or so. Terry was fascinated with all the farm machinery and loved going to the workshop, watching all that went on there. Ian was working on the lands one afternoon and I was having a lie-down after lunch when unbeknown to me Terry and Beryl went exploring. Since Keith had disappeared when he was little and been found in Ben's paddock, it was a rule in our home that the children had to tell one of the adults where they were going so we'd know where to find them. Perhaps on this occasion, they felt they didn't want to disturb my afternoon rest so simply went off. I don't know exactly what happened. Beryl informed me later they'd stopped at the diesel pumps near the workshop where Terry had told her to put the fuel nozzle in her mouth, which she did. He then gave a few pumps on the handle, the diesel going into Beryl's mouth and lungs. She came running to the house vomiting it up, breathing out the fumes. I was frantic and rushed her to Kitale Hospital. When the doctor had seen and treated her and she seemed all right again, we were able to come home. It took a few days for her to recover completely.

As a baby, Beryl had refused a dummy and instead sucked her right thumb in such a way that when her top front permanent teeth emerged they stuck out at an ugly angle, distorting her gum. We thought she'd eventually stop her thumb sucking. This didn't happen, so I took her (at an exorbitant cost) to the only orthodontist in Nairobi, Dr Vickers. Being so busy and booked up, he wasn't able to give us an appointment, but could fit us in between other patients. This meant we had to leave the farm before dawn, returning home on a long night drive once a month for 3 months. After an x-ray, it was found that the way in which Beryl sucked her thumb had parted her palate on the roof of her mouth. She was fitted with a contraption rather like the bridle of a horse which was intended to pull her top front teeth back into place – a metal brace over her top front teeth connected to a strap going around the back of her head. Beryl had to wear this at night while she slept. She became so stressed with this horrible treatment that I decided to take her to Nakuru to my old school dentist, Dr Williamson. Despite terrifying me when I was a girl, he appeared in hindsight to have been a good dentist. Dr Williamson had one look at Beryl's teeth and said, "Leave her alone and discontinue the treatment. When she stops sucking her thumb the teeth will go back into their natural position."

We were in this phase of waiting for her to stop sucking her thumb when we happened to visit Marge and Harold. Somehow, the back door of the Mercedes slammed after the children alighted. Beryl's thumb got caught in the door – it was almost flattened and so painful she could no longer suck it. To our surprise, Dr Williamson was correct. Within weeks, Beryl's teeth had straightened, the gum returned to normal and her palate had grown together perfectly. The end result was that Beryl had amazingly beautiful, straight teeth. On the farm, our children never knew Coca-Cola or other fizzy drinks. They ate little in the way of sugar, ice-cream or sweets, being allowed only 4 sweets a day after lunch, chosen from a big round biscuit tin. Ian gave us as much milk as we wanted to drink or cook with, fresh cream for porridge and the puddings I sometimes made. All 4 children had good teeth with few fillings later on in their lives. Drinking so much milk himself, Ian once got severe gout in his big toes and could hardly walk. The doctor advised him to cut back drastically on milk, which he did. He never again suffered from gout.

Having children is a real responsibility as I found out. Despite the greatest care possible and best of intentions sometimes accidents in one form or another did happen. I think most families have probably had something untoward go wrong as they raised their children.

We had 2 British paratroopers, Chay Blythe and John Ridgeway, based in Aden (a seaport city in Yemen) spending one week leave with us. They were later famous for their sailing around the world in a small craft. Ian was out working on the farm and the 3 of us were having a late breakfast. Lindsay, who was 3, came to the dining table. She was very pale, and told me she'd swallowed some pills. Showing me the Daraprim (malaria tablet) bottle, she said she'd found it in my drawer. There was about half a bottle of pills left. Daraprim was a newly recommended product. The small white tablets were tasteless and about the size of sugar sweeteners, so dosing the children was easy. I rushed Lindsay to the bathroom. Putting my finger inside a well-soaped flannel then down her throat, she luckily vomited up the tablets and shortly afterwards was all right. We'd switched to Daraprim because the children found it difficult to swallow the bitter quinine-based tablets. After this frightening instance, I changed to the newest medicine, Nivaquine. It was equably horrible, but far more effective against malaria, as it reached the liver. I put the tablet inside a gelatine capsule so the children had no further difficulty tasting bitter medication. Nivaquine made us all feel a bit nauseous for a short while afterwards, but as malaria was a big problem in Western Kenya there was no option. Ian was the only one of us who had a serious bout of malaria, but this was before we went onto Nivaquine.

I remember finding Asha once letting Stuart suckle on her shrunken, shrivelled breast. On another occasion, I found him latched onto one of Dingo's teats with his mouth as she fed her puppies!

Our hobby of the Ayrshire cattle worked out well. We built up an impressive herd, some animals being exhibited at shows, the main one being the Eldoret Royal Agricultural Show of 1962. The Queen Mother, Elizabeth, had been invited. Ian was awarded the only gold medal ever presented by the South African Farmers' Weekly for the outstanding quality of his Ayrshires. Afterwards, the Queen Mother spent some time chatting to Ian at length since our breeding stock had originally come from that of her own line of Kirriemuir cattle. This greatly interested her.

Stuart went through stages from about the age of 2 when all he wanted to eat for breakfast, lunch and supper was either pork sausages, Maltabella porridge or roast potatoes. Nothing else I offered him swayed him from this craze. So I let him continue with these single-food diets until he gave them up himself. They didn't last long enough to make me worried about his health.

Late one evening, just after dark, Ian decided to go and check one maize shamba as he was worried about the rodent situation. He told Keith, Beryl and Lindsay they could go with him. The children, all very excited, piled onto the back of the long-wheel base Land Rover. Keith was behind the cab on the driver's side, Lindsay in the middle and Beryl on the left. Stuart stayed home with me and while he was asleep, I decided to wash my hair. With my head over the basin and shampoo foam all over my scalp, Ian suddenly rushed into the house shouting for me. He was carrying Keith and put him down on our bed. I had a terrible shock to see Keith with a hole in his stomach, plasma bubbling out of the wound. Hurriedly, Ian told me there'd been an accident. Keith had jumped off the back of the Land Rover just as Ian opened his driver's side door and been impaled on the very sharp point at the top of the car door frame, suffering a v-shaped gaping wound. We were all traumatised looking at Keith lying inert on our bed. I told Beryl and Lindsay that we'd have to leave them to look after Stuart because we had to get Keith to Kitale Hospital about 24 miles away. With no time to rinse my hair, I gave it a quick rub with a towel and combed it through.

Lindsay, standing at the bottom of our bed, staring in disbelief at Keith so badly injured from what was supposed to be an exciting outing said gravely, "Mummy, I hope Keith doesn't die."

Beryl was so shattered she couldn't speak at all. This was the only occasion we ever left our children alone at home day or night. Stuart was still asleep – Beryl and Lindsay would keep watch over him. When we arrived at the little country hospital, I rushed inside ahead of Ian to inform the staff. Ian carried Keith from the Mercedes. A gurney was always kept ready for patient admittances. Ian laid Keith down gently. With me standing on one side of the gurney, and the nun nursing sister on the other, she said that Keith would be taken into theatre immediately, while the other nursing sister on duty telephoned Dr Leach to inform her of our emergency. Just as the sister and I were wheeling the gurney down the passage, never taking my eyes off Keith, suddenly to my shame and embarrassment I noticed a big fat flea on

Keith's dirty shorts. I knew the nun had seen it too. This was a place of healing, medical care and the most stringent hygienic conditions possible. Patients weren't supposed to arrive with fleas! Before I had a chance to catch and squash it, the flea had jumped, and I didn't know where to! In that moment, I decided there was nothing I could do about it. Keith's grave condition was of greater importance. So I never mentioned the flea, and very much appreciated that the nursing sister didn't say a word about it either.

Dr Leach arrived within minutes and went straight to the theatre. She later told us she'd stitched Keith's stomach wound and that he was very lucky as, miraculously, no organs had been pierced. We waited for Keith to recover from the anaesthesia before leaving for Westlands, arriving back home at about one o'clock in the morning to find Beryl and Lindsay hadn't slept at all, anxiously waiting up for us. I remained mystified as to where that flea came from as Ian dipped the dogs about once a fortnight in the cattle dip. It might have come from the back of the Land Rover as this was a work vehicle, going all over the farm with Jock on the back. After a couple of days, Keith was up and about. His wound healed amazingly quickly, but left him with a clear v-shaped scar on his stomach.

Stuart had a pet Large White piglet given to him by Jim Roberts, a pig-farmer and friend, living at Soy. Kamau would help Stuart bath 'Piggy' since he was allowed in the house and on the chairs and beds. Piggy's favourite sleeping place was on the bottom shelf of the tea-trolley where he'd stretch out and be wheeled around the homestead by Stuart. 'Patsy' was Stuart's pet goat. She slept on the beds and would jump up onto the mantelpiece. Patsy really annoyed Ian by jumping onto the bonnet of the Mercedes, clattering over the roof, then running down the boot onto the ground, where she'd start the whole procedure over again. She liked the fun and noise of this though she knew she was misbehaving. Cleverly, she'd first check to see if Ian was anywhere around. Left on her own, Patsy would run up and down the seesaw. Sometimes, she'd get the balance right and would stay in the middle. She thoroughly enjoyed life, this being one long playtime. Both animals grew up to be adults and were returned to their own kind. Patsy never forgot us, and would leave the flock and come running over to say hello when we visited her back on Merrowdown. At an early age, Stuart took a great interest in insects and creepy-crawlies and kept a number of chameleons of all sizes, some of which occasionally accompanied him in the car. Three, unfortunately, climbed under the long all-in-one front seat of the Mercedes making it well-nigh impossible to locate them. It was a couple of weeks later that we finally managed to retrieve the chameleons, by then very pale and extremely weak though they thankfully survived, and wobbled off when I put them on to a garden shrub.

On 12th December 1963 the world was told of Kenya's Independence *UHURU* (freedom). Sixty-eight years of British rule ended when the Duke of Edinburgh, representing the Queen, attended the ceremony. The Union Jack was lowered while the bands played the anthem, 'God Save The Queen'.

The following satirical song, written out and passed along, did the rounds though I don't know who wrote the words:

THE KENYA FREEDOM SONG

We'll have the white man's shamba,
We'll drive his shiny car,
We'll drive all over the place till we don't know where we are,
We'll travel free, for nothing, on the buses and the trains,
And all the leading citizens will have their private planes.
We'll drive on both sides of the road…
Why should we stick to one?
The roundabouts and crossings - smashing fun!
There will be no need for taxes –
There will be no need for rent –
These things will be arranged for, by our Government.

And when the money's gone, and the country's on the floor
We'll get the Government Printing Press to turn out some more.
The labour leaders promised us that when the battle is won
There will be no need to go to work.
We can lie in the sun.
Our women will do the work (that's what they're there for)

And if one (woman) can't do the lot, we'll buy a whole lot more!
With Sterling from Great Britain and Roubles from the Reds
And Dollars from America to turn our trusty heads,
We'll be so bloody wealthy that we'll be a Welfare State.
Then we'll phone up Mr Wilson to say
"Come out and join us, mate."

Jomo Kenyatta, a well-educated Kikuyu, who'd been arrested along with 5 others a day after the State of Emergency was declared in 1952 for organising Mau Mau, served 7 years in prison until 1959. He was detained at Lodwar. On 12th January 1960, the State of Emergency was lifted, and Kenyatta became the founding father of the Kenya nation. He was Prime Minister from Independence in 1963 to 1964, then President from 1964 until his death in 1978. Kenyatta married 4 times (his 2nd short marriage to an Englishwoman) and had 8 children. He was also the author of 7 books. There were several phrases Jomo Kenyatta liked to say, some of which caught world attention:

"The British are like a bull-dog with no teeth";

"A leopard cannot change its spots";

"When the missionaries arrived, the African had the land and the missionaries had the Bible. They taught us to pray with our eyes closed. When we opened them, they had the land and we had the Bible." Kenyatta was never seen publicly without his gnu-tail fly whisk. I remember him at a public address exhorting his people to breed a child a year.

Through the post one day, we received by registered letter a notification that evaluators would arrive to check out the whole farm, what was on it and what improvements had been made to the property, ascertain the livestock and machinery we owned. The British Government, Lancaster House specifically, was upon us. A 'wind of change' would blow dramatically, not only for us, but for many disillusioned native Kenyans. We had some knowledge of this procedure already, Lancaster House having bought out Anchorage after Daisy's death, as well as Vi and Bertie Case's farm also in the Ol'Kalou district. Bertie was an excellent farmer, producing oats, wheat, maize, turnips, beef and dairy. They moved permanently to their Malindi holiday home which they later sold, buying a very nice house in the popular tourist hotel area. Neville dealt with the sale of Anchorage. I was so relieved at the time that my mother's death spared her this traumatic ordeal. She could not have borne losing the home and farm she so dearly loved and had worked so hard for years to build up. People had no option than to sell to the British Government per an agreement with the new Kenya Government regarding the restitution of land. If they chose not to sell it was at their own risk.

Now we faced the same situation ourselves on Westlands. Ian and I were filled with trepidation and an uncertain future for ourselves and our children. Like it or lump it, the message was clear, either way we'd have to move on regardless. There being so many emotional attachments for us in this process, we decided it would be better not to be present but to engage the services of an arbitrator instead for the farm inspection. We appointed Alistair Burns, a Land and Estate Agent from Kitale to act in our best interests while we went away for a long weekend of camping and trout fishing at Uruku from the Friday to the following Tuesday. Ian arranged with our cousin, Peter Smith, living on Ol Morijo (who now owned neighbouring Uruku as well) for our few days away. Peter said we were most welcome. Marge kindly looked after Lindsay and Stuart for us, Keith and Beryl being at St Andrew's boarding school in the village of Turi (between Eldoret and Molo) about 2 hours drive from the farm.

The whole idea of having to give up our farming work again, hopes, home and whole life was hideous, especially as minimal prices were being paid for the land of those farmers who'd already been forced to sell. The price paid was just for the land. It would not include what we'd had to pay in costs for terracing and fencing or water piping, pumps, tanks and troughs and relevant building costs thereof. Neither was the cost of the electricity generator taken into account or new buildings for cattle milking, calf and horse stabling, barns, stores, the tool shed and machinery store. Expenses for the extensions we'd made to the farmhouse and workshop weren't included or even improvements to farm roads plus clearing of land for further agricultural development. Word was out that the machinery you couldn't manage to sell would just have to be left on the property. Farmers were told to get rid of their livestock.

The intensity and gravity of the impending takeover weighed heavily on our minds. I imagine anyone not being a farmer would more than likely not fully comprehend the magnitude or implications of the situation. We didn't know how to reconcile our hearts and minds to the ordeal that lay ahead. Both of us needed to get away for a few days to Uruku, and try to find some sense of direction within ourselves of the path forward. Although we knew the Pesi River well having lived on Uruku, it was a different and serenely pleasant experience for us to camp along the upper reaches of the river. The freshwater was beautifully clear and cool. We spent the days walking to new places suitable for trout fishing. One night, we heard a leopard sharpening its claws on a tree not far from our tent. On another occasion, I had an unforgettable experience in a glade near a pool. Ian had moved off to cast his line a little further upstream. I'd picked a spot to sit down close to the water's edge. After a short while, I got the distinct feeling I was being watched. It took a few moments for me to realise I'd sat down beside a broody duck on eggs, her surroundings so incredibly well camouflaging her, not 2 feet from me, her beak tucked under her wing, beady eyes steady on me. She made no sound or movement. Instantly, I understood I shouldn't speak or fish lest I frighten her away. Eventually, when Ian moved still further upstream, I managed to do the same without causing distress or disturbance to the duck. I left her as I'd found her, grateful for this 'silent meeting of 2 mothers' so very calming to my worried mind – a cherished experience forever in my memory.

On our return to Westlands, we were dismayed to hear what had been offered for the farm. We declined, but agreed to have a revaluation done at a later date. Alistair Burns met the men assessing the farm (which lasted a day). He dealt exclusively with the whole situation, the negotiations conducted between himself and the Lancaster House Agent, being the Central Land Board. Alistair had done his best on our behalf.

Kamau received news via the grapevine that his brother had died, and asked Ian for leave to go to his Kikuyu homeland immediately.

Kamau was shaken up, saying he'd been told that a dead pigeon had been placed in front of his brother's closed hut door and it was this curse that had caused his brother's death. It was the only occasion Kamau ever asked for leave. It reminded me of the instances during my childhood at Anchorage where the same superstitious 'curse' involving a dead pigeon resulted in mysterious deaths.

Zoe and Sally (Don and Mary Rooken-Smith's daughters, living on Merrowdown) came to stay for 2 months while their parents were away in England and India for Don to play international polo. Their ayah, elderly Elizabeth, came as well. She and Asha became best of friends and had a wonderful time together.

Chalagut, our dedicated old Tiriki cattleman, came hurrying across to the house one day from the river to tell Ian that the steers had surrounded a python and were trying to stamp it to death. Ian took his Mauser rifle and drove to the cattle with Chalagut to find the steers crowding around the python which he then had to shoot. It measured 17 foot 3 inches long. The python was brought back to the house and put in the backyard later to be skinned by Kamau. He soon rushed into the kitchen saying the snake had come to life and was "going." Ian went to check and found the supposedly dead python now alive which had somehow got into the duck pen. The ducks were all totally mesmerised, standing about in a trance. Ian shot the snake again. Finally, it was skinned and Kamau asked if he could take the snake fat which would be used as *dawa* (medicine) for the witch doctor.

I didn't know at the time that the snake's head had been cut off and was still outside in the backyard. Later that afternoon, Simon the Siamese cat, dragged the head through the kitchen and past Kasuku parrot who was minding her own business eating shelled peanuts. All of a sudden, Kasuku noticed the large snake head and fell about screaming and squawking at the 'apparition'. I had to rescue and pacify her. Her heart was racing and she was utterly terrified. Kamau took away the python's head after this. Or so I now thought. That evening as was our custom, we lit the Tilley lamps at sunset and carried one to the bedroom. Witsy, the other Siamese cat, was fast asleep on our bed when she suddenly espied Simon with the snake's head. I could hardly believe my eyes to see it back again! Leaping up and down, Witsy landed on the Tilley lamp which overturned. One way or another, the python's head created a fair amount of pandemonium in our home that day. It was lucky the house wasn't set alight! For a few days, Ian continued teasing the cats by tying a string to one of his stockings stuffed with a sock in the toe end, and pulling this over the bed. The cats soon twigged on!

Chapter Eight
Croc-infested Lake Rudolf

Gill Buswell, and her husband, Richard – brother to Micky, farming near to one another in the Lugari area – lived less than 30 miles from us. They were our best friends. Richard was Stuart's godfather. We took it in turns visiting each other about once a fortnight. Ian and Richard decided we should go to Lake Rudolf in the semi-desert region of northern Kenya for a fishing holiday. Because Lake Rudolf is so remote – 3 days journey – preparing for the safari took several weeks as there was no margin for error in forgetting things. Richard and Ian shared the cost of a second-hand 16 foot fibreglass fishing boat with a small Evinrude petrol-powered outboard motor and a boat trailer which Ian built. The boat, named *Samaki* (fish) had 3 wooden benches, space for one's gear and picnic items and a good keel making it safe in choppy water.

Gill and I spent considerable time discussing grocery lists, carefully checking off every item when shopping. She ordered a substantial quantity of fresh eggs in cartons of 18, packed in a special wooden box to prevent breakages. I baked a considerable variety of biscuits. The majority of the grocery items were tinned fruit and vegetables, bully beef, condensed and ideal milk, and plenty of powdered cool drink. We wouldn't be able to bake bread so cream-crackers were the replacement. A cured ham for the first few days was on the list. We made sure we had an ample supply of salted smoked bacon for breakfasts, loose wrapped sweets, rice, potatoes, onions, cabbages, bottles of pickles in mustard sauce, sugar, maize meal, spaghetti, cooking oil, tea and coffee. A round cheddar cheese weighing about 10 pounds was packed, plus condiments etc.

Richard went to Kitale to the Parks Board Offices to obtain the required camping and fishing licences. He told us he'd been strongly advised to get saw-scaled viper anti-venom in case of snake bite. So I was assigned the duty of contacting the Nairobi Snake Park for the serum, which was posted to me for collection at Soy Post Office. We also heard via Richard (who knew the family concerned) about a crocodile attack that occurred about 2 years before our planned trip. A

Kitale father and his 17 year old son had gone to Ferguson's Gulf, the area of Lake Rudolf where we also planned to camp. Standing on the beach, the father was shore-fishing while his son walked along the water's edge. In a flash, a croc took the teenager, his father witnessing in horror the split-second fatal attack. His son was never seen again. The best we could do regarding the crocs was to keep our eyes peeled, be ever-vigilant, and hope such a terrifying incident didn't happen to any of the children or adults with us.

A large group of us would be making the Rudolf trip and all the vehicles were 4-wheel drive. A few days before we were due to leave, Richard came over in his 5-ton Bedford lorry and loaded up most of our holiday equipment and supplies. The lorry had an open top with high side railings. Richard and Gill with their 2 sons, Budgie (his nickname for Richard junior) and Bruce, plus a young English tourist they'd befriended in Kitale named, Sue (she was staying with them temporarily), travelled in their lorry. *Mpishi,* their cook also accompanied them.

Carol and John Chart (family of ours, he was Lindsay's godfather) farmed on a large scale with dairy and beef cattle and extensive wheat production on the Eburru Range, which apart from being agricultural land had dense forests and plenty of buffalo. John and Ian played polo together. The 4 of us were about the same age and thoroughly enjoyed each other's company so going on safari was an opportunity not to be missed.

We went in our long-wheelbase Land Rover towing the boat-trailer. Wambugu, our houseman, was with us. We'd also invited Janet (Marge and Harold's daughter) and 5 year old Mark (Neville's son). Mark had broken his arm – now healed, the plaster cast had recently been removed.

Robert Foster took Barsindet, a senior staff member, with him. Robert and his brother, Fuzz (Francis) farmed at Kaptagat about 15 miles from Eldoret. Their sister, Mary, was married to our nephew, Don Rooken-Smith, who was running Merrowdown for his parents, Marge & Harold. Fuzz stayed home to look after the place.

Leaving Westlands at sunrise, we all met up in Kitale. Adults and children alike were in high spirits for this much-anticipated safari. Here, most of the paraphernalia was transferred from the vehicles to the lorry – fuel, paraffin, tents, clothing, bedding, fishing and camping equipment, food, beverages, drinking water, gas cylinders, 2 portable gas cookers, Dietz lamps and gas lamps. Each vehicle carried extra spare tyres, a spade, a basic First Aid kit, tools plus fan belts in case of breakdowns. Ian had put together a comprehensive toolbox for the Land Rover. Wambugu joined Mpishi from Kitale, journeying on the back of the lorry with him to help with possible flat tyres or suchlike, loading and unloading of the lorry and generally taking care of everything. All of us, including the children, valued and respected our staff and although they were on a 'working holiday' were made to feel welcome as part of our large group. Not having ventured far from their homes on the farms before, all 3 staff initially appeared somewhat apprehensive as to where they were headed. It wouldn't be until we set up camp at Ferguson's Gulf that they'd totally relax though they learnt and saw many things along the way that made them smile and have animated conversations amongst themselves. Now and again for short stints along the way, Keith, Beryl and Lindsay would join Mpishi, Wambugu, Budgie (pronounced *Boojie*) and Bruce on the back of the lorry, perched on top of all the gear.

With the low rumble and slow roll of the powerful 5-ton Bedford sparking in all of us the beginning of the big adventure now underway, we drove through the picturesque, intense farming area of Kitale (mostly wheat and cattle) north to Kapenguria, the tribal homeland of the Pokot. Then we continued on to the Turkwel River where we had to halt for the night as the water was in raging flood. Little Mark had a nervous disposition. Never having experienced a camping trip of this distance or duration, he required considerable attention, hovering around me or clinging to my legs most of the time while the other children eagerly went off with the staff gathering firewood to boil the kettle as usually happened at every stop. Our camp beds were put up in the open as there were no big shady trees around, though plenty of small thorn trees and scrub. Gill and Mpishi were in charge of the cooking, though in this instance we had picnic supper. Sitting on their camp beds trying to keep their feet away from scuttling scorpions kept the children on tenterhooks and thoroughly engrossed for some hours.

Exhausted after much chatter of the day's encounters, we all fell asleep under the stars with Mpishi, Wambugu and Barsindet sleeping on the back of the lorry. Rising at dawn due to the heat, we started the day sipping on delicious sweet hot coffee made with condensed milk, looking forward to the next leg of the journey. Most annoying though, were the hundreds of very small bush flies that clung to our faces and got into our eyes. We were constantly brushing them off with our hands. After breakfast, Ian slowly walked into the river, the water now having subsided a bit. The crossing was about 60 yards wide. He needed to gauge the very narrow concrete causeway which couldn't properly be seen due to the muddy flowing water.

The causeway turned out to be about 2 foot higher than the river bottom. So without being able to see the edges, the driver of a vehicle could easily misjudge the width, but based on the flow of the current, Ian felt all the vehicles would make it through; otherwise we'd be held up. Telling Wambugu not to worry and to sit tight on the back of the lorry, we were the first vehicle to cross the river. Based on the feelings of trepidation, visible wide-eyes and absolute silence broken now and then only by audible gasps from us passengers in the Land Rover (Ian never flinched), particularly when the water reached the bonnet and came in through the doors, covering the floor, I can only imagine how Wambugu must have felt watching us from the lorry knowing it would be their turn next! It was an adrenaline pumping yet incredibly thrilling experience. There were loud cheers and plenty of clapping from our children, out of sheer relief, when the wheels of the Land Rover hit dry land on the other side and we pulled over to watch the other vehicles cross. It took time for even my pulse to slow. For hours afterwards, this crossing gave us non-stop conversation as everyone relived their heart-stopping memories and terrifying moments as the heavily laden lorry slowly ploughed through the flowing water. Could Richard manage to keep the big, wide wheels on the concrete? Barsindet, Mpishi and Wambugu alternated between first shaking their heads and erupting in a torrent of Swahili, then breaking into beaming smiles and laughter as they applauded in their own way a feat well accomplished. It was good to see them starting to get excited about the trip.

To keep the children occupied while travelling, we sang a lot of nursery rhymes, played 'I spy', counted various objects of scenery or told stories. Ian would stop about every 2 hours to stretch his legs and give us all a break from being in the car which was always a delight for the children who'd investigate the new surroundings. On this occasion, he lay down on the road and even managed to get a half-hour's sleep as we waited for the lorry to catch up. Every vehicle carried a spade for anyone who needed the 'toilet', and the rule was rigidly followed that a hole was dug and afterwards was covered properly. One simply asked for 'the cat's paw'.

We were now onto a long yellow, corrugated, dusty road the landscape having changed to semi-desert when the back universal joint on the Land Rover came to grief. Ian had to get out his tools, take it off and with some miraculous workmanship put the front universal onto the back, meaning we no longer had 4-wheel drive as only the back wheels now had traction. There was plenty to keep us all occupied while Ian fixed the Land Rover. The scenery was magnificent. Starkly contrasting colours were a wonder to behold and stuck in my mind. In the far background was a long range of low hills in indigo blue with white cotton-woolly clouds above and shallow valleys of yellow. Wild camels amongst green semi-desert shrubs growing here and there were in the foreground. Dotted around were bits of blackish lava. The sky was a pale blue.

The camels were quite unperturbed by our presence, meandering around small dunes – babies and mothers and families, their hides in varying shades of brown to cream to dusty white, with stubbly chins and long eyelashes shading their eyes. They nibbled on the bright green leaves of stunted thorn trees and desert shrubs that came up to the knobbly knees of the adults. Our children were enthralled with these 'ships of the desert', falling in love with them instantly. There's a kind of mesmerising, almost transfixing relaxation in watching a camel – one's gaze is drawn to the movement of its hump in direct relation to the animals' gait. Interspersed in the scenery were reddish-brown anthills, some taller than Ian, up to 8 foot. Quite a number had more pointed tops, others were rounded or odd shapes in various sizes. All were as solid as concrete. One couldn't detect any sign of crumbling in the sand texture of the anthills. We marvelled at the skill and commitment of such small creatures. As a combined workforce, they were capable of this exceptional structural engineering, creating intriguing works of art in the silent semi-desert landscape. The children climbed up and down the anthills to play on them and have photos taken, full of questions about the ant master-builders and the camels. This area was devoid of human habitation.

Back on the road again, still in semi-desert, all of us felt rejuvenated from a stint in the open. Suddenly, a wheel flew through the air like a missile, luckily missing my front passenger door, and went hurtling off to the side of the Land Rover. Ian stopped the car immediately. Thankfully, Richard was behind us and had seen it happen. One of the wheels had come off the boat trailer. The men went off in search, finding it lying against a small sand dune. Fixing it securely back on the trailer, we were on our way once more when the road came to a dry river bed with a lugga (a stretch of loose dry sand) about 50 yards wide with some lovely tall trees on the far side. We decided to camp there overnight. The Land Rover went through the lugga with no problem, but one of the back wheels on the heavily laden Bedford sank a bit when the top-sand gave way into a hole beneath it. This created a lot of excitement in the extreme heat of the day as every able and big enough member of the group came to the rescue. Pushing the lorry forwards then backwards, we'd dash madly from the front to the back, trying to create a rocking motion for the big tyres to gain traction in the sand. There were a lot of instructions shouted by the men. Everyone, including the children, joined in the encouraging chorus of, "Harambee," as we pushed and heaved in unison, sand flying every which way. All of a sudden, the lorry tyres got a grip and were out. On drove Richard, straight to the trees with all of us in a sweat running behind! The priority now was to get some water into everyone as we were parched from our efforts. The staff and children found the whole episode great fun and entertainment. Everyone was grateful to be in the pleasantly cool shade of the trees with their smooth trunks. It was a memorable camping spot, the children running around playing in the soft, pristine clean, fine-grained golden sand of the shallow river bed.

Not a sign of litter anywhere. In the morning, we were on our way again.

The dusty, yellow corrugated road continued to Lodwar. Reaching this far north destination signified that our long journey was almost at an end; it wouldn't be that far now till we reached Lake Rudolf. Being well-equipped, we had no need to shop at the dukas so made straight for the Government Offices on the outskirts of the town. It was etiquette to pay one's respects to the Resident District Officer, apart from which we were required to show our camping and fishing permits to be able to go through the Turkana village of Kalokol at Ferguson's Gulf. Ian and Richard went in to conduct matters while the rest of us waited in our vehicles. I had quite a time trying to ward off young Turkana men dressed in loincloths, fascinated by their reflections in the Land Rover side mirrors, even trying to break them off. Lucky for me, an American missionary passing by who spoke their language came to my rescue, after which the youths went away. The Government Offices compound, situated in a dusty, grey sandy area was surrounded by a stone wall. It comprised the Police Station, District Commissioner's Residence and Prison (where Jomo Kenyatta had been detained). The Askari (sentry-policeman) standing on the corner of the wall I found impressive, and studied him intently. He was an imposing sight, impeccably dressed in his red fez with tassel, uniform of navy blue tunic with long sleeves and a brown belt, beautifully ironed knee-length khaki shorts and puttees. The Askari stood stock still on guard, exceptionally smart and proud, every now and again raising and lowering his rifle then marching from one end of the wall to the other.

Richard had been advised in Kitale to take some kind of rations to give to the Turkana Chief as a gift so we were prepared in this respect with sugar and maize meal. On hearing our vehicle engines as we arrived at Kalokol on the western shores of the Lake at Ferguson's Gulf, Turkana men came rushing out to greet us. Richard and Ian got out to salute the Chief who was naked, though bedecked with bead necklaces, bangles and leg ornaments of tufts of hair (perhaps from goat tails) and white ostrich feathers in his dried mud hair-do. He stood on one leg while leaning on his spear (as is the custom of mature Turkana men). Although he didn't speak any Swahili, and Richard and Ian no

Turkana, the 3 men exchanged some sort of pleasantries. A young boy, also standing on one leg next to the Chief, unperturbed and quite naturally held onto the Chief's very long flaccid penis. The youngster, still a child, had a thin leather thong tied to his own penis with a little stone on the end. We would learn this was another of their customs whereby from a very young age a boy has a stone on a string or leather thong tied to the penis, the stone being replaced with a bigger one as the boy gets older and the penis longer. The pleasantries concluded a retinue of male youngsters came forward to receive our gifts handed over by Richard and gratefully accepted by the Chief. Our arrival seemed to cause quite a stir. Some of the Turkana men appeared never to have seen white women and blond-haired children before, or our western dress. Even Wambugu, Barsindet and Mpishi were of great interest to them being from different Kenya tribes.

We parked our vehicles in the shade of some palm trees at Kalokol, an oasis with lots of Doum Palms and a number of large water puddles. Looking across the water of Ferguson's Gulf, we could see the high sandbank on the opposite side known as The Spit, our proposed camping site. Our men launched Samaki ready to begin the process of transferring everyone and all the equipment across to The Spit. Thankfully, we were kindly assisted by young Turkana who willingly came to offload and carry our gear to the boat. It was about a 20 minute trip either way across the water. Numerous boat loads were taken and once on the other side at The Spit, we again found Turkana only too pleased to help get our goods to the camp site. All of us, children included, in one way or another, did our bit getting everything up the high sandbank.

Standing on The Spit – a natural sandbank about 16 foot high above the desert Lake, giving a bird's eye view of the area – one was at the mouth of Ferguson's Gulf. On the left side of The Spit was the bay below with the beach shoreline stretching all the way around to Kalakol village where we'd left the vehicles and fuel drums. The section of bay below us was usually a hive of activity where the Turkana fished. Not far from our camp was a rather smelly area where they cleaned and cut up the fish to dry it in the sun. Directly below our campsite on this same side, the beach narrowed to about 5 yards wide, where we'd swim and pull the boat up at night to anchor it. On the right side of The Spit, we had a direct view across to Central Island in the middle of the Lake with the waters stretching beyond to the eastern shores that we couldn't see because the Lake is so wide. On this right side of The Spit, the sandbank gradually tapered down to beach level some way off along the shore line. We never swam or fished this area due to the Nile crocodiles. The Lake is also known for frequent howling gales that whip up huge and dangerous waves. Camping above the Lake on The Spit gave a measure of respite from weather coming directly off the water. Every day, the wind changed the formation of the big sandbank in some way.

Our camp set-up was primitive, though exactly right for this type of holiday. Sufficient tents, all with groundsheets, had been brought for everyone to sleep undercover, and a large tarpaulin awning stretched over poles gave us essential shade from the burning sun to sit in deck chairs or eat at trestle tables. The tents and awning were all anchored with necessary guy ropes. Even so, Robert's lightweight blow-up igloo-shaped tent often had us running after it during daytime as the wind now and then rolled it away across the sand. The staff tent had a side flap giving shade. While everyone else was in a dreamland of exhausted holiday slumber, I was the only one who got up during the night because of the strong winds and went around checking all the guy ropes, pulling them tight again if they'd slackened too much. We never had a tent collapse.

The kitchen tent housed all the food supplies, beverages, both small portable two-plate safari gas cookers and the gas cylinders. A little to the outside was a large tin bath for washing-up dishes. The dish water poured onto the sand disappeared almost at once. All the groceries were combined with everyone sharing what they'd brought. For washing we had a big plastic bucket, though Ian washed and shaved in my father's tarpaulin camping basin. The bit of laundry was done in the tin bucket and then hung on the tent guy ropes, drying in no time at all. Now and then, our men would go across to Kalokol to fill up our containers with fresh drinking water and petrol. There was a roofless long-drop toilet some way from the camping site, which was merely a 44 gallon drum that had been lowered into a hole in the sand with a weather-worn box-seat with a hole in it on the top. To give some privacy, upright wooden poles had been placed on 3 sides around the toilet then covered across with hessian sacking. But by this stage, the poles were no longer completely straight up and the hessian was torn and flapping in the breeze.

Bob McConnell (who'd been at Nakuru School with John Chart and me) was the Fisheries Officer in charge of Lake Rudolf and came to see us the following morning. Most days he'd visit for a short while, sometimes having a cup of coffee. He told us that the long-drop toilet had been built a while back for Prince Phillip's use when he was on safari at Ferguson's Gulf. Bob also related to us the story about a woman who'd been bitten by a saw-scaled viper (Echis pyramidum – also known as the North-east African carpet viper), a snake that burrows in the sand, the venom of which coagulates the blood. This occurred before Bob was working at the Lake. Apparently, one night she'd been sitting on the sandbank (where we were camped) looking at the starlit sky, twiddling her toes in the sand when she felt a tiny prick on her big toe. She thought nothing of it at the time. The following morning, her body had started turning black. She was rushed as fast as possible to Nairobi where, unable to treat her condition as it was so far advanced, she was flown to England. The saw-scaled viper is a small snake (no more than 60cm, the length of 2 rulers), has a side-winding movement and is responsible for many snakebite cases and often deaths.

Each day, our menfolk (and I was the only woman who enjoyed fishing) would be out in Samaki trolling for big Nile Perch which have a lovely flaky flesh. With such a large family of campers and our diet consisting mostly of fresh fish, we tried to catch enough every day and did. Wambugu, Barsindet and Mpishi didn't want to go on the boat or be near the water, I think due to the crocodiles and perhaps they'd not learnt to swim, though they helped with carting things to and from the boat. Ian and Richard taught them how to gut, scale and cut up the fish then hang out to dry what we weren't eating fresh. The 3 men had plenty of time to relax and mosey about as their duties were minimal. They'd sweep out the tents, wash dishes, do the laundry, fetch water from the lake, and clean out the pots using sand as an abrasive scouring agent. All 3 got on well together. Hardly any of the Turkana men spoke Swahili and even then only a few words, so mostly Mpishi, Wambugu and Barsindet kept to themselves.

The faint glow of pearly pink sunrises accompanying the dawn heat had us awake early. Gill and I would make cups of coffee and tea for everyone then breakfast of tinned fruit and sizzling bacon and eggs. Soon the burning sun would appear and the temperatures quickly rose to scorching.

Lake Rudolf has the largest population of Nile crocodiles in the world. Thousands of them! It was vital that the children swim only under adult supervision and their time in the water was restricted, though they swam on and off all day. The Lake water is soft and silky smooth with a sort of soapy feel to it. When it was calm, we'd slide down the sandbank to swim and play around on inflated car inner tubes and a big tractor tyre inner tube. Robert and Sue were marvellous about swimming with the children. Everyone was excited and having fun extremely noisily and doing much splashing so it was easy to swim or drift too far out, all of which could attract crocodiles. Two adults would sit on the bank of The Spit having a better view of the crocs about 50 yards from us, just floating about, lazily swimming around or heading off to Central Island, their breeding grounds. Carol was an excellent croc-watcher! The water in the Lake depths seemed a sort of khaki-green, but appeared quite clear when put into a bottle. On hot windless days there was some reflection of blue sky turning the Lake a greeny-blue, though during gales the water appeared quite grey, the high waves topped with white crests would break on the beach bringing in more sand. We'd been advised not to drink from the Lake as it could result in tummy upsets.

Lunch consisted of easy foods like tinned bully beef with baked beans or butterbeans and pickles with cream crackers and cheese. Robert had a hankering for cheese – the smellier the better – and was known to ripen it in the cubbyhole of his car. When taking the lid off the container, we'd all have to hold our noses! Sometimes, he'd jokingly say he'd given up women for cheese. He never married and didn't have children, but was godfather to about 50 kids, and was as much-loved and popular amongst the adults as he was with the youngsters. His Mpishi back home made sure Robert had a good supply of savoury biscuits specially baked to go with his cheese. After lunch, it was usual for all of us to take a nap with a couple of sweets to suck. We always had morning and afternoon tea with biscuits.

Watching the last two-and-a-quarter minutes of the sinking sun was truly wonderful, the sky again filled with glorious pinkish-gold colours. Then would come the twilight and respite from the heat of the day. Sundowner time was amazing before the dark of night set in, and moonlit nights magical as the glow gave clearer vision than at twilight. Supper was delicious fresh fried fish with variations of potatoes, rice or spaghetti, cabbage, onions and tinned peas. Mpishi always cooked up a good pot of *posho* (maize meal) for the staff (a staple food they loved) and together with the fish, a real treat for them. They thoroughly enjoyed mealtimes.

There were some basic camp rules. No-one in the water without a lookout; children not to wander off; litter forbidden; hats worn at all times in the sun; no children on the boat in case of sudden squalls and crocodiles; children accompanied to the long-drop toilet; going barefoot allowed only on the beach (snakes and scorpions); everyone had to be in bed by 10 at night to save on paraffin and gas in the lamps.

It was only natural that the Turkana people came to watch the 'antics of the white man' as they were particularly fascinated with mirrors and all our other objects, mannerisms and behaviour in and around the camp site. There never was a problem with them – no stealing, they were always respectful and polite, and never expected anything. They just watched.

Young Turkana under the supervision of Bob McConnell were supplied with large-weave fishing nets and taught that fish under a certain size had to be released. Nets were pulled out of the water twice a day and the catch given to the villagers. When there was a surplus, the fish was dried. The Parks and Fisheries had an old boat about 30 feet or so long called the African Queen. Mature men all had spears which they leant on while standing on one leg. They also carried strange looking, very small two-legged stools for sitting on that served as head rests as well when placed at the back of the neck so that their mud hair-do's weren't damaged. Bob told the Chief we had dried fish for them, and one day he visited us, quite naked, greeting our menfolk only. Sitting on his little stool, we couldn't help noticing the length of the Chief's penis lying on the sand. Amongst ourselves, we named him 'Chief Longtool'. Sometimes, we saw Turkana maidens, though hardly ever adult women. Turkana adults and youths with spears or long sharpened sticks would often stand stock still in shallow water waiting for fish to swim past. Some men had lines and hooks that they'd throw in from the water's edge. They found our methods of using sea-fishing lures intriguing. Though the majority of them were naked, some wore loincloths which were removed before going into the Lake. They also liked to help us with cutting up our fish then laying the strips out in the baking sun. In a couple of days, it was dry enough to be packed into bags to start building up a sufficient supply to take back home as a treat for the farm staff. In return for the help from the Turkana, we gave them dried fish.

Bob told us about a teenager we'd named 'Bootlace', who after all the unloading on our arrival at Kalokol had frequented our campsite. Even though he spoke no Swahili we'd understood by his actions that he wanted to continue being with us and happily doing anything to help around the camp. Richard loved Bootlace, who was perpetually dunking his entire body in the soft water of the Lake. Bob informed us of his medical condition called Ectodermal Dysplasia, an inherited disorder that resulted in defective sweat glands. So at least every half-hour or so, he'd be in and out the water. Bootlace was such a willing youngster, helpful in every way and played with the children. We'd noticed he was ostracised by his people. Perhaps they didn't understand his medical condition. He was so glad when we accepted him into our group and treated him normally.

One morning at breakfast time, Janet couldn't find the tin-opener but spied Uncle Robert's special carving knife, which was always honed to the sharpest degree and went everywhere with him. She quickly used it to pierce two holes in the condensed milk tin. Unfortunately, Uncle Robert just happened to walk past. His usual laid-back character was such that we only ever knew him as a totally unfazed person, to the extent that if it had snowed ink he wouldn't have batted an eyelid. However, we all learnt this particular morning, that when it came to Robert's carving knife things were different. He made such a fuss and was quite unforgiving. That night the children got together and found a very smelly 4 foot long Nile perch fish skeleton and put it in his sleeping bag with the unsightly head on his pillow. Robert neither saw nor smelt the fish skeleton when going to bed and climbed into his sleeping bag before realising it was there. He had no sense of smell. Knowing it was the children who'd done this he raked them out of bed. They all owned up! Thankfully, Robert saw the funny side and we all had a good laugh. Other times, the children would let the air out of his igloo tent, which had tubes like bicycle tyres as supports to lift and hold the light-weight fabric. These tubes had to be pumped daily which the children loved doing for Uncle Robert. Apart from spending so much time swimming with the youngsters, Robert was fun, playing with them a lot and was marvellous about reading bedtime stories. He was a very favourite Uncle.

One day, 2 young Americans, Tom and Jerry from the Peace Corps, came over to our camp to introduce themselves. They'd arrived at one in the morning. Unknowingly, they'd pitched their tiny tent a distance from us, but at exactly the spot where crocodiles habitually sunbathed. This was the place where the Turkana did their fish scaling and chopping up so there were fish carcasses and bones littered around, and it smelt revolting. On waking up and finding the unpleasant surroundings, Tom and Jerry had moved to a cleaner spot. Considering where they'd slept the night, we found it amazing they'd not had a visit from a croc! It was their first trip to Ferguson's Gulf and their initiation to fishing, so Ian gave them the general rundown and showed them how to put traces onto fishing lines etc., and also gave them some fishing lures as they had none. Tom was a mathematics teacher and Jerry taught English at the Mission School in Lodwar. Bob had given permission for them to use the old Fisheries boat, the African Queen, so they could have a couple of days on the Lake. They'd borrowed a fishing rod and a few hooks. On their first attempt at fishing they caught several Nile Perch, and then had lost all the lures. But they'd become so keen on fishing that they improvised a lure by using one of their old canvas sandshoes. As luck would have it, they caught and landed a Nile Perch weighing 364 pounds – a record that stood for a number of years! None of us had caught a fish anywhere near that size at Lake Rudolf. Tom and Jerry departed just as suddenly as they'd appeared. We never saw them leave so unfortunately weren't able to say goodbye.

Late one afternoon, with all of us back in camp having finished our tea and biscuits, we were just chatting, sitting under the awning, winding down in a relaxed mood after a hot and busy day of sun, swimming and fishing. Suddenly, we heard an almighty commotion coming from the beach below us and a Turkana came running up the sandbank shouting and waving his arms hysterically. We all rushed to the edge of The Spit to see what was going on. A crocodile had bitten off a young Turkana's leg. As luck would have it, John Chart had brought his rifle with him. Bob McConnell had gone home already as he'd finished his working day. Our men hurriedly scrambled down to the beach to help while Gill and I herded the children away from the edge of The Spit so they wouldn't see the gory scene. I knew from past Mau Mau happenings that Ian always shielded me from witnessing trauma and bloody scenes, so he certainly wouldn't want the children to experience anything of the kind. Up on the campsite, we could hear the continued commotion below, everything happening so fast. Then the gun fire, followed by wild cheers and whooping indicating to us that John had managed to shoot the crocodile. We made our way down to the beach with the children to find that Richard and Ian had already left in the boat with the injured teenager. The Turkana were busy pulling the massive dead croc onto the sand with a rope. Part of its tail was missing, an old wound that had healed. By John's reckoning, taking into account the missing section, it was a whopping 15-footer. More than likely, because of its unnatural short tail the croc's characteristic lethal lunging ability was severely impaired hence the youngster's miraculous survival. He'd been fishing standing in the water quite near our part of the beach when the attack happened. Fortunately, there were a number of other Turkana youths loitering nearby who witnessed the croc lunge and went to his rescue.

The children all climbed on the back of the dead crocodile, its enormous mouth propped open with a stick so the huge teeth and powerful jaws were clearly visible. We took several photos. The bush telegraph had spread the word fast, and in as little as 20 minutes the carcass of the big crocodile was chopped up into chunks with pangas and carried away by a horde of meat-hungry Turkana men with their delighted male children looking on. Richard and Ian arrived back after nightfall having been guided across the water to our camp by the bright gas lamps hanging from the cross-poles of the awning. We'd decided to have supper, and were very relieved to see them safely home as we'd started worrying, especially with no way for them to have a clear view in the dark of the many crocs lurking about! At night, they can be spotted if you have a torch or some sort of light to shine on the water and pick up the gleam of their eyes. Ian and Richard had transferred the young Turkana from the boat into the Land Rover at Kalokol and rushed him to the Mission in Lodwar. Perhaps our men discussed the incident further amongst themselves, but I didn't ask Ian anything else about it. We never heard about the young man again. I don't know if his life was saved or not.

Lake Rudolf was an unforgettable and sometimes almost heart-stopping adventure. It proved so popular with our children that we made another memorable trip there a year later.

Renamed Lake Turkana in 1975, it is also referred to as the Jade Sea. The colour of the water is caused by algae rising to the surface in calm weather. It is the world's largest alkaline lake and also the largest permanent desert lake, with the far northern end crossing into Ethiopia. North to south, the Lake is 294km long and 44km at its widest point with a depth of 30 metres.

In 1997, the Lake Turkana National Parks were listed as a UNESCO World Heritage Site. Many anthropologists regard the Lake Turkana area as the cradle of humankind.

Chapter Nine
Climbing Kilimanjaro

On the 3rd and final farm evaluation regarding the 'Buy-Out' Scheme carried out by the Central Land Board, Nairobi, and having no other option, we accepted their price of £10 per acre. A document signed by Ian, showing details of our property and assets was sent to us by the Settlement Fund Trustees. Page 2, Paragraph V partly read: '…All fixed and loose assets including livestock and machinery will be checked at the time of takeover and if there are any items missing or which have seriously deteriorated in value, the full value or other appropriate amount as assessed by the Trustees, will be deducted from the price of the farm'. The Title Deeds of Westlands then had to be sent to the Commissioner of Lands, Land Department, Nairobi. As our future was undecided, the furniture and curtains in the house were included in the sale. With so many different aspects to see to, it would take some time to wind down Westlands.

When Lindsay turned 6 in January 1964, she joined Keith and Beryl as a boarder at St Andrew's School. It was privately owned and run by Pa and Ma Lavers, an elderly couple with old-fashioned ethics whose entire lives revolved around their pupils. The school enrolled boys and girls up to the end of their primary tuition. There were 3 school terms and 3 one-month holidays a year. Extra-curricular activities were provided such as boxing, music, dancing and a variety of sports. Parents were allowed to visit their children at mid-term. During the school holidays, I took the children and Asha to the cinema in Kitale. We saw 'Anna and the King of Siam', 'Goldfinger', and a Japanese-made film which was supposed to be scary, about a giant rattling metal worm-like monster with huge eyes which apparently lived in a mine. Every now and then it would emerge from underground and terrorise the population. This was the only film that made any lasting impression on Asha. I often wondered how she'd relate this story to her husband, Chalagut, who wouldn't have had the foggiest clue what she was talking about.

Ian and Vi felt uncertain about the children's long-term future and decided it would be best if they all went to boarding school in South

Africa. I was unhappy with the idea. Mater, Ian's mother, was still living in her flat in East London. King William's Town wasn't far from her and offered good schooling and hostels. I made the relevant arrangements for the 1st term in January 1965. Keith and Tony would go to Dale College for boys. Hazel, Beryl and Lindsay would go to Kaffrarian High School for girls which also had a primary school.

We attended the St Andrew's School annual sports day at the end of the year. All 3 of our children attained good reports. Keith was particularly happy there, so it was with a sad heart that he said goodbye to his friends.

Before mid-January 1965, I flew with the 5 children and young Stuart from Nairobi to Johannesburg where we had an overnight stop and caught the plane to East London the following day to stay with Mater. King William's Town was a train trip away. With so many things to see to there was no time to waste. School uniforms, shoes and sports clothes needed to be fitted and bought, name-tapes ordered and sewn on. Every item had to be marked. Tuck boxes and tuck, doctors and dentists, school and hostel fees as well as pocket-money had to be arranged. Spare finances had to be made available to the Hostel staff in case of any other eventualities. Having settled the children into boarding school as best I could, I flew back to Nairobi with Stuart. South African schools had 4 terms a year with 2 long holidays in June and December, and 2 shorter holidays at Easter and again in September. For the 2 long holidays, the children would fly home to Kenya, but for the 2 short holidays they would either stay with Mater or go home with friends if they were invited. As can be expected, being so far from home all 5 had serious bouts of homesickness. Vi and I kept a regular correspondence with them. In time, they settled into the South African schooling system. I was often in tears and Asha would ask me why I was crying. My reply was that I missed my children very much.

I'd been invited by a friend of mine, Julia Rutherfurd (a year younger than me), to climb Mount Kilimanjaro with her. With our imminent departure from Westlands looming, we had a mountain to climb and I a promise to keep before the opportunity was lost. Jock (Julia's husband) and Ian had been in the Kenya Regiment together. The couple had very kindly lent us Cinderella, a lovely dappled grey pony, for Lindsay to ride.

Julia had first brought up the subject of climbing Kilimanjaro when they were managing a farm near Soy for an elderly gentleman, Alec Douglas. The British Government, Lancaster House, had bought-out Mr Douglas' farm so Jock and Julia had arranged for game catchers with the intention of relocating a small herd of rare Rothschild's giraffe before the farm had to be vacated. There'd been an incident where one of the bull giraffes had caused extensive damage to a car by beating its hooves on the hood and bonnet when the driver had stopped to admire them crossing the road in front of him.

Watching the giraffe catching, Jock and Ian were standing talking and Julia and I were sitting on blankets under a thorn tree. Men holding long poles with nooses on the end were standing on the open-back lorries of the game capture company trying to get the nooses around the necks of the giraffe, when Julia suddenly asked, "Would you like to climb Kili with me, Heather?"

The question took me completely by surprise. I'd never given it a thought before. Just to make sure I'd heard right, I queried, "Kilimanjaro?"

"Yes," she said, "why not? We're young enough to make it up and down."

I gave it a few quick moments thought. I'd climbed plenty of trees as a girl and hadn't been called Nugu for nothing. Add in some fences, small hills and the garage roof at Anchorage and I'd done a fair amount of walking at Daisy's, Uruku and Westlands. But, as a farmwife, the most I'd climbed was up and down a ladder to hang curtains. I had to admit though, it did sound incredibly exciting tackling Africa's greatest mountain.

"All right, Julia," I said, smiling, "I'll go with you. What's the plan?"

"Stamina is the first thing we'd need to work on before we even attempt to climb Kili. We'd have to get together regularly beforehand to work on that."

Jock and Julia had since taken over running the Soy Club. Soy, a small village with a Post Office, a duka and the Soy Club (an upmarket establishment) was about 15 miles from Westlands. Patronising the Soy Club was beyond our financial means so the only time we went there was to attend a wedding. The occasion was memorable because Lindsay, in her pretty pink party dress, was pecked in the eye by one of the very beautiful Kavirondo Cranes (also known as Crested Cranes) wandering around the garden.

What with sorting out our children's schooling and tying up various matters regarding Westlands, I'd not had the time to attempt a climb of Kilimanjaro. With my diary relatively clear for a few weeks it was now or never. Julia was still as enthusiastic. To build up our stamina and leg muscles and get us used to walking for long hours, Julia drove over to us very early every Saturday morning so that we had ample opportunity to hike up *Soysambu*, a beautiful hill made of giant rocks piled one on top of the other which was partly on Westlands. We'd return home by noon. Soysambu – meaning striated rock in Maasai – was a snake paradise; lots of puff adders and cobras, so we stepped very gingerly and avoided any crevices. It wasn't long before Peter Smith heard of our proposed climb of Kili and readily opted to join in, though he was too far away on Ol Morijo to participate in our Soysambu training excursions. When Julia and I thought we were ready to do the Kili climb (truth is we'd not the faintest notion of what this trip entailed), I made the bookings for hotel accommodation and the climb with the management of the Moshi Hotel in Tanzania situated on the foothills of Mount Kilimanjaro. Just the idea of getting to the top of Africa was enough for me to want to have the experience.

I had the local Eldoret Indian shoemaker *fundi* (meaning expert) make me a pair of sheepskin-lined boots with the outer covering being plain black leather. Shopping in the same town at an Indian clothing duka, I bought what I could find in suitable warm clothing – a heavy-duty jacket, corduroy trousers, some thick socks and a bush hat. The Moshi Hotel manager wrote telling me that they provided extra clothing, gloves and balaclavas so there was no need for us to worry about having the correct outfits for extreme conditions of cold. With that in mind, I took out smart clothing and shoes to wear on the trip there and back, underwear, a thick jersey with a polo-neck that I'd knitted myself and a suitable outfit for dinner. Together with the heavy clothing it all fitted into a medium-sized suitcase. In my small beauty case, I packed lip-salve, moisturising cream, toothbrush and paste, toilet soap and flannel, dark glasses and a tube of special ultra-violet cream that our Kitale doctor, Irene Leach, had advised I take as a precaution against snow-burn. Last on my list, but vital, was my good Optima camera.

Ian made no comment about whether or not attempting to climb Kili was a crazy idea since we'd never been mountaineering before, or even whether Julia and I would reach the summit. Neither did he remark on us going off walking up Soysambu. He was just so busy with the farm that he felt if I was happy then he was too and gladly let me take the Mercedes for the trip to Moshi and back. Keith, Beryl and Lindsay were at boarding school in South Africa. Stuart (four-and-a-half) was now old enough to stay at home with Ian and Asha.

Julia and I travelled to Naivasha, had a pit stop then went straight on to Nairobi, continuing till eventually the road branched off from good tarmac onto the most appalling corrugated dirt road I've ever been on, all the way to Namanga, the Kenya-Tanzania border-post. I felt sorry for Ian's Merc travelling over the horrendous dirt roads. The very pleasant African border guard took the Moshi Hotel booking confirmation letter, turned it upside down and then using his index finger went along slowly reading each word. Julia and I were flummoxed. Seemingly completely satisfied with our paperwork, he then let us through the barrier. This was the 2nd time – after Asha who could only look at pictures upside down – that I'd come across this phenomenon. In this instance, the man was actually reading upside down. It was apparent to us that he found it quite normal. We arrived at Moshi Hotel shortly before dark on 21st July 1965. Peter was already there. Almost immediately after being shown the en suite room Julia and I would share, we had dinner. Meals were included in the tariff and the excellent cuisine consisted of several courses. The tables were beautifully set with good quality cutlery and crockery and the service excellent. Drinks were extra. Although we felt dead tired, Julia and I went to sleep that night like 2 kids on Christmas Eve hardly able to contain their excitement of what the morning might bring.

At sun-up, a Canadian (whose name now eludes me!), and a New Zealander, Dan Brown, joined our party, making 5 of us. We were briefed on the climb by the white manager who also ran the tour business, giving us an idea of what we would be facing. Three days up the mountain sleeping overnight in huts, then the easier days of coming down sleeping 2 nights, returning to the hotel on the last day.

Kilimanjaro is classified as a giant stratovolcano (a conical volcano built up of many layers of strata, being hardened lava, tephra, pumice and volcanic ash) and consists of 3 distinct volcanic cones – Kibo, Mawenzi and Shira. Not only is it the highest mountain on the African continent, but it is also the highest free-standing mountain in the world. Kibo, the highest and youngest, is 19,341 feet (5,895 metres) at Uhuru Peak on the summit of its crater rim and is dormant though it could erupt again. Mawenzi (16,893 feet or 5,149 metres) and Shira, the oldest (13,000 feet or 3,962 metres) are extinct. The name *Kilimanjaro* (Kilima-Njaro) is generally understood to mean *Kilima* (Mountain) *Njaro* (of Greatness) though *Njaro* may also mean 'White' or 'Whiteness' referring to its snow-capped peak. There are 7 official climbing routes to ascend and descend Kilimanjaro. The base of Kilimanjaro is about 40 km across and covers an area of approximately 388,500 ha.

The hotel loaned each of us a knapsack and raincoat, some extra-warm under-clothing, balaclavas and gloves all of which looked as though they could have previously been navy or military clothing. I was instructed to wear a pair of sailor's long johns under my corduroy slacks when we reached the colder altitude. We were all advised to wear sunglasses while climbing. The Canadian had brought goggles with him. To protect the lenses of our cameras, we were told to keep them under our clothing next to our skin as the lens could crack from the extreme cold. I kept my Optima against my midriff.

Next, we were introduced to the tour staff who'd accompany us. Then the expedition began. The porters, including the cook (being one staff member for each of us hikers), carried our small knapsacks of basic requirements, cooking utensils, sleeping bags and a thin pillow each, other climbing equipment, pangas, tents for the staff and cut wood for making the fires for cooking and warmth. Mpishi (yes, another

Mpishi, rather like the 2 Mwangis – it was a generally acknowledged sign of respect to address the cook as Mpishi instead of by his name) seemed to be in charge of everyone and led the way, the porters and we climbers obeying him completely. We spoke to the staff in Swahili, the lingua franca throughout Kenya, Tanzania, East and Central Africa, though it differs slightly depending on where one is born. Everything about the trip so far appeared well organised. The porters, of their own accord, kept a dignified distance yet were always quietly at hand and highly efficient.

Having started off early on the morning of 22nd July, it wasn't long before the African sun became hot. I tied my jersey around my waist, to be replaced about half-way through the first day with warmer clothing as the chill air began to set in. Mpishi walked in front, followed by the Canadian, then Peter, Julia and me next, with Dan at the rear of our group. One behind the other, we followed a well-worn foot path. The porters carrying the baggage were the last in the 'crocodile' single file column. At the start, we hiked through lovely woodland and grassy grazing areas with the occasional big shady tree and small herds of goats and sheep contentedly munching away and bleating, watched by their child herders. It was obvious the staff and child herders knew each other. We all waved and received friendly gestures in return. The young Canadian was very confident and told us as we walked along that his country had plenty of mountain climbing and snow. Dan, the New Zealander, was a very decent 35 year old, a quiet, unassuming chap who said coming to Africa was the experience of a lifetime for him. We were a happy bunch getting on well.

Still walking for many hours on the gentle elevation of the lower slopes, but now on a dusty car track that was hard on the feet with lots of pebbles, we saw scattered African rural settlements of round mud huts. Thin wisps of swirling acrid smoke wafted from the thatched roofs, the homesteads enclosed by brush fencing to keep in the livestock at night. We stopped only when Mpishi gave us picnic sandwiches and something cool to drink, otherwise we were on the march with no slacking. By that evening, Julia and I were whacked from a day of foot-slogging for hours on end and ready for a good night's sleep, due not only to the tedious hiking but also the long car journey to the Moshi

Hotel. The first Hut, Bismarck (also known as Mandara Hut), was made of stone with a tin roof, a very basic single room with an entrance door, windows and sufficient space for us 5 climbers to sleep. The toilet was a long-drop just a way off from the Hut. There were no washing facilities. In no time at all, Mpishi had a kettle on the boil and produced a meal from his store of tinned food which he heated in a pot over a very smoky open fire made from the ready chopped wood the porters had carried, and bits of dry grass kindling collected from around the Hut. Mpishi and the porters never said a word to us about how well we'd done or hadn't done that day. They just got on with their job of taking care of us, seeing we had what we needed and keeping a strict eye on the time. All of them were well experienced having been up and down the mountain many times as guides so we did as we were told with never a murmur of dissent. By 7.30, we were all in our sleeping bags grateful for rest. The porters and Mpishi slept in tents.

We were woken at dawn on the 2nd day by Mpishi, who gave us a tin mug of hot coffee and a tin plate of oatmeal porridge with sugar, after which we were given minimal time to be ready to move on. There was no relaxing going to the toilet or the like. If you hadn't been it was just bad luck. By this stage, I had the distinct impression that the tour was a regimented time schedule, the sole intention being to get hikers up the mountain and back down as quickly as possible so that the next group could get going. During walking on the first day, no information was volunteered regarding points of interest of our surroundings. I felt a little disappointed that we could only take photos whilst hiking without being given a bit of extra time to stop now and then along the way. On numerous occasions, I had to run to catch up with the others.

The gentle rolling slopes were now gone as the climb unexpectedly became a steep incline into rainforest that left a lasting impression on my mind. We were instructed to put on our raincoats, and I was glad to have my bush hat as the heavy mist gently dripped big fat drops from the dense dark-green canopy of trees above. The sudden change in visibility and temperature was dramatic – from bright sunshine to dank cold forest with hardly any light. Swathes of pale grey-green 'old man's beard' hung from stretching branches, and jungle green lianas clinging in thick creeper-cords wound around the tree trunks. The narrow slippery path of red clay with a trickle of water was about a foot deep from so many climbers over the years. The clay stuck heavily to our boots as we slogged one step in front of the other in and out of the maze of trees, carefully clambering over thick brown roots in our way. Had it been a leisurely hike, I would have welcomed the opportunity of spending a little time examining the trees, considering my childhood of enchanting forests at Anchorage and the Wanjohi Valley.

We suddenly came into bright sunlight onto open moorland, an area with large clumps of tall reeds and rivulets of water, a kind of bog-land, still with the single path winding around and about. Having been walking for a long time, I now fell behind the others as I managed to take about 3 photos of this area. Despite the steep ascent, the moorland was to me the most tedious and uninteresting but easiest part of the climb. Making up for the monotony of this part of the hike was the magnificence of Mawenzi looming ahead and above. A spectacular jagged mountain of black lava rock peaks forming part of the Kilimanjaro panorama. We made straight for Peter's Hut. The accommodation was an absolutely basic one-roomed rectangular corrugated-iron tin shanty standing alone on stony ground surrounded by some hardy species of Erica plants. Again, there was an outside long-drop toilet. The Hut had a door, 2 little windows (never open, more for light than air), wooden double bunks against the sides, a cement floor and tin roof. All of us were weary and relieved to go to bed fully dressed in our warmest clothing, glad to get into our sleeping bags. With no ceiling, the only thing separating us from the severe chill of the black mountain sky above, were a few sheets of rusted corrugated-iron. There being no facilities again, none of us washed or cleaned our teeth. As it had been my daily habit instilled in me by my mother since I was tiny, it bothered me. I went to sleep once more feeling unclean.

No-one complained about anything. There didn't seem any point as the goal by this stage was simply to remain focused and get to the top of Kilimanjaro. I don't remember even trying to turn over on the bottom wooden bunk. The moment I was in my thin sleeping bag, I curled up in a ball to retain body heat as the rough, bare cement floor was about 18 inches beneath me. Stiff and sore from no mattress to cover the gaps between the hard planks or stop the chill from the floor, the intense cold of the night at 12,340 feet (3,780 metres) was exacerbated and soon penetrated to the marrow of my bones. I was grateful for the small, thin pillow and balaclava provided by the hotel, and couldn't imagine how the night would have been without my gloves.

At early morning sunrise, my body stiff and my finger joints locked from the cold, we were woken by Mpishi who had coffee and our porridge ready. We gobbled our breakfast then I went to an outside pool of groundwater with my flannel and handkerchief as by this stage I felt dirty and it was beginning to upset me. There were a few gorse bushes nearby for privacy. The water was so cold that I couldn't even dip my flannel in, but merely dampened it and quickly gave my face a wipe. Then I wet my handkerchief in the same way and ducked behind the bushes while I got my trousers down to wipe my nether end. Later, I would understand the gravity of my mistake.

Leaving most of our clobber at Peter's Hut, we wore our warmest clothes for the night's stay at the last Hut, Kibo, and the final part of the climb to Kilimanjaro's summit. The porters carried only our food, firewood and sleeping bags. We started the 3rd day climbing steeply to the base of Mawenzi, the sun shining brightly and the air chilly, and were then allowed a short respite to attempt some rock climbing. The soles of my boots were smooth, and unable to get any grip on the sharp, brittle rock ledges I started feeling afraid and didn't get higher than about 20 feet. Realising it was hazardous and foolish to continue further, I turned back. Even the Canadian had doubts about tackling the jagged rock-face of Mawenzi, as did the others, everyone descending shortly after me.

Regrouping, we set off again into what is known as the 'saddle' of Kilimanjaro, a flattish area between Mawenzi and the start of the really difficult part of the climb to the top of the mountain. It was a vast stretch of bleak, desolate and dusty-grey alpine desert not unlike what one imagines the surface of the moon to be, devoid of vegetation, with huge boulders lying around. I started vomiting with diarrhoea and had to keep disappearing behind large boulders, very embarrassing for me, to keep out of sight of Dan Brown who opted to stay and keep me company which was very noble of him. Feeling really grim, I had to remove my balaclava for vomiting. This very unpleasant phase lasted a couple of hours and left me feeling drained of energy. For supper the night before we'd been given tinned ham which I have avoided ever since. It could also have been something to do with mountain sickness, the signs being nausea and shortness of breath from climbing at high altitudes. Finally, I got over this difficult period and Dan was free to go on at his own pace and quickly caught up with the others who were now quite some way ahead. Even the porters were just ahead of me but within calling distance.

Eventually, I caught up with the group, and Mpishi pointed out to us the wreckage of a plane lying in a sandy patch between jagged peaks of Mawenzi and I took several photos. In May 1955, an East African Airways Dakota flying in thick cloud hit the south-eastern face, killing everyone on board. Tragically, had the pilot been flying 10 metres higher, the plane would have just made it over the summit ridge of Mawenzi. The alpine terrain now suddenly changed and we had to thread our way through and over large boulders and rocks packed closely together which seemed to be settled into sand and shale. More energy was spent on breathing, and the chill was severe. Thankfully, I had my balaclava on again as my nose felt distinctly numb.

Much to our relief, we reached Kibo Hut just at sunset, an even smaller corrugated-iron shack set on a cleared space among the rocks with a long-drop toilet nearby. There were again the basic wooden double bunks and cement floor. At this altitude, it was freezing cold inside and outside. The porters made a fire and lit a Dietz paraffin lamp for light inside the Hut. Then Mpishi dished out a quick hot meal of tinned baked beans and bully beef with a mug of hot cocoa each, handed out the sleeping bags, and we had a last visit to the long-drop. A baked bean tin with a jagged edge had been left in the Hut in case anyone needed the toilet during the night. All of us were glad to end the day, just said goodnight and curled up. Fully dressed in my thickest, warm clothing, no matter how I snuggled, I still couldn't get warm. Before I could fall asleep, I suddenly needed to wee again and became desperate from struggling with my clothes, my fingers stiff and clumsy. Using the baked bean tin was not an entirely successful manoeuvre with so many layers of clothing. Some wee, unfortunately, went on the floor.

I felt very self-conscious knowing everyone could hear me, but no-one said a word or moved. Afterwards, my bladder much relieved, I quickly opened the door just enough to empty out the tin, put it back on the floor then climbed into my sleeping bag again.

Seemed like the next thing I knew, Mpishi came in with a Dietz paraffin lamp, woke us, and in the soft lighting said we should get up. I think I was in some sort of torpor as I'd had a rotten night and needed more sleep. The vomiting and diarrhoea of the day before had sapped my energy and every bone in my body seemed to be aching. Apart from which, I felt almost frozen stiff from lying in a curled-up foetal position due to the freezing cold and my nose was swollen. It was 1.30 – to me, still the middle of the night. Mpishi watched us closely eating our oatmeal porridge with sugar insisting we finish every mouthful. Then holding a Dietz lamp, he gave each of us a small hand-torch and we followed him into the darkness at 2 o'clock in the morning. Numbly we followed one behind the other without speaking, and made our way through big boulders and smaller rocks with loose shale beneath our feet, our breathing shallow. It was a very steep ascent in the freezing darkness, our minds concentrated on Mpishi's lamp ahead and our torchlight to guide each step.

Eventually, the pale light of early morn was upon us as we reached the base of the massif. Looking up, the mountain loomed so sheer I couldn't see the summit. Neither could I grasp the enormity of what was ahead of me in conquering this last hurdle to the top of mighty Kilimanjaro. Beneath our feet our boots crunched heavily in loose deep grey shale mixed with scree and dust, making every step a monumental challenge. It was impossible to walk directly upwards, my thigh quadriceps burned from the effort. Mpishi had given each of us a tall alpenstock with a metal spike on the one end which was of significant assistance in getting us up this final, very challenging section and at this critical point I felt particularly grateful. Even so, everyone struggled with the 4,000 feet of shale. But, I kept going. There was no choice. I couldn't go back down the mountain at this late stage, I just had to go on and wouldn't give up, my mind on auto, two steps upward, slide one backwards, most times my body bent over using my free hand to steady myself – two up, one back.

Finally, I reached the top of Kibo and stood up straight at last, in relief and enraptured awe, looking down at the world far below, a vast expanse in all directions of varied African landscape stretching across into Kenya. The others were sitting on a rocky outcrop exhausted, catching their breath, huddled together against the bitterly cold wind on this part of the summit known as Gilman's Point (5,681 metres). I walked over, grateful to join them and be able to sit down and rest. Yes, my heart felt elated at having attained my goal in climbing this magnificent mountain and it felt like a miracle at that moment, but my body wasn't up to any physical celebration as I'd taken quite a hammering and hadn't the strength to leap up and down in excitement or even shout for joy. I was just too drained. Mpishi then gave each of us a bar of plain chocolate for extra energy and told us we only had 20 minutes to rest after which we'd have to keep moving. He also emphasised the danger of removing our sunglasses which could result in snow-blindness.

Standing on the top of Africa, every exhale of our breath resembled the proverbial dragon's, rising in white puffs into the cold air. We took it in turns taking group photos, sitting on bare, sharp rocks surrounded by enormous brown boulders and blindingly white snow that I found incredible. It wasn't soft as I'd expected, lying in a blanket covering the ground where one could build a snowman or throw snowballs. Instead, it was tightly-packed, hard white huge pieces of snow with flat tops, some exceptionally large, others smaller, not joined together, about 3 foot high in thickness with vertical sides that looked as if they'd suddenly been sliced off with a big, sharp knife. The scene of white interspersed with sections of brown moonscape was absolutely fascinating and resembled to me a giant upside-down Christmas pudding with generous dollops of hard Royal Icing decorating the top.

Walking towards the crater of the gigantic volcano, I stopped a safe distance from the edge, terrified of slipping on the small, loose stones of scree and falling in, or becoming light-headed, even disorientated, and suffering some catastrophe. Awaiting me was the most wondrous sight I could ever have imagined, indelibly etched in my mind's eye for eternity and an experience I'll never forget. It was worth every arduous step and ounce of effort I'd endured to behold the stupendous wonders of Kilimanjaro's summit. The sky was a cloudless pale blue and the early morning rays of sun fell on translucent glacier creations of solid ice filling the enormous round crater, some as great and tall as city buildings, stacked next to and on top of one another, the play of light giving an impression of architecturally sculpted frozen blocks in the palest of shimmering green. I stood mesmerised at the sight, realising too how absolutely deadly and easy it would be to fall into this, so deep it was, with no way of rescue.

Julia, the Canadian and Mpishi said they were walking to Uhuru Peak where the Tanzanian flag flies. The rest of us opted to stay and wander around taking photos.

I remained in the vicinity of the crater rim, walking about spellbound with my camera, lost in this time of ethereal wonderment and gratified peace within myself, surrounded by the purest gift of silence as I gazed at the incredible ice-magic hidden like a secret in the belly of the volcano.

Mpishi returned with the others and we started the descent as a group, but the young Canadian immediately dashed off down on his own and that was the last we saw of him. Because the shale section was loose the best way over it was to run. This sounds easy, but with your legs moving very fast there was the possibility of tripping and rolling down without stopping so there was a certain amount of agility and concentration involved in keeping unhindered momentum, especially when wearing boots and heavy clothing. Also going down the mountain was a Japanese hiker and another inert person on a stretcher, being carried by porters who shouted something as they passed us about the individual being sick. For a change, I seemed to have the advantage with my short legs and made it first to the end of the shale under half-an-hour and back onto solid ground. Even though we followed the same route, there was a huge difference time-wise in coming down the mountain as opposed to climbing up. When everyone was together, we set off for Kibo Hut where we had something light to eat. Joined up with the porters once more, we continued on to Peter's Hut for the night. I never thought I'd say this, but it was a distinctly blessed relief to climb onto the hard wooden bunk once more and into my thin sleeping bag for some much-needed rest and 'shut-eye'. I'd reached a point where just getting sleep was bliss. By this stage, aches and pains of one kind or another, or locked finger joints from the cold were understood to be par for the course.

Early morning came with Mpishi waking us for the usual breakfast, after which we lined up in front of the shack. He presented each of us with a small posy of pale pink alpine flowers and told us the alpenstocks were ours to keep as a memento for having made it to the top of Kilimanjaro. Then the very long foot-slog back to the hotel started, luckily on downhill slopes. I was really exhausted and mentally weary, my main thought being to get back to civilisation, have a luxury bath and hair wash. My nose had become seriously painful and felt very different, so the first thing I did on getting back to our hotel room towards evening was to look in the mirror. What a shock I got! My nose was not only swollen, but ugly too, and a distinctly maroon-brown colour! Later, we had another memorably pleasant dinner, said our goodbyes to Peter and Dan, left a *bakshishi* (it was customary to leave a tip) for Mpishi and his gang, and had a blissful night on comfy beds with sweet-smelling linen and eiderdowns. I realised, with a quiet and grateful smile to myself, that a little bit of Heaven on earth is having a mattress to lie on!

We left for home in the morning, driving on the jarring, dusty corrugated road till just outside Nairobi where travelling became easier on the good tarmac for the last long leg of our trip back to Soy. There'd been little time or opportunity to chat while climbing Kilimanjaro so it was nice to spend time again with Julia. We had plenty of hours in the car to catch up on conversation. Both of us were proud to have made it to the top of this great mountain and I was glad she'd invited me to join her. I dropped Julia off at Soy Club then continued on to Westlands.

Ian, Stuart and Asha were pleased I was home again. I knew Ian was also relieved to have his Mercedes returned in one piece, and he didn't say a word about my unsightly nose! Unpacking later, I realised that the Indian fundi shoemaker had done an excellent job making my sheepskin-lined boots – neither pebbles nor dust had got in, and not a sign of a blister anywhere on my feet. My Optima camera never worked properly again, yet the Eldoret photo-shop people could find nothing wrong with it. The frostbite of my whole nose, I think, started from wiping my face with my flannel in the severe cold of the high altitude during the latter stages of the climb and was then exacerbated by my not being able to wear my balaclava for some hours the same day during the period I was vomiting for some hours. Then, more than likely adding to the problem was walking around on Kibo's freezing cold summit taking photos. The way my nose looked, I felt like Rudyard Kipling's Elephant's Child must have done when his trunk shrank in the great grey-green Limpopo River! Luckily, my condition healed in 6 weeks living at a normal altitude. The brown and ugly hardened leather-like skin finally curled up in small patches, and by me carefully picking at it, left me with a new pink nose.

Since 1912, Kilimanjaro has lost 82% of its ice-cap, and since 1962 has lost 55% of its remaining glaciers. Kilimanjaro National Park was designated a World Heritage Site in 1987. By 2040, it is estimated that most of the ice on Kilimanjaro will have disappeared, and after 2060 it is unlikely any ice will remain.

Chapter Ten
Malindi

Our staff and Asha particularly, were shock-stricken when we'd told them sometime earlier that we were leaving Westlands forever. None of them understood politics and couldn't remotely comprehend any of the business of the Lancaster House Agreement. It didn't make any sense to them. Looking at it from their point of view, I could see why they felt confused suddenly facing no longer having work, after all, what had it really got to do with them? They could not understand that we had no option, being forced to sell the farm and had to get out whether we wanted to or not. It was extremely sad contemplating having to leave them. As each day passed until it was time to say our farewells, Ian and I had heavy hearts as we counted down the days.

We were the last farm in the first million acre Buy-Out Scheme and were already surrounded by properties that had been taken over by Lancaster House and handed to the Kenya Government. All these properties were non-productive because, as yet, they'd not been settled with new occupants due to resident farm labour who were not earning a salary. The Government was arranging for surveyors to divide up the land into 15 acre plots for Kenyan African new owners (a further cost paid for by the British Government, ultimately being the British tax-payer). Merrowdown was bought out before Westlands – Don and Mary Rooken-Smith moved to Northern Kenya with their children. Marge and Harold left their small-holding, Ellegerini, for South Africa in 1965. Before their departure they made a special trip to see what was left of our Granny Marjorie Aggett's old homestead. Only the intact stone chimney stood tall and bare on the edge of the Maasai Mara Reserve.

Maize of the highest quality we'd grown from registered seed number SR52, cultivated in and imported from Southern Rhodesia (now Zimbabwe), a most progressive agricultural farming country outdoing all others with their yields of maize and soya bean. SR52 seed considerably increased the yield of the plant producing 4 to 5 good cobs per sturdy stalk. Our best crop yielded a phenomenal 20,000 bags, each containing 200 pounds of shelled maize.

As our cattle livestock was vastly undervalued, we'd been given permission to sell the Friesian Dairy Herd to Makerere College in Uganda. Professor Lule himself came with his entourage, signed the sale and export papers and paid the money. Then all of a sudden, the Kenya Government reneged and stopped the sale and we had to refund the Professor. With no other buyer and no time to source an alternative, Ian was forced to send all our highly bred Friesian dairy cattle, plus our pedigree Ayrshire herd (which he'd received awards for) as well as the bulls from both herds, to the Kenya Meat Commission where they were slaughtered. We were paid a reasonable beef price for this stock, but what truly upset us and which was unforgivable then and still is and absolutely broke our hearts, was to have to send these exquisite cattle to their deaths when they could have gone to Uganda and carried on their excellent bloodline. Ian was bereft loading these prized animals of his for their trip to the abattoir. I will always remember his heartache reflected deep in his eyes on this day of utter devastation for a devoted and proud farmer who loved and cared for his livestock beyond words. Not long after this, Professor Lule was assassinated in Uganda. Despite investigation, we never heard anything further regarding the dubious circumstances of his death.

Other farmers in the two Buy-Out Schemes were also experiencing the same behaviour from the Central Land Board. One or two white farmers were given a fair deal for the price of their land, but on the whole it was an utterly shabby disgrace. A Government Minister bought our house and 100 acres around it from the new Kenya Government under Jomo Kenyatta. The deal had nothing to do with us.

Ian managed to sell the machinery cheaply, and we returned Cinderella to Jock and Julia, grateful to have been lent the pony for Lindsay to ride. No animals belonging to us were left on the farm. Ian found buyers for his polo ponies, making sure his horses only went to good owners – another very painful experience for him that signalled the end to his much-treasured polo-playing days. Before Harold and Marge moved to Merrowdown in Western Kenya, Harold had started the Ol'Kalou Polo Club, the sport being played by various clubs from all over the country. Ian started playing polo at Westlands and was in one of the Kenya Regiment teams along with Don Rooken-Smith, Tony

Barkas and Mike Keane playing at Moiben. Our Rooken-Smith polo team comprised Ian, Harold, Don and Bruce. Marge knitted the 4 team jerseys in a striking colour combination of dark green with a broad silver stripe across the front and back. Polo tournaments were played in several Provinces with major events held in Nairobi where Ian twice won the Macmillan Cup playing in our Rooken-Smith team.

Stuart, now approaching 5 years old, became upset on hearing that we'd have to leave the farm. He showed extreme anxiety when he understood that his bed would not be taken with us. To his young mind, there was no valid reasoning why we should have to move from our home and animals we loved so much. To ensure we only had the basics to transport in our vehicles the day we departed from Westlands, we packed and moved the majority of our personal belongings a few weeks earlier to Ellegerini where Marge and Harold had storage space. They'd left an elderly gentleman, Bud Woodley, managing the small-holding. I would have to conclude the sale of Marge's large dining room table and chairs on her behalf. Some time later, Ellegerini would also be sold.

I shared out many kitchen, pantry and household items between Asha and our houseman, Wambugu, and gave Asha all our double bed linen. Ian always dealt with staff remunerations and farm finances. They both received their salary and a substantial bonus. Asha had been a wonderful companion and greatly loved nanny – Wambugu a truly decent, good man. None of our staff ever asked us for anything. They'd remained always grateful to have employment, going about their work with dedication and respect.

Old Kamau died before we left Westlands. One morning, our farm Headman, Twiga (his name meaning 'giraffe'), a proud Abaluhya, 6 foot 3 inches tall and well-built, informed Ian that Kamau couldn't come to work as he was feeling sick. So I took the old fellow to the State Hospital in Eldoret. We had no farm telephone line. A week later, I went back to the hospital to find out how Kamau was, only to hear the shocking and very sad news that he'd died. I wasn't given any medical explanation regarding the cause of his passing. Since Westlands was in the throes of Government takeover, Kamau was not permitted burial on the farm. The hospital authorities dealt with the matter. Regardless of where we would live in all the following years, I kept framed photos of

Kamau and Asha on display in the house so I could see them as I went about my day. They both remained firmly ensconced in the memory of our children – Kamau a special and loyal man, and Asha a gem.

Chalagut, Asha's husband, this naturally gifted devoted cattleman, apart from his salary received a double-bonus as well as a going away gift from Ian.

Twiga's word as Headman was law and he was respected by all our staff – a handsome, quiet and utterly reliable man, very conscious of his status. We could go away to Malindi at the coast knowing that Twiga would carry on with the dairy and whole milk supply, manage the veterinary work and keep the Land Rover in good nick, just as Ian had trained him. Ian gave Twiga the long-wheel base Land Rover and Ian's Harley motorcycle, plus he was paid a bonus with his salary. I don't know what went on with Ian and Twiga the day we left. As with all Ian's male staff and the excellent working relationship they had, I know there was mutual heartache and sorrow as they said their goodbyes. All Ian told me was that Twiga said he'd be returning to his tribal lands.

Mwangi was a young, unmarried Kikuyu man. His daily work had been taking care of the bulls, cleaning each stable, putting in new hay etc., grooming and feeding, and taking them into their own paddock. He loved his bulls and there seemed to be a mutual understanding because they amazingly never showed any aggressiveness towards him. I've no knowledge of what Ian gave Mwangi when we left. This was between the 2 men, but knowing how highly he valued Mwangi's work and that Ian firmly believed in recognition for dedication and commitment, I'm sure Ian remunerated him generously.

When the day came to pack our cars and finally leave Westlands in late 1965, we were relieved to be gone from all the extreme stress and unpleasantness of everything to do with the Central Land Board in Nairobi and the people affiliated with it. Some goodbyes are particularly traumatic. In writing 'Daisy's Daughter', I hope to have paid due honour to our staff, for each in their own way significantly contributed to turning Westlands from a run-down property into a highly successful farming operation. None of our staff knew what their fate would be. The new Government took over the day we left. The maize harvest was in and had been marketed, and Ian had already been paid. Later on we would receive a whopping Income Tax bill to pay.

Ian drove the packed Land Rover and took Jock with him. I followed in the Mercedes with the cats and Kasuku parrot, and Stuart sitting on the front seat understandably distressed. To take his mind off the sad happenings of the day, I handed him Daisy's large oak mantelpiece clock she'd given me, after first removing the pendulum.

"Hold Granny's special clock tight," I said, his forlorn little face looking up at me, "and take good care of it for Mummy, please."

After a few minutes drive, as we turned from the dirt farm road onto the tar on our way through Soy then Eldoret and on to Kaptagat, with teary eyes and my heart and mind waving a quiet goodbye to 12 wonderful years of happiness at Westlands, a little voice suddenly spoke from the seat beside me.

"Mummy," Stuart said solemnly, clutching Daisy's clock, "when you get a feeling to die, please can I have this clock?"

Not long after our arrival at Ellegerini, the South African schools started their end of year holidays. We flew Keith, Beryl and Lindsay from East London to Johannesburg then on to Nairobi with the last leg of their journey being a flight to Malindi. We met them at the airport and all holidayed again with Vi and Bertie. The 3 children flew back to school via the same route late in January.

Arriving back at Ellegerini, Bud Woodley broke the traumatic news to us that our wonderful dog, Jock, had been slashed to death by panga. He'd suffered the same hideous death as Danny had when we'd been living at Uruku in the early Mau Mau days, by men who brought a bitch in season to be mated with him. Twice while we'd been away, there were attacks on whites living close to Ellegerini. One was an elderly South African man who'd moved to Kenya many years before, known to everyone as Uncle Tom Louw, and a dear friend of the family, shockingly murdered by panga in his sleep.

The second horrific attack was on Neville Rowan (sister to Robert, Fuzz and Mary Foster), a much-loved family relative. The entire district was shattered. As a family, the impact on us all was profound. Neville's husband, Simon, was away in New Zealand playing cricket, the 2 older children were at boarding school and the youngest son, Anthony, was upstairs in bed asleep. Neville was in her usual place in the evenings, sitting knitting in front of the fire in the lounge, their dog lying on the floor next to her chair. The night watchman was on duty. Suddenly, 3 men entered the room. Most peculiarly, the normally vigilant and protective family dog hadn't even sounded the alarm or displayed any behaviour of unfamiliar people around. Neville was brutally hacked by panga, mostly on her arms. She bravely defended herself using her knitting needles then she was struck on the back of the head. The attackers took off. Neville managed to get to the telephone and rang her mother's home. Robert rushed to her assistance otherwise she'd have bled to death. The wall next to the telephone was covered in blood spatter. Her injuries were severe. She had many scars and never regained the full use of her one arm. Later on, she developed a tumour in the back of her head which had to be removed. For the rest of her life, Neville suffered acute and severe anxiety in certain situations which in any way reminded her of her attackers.

We were in a sort of state of limbo regarding our future. Two years previously, Ian had bought 3 plots in Malindi, as well as a deep-sea fishing boat with a cabin and diesel engine, named Hiltonian, that he got at a fair price. I was somewhat still unsettled in my mind with the 3 older children so far away at school, so Ian felt we should have a holiday in South Africa and check out possibilities while we were there. Putting the Mercedes aboard the SS Uganda (her last trip) at Mombasa, Ian, Stuart and I voyaged as far as Durban, where we disembarked. Collecting the children from boarding school in the Cape, we had a happy 3 week holiday at Kidd's Beach near East London and spent some time with Mater. For 2 months, we travelled around Natal and the Cape looking at farmland, but Ian wasn't taken by conditions in South Africa, particularly the apartheid circumstances which appeared to have made no progress and which he'd always disagreed with. Good farms simply weren't for sale and had been owned by families for generations. Other farms brought in little return, so Ian decided we should return to Kenya and set up a sport fishing business at Malindi.

Headed for the coast and the start of our new life at Malindi, Stuart started misbehaving in the car. Understandably, it was a tiring, hot journey for him of many hours. Although we'd done the trip many times for our holidays at Malindi, Stuart in this instance had become uncontrollably irritable and unruly, probably mainly from boredom. With some mileage still to cover, Ian's patience was wearing thin. On a long, straight stretch of road we suddenly came upon a pack of elusive and mysterious African wild dogs, and Ian had to bring the Merc to a halt. They were on the move, baying and squealing, keenly fixated on whatever their quest was and took no notice of us or the car, crossing the road right in front of the Merc. The timing of the incident was most opportune as it caught Stuart's attention immediately and had him riveted. He'd only ever known tame domesticated dogs. This pack had a sinister look about them. Lean, scruffy-looking wild animals with bristly, mottled hair in black, brown, red, white and yellow and huge rounded fox-like ears, they can make the hair on your neck stand up and instil in one a sense of trepidation with their almost maniacal eerie sounds which carry for miles. Ian told Stuart he'd put him out with the wild dogs if there was any more nonsense. From then on, whenever we travelled this road, Stuart remembered this exact spot as 'Wild Dog Hill' and would become absolutely silent and as good as gold.

Knowing the children so enjoyed the thrill and hum of activity at the ferry crossings and to give Stuart some excitement, we took the longer road and stopped for a while at the Snake Exhibit housed in a small building close to the edge of the creek at Shimo-La-Tewa Ferry. He'd already shown a keen interest in creepy-crawlies from a young age so we felt he might be interested in reptiles. Although Ian and I were fascinated by them we had no desire to handle snakes. The building was made of mud and wattle with white-washed walls inside and out and a makuti (palm frond) roof. With the sea breeze and overhanging trees, the inside temperature was surprisingly cool. Stuart was immediately fascinated as we slowly walked to each snake exhibit, the reptiles housed in safe rectangular glass cases with lids. Noticing how keen this youngster was, the snake-catcher owner with snakes for sale, let Stuart handle a juvenile grey-coloured 4 foot python. From that moment on, Stuart was hooked on snakes and we never by-passed Shimo-La-Tewa ferry.

We lived with Vi and Bertie for 6 months while our house was being built by Bakari, an Arab builder and delightful man, on the 2nd row behind Silversands Beach. A lovely, big L-shaped structure we designed it to be airy from the sea and hinterland breezes with louvre windows, a cooling makuti roof and wide verandah along the kitchen, dining room and lounge. Bringing in tons of sand and rubble, we raised the level of the house to be above the double garage and Ian's workshop that were at ground level. Having 3 adjoining plots we were surrounded by bush with no residences either side of us. The Kiswahili spoken at the coast was a different version to our upcountry Settler Swahili, though it wasn't a problem as whatever we said was understood.

Malindi, a little south of the equator with a tropical climate, had wide, clean and beautiful beaches. The town became famous for sea, sun, surfing, deep-sea fishing and scuba-diving, sailing, snorkelling, waterskiing and horse-riding. Due to there being no reef along the Bay, occasionally heavy seas brought in flotsam and every now and then prisoners were taken out under supervision to pick up any debris and rubbish in front of the beachfront hotels. Only the Bay had breakers. Surfers could ride the waves any time of day, though sometimes the rollers became dumpers and too dangerous. The overall impression of the stretching town and surrounds which left an indelible, lifelong mark on my mind was an Eden of floral colours and scents and coral creepers, impervious to salt air and growing along residence walls. A multitude of glossy trees ranging from shady mangoes to tall coconut palms; masses of sea and garden birds, especially the Lilac-breasted Roller; unspoiled beaches, the ebb and flow of tides revealing mysteries of a delicate coral reef; hairy coconuts with sweet flesh; boats bobbing about in the harbour and dhows on a shimmering horizon.

Taking the road south – to the right from our Silversands home – beachfront residences extended for several miles with a dense row of Casuarina trees fringing the high-water beach mark. Behind these homes and facing onto the dirt road were their pretty gardens filled with wild fig trees, their spreading canopies held aloft by supporting shoots; frangipani trees with their unmistakable flowers and memorable scent; many shades of large-blossomed hibiscus; and bright red-orange Pride of Barbados. Bougainvilleas grew profusely in every colour – a spectacular sight almost everywhere one looked – in white, cream, yellow, orange, pale pink, dusky pink, rust, red and crimson, some with variegated white and cerise bracts, others with variegated leaves. To get to Silversands Beach from our home was a walk of about 4 minutes on a designated public area between two beachfront properties. When the tide was out, the coral reef stretched either side north and south of Silversands Beach, very popular for goggling.

Malindi town was to the left of our property, only a few minutes drive past the Driftwood Club, a very popular holiday resort not as expensive as the upmarket hotels. Immediately after this was the Silversands Camping Ground and Cafeteria on a long stretch of pristine seashore with abundant coconut palms, various mango trees and Casuarinas. Approaching town, one first came to the Hospital (where our family general practitioner, Dr Zoltan Rozinger, worked), followed by Vasco da Gama Point and the Engineering Yard. After this was the little Portuguese Chapel with its fresco built before 1542, then on to the sweeping Bay with its sea wall, harbour and jetty next to the Fish Market and gantry. A few metres further were the Malindi Sea Fishing Club and Gilani's Hotel. As the road curved and climbed, the Mosque was on the left just before one got to Malindi Old Town. Continuing with the main seafront tar road first was the double-story District Commissioner's Office and Residence enjoying a splendid ocean view. On a gentle downward slope, the tourist hotels were in a row along the beachfront with houses in between – Lawfords Hotel, the Blue Marlin (with a Swedish sauna) then the Sindbad and lastly the Eden Roc built above the cliff-face with a large freshwater pool. Tourists en masse arrived every 8 days, flying to Malindi or Mombasa Airports where the hotels provided everything needed for a carefree, memorable and relaxing holiday including evenings of entertainment with discos, parties and shows. A Touring Company run excellently by George Crossley proved to be a most successful enterprise and convenient way for tourists to get around – either by safari or hiring mini-motor vehicles painted in black and white zebra stripes with overhead awnings. George's wife, Chris, was an artist, painting mostly landscapes.

Vi and Bertie's home was behind the Blue Marlin Hotel, on a long straight stretch of the main tarred road shaded either side by impressive trees including Wild Almond, Mango, spectacular Flame Trees, Pride of India and Jacarandas, dotted in between with lush green shrubs and an abundance of colourful bougainvilleas. This was an exceptionally beautiful area of town. We visited Vi and Bertie often as nearby was the Post Office, our bank and Malindi Hardware store run by a very nice young Arab, Salim, and his family. Fairly often, we'd pop in as well at Marge and Brian Jenkins' beachfront home in the same area. Sitting on the verandah for a chat, we'd watch the breakers whilst sipping a wonderfully cooling glass of Marge's much renowned freshly squeezed lime juice – lime trees flourishing in this climate. Heading north out of town, was Kisima Farm supplying dairy and meat needs. Lastly came the Golf Club offering bar facilities and regular Sunday evening cinema shows for residents and their children. Malindi airport was a short distance from town on the Watamu-Mombasa road.

Many Silversands residents were spoilt in that they could buy freshly caught coral reef fish – particularly the most delicious parrotfish – lobsters and crabs delivered to their homes. Some folk even placed orders for specific types of coral reef fish. Reef-fishermen in dug-out *horis* or *ngalawas* would paddle out according to the tides to the shallow reefs and spearfish or troll several fishing lines. One line was usually tied to their big toe to give them both hands free. They would also free-dive for crustaceans. A *hori* is a basic canoe-like craft roughly chipped from tropical hardwood tree trunks. An *ngalawa* is a *hori* with one or two outriggers, rather like a basic catamaran. Returning home, the fisherman would hoist a sheet-like cloth to a rather rickety centre pole in their horis or ngalawas to catch the onshore wind then pull their craft onto the beach up to the high-water mark. Residents kept a small scale to weigh their purchase which they paid the reef-fishermen for on the spot. Everyone was happy with the transaction. We often bought fish and crustaceans from them though I, personally, was unable to eat any kind of shell-fish. I'd developed an immediate life-threatening allergic reaction some years earlier during our initial holiday at Malindi when I'd eaten some lobster for supper.

In the meantime, Ian, with our 26 foot boat Hiltonian, went into a deep-sea sport fishing business partnership with HB Swann (called 'HB' by everyone and known as 'The Old Man of the Sea'). He owned 2 similar sized vessels, Hunter and Gem, and lived on the seafront close to Malindi Old Town. HB was acknowledged as having started the income generating professional deep-sea fishing business in Malindi. Ian learnt a great deal about the ocean and fishing techniques from this elderly friend. Bertie and HB had been in the East African Armoured Car Regiment (EAACR) together during WWII. Our boat, Shrimp, that we'd built, was unsuitable for fishing clients as she had no cabin and didn't meet the charter boat requirements. We kept her on the trailer and launched her at Silversands Beach whenever we wanted to go water-skiing at high tide.

My involvement in the partnership was fetching our international fishing clients from the various hotels (all with their pre-packed hotel sandwiches and drinks for the day) around 6 in the morning. From there, I'd take them to the harbour jetty where at low tide they could wade in shallow water to reach the waiting Malindi Sea Fishing Club dinghy that would take them to the anchored boat they'd chosen to fish from that day. Around 2 in the afternoons, I'd be waiting to collect the clients after about an 8 hour excursion when the dinghy returned them to the jetty. Bystanders milled around as fish catches were offloaded from the dinghy and dragged ashore. Big fish were first weighed at the Fish Market otherwise Ian had his own scale at the gantry where ropes were used to hoist the catch. Details of the angler, fish weights and dates, boat and captain's name were chalked onto our board, all the photographs taken by myself. Lively auctions took place at the Fish Market every day, attracting a swarm of noisy, keenly interested local onlookers and buyers, including fish merchants from various areas as well as Mombasa. Fresh prawns could be bought here as well – one of Ian's favourite dishes. Income from fish sales was paid directly to the boat owners which firstly covered the cost of fresh bait for the following day's fishing and also contributed towards heavy maintenance costs. Some clients wanted their catch taken back to the hotel where the chef prepared it for dinner. Others requested their trophy fish-heads be sent by air to a Nairobi taxidermist, which I arranged. After each fishing trip, the boats were thoroughly cleaned and scrubbed down, all equipment and fishing tackle checked and supplies replenished. Later, Ian or I took the empty metal jerry cans to the petrol station for refuelling the boat engines.

The Malindi Sea Fishing Club was situated on the 2nd floor of a building overlooking the bay and was supported by Members or temporary Members. Boat owners often brought their angling clients. The Club offered bar facilities with hot and cold beverages and simple meals like bacon and eggs. Clement, the African Barman, was excellent, highly proficient in his job and much liked by everybody. He was a vital part of the Club's charisma. Fluent in English, he had a naturally friendly manner with people, chatting easily on a variety of subjects including the local fishing industry. Clement was always perfectly attired in a precisely pressed long-sleeved white shirt with black bow-tie and long black trousers.

Gilani's Hotel, run by Mrs Gilani and her son, was open to the public every day, all hours till after dark, and was extremely popular with the Indian community. The Gilani's produced mild to hot curries from both meat and fish, and on request delivered to the Club. On several occasions when I had visitors, I bought Mrs Gilani's basic curry sauce to enhance my own special dish. Her delicious pure fresh mango juice was a favourite with my children and their friends. Mrs Gilani's curries were firm favourites. With her genial character and aiming to please her patrons, I think she was sometimes long-suffering. A good fishing client and close friend, Maurice Brown, and his wife would stay with us on their Malindi trips. Maurice was the East African and Pakistan representative for Harrier jets (he was based in Nairobi), and spoke *Urdu* fluently (an official language of Pakistan). He also liked burning hot curries. Robert Foster often stayed with us as well – of course, bringing his supply of ripe cheese in his car cubby-hole! After a billfish tournament, the men really enjoyed a rather rowdy lunch party of Mrs Gilani's special hot curry with beer. Not to be outdone by Maurice who ploughed through his bowl of 'fire' with apparent ease – watching the scenario, we women got the impression this was quite some contest – the other men suffered distinctly flushed features and dripped sweat, but none would give up until their plate was clean. Considering the already high weather temperatures plus the heat of the chilli-spiced curry, the women left this 'realm of hot-curry contests' to the men!

Once, on a quick trip to Malindi, Maurice brought his UK counterpart, Johnnie Johnson (one of Britain's renowned WWII ace fighter-pilots, flying more than 60 operations against German targets), to stay with us. They'd just been to Uganda demonstrating the qualities of a Harrier jet to Idi Amin, and showed me the amusing photos of Amin chasing his cap down the runway after the jet engine turbulence blew it off. Leaving for their next stop Pakistan, a real thrill for Keith was finding a 20 shilling note under his pillow from Johnnie.

Ian thrived at Malindi. He'd always loved fishing and being out on the ocean every day was idyllic for him, plus his psoriasis skin condition improved considerably. On the other hand, due to the high humidity I suffered painful, chronic middle-ear problems (commonly known as 'coral-ear'), once landing up in the Nairobi Hospital for 10 days. Advice of the doctors was that I move away from the coast!

Stuart's new interest in snakes remained strong. On a subsequent visit to Mombasa we stopped again at the Snake Exhibit. The owner remembered him immediately and Stuart became lost in his own world holding various snakes that crawled inside his shirt or out the legs of his shorts! The outcome of this visit was that Ian bought him the young python that had originally ignited his snake passion. Some time later at home, in a rush to be off with his friend, Stuart quickly put his python into his cupboard. Gideon, our houseman, went to put Stuart's ironed clothes away. There was a great commotion when he opened the cupboard door! Luckily, the Giriama (a Kenya coastal tribe) are very used to snakes, so after the initial fright Gideon calmed down, but he complained bitterly to me that he did not like snakes in the house! Gideon loved Stuart and put up with a lot from this small boy.

Mark Easterbrook (known as 'Snakey') started a successful tourist venture called 'Strolling Safaris' whereby he'd take a number of people and stroll around Malindi, Silversands and along the beach fronts and nearby plantations. The trees in and around these areas are huge and full of foliage.

Mark would say, "I can go to any mango tree and guarantee you I'll find a snake."

German tourists particularly were fascinated and spellbound by the reptiles. Malindi had many species including venomous cobras, mambas, puff adders and coral snakes. The clients had difficulty seeing the snakes in the trees, but Mark spotted them easily. He'd catch one, demonstrate how to handle it and give on-the-spot lectures. Mark kept a number of snakes in his house. One day, a large python escaped which was found days later in someone's garden and re-captured without being harmed. On one of these strolling safaris, Stuart was bitten on the index finger by a back-fanged whip snake. He suffered a swollen hand and a severe headache for 3 days, but this didn't dampen his interest whatsoever. We had 2 incidences of cobras at home. The first was a 5 foot greyish cobra under one of the dressing tables that luckily the cat alerted me to. The other was a smaller black cobra on the verandah that slithered into the nest of our broody Bantam hen, first swallowing an egg before biting her on the thigh. She died quickly in my arms. Ian killed a very fat, 6 foot yellow-and-black patterned puff adder outside the garage. Measuring its fangs they were three-quarters of an inch long. We've never seen a bigger one since.

At the entrance to Vi and Bertie's driveway, was a Bajuni street vendor with a makeshift makuti stall who sold shells and always dressed in an off-white kanzu and embroidered Arab cap. The Bajuni are a minority ethnic people from the tiny Bajuni Islands in the Indian Ocean, many of whom traditionally reside in Kenya mostly along the coast. A very animated character, somewhat on the lean side, there was never a dull moment in his company. His proper name was never known to us. Often in one another's company due to their mutual yet diverse interest in seashells, Vi affectionately nick-named him 'Hoppy'. He suffered from a disability in one hip and permanently walked awkwardly in a sideways manner, his one leg considerably shorter than the other. Hoppy took to his new nickname instantly and everyone called him this. Hoppy employed his own beach-combers and snorkelers for collecting both dead and live seashells which he'd sell door-to-door, especially to the tourists at the hotels, who had no idea whether a shell had been collected dead or alive. The difference being that a shell collected alive continued to keep its colour and sheen. Sometimes fishermen would bring him live shells, in which instance he'd immediately go to Vi. She was the only serious shell collector in Malindi I knew of, meticulous and going by the book. Vi always bought from Hoppy any shell she didn't have, and would show him in the book the shells she was looking for.

When Hoppy had a really good day of shell sales he liked to visit Vi for a chat and a cup of coffee, and would metaphorically describe his negotiations thus, "I cut their throats and drink their blood!" This was Hoppy's way of saying he'd sold for good prices pretty worthless shells.

Vi kept all her shells polished and out of the light in a specially made wooden chest, each drawer lined in damp-proof felt, every shell from smallest to biggest labelled precisely in her naturally neat writing. Having been forced to leave their farm life where Vi was an excellent baker, sweet-maker and beautiful knitter, her coastal interests were shells and her glass sea water aquarium which was on their front verandah. Both these hobbies were vastly time-consuming. Having a full-time houseman and cook, and Bertie taking care of the extensive garden and shopping, Vi was able to devote the remainder of her time to snorkelling to look for shells and an assortment of saltwater aquatic life for her aquarium. She rotated the aquatic sea-life every 2 weeks or so back to the ocean, replacing it with other species, mostly exquisitely coloured tiny coral fish. Before she'd married Bertie, Vi had qualified as an accountant. Bertie, having always been a busy farmer, now kept himself constantly occupied in various ways apart from gardening. He even made a solar heating system out of broken mirrors that kept their home permanently supplied with hot water.

The Old Town of Malindi was positioned above the Bay on a naturally higher lay of the land but without a direct view of the beach or Indian Ocean. It was a paradise of ancient eastern mystique – a maze of narrow winding streets lined on either side by high-walled homes of Arab influence, many of which also served as shops run by their owners. Adjoining the Old Town were spread-out villages of traditional dwellings where the majority of residents lived. Plantations of coconuts, bananas, mangoes, and cotton and kapok trees came right up to the houses. Regardless of one's religion, race or ethnicity, everyone lived side by side in amicable harmony. Boat owners were always invited to and attended Arab ceremonies, being treated with utmost respect like honoured guests. Jasmine and frangipani blossoms were used extensively as garlands, and customary pieces of sweet *halwa* (an Arab form of Turkish delight) were given to everyone attending a ceremony.

Malindi Old Town was a world of its own, an instant awakening to a glorious fusion of colours and essences. Creepers of waxy, delicate pink-white flowered jasmine and frangipani trees in pretty yellow-and-white blossoms left a distinct and lingering floral fragrance. Combined with the humidity and Attar of Roses (a sweet-smelling feminine Arab perfume) as well as the aroma of lit incense wafting from shop doorways there was a permanent almost heady scent in the air. The Arab bakery operated throughout the day producing batches of hot, fresh sweet-dough bread rolls, mingling with the smell of strong percolating coffee coming from the street vendor, a little old man dressed in white flowing garments. He'd do his rounds holding two handle-less small cups in one hand, whilst in the other hand he'd swing his brass-engraved conical coffee-pot suspended on a triangular device that allowed the base to be kept on glowing coals. The aroma of the bread rolls mixed with the fresh coffee brew was a sensory delight. Dukas were permeated by the strong aromatic assortment of spices – cinnamon, cloves, nutmeg, vanilla, turmeric, curry powders, cardamom, paprika and cumin to name a few, a kind of strong perfume on their own. Dry foodstuffs, materials, fruit and vegetables, curios and knick-knacks were also sold in these shops. The affluent Arab community obscured their daily family lives behind heavy wooden iron-studded or carved doors opening onto small courtyards for privacy. Street-front business sections of homes were separated by curtained-throughways. Very thick walls, high ceilings, cement floors and small shuttered windows made rather dark interiors of these buildings, but kept the premises cool.

I did my grocery shopping at Abbas, the general dealer, whose family had been in Malindi for generations. They gave an excellent service to residents and stocked everything for the pantry, as well as a wide range of other household commodities such as paraffin, mothballs, newspapers and even bacon (only ever handled by their Bajuni assistant). Abbas was next door to Mulla's that sold a jumble of miscellaneous items in heaps everywhere in the 2 rooms that comprised this duka. All sorts of things could be found from toys to watches, clocks, hand-mirrors, plastic mugs etc. It was quite in order to sift through the horde of stuff. Everyone referred to the shop as 'Mulla

Taka-Taka' (loose term for 'junk' or 'cheap' items) and Mr Mulla didn't mind in the least. At his shop entrance, he had 2 Swahili sewing fundis at their Singer machines.

Our cousin, Hector Bastard, started an informal-wear craze amongst our family men of donning cool, comfortable *bombis* (based on the Burmese traditional wide-legged trousers known as *longyis).* Very wide in the waistband and legs basically 2 men could fit into a pair of bombis, the waistband then being folded across and tied in a certain way to keep the trousers up. Well-suited to the heat and humidity at the coast, I took the pattern with me and asked Mulla Taka-Taka's sewing fundi to make 3 pairs of bombis for Ian. His curiosity got the better of him when I paid. "But memsahib," he said, "your husband must be a very fat man."

Abbas and Mulla's 2 enterprises were pretty much the central hub of shopping in the Old Town – devout Muslims, for whom we all had the deepest respect. There was an Indian shoe-repairman who was always busy, sitting cross-legged on the floor to do his work. He stitched my old, worn stuffed koala bear my father had given me way back, the last day I'd seen him when I was 9 years old.

"Madam," he enquired ever so politely when he'd finished his careful leatherwork mending, "what sort of animal is this?"

As he was so intrigued, I tried as best I could to explain to him about koala's living on another continent called Australia. He listened carefully but it was apparent he hadn't a clue what I was talking about. Around the corner was the tiny barber's salon in a narrow alley. It had a mirror and only enough room for a rickety bench and an extremely old dentist's chair for clients. There was a board across the arms of the chair for smaller customers to sit on. Keith and Stuart were regulars for crew-cuts. I had my hair cut by a professional Goanese girl who had a little parlour near the Standard Bank. Ian's hair I'd always cut myself.

Busy tailors with whirring treadle machines were at many duka entrances. Hanging from the doorways were lengths of brightly coloured cotton materials. For more specific fabrics, such as the exotic and beautifully embroidered saris, there was an Indian shop especially for the ladies opposite Abbas. A Sikh owned the photography shop and gave an excellent service. He always had my black and white photographs done in time to hand over to clients before they returned home. The ice-cream shop, situated on a corner of the Old Town main road across from HB's residence, belonged to an Indian family. It was a favourite quick stop with our children as it was easy to just pull-over and buy twirly-whirly vanilla ice-cream cones when going towards the hotel side of Malindi. One of the best recipes we'd ever tasted, the ice-cream was deliciously sweet and creamy, but melted fast in the heat so there was a lot of finger-licking and lip-smacking. A big, fat Arab affectionately nicknamed Professor Ali – a delightfully jovial character – ran a disco. As a dancer, he was 'as light as a feather on his feet'. Before tourists even arrived in Malindi, they'd have his telephone number and he'd obligingly fix them up with dance partners. Professor Ali was very much a part of Malindi, a real entrepreneur. He had tremendous initiative and was involved in several lucrative business ventures all to do with the tourist industry. Ali and Barbara (wife of a young, newly married Canadian couple who'd come to Malindi for deep-sea fishing), won a jiving competition. Not 2 years later, Barbara's husband, David, was tragically severely mauled by a brown bear while on a hunting safari in Alaska and died a couple of months later.

On a dusty, rough road on the periphery of the town villages under big, shady trees were groups of gifted Wa-Kamba (Kenya tribe) wood-carvers, squatting on their haunches inches deep in wood chips as they worked. Using adzes (a carpentry tool) on lumps of soft wood, they churned out beautiful wildlife and animal wood carvings, traditional masks, bowls of every size and many other objects then polished their carvings with black or brown shoe polish. Catering to the needs of the locals were large open-air vegetable, fruit, fish and meat markets where much bartering took place. Everyone was busily going to and fro, mostly on foot, many on bicycles, some on donkey carts, others by motor vehicle. Very popular amongst tourists for photographs were the bare-breasted Giriama women in their traditional thick, combed-cotton skirts (known as *hondos*). They regularly came into all areas of Malindi town to sell their produce either on the streets or in the local markets. Various types, sizes and shapes of mangoes were available throughout the year. Only the Boribo, the expensive mango, was free of stringy flesh. Our children especially loved eating the big, sweet variety. The best place to do this was in the sea-surf to overcome the messiness of the dripping mango juice. Somehow the saltwater also enhanced the flavour. An absolutely delicious, cooling drink was the milk from green coconuts. When my mother was so ill one of her longings was to eat a Malindi orange, a most unusual variety that had a green skin yet the sweetest, juicy flesh.

At Formosa Bay (now Ungwana Bay), 31 km north of Malindi, the Italian-built San Marco-B satellite was launched from the San Marco Equatorial Mobile Range (SMER) and placed in direct equatorial orbit on 26th April 1967, making headline news. This was in the wake of the 1964 launch from a USA range (by the same Italian team) of San Marco-A, whereby Italy became the 3rd country (after USSR & USA) to put in orbit its own satellite. The SMER consisted of 2 (now 3) offshore platforms, 2 fixed rigs, and a shore base camp. Conceived by Prof. Luigi Broglio, the SMER (owned and operated by Italy per an Agreement with Kenya) was active in satellite and sounding rocket launch operations from 1967 to 1988 during which time 9 scientific satellites were orbited with a 100% success rate for 3 countries: Italy (4), USA (4) and UK (1). All launches were carried out by an Italian team utilizing the NASA-supplied 4-stage Scout rocket vehicle. The SMER (renamed Broglio Space Centre in 2001) is engaged in satellite tracking and data acquisition, remote sensing and other projects for peaceful purposes. (Contributed by: Bruno Bernabei, Scout Mechanical Assembly Engineer 1964 – 1988. www.progettosanmarco.it)

Towards the end of January 1968, Stuart joined Keith, Beryl and Lindsay at boarding school in King William's Town, South Africa. With all our children gone from home, I missed them terribly. Stuart, understanding it was time to join his siblings at school, realised the most satisfactory solution regarding his pet python was to give it to 'Snakey' Easterbrook. Communications from hostel staff were that Stuart had a great passion for his East African heritage. He was apparently full of wild African adventures. His young mind conjured up images for his boarding school pals of 'crocodiles in the bath' and 'lions wandering around outside his home in Kenya' and on one occasion said 'he had a pet elephant!' On hostel out-weekends when the children stayed with Mater in East London, Stuart would sit entranced at his grandmother's feet listening to her riveting accounts of times long gone. She'd relate how she and William travelled by ox wagon carrying supplies to the Cape Coast, encountering many wild animals along the way. Stuart never tired of Mater's wondrous, brave tales. No sooner had she finished, he'd beg her, "Please tell me the story again!"

Ian had built up a sufficient fishing clientele and with HB's blessing they amicably agreed to end their partnership. Starting our own company, Malindi Sport Fishing, we bought a 2nd boat, Nafika, and signed up with a German Tourist Company. For a short time, Ian also ran 'Pelican' for a farming friend, David Broatch. Every day we had clients, most of whom were new to the sport. The German Group donated an annual prize of a holiday to Corsica or the like for landing the biggest fish of the year. Ian skippered Pelican. Abdu captained Nafika. Kombo was captain on Hiltonian, plus each boat also had a First Mate. Boat crews were always on the alert to the various sea conditions. They also harnessed clients into the chairs as well as baiting the hooks and setting up the rods and trolling lines. Some clients took a while to get the hang of seeing the bait or lures just under the surface of the water in order to make a strike when a fish took the bait. Others were careless or so excited they damaged or broke fishing rods. 'Bird's nests' entanglements of fishing line on expensive reels took ages to undo and rewind. There were clients who had little or no luck while others had fantastic fishing. One thing in common for everyone on board was to keep a sharp lookout for seagull activity which usually meant there were fish around.

We met many interesting people and made a lot of friends in this hectic, hard work and highly social life constantly entertaining clients. 'Burning the candle at both ends', sometimes we had no sleep at all only getting home in the early morning hours. With just enough time to bath and dress we'd be off again at 5.30 to start another day of fishing, with me collecting the clients from their hotels. I also did the office work for the company.

Some people loved going to Robinson Island with its unique 'restaurant' run by David Hurd, 36 kilometres north of Malindi. One Christmas morning, early and on the spur of the moment, we decided

Robinson Island would make a new and memorable festive experience. David wasn't there that day, but disappointed we certainly were not. Arriving by car, you'd have to toot the horn then wait for a Giriama African man in a very small dinghy to row a short distance across the channel that was too deep to walk through. He'd take you over to the island dining area, which was a truly 'Robinson Crusoe' set-up consisting of a weather-worn, palm-frond flat roof-covering tied onto Boriti poles dug into the sand. In the shade beneath (a most welcome and necessary respite from the scorching sun) on deep, loose sand were a couple of dilapidated, low-slung and higgledy-piggledy lopsided wooden chairs to relax in. There was as a long, bare narrow table of chopped off Boriti poles for legs with rough planks across the top, and equally basic benches either side. The dinghy driver was a man of various talents as he was also the waiter-cum-fisherman-cum-cook. There was no fridge to make ice so all drinks were served in their bottles at the temperature of the day – the children had warm bottled fizzy drinks. Ian and I indulged in locally brewed palm-wine (the restaurant 'special') sipped from half-coconut shells. The waiter took our lunch order then while we enjoyed the ambiance and mellowed in the heat of the day and our warm alcoholic wine, he now became the fisherman. Walking to the creek to first catch the lobster, fish or crab per our request, he then came back and prepared it, followed by putting it on the already burning charcoal-filled half-drums to barbeque. Hey-presto, we had a really scrumptious, sumptuous meal served on banana leaves! No cutlery was produced, and after the meal, having used fingers only, the waiter brought around an old dirty, wet cloth hanging on his shoulder to clean our hands. We all politely declined! A short way from the rudimentary restaurant structure was the long-drop toilet that had only 3 sides around it made of palm tree fronds for privacy.

Guests to David's restaurant gave the Island the name, Robinson Island, to acknowledge David's Robinson Crusoe-like appearance and living style. David had a very interesting life. On 6th February 1964, while visiting a coastal village on the shared Kenya-Somalia border to check on the repairs being done to his boat, David had been captured by the Somali Shifta. He'd been their captive for about a two-week march into the desert, saying his prayers perfectly when his captors stopped to face the East. Then their radio 'broke'. David was a devout Muslim. Apparently, he fixed the radio and because of this, his life was spared. I was told the American Consul took some responsibility for David's release and return to Malindi. His book, 'Kidnap at Kiunga', tells of this harrowing experience. David died later in a car accident in 1986 after a trip to Malindi to get supplies. His second book, 'The Coconut Comes in Due Season', was published posthumously.

Travelling 20 miles by road north of Malindi was the totally Arab village of Ngomeni. Here, each Arab child had his own little blackboard (I never saw girl children) on which was written the daily lesson to be learnt by heart. The sea around Ngomeni is shallow and warm, and was best known for bonefishing (a sport-fishing for bonefish not many people practiced).

My first trip to Lamu was with a long-time farming friend, Adrienne Richardson. Our flight north of Malindi took half-an-hour. We spent the day, much like any other tourist, visiting important Arab buildings and buying a few silver and brass trinkets in the very old, fascinating town of narrow streets, once again with many scents of spice shops. Lamu Old Town is one of an archipelago of several islands. At the time of our visit it was totally unspoiled. History records battles between the Portuguese and Arabs on the hills behind Lamu. The buzz was that if one dug deep in the many dune hills, relics could be found. We were aware of only one hotel at the time, Petleys, the owner a Colonel Pink who'd been murdered a while before. His surname 'Pink' intrigued me.

We'd had some requests from clients to go considerably further north towards Lamu for fishing. As the distance was too great to get there and back in a day by boat, it entailed camping overnight somewhere safe with suitable mooring. The ideal opportunity arose to test this kind of excursion when Ian made friends with an English couple, Mike and Anne Watson. They had 2 children and said they'd be keen to join us. Heading for one of the many sheltered islands half-way to Lamu, we were in 2 boats; Ian and me on Pelican, and our guests on Hiltonian with Kombo as their captain. Relaxed and looking forward to an overnight boating and camping adventure, we dropped anchor in the afternoon at the shallow shoreline of a large treeless yellow-sand island with beautiful, clear waters around it. The silence was amazing and the view breathtaking with the ocean gently lapping the beach – quite a paradise. We'd just unpacked the chairs when we heard a voice carried on the wind though we couldn't make out or understand any of the words. Suddenly, a boat, like a long dug-out, came around the far end of the island towards us, making quick headway on the calm water. Standing on the prow, the captain's body language, loud and harsh tone of voice portrayed fearsome intent to us. With no greeting or even slight gesture of a friendly nature, he was beating the air with his fist to keep disciplined rhythm while urging on about 8 men to row hard, fast and totally in unison in our direction.

Kombo's distress was instantaneous and noticeable to all of us. They were Somalis, and he was afraid. He told Ian we must quickly pack and start moving our boats out of reach. "These are very bad people," Kombo warned.

It was clear that staying would be dangerous. Kombo gave no further explanation and Ian obeyed him without question. A sense of dread rushed over me – my first thought was that David Hurd had experienced being kidnapped by Somali pirates and I was terrified that the same could happen to us. Everyone doubled-to immediately, throwing the camp chairs any old how on board. Then it was anchors up, engines full-throttle and away we went, passing them as we moved fast to deeper water, the brigands shouting, "Kiberiti, kiberiti!" (Swahili for matches) as the wake from our boats bobbed their dug-out. Ian told me to put matches in a plastic packet, which I did, tied a knot and threw it overboard for them to pick up. Whether or not they did we don't know; we were headed around the corner of the island into open sea. Pirates have long been known on the Indian Ocean. We had a lucky escape that day.

Camping overnight on Manda Island across the channel from Lamu, there was plenty of driftwood around for making a fire. Supper was fresh barbequed reef fish. By now, we were all recovered from the Somali scare. The following morning, we spent some time wandering around the ruins on Manda, and decided in the afternoon to go goggling. Leaving Hiltonian anchored safely, we all went on Pelican, and had another nail-biting yet thrilling experience. Kombo remained on the boat doing some bottom fishing and looked after the children.

Mike, Anne, Ian and I were in the water with our goggles, snorkels and flippers on, just lazily swimming about looking at the fish and sea bottom, when Ian heard Kombo shouting. Looking up, Kombo pointed out to him a massive water-spout on the horizon. Literally, a column of water, rotating and rising into the sky ending in a great cloud of vapour and seeming to be moving at speed towards us. Hastily, the 4 of us swam back to Pelican, removed our flippers and goggling gear and climbed up the ladder. Ian started the engines, we upped anchor and headed straight for camp and the safety of land. None of us had ever heard of or seen such a thing before, and we'd not met anyone who'd mentioned such a happening, let alone witnessed something like this. A land whirlwind, yes, but this looked liked a sea-tornado. It was very frightening indeed. I was really scared because we at least had a chance to get away from the Somalis, but there wouldn't have been any escaping this had it borne down on us. Shortly after we'd made it back to land, the water-spout had moved on. Much relieved we all were.

Back at Malindi, we discovered residents had seen the water-spout as well which was at least 100 miles away. Being in the water when we first saw it made the water-spout appear to us as though we were in its direct path, and we panicked. There are 2 types of water-spouts. This was a fair-weather sea water-spout (different to a tornado water-spout) which occurs in calmer weather and only over open water, developing at the surface and becoming a visible tunnel of water reaching many hundreds of feet skywards ending in condensation. They can be hazardous to ships, boats, swimmers and even aircraft, if in their path. Water-spouts can move onto land, some having dumped shoals of fish. Apparently, modern ships on encountering a water-spout will even attempt to break it up by firing a cannon into it. As heart-stopping as this experience was for me, it was also a tremendous, unforgettable spectacle.

Charo's daughter (he was Marge Jenkins' cook), was kidnapped and said to be taken to Arabia. He spent a lot of time working with the police, but his daughter was never seen again. It seemed to be common knowledge amongst the local community that this evil was still taking place with no way of overcoming the problem.

Beryl ran away from hostel in early high school, followed a year or so later by Keith doing the same thing. Both children had found the South African Afrikaans language difficult and the religious Christian practices too fervent and stifling. They were sent back to us in Malindi and I continued their tuition through correspondence courses. Life has many challenges. We had to make the best of the situation. Lindsay and Stuart continued at school in South Africa.

On a trip back from Mombasa to buy fishing tackle, Ian and I were on the Shimo-La-Tewa ferry when we noticed 2 young girls carrying back-packs. One of them appeared to be very ill, being supported upright by her friend. Speaking to them – Anita and Pammy – they said they were on their way to Malindi having seen a doctor in Mombasa. We took them home with us and they stayed about 10 days, leaving a note in our Visitor's Book: 'We were two little waifs, alone and ill … and you took us under your wing! Thank you for your kindness and hospitality'. Anita and Pammy S, 74 Holtspur Top Lane, Beaconsfield, Bucks., UK.

Chapter Eleven
Saving Apple Pie

Sixteen inches of rain had fallen over a period of 4 days and Malindi was awash. Great pools of water lay everywhere, and the storm drains that ran out to sea were clogged full of sticks, dry grass, palm fronds and other floating garden and household refuse. While clearing the sunken patio garden drain at the Sindbad Hotel, the Manager, Clive Walker, was shown a near lifeless body of a 'rat-like' animal. He telephoned me, and Beryl and I rushed to town.

Beryl cradled the tiny, foul smelling body covered in viscous mud close to her chest. As soon as we were home, we bathed the tiny male baby mongoose and dried him. He was about 6 inches long. Keith immediately named him 'Pong'. We fed him small amounts of warmed Ideal milk through an eye-dropper and soon Pong's eyes opened. It was no struggle whatsoever to tame him, he was quite at home from the start, and Beryl carried him around close to her body everywhere and anywhere we went. She also slept with him.

Once his strength had returned, we made Pong a nest in my old black handbag that had a long shoulder strap. This proved to be safe and snug, and if curiosity got the better of Pong he could sit up and peep over the rim to check on things around him. He slept most of the day, getting all the cuddles, love and play at feeding time, then it was 'toilet time' and never was there any mishap. The technique used was a warm-water rag to rub his private parts and within seconds he'd relieved himself. Now we progressed to new menus, and the family had to look for and catch grasshoppers, moths and other insects for this tiny, dear little mongoose.

Pong grew into a handsome grey-coloured teenager with a long, bushy tail that had a white tip on the end, and measured one metre from nose to tail-tip. He had long, curved slender needle-sharp teeth and strong claws, intelligent beady eyes, was ever alert and had become incredibly agile. Pong had the run of the house, garden and surrounding bush. He took to sleeping under the guest bath where he could catch frogs, moths, geckos and scorpions that came in at night, drawn by the indoor electric light left burning in the passage. As part of the design of our L-shaped home, to allow for cooling breezes, were fairly large open square holes in the outside walls of the 2 passageways, one along the lounge, dining room and kitchen, and the other along the bedrooms and guest bathroom. These holes in the passage walls also allowed Pong unrestricted access in and out of the house whenever he felt like it.

Our Alsatian dog, Teddy, and Dachshund, Dumbo, as well as the cats, parrot Kasuku and a flock of free-range bantam chickens all lived happily together with Pong. The trouble began when Pong's friends and relations from the wild started visiting at night. Then there'd be fearsome noises and fierce fights lasting hours which soon started taking place in the passages.

We decided the only way to end these skirmishes was to have Pong castrated, so Beryl and I drove the 80 miles and crossed the Kilifi Ferry to Mombasa mainland. We had lunch at the Manor Hotel where Pong wandered amongst the astonished patrons then back to us, settling in his basket. At 2 o'clock, we were with the veterinary surgeon for half-an-hour and left immediately Pong's surgery was complete, arriving home by dark. The following day was just like any other, Pong showing no sign of discomfort.

The mongoose is known for being very agile, cunning and unafraid when it comes to catching snakes. Our Giriama gardener, Charo, let it be known that I'd buy any small live snakes that could be found as it was necessary for Pong to learn natural hunting skills of his kind. We were soon brought small snakes and found that Pong needed no teaching. He quickly knew how to catch the head first, kill, and munch up a 12 inch snake in 2 or 3 minutes. We also gave him eggs. Once again, he knew how to crack the shell. He'd manoeuvre the egg, the broad end between his back legs, and get close to a wall. Then with his front paws he'd throw the egg which would impact against the hard wall. Pong would lick up the yolk, not caring much about eating the white albumen. There was always a bit of mess to clean up afterwards.

Pong was naturally inquisitive of everything going on around him and came and went as he pleased, exploring and getting up to mongoose-things. He was well-known amongst residents, and knew how to catch his own food and also to avoid our vehicles coming in or out of the garage. Unafraid of people, Pong always came to say hello to visitors and check them out. Friends of ours from Westlands days, Nick and Wendy Allen, who lived in the Kitale area, came to stay for about 3 weeks. Nick had an artificial leg up to the thigh that he'd remove during his afternoon rest on the verandah. Much to Nick's amusement, this became a favourite plaything of Pong's, going in nose first then reversing out again, over and over, and rolling about with all sorts of play and antics.

We were employed by Al Killeen (an American fishing client of Ian's who was 3rd in Senior Management of Coca-Cola worldwide) to run his beautiful 31 foot Bertram with a flying-bridge, Apple Pie, imported from the United States. Her clients were mostly seasoned international fishermen. Across her beam, written in beautiful, large yellow-and-red italics was her name, 'Apple Pie'. Pelican wasn't making money and Ian couldn't skipper 2 boats at the same time so her owner made new arrangements and she was no longer a Malindi harbour vessel. Ian now skippered Apple Pie. Abdu was captain on Nafika; and Awuni on Hiltonian. Ian once took the Coca-Cola people to Robinson Island. They flew from America in a Lear Jet to Nairobi then onto Malindi, specifying that Robinson Island was where they wanted to go for a crustacean meal, and they loved this unique experience.

Malindi had been famous for sailfish. Our best sailfish catch for one day of fishing was 13. HB's was a record of 20. Ian had some Australian clients from Cairns who'd advised him regarding their methods for catching black or blue marlin. Ian had then introduced his own marlin fishing technique which was very successful, making him the 1st Malindi boat owner to hook and land marlin.

George Dove, a well-known white hunter from Tanganyika (Tanzania) came to Malindi for a week's sport fishing with Ian on Apple Pie before leaving permanently to make a new life on a ranch in Mexico. We'd invited him over one evening to have dinner with us. Some hunters, for example, have a hat or an ammo-belt as a kind of trademark. George, instead, was known for his prestigious moustache, which was gingery-coloured, well-groomed and of some considerable length. He meticulously waxed it to fine points that curled up either side to his cheekbones, and very proud of it he was!

At the end of this perfect day of excellent fishing during which George had landed a 232 pound black marlin and was as pleased as punch, we were sitting in the lounge enjoying good Scotch whiskies, chatting over old times and people we knew. Every now and then, conscious of keeping his moustache curled to perfection at all times, George would twirl the ends. Suddenly, Pong leapt up onto his shoulder and in one fell swoop nipped off one side of his famous moustache! It all happened so very quickly. We were completely taken by surprise though not as much as George! Ian and I could only surmise that Pong had been intently watching this 'thing' that kept moving about as George spoke or laughed and decided it was something to be caught. George was very good natured about his loss, seeing the funny side. Despite a thorough search, we never found the missing piece of moustache! When I dropped him off at his hotel later that night, George was still a proud marlin fisherman, but the bearer of a now lop-sided moustache.

My personal best fish catch was a yellow-fin tunny (tuna) weighing 104 pounds and 8 ounces on 50 pound breaking-strain line, a record that I held for a few years. The 1967 December Children's Fishing Competition was won by Lindsay, aged 9, when she single-handedly landed a 131 pound black marlin on 50 pound line, fighting the fish for an hour and getting blisters on her hands, while Stuart landed a 20 pound wahoo. He was most aggrieved not to have caught the marlin, because they'd only just swapped rods on the allotted half-hour when the marlin took the hook on Lindsay's line. She received a cup with 100 shillings under the lid (Rand 10) and had a wonderful spending spree in Malindi. Stuart, however, had a stroke of luck on another occasion. Al Killeen didn't pitch up for a billfish tournament, so at the last moment Ian put Stuart in his place, and he proudly and ably brought in a 70 pound sailfish. Ian landed a 24 pound Dorado (also known as a Falusi/ Feruzi) caught on 12 pound line and received a certificate, the significance being the skill involved in playing a fish of this weight on such a low breaking strain line. This record stood for a few years.

I was with Ian when he landed a 367 pound black marlin on 24.08.1969 hooked towards the Watamu waters. This caused a sensation in Malindi. He was the 1st recipient of the Marlin Cup presented by the Malindi Sea Fishing Club. Club members and their guests enjoyed the sea breeze as they watched the horizon from the long, cool verandah for fishing boats returning home. Each boat had its name and Marine Registration number painted on the bows. All boats flew flags according to their billfish catches – blue for marlin, red for sailfish. The Club held annual competitions during the north-east monsoon which normally occurs from early November to the end of March. It was usually during this period when the most and biggest fish were landed. The success of the Club was due to Barbara and Monty Brown's untiring, passionate work as well as the Club Committee's, including Ian's.

Some fish catches of friends that I remember well were Maurice Brown who landed a 332 pound black marlin on Apple Pie. Jack Block, the owner of the New Stanley and Norfolk Hotels in Nairobi, caught a 207 pound blue marlin. Hans Breede pulled in a Karambesi weighing 80 pounds. Richard Magor, a coffee farmer on the slopes of Kilimanjaro, also a 232 pound black marlin. Klaus Drabert was a keen fisherman with numerous sailfish catches. Ludwig van de Loo was elated with his 748 pound tiger shark. Robert Foster often fished with us, landing many sailfish.

One year, at a Billfish Tournament that happened to be on my birthday in November, all Ian's boats were booked. Not to leave Robert and myself out of the competition, Ian said we could use Shrimp with Mohammed as our captain. With no shade cover or cabin, we wore long-sleeve shirts and trousers and big, floppy hats to protect us from hours of scorching sun and glare off the water. Thankfully, all boats had to be back in the harbour by 2 in the afternoon. Robert hooked and played a big black marlin for 3 hours bringing it to the boat 3 times, but it broke the line. He was exhausted though a good sport about losing the marlin, and I was very relieved as there was no way we could have gaffed it, brought it on board and had place for it, Shrimp being only 13 foot. This birthday I remember well as Robert bought me a beautiful old Lamu Arab chest with brass fittings that I've cherished ever since.

There was a time when Hiltonian had a run of 17 days without even a fish strike. This was during the period between the *Kaskazi* and *Kusi* monsoons known as the *mallalahal* when the seas are flat and totally calm with hot temperatures and no wind, resulting in poor fishing. Abdu approached Ian and said that all the boat staff had discussed the matter, and to overcome this run of bad luck it was essential to sacrifice a goat. Respecting their customs, Ian agreed, and the staff made the relevant arrangements. The ritual took place at the slip-yard of Malindi Engineering Works where Hiltonian was sprinkled with goat's blood. Everyone was satisfied. A few days later, the monsoon winds changed and once again, Hiltonian started bringing in fish, and began to be known as a 'lucky boat' and remained so. However, at the same time, Ian had started using brightly coloured feather jigs in jewel-reds, yellows and pinks as lures.

I used to do the English office typing for the Eden Roc Hotel. In return, our children had free access to the huge pool with its diving boards so when Lindsay and Stuart were home from South Africa for holidays, I often dropped them off while I was in town, or they swam while Elsa dictated the English typing to me. Otherwise, Stuart spent the majority of his time with his great friend, Robert Slingsby, son of Bob and Clara who ran the Silversands Camping Ground. Both boys were happiest in the water and swam like fish for hours on end, Robert even going out with the reef-fishermen. The chlorine content of the Blue Marlin swimming pool was so high that Stuart's eyes were red and sore and his fair hair tinged green, but he wasn't deterred even though I worried about his eyes.

Sometimes we visited places of interest in and around Malindi during schoolholidays. Behind the Mosque stood 3 tall weathered statues resembling phalluses thought to have originated in Somalia (something to do with fertility rites) when tribes took over Swahili towns. It's a mystery how the phalluses came to be grafted onto Muslim tombs.

Ten miles from Malindi in the forest and built of rock and coral, is the ancient city of Gedi founded in the late 13th century; the reasons for abandonment are not known. Strangely, Gedi was never mentioned by the Portuguese historians who occupied Malindi from 1512 to 1593. Vasco da Gama, their intrepid explorer, erected a pillar at Milindi in 1499. The present old, grey conical pillar of coral with the cross atop replaced the original and was erected in a later century by the

Portuguese. It is a renowned landmark and since then known as Vasco da Gama Point (tabled in the Africa Pilot manual used for navigational purposes along the African eastern shores, and which we ourselves used for sea safaris).

Gedi was declared a National Park in 1948 and we visited it several times. It was and remains unique and magical with a sense of great mystique. Tall wild figs, baobabs, tamarinds and indigenous trees made a canopy over the ruins through which dappled sunlight reached to the ground. The leaf litter was soft and thick with an odour of damp topsoil. At every step we were extra watchful about snakes underfoot, in particular puff adders. On one occasion and an absolute treat for us, we happened to glance over to the bush that came right up to the ruins, and there standing dead still for a fleeting moment was a male Sunni (also spelt 'Suni'), a dwarf forest antelope that fully-grown stands 12 to 17 inches high. Only the males have horns. The natural camouflage, forest flora and leaf litter surrounding Gedi provided the perfect cover and diet for the little Sunni.

Another favourite place of interest and great fun for our children and their friends was what we called the Grand Canyon (correctly known as the Marafa Depression or Hell's Kitchen) in the Dakatacha Woodland about a half-an-hour Land Rover drive from Malindi. Stuart had his 7th birthday party there, the only parent joining us being Shirley Brown. Made up of different coloured layers of rock and softer sections of crumbly sandstone, each layer clearly visible in hues of russet, beige, and tan to creamy-yellow, the picturesque maze of naturally eroded ravines, some steep or with high walls and sharp outcrops seemed surreal. The children were enraptured with this wonderland where they could explore, climb up or slide down, run around uninhibited and make as much noise as they wished. In the surrounding woodland, I found many wonderfully shaped fungi clinging to dead tree trunks.

We made a couple of trips inland to Tsavo National Park taking the back road from Malindi. Up before daylight, we left very early packing plenty of sandwiches, hard-boiled eggs, salt and pepper in little paper rolls, sandwich-spread, condensed milk and Marie biscuits, water and flasks of coffee. We were assured of seeing plenty of game such as zebra, giraffe and lions lying under trees during the midday heat, or with a bit of luck a bull elephant crossing the road and were never disappointed. The distance travelled was well worth every experience and the return trip was a reminiscence of the exciting day of who saw what animal first and 'I spy with my little eye' being a game we'd played since the children were little. We arrived home some time after nightfall. Completely whacked out, everyone was ready to fall into bed after a memorable day viewing Africa's exquisite and wonderful wildlife.

Some incidents with fishing clients were unforgettable – one being a Doctor, his wife and 4 children from Hannover, Germany, who booked Apple Pie. The 2 younger children were boisterous and undisciplined to such an extent that Ian felt it wiser to tie them to the outrigger poles on the gunwales, in case they fell overboard. Better to be safe than sorry and accidents happen in seconds. Although they were wearing life-jackets, Apple Pie was a fast boat and the powerful twin engines churned up the sea. Sharks were plentiful and could arrive in no time, sometimes even attacking the engine propeller blades, so the dangers of falling overboard were very real. Ian had first hand experience. I was with him when a black marlin he'd hooked and brought alongside the boat to gaff was suddenly taken by sharks leaving the head which alone weighed 167 pounds. We sent it to the taxidermist in Nairobi to be mounted. Joan Wedekind, an artist and expert at painting on fish moulds, put on the beautiful pearly finishing touches.

On holiday at the same time as the Doctor was a friend of his fishing on Nafika – he was the local postman in their home town in Germany. They had a wager as to who would catch the biggest fish. The Doctor, on Apple Pie, hooked and landed a black marlin weighing 205 pounds 8 ounces, and a 64 pound kingfish, so he easily won the bet. The postman had been telling the Doctor all about his latest adventure with a 'lady of the night' in Malindi. It was such a laugh that the Doctor said the bet was more than paid! Apparently, the 'lady' had taken the postman to her abode which was downtown somewhere, a square, windowless room with an earth floor and a thatched palm-leaf roof. The bed was 4 rickety poles on a frame, stranded across and lengthwise with plaited palm fronds forming a base to lie on and which sagged in the middle owing to the stretching of the palm fronds. There was no mattress, and the end of the bed was where the chickens normally roosted at night! The descriptions and graphics of the postman regarding this entire evening's experiences were so hilarious that the Doctor said he'd not heard anything so funny in years!

Stormy weather at the monsoon changes often brought heavy thundering seas. A number of fishing boats in the bay had at one time or another been sunk or completely smashed to pieces against the concrete of the long sea-wall protecting the length of the esplanade road, the Fish Market and other buildings.

The telephone in our bedroom rang at about 5 one morning and I answered.

"Good morning, Mrs Smith," Abdu greeted politely on the other end.

Although he was the senior captain of our boat crews and often telephoned regarding work, it was odd for him to call so early and I thought his voice sounded very sombre. By this time, he'd usually be on board Nafika and Awuni on Hiltonian awaiting Ian at 5.30 to skipper Apple Pie.

"Good morning …," I started to reply, but before I could finish my sentence, Abdu interjected, "Mrs Smith, Apple Pie has sunk. I can see only the top of one outrigger."

You could have knocked me over such was my shock. Abdu realised I was at a loss for words and asked to speak to Ian. My mind instantly went back to a few days earlier when HB's boat, Hunter, had lost her moorings due to the high seas and been smashed to smithereens against the sea-wall. Everyone in Malindi who passed the scene of floating timbers was aghast and saddened by it – the 'death of this lucky-and-happy boat'. They were especially sad for HB, 'The Old Man of the Sea', because his other wooden boat, Gem, had also met with complete disaster under similar circumstances in Malindi harbour some years before (Abdu had previously captained Gem before joining us on Nafika).

During the night, Abdu said the seas had been rough and high and Apple Pie had sunk. Ian left immediately in the Land Rover to assess the situation and put into action a plan to resolve it. I could see how worried he was. It was a terrible shock for him as well. I went in the Merc to collect the day's fishing clients from their hotels, stopping on the way to look for Apple Pie's outrigger tip. Sure enough, every now and then as the currents rocked her on the harbour sea-bed, the lapping waves above would reveal perhaps a few inches of one or other of her outrigger tips, hardly discernible if you didn't know what you were looking for. Although I was now witnessing as a fact that Apple Pie had sunk, at the same time I felt numb with disbelief, the scene before my eyes quite surreal. I had some idea how devastated HB must have felt, and realised that I'd have to take over the running of the business completely until Ian could float Apple Pie and get her back in shape again for clients. Right now, he needed to be able to concentrate all his efforts on raising her.

Hiltonian and Nafika's clients went off for the day as usual with Abdu and Awuni as their captains. Mohammed, the First Mate on Apple Pie, helped Ian. Luckily, Apple Pie didn't have clients booked that day. Ian had never experienced anything like this before and had to have his wits about him, though as was his way, he remained calm and positive throughout. It was such a traumatic day that I'm unable to recollect precisely the order of events that followed, though I was the one that morning to telephone Al Killeen, Apple Pie's owner, who was in Johannesburg at the time. He took the news in his stride, never making any fuss.

"Leave it to me," he said, "I'll get in touch with Lee Harrigan in Nairobi regarding the insurance."

I have always been grateful for Al's acceptance, and for leaving Ian to get on with raising and renovating Apple Pie. Ian returned home quickly to fetch his goggling equipment and soon discovered that Apple Pie was, thankfully, in one piece. Salim at Malindi Hardware was extremely efficient, finding empty, watertight 44 gallon drums, supplying rope and chain, mechanical pumps and some extra men. The Club dinghy (per Club Rules) was only permitted to take fishing clients to and from boats so Ian had to wait some hours for authorisation from Monty Brown. It was imperative to get Apple Pie to the surface as soon as possible because of sea water damage to the twin Detroit diesel engines. We fell into bed that night exhausted, both of us racked with guilt, particularly Ian, as Apple Pie wasn't even our boat. Ian knew the responsibility of lifting her rested on him and he was absolutely determined to do it. Al Killeen and Ian discussed the recovery and Al was confident of Ian's abilities and would go along with his decisions.

Jack Block, a mutual and long-time good friend in Nairobi who'd often fished on Apple Pie, soon became aware of events. Very concerned and so wanting to be of some benefit to Ian, of his own initiative and generously carrying the cost himself, arranged for an Israeli under-water team to fly from Nairobi to help raise Apple Pie.

David Taylor and his wife, Anne, complete strangers, came forward of their own free will and kindly offered their assistance as well, forming a new and lasting friendship. In troubled times, the incredible kindness of others really lifts one's heart.

The Israeli team arrived 6 days later at Malindi Airport at 8 in the morning. I collected them – such a pleasant group of men. We first had breakfast at our house before going to the harbour. On our arrival at the jetty, we found that Ian had successfully brought Apple Pie to the surface, quite remarkably, as he'd had to work in poor visibility underwater. The Sabaki River entered the sea north of the bay and, as a result of heavy cultivation along its banks, had muddied Malindi harbour. Next was to empty Apple Pie of water using pumps, take out the sodden cabin upholstery and all other loose items. Then she was towed to the Engineering Yard slipway where she was floated onto her cradle and pulled up onto the concrete ramp and work area to check her fibreglass hull infrastructure, exhausts, portholes, toilet etc.

Al Killeen phoned us that evening and congratulated Ian on raising Apple Pie without the assistance of the Israeli team.

The rough, heavy seas of the night Apple Pie had sunk had shipped water through the twin exhausts as she was lifted on the high waves then dropped low into the sea troughs filling the bilge till she was eventually so heavy that she sank. There was a blessing in that – at least she'd remained in one piece. Another was that her anchor had held and she hadn't drifted and been smashed against the concrete sea-wall. Also, it was lucky that no rods, reels or fishing tackle were ever left on our boats overnight. Ian worked on the Detroit diesel engines himself, stripping them completely. Although he regularly checked the exhausts of all our boats, closer inspection revealed a small hole in one of Apple Pie's twin exhausts and Ian replaced them with a superior quality. Dan, a Seychellois living in Mombasa, restored the cabin, woodwork and paintwork. Ian had new cabin upholstery and curtains made in Mombasa and the 'fighting chair' was completely re-upholstered. Everyone did a good job. After 2 months of gruelling work from daylight to dusk, Apple Pie was once again shipshape, ready for fishing clients.

Salim's excellent assistance when Apple Pie sank reminded me of another occasion he and Ian had shared. One evening, Ian returned home from work and told me he'd gone to Salim's that day for some hardware items. He'd found Salim feeling somewhat faint on the front verandah looking at a local fisherman with a really nasty 6 inch barbed shark hook right through the calf of his leg. Dr Rozinger at the Hospital had sent the man specifically to Salim saying to tell him to use a bolt cutter to cut off the shaft of the big hook. Salim was dithering, feeling somewhat 'green about the gills' at the thought of carrying out this procedure, and asked Ian to help him. Ian immediately took the big bolt cutter, positioned it correctly then cut through the shaft at the barbed end and withdrew it from the man's calf muscle. Throughout, the fisherman remained quiet and kept still.

Dr Zoltan Rozinger, an Austro-Hungarian, was originally a highly qualified brain surgeon in his native country. He was not able to practice as a brain surgeon in Malindi as he was not sufficiently fluent in English to be able to write the required exam. Three young European men decided to go spear-fishing off Ngomeni. One of them was a professional scuba diver. While they were in the water, one of the other two men let fly with his spear gun and the harpoon found its target in the nape of the professional scuba diver's neck. As medical assistance was paramount, the shaft of the harpoon was unscrewed and the scuba diver taken to Malindi Hospital where Dr Rozinger tended to him and alerted Mombasa Hospital to expect the patient as he required surgery. The story goes that Rozinger was at the time writing a book on Marine Accidents during his spare time and quickly buzzed off home in his pale blue Peugeot to fetch his camera for taking some photos of the man's neck injury. The scuba diver was successfully operated on at Mombasa Hospital. Luckily for him, the harpoon just missed his spinal cord.

We all loved Zoltan Rozinger. He was a great character and a top-class doctor. His wife, Joan, was a very sweet, gentle woman with beautiful blue eyes. The locums from Germany who worked with Rozinger were amazed at the conditions under which he practised and the cases successfully attended. Lindsay needed Doc Rozinger's expertise on 3 occasions – the first, an emergency appendectomy for which he sent us through to Mombasa, Lindsay staying that Christmas in hospital. Stitching her leg when a coke bottle broke on her shin was the 2nd occasion. The 3rd time was for removing a third-degree burn blister from across her foot while making toffee at her friend's house. The pot of boiling toffee had tipped over on the stove and Lindsay grabbed the wooden spoon, the scalding hot toffee going across her foot. Dr. Rozinger had an enormous, deadly poisonous stone-fish preserved in formalin in the steriliser. His patients were intrigued while he attended to them. He would always say, "Do you want to see my stone-fish?"

Many European tourists complained bitterly to hotel managements that there were crocodiles in their bedrooms. They'd confused crocodiles with 'geckos' which are a common, completely harmless type of little lizard. Geckos were naturally found everywhere day and night in Malindi, particularly on inner and outer walls of buildings, hunting for moths attracted at night by lights and lamps so they were often in guest rooms. On a goggling trip, a tourist cut one of his feet on a piece of coral. His foot bled quite badly. He was convinced a shark had bitten him. This caused a bit of mayhem in the Blue Marlin Hotel as his story scared the other guests who then became afraid of going on goggling trips.

Mrs Fernandes, a Goanese lady and gifted dressmaker living on the north-end of town near Kisima Farm, made many of Beryl's and Lindsay's frocks. She never needed a pattern, and only took measurements – you simply explained to her what you wanted. There was a wide variety of materials readily available in Malindi, so we had several dresses made at a time, 2 being beautiful long evening dresses cut from exquisite sari fabric with layered cotton petticoats. Beryl's was in white and Lindsay's in pink. We were often at Mrs Fernandes' home for fittings. On one occasion, I asked Mrs Fernandes why her son wasn't at school. She said he had this continual awful cough that no medical treatment alleviated so she was keeping him home. They'd seen doctors and he'd had chest x-rays in Mombasa as there was no radiography unit in Malindi, but nothing showed up in his lungs. Perhaps a year later when I saw Mrs Fernandes again, she said they were going to India and would take their son to the Bombay University to see if someone could investigate his constant, baffling cough. The story had a positive ending. Doctors in Bombay had operated and found buried in the lung tissue a mysterious foreign object. It was amazingly revealed to be a metal Coca-Cola bottle top and the mysterious constant cough vanished.

One day, Ian suddenly informed me – a shock and a surprise – that he'd agreed with the owner of the Driftwood Club, Dick Soames, that we'd take over control of the holiday establishment as it was 'in the red', and that I'd be doing the catering and office work. Running our fishing business at the same time meant we'd have to be super-efficient if we were to have any time for our home, children, pets, parrot and garden every day. Up at 5 in the morning, I'd wake Ian and make his sandwiches and coffee while he bathed, see him off, then fetch the fishing clients from their hotels and take them to the jetty, return home, bath myself and be at the Driftwood Club by 7. We did a complete overhaul of all the Driftwood facilities, routines, bar, kitchen, bookkeeping, banking and guest bookings. It was a very popular holiday venue with a freshwater pool and squash court, the great attraction for people being the casual ambience, informal dress code and general layout of the Club. Guests could spend their days in shorts, bathing attire, kikois and kitenges.

The front of the Driftwood faced onto a sandy area with the pool surrounded by several big, shady trees and coconut palms, leading directly onto the beautiful clean beach with the reef beyond. A short distance from the pool was the large, open-air main area of the Club with the bar and dining niche under the coolness of makuti roofing. Much of the décor came from the sea having been picked up on the beach – pieces of driftwood, coral, shells, fishing nets and glass fishing buoys etc. With clever lighting, the Driftwood had a charm of its own for evenings out or impromptu parties. During daylight hours when patrons could be under the trees at the swimming pool near enough to all the facilities, meals and bar, it was a most pleasant and inviting place to relax. Guest accommodation was rustic in separate bungalows also with makuti-roofs. When I found a mouse-nest in one of the guest bed-pillows, I bought new pillows for all the bungalows from Mulla Taka-Taka. I also brought in Awuni's wife (one of our skipper's wives) to make curtains and do mending on my Singer hand-sewing machine that I'd brought from home.

Ian employed a young African barman, David, for the day shift who proved excellent. There were 2 cooks. After discussing the day's menus with them, they told me what was required then Said, the driver, would go into town to Abbas, the Arab green grocer and the bakery. Daytime meals mostly consisted of easy catering like fruit, bacon and eggs, toast, coffee and tea, and toasted sandwiches. Evenings, hot dinners of generous portions were served – spaghetti bolognaise, fried fish, steak or curry and special orders for shellfish – again, simple yet tasty filling food. The Driftwood became known for meals that were value for money. We introduced free bread rolls at evening mealtimes which were immensely popular. If we ran out of rolls, Said would nip into town as the bakery kept open till after dark. I'd help in the kitchen most evenings. Said, a middle-aged Lebanese man with a crew-cut and many missing teeth was a favourite of mine. He often told me interesting snippets of information about goings-on, was absolutely dependable and never complained of the long hours or of being on the go all day long. He even went to Mombasa when necessary, and also collected guests from the airport. On one occasion, he rushed a young American girl to Mombasa hospital as she'd somehow managed to get sand underneath her contact lenses then fetched her a few days later.

Ian ran the bar after his day's fishing and on several occasions, he did bar duty throughout the night, having no sleep. Returning home, he'd have a quick bath and change of clothes then go straight to the boats for that day's clients.

Discos at the Driftwood became popular, particularly amongst the younger crowd, as did the squash court and scuba-diving (run very successfully by Roy, an Irishman). Most times the Driftwood was fully booked by up-country folk. In our time, the Club also catered for 2 weddings, Christmases, New Year's and birthday parties. The bar did a roaring trade especially at night as Ian was able to converse on all sorts of subjects. Some guests enjoyed many relaxing hours telling their stories, particularly long yarns about 'the fish that got away'. However, there was also a downside to this new success and turnaround of the Driftwood Club which was now running 'in the black'. Regardless of how organised we were, Ian and I had no home life. We no longer had visitors to stay and never went goggling any more. Our children had to amuse themselves. We never visited any of our friends nor they us. Often, I'd be up at 3 in the morning to be able to do a few necessary things in our garden. A friend of mine, Paddy Taylor, once remarked to me that I was always tired.

A British woman – unfortunately, I've forgotten her name – had lunch at the Driftwood one day and I chatted to her for a time. She was forty-ish and had a teaching post in Mombasa. She related to me her nightmare experience and escape when she was an English teacher in Zanzibar (an archipelago of beautiful islands known for spices, world famous particularly for cloves), lying off the East African coast in the Indian Ocean about 22 miles north-east of Dar es Salaam (in Tanzania). The Zanzibar Revolution broke out on 12th January 1964 (also known as 'Africa's Forgotten Genocide'), taking everyone by surprise. She said about 4,000 Arabs, women and children included, had been herded into the main square and mown down in a horror bloodbath. Two ships, a frigate the HMS Owen, and the USS Manley, were the first to arrive, and lay about 400 yards off-shore to evacuate their citizens. She swam out to the HMS Owen and was taken aboard, a remarkable feat in itself as those waters are shark infested. All she could think of, she said, was getting to the ship and to safety and never gave a thought to the terror of sharks. Docking at Mombasa she decided to disembark and sought a teaching post. The other interesting detail she gave was that the HMS Owen later, after leaving Zanzibar waters, had picked up the Sultan of Zanzibar, Jamshid bin Abdullah, and his family who'd escaped on their private yacht.

At the time of the Zanzibar Revolution, we were still at Westlands and had heard the news on the radio, but being so engrossed in the farm Government takeover we'd paid little attention. It was a real shock to me to comprehend how intensely brutal this slaughter had been. I am now more than ever horrified at the savagery. John Okello (a Ugandan by birth), was the instigator of 'the death machine' in Zanzibar, believing God had chosen him to remove the Arabs from the island by 'guns and knives' though he specifically instructed that Europeans were not to be attacked. From 1698, Zanzibar was ruled by the Sultan of Oman. In 1890 it became a protectorate of Britain then gained Independence from the United Kingdom on 10th December 1963. After the Revolution, it became the People's Republic of Zanzibar & Pemba, and shortly afterwards became part of the United Republic of Tanzania. Zanzibar had been heavily involved in the slave and ivory trades. An Italian film crew in a helicopter recorded the horror of the 1964 Zanzibar slaughter in the main square. The footage was included in 'Africa Addio', a 1966 Italian documentary.

I was fascinated by the Arab *dhows* and my knowledge was substantially increased by Dr Jacobson, a fundi on the subject having studied the history of these ancient vessels. I'd met him at Mombasa Hospital when I'd been admitted with a serious bout of salmonella I'd picked up at one of the hotels. The term *dhow* is commonly used for a vessel with lateen-rigging (triangular-shaped sail or sails). Built from heavy, durable timber there are many different types and sizes of dhows with long or short rudders. All have decks and a poop, the latter covered with canvas awnings. We could often see great Boom Dhows with their white lateen sails billowed out by the *Kaskazi* (north-easterly) monsoon winds, sailing majestically down the East African coast, ploughing their way across the Indian Ocean. They've been sailing these routes since the days of the Queen of Sheba and King Solomon in search of 'gold, silver, ivory and apes' (First Kings 10-22). After Lamu, they'd call in at Malindi then wait for the high tides before setting sail southwards to the Old Port of Mombasa, then onto Tanga, Dar es Salaam (Haven of Peace) and Zanzibar. When the strong *Kusi* (south-easterly) monsoon winds blew, the dhows put out to sea again, conveniently blown homeward whence they came. As soon as a dhow sail was sighted on the horizon, the Malindi conch shell blowers would alert the general public by booming out its imminent arrival. Then there'd be great excitement as people rushed to the beach, whooping and shouting with jollification as they waited for the unloading of the long-awaited cargoes. Not only did the dhows transport dates, salt, Persian carpets, brass, silver trinkets and copperware, dried fruits, almonds, salted fish, fabrics and many other commodities (some smuggled), but importantly, they also relayed news from faraway lands. In days gone by, the slave trade via dhow was brisk.

Maintenance on Malindi dhows took place only at certain times of the year depending on the tides and had to be done on a flat beach (known as a 'careening beach'), usually near the Fish Market. Emptied of cargoes and dismasted, the heavy dhows were masterfully floated onto the fine-sanded, hard beach, and gins and sheerlegs were speedily lashed into position so that the dhow settled upright on the keel. The under-water timbers were hurriedly, but meticulously cleaned and crevices filled manually with a mixture of lime and heated beef or camel fat. The upper parts of the dhow are thickly coated with sticky, vile smelling shark or fish oils. This leaves a gleaming reddish-brown colour to the wood whilst protecting it against Teredo shipworm – a marine bivalve mollusc that grows up to a metre long and bores into ships' timbers spreading the rot rapidly – so maintenance is done regularly. The *Nakhoda* (Captain) carries aboard a special Arab chest. Some are quite plain while others are ornamental – brass fittings are popular and most even have secret compartments known only to the owners, in which documents, valuables, pens and so forth are kept. In the Arab household this chest is the family 'safe'. Dhows are considered to be male and can be named after an individual, but mostly they are given lyrical names denoting strength, endurance, determination and so on. Many are given names with a divine or symbolic significance (never female names). Dhow crews and Nakhodas hand down their traditions from father to son. Their navigational skills are excellent, discipline on board ship is absolute, and competition amongst the dhows is strong. They are proud seamen. Outgoing cargoes consisted mainly of Boriti (mangrove) poles used for buildings, charcoal, coconut and sim oil (also known as sim sum oil from the Sesasum Indicum plant, used for many things), firewood, ghee (clarified butter) and coffee.

Our neighbour over the road, Dodo Allen (no relation to Nick and Wendy), employed a new gardener. Whilst working, he noticed an animal rootling around the compost heap in the far corner of their garden and killed it with a pitchfork. It was Pong. The gardener had not yet been told about him. It was a terrible day for us. Our sadness knew no bounds at the loss of our precious and beloved mongoose who'd given us 4 years of utter delight, pleasure and interest. Pong had been painted by artists, photographed and loved by many people. I'd written about him to friends all over the world. He will always be remembered with the greatest love and we're grateful to have been part of his life.

During our years at Malindi, we received a number of letters from several of our Westlands farm staff, and wondered how they'd got our address – perhaps through the Post Office as we'd left them our forwarding details. One staff member wrote to ask if we had work for him. Others complained they'd never been allocated any land that had been promised by the Kenya Government, nor could they find employment. Part of one sad letter read, "…since you have left we have not seen any single cent." Word of mouth news confirmed that Westlands had indeed been divided into 15 acre plots on which entire families settled together with their livestock. The irony of the situation was that apparently mostly Kikuyu people were given plots whilst the Abaluhya, for example, who were indigenous to the area, didn't fare so well. All terracing of agricultural land had been bulldozed flat and every bit of fencing removed. I received a letter too from Daisy's Mwangi, whose dream it had been to start up his own café after my mother's death, this ambition of his helped by her various kitchen appliances, crockery and cutlery. Tears came to my eyes as I read his sorrowful words and I empathised with his heartache. His own people, jealous villagers, had trashed his café leaving his life broken. Shortly after receiving Mwangi's letter, I heard he'd passed away.

Carol, a Canadian girl, also came under our wing while we ran the Driftwood Club. She'd been staying free of charge for some time at the Silversands Camping Ground per kind favour of Clara and Bob Slingsby, and had now run out of money, unable to buy or pay for her food. Clara came to see me to ask if we could give a helping hand. I at once agreed, as did Ian when I asked him later. So Carol walked the short distance to the Driftwood for her meals and Ian carried the cost. Strangely, I never learned Carol's surname. A very sweet person, no trouble at all, with short blonde hair and very fair skin, I think about 20 years old, she spent quite a lot of time around me quietly sitting reading a book or lying on the bench outside my office. I don't recall seeing Carol in a bathing costume, she always wore shorts and a top, and I never noticed her swimming in the pool or the sea. She didn't appear to have any interest in boyfriends, didn't engage in conversation with others, wasn't outwardly jolly or happy and never sat at the bar or drank alcohol in our company. I didn't pry or ask her questions, I rather just let her be as whatever her private issues were I felt she'd talk to me if she wanted to. She never confided in Clara either. I got the feeling that basically, Carol was just so grateful to have a safe haven to stay and food to eat from people that didn't put any pressure on her. After a few days, Carol approached me and said she didn't have the money for an airfare back to Canada, so I telephoned her mother and we both spoke to her – she was difficult and unwilling about sending funds for an air-ticket. Twice more I called her mother and she eventually agreed to send the money. The arrangement for Carol's flights had nothing to do with me, being done directly through Gary Cook of East African Airways in Malindi. We knew Gary well, his office was near the Standard Bank, plus he was Weigh Master for the Malindi Sea Fishing Club.

After about 6 weeks or so, Said took Carol to Malindi Airport to fly to Nairobi and catch her onward flights via Addis Ababa (Ethiopia) etc. We'd had a fond farewell of hugs and good wishes at the Driftwood Club beforehand with Carol thanking us for our kindness and help. Then she was off in the Kombi with Said. I felt glad her mother had paid for her airfare so she could at last get home and I really hoped things would go well for Carol. That was that, my days were so busy I never gave it another thought. Via Gary, we heard news that had us reeling with shock, myself particularly. There'd been a horrific VC10 plane crash at Addis Ababa on 18th April 1972. It was Carol's flight. I was stupefied, unable to think straight. How could it be? Carol? Perhaps Gary had made a mistake? He assured me he had not. It definitely was Carol's plane. I felt terrible. If I hadn't got her mother to send the money maybe Carol wouldn't have been on that aircraft. I felt torn about the situation. Later, Gary advised me Carol hadn't survived, but that there'd also been a Malindi resident on board the fateful aircraft who'd made it – the son of the Indian owner, Dolly's Supermarket, a fairly new business in town.

I gave it a few days then went to Dolly's to ask whether I could speak to the young man. His father was at the front of the shop and said this would be quite in order, and that I'd find him at the end of one of the aisles packing out some items. The young man was instantly responsive and more than willing to tell me his story. He'd been on his way to London and said I was the only outsider who'd asked him about the crash. I found his story to be miraculous and terrifying and I was awestruck at what he'd lived through. He said as the VC10 rolled fast down the runway ready to lift off he felt the plane suddenly shudder so badly, to the extent he knew immediately something was very wrong. Determined to survive, he instinctively unbuckled and threw off his seat belt grabbing his Passport and ran down the aisle towards the back of the plane. He said he just kept running as he knew he had to keep his legs moving, his only thought being to hold his British Passport tightly. Suddenly, the back of the plane broke off and he just kept running in mid-air, landing on the ground in a pool of jet fuel, luckily not yet alight. The young man said his intuition was just to keep the motion of running. I found him to be incredibly brave. How he managed to remain upright when he hit the runway below and didn't break his legs he didn't know. Uppermost in his mind was to just keep on running, the fear and will to survive keeping his legs in motion. When he felt safe, he glanced back and saw the fireball behind him.

Maurice Brown, our Nairobi Aviation friend, would spend a few days with us quite often, and arrived not long after this VC10 disaster. He'd attended the air-crash investigation together with his Addis Ababa counterpart, Dick Floer. Maurice said the fire was so intense passengers had been incinerated, melded in their seats. Official Investigation findings report several factors that contributed to the crash. A Cessna 185 had taken off earlier with an improperly stowed jacking pad that had fallen onto the runway. When the VC10 (bound for Rome and London) was half-way along the runway, the jacking pad punctured its right-hand nose wheel causing the tyre to burst and the pilots aborted the take-off. Unbeknown to them, there were significant problems with some of the braking-power systems which resulted in another tyre bursting. With insufficient brakes to stop the aircraft, the VC10 overshot the end of the runway falling down a 10 metre drop. Broken in 3 pieces and with a major fuel rupture the aircraft burst into flames. Of the 107 people on board, 43 died and 15 were injured. The examination concluded that abandoning take-off was the right decision and had been done in time with sufficient runway. All my life since then, this has been a kind of haunting memory for me. Every now and then I think of Carol and ask myself, what is fate? What's it about? It seems we can choose our destiny, but we've no control over our fate.

Marge and her daughter, Janet, returned to Kenya for a visit after being in South Africa some years. They specially went to Ol'Kalou and to Daisy's old farm, Anchorage, to see what had become of them. The homestead was a relic of days gone by when it was appreciated, loved and cared for. Now standing empty, it was stripped bare, the beautiful cedar floorboards ripped up. Daisy's orchards which she'd planted and tended so carefully, the trees having borne copious fruit and filled many bottles of preserves for years, had been bulldozed to obliteration. Marge said, looking out across the valley to what used to be a scene we'd all loved of paddocks and productive wheat fields that contributed towards feeding the nation, was now a mass of tin-roofed shacks stretching as far as the eye could see. In what had been the small, neat village of Ol'Kalou, Marge and Janet had struggled to locate St Peter's Church and had to ask someone for directions, as again, this was now a confusion of roads in and out of a maze of tightly clustered corrugated-iron dwellings. Daisy's and Mr Golding's graves were still intact in the cemetery, but the pretty gardens surrounding the Church were gone – goats and sheep wandered around the premises which was fenced in by unattractive haphazard wooden poles. At this time, Kenya was heading the list as the world's fastest growing population, statistics indicating that every wife had a child every year, the average family having 9 children. Apparently, one or two spectacular homes with exquisite gardens had been left intact for show purposes in the Central Highlands. When I read Marge's letter to Ian about her Kenya visit, he stood still a moment then quietly said, "It took sixty long, hard years of work to build Kenya, and only six months to tear it down."

Our time of running the Driftwood Club came to an abrupt halt one evening. It was entirely my fault. At supper times, one of the dishes we usually served was a hot lobster thermidor. During the day, guests could order lobster salad. A couple had come to the Driftwood for supper and ordered a lobster salad. It being the evening meal, I'd erroneously instructed the cook to make lobster thermidor, which the guests complained to me about before eating the thermidor though they nevertheless enjoyed it. They said they'd be back a few evenings later for the lobster salad. That day, fresh lobster was unobtainable, even from the reef-fishermen, but I managed to source a frozen lobster at one of the hotels and decided it would be better to serve it hot than cold. What I forgot about though amongst the multitude of things I had to do running the Driftwood and doing the accounts, whilst at the same time seeing to our fishing business, was to tell the expected supper guests that I'd have to again serve the lobster hot. It completely slipped my mind. I have no excuse for it, I simply forgot. When the hot thermidor arrived the second time they again called me over. I apologised sincerely and tried to explain why we'd served it hot and not cold. They'd have none of it and made a loud scene in front of the bar guests and other supper patrons, to the extent that Dick Soames heard the drama. He walked over to the guests' table and in front of everyone yelled loudly at me, "You're fired!"

Ian had heard and seen everything as he was Barman at the time, only a few feet away. He was exceptionally annoyed at Dick Soames for the manner in which he'd handled the matter by belittling and firing me on the spot so everyone could hear. Ian was further fed-up because we'd dedicated our lives for about 2 years to running the Driftwood and turning it around from a business running at a loss to a now profitable concern. In no uncertain terms, Ian told Dick Soames he could 'keep his job'. We went through to the office, handed over the files and left immediately. Ian never in any way had a go at me regarding this. Though I naturally felt bad having 'messed up', it was a sort of relief for both of us to be able to have some 'life for ourselves' again.

Both Keith and Beryl did very well with their home studies, writing their matriculation exams in Mombasa. Maurice Brown represented the UK Hawker Siddeley Company and was a friend of ours, and through his contacts Keith was accepted for a 5 year engineering degree. Thrilled and excited regarding his future prospects, we flew him to England. Beryl, thanks to Al Killeen's assistance, started at an exclusive finishing school in Johannesburg, after which she'd be able to take an office job. Things had worked out well for them both in the long run and we were delighted. Lindsay achieved well academically and in sport at school obtaining both junior and senior swimming colours, broke an Under Eleven Border backstroke record, swam at SA Schools and was swimming captain in high school. She also played in the first teams for netball and hockey, and was junior tennis champ. We moved Stuart to Treverton College in Mooi River, Natal, where he made many friends, was very happy and received excellent character references from the Headmaster and teachers who felt he had strong leadership abilities. Our hearts were content regarding our children.

As time passed, sport fishing in Malindi became too competitive, expenses heavy and charter income minimal in comparison to costs. So we decided to sell our Malindi Sport Fishing business and our home, and move further south on the African continent, perhaps to South Africa or Rhodesia. We'd have to check out our possibilities before coming to a final decision. A German friend bought out our fishing business keeping our employees – it was a relief to us knowing that all of them would still have work. A Kenya woman with an Australian husband became the new owners of our home – it was virtually a 'walk-in walk-out' house sale that included all the furniture, linen, kitchen utensils, fridge, freezer, stove, almost all the wall pictures, curtains, gardening and garage equipment etc.

Unexpectedly and most thoughtfully, Abdu handed us a typed invitation to join him and his family at their home a few days later for an afternoon tea-party. What a great surprise we got when we arrived. Our boat crews and some of our boat-owner friends were in attendance, as well as Vi and Bertie, HB, Paddy Taylor, Pip and Charmian Beverley, and Monty and Barbara Brown. It was a wonderful farewell party with speeches from Abdu and Ian, beautiful garlands of sweet-smelling frangipani flowers draped around our necks and a precious gift of an exquisite antique brass, copper and silver coffee-pot from Abdu. There were tears and emotional moments as we bid goodbye to our staff and friends before leaving Kenya forever.

Afterwards, Abdu let us have a copy of his speech:

"I am standing here on behalf of my wife and on my own behalf and I would first thank you all for responding to my humble invitation to this sad occasion to both of us, of bidding farewell to our old acquaintances Mr and Mrs Rooken-Smith who are leaving Malindi. Speaking from the bottom of my heart parting with Mr Rooken-Smith my employer and friend and his lovely wife, is one of the saddest experiences in life. The relation between us has been nothing of a boss and servant type I can never recalled any unsatisfactory remarks or mishaps between us, and life amongst us has been full of happiness and good experiences. Such has been Mr Smith's attitude to all his staff. I am very serious when I say Mr Smith has taught me lots of skill and has tremendously improved my fishing talent. I am sad to see the couple leave Kenya, but I am very proud to say Mr Smith is only leaving after blessing me with both material and moral assets to enable me to continue with the fishing business of which I have interest. I am sure it will please Mr Smith to hear I shall employ all the resources and techniques he has bestowed me with, to make my job a success and to keep his name up. Finally, I thank you once again for coming and I would ask Almighty to keep Mr and Mrs Rooken-Smith safe on their journey and I wish them all the happiness in their new life. Thanking you. Abdu Khalid."

Abdu had proven himself to be a superb sport fisherman. We had confidence in his and the other staff's abilities. I would like to give due credit here to our captains and boat crews who over the years of our lives in Malindi, worked long and hard hours, dedicated to making our company, Malindi Sport Fishing, a successful enterprise. They were trusted, respected and valued by us both. We had many fond memories of our times together and greatly appreciated their expertise and professional manner.

Joan Wedekind kindly offered to have Kasuku parrot as we'd been unable to get an export permit to take her with us. By this time, we calculated her to be 80 years old. She suffered from severe arthritis in her leg joints and was totally blind in one eye. Some months before Beryl had left for Johannesburg, our dog Dumbo contracted hepatitis and the vet did his best, but was unable to save her. Even Dr Rozinger had tried to help. We were unable to find a home for our Alsatian,

Teddy, and as we didn't know where we'd be living, sadly we had to have her put to sleep.

We'd packed 5 wooden crates – each a little bigger than a linen chest – of personal family items that we just couldn't bear to part with and sent them by ship to Durban. It was heart-wrenching to leave our animals and home and the country where we'd both been born. So many memories – I had fleeting moments when I found it difficult to comprehend properly the finality of saying goodbye to Kenya.

With only a suitcase each, Ian and I flew from Malindi to Nairobi then caught a flight via Malawi to Durban. Settled in our seats for some hours of flying as we headed for South Africa, a country of considerable wealth and mining, my mind turned back down the corridors of time to when Mater told me about one of her late husband's patents. Thank you, again, William, for enlightening us with the story regarding your Patent 163 of 1903:

'But the hand of God was heavy on me for several years after enduring the Boer War. I invented an adjustable front foresight and gave it to Colonel of the Oxford Regiment who at the time was Commandant of Cathcart. He promised to let me know if it was any use to the military but never heard from him after he left our camp at Fall Kop. It was also during the Second Boer War that I invented the unwearable axle which was a very simple affair.

It consisted of a tube within a tube, the inner tube fitted onto the axle for the outer tube fitted into the hub or what is known as the nave. So these two tubes took the friction on both axle and hub and made both unwearable as the tube took the friction.

I patented it in Cape Colony and sent the model to the patent office, Cape Town with my specifications. I also patented it in Natal, Free State and England. I received a letter from King Edward VII which read something like this: 'King Edward VII of Great Britain and our dependencies beyond the sea do hereby send greetings to William Alexander Smith of Cathcart in the Colony of the Cape of Good Hope' and some more old-fashioned words that I don't remember. Owing to the Boer War the patent office in the Transvaal was closed so was unable to lodge the patent. But as soon as the patent office opened I applied for the patent in Transvaal but was too late. The mines had sent an engineer who saw my model and specifications and went to Johannesburg about it. They had my patent working on the skips dealing with the quartz coming out of the mines and also taking the crushed quartz to dumps.

The quartz being hard and sharp quickly wore out the axles and bearings.

I was advised by my lawyer to come to Johannesburg and see the engineers; so to Johannesburg where I was for about a week. The first two days they dodged about putting me off and during this time I was being told to look out for Salmon. He was a lawyer of great repute and was addicted to using very bad language. Therefore I was to be careful not to offend him lest he should let off a volley of abuse on me.

I told them that I had no fear of him; I would not purposely offend.

On the morning of the third day I was asked to meet the engineers at a certain long building at 9 a.m. My lawyer took me to the place and left me to be ambushed by half a dozen engineers who had an exceedingly long table covered with maps and diagrams of which I knew little. At last, one who had not spoken tried to knock me out by saying I was trying to claim the same thing as was used in pulverisers known as disc harrows. Then I had to point out that a disc harrow had a square shaft that revolved in bearings and the shaft was not in the bearings; and I was claiming an unwearable axle. Some of the others had a grin at the would-be clever one and said I was quite right and so we argued till lunch time.

At 2 p.m. we again met but now the head engineer a Mr. Roulstone was present. He said, "We are not going to waste any more time over this matter; you are quite right we saw your model and specifications in Cape Town and have your invention on our skips and as we have it working we will oppose your application for mining machinery; we cannot allow the mines to be burdened with a royalty but you are fully entitled to the invention and will not oppose you in anything other than mining machinery.'

So there, I had lost the best patent of the lot!'

**First Boer War (also known as First Anglo-Boer War or Transvaal War) was from 16th December 1880 to 23rd March 1881. The Second Boer War was from 11th October 1899 to 31st May 1902.*

Little did we realise how much Abdu's blessings and prayers to the Almighty 'to keep us safe' would be needed when we finally found somewhere we thought would be our new home.

Chapter Twelve
Africa's Breadbasket

Our plane touched down in Durban in May 1973, coinciding with the onset of South Africa's coldest winter months. First on the list was to buy warm clothing, blankets, a safari gas stove, cooking utensils, pots and a supply of food. We picked up a new VW Kombi with a canvas side-tent and had a roof carrier fitted enabling us to camp safari-style throughout what we envisaged would be extensive travels until we could find somewhere to settle. The 5 crates arrived at Durban harbour and were put in storage.

The car side-tent with a ground sheet could sleep 4 quite comfortably in sleeping bags on camp mattresses leaving space for suitcases and toilet bags etc. and we could be zipped up tight against the freezing winter nights. Our suitcases, camp chairs and table, small two-burner gas stove and gas lamps in their containers fitted easily onto the roof-rack. Two tin trunks containing all the cooking utensils and food were stacked into the storage space behind the back seats. Camping grounds were splendid with well kept lawns and provided ablution blocks with hot and cold water. There were stone barbeques with grids and gas was available wherever we went. Each day, we bought a bundle of wood for the nightly camp fire, our daily food requirements and had our usual sundowners each evening.

In Natal we visited my brother, Ken, and his wife, Jean. They owned a banana plantation on the South Coast. Then we went on to see Janet (Marge and Harold's daughter) and her husband, Ted, living in Howick. Having toured Natal extensively, we moved south to the Eastern Cape to spend a few days with Mater in East London. Still living in her ground floor flat, she appeared quite capable of coping alone and was in good health, apart from her varicose veins and arthritis. She continued her church interests and generally seemed happy. From our sight-seeing in the Cape and Natal looking for property, Ian found he still had no wish to stay in South Africa so we didn't check out possibilities in the Orange Free State or Transvaal. Ian detested the country's politics. In his opinion, nothing in that regard seemed to have changed. He felt we couldn't live in an apartheid country having not experienced a legislated segregated society in Kenya. For my part, I only hoped we could stay in South Africa to be near our 2 youngest children still at school.

Collecting Lindsay and Stuart from their boarding hostels for the 3 week June holidays, and a friend each, Jenny and Jonathan, we took a long safari starting in Mozambique on the southern African east coast. After this, we travelled inland up through Botswana and back down again. It turned out to be the most wonderful, memorable adventure. All 4 children thoroughly enjoyed themselves, as did we. There were some amusing times when on waking in the morning and needing to go to the public ablution blocks, we found the tent zip frozen and had to wait a while for the sun to thaw it out. On a few occasions, the milk we'd left outside the tent overnight was also frozen in the morning. I'd never experienced cold to this degree.

In Mozambique we headed for Beira where we'd been offered work in a sport fishing business at one of their well-known coastal destinations. Having discussed the political situation with our host, we decided that any enterprise would fail since it was unstable. Our time on the Mozambique coast at Inhassora and Paradise Island, just north of Vilanculos, was fantastic with plenty of superb crayfish, seafood and fish. It was here in a dusty little shanty shop that I bought a very old bottle of green wine with a coat of arms on the label that took my fancy. It was covered in dust on a top shelf, and produced in Portugal for the King of Portugal. We knew nothing about wine, but drank it anyway, though it tasted dreadful. Amazingly, later on I was paid Rand 35 just for the empty bottle!

Botswana was a big, bare, brown country that winter holiday, not attractive to us because of the season and the way we were made to feel unwelcome on our arrival in Maun. It had been an exhaustingly long trip from Francistown for Ian to find out about an employment offer. The appointment for the interview had been set up by Jack Block. We literally turned around after a few hours and started the drive back again. Botswana was a closed book – the people didn't want newcomers upsetting the applecart. It was days of dusty drive over many rough, dirt roads mostly camping nights along the river where millions of mosquitoes devoured us at night. Ian became a fundi at cooking our supper on the camp fire in a big, cast-iron 3 legged pot. Breakfast, prepared in the same way, was oatmeal porridge with delicious, steaming hot coffee made with condensed milk. For lunch, we'd stop somewhere along the way and have simple, easy meals like peanut-butter or bully beef sandwiches. We were 'lent' a supposedly haunted house in Francistown for one night on our trip up to Maun and another night on our drive back. The 4 children were scared stiff! It was this June holiday trip that really had an impact on Stuart. From then on he was bitten by the adventure bug in a big way, loving every minute of the great African outdoors.

Having returned the children to boarding school, we decided to move on to where Harold and Marge had bought a cattle ranch not far from the tiny village of Lalapanzi near Gwelo in Southern Rhodesia (now Zimbabwe – Northern Rhodesia became Zambia). Although they hadn't been on the farm that long they were content in their new life with good, reliable staff. Gwelo, a small but spacious town was their main shopping centre. Harold was busy building up the farm while Marge was creating another beautiful garden and growing sufficient vegetables. Of their 3 sons, Don and his family were still in Kenya though he'd made a trip to Brazil to look into cattle ranching. Bruce was a Major in the Rhodesian Army living in Salisbury. Rob was managing a farm nearby. Lex (Harold's elder brother from the *second litter*, being Ian's elder half-brother), was living with Harold and Marge. Between us 3 brothers and 2 sisters, we spent very happy days together. Ian had a particularly strong bond with Lex and Harold as they were the 2 siblings William sent off in different directions to fetch the doctor and nurse in Kenya in 1930 the day Ian was born.

An ex-Kenya and polo friend, George Knaggs, had an Estate Agency. Searching for a farm, we travelled with him the length and breadth of the beautiful land-locked country with its diverse features – from scenic rugged hills and lush valleys to natural dense forests of tall trees, fertile red-soiled arable land, and expanses of sugar cane to wide savannahs for beef farming. Ian was delighted to find rainbow trout-fishing rivers and streams in the hills. There were great fruit orchards, the orange groves in Mazoe stretched for miles. We saw artesian boreholes that were very impressive spontaneously spurting incredible amounts of water into the air. This water was channelled and used for irrigating maize. Another bonus was that if one felt like a holiday at the seaside, the Mozambique coast was easily accessible.

Every farm we either visited or drove through was well designed and maintained, with highly productive, impressive looking crops, beef cattle of quality, dairy stock and piggeries. Southern Rhodesia became self-sufficient. The farmers were the star-turns. Their absolutely stupendous contribution to the agricultural world made them famous for maize, tobacco and soya bean production, taking 1st prizes in world shows before sanctions were imposed. Despite many difficulties and hurdles, the farmers kept Southern Rhodesia going strong and healthily, the country becoming known as the 'Breadbasket of Africa'. We were invited to meet many white farmers, even a Russian couple who'd left their motherland some years before to start in Southern Rhodesia. On one occasion when we were invited to have lunch with a farming couple, eleven different vegetables were served, all of which were grown on the property. Everyone was dedicated to taking care of their land.

Umtali we found to be the most picturesque part of the country and luckily found a property we both liked in that area. So certain were we of getting this farm that we bought two good fold-up single beds with mattresses and a standing lamp from the owners and even adopted their dog, a black Schipperke named Cricket. We stored the beds and lamp at Marge and Harold's. For some reason, the Government didn't allow the farm sale to go through. The elderly couple, due to retire, were as disappointed as we were. However, the Government was going to be putting tracts of undeveloped land up for sale in the Tuli district and people were invited to put in bids. Ian was keen and offered substantially more than the recognised value for a piece of land. We were advised it would take some time before we heard the outcome and in the meantime, the Government kindly let us have a flat free of charge in the capital Salisbury, more or less centrally situated in the country. To help sustain us while we waited, both of us found jobs in the same company, a lucrative business that repaired radiator grilles of all types of machinery. Ian was employed in the workshop and I did office work.

Our stay in Southern Rhodesia was an eye-opener. There were world sanctions against the country, yet it seemed as though only the luxury items were missing from shelves of shops and supermarkets. The country produced its own nylon stockings; the clothing industry was extremely busy and produced good clothing which was exported to South Africa. Crockery and kitchenware was made; and exceptionally good farm machinery was manufactured. Gold and gem-stones were mined. Tea, coffee, sugar, maize meal and flour, dairy products, wines, meat, fish, vegetables, fruits and juices, honey, toilet paper, and fantastic steak and kidney pies in tins – all were available in the various shops.

The Salisbury flower-market was ablaze with colour every day. All the flower sellers were Africans lining the avenue in front of the well-known Meikles Hotel. From them I learnt how to tint and paint white fresh flowers any colour I chose, 2 good examples being white daisies and white arum lilies. On the daisy petals one simply used any shade of eye-shadow, blue was popular; on the arums, any colour of water-based paint. Salisbury's avenues were lined with the most magnificent Jacaranda trees I'd ever seen, the pavements covered in fallen lavender-coloured petals, truly a most beautiful sight. Streets were wide – we were told this was because in the early days a wagon and team of oxen needed to be able to turn easily in the road. Many other towns and gardens also had Jacaranda trees, a sight to behold.

Pharmacies supplied necessary drugs; hospitals were well maintained and running efficiently. National Roads crisscrossing the country were tarred, and gravel roads were well-graded and kept in good order. Petrol was in short supply, yet we managed to traverse the country any day we wished. Good Scotch was difficult to find, but was obtainable at a price, as we found out. We tried their 'Spirit of Independence', a label with the head of a kudu as a logo, and found it too strong and raw. After sampling a bottle of this, we preferred paying a heavier price for real Scotch.

Bata Shoe Company had one of their biggest factories in Gwelo, and supplied cheap shoes for world markets. People were innovative and created all sorts of items for the gift shops and tourist industry. Second-hand car businesses thrived because they simply had to supply workable vehicles, and spare parts had to be manufactured wherever possible.

We even tried the train from Salisbury to Umtali, which was a similar experience to the trains we'd been on in Kenya in that schedules were adhered to, locomotives worked, carriages were in good condition and there were very pleasant and efficient Station Masters and porters. Our trip was overnight, the weather freezing cold. We had our own compartment with 4 bunks for the 12 hour journey and I'd bought a chicken supper for us at Salisbury Station.

There was no food shortage that we experienced at any time during our stay in Southern Rhodesia, and one could safely walk the streets late at night in Salisbury or any other town. We stayed at a number of spectacular hotels and had excellent meals in different restaurants, meeting all kinds of people, always being treated with respect, civility, kindness and help when needed. Particularly noticeable was how well-spoken and politely mannered the Africans were, and those who'd been to Prince Edward school in Salisbury made sure to mention this fact.

We also visited other Rooken-Smith family members living in Salisbury – Bruce and his wife, Jenny, and Brien and Lise. Brien (Lex's son) had been Rhodesian Prime Minister, Ian Douglas Smith's, Principal Private Secretary (which included backup bodyguard role), since May 1970, remaining so till October 1973.

On the Griffin side of our family, it was nice to see how well my brother, Ken's son, Terry, was doing. Also in the Rhodesian Army and based in Salisbury, Terry was a Lieutenant, commanding a troop in a Combat Engineer Squadron. My eldest brother, Neville, and his wife, Frieda, lived on a property not far from Darwendale, an area known for chromite mining. Neville was in a managerial position with a local company. We spent an enjoyable weekend with them. Neville's wit was as sharp as ever. As religious as Frieda was, so Neville was not. Standing quietly behind our chairs at the dining room table one lunchtime to say Grace, Ian and I were completely taken by surprise and could hardly contain our mirth at Neville's words which replaced the better-known version:

"For what we are about to receive, make us truly grateful to Neville Griffin for providing it."

Having not seen so many of our family for a time, and in some instances years, as they'd moved from Kenya well before we did, there was a lot of news to catch up on. We reminisced plenty about old times and stories we recalled, with lots of laughter and quality time spent together. It was wonderful 'to be a united family' again after the tragic events in Kenya had forced us to scatter. This togetherness formed a special part of our travel memories as the value and bond of nearest and dearest had always been deemed vital as taught to us by our parents. Neville had been Ian's best man at our wedding in 1952, so again this was a special relationship. In trying to get an all-round feel of Southern Rhodesia, Ian and I even took a day outing to Wankie, a National Game Park, seeing elephant, plenty of kudu and other game. We reckoned we'd traversed the country far more than we'd ever done Kenya. Added to going to and from South Africa, touring that country, our Mozambique and Botswana trips, we'd notched up a substantial mileage.

After some months, the Minister of Agriculture advised that due to us being considered foreigners, Ian's bid for land in the Tuli area had, unfortunately, not been successful. He instead suggested we return to South Africa and consider buying a block of flats to rent out as a steady income. Ian was very disappointed – he had no interest in South Africa let alone owning a block of flats there. What he wanted to do was farm again. I felt his despondency. We both loved Southern Rhodesia and the people. As we no longer had the use of the Government flat in Salisbury, we gave up our temporary employment at the radiator workshop and returned to Harold and Marge's.

Quite suddenly one evening, there was optimistic news which brought us some hope. Peter Gill, and his wife Barbie, came over to see Rob (Marge & Harold's youngest son). They told us they were going to take up the offer of the Portuguese Angolan Government who'd asked for 6 new farmers to come to Angola and open up land for the production of tobacco. At heart Ian was a farmer: it was his ultimate goal to work again at cultivating land. This surprise turn gave him new hope though he was cautious as we knew nothing about Angola. Peter assured Ian that in his opinion the political situation in Angola was stable and invited Ian to seriously consider this possibility. Later, the men of the family – Lex, Harold, Ian and Rob – got together for an in-depth discussion on the matter. Both Rob and Ian decided to look into the Angolan offer. With no further delay, Rob and Ian made their separate plans to go and see this sizeable mainly untamed country.

With the December school holidays upon us, we fetched Lindsay and Stuart from South Africa, returning after another long drive back to Marge and Harold at Lalapanzi to be with our extended family for Christmas 1973. Stuart spent all his time fishing in the dam, making models of fish out of putty, and adventuring in the bush. Beryl had since completed finishing school in Johannesburg, spent a time in Germany, and joined us in Southern Rhodesia. Keith continued his diesel engineering training in England. Though he missed Africa, he was doing well, and had found new interests in his spare time joining a rowing team that competed on the River Thames, and a rugby team.

In early January 1974, Ian flew to Serpa Pinto in southern Angola where some of the new land in the Cuando Cubango Province was to be sold to would-be farmers. Two weeks later her returned, and told us he'd been with both the Governor and the Minister of Agriculture for the Province. Ian had bought 21,000 acres with the River Luauca flowing through the property and any number of springs, shown to him from a small aircraft, which under years of Portuguese rule was still untouched, totally uninhabited and undeveloped in any way.

Going to Salisbury, Ian made arrangements to spend 4 full days with Professor Papenfus at the Rhodesian Tobacco Research Station where he learnt everything about the growing and cultivation of Virginia tobacco. Ian saw, watched and was told every stage, and was reminded again and again that he must follow precisely the instructions in the tobacco manuals and literature which he bought. Professor Papenfus then sent us to Penhalonga to visit a young couple who'd become millionaires within a couple of years from tobacco sales. On this trip, we also visited the famous grove of exceptionally tall Eucalyptus Grandis trees planted in 1905, and were told they were measured every so often by someone sent specially from Australia to record their growth.

For the cost of one Rhodesian dollar, Ian also bought a small black comprehensive handbook known as the Farmer's Bible. This contained precisely any and everything a farmer should need or want to know, and was invaluable.

There were decisions to make regarding the 3 children. Beryl we found a filing job for in an attorney's office in Salisbury. Lindsay was more difficult to sort out. In 1973, in Standard 8, she'd been at a Secretarial High School in Port Shepstone, Natal, but Rhodesia didn't have any similar secretarial schools. The only option was a full-year's Secretarial College in Salisbury, but as she'd only turn 16 in January 1974, the College wouldn't enrol her until she'd been tested by a psychologist and confirmed to be ready. Thankfully, she was approved and accepted. We found board and lodging for Beryl and Lindsay with a very nice family in Salisbury. Stuart would come with us and on the way we'd put him into school in Windhoek, South West Africa, this being the closest English school with hostel facilities to where we'd be based in Angola.

Having made the decision to invest and start a new farming venture with tobacco and cattle in Angola, we once more packed our Kombi, Stuart bringing his 2 snakes along. He was sad to leave his friends at Treverton College in Natal, but at the same time he was raring to get stuck into another African safari.

We left Southern Rhodesia full of enthusiasm, hope and willingness no matter how difficult we'd find the new life, language, customs and people of Angola – a great, exciting challenge lay ahead. Rob had also checked out the country and bought land. We considered the Angolan offer to be a tremendous opportunity and couldn't foresee a collapse of the Portuguese Angolan Government since there was total integration of the peoples with no apartheid. How the future of Rhodesia would unfold we'd no idea, though we suspected it would have to be majority rule.

Stopping off at East London, we stayed some days with Mater to say goodbye. She was very interested in the new life we were going to forge from untamed African bush and wished us well. I think this brought back a lot of memories for her of her early life with William as they traversed together great distances by ox wagon to build their lives. Ian bought a good second-hand cream-coloured Chevrolet bakkie and trailer and we headed to Durban to load up our wooden crates from storage.

Finally, we were on our way, headed to the South West African border. It had taken about 8 months in all to find somewhere to call home and be able to settle down again. The old saying, "When one door closes another one opens," proved true in this instance. I was relieved to see Ian's positive mindset return, his determination renewed with a farming goal to look forward to and achieve after being forced to sell Westlands. Many of our family Smith and Rooken-Smith men took after their father, William, his pioneering spirit definitely part of his sons' characters. It was firmly ensconced in William's grandson, our Stuart, as well.

"Angola here we come," Stuart said happily, his face lighting up in a broad grin as he let out a "Whoopee!" of joy.

Chapter Thirteen
Fazenda Esperança, Angola

Although we'd not the faintest idea of the enormity of what lay ahead of us in deciding to buy land in Angola, we did not at any time think we could or would fail in our proposed agricultural venture in this foreign country. From farming dairy and maize in Kenya, a country situated towards the Horn of Africa on the East side of the continent with a coastline facing onto the warm waters of the Indian Ocean, we would now start cultivating tobacco from virgin bush in Angola, a country on the West side of Africa with a coastline facing onto the colder waters of the South Atlantic Ocean. Situated directly north of South West Africa (now Namibia), the northern-most border of Angola is almost in line with the southern-most tip of Kenya's border. Considerably larger than Kenya, Angola is the 23rd biggest country in the world and 7th in size in Africa, whereas Kenya's landmass is 23rd largest on the continent.

Stuart was ecstatic at the idea of the long trip from Rhodesia, passing through South Africa then crossing into South West Africa and finally into Angola to settle on our new farmland in the large, most southerly Province of Cuando Cubango. We carried a permit issued by the Angolan Luanda Veterinary Department for Stuart's two snakes – they hadn't seemed worried about papers for our dog, Cricket. Whip snakes are back-fanged and have to really get a grip to inject their poison so are not considered dangerous to humans.

We crossed the South African border over the Orange River with dramatic sheer cliff scenery in colours ranging from deep violet to browns, pinks and beiges at Vioolsdrif and Noordoewer into South West Africa. Since then, I've remained awed by this scenery. Driving up the 40 kilometre steep climb felt like 'being on top of the world', but the wind began blowing a gale, forcing the packed VW Kombi to slow to a snail's pace. At one point, having a broad flat front, the Kombi simply wouldn't go any further against the buffeting gust so we stopped on the roadside for several hours before being able to continue. Ian in the fully loaded Chevrolet bakkie towing the packed heavy-duty trailer had also been battling the wind.

Our long journey took us through the southern part of South West Africa. The tarred roads were wonderful, long and straight, and the countryside was looking beautiful – great expanses of tall swaying grass with the occasional big thorn tree. We didn't know there'd been heavier than normal rainfall. When we reached our half-way mark, Keetmanshoop, we found this vast area just about under water. Railway lines for miles, roads and minor bridges had been washed away. In previously dry river-beds were rushing volumes of brown frothy water, taking away yet more soil and vegetation, causing further erosion. The rains had been the heaviest for 67 years and the camping ground was closed – the only place that would accept us for overnight camping was a big petrol station which was 'high and dry' from all the surrounding wet. Having to forego the tent and sleep right up against the inside roof of the Kombi on top of our bulky possessions was most uncomfortable. The mosquitoes drove us mad all night, but at least there were good, clean toilet facilities.

The tiring journey, slowed by the heavily loaded vehicles, continued for another day to Mariental. Here also, we found that huge rains had fallen and the dry river beds were flowing strongly. The scenery was stunning – far away deep-blue craggy mountains and stretching plains of rippling, tall green grass. It crossed my mind that this would be the perfect backdrop for making cowboy films. I could visualise 'Red Indians' on their ponies coming up over the mesas – all flat topped mountains above sheer ridges. This magnificent view continued right up to Rehoboth where the river had burst its banks. Sun-bronzed children, some with blond curly hair, were playing in the shallows around newly created sandbanks under the shade of large, attractive thorn trees. I learnt many years later that Rehoboth was a sort of Enclave, and belonged to the Baster (bastard) people, a name they themselves chose, and also opted to be a different people to the coloured people of South West Africa/Namibia. They'd always been accepted as a kind of independent state within a state. When South West Africa gained Independence some years later and became Namibia, there was a lot of ill-feeling towards the new Government, but finally everything was settled, and they became a definite part of the Republic of Namibia.

From Rehoboth we continued to Windhoek, the capital, which lies in a valley surrounded by spectacular ever-changing blue-grey, almost barren mountain ranges – a most attractive city with a good climate. We found a lovely camping ground with full facilities, and the next thing to do was go to the supermarket in the town centre. The shopping was excellent and everything was available. I also stocked up on medicines and first aid items I thought we'd perhaps need on our Angolan farm. Ian had the 2 cars serviced.

Stuart needed to be enrolled in a primary school. We contacted the Education Department and were given names and telephone numbers. It all seemed quite simple. There were no hitches or hurdles. South West Africa/Namibia is a trilingual country – English, Afrikaans and German (being the business languages as well), and all 3 are spoken fluently by Windhoekers. Some words from each language have crept into and stayed in the speech of all 3. Windhoek provided both private and state-run English-medium schools. We chose Emma Hoogenhout Primary which had a boarding hostel for scholars, and had an immediate rapport with the Headmaster which set our minds at ease, Stuart being so far from us. He'd later attend a High School with boarding. That was the plan. The great rush now was to have name tapes made and sewn onto Stuart's new clothing, get him completely kitted out and settled as much as possible into hostel before Ian and I left to continue our journey through to Angola.

Cricket was not a young dog, so we decided that whilst in Windhoek we'd look for another dog to take with us to Angola. Stuart and I went to the SPCA (Society for the Prevention of Cruelty to Animals) and found a beautiful, young male Keeshond we named 'Pepu'. There was an immediate bond between Stuart and Pepu.

It was also essential to buy a Portuguese/English dictionary and a set of cassettes of the Portuguese language, grammar and accent. Four days later, after making the vital arrangements for Stuart regarding money, doctor, dentist and flights for holidays home to Angola, we said goodbye. Two day's travel still lay ahead of us in South West Africa before reaching the Angolan border, with Cricket, Pepu and Stuart's 2 snakes as companions.

Just on one o'clock in the afternoon, we drove beneath the big painted signboard above the entry point which said PORTUGAL/ANGOLA and arrived at Santa Clara Border Post. The two Border Post Officials just couldn't make head or tail of what we were about. They could not or would not understand the gist of the Governor of Serpa Pinto's letter stating that we were new landowners to Angola and should be given safe passage. I showed them the Veterinary Permits for the 2 snakes, but this was altogether too much of a headache for them. With many graphic hand and mouth motions they said, "Chop-chop," and pointed to the time so we understood that during the lunch hour the place closed down.

It was unbearably hot and we didn't feel like eating lunch, so I opened the new dictionary and tried to write and piece together the little I could imagine, which I hoped would make some sense to the 2 Officials. I realised we didn't even know how to make the polite and correct greetings in the Portuguese language. This was a big mistake, as we quickly learned. My writing efforts didn't help much. Instead, the Officials turned their attention to our 5 crates of possessions and indicated they should be opened for inspection. Ian gladly got out the screwdriver from the tool kit he always kept handy, and invited the 2 men to go ahead. They declined, and had some sort of discussion in a secretive way, and within a half-hour had stamped our documents and waved us through without further ado. They'd shown no interest in our dogs or snakes and didn't bother with the permits.

We drove the short distance to Pereira D'Eça (now Ondjiva), a fly-ridden, dusty and scruffy village, to have coffee. This was my first experience of the most unsanitary public toilet facilities imaginable – not in working order, broken and filthy dirty. The scenario was so bad that I felt I couldn't use the ablutions provided, preferring to wait till we were once more on the road, in the privacy of the bush. It was with huge relief that we left Pereira D'Eça – for me, a dreadful place. Driving on the right-hand side of the road was a slight mental adjustment. We travelled on a narrow, tarred main highway through uninhabited country with bush coming right to the edge of the road. The man-high telephone poles were strung with very slack wires, hanging exceedingly limply between the poles – another slight shock to us.

Starting at daybreak the following day, we headed north and veered off to the central part of southern Angola, stopping in the late evenings to camp for 3 nights, and having no idea of the next hurdle. Thank goodness I'd stocked up with so many tinned, easy to prepare and delicious Rhodesian steak and kidney pies!

Behind the wheel again, and surrounded at most times by dense bush, we were soon onto dirt roads which were extremely rough and stone-strewn in many places. Both of us were definitely beginning to tire from the practically non-stop long-distance driving. Ian decided we shouldn't camp again, but push on. It was after 9 at night when at last we saw the lights of a big town, hoping it would be our 'home town', Serpa Pinto (now Menongue), which as the crow flies, lies approximately 700 kilometres from the border. It was indeed, and at last the tarmac was back. After driving around, we stopped just after 10 at a prominent hotel (that turned out to be the only hotel, and most pleasant) and wearily went in to make ourselves known and ask for the Banco Totta Manager, a man named Manuel.

Everyone knew who we were and had been waiting for our arrival. Manuel was the Bank Manager Ian had met and through whom all the financial arrangements had been made on Ian's first trip by plane to Serpa Pinto to check out the farmland. In no time at all, the hotel people had accepted us and made us feel welcome. They pressed upon us a whisky, and then so hungry that we couldn't wait any longer, we indicated that we'd like to eat something. Since we couldn't read the menu, I merely used singular words from the dictionary which I now kept with me permanently. At the same time, the maitre d' was trying to tell us something. Eventually we got the hang of the problem – the gas in the cylinders had run out, but they would make arrangements for a private home to deliver scrambled eggs, sausage and chips for our meal. We had our supper about an hour later. Manuel arrived and with his passable English we had a couple more drinks (that being the custom), then said we simply had to get to bed. We were both utterly exhausted. Cricket and Pepu were allowed to stay in the room with us. Ian could hardly wait for the morrow as he was so anxious to get to the farm, which we'd have to pinpoint and find. We were unaware that as soon as the Portuguese learnt we wished to live on the land we'd been dubbed 'the mad strangers', and the nickname stuck! It was the 'done thing' to own and live in a smart town house, and visit one's farm as and when necessary.

Our breakfast was wonderful, strong sweet black Angolan coffee and Portuguese bread rolls with butter and jam. Then Ian decided I should see the town and do some shopping before setting off to find our farm, which we'd named 'Fazenda Esperança', meaning 'Hope Farm'. The Governor's pink palace was a fairytale sight – a long imposing double-storey building with tiled roof set on a slight hill. It was surrounded by green well-manicured lawns with shrubs, trees and gardens leading down to one of Serpa Pinto's pristine clean, fast flowing rivers. The railway station was a short way from the centre of town, as was the airport which had a very long runway. The important buildings all had marble facades. There were 3 banks, supermarkets, butchers, bakeries, petrol stations, attorneys, doctors and dentist, hospital and heliport, school, pharmacies, gift shops and salons – absolutely everything needed for a population of 4,000 people. However, there was no pet shop where we could buy mice to feed Stuart's 2 snakes. The problem I had was to find which shop I needed for a particular purchase. It took me a few weeks and learning some Portuguese to correctly identify the shops. In the beginning, the only places I was absolutely certain about were the bank, the supermarket, hotel and the petrol station. We'd had no difficulty driving right-hand-drive vehicles on the right-hand side of the road.

There were many coloured, prettily painted houses all of which had continental shutters, walled small front gardens and large backyards where vegetables were grown in neat rows, plus a dog or 2. Then there were the suburbs where the not so affluent people lived, and lastly the shanties. On the perimeters of town were small-holdings where turkeys, chickens, rabbits, pigs and cows were kept, supplying Serpa Pinto. Just outside town was the huge Agricultural Department, and this included the Forestry Offices and the extensive tree plantations. Indigenous Angolan trees were propagated, and sawmilling was an important business, the different types of cut timber magnificent.

Before leaving this delightfully pretty town of Serpa Pinto, the friendly people and civilisation, we had to go to the big supermarket for supplies. My 'chop-box' was almost empty and I didn't want to use up the remainder of the Rhodesian steak and kidney pies. This was the first test for the 'malucos estrangeiros' (mad strangers). Few of the town's residents spoke English and of those that did many knew only a few words, but I managed to buy sufficient groceries to carry us through the next few days. On the whole, we did pretty well finding margarine in one litre tins; wonderful ground coffee and an aluminium pot for coffee percolating with a really heavy filter cloth; good cheese; a 5 litre tin of Nestle full-cream dried milk powder; the most delicious uncut ham cured in white wine; and thick granadilla juice which came in foil-lined 2 litre cartons, as well as all sorts of other things. The nearest I could find to marmalade was orange jam, overly sweet, as we would soon find out. There'd been no real difficulty doing this shopping, it was fun, and took the minimum of imagination to know what one was looking at on the shelves. Everyone was exceptionally tolerant.

Next stop was the bakery, where we bought a bag full of Portuguese bread rolls. This was easy as we merely pointed to what we needed. In time, we came to know Daniel, the baker. The butchery followed, which was something of a shock! A number of beef and skinned pork carcasses were hanging close together from ceiling hooks behind the counter. The butcher was a big, stout man, wearing a well-bloodied white coat, and constantly honed an evil-looking large knife. Made of wood, the counter was definitely not spotlessly clean and shining. When we pointed to the beef, the butcher grabbed a carcass, cut off a chunk and slapped it onto the scales. This, I was told, was 'bife simples', which as I understood it in all our time in Angola meant 'simple beef steak'. Meat for our dogs was exactly the same cut. I think the butcher thought we were mad giving our dogs the same meat as we ate. Pork skin was sold separately, then cut into tiny pieces and fried at very high heat and served as titbits like 'crackly' with evening drinks. It was crispy and actually quite nice. There were skinned cattle heads propped up against the counter on the side where customers stood, all quite gruesome. We immediately knew, since we were to live in Angola that we'd have to learn to accept this sort of situation. I expect the butcher could see our reaction, even though we did try to be as polite as possible and not let our emotions show on our faces. This first-time butcher experience, and one which would be repeated many times while we lived in Angola, always left me with the same feelings of revulsion.

I was using single words from the Portuguese/English dictionary, having to turn pages and scrutinise each word every time we needed to know what to say for what we wanted. Everyone we came in contact with was very patient and tolerated my accent, and most times were faintly amused. Ian mostly left me to do the talking, such as it was. Luckily for him, most of the businessmen in Serpa Pinto knew a few words of English, so it was quite simply merely signing a cheque having filled in the correct numerals then letting the company representative complete the wording and use their official rubber stamp for the payee. All official documentation had one original and 4 copies – one copy was sent to Luanda and the other to Portugal. Our timber merchant and his wife became visiting friends. They spoke fluent French and some English so our conversations were easier to manage. The Agricultural Minister, Senhor Gil Vieira, and his wife both spoke fluent English. He had given Ian an official Government map of where our farm lay, so we set out on a district dirt road and soon came to woodland and several valleys which had trickles of water running through them. We had just passed a *kimbo* (a spotlessly clean African village), where hordes of Angolans came out to cheer us, shout and dance, and run after the 2 cars. Waving back, we noticed a small group was following us a short distance behind the cars, determined to keep up with us.

Ian, in the Chevrolet bakkie with trailer, stopped to tell me that by his reckoning we were adjacent to our farm and should now turn off and drive very slowly the remainder of the distance, being about 3 miles further in through bush and woodland. The speedometer showed us to be 21 miles from the district dirt road turn-off to Serpa Pinto town. We'd only gone a short distance when the cars bogged down in black cotton soil – thick black viscous soil well known to farmers and pretty much found anywhere in the world, probably mostly known in the great cotton areas of Australia and USA; we had plenty in Kenya. Without the help of the few curious onlookers who, luckily, had persistently run after us, we'd never have got the cars out by ourselves. We continued through these patches then into the woodland emerging onto sparse grassland along the shoulder of a shallow valley. In the distance, we could make out the meandering Luauca River.

By now, it was nearly 5 in the afternoon on a day in February 1974. We'd reached a point dead-centre of the farm, so stopped to erect our big Aruba tent. It had a fitted ground sheet covering the entire tented area, a fly (a flap with zips forming the entrance to the tent that also covered the 2 mosquito gauze windows), all of which zipped up snugly. There was plenty of space inside for the 2 beds and mattresses we'd bought in Rhodesia with a make-shift bedside table in between, and space for our suitcases and other personal items. While I made supper on the portable safari two-burner gas stove (that folded down to a flat box), we had a whisky. I fried eggs which we had with slices of the marvellous fiambre ham, rolls, butter and coffee. Cricket and Pepu had some chopped raw meat. The Portuguese had mentioned something about malaria, and said that to make sure we didn't get the disease we should drink plenty of coffee and whisky! I had bought a stock of quinine tablets in Windhoek so we had the medication if necessary. We were so dead-beat we didn't even undress, just simply fell into bed and slept without waking till the first pale pink rays of the sun suddenly shone brightly through the small square tent window onto my face.

I woke slowly, knowing this was the first day in the great challenge and birth of Fazenda Esperança and most likely, many trials of which I'd no idea. Ian continued sleeping soundly. I felt loath to wake him after all our long travels. Lying in the toasty warmness of my bed and wallowing in the satisfaction of a peaceful good night's sleep, the world outside seemed quiet and content. My thoughts kept turning to what sort of effort I must make to learn and understand the Portuguese language. I'd just decided I must write down 20 nouns a day and learn them perfectly, when I got the distinct feeling our idyllic Fazenda Esperança first sunrise was not being spent alone. We were being 'watched'. Turning my head, I looked through the tent window to see 2 African men in ragged clothing standing stock-still, watching us while we slept. With this first glance, I noticed they each carried across their shoulders a dreadful looking weapon, known as a machete, and that one man also had a shotgun. 'Terrorists' was the instant thought that blazed through my mind! The 2 dogs, also exhausted from the days of travel, were sound asleep on the floor well below the tent window. They neither smelt nor heard the 2 men. As loudly as I dared, I whispered to Ian, urging him to wake up, saying we had 2 terrorists just outside the tent. He could hardly believe, or take in what I was saying, but within seconds he quietly got out of bed and opened the tent flap not really knowing how he would deal with the situation. I was now immensely relieved we'd gone to sleep fully clothed.

Imagine our complete surprise when the man with the shotgun brightly said, "Môre, Baas," which in the South African Afrikaans language means, "Morning, Boss."

Ian's immediate friendly reply was, "Môre, kerels," meaning, "Morning, young fellows." Ian had a smattering of Afrikaans left over from his school days in the Eastern Cape, South Africa while he was at Selborne College in the 1940s. The man with the shotgun then went into reels of a story. His name was José, he was an Angolan (born in Angola), but he'd worked in the copper smelting mines at Tsumeb in South West Africa and could speak Afrikaans. He and all the others in the kimbo we'd passed the day before had heard that 'estrangeiros' would be taking up farming land and everyone was so excited as they wanted and needed work. Since the uprising in 1960, the Portuguese Government had moved all the people into various villages scattered across the country for security reasons. Ian explained to José in Afrikaans, who interpreted to the other man, named João, that first he had to get our camp properly erected where there was an easily accessible water supply, after which he'd make his farming plan and be looking for a large labour force. The 2 men then asked if there was something they could do for us, just anything. I came up with the idea that maybe they could capture 2 mice so we could feed Stuart's snakes.

"Não problema," they said, "we'll be back later."

We spent the morning driving all over the farm looking for what we considered would be a good site for our homestead, deciding on a flat area at the edge of woodland leading down to a spring which was running strongly. By early afternoon we were back at camp, where to our astonishment, José and João were waiting with 2 live field mice in a flour sack.

Ian asked them, "How did you catch the mice so quickly?"

They explained they did this all the time as field mice were plentiful. First of all, they sliced off the very top of an ant-hill then propped this up with pieces of sturdy dried grass stalks, followed by sprinkling a little maize meal well under the ant hill top, and then merely waited. The mice would come in and mosey around, disturb the dry grass stalks and, wham, down would come the fairly heavy earthen ant-hill 'lid' and stun the rodents. We offered money to pay for the mice, but were asked, please, they would rather be paid with food. So, I looked through the chop-box and handed out several tins of our supplies. We would later learn field mice were a source of food, as were Mopane worms which were actually big caterpillars. Being a great delicacy, the Mopane worms were available only at certain times and found only on the Mopane trees. Sometimes the trees were even cut down to collect the worms which were then cooked in small cast-iron pots over wood fires and much enjoyed by the people.

We packed up what was to be our last camp and José and João happily accompanied us to the new homestead site we'd chosen. While Ian was once more setting up the Aruba tent, José told him in Afrikaans all about himself and the people, and how desperate they were to earn money to buy clothes and food from the shops. They were sorely deprived he said, and we would be 'their father and mother', and we'd bring hope to them, something that had been missing for a long time. The Afrikaans language – by no means fluently, but rather such as was needed – now came back relatively easily to Ian. I was unable to understand or speak it except for a few slang words, nothing worthwhile for conversation, having been born and schooled only in Kenya. The very sturdy waterproof Aruba tent contained our ample sleeping quarters, and the verandah with the fly-flap would be our sitting and eating area where the table, gas lamp and 2 camping chairs were placed. From the centre rod of the tent awning we hung the cooler bag containing the uncooked chicken and butter, as well as the water bag, all kept cool by the breeze and shade. The orange-coloured VW Kombi tent was erected and used as a kitchen and pantry. Then 3 round, reasonably sized stones found somewhere in the woodland were put down to make an open fireplace, which kept a very large camping cast-iron kettle on the boil, giving us an enjoyable fire at night while we had our sundowners. The stones, with the heat from the fire, often split in half with a sharp crack like rifle fire and we'd have to search for more.

Using the black cotton soil, we shored-up an area just below the trickling spring water, making a small dam. Since we were entirely alone, we could bathe completely naked in the hot sunshine and luxuriate in the sparkling soft water. Soap and shampoo lathered and frothed excessively. Our hair and skin was always fresh and soft after these ablutions. A little lower from the first dam, we made another which, once again, quickly filled with fresh running water. I'd put all the things for washing into a large red plastic basin and we'd carry this down to the second dam, where I washed the pots, dishes and kitchen utensils, also our clothes. It wasn't long before we noticed tiny fish, not an inch long that appeared to thoroughly enjoy all the bubbles and fed on the waste matter in the dishwater.

José and João came a few days later with a number of other men. Ian immediately put them to work digging a deep pit, while he went off to Serpa Pinto to buy timber, corrugated iron and other bits and pieces to make an outside long-drop lavatory. Once the pit was dug, Ian made the entire box-like seating arrangement to fit over it safely. Then using clay and thin sticks as supports, three walls were built around it for privacy and a tin roof was added. I strung up an old blue curtain as a doorway, and Ian cordoned off the entrance with a trellis made of sticks cut from woodland saplings and we had a private, satisfactory and attractive 'little out-house'. To keep our 'loo' sweet smelling I sprinkled in chlorine powder weekly. Both Ian and I had grown up having, at one time or another, a long-drop toilet so it didn't bother us in the slightest. One day he would install a flushing toilet in the homestead he'd build for us when he was able to get to that part of the construction.

After this, Ian had to hurriedly erect a large thatched structure as accommodation for the 2 Portuguese Caterpillar tractor drivers. They would spend from Mondays to Fridays on the farm clearing 12 acres of land in thin strips, with woodland between each one as a windbreak for the cultivation of tobacco. This arrangement had been made with the Agricultural Officer on our arrival, so everything ran like clockwork.

We were also told in no uncertain terms by an Official of the Agricultural Department that the Luauca River, part of which ran through our property, had plenty of alluvial diamonds and that picking up or buying illicit diamonds was such a serious crime that one could be sentenced to death for it. Over time, we would hear of many murders as a result of people becoming involved in diamond buying and smuggling. Several people came to us with tiny parcels of old newspaper in which were wrapped uncut diamonds – I never looked in these parcels, but the sellers were persuasive and showed Ian who categorically refused to have anything to do with them.

A lazily flowing river about 20 or 30 feet wide and about 10 feet deep, the River Luauca was treeless along its banks with crystal clear water so one could see the black cotton soil river floor clearly. Along the sandy edges grew sparse clumps of reeds, now and then interspersed with knee-high coarse-leafed grass surrounded by short grass, the stalks of which were as straight and fine as a thin sewing needle – perfect for use on the tobacco seed beds later on. At one section of the river there was quite a large central rock island where I visualised my eventual home to be.

While living in the tents, we discovered that porcupines regularly visited, shaking their quills and rummaging through the camp site under cover of darkness. The dogs slept in the Aruba tent with us and were unperturbed. We had now also acquired a very large and magnificent dog named 'Cubango'. He looked like a Rottweiler, but was mainly white, with one or two grey and brown patches all over him, and was loving and affectionate. Cubango had been found wandering in Serpa Pinto, and Senhor Gil Vieira asked us to give him a home. Every now and again, Cubango would walk the 21 miles back to town in search of his previous owner – the local Vet, Dr Sá, who'd gone to Brazil and decided to stay – and then return to us.

Building plans had been drawn up by Ian for the huge reservoir and the tobacco barns which comprised outbuildings on both sides of the one enormously long structure, each much bigger and longer than a tennis court, with high walls. The first 100,000 bricks had been ordered with some 100,000 more to follow. Lorries began arriving, delivering corrugated iron sheets, cement, bricks, lime, nails, a wide variety of tools and piping (both black heavy plastic and metal), various sizes of cut and treated timber, and all the items needed for building on a huge scale.

Ian started employing his labour force by going to the kimbo and interviewing some men, then choosing a suitable headman capable of handling labour and commanding their respect. Fernando, a middle-aged man and father of 22 children, being more senior and well-respected by the community, seemed to be the right person. From then on it was his job to do the actual recruiting of labour as and when required and see that Ian's orders were carried out. There was no shortage of staff. They worked exceptionally well and were satisfied with their wages, eagerly ready and waiting each day. Ian had bought a grey second-hand 5-ton Ford lorry and each morning at 7 the workforce were collected from their kimbo situated just off the main district dirt road which was at the end of our farm road turn-off. They were returned home each evening at 5, a distance of about 7 kilometres each way. Later, when the time came for harvesting the first tobacco crop, the labour required for this enormous task alone would number at least 200, many of them being women.

A priority was to cut a straight road leading from our campsite and the area designated for the tobacco barns directly to the main district road. This didn't take too long to complete as the soil was very sandy and without stones, so the work really meant only felling trees on that line and removing the roots. This cut timber was taken away and stored to dry out, later to be used as fuel for the tobacco barn furnaces. The amount of traffic on this bush road soon turned it into a permanent highway. I picked out a piece of new sawn timber and painted on it in large black lettering, 'Fazenda Esperança', and Ian erected the signboard at the entrance of our road.

We found that we had to go to Serpa Pinto at least once a week. One morning at dawn on a perfect Angolan summer's day, Ian and I left the fazenda in the Chev bakkie for a day of banking business and shopping at the supermarket in our beautiful little pink and white town. Nearing the end of our farm road yet still in dappled tree shadow and swathed in early morning steam, the heat rising from the dampness of the woodland floor, we saw ahead what appeared to be a buffalo lying in the centre of the car tracks. Throughout our marriage, Ian had always relied on me to be the lookout for unlikely things on the road while he concentrated on the driving. So when I saw what appeared to be a buffalo, I yelled out and he approached cautiously. Not till we were almost upon it did we realise it was a huge thick snake, a cobra, caught and held by the powerful talons of a snake eagle. These cobras are as thick as a man's forearm, dullish grey/green in colour, grow to at least 6 feet and are known by the name 'Naja Haje Anchietae'. The eagle had its wings outspread with the tips resting on the ground, while the cobra's coils were draped across the eagle's shoulders, both locked in deadly combat to such an extent that they neither saw nor heard our car approaching. After watching them for a few minutes, Ian honked the horn which made no difference, so I banged on the outside of the car door several times with my closed fist. Finally, the eagle disengaged, shook itself, shrugged off the cobra's coils and casually flew off. We watched the big snake, obviously painfully injured because it moved off very slowly in an unnatural manner and disappeared into the long grass along the verge. I felt certain that never again would I witness such an incredible sight of nature.

Living in the tents, I had practically no house-cleaning or housekeeping to do so found time to write many letters to family and friends, especially to Jack Block in Nairobi, giving details of everything we encountered and the progress of our lives. Jack was an excellent correspondent so we both had regular news.

During the many walks through the virgin woodland, I'd collected 17 types of grass, unfortunately none of which were suitable for livestock grazing. There were a variety of truly large and exquisite butterflies as well, so I sent to a Durban Bookshop for 'A Field Guide to the Butterflies of Africa'. I'd also found beautiful ground creeping Protea plants, and lots of different orchids on the trees. Sometimes the early morning mists swirled off the River Luauca yet didn't penetrate the nearby woodlands. According to Guggisberg, a world-renowned expert, the forests in the southern part of Angola where we lived were classified as 'woodlands' and not forest. In true forest sunlight does not penetrate the tree-canopy to the forest floor. Where we were the canopy of trees was sufficiently spaced to allow sun to fall to the floor so that indigenous grasses, flowers and plants could grow.

On the main district dirt road to Serpa Pinto was a chana – a stretch of black cotton soil, usually in a lower-lying section of land, such as a valley, gully, river bed, or dip in the road through which runs spring water. When the rains come the chana turns into thick black sludge, usually impassable by vehicle until the water subsides. As it was the rainy season, the chana 'floor' (about 100 yards wide) became a black cotton soil morass of mud 18 inches deep, so for trips to town we left the Kombi on the farm side of the chana and the Chev bakkie on the Serpa Pinto side. We always took one of the staff with us to help carry across the supplies we'd bought as the banks on both sides of the chana were steep and one had to wade through the muddy mess in the middle. Once in Serpa Pinto, we'd go straight to the hotel to clean up then do our shopping. The trip home was the reverse.

On 7th April 1974, we made such a trip to town and on our return found a forked stick with a white business card attached to it standing up against the Aruba tent door. On the front of the card printed in black was 'Robert Hudson Ford Agents Luanda' and written on the back in Swahili was, "Bw. Ian Rooken-Smith. Salaam sana. Hodi. Iko whisky. James Walker. Harry Parsons." Translated this reads, "Mr Ian Rooken-Smith. Many greetings. Knock. Have you whisky. James Walker. Harry Parsons." We were so delighted and happy to have old Kenya friends to visit. We'd been without company for weeks on end and every daylight hour had been non-stop farm work. It was incredible and an absolute joy to find the message awaiting us. You could have knocked Ian and me over with a feather!

The following day we went into Serpa Pinto through the chana again and drove straight to the hotel, the only place where the 2 chaps could possibly be staying. And there they were! Realising the chana was impassable, they'd found a man, written the note attaching it to a newly cut bush stick and sent him to deliver it. Not finding us home, the runner had left the message at the zipped tent door. Ian and I had a shower, followed by a wonderful lunch with James and Harry, lots of fun, wine and early whisky. Harry Parsons had been one of Ian's Malindi deep-sea fishing clients and become a friend. He was based in the UK, many times fishing with Ian off Apple Pie. James Walker, like us, was also a friend of Jack Block's in Nairobi. It turned out that the

Ford Motor Company UK had also taken up the Government's offer of farming land and bought a property next to us. Representing Ford, James had come to check out the feasibility of a sisal plantation as opposed to growing tobacco. Harry had accompanied James as a companion on the trip. The day was spent catching up with all their Kenya news – Jack Block had obviously filled them in about us to a certain extent. We talked about the good old fishing days in Malindi and told James and Harry what we were now doing and how we were achieving our aims. Since the chana made the road to their farmland impassable they decided to return to Luanda. It was a most enjoyable outing in the presence of excellent, valued company, 'just what the doctor ordered'. We arrived back at the fazenda around 5 in the afternoon, had a lovely hot bath in the big red plastic bucket and went to bed feeling rejuvenated, peaceful and content.

Of the 6 farmers the Portuguese Angolan Government had been looking for and who'd bought land at our time were the 4 of us in our Cuando Cubango Province – 2 Germans, Franz Josef Nachtsheim and his farming partner, August; a 'predikant' (Afrikaans word for church minister) by the surname of De Jager, from Tsumeb, South West Africa; Ford Motor Co UK; and us on Fazenda Esperança. In neighbouring Bié Province was our nephew, Rob Rooken-Smith, and Peter and Barbie Gill.

In the colder mid-year months when the first frosts came the fields were covered in shiny white layers. On either side of each tobacco land was a strip of woodland and the winter scenes were very pretty with the dappled sun shining through the canopy. Many of the trees had flowers (honey, wax, timber, oil and coffee were some of the top 10 exports from Angola). By 9 o'clock, the morning sun had completely melted away any sign of frost and we'd be back to the African warmth, shedding jerseys and warm clothing. Whilst out on these excursions, I often came across pairs of Ground Hornbills – large birds, commonly known as turkey buzzards – which weren't in the least afraid of me. They are more terrestrial (being of land and air, though more so of land than other species of smaller hornbills) and look like big black turkeys. The ground hornbills meandered through open grassy terrain and under the trees, digging and poking into the ground with their significantly powerful beaks in search of insects, frogs, small reptiles, mice and rats. They will even take small fish out of shallow pools (as I was to later find out). I remembered Robert Foster once had a ground hornbill at Kaptagat, Kenya, which had given the family enormous pleasure. So I asked João and José if they could sometime in the future, being very careful not to cause a disturbance to the nest, perhaps find me a ground hornbill chick, for which I would pay them.

Water was crucial to Fazenda Esperança and had to be a sufficient supply for all the buildings and had to be gravity fed. The first construction task was to erect the massive reservoir some way behind and at a higher elevation than the sites chosen for the homestead and tobacco barns. Ian and I had returned to Rhodesia once in the Chevrolet bakkie to buy a dam scoop. Using this implement, Ian built a really good, long dam wall across the valley, with a spillway. This big new dam filled up quickly from the natural spring and supplied, for the time being, the necessary water. Once the dam had filled, a diesel engine and pump were installed, and underground piping was laid to reach every point. Now beautiful natural water filled the reservoir and reached everywhere building was taking place.

Ian and I decided to take a Saturday off and go to Chitembo, the capital of neighbouring Bié Province, to visit Peter and Barbie Gill, and Rob. Peter and Barbie had built themselves a nice house, but had so far done little with the land. On Rob's farm the bracken was tall and thick as real forest, an impossible task to cut through. Slashing and burning was the only answer, but as soon as the rains fell up came the bracken again, thicker than ever. In most places, a horse couldn't be ridden through the dense growth. We learnt later that fire destroyed only the growth, but still left the root system free to regenerate. Rob also had on his farm the most wonderful patches of incredibly tall, big ironwood trees (a variety of the Betulaceous Tree), a sight worth seeing.

As Rob was unable to accommodate us in his small abode, we spent the night at the Chitembo Hotel, approximately 80 miles from our home. Our 2 dogs weren't allowed to sleep in our bedroom on the 2nd floor, but were allowed a twin-bedroom of their own on the ground floor, a luxury night sleeping on ready-made human beds. This was difficult for us to understand. We'd travelled through heavy rain that had soaked the dogs as they'd been on the open back of the Chevrolet bakkie. Again, I expect we were considered the 'malucos estrangeiros' paying for a room for their dogs! We, equally, thought it stupidity as the dogs could have happily slept on the floor in our room. Hennie and Martha van Rensburg also lived in that area. They were the first and very successful tobacco farmers, having already had 3 or 4 harvests, and willingly gave out free advice. Hennie's brother, Janse, and his wife, Elsie, also lived on their farm helping with the workload. The 4 of them had visited us before on Fazenda Esperança. On our way back home, we stopped in for lunch at predikant De Jager's farm in our Cuando Cubango Province. He'd brought in goats, though I don't recall he'd started the actual tobacco farming in any way. It was interesting seeing how some of the other farmers were doing and coping with the many difficulties and language. We felt so pleased and happy that we were making a good success of everything we'd undertaken.

The task of turning 21,000 acres of virgin bush on Fazenda Esperança into a viable agricultural venture was massive since we planned not only to cultivate tobacco, but also maize, fatten cattle for beef, and have a small dairy herd for our own milk supply. Bearing this in mind, we invited our eldest son, Keith, his wife, Mary, and their baby daughter, Debbie, living in England, to come and join us. Writing a long letter to them we gave the gist of what we planned. By return, they said they'd come and would start winding things up in England.

Mary fills us in a little here: "Keith had finished his training in April 1974. He then went into refrigeration, but England and the weather was getting to him. He wanted to return to a similar life to what he'd known in Africa. He'd thought about Chile at one time, but after his training we went to Australia House in London and asked about immigration. We were accepted and had packed up ready to leave when his father suggested that instead of going to Australia, we join them on the farm in Angola." They planned to bring only their luggage and 3 items which I asked them to buy for me – a double-bed blanket, a grater with several blades, and because most of my recipes are in pounds and ounces, a scale with its weights.

Ian heeded Professor Papenfus' advice. He carefully studied and carried out the tobacco manual's instruction to the letter, so that when the time came to prepare the seed beds for the Virginia tobacco, they were made and planted in a very short period of time. Two men were put to making the long seed beds, each being about a yard wide and constructed of raised sifted soil. Tobacco seed is extremely fine, similar to ground pepper – it was carefully and evenly sprinkled over the beds. Then came a fine layer of sifted soil, and lastly a light covering of the chopped fine grass from the Luauca River-banks laid over the whole structure, so that the twice-daily watering did not disturb the seed, but held it firmly in place. The chopped fine grass also kept the African sun from wilting the germinating tobacco. Watering was done by a hose and fine rose-attachment, such as is found in bathroom showerheads. Once the seedlings reached the size of an ordinary pencil, they were exactly right for transplanting into the already prepared high rills on the lands. To avoid failure it meant that everything had to be ready by the onset of the rains that fell on regular and expected dates.

In preparation for the arrival of Keith, Mary and little Debbie, Ian had built the main house so that we each had our own bedrooms. The long-drop was still the lavatory. The enormous amount of work to be done on the farm was priority, so although the exterior and main walls of the house were complete, proper doors and windows, kitchen fittings and the cosmetic finishes had yet to be completed. It was a square house with 4 bedrooms, kitchen and bathroom all leading off a large centre lounge-cum-dining room with 2 main entrance doors, front and back. Hot water for ablutions, cooking and laundry was an absolute necessity. Having already put in proven, reliable hot-water systems at Uruku and Westlands, Ian soon had the matter perfectly resolved at our fazenda home. Using the same plan and structure of bricks and concrete with a base, he built a boiler with a closed-in top and chimney, 3 closed sides and an open front. A log fire was kept burning that heated the water in the large drum above. It gave a constant supply of hot water as long as the fire was going – as simple as that.

Mary tells us about their trip from the UK: "We spent a few days in Portugal waiting for our tickets. For us, the weather was wonderful, but being November, to the Portuguese people it was cold and miserable. Debbie would only eat chips and chocolate mousse. When we landed in Luanda, Angola in November 1974 (a month before Debbie's 2nd birthday), on the first stage of our journey to the farm, I think we were all in a bit of a daze after the 14 hour flight."

I'd flown from Serpa Pinto airport in the central south with TAAG Portuguese Airways (that had an excellent aviation record) to the capital, Luanda, on the north-west coast. It was at least an hour-and-a-half flight time. Keith, Mary and Debbie arrived via TAP, the Portuguese Airline from Lisbon. While we were at a cheap hotel overnight, sitting together having a drink and engrossed in conversation with so much to catch up on, I was tapped lightly on the shoulder. Before I even had time to look properly at the person, a scrap of paper was put into my hand by an African who then immediately vanished, giving me no opportunity to take proper notice of the bearer.

Unfolding the note quietly, in very poorly written lettering it said, "Don't be afraid, we will never hurt you because you are English."

I was extremely worried, and although it was deceitful, I felt it unwise to convey the contents of the note at this time to Keith and Mary. They'd just arrived from the UK. I put the note away until I could give it to Ian when we arrived back home. Someone was definitely watching us, but who and why, especially my movements otherwise how would they have known I'd flown from Serpa Pinto to Luanda to meet arriving family members and hand me the note here? Why did they choose to give the note to me and not to Ian? And, why should we be afraid, who would want to hurt or harm us anyway? We'd done nothing wrong. Certainly, we hadn't taken land from the people, neither had anyone been thrown off their property. We provided employment for hundreds of the local citizens and were here at the specific invitation of the Government. We had legally bought and paid for our farm and invested all our financial assets in ensuring agricultural success of our venture, which was to the country's advantage. Everything we'd done had been transparent and 'by the book'. As for 'them' writing they wouldn't hurt us because we were English, I had no idea what this could refer to. Yes, we'd been nicknamed the 'mad strangers', but I felt sure that had nothing to do with the sinister written message. The contents of the note gnawed anxiously at my gut all night long – this uneasy feeling in the pit of my stomach, memories of Mau Mau and Kenya's turbulent, terrorist years leading up to Independence.

Chapter Fourteen
Protetor, Donna Eeffa & Humpy Hornbill

Ian was called *'Protetor'* (Protector) or *'Pai'* (father) by our labour force and referred to as *'Senhor* Smith' by the townsfolk and our friends. I was spoken to as *'Mãe'* (mother) by our staff, otherwise I was known as '*Donna Eeffa*', much like 'Eva' because the pronunciation of my first name, 'Heather', was difficult for them. Mary was known by her name, familiar to them though in the Portuguese equivalent, being '*Donna Maria*'. Keith's name they also had difficulty with the 'th' so he became 'Mister' or '*Senhor Keef*'.

'*Donna*' is Italian. In Portuguese it would be '*Dona*'. From the outset of trying to learn Portuguese, most times I would spell the word according to the way it sounded to my ear. On numerous occasions, Manuel would correct the Portuguese spelling in my notebook, but quite amusingly, the Italian '*Donna*' stuck in my mind!

Often our staff would say to Ian and me, *"Vocês são nosso pai e nossa mãe"* ("You are our father and mother").

All 4 of us appreciated the polite and respectful way we were addressed, that being the Portuguese custom, and felt particularly honoured by the term of endearment our staff gave us. They all had a Catholic upbringing. Near or adjacent to every kimbo I saw there were little buildings made of mud and wattle with a cross atop at one end. Our people were so enthusiastic and willing about building up Fazenda Esperança and were proud of their achievements, the likes of which they'd never seen. Without their help, we would not have achieved our Angolan dream. To our knowledge, in 510 years no-one had lived on the land we'd bought and named Fazenda Esperança (Hope Farm). We rose early and went to bed early. Usually at evening meal times, Ian would discuss the following day's planning. Paraffin lamps provided light at night.

A farmer's wife's life can be lonely so I appreciated Mary's company. I thoroughly enjoyed being able to chat to her or discuss housekeeping, meals, lists of necessities and groceries for the house, or go to Serpa Pinto together for shopping. The men had no use for any of these topics. I always made English scones for tea. Mary took over most of the housekeeping and cooking, and did wonderfully with whatever meal she decided upon. She also had little Debbie to care for. Several times a day, Mary would make a bottle of coffee for Ian and send it to the barns or wherever he was working. Sometimes he'd send a note to her asking for a bottle. We never lacked meat, but did have to buy vegetables and fruit which were plentiful in the beginning in Serpa Pinto. None of these commodities in the shops were packaged so the housewife could be fussy and pick and choose. As Mary had no driver's licence and took over many of my usual home responsibilities, my time was freed to do other things such as running many errands for the farm to Serpa Pinto which helped Ian as he could get on with other farm projects. I also had the opportunity to get started on our garden.

We had a weekly '*lavandeira*' (the Portuguese word for 'washer-woman') which was the custom in Angola. She was addressed as '*lavandeira*' and not by her first name, and did the laundry perfectly, washing the garments down at the river and drying them flat on the spiky grass in the sun. I can't remember ever having to iron anything. When Ian later put up a washing line for me, our '*lavandeira*' taught me how to hang washing on the line correctly, using wooden pegs (the simple kind without any metal spring in them).

Dominga (her name the feminine for 'Sunday' in Portuguese), a 16 year old girl from the kimbo was employed to watch over little Debbie. They'd wander around, hand in hand, to see all that was taking place in the barns and visit the animals, but never went into the woodland. Dominga also spent time in the house as company for Debbie when it was raining. Generally, they just had playtime together with Debbie's toys and books. A tall girl, Dominga was always neat and clean and a very personable teenager, treating Debbie with gentleness.

José arrived one morning with a big, grey fluffy chick, his black feathers just starting to peep out of his down, unmistakably a baby ground hornbill. I'd asked José and João some time back to try to find one for me, so I was thrilled. I gave José one conto (approximately Rand 25) and named my new baby ground hornbill, 'Humpy'. He was the greatest delight, highly intelligent and became a central part of our home and family. I made a comfortable nest-bed from a large shallow cardboard box with plentiful soft dry grass where Humpy remained for a month till he could waddle around. His food was minced raw beef mixed in with cooked mealie meal and shaped into chipolata-sized 'sausages' which he willingly took without coaxing and swallowed with no trouble at all. This was complemented by an abundance of insects, especially grasshoppers, which were always to be found. He had a voracious appetite.

From the first, Humpy was 'potty-trained' and never messed his nest. We knew when he was ready to defecate because he'd waggle backwards to the edge of the box, position his rear well over the rim and relieve himself on the sand I scattered around the box, which was then replaced with clean soil. Humpy and his box-nest went with us all over the place, except to town. Mary and Keith took care of him if I was ever away. When he was ready to take his first unsteady steps, I took him from the nest-box, held him high so he could stretch his legs and get the feel of the earth with his feet. It was a couple of days before he could manage to stand, and then walk, alone.

Franz Nachtsheim and his farming partner, August, came to see us on Fazenda Esperança on 2 occasions. Keith and Mary had previously visited them on their fazenda. They spoke at length with Ian about tobacco farming techniques and wanted to see how Ian was carrying out his methods. Franz spoke English, was a strongly-built blonde haired man and such a happy chap. We had an instant rapport with him. August had more of a reserved nature and only spoke German.

Everything we'd accomplished so far had taken a great deal of organising and managing. We'd been kept extremely busy building the massive tobacco barns and getting the furnaces to correct heat specifications using tobacco thermometers, and preparing the lands for the seedlings. Then there were the trips to and from Serpa Pinto; the delivery of the tractors and hydraulic equipment; installing the water supply; analysing the soil and ordering the supplies and correct fertiliser for maize production. Overseeing the labour who'd never before worked anywhere except to dig up very small unproductive patches of ground in nearby woodlands; building a 4 bedroom house; importing Boer Goats from South Africa, buying in native Angolan cattle as a beef herd and a small Brown Swiss dairy herd, establishing poultry for eggs and turkeys, and keeping a few pigs and sheep – the administration was huge. The goats were not a good idea as we soon learned, though they thrived in summer and bred. However, come the heavy rainfalls followed by winter, death also came. They developed pleuro-pneumonia, a condition which could not be stopped and they died very quickly, medication hardly helped. Quite simply, it was the wrong climate for goats. This distressed Mary very much. The sheep were able to cope though.

On top of all this was the red tape for which Portugal is famous! Money from Ian's bank account in England provided the funds. Ability to speak the language helped tremendously. I really have to thank my high school teachers, Miss Dorothy Gunn for the French, and Mrs La Fontaine for the Latin. Without these 2 languages learnt in the 1940s, it would have been more difficult for me to converse with our friends and business associates. I shall never forget our Portuguese friends. They were so pleased that we tried to learn their language, and that I particularly took a keen interest and made such an effort. Even if I did not always correctly enunciate the Portuguese words they would tell me, "It is delightful to hear your accent."

Since we'd been allotted the 2 Portuguese Caterpillar drivers for a certain time period only, they returned with their tractors to the Serpa Pinto Agricultural Department not long after Keith and Mary's arrival. Keith took over the entire machinery maintenance side of the farm – no mean task – for the old grey 5-ton and new 7-ton green Ford lorries, the Kombi, Chev, new Massey-Ferguson tractor, new big Ford tractor, all the many new implements used for the agricultural work, including the bulldozer.

Ian had bought his own new Komatsu bulldozer with which Keith cleared and broke new land for further cultivation of maize (both white and yellow) and harrowed the newly prepared tobacco lands. There was no workshop for Keith and no electricity for power tools. Machinery was assembled each evening on a large area behind and to the side of the house, an open space before reaching the Brown Swiss herd stalls. Here Keith worked, using his technical maintenance skills on bare ground. Without a doubt, we'd never have managed in Angola without Keith and Mary.

Grazing in our area of the Cubango Province was poor, the sour veld grass not nutritious for cattle. The idea was to plough and plant maize and under-sow with Rhodes grass seed, excellent for grazing, with which we were successful at Westlands in Kenya.

Great logs were cut and stacked, giving them time to dry out for when the tobacco barn furnaces would be in use. The tobacco seedlings were planted and there was visible daily growth as they took root immediately, each having received a pint of water to carry them through till the time when the expected rains came in torrents. Ian bought two small 'monkey' 2-wheeler motorbikes, used for driving up and down the rows of tobacco and supervising the picking of the correct-sized leaf by the 200 strong, mostly women, labour force.

One day, on his return from clearing a new 12 acre stretch of land, Keith almost went over a young brightly coloured cobra about 20 centimetres long. It spread its hood and stood up to the great steel blade of the Komatsu with such bravery that he waited for the little snake to escape. A newly hatched cobra is as lethal as an adult. On another occasion, driving the big Fordson Major tractor, about 100 yards behind an Angolan driver on a small Massey-Ferguson, Keith was amazed to hear shrill, piercing screams and see the driver leaping off and haring into the surrounding trees. Reaching the stalled Massey-Ferguson, Keith saw an enormous bright-skinned python slowly undulating its way over the rills, leaving a distinct track in the newly-turned slightly damp soil, eventually disappearing into the woodland. The tractor driver later told Ian that he'd never before seen such a huge snake and had been terrified. Some African superstitions deem it bad luck to look upon snakes, chameleons, even geckos and iguanas. Later we learnt they also felt, on hearing the eerie call of ground hornbills, that this augured bad luck.

On a trip to Serpa Pinto one day, we met our Bank Manager coming out to our fazenda. With him he had our eldest daughter, Beryl, and her boyfriend, unexpectedly arrived from Rhodesia (Zimbabwe). We were somewhat perplexed. All soon became clear. Beryl was pregnant, and her boyfriend needed the safety of a job, in a faraway place, as we later learnt he'd bought a car, exporting it from Britain and had somehow managed to get it into Rhodesia without paying for it.

Christmas 1974, all our children were with us and we enjoyed traditional English fare including our own pork with crispy crackling, the other indulgences of the festivities, and the giving and receiving of presents. It was a happy occasion and wonderful to be together again as a family on our new farm in Angola. The house still needed glass window panes, the kitchen and bathroom awaited finer finishing touches and the cooking and washing-up area was still in the 2 outside tents. Everyone continued walking to the long-drop lavatory. Lindsay and her German boyfriend, Heinz, had flown from Salisbury, Rhodesia, for a few weeks holiday. She'd finished her year at Secretarial College and would return again in January 1975 to work there.

Regardless of the amount of work involved or how tired we were each evening, our Angolan farming dreams were coming to fruition before our eyes and becoming a reality. It gave all of us an enormous sense of personal satisfaction to see what had once been virgin bush turned into a viable agricultural future for our family.

Ian had several sayings, 2 of which were, "No pleasure without pain," and, "If you're going to do something then you may as well do it properly." Both rang so true of our enormous efforts in Angola. Every one of us gave 110% commitment each day to the farm and to one another, in ensuring every cent of money spent, drop of sweat, aching muscle or worries through many struggles was absolutely worthwhile. Each of us understood perfectly that it would be only what we put in that would result in the ultimate payment of what we would get in this venture.

It also gave us immense pleasure to be able to provide work for so many of the struggling local Angolan people. They in turn showed their appreciation as loyal, hardworking individuals and felt their own sense of pride seeing Fazenda Esperança come to life through their hours of dedicated toil. Regardless of where we'd lived in Africa, Ian had a natural ability to work in harmony with his staff, always gaining their respect by recognising their right to be respected as individuals, paying a fair wage, giving credit where credit was due and bonuses for a job well done. He always had an 'open door policy' with his workforce whereby they could approach him with the problems or struggles they faced in their daily lives.

João was a young adult of quiet demeanour, well-spoken, responsible and reliable. The growing of tobacco is precise work and the timing of the cutting of leaf is vitally important. Ian taught a number of specifically chosen men, João one of them, who in turn taught the women workers how to cut the tobacco leaf when ready from the parent plant. It was then delivered by men carrying huge bundles to the lorry waiting alongside the tobacco fields, then from the lorry again by men and put into piles on the tobacco barn floors. Women then picked leaves from the piles and sorted them into further new piles in rows on the long narrow barn tables. Each leaf was laid flat down one on top of the other in groups of uniform size and weight and tied into bundles ready for the hanging up and drying process from the wood-fired barn furnaces. These had to be kept at certain temperatures – this meant either adding in more timber or pulling out timber to raise or lower the air temperature. The furnaces had to be kept going 24 hours a day during the drying process. Ian, Keith and I took it in turns to get up hourly at night to check the furnace temperatures – quite exhausting work.

José was Ian's interpreter, translating Ian's Afrikaans instructions into Portuguese for the staff, and stayed by his side. A chatty, happy chap, José was very willing to work and always sent a message with someone if he was to be absent for the day, which was seldom.

Then there was Angelo. He was very old, or so it seemed, but probably he was only about 60. He said he wanted any work. Ian put him onto keeping the hot-water system going, generally making sure the area surrounding the house was clean and tidy, and checking that the home livestock didn't stray too far away. He was an expert at collecting Mopane worms and was the man chosen by the labour to cook this delicacy in a small iron pot over hot coals, which they then enjoyed eating cold. It looked most unappetising to me! Old Angelo would arrive for work and say in Portuguese, "Good morning, father. How are you this day?" to Ian; and to me, "Good morning, mother, and how are you this day?"

The correct way to reply is, "I am well, thank you, and how are you?" after which any work instructions were given. This greeting never changed with Angelo and we realised this was a ritual that must not be broken. He had no shoes, and his feet were covered in thick ghastly looking leathery skin, so deeply cracked and filled with old black mud probably from the cotton soil, and for me so very shocking to see. He must have suffered great pain in the winter months. When he came to us he was in ragged attire. Because of this, Ian realised the labour needed clothing so he bought from a warehouse in Serpa Pinto 2 huge bales of good second-hand garments imported from USA. Each staff member could choose any items they fancied for which they paid the equivalent of one South African Rand or ten Escudos per garment. Soon they were better clad, had warm coats for the cold months and were 'tickled pink', delighted and very grateful.

Simão was my garden-man. He worked only with me and had never done any gardening before. He was forty-ish with a pock-marked face and had all his front top and bottom teeth filed to sharp points. Simão said it was the custom with his particular branch of a tribe living in the area, and told me a file was used on either side of the tooth to make a sharp point at the end. He was the only one of our homestead staff with this tooth-filing (I don't know about the other labour force members as they worked with Ian).

We started with clearing bush behind the house to levelling the ground in the front in order to make a really big lawn sloping down towards the dam Ian had built. Then we planted Kikuyu grass runners which I was given by our Vieira friends in Serpa Pinto. During these gardening hours, Simão would teach me how to speak Portuguese. I'd learn 20 nouns each night while in bed before putting out the paraffin lamps and going to sleep. Next morning when Simão arrived, I'd put on my hat and an apron with a pocket in which I kept the green Collins Portuguese/ English dictionary I'd bought in Windhoek, notebook and pencil, and while we worked I'd be tested.

Simão was quite strict with me. "Donna Eeffa, say that again like this… not like that, say it again," most times, over and over. He was the only one of the staff to call me by name.

Having realised I should first note the word phonetically in English to get the right pronunciation of Portuguese, I later corrected the spelling – I remembered the conjugations of verbs from Latin so those came easily, but the grammar was more difficult. Whilst working together, Simão and I had many short-sentenced conversations. Later, when there was time, I'd listen to the cassette tapes I'd bought in Windhoek on our battery-operated radio/tape deck to get the correct accents, but my best teaching came from Simão who was patient and taught me the necessary language of everyday things and usage.

We'd given a home to yet another dog, a naturally very energetic, bouncy and curious Fox-terrier named Tintin, who took to exploring the surrounding bush and forest. When Tintin didn't come home one evening we searched everywhere and continued looking the following day, but were unable to track or find a trace of him anywhere. Deep in the woodland, we found the massive hole where an exceptionally large python had its lair. It's quite probable Tintin, unfortunately and sadly, found the hole and the reptile took him. A trench had been scored deeply into the earth by the python's body continually going in and out of the lair the same way. The last 3 feet of its tail was sticking out. Probably there was no more room in its home! Close by and scattered all around were ragged remnants of its old skin, some short intact pieces were bigger in width than Ian's thigh. There was no way in which to measure the python's length accurately, but we remembered vividly Uncle George Aggett's 2 python skins on his dining room wall in Laikipia, Kenya, the one being 28 foot and the other 24 foot long. The middle of the 28 foot python skin was 3 feet wide! Often when we'd visited Uncle George for tea, I'd sat mesmerised, staring at those 2 enormous snake skins. Bearing this in mind, we measured the width of the clear underbelly spoor left on the tobacco rills by our big snake, which measured one of Ian's size ten-and-a-half boots, multiplied by 2 for the circumference of the belly. Ian estimated our python's length to be approximately 24 feet. The word soon spread. Trophy hunters kept coming to the farm, pleading with us to allow them to shoot our massive snake, which we categorically refused. While we lived on Fazenda Esperança, we'd do our best to ensure the python was safe and would live to a great age. I'm also given to believe that the tallest recorded African elephant was in Angola.

In the utter stillness of the vast surrounding land and the great black star-flecked Angolan nights, large packs of wild dogs (correctly known as African hunting dogs) made the most terrifying sounds. Faintly at first from far away, maybe 10 miles, but as they came closer and closer their whining, squealing and howling was spine-chilling and positively unnerving in the extreme, exacerbated by the sense of remoteness and aloneness one felt in the all encompassing, unyielding stark darkness outside the bedroom window. What Mary must have felt hearing these wild dogs, I've never found out. Then the sounds would become fainter and fainter as they moved further away on their hunting quest, and you could literally feel your body physically unwind in a silent ripple effect of relief and relaxation, till you finally drifted off to sleep once more.

Our small Brown Swiss dairy herd of 6 was kept near the house and stall fed only at milking times (a mixture of maize, bran and cattle feed bought from the Serpa Pinto Farmer's Co-Op), otherwise they were free to graze in the area around the house. Ian personally did the milking every day, the milk for our own use only. We had at least 40 long-horn Angolan cattle (their horns are massive, not unlike the Texas long-horn breed) for beef to be fattened and eventually sold to the Serpa Pinto abattoir – hardy livestock to survive the Angolan countryside, and very tall at the shoulder.

It happened one midday that a pack of wild dogs attacked one of the Angolan oxen grazing peacefully with the herd on open land at the verge of the woodland, across the valley, and easily seen from the house. The cattle-herder rushed over the dam wall to tell us. Ian grabbed his rifle and we drove pell-mell to the spot, where I witnessed for the first time how a wild dog pack pulls down an enormous animal, and saw how rangy, tall and unafraid the Angolan wild dogs were. Maybe it was hunger that made them so fearless. With many rifle shots into the air and much yelling and chasing from the cattle-herder, the pack was scared off. I'll never forget the absolute eeriness of the wild dogs' shrill howling, quite haunting to this day. On another occasion, the herdsman came rushing over to say he'd speared a big snake which had bitten one of the fully-grown steers. Within 20 minutes, Ian got to where the cattle were grazing and found the animal already dead. The herdsman dug the snake out of a hole and found that it too was dead. Angolan cobras are not only very large, but deadly.

I decided turkeys would do well as free-range poultry on our fazenda, so when next in Serpa Pinto our inquiries led us to the cleaning lady of the town's 3 Banks, who also bred and sold turkeys. She'd heard about the 'mad strangers'. It was with some difficulty that I explained and negotiated in my poor Portuguese that we wished to buy 2 hens, a gobbler and a broody hen with a clutch of eggs. Back on the farm, we released the turkeys and soon they were quite at home, roosting in low branches of the trees at night. The broody hen and her eggs I put in what I thought was a safe place. The small flock grazed contentedly around the farmyard and house, and came for their daily hand-out of maize. Mother turkey-hen had been sitting on her eggs for more than 2 weeks when disaster struck. On going to her nest in the morning, she was dead and most of her eggs gone. We carefully examined her corpse and found the tell-tale marks of a snake bite on one thigh, and knew we had a cobra living not too far from the house.

It was the turkeys themselves that sounded the alarm not long after. Keith and Ian rushed out to find a very large cobra, which soon spotted them and hurriedly slithered down a hole in the ground right near to where the vehicles were parked. Keith fetched a piece of hose, attached one end to the old lorry exhaust pipe and the other end he inserted well into the snake's hole, then revved up the lorry engine a short time, followed by letting it idle for about 10 minutes. The hose was withdrawn and we waited with bated breath, the turkeys acting in a very agitated manner, gobbling and squawking. In due course, out came a very woozy cobra, swaying from side to side. The turkeys instantly reacted with a cacophony of noise and the cobra was hit on the head with a dropper (a wooden fencing pole). With much chatting and gobbling, all the turkeys examined the dead reptile then sat around it and simply couldn't talk enough about it! We left the snake there for them and after 3 days the turkeys were convinced the evil monster was really dead and once again took to their normal grazing habits. Maybe they even forgot how terrified they'd been.

Stuart came home each end of term holiday flying from school in Windhoek to Sá Da Bandeira about 2 hours drive from the farm (international flights landed at either Luanda or Sá Da Bandeira). I fetched him from there, Sá Da Bandeira (now known as Lubango) being a beautifully built and large town with street facades of marble, the quarries situated not so far away. Stuart was completely in love with

Angola, the farm and woodlands, our way of life his ultimate dream come true. His days were spent in teenage ecstasy of non-stop adventure and freedom. He'd be out monkey-bike riding between the rows of tobacco, ducking his head under the huge green leaves as the plants reached maturity, and checking farm building and general progress. Nights were spent around the outside fire. He loved the different farm animals and wildlife, and helping his elder brother, Keith, with the machinery. Stuart constantly explored the bush on the farm with Pepu, his Keeshond, always faithfully at his side, the 2 quite inseparable.

Over the months, many Portuguese visitors came to check-out the 'malucos estrangeiros' curious to see how we lived in the bush, what we were doing, and later on to get dried tobacco. Mostly, they were surprised to find we were quite self-sufficient, having daily fresh milk, even making ham and bacon. Both these were a great success, thanks to my mother's cookery book and a recipe from the Scientific American Cyclopedia of Formulas, Page 762.

There were no telephone lines to the farm. Our only communication with the outside world or getting news to or from anyone was by going to Serpa Pinto or from visitors, the 'bush-telegraph' daily labour force from the kimbo, and by listening in daily to BBC radio, the only station we could understand.

Keith was managing efficiently with the huge amount of machinery that had to be kept in tip-top condition, and Mary had picked up the Portuguese language with a delightful Irish accent. Everything was going smoothly and like clockwork. We'd been accepted into the Portuguese society with great friendliness.

A handsome lad Humpy had certainly become. He had dense, long and stiff eyelashes that gently turned up at the ends, probably to protect his eyes from the harsh African sun and rain, very beady, intelligent eyes with pale irises which missed nothing, and bristles sticking out of his nostrils. His hearing was excellent and he had plenty of courage. On one occasion, he took on the adult pedigree Brown Swiss bull which charged, Humpy merely giving him a dose of his own medicine by an enormous stab with his powerful beak, closing that affair with the bull backing off suffering a bleeding nose! Humpy's feathers were metallic coal-black, his wing feathers particularly strong, though we never measured the span. A photo of him sitting on the seat of one of the monkey-motorbikes shows the enormous size he'd grown to. His long, heavy beak was slightly curved near the hairy nostrils, and came to a sharp pointed end. Humpy could dig and enlarge a hole that he'd made simply by opening his beak and forcing the soil loose. One of his favourite games was to play football. Keith and Stuart would ride their Honda monkey-motorbikes while kicking a football around and Humpy always joined in the fun chasing the ball. Keith's job, being the maintenance of farm machinery, sometimes meant he'd be working near the house and Humpy would saunter over, squat down beside Keith and take a keen interest in all that was being done, picking up each nut or bolt, all the while having a soft undertone conversation, then putting the items back where Keith originally had them. He found Stuart's fishpond, and within a few weeks had devoured all the fish. Quite often, Humpy would bring in frogs that he'd caught and present them to us.

One afternoon, while we were having tea and freshly made scones with butter and jam, Humpy came in and stood beside the table. He could quite easily see what was on the plates. Then he began salivating profusely and drooling from his beak. It was frightening. We thought he'd maybe eaten a poisonous frog, so I immediately picked him up, rushed him to the bathroom and with a flannel washed out the saliva, which was all over the inside of his mouth and on his tongue. Cleaned up, he was free to go and I went back to finish my tea. No sooner was I seated, than Humpy was back, drooling profusely again – we now realised because he wanted what he saw us eating, so we gave him his scone! From then on he was present at afternoon tea. Humpy was able to fly and cruise around, and was going further from the house. He knew when we'd be going in the VW Kombi to Serpa Pinto, and shortly after we drove off he'd fly alongside then hop onto the roof luggage carrier for a free ride till we reached the end of the farm road. As we turned onto the main district road, he'd take off and fly home to sit on the ridging of the house. On our return from town, at the farm turn-off, there would be Humpy again, flying alongside. How he knew when we'd be there was amazing. With a sudden swoop, he'd settle on the luggage carrier once more and hitch a lift home. He was such a dear and greatly loved member of our family.

None of us, including the staff, was able to get along with Beryl's boyfriend, Terry, for many reasons. He thought only of soccer, frequented the pubs in Serpa Pinto where we would have to hunt for him, and was given to drunkenness, fighting and brawling. The crunch came when he physically assaulted Beryl when she was 6 months pregnant. Without further ado, we paid for his return ticket, took him to the airport at Serpa Pinto where he flew on to Luanda then to Rhodesia. There was no further contact between any of us. Beryl wanted her own little place, so Ian built her a small two-roomed mud cottage with a verandah, not far from our house. Here she waited out her pregnancy painting and had a dog companion. Then José brought her a crow chick she named 'Squawky'. Bringing him up gave her a lot of pleasure. Beryl was totally unafraid of living alone, and just came over to us for meals. She kept very healthy, and I made baby clothes by hand.

Yet another dog, Bidou, was given to us, a little, woolly white bundle. His owners were leaving the country. With the Veterinary Officer gone to Brazil and not having returned, those folks who now started leaving Angola had no way of putting down their animals. All this brought a kind of uneasiness to us.

A further rather ill-written note was delivered to Ian. This time it said, "If you are South African or Rhodesian you must go or we will kill you." Understandably, this 2nd note was also somewhat unnerving, but we chose to ignore it. There was nothing we could do about these anonymous messages. We were advanced in all our farming plans and projects, were well-settled and had established a home. Most definitely, we were not about to leave due to a handwritten threatening message.

The following is a short-story written by Stuart, aged 14, in 1975 and titled, 'A Day Fishing Trip in Angola':

'We left home at about 11 o'clock that morning. With the rumble of the old 5-ton lorry, and a-bumping-along on the body of the lorry where the seat ought to have been and where I was sitting, we left Fazenda Esperança for a day or two of fishing on the Cuelei River, some 30 kilometres distant. I sat with my brother, Keith's, Jeffery .404-rifle between my knees as we bumped along sandy roads. When we reached Kalulu kimbo (village), about 8 or 10 kilometres from our farm, we turned a left along a broad sandy road still under construction. We stopped about another 5 kilometres further on to pick up Paulo's possessions. Paulo was one of the foremen on the farm. From here we turned right onto a dirt track used by people on foot.

We passed over a few broken bridges in the forest, and eventually came to another kimbo, where we asked the way to the Cuelei River. We had to cross another stream where there were signs of vehicles having been stuck before. Then we followed a bulldozer cutting to within about 2 kilometres from the Cuelei, and in trying to reach the River, we got stuck trying to cross another stream. Having got the lorry stuck in the muddy black cotton soil, we moved our sleeping bags and cooking utensils into the forest, about 40 metres from the lorry. We found a nice and somewhat sheltered spot among the trees. Later on, we tried unsuccessfully to get the lorry out. It was nearing darkness so we decided to go off and see if we could shoot some game for the pot.

After 20 minutes of walking, in the on-coming darkness, we saw 2 red Lechwe about 200 or 300 yards away and on the other side of the stream. It was now already too dark to see the front sights of the Jeffery, so my brother took a chance shot. From where I was sitting, I saw flame spurt out from the barrel and the kick of dust from the heavy slug as it ploughed into the earth a few feet from the Lechwe, which took off in fright. Immediately after Keith had fired, there were answering shots in quick succession from the opposite stretch of forest. We heard a few more shorts fired, which we thought were at the lorry, so we quickly started back to camp, walking in single file. On the way back, we passed numerous piles of elephant dung and tall flattened grass, which proved that fairly recently small herds had been in the vicinity. We cautiously walked into camp, cooked some maize meal, talked a bit and then huddled closer to the fire, and went to sleep.

The following morning we woke early, and decided we would go fishing after breakfast. We followed a foot path down to the River and on the way saw a duiker, and a lot more elephant dung. Having now reached the Cuelei, we assembled our fishing tackle and began to fish. We saw an otter cross the River, which at this particular place was very swampy; after a few more casts I had a large tiger fish follow up. We fished till midday, and caught nothing but a crab, which Keith could not stop boasting about! We arrived back at the lorry, and again tried to get it out of the mud, with no more success. So, we decided to leave the tool boxes and sleeping bags with some *Angolanos* (Portuguese term for Angolan/s) who were clearing the forest a little way from where we were camped. We left at about 2 o'clock in the afternoon, heading in the general direction of our farm Fazenda Esperança. A short time later, we came across 2 grass and mud huts, where a wedding ceremony was taking place. A single Angolano was having a double marriage. They had been celebrating for 3 days and nights by the time we passed by. The night before we left, they would send up occasional red flares over our camp while we were trying to sleep, just to let us know they were still celebrating.

We cut across the forest until we came to the road which had led us to the kimbo before our trip, along the boundary clearing. While walking through the forest we came across buffalo tracks, and luckily did not see any. Once on the road, we walked about an hour-and-a- half. By this time, I was very thirsty. At the next stream I dived in, and put my head into a column of red ants, which I thought was floating weed. After about 20 seconds something bit me in the nose, and I came up doing a merry dance, slapping and brushing, which only caused the ants to become more frantic and biting. My hair was full of red ants, but 10 minutes later, all was well. We carried on walking, and just before dark, we reached Paulo's kimbo, where we had left him. We made a detour round the kimbo as we did not wish to be seen carrying the Jeffery .404 as we would probably have been asked a lot of questions by UNITA. About 400 metres from the kimbo, Keith and I sat down to eat and drink what we had left.

We now had to make for Kalulu, where we came across one of our farm workers, and a UNITA soldier who was very humble as he had forgotten his rifle at the kimbo, and he saw we were armed. After a few minutes of chat, we passed them and continued on our way. We ambled down the last few hundred metres to Kalulu trying to look as casual as possible, so as to attract no attention. We turned right at Kalulu and slowly walked past a group of UNITA soldiers, who were having some

Mary and I went shopping one day in Serpa Pinto, and as usual, had to go to the butcher. Here we bought meat for the dogs and Humpy. Once again, the butcher just hacked off chunks and openly thought we were mad to feed good meat to our dogs and a bird. Mary was appalled at the street dogs that came into the shop to scavenge and pee against the skinned cow heads which were stacked, horns up, eyes still in the heads, and lined up against the counter base – an awful sight. I then took my mother's ladies Rolex gold watch to the jeweller to have a new glass fitted as it had become so scratched and pitted, I was afraid it would fall out. After our shopping and chores, we went to the hotel, our favourite place for Angolan coffee and baked custard tarts. Here, Mary was accosted by a hostile African man who, in broken English, insisted she was a South African. Luckily, Mary always carried her Irish Passport. That calmed down a potentially ugly situation. Once more, we felt pangs of anxiety.

By this time, with the sense of unease that kept surfacing because we constantly heard that many people had started to leave the country, we were living a day at a time. The big firms in Serpa Pinto were still in business, their owners still in command. Most disturbing to us was that a number of Portuguese people kept coming to the farm asking whether we had any foreign currency we would like to exchange for their Contos, the Portuguese-Angolan money. We still had some Rands from our trips to South Africa and had luckily managed to retain a little of it.

UNITA, one of the political parties, had also been to see us on an 'Official visit'. The spokesman, a very black-skinned, arrogant and dandy gentleman wearing pitch-black sunglasses which he never removed, sat in a chair in our sitting room. He spoke English and demanded we give him a lorry 'for their cause', and that someone would soon be coming to collect the vehicle. We were also told, without elaboration or the remotest sense of compassion or emotion from this 'gentleman', that we had to become members of UNITA otherwise we would be killed. Just like that – killed. Humpy strongly objected to the presence of this cold, heartless and undoubtedly ruthless man, and kept pacing around the sitting room floor in a state of extreme agitation, stretching and folding his great wings and opening and shutting his large sharp beak, his beady eyes ever watchful. Our Angolan visitor, extremely superstitious about ground hornbills, believing them to be harbingers of bad luck, was distinctly unnerved by our large pet bird and didn't stay long. Humpy was correct in summing up the character of this individual!

There were 3 political parties in Angola, all of them with contingents stationed in Serpa Pinto – FNLA, MPLA and UNITA – each demarcating their own area, and proving to be a nuisance to every citizen. On the next trip to town, we were all enrolled as UNITA members, had to carry our cheap cardboard cards, and show them wherever we went. Just getting to town was now a bit hair-raising. At the end of our farm road we'd turn onto the main district dirt road and at a short distance further a barrier had been erected so that one couldn't pass through. It was manned by armed, adult UNITA soldiers wearing camouflage uniforms. In the background, just off the side of the road, was a large scruffy camp with smouldering camp fires, some women camp-followers, and raggedly-dressed child-soldiers, some as young as 7, each with a stick across the shoulder. They were being relentlessly drilled on a bare piece of ground by a noisy uniformed army man. We were stopped both coming and going, and all our documents scrutinised; only then could we pass. I cannot say these roadblock people were in any way friendly. Mostly, they were aggressive in their attitude despite the fact that we were UNITA members. Showing their authority was what they intended.

One day in Serpa Pinto, quite by accident, we met the CSIR (Council for Scientific and Industrial Research) pilot from Johannesburg. He was using the company small aircraft and had specifically been sent to Angola to fetch someone from their department. As the aircraft was returning via Windhoek, he willingly took Beryl. We realised we'd have to get her out of Angola, and this was an opportunity not to be missed. All we could do was hope she'd manage on her own. We advised her to take the first job she could get. Later, we learned she was employed immediately as a barmaid by the modern and new Kalahari Sands Hotel set in the Windhoek city centre. Here she was given her accommodation, food and a small salary. At least it was a start, and she could contact Stuart who was within walking distance of the Hotel, having started his 1st year of high school. We could only hope the 2 of them were all right, since by now communication had become difficult. Lindsay was still working in Salisbury, Rhodesia.

We had occasion to go to another area of the country to check out some cattle which were for sale. On the road, we came to a barrier manned by MPLA soldiers. They were a truly dreadful and frightening bunch of bullies. We were lucky to escape their grip. First of all, they confiscated Ian's half-brother, Willie's, WWI bayonet (Willie from William's *first litter*, the son who was shot by a German sniper at Longido, Tanganyika in WWI), which we always carried. It was the tool we used when in difficulties with the vehicle sinking in mud and rock on the back roads. Secondly, they espied our little dog, Minnie, and demanded we hand her over. We refused point blank. I was so distressed at the MPLA soldiers demanding Minnie, and clutching her tightly to me, that I can't, to this day, remember what Ian said that eventually let them decide we could keep her. Minnie had been given to us by the dentist who'd made Ian's dentures, a real work of art. He'd required us to spend 3 days with him to check out the dentures and make any necessary adjustments. During this time, he told us he'd be leaving for Portugal and asked if we'd take Minnie, his beloved little Miniature Pinscher and give her a home, which we did.

Everything in Angola now became so uncertain that Ian and Keith, very wisely, hid several drums of fuel deep in the woodlands, away from any beaten-track footpath, together with our new 7-ton Ford lorry. Neither Mary nor I knew the place chosen.

On yet another day, UNITA came to the farm while we were away, and threatened Keith and Mary. It was João who probably saved their lives with his placating and begging on their behalf and they were left unmolested. Mary understandably was severely shaken. Keith had managed the unpleasant instance well, but we felt the situation was becoming out of our control. We'd have to wait and see what the next turn of events would bring.

One night, we'd all gone to bed and been asleep for a couple of hours when we were awoken, in the eerie stillness of the black Angolan night, there being no moon, by the sound of a vehicle with no silencer. The engine noise carried clearly, getting louder as it slowly approached our house. I felt my blood freeze, wondering just what was about to confront us. For the first time in my life, I can say without shame that I was mortally afraid, overwhelmingly panic-stricken and rendered almost immobile from dread. At this point, I remembered Mrs Hauschild during Kenya Mau Mau days when she would suddenly sit up in bed in the room we shared, shouting "Now they are coming! Now they are coming!" I only now understood perfectly what her utter terror had been. We all arose from our beds. None of us said anything. We just waited.

I can't describe the sense of sheer relief we all felt when it wasn't armed soldiers from one of the factions arriving, but turned out to be Peter and Barbie Gill from Chitembo some 80 miles away, in their Land Rover. They'd arrived at midnight with their 2 very young children and only their suitcases to their names. Everything else was left behind on their farm. They stopped long enough for a very quick cup of tea and to tell us they were getting out of Angola. It was winter 1975. Barbie was shivering with the cold so I gave her my lovely pink mohair shawl which Marge had given me when we left Rhodesia. Their Land Rover had a tarpaulin cover over the back so it wasn't a snug, warm car for their long journey ahead to South Africa. They'd faced a tragedy of their own already with the loss of a third baby while on their farm at Chitembo.

Being so alienated out on the fazenda, and what with the political unrest in the country, we had no news of the other farmers Franz and August, De Jager or the van Rensburgs. Even Peter and Barbie had no idea how they were faring, though we'd heard some time before that Rob had gone to South Africa returning with a truck-like vehicle then left the country. He hadn't stopped in to say goodbye to us. Without telephones or other means of communication, each farmer had to fend for himself and make the decision if or when to leave according to his own circumstances.

A South African mining company sent out their man, Alec Medlycott, who came via us. He said the company was pulling out, and that a very long lorry convoy had gone on ahead.

Still we stuck it out.

Every cent of our money was in Fazenda Esperança. It was just the greatest achievement of our entire lives. In our 1st crop alone, we'd reaped the finest and heaviest leaf ever of tobacco grown at that time in Southern Africa. Silal Tobacco Auctioneers had paid money into our bank for the 1st delivery of baled tobacco and there was more in the barns awaiting transport to Chitembo for export by Silal – exactly what Portuguese-Angola had specifically wanted from us farmers. And, we'd paved the way for Rhodesian tobacco to be exported to world markets via Angola, thereby bringing financial gain to that country in the face of sanctions.

The 4 of us now realised the desperate situation we found ourselves in. The thought crossed our minds that we too might have to flee. But, while there was hope, we would stay and protect our property, home and animals. Fazenda Esperança was the name we'd deliberately chosen for our new Angolan life. We'd hang on to the last.

Then came the morning when a runner arrived saying he'd been sent from the kimbo. He told us that the war in Serpa Pinto had started and that we must not, for any reason whatsoever, go into town, that no-one was coming to work, everyone was too afraid and that when it was safe enough to go to town, someone would be sent to inform us. We never discovered who sent the message, but we were grateful and heeded it. We began to hear the intermittent heavy thud of mortar fire from distant Serpa Pinto.

José sneaked in around about this time. Probably he risked his life. He came to tell us that he was suddenly going blind and could no longer be of any help to us, and thanked us for all we'd done for him.

Despite the civil war, of which so far we'd not seen or received any official report, João stayed to help out. He and Keith had a good rapport. With hindsight, I think he probably felt he would have liked to keep close to us knowing that at some time or other we would have to make the decision to flee the country, and that he could come too. He was a brave man. What's more, he fully understood and appreciated our farming aims, not only for our own gain, but for his country and his people.

Towards midday, we could quite clearly every now and again, hear the sounds of rapid artillery fire and great booming sounds of mortars.

In 2 or 3 days all was quiet once more.

Some of the labour returned. Their plea was again, "You are our mother and father. What shall we do without you? We have no food or money."

Simão, my Portuguese teacher and gardener, told us that all but 8 inhabitants of Serpa Pinto had left town.

A week later, we received a message saying that UNITA would allow us to pass through their barrier to go to Serpa Pinto. Ian and I left in the Chevrolet bakkie. We were starting to get low on provisions. Keith, Mary and little Debbie stayed on the farm.

What follows – the Shelling of Serpa Pinto – by UNITA, FNLA and MPLA, is taken from my diary.

Chapter Fifteen
The Shelling of Serpa Pinto

FNLA
Frente Nacional de Libertação de Angola
National Front for the Liberation of Angola

MPLA
Movimento Popular de Libertação de Angola
People's Movement for the Liberation of Angola

UNITA
União Nacional para a Independência Total de Angola
National Union for the Total Independence of Angola

The beautiful little town of Serpa Pinto (now Menongue) in the Cuando Cubango Province of Angola experienced a bloody battle on 1st August 1975. It was left devastated, bullet and mortar-ridden. Miraculously, no white Portuguese were killed.

It seems that by pre-arrangement between the 3 factions, UNITA (Angolan), MPLA (Zambian) and FNLA (Congo), that a battle for supremacy was designated to begin at midnight on August 1st.

A very rich *mulato* (one parent being white and the other black) businessman by the name of Miranda, owner of shops and workshops etc. and the most beautiful home, married to a Portuguese lady and with 2 children, was also the Chief of the MPLA in Serpa Pinto. He most cunningly and secretly arranged for a further 200 soldiers to arrive from Moçâmedes (now Namibe, situated on the Angolan coast) on the 8 o'clock night train, after which he'd surreptitiously planned that the battle would begin earlier than arranged, 2 hours ahead at 10, to take the other factions by surprise. Unbeknown to anyone else, he and his family would do a cowardly bolt. These plans went awry and left many of Serpa Pinto's inhabitants angry and disgusted.

Unfortunately for the rival soldiers, but most fortunately for the inhabitants of Serpa Pinto, somebody, whilst enthusiastically cleaning or getting ready his gun, unintentionally let off a shot at 5 minutes before 10 that night.

This, of course, seemed to be a signal to open fire and all hell broke loose. We were told that Miranda went to the town water tower where he fired a mortar bomb. From there, he went to Dr Pôtes' house (the Government Veterinary Surgeon) and asked for protection. Dr Pôtes, so the Portuguese say, threw Miranda out. He then went to the TASA pilot's house (TAAG was the national airline, perhaps TASA may have been their agency – I've no idea what the letters TASA stood for), where he remained for 3 hours before Cabral asked him to leave as he was endangering their lives.

The story continues with Miranda going to UNITA saying he'd like to change his allegiance and be one of them. Their reply was to shoot him at point blank range through the back of the head. FNLA added to the fracas then by also wanting to disembowel him. UNITA then threw the body into one of the rivers flowing through the town.

Meanwhile, all and sundry of the 3 armed militia were haphazardly firing in every direction, in the mayhem killing one another. Various groups of the factions got themselves into civilian homes, set up their mortars etc. and had a glorious shoot-out for at least 42 hours. Many bodies were thrown into the rivers.

Civilians en masse, at the onset of the shooting and mortaring, had taken their ready-packed supplies and escaped in their cars, leaving their animals and made straight for the Forest Department Reserve, 16 miles out of town, where there was water, buildings and shelters with facilities, and plenty of cover from the forests. This pre-arrangement had been decided upon because of a good or reasonable measure of safety. Here they spent 5 days living off packets of baby food and suchlike which they'd been storing for some weeks. Supermarkets had been getting low on supplies, so the people had prudently been buying what they could in case of siege – the Portuguese in town knew far more than we did about the situation.

When the people eventually returned to their homes, there was very little left. Most houses were bullet-ridden shells, the contents stolen, deliberately smashed or shot to pieces.

The battle raged so long because each faction had a good 'hang-out' – there they stayed and could not be budged. It seemed that no-one actually ventured out to do any commando tricks. They relied solely upon the indiscriminate firing in any direction within the range of their weapons.

MPLA also had a bazooka, so with the firing, cross-firing, and doing nothing except shooting up the town's buildings and houses, an incredible amount of damage was done to the infrastructure. Even anti-aircraft artillery was used. There apparently had been an inexhaustible supply of ammunition.

On this, our first trip to Serpa Pinto for provisions since the war between the 3 factions, Ian and I were met by a brave young man, Edgar Carmo. He filled us in on all the details of the battle. Then in the Chev we followed Edgar in his car on a slow and quiet drive down the main street of our once pretty town, and went into a few homes. Edgar said it was inadvisable to go snooping further. The streets were deserted of townsfolk.

Driving past, one could see virtually all the houses had smashed windows. According to Edgar, hundreds of bullet holes scarred inside walls and ceilings, proving how indiscriminately and frighteningly the crazed factions meted out their frenzied bombardment. Aside from this utterly senseless destruction, vehicles had been carting away as much as they could from houses and shops, including my mother's gold watch from the jeweller. Edgar divulged it was not only members of the 3 factions that were guilty of looting, but also some of the town's residents as well – private possessions, foodstuffs, robbing the banks and Government Departments, tossing important papers all over the streets and commandeering vehicles (including tractors). There'd been much inane lunatic racing in and about the town for no apparent reason. Ian and I saw vehicles belonging to the various factions racing about in their designated areas.

Slowly driving past the now abandoned and once superb bank buildings with their great and magnificent marble facades we were shocked to see how particularly battle-scarred they were – bullet-ridden and with gaping holes from anti-aircraft munitions, the huge doors open and the enormous glass windows smashed, destroyed office furniture and machines visibly lying around. In the street, bank micro-film and papers were strewn all about, being blown by the wind every which way to be driven over by vehicles, including our own.

Ian's UK funds which had been regularly transferred to our Angolan bank account were by now, unfortunately, exhausted. Of some small consolation, Ian had realised the seriousness of the political situation and on a previous trip to town had sensibly had the foresight to draw out a substantial amount of cash. It was clear to us now from the state of the destroyed bank buildings that there would be no probability of ever getting any further money or of having any possibility of bank dealings regarding any form of our financial assets. Discussing this matter later with Edgar, he confirmed that whatever one had previously had in the Serpa Pinto banks was now lost indefinitely.

Surprisingly, the bakery was intact having escaped the shelling and looting, ironically deliberately kept in working order for the production of bread to feed the fighting factions. That was lucky for us, as I could buy a pillowcase full of Portuguese bread rolls, which for some reason don't go mouldy.

Our Supermercado (Supermarket) was deserted and bullet-ridden so we were unable to get any provisions there.

Edgar took us into 3 houses to see for ourselves the state they were in. One was a beautifully furnished, opulent home with heavy and lovely coloured brocade curtains. In this house, we saw no interior artillery or weaponry destruction, but were appalled and horrified at how, whichever faction it was or all 3 of them perhaps, had deliberately defecated in every conceivable and unbelievable place. Great mounds of human faeces anywhere one looked – on the back of chairs, in the bath, on the Persian rugs, beds and tables, even on the fireplace mantle-piece, obviously deliberately put there. Apart from the sight of this abhorrent stinking human excrement, some of which it was obvious had been strategically placed, there was the 'zizz' of hordes of buzzing flies attracted by the putrefying stench. It is a common phenomenon, this 'vulgar practice of evacuating the human bowels on another's property or possessions' and witnessed in other parts of colonised Africa, aptly named 'shitting on the white man', examples I've personally and factually known of being in Kenya and Rhodesia. In surveys done it was found that mealie-meal eaters, who at one sitting consume large quantities of this high roughage food, evacuate huge quantities of faeces when emptying their bowels.

Another residence we entered was now unliveable owing to the destruction of the walls and ceilings by anti-aircraft munitions, empty shells lying around in enormous quantities, the possessions looted.

A 3rd home had 26 (mixed race) people living in it, forced to shack up together, their houses having been completely destroyed. A few were cheerful, others completely shattered, with no hope at all and some said they'd never have believed such things could possibly happen. Then there were those who were utterly disgusted to have to acknowledge that amongst the town's residents were some peasant-type white Portuguese who'd actually taken part in the looting of other people's homes or businesses.

Still following Edgar, our return route took us over a bridge spanning one of the 2, what used to be, pristine and gently flowing rivers. Edgar had warned us that bodies had been flung into the water at several points. Glancing over the side as we drove over the bridge, we saw the gruesome sight of 3 naked bloated bodies floating together, washed up against the river-bank.

Driving past, we could see the Governor's Pink Palace was mercifully not affected by the warring factions, there being no sign of attack, the manicured lawns and gardens remaining intact.

FNLA had a monstrous-looking slow-moving truck, with a huge so-called gun protruding menacingly from the rear, which was well-covered with a tarpaulin. It was in fact, an asbestos pipe painted in camouflage colours, and looked authentic enough. It probably scared the hell out of the naive population, but did not fool us. The ironic side of this is that the truck always had to be parked on a down-slope enabling it to roll to be started – we witnessed this and made sure we kept a straight face.

The war for supremacy had ended with the deaths of many people – some had been rounded up and then shot, and bodies thrown into the rivers.

After the initial battle, some of the MPLA, and including one white Portuguese by the name of Bianco, were transported to a place about 45 kilometres from Serpa Pinto on the road to Chitembo, called Aldeia Dumbo. Here they had their throats cut, and we were told, later were burnt en masse. It appeared that nearly all the mulato members of the community in Serpa Pinto were MPLA.

Another important mulato to be killed was the Notario Publico. He'd always been helpful to us. The odd hundreds of escudos we always had to pay for legalisation of various documents, I personally found worth the cost merely from seeing the man, in all seriousness, make his quite fantastic signature. This consisted of 17 scribbled circles within each other, 5 dots and a line below, all the while gazing out the window or importantly giving himself airs. With the greatest of difficulty, I always managed to keep a straight face, while the Notario Publico's 'man Friday' was dutifully impressed with this great show of learning and importance.

The senseless destruction of our once charming town was utterly depressing and incomprehensible to all law-abiding citizens, and the vast majority of the inhabitants decided to salvage what they could and leave. The same situation had occurred in other towns bigger than Serpa Pinto.

Pre-civil war, people had become very nervous of the political situation, and it was then that 25 tough Portuguese men from Nova Lisboa (now Huambo) in the neighbouring Bié Province formed a group, and by any and every means possible armed themselves with whatever came to hand. Together with some organisers, Edgar being one of them, they spread the word that they would escort people out of the country via South West Africa. For this service fees had to be paid – apparently the total amounted to the price it would cost to buy a jumbo jet. Many people in Serpa Pinto had already contributed, well before the idiocy of the civil war began. At the time, we were totally unaware of these plans.

Edgar Carmo having physically taken us to see the widespread destruction vehemently pointed out to us that our family must leave with the convoy, escorted by the mercenaries in their Land Rovers from Nova Lisboa which would be passing through our town any time soon. He also said we wouldn't have to pay anything because we were 'estrangeiros'. We learnt too that about 10 days before the great battle,

could, doing the milking and feeding the livestock, but it was now impossible to work the tobacco or the barns.

Eight days after the start of the war, around 10 o'clock at night, our dogs went mad barking. Keith and Ian went outside to look, but couldn't see anything. After a short while, the same thing happened again, but this time 2 black strangers were at the back door. Their body language showed us they were in a highly nervous state. We invited them inside, and attempted to fully understand the problem. They jabbered in Afrikaans. Only Ian spoke the language but not fluently. What we understood was that they were cold and hungry and were brothers from the UNITA camp. The elder brother was dressed in army uniform and had come to commandeer our old lorry which would be used to transport more troops to Cuchi where more trouble was expected. Their 'plan', they said, was that the younger brother was to stay and guard us, and to prove this, he nonchalantly brought out a hand-grenade which he was carrying in a small briefcase, and said he would 'protect' us.

We refused their offer, so after demanding the keys from Ian, off the 2 men went in our old, grey 5-ton lorry that Ian had used for transporting the labour to and from the kimbo. Luckily, and unbeknown to them, our new 7-ton lorry was still in the woodlands where Ian and Keith had earlier hidden it along with the drums of fuel.

Next morning – and we suspected the previous night's tale was another 'cooked up sham' – back came a weary and sorry looking younger brother with a new story. He said he'd, "Run over a rabbit and while collecting it the MPLA had opened fire on them not far from our farm." The smart and saucy young man of the night before was no longer! He now, after probing questioning, admitted he was a SWAPO (South West African Peoples Organisation) member and had joined MPLA. His elder brother, who was a UNITA member, was trying to hide him by sending him to us. The hunt by UNITA for MPLA was still very much in force. Both brothers originally came from Rundu, South West Africa.

So much which had been unclear from the night before now made sense. The SWAPO-now-turned-MPLA younger brother had been captured by UNITA, and the older UNITA-member brother was trying to keep him safe. The vehicle, our old lorry, was needed to initially transport the younger brother to safety and then later others to Aldei Dumbo for execution. Older brother had decided he'd leave his younger sibling in our care, in so doing, counting on the chance that he wouldn't be discovered hidden by us and that the 'estrangeiros' would save him.

For 4 days this man stayed in the camp we'd specially made for the 2 Portuguese Caterpillar drivers, a little way off from our house near the Brown Swiss cattle feeding stalls. We gave him food and Ian spoke very kindly and at length with him. Ian offered the youngster money and food and told him to hide in the woodlands and to eventually make his way back into South West Africa, but he seemed to have implicit faith that the 'estrangeiros' were the only ones who could save him from execution.

We realised that sooner or later something would happen. It did. Someone leaked information that there was a stranger hiding on Fazenda Esperança! Back came our old 5-ton lorry, in the morning 4 days later, rumbling into the yard. It was jam-packed tightly with soldiers and a bunch of men and women 'rabble hangers-on', the latter wearing red-cloth headbands and raggedly dressed. We soon would witness that they'd come for the 'human sport'. Everyone, with much shouting and wild frenzied gesticulating, leapt off the lorry and surrounded our house.

Mainly, they were a bunch of armed cut-throats, their leader an Officer in the uniform of UNITA. He told us in no uncertain terms, to get into the house, together with our dogs, which we did, closing only the bottom half of the stable door so that we could watch the 'goings-on'.

We'd been taken by surprise and didn't know what to expect or how serious the situation would become because of the rowdy and undisciplined bunch. We told them to get off our lawn, which we were struggling to grow. The Officer in charge, once the rabble had moved off the grass to the perimeter, then came towards the house where Ian met him. He told Ian that everyone must stay inside the house. Since I was the most fluent in Portuguese, I did the interpreting. The Officer was pleasant and courteous, described who they had come to fetch and asked if he was on our farm. Much as Ian didn't want harm to come to the young SWAPO-turned-MPLA fugitive, he had no alternative but to say, "Yes."

The so-called troops, then thirsting for blood, dashed off towards the river swamps with much whooping, while the Officer made it quite clear to the armed rabble surrounding our house that no-one should make a sound. Shortly afterwards, we heard 5 shots.

Meanwhile, our ever-faithful pet ground hornbill, Humpy, put the war-savages to shame that day.

Humpy had earlier on done his disappearing trick, and not till the rabble had surrounded our house and there was a deathly hush all around, did he suddenly ever so quietly appear again, clearly seen only by us. With what seemed to be an innate perception of the bad-luck superstition of locals regarding ground hornbill birds, Humpy unobtrusively sneaked up behind one of the rabble rousers and gave his best God-Almighty peck with his easily 5-inch, needle-sharp beak on the man's bare bottom showing through his worn-out trousers! Humpy's beak, with just one well-aimed stab to the nose had expertly and fearlessly driven off our charging Brown Swiss bull. I've no doubt this individual felt with considerable pain the full extent of the physical damage Humpy's beak could deliver in one powerful attack on his exposed buttock!

The rebel-savage instantly thought he'd been shot. He screamed, yelled and fell to the ground in a show of heightened agony, writhing about.

Humpy momentarily stood by ever so pleased with himself then managed to get in a few more painful and vicious pecks at legs and backsides of rabble-rousers caught off guard, now running around in a daze wondering what sudden and unsuspected attack was taking place.

Quite simply, Humpy had taken exception to these threatening strangers invading his domain.

As soon as the other men realised their comrade had not been shot, they in turn fell about laughing hilariously. One man nearly collapsed from hysteria at the pathetic spectacle of the 'so-called shot soldier' who had instead been pecked in the nether end by a bird!

Humpy now, with great intelligence, took the hint and flew off, well away from the house. We privately indulged in a sense of satisfied smugness and pride. Humpy, with fearsome determination and his reliable weapon, had quietly and mercilessly attacked a 'brave' rebel, wounding and reducing him to an embarrassingly laughing stock amongst his war-mongering comrades!

During this time of tension and until Humpy had defused the situation with his excruciating pecks, the SWAPO-turned-MPLA man had managed to escape towards the swampy area of the River Luauca, about a mile distant. He was caught an hour later.

The rabble troops, with much glee and shouting, brought back the exhausted young man they'd hunted. He'd been stripped naked and his elbows were pulled behind his back and tied together with thin strips of pliable bark. All the while, he was being lashed with sapling boughs or brutally beaten in the face with the butt of a rifle, or someone would take a leap and kick out at him. He took the vicious assault without a murmur or show of any emotion.

Ian had told Mary and me not to watch, but given that the situation could in some way possibly affect our lives if things got out of control and we also became focused targets, sadly we did observe the punishment meted out on this man. The memory caused us many sleepless nights.

The young captive was then brought around to the rear of the house to where the lorry stood. Ian together with Keith, were asked to identify him. Mau Mau atrocities in Kenya were something Ian would never forget. The stakes were – our family – or the man. There was no alternative but for Ian to identify him. Now the broken figure was flung onto the lorry, which then drove away with much shouting and brandishing of weapons by the victorious rebel-savages.

In my heart, there's no doubt that Humpy's bravery saved our lives that day by turning an extremely volatile situation into what I felt sure would become a much repeated 'hilarious war story' amongst the gun-happy soldiers and their rabble hangers-on.

FNLA then visited us for maize as they were short of food and spoke of the situation, making a great pretence that they needed more good white farmers to come in and farm productively. They were a far better disciplined bunch than UNITA of that area, but had a worse reputation for extreme cruelty to their captives. They were mainly troops from

Congo. The MPLA, who'd molested us either on the roads or in the town before the war, were from Zambia and spoke English. FNLA spoke French, a small amount of Portuguese, and very little English. UNITA truly seemed to represent the people from the country of Angola and spoke Portuguese, though we never came to understand why troops from other countries took up the civil war in Angola. Perhaps they were mercenaries brought in, and had we known, it wouldn't have made any difference to our situation.

We now learnt of a man having been shot simply because he wasn't carrying a 'Carta', an Identification Document. We were told many times that no bullet could 'pierce' Jonas Savimbi, a great nationalist and the leader of UNITA. He was a large African man, born and bred in Angola and had been much revered by the Angolan people. He is reputed to have been able to speak 5 or 6 languages.

We had no gas for cooking or for the fridge. The diesel fuel we used in the night light paraffin lamps was so awful that we had to put in a good number of naphthalene mothballs which improved the quality of the flame and diminished the distinctly unpleasant, cloudy smoke given off from the diesel.

Keith made us a most handsome, solid outdoor fireplace-cum-oven-stove near the hot-water heating system, the sides of which were built with bricks. The cooking top was an old lorry door, and any baking etc. that normally required an oven was done on top of the lorry door in a well-cleaned oil drum with a piece of iron as a lid, held down with a brick. A good fire underneath kept the 'stove' sufficiently hot for cooking.

Our flour supply had now run out as well, and rather unsuccessfully, we tried to make some sort of bread, quite hard and unappetising, out of maize meal. Luckily, the Brown Swiss cow was giving so much milk we had enough for us and the dogs. The sugar gift was a godsend, and the dried bacalhau fish from Edgar's family we decided to keep in case of really dire food circumstances. By this stage, we had about 50 turkeys which kept us in plenty of eggs. We had sufficient meat, so at no time did we go short of food while we lived on Fazenda Esperança.

Ian, unable to buy cigarettes, had to smoke his own grown-and-dried tobacco, which was carefully selected, finely shredded and sprinkled with honey and rum or vanilla, and steamed in a cloth over a pot of boiling water. It smelt really inviting and the aroma was wonderful. He said it was the best ever pipe smoking he'd had.

Two of our Angolan staff from the kimbo, and João came to live in the camp we'd originally built for the Portuguese Caterpillar drivers – mud and wattle rooms with thatched roof, outdoor fireplace, long-drop lavatory, piped water and stand-up tap connected to the main water supply. With their help, Ian and Keith tried to continue as best they could with the farm work, but it was well-nigh impossible to do much except odd jobs without a full labour force. With the exception of these 3 men, the Angolan workers preferred to live at their communal kimbo.

José by this time was completely blind. We were told by João that he'd lost all hope and just sat in the sun outside his hut not wanting to communicate with anyone. Why he'd suddenly gone blind we had no idea. Personally, I think this affliction was something to do with a particular small species of fly found in Angola that reminded me of the flies which caused blindness in the Turkana people of Northern Kenya.

One midnight, we heard the rumble of vehicles on the main district road near our farm turn-off, an all too familiar sound invoking dread. None of us said anything, but I sensed that the unease we all felt at that time had each of us entertaining the idea of making a dash to hide in the bush if necessary. With great relief, it turned out to be a false alarm – we learnt later that it had been a convoy of heavily laden lorries passing through en route to the border.

It was a Friday when Ian and I went to Serpa Pinto again for any sort of supplies. We'd paid our labour force up to the time of the war. Since then, they'd stayed at their kimbo afraid to come to work except for João and the 2 men who were helping out with odd jobs. We didn't hold out much hope of finding money in Serpa Pinto and when we'd tried explaining to the staff following our first trip to town shortly after the battle, that the banks had been blown-up and there was no money left in them, our workers found this utterly incomprehensible.

There was no fuel left in Serpa Pinto, no gas, paraffin, diesel or petrol. Some of the civilian population had already been disarmed months before when Portugal itself had been shocked and blasted by the book written by General Spinola – at that time coming to be known as

'Coup de Abril 25' (Golpe de 25 de Abril) – and crudely known by the locals as 'Spinola's Wet Dream'.

Now there was more distressing gloom with the news that a batch of 4 battalions of Portuguese soldiers had arrived from Portugal to help MPLA. Added to which, Silal, the tobacco auctioneers in Chitembo, Bié Province, still owed us thousands of Contos for delivered tobacco. Everything we knew of had come to a dead stop.

During our absence that day, FNLA from the neighbouring Province of Bié came to the farm and demanded machinery. It was a most frightening experience for Keith, who sent Mary and little Debbie to the tobacco barns for some sort of cover, because not only did FNLA soldiers threaten Keith's life, but they also beat up one of the labour who explained that the owner, Ian, was in Serpa Pinto. These men invaded our house and made themselves comfortable – just another bunch of ill-disciplined, 'loose-cannon' rabble trading on the authority of their uniforms. FNLA soldiers were well-known by all Angolan people for their cruel behaviour. The whole episode was nasty in the extreme. Had it not been for João again, anything could have happened, as he took over the negotiating from Keith whose temper was beginning to fray.

Later, arriving back home empty handed having found no supplies, both Keith and João told us what had happened. This incident had shaken them both. Discussing this later between ourselves, we came to the conclusion that Bié FNLA was taking a huge chance by coming into another Province. They'd used the excuse of looking for and demanding machinery as a cover up for 'snooping' to see what was going on and what 'spoils' they were hoping to get later on, counting on the fact that we would probably leave like so many other people.

The following day, once we'd first again ascertained all the correct facts from Keith, Mary and João regarding the unpleasant FNLA visit to our farm, Ian and I went to see the Chief of FNLA in Serpa Pinto, a man reputed to be reasonable. We took João with us to corroborate details of the incident. The FNLA Chief provided Ian with a letter for the Catota branch of FNLA in Bié Province, stating that they had no right to enter another province, and that he was not amused!

On our way home at about 7 in the evening, still on the main tarmac road and only a short distance from Serpa Pinto, we were stopped by Edgar Carmo. He was returning from Nova Lisboa (now Huambo) in Bié Province where he'd been negotiating with the mercenaries about the planned exodus. We informed him of all recent developments and João again verified the FNLA incident.

Edgar told us that a massive convoy of 2,000 vehicles was on its way from Nova Lisboa picking up vehicles from Chitembo and other towns en route, being escorted by the same mercenaries he'd earlier told us about in Serpa Pinto. He said that the convoy should reach our little town the next morning and that this was *our last chance* to leave the farm. He urged and begged us to please listen, reiterating that this truly was the only opportunity left to leave Angola with protection.

Arriving back late at Fazenda Esperança, we had a hurried supper Mary had prepared, followed by a life-or-death conference between ourselves.

The thought crossed our minds that as frightening as the Bié FNLA incident had been, had it not occurred forcing Ian and me to make the trip into town to see the FNLA Chief, thereby returning home so late and luckily meeting up with Edgar on the road, it may well have been that we wouldn't have known about the last convoy out of Angola in the morning or heard about it in time to join it.

We all agreed that despite anything we could possibly ever do or had done to change the situation and remain on our farm, circumstances were now completely and devastatingly, sadly and seriously beyond our control in Angola. The time had come to make the extremely agonising decision to heed Edgar's advice and desert our farm, animals and the last shred of hope we'd held onto.

It was a chilling realisation for the 4 of us.

Foremost and above any of our material possessions, even our home and farm buildings or the crops in the fields and tobacco in the barns, abandoning our animals went against everything in our beings. It was the biggest and hardest decision any of us had ever had to make and weighed heavily on us emotionally. We felt overwhelmingly racked with guilt and heartache.

The saying, "The Captain of a ship is a lonely man," was truly poignant. Ian, as our 'captain' and ultimate guardian of our lives and those of our animals and livestock, bore the greatest and final responsibility of the decision. It was painful to see the heartbreak etched on his face and in his eyes.

Now, with such short notice and so few hours to prepare for meeting up with the convoy, and the allotted time hours of darkness only, coupled with the UNITA roadblock not far from our house, Ian was caught in a personal dilemma of not being able even to put some of our animals down. Firing off just one shot was tantamount to summoning disaster with loss of our lives had we been besieged by trigger-happy soldiers in response to any gunfire in the night.

Ian kept saying he'd return one day. My heart pained much seeing him having to leave his animals, farm and the work he so loved, again – a déjà vu now of Westlands, Kenya, but worse and almost incomprehensible being the 2nd time around after his dedication in Angola to ensure success.

I really don't know what Keith and Mary felt while packing. We all had a job to tackle within a certain period of some hours and that is what we set our minds to. None of us cried. Time on this particular night, unfortunately, didn't allow for such indulgences of the heart.

Frantically, from 9 that night, we started packing to be absolutely ready to leave the farm by 6 o'clock in the morning in order to be in Serpa Pinto by 8.

Each of us understood perfectly that we had a vital deadline to meet, and that we'd fare better in the little time we had without succumbing to emotions that could even temporarily hinder our progress. The situation required total acceptance yet a realistic view of what we might require for the journey ahead, not forgetting too those most meaningful possessions of ours to be packed as best we could manage.

Our personal belongings went into several suitcases and the 5 crates we'd arrived with in Angola. Two of the crates were items of real value that had never actually been unpacked since we left Kenya in 1973 as our fazenda-house wasn't yet completely finished.

As all arms and ammunition had already been taken from the civilian population in Serpa Pinto in April 1975 – and we don't know why, but at the time no-one came to our farm to disarm us – Keith dismantled his .404 Jeffery rifle. Together with the ammunition, he packed it all in grease and sealed it in PVC toilet piping that had been surplus when installing the inside bathroom. This package he put down the outside long-drop toilet per Ian's instructions – there to remain for eternity, I imagine.

Ian and Keith then removed all vital working parts from the farm machinery. There was still 170 tons of shelled maize, and the yellow maize was not yet completely harvested, much of it still on the cob and stored in the barns. Apart from the delivered crop of tobacco awaiting auction at Silal in Chitembo, there was yet another lorry load of sorted, compressed and ready-packed baled tobacco, stamped with our logo, 'Crown Tobacco Fazenda Esperança', in our sheds ready for transport. Huge piles of unsorted leaf were lying on the tobacco barn tables.

We packed constantly and with great urgency throughout the night, without pause, sit-downs or sleep. Ian and Keith were mostly outside in the darkness by paraffin lamps seeing to vehicles, machinery, fuel, water containers etc. Mary and I concentrated on the house and women's tasks, one of which was to break the glass of pictures and remove the frames as glass was extra weight and picture-frames took up too much space.

At one time or another, we all had difficulty deciding about items to take and what not to, trying to make the right decisions, and really not knowing how to go about packing up our lives in a few short hours. We tried to think what we'd need on an unknown convoy route. Throughout there was total co-operation amongst the 4 of us.

Mary and I packed the VW Kombi with blankets, bedding, food and clothes for the 5 of us. Then Ian and Keith drove the Kombi to the loading ramp against which the new 7-ton green Ford lorry – now retrieved from its hiding place in the woodlands – was backed-up. They'd already loaded onto it the last two 44 gallon steel drums of diesel fuel that had been half-hidden in the ground and covered with foliage. Keith and Ian had levered the drums onto the back of the lorry using 3 planks then stood the drums up behind the cab. Our double-bed mattress was used as a buffer between the diesel drums and the Kombi once it was driven onto the back of the lorry. The mattresses from

Keith, Mary, Beryl and Stuart's beds were packed along the sides of the lorry, and as many of our possessions as possible were pushed under the Kombi. The Chevrolet bakkie was also fully loaded and space was made to safely stand the 2 monkey-motorbikes on the back as well. We left a red VW Beetle, without its rotor.

The plan was that Keith, Mary and Debbie would be in the Ford lorry. Ian and I and our 4 'inside-house' dogs, Cricket, Pepu, Minnie and Bidou would be in the Chevrolet bakkie which had sufficient petrol to get us well beyond Serpa Pinto. After that, if we weren't able to find more petrol, the Chev would have to be towed by the diesel lorry. We hoped the 2 drums of diesel were sufficient for us to make it to the South West African border.

Edgar Carmo's specific instructions were that we should be at a certain place behind their now abandoned family's machinery workshops by 8 in the morning at the latest, and that we should keep a very low profile. Any undue noise would surely bring one of the armed factions, guns at the ready for further 'blood-letting'.

We realised that we'd need some extra time since we were forced to pass through 3 roadblocks – UNITA, not far from our home; the 2nd, MPLA, which could not be by-passed was just outside Serpa Pinto's perimeter housing; the 3rd the FNLA bridge roadblock on the national road at the entrance to the town. At this stage, the men manning the roadblocks were all very tricky, nervy, quite unpredictable and armed – in short, gun-happy and irrational, as Keith had experienced.

Before even the first faint morning light and still using paraffin lamps, we'd all had our last hot baths. While having a quick breakfast of oatmeal porridge and coffee, we tuned into BBC and heard for the second and last time a message which roughly said, "All British subjects to be airlifted must get to Luanda Airport by 06h00 tomorrow morning…"

Fat chance, we knew. Luanda was at least 1,000 miles north of us. Bridges had been destroyed and people with guns were roaming the countryside shooting at anything that moved. Even if we'd managed to get to Luanda airport, it was highly unlikely we'd have been able to take anything with us apart from a suitcase of clothes. So broken-down like this, perhaps being in the south of the country and leaving with the convoy was the better of the 2 options.

João and the 2 labourers turned up to give a helping hand to Ian and Keith outside. Under normal circumstances, arriving this early would have been exceptionally unusual for our staff, though João had been with us the night before when we'd met up with Edgar on our way home and he'd told us about the convoy.

I had a feeling the 3 men had been quietly watching us during the night with the comings and goings from the house and the paraffin lamps burning. Quite possibly, they'd been keeping an eye on us for some weeks already for any signs that we might also be leaving, along with so many others who'd already fled the country. Apart from this, the kimbo was situated just off the main district road at the end of our farm road turn-off and the workforce would have seen and heard vehicles leaving Angola and received news via the 'grapevine'.

The 3 men were devastated and confounded to learn that we were abandoning them. *"Vocês são nosso pai e nossa mãe, e vocês vão e deixam-nos,"* they said ("You are our father and mother, and you are going and leaving us").

What they said was true. Added to our animals, the farm and everything else, leaving our staff was a further dimension to the burden of guilt we felt, but there were no other options left to us.

By this time, Ian had learnt a little Portuguese and Keith had picked up the language though by no means fluently. With Keith's help, Ian explained to the men that the time had come when we had to leave due to the warring factions and the highly unsafe situation in the country, and that we had already been threatened several times ourselves, that he and Keith hoped to return in the not too distant future. They could see the house was still fully equipped with beds, furniture, stove and fridge etc. Ian had bought me the best quality on the market 6-plate gas stove made in Spain and gas fridge from Switzerland. We'd only been using our household appliances several weeks when the gas and paraffin had run out in Serpa Pinto.

Ian then carefully instructed the men that as soon as we'd driven off the fazenda that the people from the kimbo were to take as much of the maize as possible before the Army came to commandeer it. He made sure the 3 of them understood that they were to share out all our poultry and livestock – turkeys, the few remaining goats, sheep, the pedigree herd of 6 Brown Swiss cattle, as well as the huge beef herd of by now approximately 80 Angolan steers. Thankfully, we didn't have any pigs at the time. Listening to Ian, it finally registered and 'hit home' with huge shock, utter dismay and broken hope to Keith, Mary and me how desperately wrenching the whole situation was.

I knew from the very quiet yet precise tone of my husband's voice as he spoke to the men giving specific clear instructions so that they properly understood to share out our animals and take the maize, that he'd been desperately fighting his own inner demons all night whilst packing up our farming life to the best of his ability with Keith in the short dark hours till morning light.

Backed into a corner not of his making and without options of staying that ensured safety for his family, I think Ian had come to the realisation and painful acceptance that Angola for us was over. His UK funds were now finished. Our first tobacco income was forever untouchable in a blown-up bank. The rest of his crops had to be left on the land and in the barns. He had no income to be able to return to Angola, without first finding work in another country – which would take who knew how long – by which stage there'd be nothing left to return to. And he now faced a convoy journey without even enough petrol in his Chev. It was better to give our livestock and crops to our workers. There were at least 300, if not more, people in the kimbo. If anyone was to have the benefit of what we were forced to leave behind then better our staff and their families than the life-threatening Army factions who'd done nothing other than terrorise and destroy people's lives, property and bring the country to a civil war standstill. Our labour had worked hard and loyally for us, always been polite and respectful, never stolen a single thing and had felt as much pride as we did in the 'building' of Fazenda Esperança. We were grateful for their many efforts. They too were suffering the hells of the civil war and would certainly fall on hard times in the future without work and food. The 4 of us knew that without us on the fazenda our livestock would be eaten, and that even if Ian hadn't told the men to take the maize and animals that soon everything would be taken anyway, if not by them, then undoubtedly by any one or all of the 3 Armies.

I understood too, the enormous pain in Ian's heart not being able to put his cattle down, particularly his pedigree Brown Swiss herd. In Kenya on Westlands, he'd at least had this option available, as painful as that decision had been, but in Angola the abattoir had already closed down a while back. Neither could he sell his cattle as there was no-one left to buy them. At the time of purchasing the Brown Swiss herd (we were thrilled to get these cattle) from the Government Agricultural Station, Ian had not been aware that the sale of the cattle was due to that Department actually closing down owing to the unstable political situation. By now, Angola had ground to a halt. Even with the remotest possibility that Ian could ever make it back to Angola, he couldn't afford to replace his cattle without first working, perhaps for the rest of our lives to save sufficient funds.

I struggle to find words to adequately explain the sheer heartbreak of the circumstances now crowded in on us in the enormity and finality of leaving our animals in fleeing Angola for our lives. These memories forever remain in our minds and hearts. In civil and tribal war, of which Africa has a plentiful and on-going history, always the innocent, both human and animal are caught in the middle, suffer hunger and huge hardship and pay the ultimate sacrifice.

In hindsight, there was so very little we were informed of regarding the political turmoil as it progressed in Angola. Perhaps this was due to us living out of town on the farm and having little to do with the Portuguese townspeople in their everyday life. Possibly this was exacerbated by being 'English strangers', maybe even 'mad strangers', as well as the language difficulty. By the time we heard news and started to gain an adequate understanding of circumstances, it was usually after events. Often over the last months of uncertainty, I'd thought back to the note I'd been handed in Luanda almost a year earlier in November 1974.

Right now though, we would forever remain grateful to Edgar Carmo for personally informing us of the dire situation and the coming convoy. He had at heart a true concern for our well-being. It was absolutely imperative, now that the decision had been made to leave, that we remain focused, reach the convoy in time and concentrate on arriving safely in South West Africa from war-torn Angola.

We knew with some certainty that we could leave Cubango since his natural dog-life was one of regularly wandering the 21 miles to Serpa Pinto and back, but we had to make the sad decision to leave 3 of Cubango's stray tag-along dog-friends too, that he'd picked up at the kimbo on his travels and brought back to the fazenda with him. They were not 'inside-house' dogs and spent most of their time lying around outside the homestead, were fed by me, and had been excellent watchdogs, particularly at night. Nevertheless, leaving any of the dogs was heart-wrenching, but Ian said under the circumstances it was impossible to take more than 4 with us.

During our frantic night's packing, we'd asked Ian the same question about putting these dogs down as we'd asked him about the Brown Swiss Cattle – we'd have preferred to shoot them rather than abandon them. His adamant, though absolutely understandable answer was the same, and the sense of guilt was emotionally crushing. We were all between a rock and a hard place. Firing off gun shots in the Angolan night was risking one's life and tempting the army from any one of the 3 factions to descend on us, in which instance the results would be catastrophic. Not forgetting the UNITA roadblock a short distance from the end of our farm road and that sound carried for miles in the vast, still quietness of the bush, particularly when all life was (supposedly) at rest.

I'd been fighting my own inner hell too, about Humpy, whilst frenziedly packing. He'd grown enormously while he was with us and had been feeding himself for some time, eating the fish in the pond, catching frogs, lizards and small snakes, and often brought these creatures into the house to show us what a clever chap he'd been. Humpy loved this attention and appreciated us petting and talking to him, knowing he was being praised, then he'd toss whatever he'd brought to us into the air, catch and swallow it. He was just beginning to get his 'wattles' (bright red-coloured fleshy, knobbly things that wobble about and hang down under the bill and on the throat of his species – females have grey-blue, sometimes pinky colour wattles). We knew he'd soon seek out a mate, more than likely joining up with a group of his kind, there being many wandering around the savannah chatting to each other. Often we'd seen them entering the woodland not far from the back of our house where they went to roost in the trees. Their booming calls are uttered from tree tops at the first sign of dawn.

In Humpy's case, when he was old enough and able to, he roosted on the ridging of our tin-roofed house and performed many antics while booming out his call – an amazing and very noisy alarm-clock – no-one could over-sleep! It was wonderful lying in bed listening to Humpy and thinking about what he was up to on top of the house. He was so full of joy every morning.

There was no way we could take Humpy out of Angola with us or subject him to being caged which he'd never experienced. It would be impossible without time to acquire the correct documentation to be able to pass him through the Veterinary Red Line on the border into South West Africa. Where would we get the authorised papers from with the country in civil war collapse? In all probability, we felt Humpy would be safer in the environment he knew and was used to. Added to which, the beliefs of the indigenous peoples regarding this specific species of bird, some taboo never fully explained to me, made it further unlikely they'd seek him out in particular. Humpy was extremely wary and untrusting of strangers. A question always in my mind though was why José had been willing in the first place to even bring the chick to me? Perhaps the money was sufficient for the risk? I remember no-one else was around the day José arrived with Humpy-chick. Now part of me felt a sense of guilt for having tamed Humpy in the first place and then not being able to take him with us. The other part of me felt an overwhelming sense of love and gratitude for so many deeply cherished, incredible memories. Still, it absolutely tore my heart to leave him, our brave and courageous pet hornbill, who'd been such a special companion and saved our lives. We'd forever be in his debt. I knew he'd initially miss us, being the only family he'd known, but given some days I fervently hoped the call of his natural habitat would prevail, and he'd seek the company of his own kind.

Keith and Mary had arrived from England with no finances and had now lost all their hard-earned money from Fazenda Esperança in the shot-up Serpa Pinto Commercial Bank. Our financial assets had been lost in the Banco Totta, as well as all our Life Insurances that we'd taken out at the time of our marriage in Kenya in 1952, which had always been stored, ironically, for safety in bank Deposit Boxes. We still owed money to our friend the timber merchant, as well as to the turkey lady, but had no idea where they were, and had we known anyway we'd have been unable to pay them. I had Senhor Gil Vieira's forwarding address. Once we reached safety and had found a home, I would try my best to ascertain the whereabouts of both these creditors so that Ian could pay our debt.

We were virtually penniless except for the few South African Rands left after exchanging most of this currency with Portuguese people fleeing the country. After we'd paid our staff, we had some escudos, mostly small change Angolan money, and had few material possessions to our names, but we knew we'd reach some sort of safety eventually. All of us fully comprehended that we were getting away from a very ugly situation held entirely in the hands of war-mongering, gun-happy savages from who we had no way of defending ourselves. I'm sure Mary felt safe with Keith, as did I with Ian, both men being level-headed, capable, calm and strong in character. They were our rock of stability in time of crisis. With them we weren't afraid to face the uncertainty of what lay ahead.

It was time to leave. The first light of day signalled the beginning of our journey as we put out the paraffin lamps.

Experiencing so many traumatic and conflicting emotions, none of us wanted drawn-out or tearful goodbyes with the staff. João and the 2 men stood sadly subdued outside the house. The powerful diesel engine of the new Ford lorry idled quietly, a rich purr of comforting positive hope to safety and a new life, contrasting strongly with the aura of despair as Keith, Mary and Debbie waited, ready in the cab. I particularly felt sorry for Keith and João; they'd been good friends apart from co-workers, had great respect for one another, and without doubt João had saved Keith's life in the terrifying experience with FNLA.

There seemed no point in locking the house. Ian simply closed the doors. As I got the 4 dogs into the Chev, I heard him say to the men that he hoped to see them in a few weeks. I could only hope the men would take the 3 stray tag-along dogs back to the kimbo with them as they'd originally come from there, and that Cubango would cope and also find a new home. Sadly, I couldn't see a long life anymore for our magnificent giant python in its lair without us on our fazenda.

On the final drive down the farm road of Fazenda Esperança, Humpy, as was his flight custom, made a couple of impressive low aerobatic swoops alongside the Chev then landed with expert grace and precision on the luggage carrier of the Kombi now atop the back of the lorry in front of us, there as usual to be our escort, proud as ever. When we reached the main district road turn-off, Ian and I watched Humpy lift with effortless beauty into the air and heard the great flap of his wing feathers as he turned and flew back on his familiar flight-path to our now deserted and desolate homestead. I felt a lump in my throat as the tears welled in my eyes to hear those dear ground hornbill wings beat one last time for us and I didn't dare look at Ian or speak to him: I knew he too was fighting back the tears. It was like a final 'goodbye'. My mind's eye could picture Humpy first landing on the roof then dropping to the ground to walk around the silent house, devoid now of normal daily comings and goings and noise, to check on matters, his sharp eyes missing nothing, his head turning from side to side.

In matters of the heart, words oftentimes prove inadequate. My only consolation is to say that we had the privilege and experience of knowing and sharing our lives with a wonderful, highly intelligent and greatly loved bird. Humpy would remain always in our thoughts daily in all the years to come – our beloved friend and guard.

Shortly after turning onto the district road, Ian and I stopped briefly at the kimbo of Camossa where our staff lived, while the lorry carried on slowly ahead. All the people came out, visibly despondent and fearful for their own futures with the civil war unrest, and really didn't know what to say about us leaving, but showed how dreadfully upset they were in this goodbye, as were we. Ian told them to go as quickly as possible to the fazenda and collect what maize they could before the Army came to take the grain and everything else. They kept waving till we could no longer see them, and I remembered how happy and excited they'd all been, running after the Chev when we first arrived not so long ago, the year before in February 1974.

In truth, we'd achieved our Angolan dream and even more than we'd originally wished for, in part due to the superb efforts of our workforce without whom we could never have coped. They'd been an absolute pleasure to work with. We took many dear memories of them all with us and had only the highest regard for their characters and abilities.

Thinking back to the first morning when I'd seen José and João watching us outside our tent, carrying a shotgun and each with a machete and I'd automatically assumed they were terrorists, I could smile a little now in retrospect in the midst of all the heartache and turmoil as we caught up with the lorry and drove towards the UNITA roadblock. For I'd come to know José and João only to be quite the opposite – truly good, hard-working, loyal, ever respectful and grateful, brave men.

Chapter Sixteen
Convoy Excepcional

Ian had told us before we left our fazenda that we should at all times purposefully project an air of calm, remain so and drive slowly, as he felt we could expect trouble from the UNITA roadblock not far from our farm.

I was filled with trepidation as the check-point came into sight.

They'd taken our old grey lorry 'for their cause', would they now notice we had a bigger new green lorry, wonder where we'd suddenly got it from and realise we'd been deceitful and hidden it somewhere?

Ian and I had been through the roadblock twice the day before in the Chev bakkie when we'd been to see the Chief of MPLA. Would they notice that the lorry was jam-packed with our possessions including the Kombi? They'd said they'd kill us if we didn't become members of UNITA.

Anything could happen. I felt my heartbeat in my throat. Escape for us was paramount.

The lorry came to a stop ahead of us and an armed soldier walked to the cab door. We could see him saying something to Keith. The conversation went on for perhaps 3 minutes during which time the soldier's frustration became obvious. He started gesticulating with one hand, gun in the other, his body language becoming aggressive giving Keith a hard time.

The big Ford engine idled in front of us. Ian had the Chev in low gear waiting to follow Keith the moment the lorry pulled off. The UNITA camp was on the right of us, fires burning, full of soldiers and rabble-rousers. As the moments ticked by, I could almost hear Ian silently willing Keith not to wait too long as every extra unnecessary second spent at the roadblock could put us all in jeopardy.

Suddenly the sound of the lorry engine changed as Keith slammed the powerful vehicle into gear and foot down, charged the barrier, the soldier on duty really shaken, just managing to get the weighted pole up in time. The moment the lorry moved Ian was right behind, both vehicles through in quick succession.

On the drive to town, I started going through a mental check-list of what we'd decided to take with us. With utter dismay, I realised that due to the stress of circumstances, exacerbated by the quick decision to leave and followed by the turmoil of packing throughout the night, that I'd forgotten 4 irreplaceable and highly valued family exercise books which were some of William's (Ian's father's) diaries pertaining to the 1930s, the early days of his 3rd marriage to Ian's mother, Mater. I'd stored the books on the rafters of our farmhouse to keep them out of harm's way. There was no way of getting them. I felt bad about it and sad too: those times in our family history were now lost, but such is life. Of greater importance was the way forward for us, to remain positive, reach safety and start anew.

Thankfully, we didn't have any trouble from the MPLA or FNLA roadblocks. The town was eerily quiet, no visible movement anywhere, yet we knew those citizens awaiting the convoy must have been ready and waiting, keeping discreetly hidden. We arrived before 8 in the morning. As instructed by Edgar, we parked our 2 vehicles below street level at his family's now empty, very large staff parking lot. It was partly roofed and well-hidden from the public eye, and situated at the entrance to town. The extensive Carmo family business showrooms, spare parts departments, workshops and other hardware materials were all at street level, closed down, looted or smashed to pieces.

We waited on tenterhooks in our hiding spot for hours. Ian and I with the dogs in the Chevrolet bakkie were luckily parked under roofing so we had some shade, but Keith, Mary and little Debbie were in full sun as the lorry couldn't fit under cover. Already dead tired from no sleep the night before, the heat was draining and further exhausting, added to which we all had to remain as quiet as possible. Being cooped up in the lorry cab was a trying time for Mary who was about one month pregnant with her 2nd child. She had to keep Debbie quietly amused by singing, telling stories and repeating nursery rhymes. Debbie had some of her toys in the cab, one being a rag doll, 'Andy Pandy', that she'd taken a fancy to before they'd left England.

After some time, Edgar arrived to speak to us, and asked whether I'd agree to drive out, on the convoy journey, a dark green diesel Mercedes saloon car that belonged to a Colonel Botha of the South African Army

Intelligence who was based at the South Windhoek Army Camp at Suiderhof, Windhoek, South West Africa (Namibia). The Merc was not marked as an Army vehicle and had been brought to the workshops parking lot awaiting someone willing and able to drive it to Windhoek. Filling the entire boot of the car, weighing it down in the rear, was a very heavy sophisticated broadcasting apparatus, the Army personnel having long since returned to South Africa by air. I said I would drive the Merc from Angola to Windhoek.

At about 3 in the afternoon the first convoy cars, maybe about 100, arrived from Nova Lisboa (now Huambo). Watching, as the mercenaries in front stopped the traffic, Ian and Keith then walked to the control and spoke to the men. The barriers were lifted without further ado, and the cars passed into Serpa Pinto town. They'd experienced no difficulty at the FNLA border control – things had suddenly changed – the FNLA had split. Several men of this new faction had offered their services to accompany our convoy and give help should any other control points prove difficult.

Finally, at a signal from Edgar Carmo, we joined the next section of the convoy. Senhor Carmo (Edgar's father, a fabulously wealthy man), Edgar (he was about 32 years old) and his sister, Isabel, the Serpa Pinto airport radio controller and Daniel, the baker, were the only people we knew of who were still in town when we left. Although Edgar had played a major role in selflessly helping organise the convoy for others, he'd told us that he planned to start again in Brazil. Senhor Carmo said he would stay hoping things would turn out all right.

Our advance was exceedingly slow, the convoy having started to move from Serpa Pinto only at 4 in the afternoon when the sun was burning hot, the cars like ovens. Along the route, all and sundry pushed in and joined the long line of vehicles. The first leg of the exodus measured a mere 100 kilometres. At midnight, the convoy halted, giving us our first most welcome stop and a quick meal.

There was no cooking that night. Mary quickly arranged tinned food, the mainstay being baked beans. We didn't attempt to eat the bacalhau (dried cod) we'd brought with us, it was most unappetising, both the smell and to the eye. Luckily, the dogs seemed to like the dried fish which they gnawed on. They'd behaved impeccably – maybe they could feel the tension all around them or sensed there'd been a great change to their lives and were fearful of what was coming next. The day before, when Ian and I had gone to see the MPLA Chief, we'd bought another pillowcase full of Portuguese bread rolls which would last for a time. Despite going stone hard after a few days, the rolls don't go mouldy and can be softened up either by steaming or pouring a little hot water over them. Mary later said the bread rolls were probably her saving on the convoy journey as they stopped her suffering too much from morning sickness.

That night there was no washing-up. Whatever utensils we'd used just went back into the black tin storage trunk which was easily lifted in and out of the Chev (I'd owned this trunk since my first Nakuru School days in Kenya and remember my mother buying it at one of the dukas in Ol'Kalou). From the packed water containers, we gratefully managed to make some delicious, strong, ground Angolan coffee the Portuguese way, in our cheap aluminium coffee pot, on a small fire of kindling collected by Ian and Keith from the roadside. Then the 2 of them had to climb up and over the lorry sides, take out the folded tarpaulin, pull out the 2 single bed mattresses from either side of the Kombi and throw them down to Mary and me. We laid them on the tarpaulin, head to toe, in the ditch next to the lorry, and had some light from the vehicle headlamps to see what we were doing. Some of the bedding had been in the boot of the Kombi, and everything had to be tidily returned to the same packing place afterwards. I'd put a blanket in the Merc.

It may sound strange to say that as a close family and considering the circumstances, we didn't talk much to one another that night. There was little to say really except ask a few simple questions, eat and say goodnight as our exhaustion was overwhelming. All we wanted was to fall as soon as possible onto our pillows and mattresses, get into our sleeping bags or pull over a blanket. Sleep was what we desperately needed, which we'd been without for 18 hours. Our four dogs, Pepu, Minnie, Cricket and Bidou were my travelling companions in the Mercedes since Serpa Pinto. Having no other option anyway, they were content to lie and sleep most of the day.

We'd been told by the mercenaries, who took it in turns to drive up and down the roadside ditches issuing various instructions, giving a helping hand, answering questions and generally monitoring, that we must be up again by 4 in the morning, do what we had to do – in our case, it was essential to make a quick pot of coffee to keep us energetic, wide awake and alert – and that everyone should be ready for the entire convoy to move forward at daybreak. This gave the 5 of us a very short night's rest and hardly any sleep. Debbie fared best, having lots of short naps during the day, and being on Mary's lap in the luxury of the lorry cab was soporific. Mary said having a small child to entertain helped keep their minds off the gravity of the situation though it was very difficult trying to keep a young child's mind constantly occupied whilst cooped up in a small space. Just getting everyone and their cars ready for departure took a couple of hours. We were never late or held up the convoy, thanks to Ian's, Keith's and Mary's efficiency.

At Serpa Pinto we'd seen some of the convoy vehicles, and were now beginning to comprehend what an incredible conglomeration of things, people, animals and cars were in this exodus, although we'd no real idea of what the entire line of vehicles looked like. We only knew there were approximately 1,500 cars of every description, and from what we'd seen they were loaded to the hilt with chickens, birds, pigs, calves, goats, dogs, cats, turkeys, household staff, and even one guinea-fowl in a cage. The latter made me feel we should've brought Humpy, but when we gave it further thought, we knew he couldn't have survived captivity as he'd always been free and he was a lot bigger than a guinea-fowl. The stress of a cage for days on end, the heat and noise would've been too much for him, perhaps he'd have flown off and not being familiar with the territory we couldn't bear to think what may have happened to him. Much as it pained our hearts to have left our dear Humpy hornbill behind, we felt his chances were better knowing the house to go back to and being able to fly free in search of food. We felt sure that when he discovered we'd definitely left our home and that nobody was around, Humpy would've automatically flown off to join up with some of his own kind.

There were lorries and trucks loaded with all sorts of furniture, coffee, maize, machinery and household goods. Fuel tankers, low-loaders carrying earth moving equipment, tractors, trailers, buses, cars, caravans, vans, every form of vehicle imaginable – just so much stuff individual to their owners who probably hoped to start business again once they reached safety, or that they could sell what they had – the most amazing assortment of possessions.

The condition of the roads was very bad which took its toll on the drivers. We went from graded roads to no roads, by now into thick bush country travelling on an extremely narrow winding dirt track, sometimes through deep sand or black cotton soil. There was no horizon ahead or to the sides except bush, no sight of the long trail of vehicles behind, nor could we see the cars way ahead, only those which were directly in front or behind us.

In our quest for safety, the only certainty we had in any 24 hours was that day would follow night; that we'd relentlessly keep driving until at some point the convoy would stop for a few hours for the night, and that sleep was craved by mind and body. When we stopped, we always managed to make our little pot of ground Angolan coffee.

The car ahead of me, a red Mini, appeared to have nothing except a young mother, her 2 little daughters, their toys and blankets, and was driven by their father, a thin and exceedingly nervous young man. A new cream-coloured Citroën had only a middle-aged married couple, presumably some luggage in the boot, and their 2 Dalmatian dogs regally sitting on the back seat. Strangely enough, I recognised these dogs from a trip I'd done to Sá Da Bandeira having particularly noticed them on leashes, being taken for a walk down a street. I so much admired these beautiful canines and vowed to myself that one day I'd have a Dalmatian in my home.

We were now informed by the mercenaries that we were on our way to a place called 'Caira'. Then we'd be going south into dense bush with hardly any habitation, to meet up with a road which was still in the making through a chana of deep black cotton soil somewhere near the Cuito River. Owing to the enormous earthworks, it would now probably be impassable due to heavy rain.

The Chevrolet bakkie, driven by Ian, now ran out of petrol and had to be attached by a long rope to the back of the Ford lorry driven by Keith. Thanks to the 2 of them thinking of everything we could possibly need, the thick rope had been included when packing the vehicles. Driving became frustratingly difficult for Ian being towed through the harsh countryside with no real tracks to keep to and little visibility because of the closely tailing convoy vehicles causing powder-like dust clouds which permeated everything, coming through every crevice in the Chev cab. Since there was no breeze to carry it up and away, and with no way to escape this dust, Ian's face, clothes and the bakkie interior were covered in a pale greyish-coloured film. Without doubt, breathing this in for so long must have had a detrimental effect on Ian's lungs.

Keith refuelled the lorry on convoy stops, siphoning diesel from the 2 upright drums on the back behind the cab by placing one end of a flexible pipe in the drum and sucking on the other end to remove air and get the fuel flowing. There is a knack to this, one has to be very quick otherwise diesel can get into the mouth and be ingested. The other end of the pipe is then immediately placed into the fuel tank and, it being lower than the diesel drum, gravity causes the fuel to flow freely from the drum to the fuel tank. Other people also refuelled their vehicles by siphoning either petrol or diesel, from their own supply or from other vehicles.

Some people and drivers were aggravating to a degree, necessitating stops. No sooner had the convoy moved on than someone would run out of petrol and have to be towed, or they had to stop for a call of nature. Other times it was a puncture. Some merely needed a break. There were even stops for those who felt they were unable to face the unknown and had to be comforted and encouraged.

Driving in some cases had become frenetic and many women were hysterical, tiny children had become fractious or were ailing in some way or another. Pregnant women and the elderly were suffering discomfort. Our faith in finding safety had to be given blindly to the mercenaries, by now numbering only 20.

By this time, Keith estimates we were now in 'survival mode' which seems exactly the right way to describe how we all must have felt, but never voiced. At our stops we still didn't talk much. The stressfulness of the situation and having to drive so slowly left us all physically, emotionally and mentally drained.

Trying to drive through the dense unmarked bush was scary. Everywhere looked exactly the same so that most of the time we felt disorientated. It was a sandy track, extremely difficult for small cars. All the vehicles would come to a stop while the mercenaries, as quickly and efficiently as possible, would sort out any problem, in many cases just giving encouragement. Most of the people had lived quiet, serene lives in a well-ordered society, amongst law-abiding citizens, and had, at the press of a button, electricity or at the turn of a tap, water, and a civil Police Force had maintained the epitome of law and order – there had been nothing to fear. Now thrust into this ghastly experience, it was, for the majority of people, a total nightmare of chaos, uncertainty and hardship. And, where were they being led? What lay ahead in the following days? No-one could give an answer, let alone an opinion. All we personally assumed was that we would at some time arrive at the South West African Border which is what Edgar had advised us of before we left Serpa Pinto.

Several of the mercenary Land Rovers had two-way radios, so messages could be passed up and down the line and sometimes we would be informed of what the messages were about. The FNLA group who had agreed, for a sum of money, to help get the convoy through the unknown bush, positioned men ahead of us along part of the route – they directed the convoy so that there would be no confusion as to which direction to take.

I had a quiet chuckle, tongue in cheek, when one 'nosey parker', seeing a woman driving alone, halted me and officiously came to the window to inspect the contents of the Mercedes. Our Keeshond dog, Pepu, had been quietly lying on a blanket on the back seat. When the intruder stuck his head through the rear window, Pepu rose up and with a fury and deep growl, threw himself into attack position. The man had one hell of a fright, shouting, "A lion, a lion!", and hurriedly waved me on to take a right turn down a bush track. Obviously, the man had never seen a lion before because Pepu was steel grey in colour not brown, and smaller, but per his canine breed, naturally did sport a huge ruff of hair around his neck not unlike a lion.

One memorable day, we did exactly 3 kilometres. The track had now become abominable. People collected firewood during this slow progress and we lost a full day of travelling. It dawned on the mercenaries that new and strict planning would have to be enforced.

From now on, the convoy would stop only at given times, there would be no jumping the queue, family and friends would stay together, and the final stop of the day would be at sundown when there would be a one car space between each vehicle. Privacy was out of the question. We still had the occasional blind panic, like the time a rumour started that the MPLA were hot on our heels. To say the least, it had been unpleasant driving at a slow pace in the heat and dust, nose to tail from the time we'd left Serpa Pinto, and nerve-wracking on many occasions. I remember only once getting out of the Mercedes to stretch my legs and have a quick look at the vehicles closest to me, then getting back in and immediately driving off again.

We were astonished to discover there was a substantial quantity of firearms amongst the Portuguese. It was amazing to think that after the entire Serpa Pinto town's homes had been searched and all weaponry confiscated in April 1975, that so many firearms had been overlooked. Now, hunters looking for game to eat went out into the surrounding bush. There was a lot of haphazard firing, which sounded fairly close to where the convoy had stopped in its tracks. We thought it very lucky there were no accidents from this indiscriminate shooting. Mary and Keith remember seeing someone returning from shooting a ground hornbill 'for the pot', dragging it along with out-spread wings, which thankfully, I did not see.

At sundown the convoy halted. Keith and Ian threw down the tarpaulin on the ground alongside our vehicles. Mary and I arranged our sleeping bags, pillows and things we needed for the night, made a small fire, brought out the basic cooking utensils and for the first time enjoyed Edgar's bacalhau (dried codfish) since we'd become hungry for protein. Bacalhau was in some ways a staple food amongst the Portuguese people – perhaps it can be called the 'local equivalent of jerky'. Up till this time I could hardly face eating this strong smelling, unappetising, crudely dried cod fish in large chunks. I think we all felt the same, but it was the only protein we had on the journey. Boiled till soft, it was then eaten by using the fingers to break it up. In the end, we were grateful for it (bacalhau in no way resembles the pre-packed, attractive looking, individually wrapped smoked haddock boxed by well-known brands, which one buys in today's modern supermarkets).

By now, we were severely lacking sleep having been deprived for days on end, and were badly in need of a total body wash as well. Ian, being used to clean clothes every day, said he couldn't stand his socks much longer. I felt I needed a complete wash down having been in the habit of bathing every day. Mary and Keith must have felt the same. Mary had brought a potty with her for Debbie's toilet use in the lorry cab. There certainly was plenty of room for some of her toys and books and other odds and ends. The men were unshaven, clothes needed changing, and body odour was something we had to live with. Truthfully, by this stage, it was hardly noticed. Whatever food Mary prepared for us was eaten quickly without further ado and little conversation. Either we had to get going or wanted to sleep. None of us remembers having chats on this journey. There were too many other important issues to deal with.

The thick rope from the lorry attached to the Chev kept breaking, and slowly got shorter and shorter. It was surprising it lasted so long. The dust cloud, just lying in the air, now so awfully thick created by the wheels of a multitude of vehicles was choking to breathe. Ian was covered in it from head to foot. I could've scraped off the layer of fine powder on his face with a knife. He could hardly see ahead, and being towed so close behind the lorry, steering the Chev for him became extremely hazardous and tiring.

On several occasions, we had to pass through almost deserted villages in the middle of nowhere, most of the thatched huts burnt to the ground, with some still smouldering blackened tree stumps, all leaving a nasty acrid smell. A wretched, frightening post-civil-war sight, leaving me personally with a sense of guilt at seeing suffering people and their starving dogs in such distress, without being able to stop and give some form of help or assistance. The few remaining ragged villagers ran after us, screaming, "You are going and leaving us like dogs." No-one stopped to pick up any of these people. About 30% of our convoy of 4,500 people was either black or mulato (of mixed colour).

Then we came to the practically impassable chana area the mercenaries had warned us about. I'd become quite used to wading through the chana mud on the main district road to Serpa Pinto in the rainy season, but in comparison at about 100 yards wide, it was minute to what we now faced. This would be an experience I'd never forget – an approximately 3 mile stretch of bulldozed, built-up sand, mud and rocks which had been worked on with the intention of eventually completing a bridge to span a huge chana. Bringing the convoy to a halt, here the organisers decided that the saloon cars should go first and I became separated from my family in the lorry and the Chev.

The sight before my eyes was appalling. A wide black ribbon stretching straight ahead and clearly an evil thick mess. Without Ian or Keith to encourage and help me, how I felt about the situation was simple – I just had to do it, drive through the chana, come hell or high water: there was no turning back. The only way was forward, being the main objective at this time, to keep moving and get onto hard ground. I didn't entertain any negative thoughts about my family left behind – Ian and Keith were competent men; Mary, capable and in charge of their welfare and little Debbie's. Each of us had our own part to play; acceptance of what had taken place and of what lay ahead – good humour, patience and no hysterics being the order we personally stuck to throughout.

After the red Mini, I was the 2nd car to attempt the drive through, but neither of our 2 vehicles went more than a few yards before sinking to their axles in this viscous smelly mud. A Land Rover and Willys Jeep were simultaneously deployed to pull and push us through. The Mini being a lighter vehicle was mostly pulled through the chana while 3 mercenaries were taking out what they could of the stones and rocks which surfaced every now and again because of the churning up of the mud.

It was one heroic effort to get all the cars moving at a snail's pace through this stretch. A lot of serious damage was done to some vehicles: their 'bottoms' were ripped out and they then had to be towed through. The Mercedes, having a heavy metal plate under the front, which saved the engine from severe damage, but being heavily weighted in the boot would only go a short distance before grinding to a halt, the wheels uselessly spinning in deep black mud, yet again needing assistance. Despite being the 2nd car to go into the cotton-soil sludge, I was one of the last cars to make it to the other side of the chana.

Once the small and low-slung vehicles were through, then the rest of the convoy attempted the morass and all were guided safely, though I wasn't there to witness their trials or progress through the foot deep rock and stone strewn mud as I was already onto hard ground and moving ahead to the line of cars. Had we not had the Land Rover and the Willys Jeep assistance, the small and low-slung cars would never have come out the other side. We would've had to wait for the chana to dry out, which may never have happened as chanas always seem to have spring water in them; added to which Angola has a significant rainfall. One never knows the amount of water that lies under black cotton-soil until one steps into it – in no time at all, it is one big glutinous mess. In Kenya, in those early days, some which I clearly remember, black cotton-soil was the worst possible terrain to encounter while travelling either by vehicle or ox wagon.

It took 36 hours to get all the convoy vehicles through the chana, mainly thanks to 2 African Angolans who had a huge Allis Chalmers crawler tractor and earth mover. They were employed on the road-building and worked non-stop to get everyone safely to the other side onto hard bush-track. Once the car section of the convoy was across the chana and assembled, a collection was made and a good sum of money given to these 2 Angolanos. Much as I wanted to, I unfortunately, couldn't contribute anything as I had no money with me in the Mercedes, the little we had being with Ian in the Chev somewhere behind me with the heavy vehicles.

Back to driving on solid terrain once more, there were people wanting to jump the convoy queue and go ahead. Fiery tempered Portuguese of all colours wanting immediate attention were shouting and gesticulating. Panic reigned as it had on other occasions. Very few patiently and quietly waited their turn.

The dogs and I had no food or water for one day and one night, totally my fault. For me, food is no problem, but lack of water is the worst. I had, unforgivably, forgotten to take water with me in the Merc. The weather was unbearably hot, the dust perfidious. Most gratefully, the Portuguese occupants in the cars in front and behind realised that I was alone and had nothing, and with thoughtfulness and generosity brought me some baby cereal mixed with water in a plastic dish that tasted really good. Then another lady brought me a hard-boiled egg and some Marie biscuits which I shared between the dogs, but because we had no drinking water my canine companions suffered more than I did. Speaking to her, she told me this was their 2nd exodus. The 1st had been when they fled the Belgian Congo (now DRC Democratic Republic of Congo).

Instantly, memories took me back to Belgian Congo times from long ago and I could empathise with their trauma and hardships. Vehicles of fleeing people had come through our shopping town of Eldoret, Kenya. My mother had died and we'd donated her clothes to the Eldoret Municipality, where shelter and food had been provided for the Belgian Congo refugees. I remember a Ford pick-up driving into the petrol station where I'd been filling up my car. The man almost collapsed, mentally broken-down. He'd been stopped, his wife and 16 year old daughter taken at gunpoint, and he'd been told to 'drive on'. He left the Congo and arrived safely in Kenya, not knowing what happened to his wife and daughter. Just a week later, Ian and I witnessed another pick-up refuelling, again a Congo car, with the windscreen and door windows securely barred. The single driver-occupant, a man, was suffering mental and emotional collapse because he'd shot dead 2 men who'd tried to pull him out of his vehicle at one of the roadblocks. Dirk Coetzee, who at the time was the Manager of the Ford Motor Company and Ford petrol station in Eldoret (an acquaintance, our Ford regularly serviced at his workshops), told us of several other instances.

Reaching a bend of the River Cuito we had a convoy stop which allowed us to collect water from the river. The dogs and I seemed not to be able to get enough into our bodies to quench our thirst. Pepu leapt in for a swim and a drink while the other dogs lapped their fill at the river's edge. I believe they were too nervous to enter the unknown dark water which had a very distinct dank smell. Pepu, with his mass of heavy soaking wet coat came out and shook himself violently, but was anxious to be back in the car so the beautiful green leather backseat was sodden and took several days to dry out completely.

The route taken roughly followed the big Cuito River which finally joins the main Cubango and Okavango river systems ending in the Okavango Swamps in Botswana. This meant that at times we were within reach of water and allowed a stop to wash pots and pans and collect water, the latter with a few hazards. Parts of the river made one feel decidedly 'on edge', slow moving dark and deep, with masses of reeds, tall bulrushes and thick swamp grass along the edges. Sometimes, the sides were so steep it was difficult to get down to the water, and the horrible mud was the kind that sucks one in. There were crocodiles too, so we were told! I never saw any, but I certainly was very wary, not liking the look of the river at this particular stop, especially as I was still travelling alone, just the dogs and me in the Mercedes, with the rest of the car section of the convoy.

When we eventually teamed up again as a family and came near to the river the water mid-stream was clear, and on the long day-stop we had a marvellous bathing session, this being our one and only chance of a body wash the entire journey. Ian was greatly relieved to be rid of the thick dust all over him. Undergarments were washed and hung on bushes to dry while we took it in turns to bathe at the only place where there was a tree with a huge root system well above the water-line overhanging the river, the roots ideal as a support to grasp onto while submerging one's body as deep as possible in the water. The only drawback was that everyone nearby needed this spot at the same time. The water was soft and lathered frothily. Theft was a problem so vehicles couldn't be left unattended. We took it in turns to bathe and apart from this one opportunity for washing and laundry we wore the same clothes continuously as the rest were packed in suitcases, too high and difficult to reach on the roof-rack of the Kombi atop the back of the lorry.

There was no privacy of any description. On this only bathing occasion, when I was completely naked standing well-soaped on the tree roots, the sounds of crashing through the reeds made me suddenly realise this was the perfect place for hippopotamus. It turned out to be 2 young men trying to get to the river-bank. They were so astonished on seeing me, and I realised it wasn't the time to be a prude; they simply turned back and I continued with my short cold bath in the softest of water, soap suds everywhere. It really felt heavenly to be clean again after the stress, exhaustion, dust and lack of body hygiene of the seemingly never-ending convoy journey. This quick bath was an opportunity not to be missed, but there was no time for luxuriating. The fear that crocodiles might be lurking deep in the black water (black, because the river ran over black cotton-soil) made it difficult to see into the depths.

Whatever the occasion the convoy halted there was no time to waste, so chores had to be done quickly. Mary had mealtime stops down to a fine art. There were many frightened people too afraid to go off the roadside into the bush to relieve themselves, so 'having to see a man about a camel' was a common example of lack of privacy. We always made sure we went as far as possible from view of the vehicles, taking Ian's Kenya Regiment army-issue spade with us, known as 'the cat's paw', so we could dig a hole in the ground when necessary and cover the spot over with sand.

We always went to sleep fully clothed. The nights were chilly, the days very hot especially for Ian, being in a vehicle with the windows closed due to the wake of another's dust. Theft usually took place while others were sleeping; clothes, shoes, food, etc. was stolen. The culprits were never caught, and the people were furious as stealing from others was most unusual amongst them. In Angola, or in fact any Portuguese country, theft had never been a problem. Presumably, now under these difficult convoy circumstances of little, it was 'every man for himself and take what you can when possible'.

I was to have my own scary experience. Two African men, one with a firearm and the other with a bow and arrows, suddenly rushed out of the bush in front of me. Slamming on the brakes, I only managed to stop the Mercedes when the radiator-grill was against the stomach of the man wielding the gun. Nothing would make him move, and there was no way for me to get my car off the deeply rutted track. Aggressively, he came around to my window, called me a few filthy names and gestured that he'd shoot me. I only had time to reply, "You must be a donkey not to see the following cars," when Keith behind me in the lorry drove around the corner and saw what happened. The armed man reckoned he'd try the same trick with the lorry driver, except that he hadn't counted on him being my son, or that Keith was able to lean out of the lorry window, reach down and catch the aggressor by the throat, dragging him a few yards before letting go. We'll never know whether this man had a loaded weapon, if the 2 were high on dagga or just plain blind drunk, or more likely trying to stop the exodus of people and vehicles.

One day, Keith picked up a good length of chain lying in the track, so the Chev bakkie could now be towed with greater ease and at a better distance from the lorry, but this beneficial stroke of luck didn't last long. The chain disappeared one night, possibly the rightful owner taking back what was his, so the short rope was reattached. With the daily driving conditions worsening, Ian was having a bad time of it, really struggling with the choking dust behind a huge high vehicle on such a short rope. For so many days, with long driving hours at any one time, he only ever saw the back of the lorry, finding it tremendously difficult to focus properly and suffering horrible disorientation. Though he never complained about this, he did about his dirty socks on numerous occasions. Seeing what Ian was going through, it dawned on me that it had actually been a blessing to have been asked to drive the Merc to South West Africa otherwise there would have been Ian, myself and 4 dogs in the cab of the Chev with all the windows closed for hours and days on end – I'm sure we would not have coped.

We were informed by the mercenaries one morning that we'd reach a fence at a designated place they termed 'Point X', and that we should stop when we got to the fence. They told us that the South African Army would be waiting to take over the convoy and that in the meantime they'd arranged for a water tanker to be sent to meet us. They said they had to get back to Nova Lisboa (Huambo) and left us to continue to 'Point X' while they returned on the route they'd brought us. Later, reports came through that 2 of these men had been shot dead in the sports stadium – I believe it was a public execution – all this information was via the grapevine.

For hours we travelled this last lap unescorted. A water tanker did indeed arrive, and as vehicles passed people were given water as we continued on tracks which wound around thorn trees and bushes with still no horizon, no sign of civilisation, buildings or populated areas, just never-ending bush back, front and sides. We'd no idea of what we'd see when we reached the fence though people took for granted there'd be South African Officials waiting for us who'd assist and allow us safe passage into South West Africa to freedom and safety, each at his own pace. It was blind faith that led the convoy forward.

At around eleven that night, the first cars arrived at the unmarked 'Point X', so assumed because there before them was a slackly hung, 4-strand barbed wire fence. Unable to go further they stopped, not knowing what else to do because there were no South African Officials of any kind and no gate in the fence. With 1,500 vehicles in the convoy they just kept coming, like a 'car-stampede', all jam-packed ever closer together, the front people stopping their vehicles right up against the fence, with the rear convoy drivers not knowing what was going on ahead or why they could go no further. It was a large open area surrounded by thick bush and thorn trees. With no organisers now to assist or direct, the rest of the vehicle line just parked haphazardly wherever space could be found as they couldn't move forward. Eventually, word filtered around that we'd reached 'Point X'.

We were packed cheek by jowl, more and more vehicles cramming up against each other and as near the barrier fence as was physically possible, everyone trying their best to get close to it because there was so much worrisome dense bush around and no mercenaries for protection should something untoward occur. To me, it was as if we were a giant shoal of fish caught in a massive net.

With no officials awaiting us at 'Point X' and only a fence with no gate many people were left flummoxed and dejected, even somewhat afraid and unnerved as to what to do. Others were utterly confused. Our family understood that a border-line can consist of just a fence, though I think many folk expected something more, perhaps a proper border control point. It being late night darkness, after hours of stressful driving desperate with hope for an end to the trauma, the huge disappointment and disarray we now faced exacerbated feelings of anxiety and tension and reduced morale to despondency.

What a dreadful remainder of the night I had being unable to lie flat for sleep. I think we all suffered the same. There was nothing we could do about it except sit out the long hours awaiting the first rays of dawn.

Everyone had to stay put in their vehicles simply because the chaotic parking didn't allow space enough between cars to get out and move around. You couldn't even open your car door properly without banging it into another vehicle.

I felt claustrophobic in the Merc. It was a sultry night, hot and oppressive, the dogs panting constantly, Pepu's thick previously water-soaked coat having now given the leather car seat a damp, dank smell. I started with the windows open and very soon closed them as we were bitten incessantly from the swarms of ravenous malarial mosquitoes. I felt particularly sorry for the dogs. The car being motionless, they naturally wanted to get out having been cooped up for hours, as did I just to stretch my cramped legs. I had to keep shushing Pepu to calm him as he became disturbed and restless as the hours dragged. Having learnt my lesson the hard way and now carrying water in the car for us, even giving Pepu a drink only temporarily eased his discomfort. It was an extremely harrowing ordeal and the noise from thousands of weary frustrated travellers continued unabated.

With lack of sufficient moonlight, a multitude of car headlights blazed, mostly stark white while others had a yellow hue, on bright or dim, going on and off, criss-crossing over the darkened spectacle of jumbled massed vehicles, creating a somewhat distorted black and white image of flickering shadows, accompanied by noise disorientation from 4,500 people in commotion and panic, hooting and shouting. Silhouettes of large thorn trees in the background completed an incredibly surreal scene.

I cannot remember another instance when I was more grateful to see the break of day. Quite early after dawn, a South African Army car arrived. The military men took one look at the multitude of varied vehicles, general chaos and myriad refugees and realised they'd only one alternative. Using a loud-speaker, they ordered everyone, each and everyone, to move back 10 kilometres in an orderly fashion, and that in due course, everyone would be seen to. Back went the massed, haphazardly parked vehicles – another mad traffic dash in the bush to find the best place to be first in line for the time when the authorities would attend to us and allow us entry into South West Africa. Our family chose to stay till the last vehicle had left, watching in wonder as the stampede receded in the distance, witnessing the most ghastly mess left behind by humanity in what would normally have been unspoiled, indigenous and pristine African bushveld. Bottles, tins, paper of every description, and reams of used toilet roll littered the surroundings including human excrement. People had being going to the toilet next to their vehicles. In all, a shocking sight, still crystal clear in my mind's eye.

The South African Army then arrived in full force setting up their headquarters on the South West Africa side of the rickety wire border fence with vertical wooden uprights, stretching as far as the eye could see. Army personnel with wire cutters made an opening, rolling back the fencing, large enough for their smaller vehicles to pass in and out when necessary. They were faced with a real headache, only they didn't know how bad it was going to be! We were at a very lonely, uninhabited place known only to the locals in distant villages as 'Katwitwi', not at that time even marked on a map (though today there is a tarmac road connecting Namibia to Angola at this point).

The first thing the Army did was put up a tented field hospital with doctors and male nurses on the Angolan side of the fence, where we were. Big 5-ton lorries rumbling into Army headquarters on the South West African side could be heard throughout the night. Our little family was so dead tired that even the constant loud noise didn't stop us from having the best sleep since joining the convoy. By this stage we'd lost track of time, reckoning it was about 10 days since leaving Fazenda Esperança.

Deciding to move from the mass of vehicles and people, we found a lovely gigantic fig tree a good way from our nearest neighbours, underneath which we cleared the grass making a reasonable sized patch to put down the tarpaulins for our mattresses – Ian and me together, Keith, Mary and Debbie on theirs. Then we cleared another patch for a big fire place, finding a couple of stones to rest pots against, and around this we set up our camp chairs and small camp table. Ian and Keith made some arrangement to collect dry wood and a large bonfire was lit. Each night was very chilly so big logs were left for warmth to burn down to glowing embers till daylight.

anyone would use them. I've no idea why, but neither did our family as we still had the 'cat's paw' to dig in the ground with and always went far into the bush. Flies were a nuisance, not to mention the ever present small bush-fly that inhabits that type of shrubby, grassland country and which seems to stick onto one's face and bare skin. Masses of ferocious mosquitoes suddenly arrived at sundown and sustained a persistent onslaught throughout the night, though the smoke-filled atmosphere from the smouldering wood while it lasted helped keep them at bay for several hours while we slept.

Each day, the refugees were supposed to collect sufficient food for the numbers in their party. This turned out to be a disastrous plan, as some people were going back to the stores 2 or 3 times a day. The problem was overcome when supplies were delivered to each camp.

The Army brought a full contingent of soldiers to their Headquarters, and also had sufficient fuel for distribution to all the vehicles belonging to the refugees which, in time, would enable everyone to get to the capital city, Windhoek. Chatting occasionally to people, it seemed as though most wanted to go to South Africa or Brazil. Very few told us they were returning to Portugal. Most of them were still inflamed at an incident en route, where the local Portuguese policeman had stopped the second part of our convoy and ordered his men to fire on anyone who tried to get across a bridge, because he said, "All vehicles belong to Angola."

We weren't witness to this event, but several people who were, graphically described what happened. A tragedy could have occurred had a couple of mercenaries not come upon the scene. The Portuguese involved in this incident never stopped talking about it, and the news spread all the way down the convoy line and reached us. Apparently, some of the men concerned were prepared to get fuel and return and 'do in' the Portuguese Policeman. Not long afterwards, news filtered down that someone did, in fact, kill this policeman, but I can't verify this as the news came via the convoy grapevine.

No sooner were we settled in our camps at the border fence, than news via the authorities came through that a further 2,000 vehicles from a different convoy section were due in. We also heard that on a second convoy coming down the coastal area, women and children were being airlifted by helicopters from bogged-down vehicles stranded at the mouth of the Cunene River. We'd been amazed at the number of vehicles and refugees in our convoy alone. This information confirmed to us how isolated we'd been, unable to hear of or comprehend the severity and scope of the political turmoil and unrest in the country as it unfolded. Later, we were told that altogether there had been 4 convoys out of Angola – 2 overland (one being ours), one by sea, and the 4th along the coastline, and that the people on the coastal route had a really rough, tough time. Hearing how monumental the exodus of people had been, it was apparent to the 4 of us that there'd been no other option than to heed Edgar's advice and seek freedom and safety in South West Africa.

Meanwhile our field hospital became busier than ever. Those who were really ill were taken immediately by the Army to the Rundu State Hospital in South West Africa. Two women had been wounded, I don't know how, and some were miscarrying.

It was heavenly going to bed at night. The mattresses were put down on the spread out tarpaulin under the great big fig tree, camp chairs and tables out, a warm log fire, in the loving company of family and new-found friends. We'd fall asleep in a clean atmosphere under clear, starry skies. On early mornings, as the pink light of dawn appeared, first thing to do was stoke up the smouldering embers of the fire from the night before and make coffee. Then came the 'great decisions' we had to make – time for ablutions, collect firewood, whether to open this tin or that, save the baked beans for another time, make breakfasts of oatmeal porridge, and simple lunches and suppers out of tinned foodstuffs. Mary was wonderful with her ability to produce tasty food from so little choice. Rice was cooked to perfection in a pot on the open fire. Somehow, we all managed to have a noggin (drink), whether ours or shared, and make it stretch so that we didn't run out. These simple daily rituals, caring companionship and gentle evenings of relaxation and rest were a balm to mind and body, an exact opposite of the endless gruelling days and nights of uncertainty, mental weariness and physical endurance.

The Portuguese couple who shared the campsite with us under the fig tree felt very sad and utterly despondent. Their 19 year old daughter and 5 year old son had been holidaying in Moçâmedes (now Namibe) with relatives when the war in Serpa Pinto started. Since then, there'd been no communication between the 2 families. Over the various blaring battery-operated radios that people had, messages were sent out to missing family and friends, requests trying to find where they could be, or information saying where they could be found. The South African camp authorities were particularly helpful regarding passing information on as a specific radio programme was aired all day from Pretoria, South Africa, purely to assist the Angolan refugees find next of kin. We were also informed that refugee camps had been set up in various towns and cities in South and South West Africa, some being Pretoria, Windhoek, Rundu and Otjiwarongo.

Each night we were still absolutely exhausted and slept soundly till daybreak. Once again, the dogs behaved impeccably. Our friends remained understandably in deep despair and heartache, and had given the details of their lost children to the authorities, but for the days we spent with them there was no news of their 2 missing children even from listening to the radio every day. From them we learnt a great deal about the professional hunting industry in Angola and shared with them our farming and Kenya deep-sea fishing experiences. Despite their great worry and sadness, our friends were marvellous company, and our time under the giant fig tree at Katwitwi remains, for us, a beautiful carefree memory.

Our field hospital had grown. There were people on iron bedsteads, and on stretchers or on the ground. Another huge tent was brought in and set up. Very elderly and frail people were now in a bad way; it was greatly disturbing to see how weak they'd become, and the intolerable heat by day and really cold nights added to their stressed health. Now it seemed everyone had dysentery. One old man died, and a new baby was born.

It was about now that our little Debbie started getting seriously sick. Then Keith followed. We all finally succumbed to the dysentery, and it lasted a while. Debbie continued being sick on and off. She'd been examined and given medication by one of the young Army doctors, but didn't seem to recover properly.

Having had our British Passports examined, we were told we could leave. We'd been about 10 days on the convoy journey and 5 under the fig tree at Katwitwi, and had delayed our departure a bit to help our Portuguese friends who spoke little English and no Afrikaans at all. The radio request programme with details of their lost children had now brought results that they'd been found in an Angolan Refugee Camp in Pretoria. The couple had been so admirably brave waiting for news. On 5th September 1975, we left to get moving to Windhoek.

Our water containers were full, our vehicles refuelled and we carried spare diesel and petrol. For most of the 45 kilometres on very sandy tracks to Kurukuru in the district of Ovamboland, South West Africa (now Namibia), the Chevrolet had to tow the Mercedes as the boot was still heavily laden with the Army radio equipment, the bottom of the car continually dragging on the built-up sand in the middle of the road. I had some small idea now of how Ian had felt being towed so far under such extreme conditions and circumstances during the traumatic exodus from Angola.

It had been an incredible and unforgettable journey, Convoy Excepcional, from the country, Angola, where we'd gone to farm tobacco with such optimism and enthusiasm in early 1974. Ahead of us lay the long road to a new future in South West Africa in late 1975 – another unknown quantity.

Without doubt, the exodus could have been a lot worse had a group of brave men not been prepared to put their own lives at risk to escort the fleeing refugees from Angola to safety.

At last, through the words of my story, for I have known of no other way to do this, I am able to pay rightful tribute and express my sincere and grateful thanks to the mercenaries.

With regret and some sadness though, I am unable to honour and acknowledge them because in their never-failing selfless courage, which protected my little family every day on this stupendous journey, we never did learn their names.

Chapter Seventeen
'Point X' Refugees

We were now travelling through Ovamboland, a large tribal area in north South West Africa, where one lorry, overloaded with Ovambos (Africans native to that part of the country), swore and cursed at us, indicating that we should go back to Angola. This was the first time we'd encountered open hostility.

On our original safari to Angola through South West Africa in early 1974, we'd taken a different road from Windhoek north to the border through Otjiwarongo and Oshakati (the main town of Ovamboland), so this route was unfamiliar to us.

Finally, the tracks reached the main road leading to the fairly big town of Rundu. We found our way to the Police Station, reported our presence and said we'd just driven in from 'Point X' before the border where the South African Army had arrived to help us, and had stayed at the Katwitwi camp they set up for the Angolan refugees.

The Police very kindly and generously offered us free of charge municipal prefabricated housing, including water and electricity, with 3 bedrooms, bathroom and toilet, which we'd have to share with other Angolan refugees already being housed there. Presumably, these Portuguese in Rundu had come through with a convoy via the coastal route into South West Africa. Unfortunately, the accommodation was in an utterly filthy state. Household refuse was everywhere, the toilet blocked-up and overflowing, the stench so awful we couldn't even enter that room, and thick clouds of flies buzzed in every direction. Apart from this, the house was chock-a-block with people – a Portuguese man, his African wife and 4 children; a Portuguese woman and her teenage daughter; a very pregnant mulato girl and another young Portuguese woman. The mulato girl and young woman had both lost their menfolk. One had been shot and wounded and then drowned while attempting to cross a river; the other had been executed in Nova Lisboa (now Huambo). The Portuguese man was in daily contact via two-way radio with other Portuguese who were still stranded in Mucosse, Angola, which was being held by UNITA.

The municipal compound had many prefabricated houses all filled with refugees, so we made our camp in the shade under the surrounding magnificent flamboyant trees covered in red blossoms. We had 2 clear, starry nights in which to relax and recuperate as it took the authorities 2 days to complete the Police and Immigration formalities with such an influx of refugees.

A day after our arrival, we heard a two-way radio message come through to the Portuguese man in the house saying that MPLA had started attacking the people at Mucosse. The man sending the message from Mucosse got this news through then the radio went dead and nothing further was heard. We could easily hear the messages as the radios were blaringly loud.

Debbie became seriously sick again and the medication didn't seem to help. Late in the evening, she seemed to be flitting in and out of consciousness then had a violent convulsion. Keith and Mary rushed her to the Rundu African State Hospital.

Mary: "It was a tough time with Debbie being so ill in Rundu. We were all a bit unwell from the dysentery. I did hate to leave her, so tiny, with strange people looking at her, speaking an unfamiliar language, but she was in good hands in that hospital. Much the same as during the convoy, I felt as though I was in an absolute daze, seeing and remembering everything, but it was as if I was looking through someone else's eyes, almost as if I wasn't there at all. I think we were all suffering some amount of trauma, unsure and not knowing where we were going or what would happen to us. For me, I'd left one African country to go to another, not knowing if the new country would be any better. With our minds constantly challenged in caring for and keeping Debbie occupied during the convoy days out of Angola, we'd had little time for brooding too much on the future, and now with her so ill in hospital in this strange town, all I focused on was getting her better. For the moment, everything else could wait."

Debbie's illness was a horrible and frightening experience for us all. The child was completely dehydrated and very weak. We knew the sooner we could get to Windhoek and civilisation and find out about Beryl and Stuart as well, the better we'd all be.

At the Ovamboland border we had trouble with the African authorities, and were just contemplating crashing the vehicles through the barriers when up walked a group of Africans to speak to us. Incredibly, 2 of them had worked for us on Fazenda Esperança! All of them were Angolan Africans, spoke to us in Portuguese, and told us that at the first sign of trouble they'd bunked across the border so had completely missed the war. Overjoyed to see us and we them (and friendly faces compared to the Border Control Officials), they wanted to know all that had happened at Serpa Pinto and the farm. They were illegally in South West Africa, whether the authorities knew about this we'd no idea, but we couldn't have had a nicer welcome.

Getting nowhere with the Border Control Authorities, Ian eventually asked to see the white superintendent. The trouble we were having was over a pair of very old kudu horns which the officials adamantly insisted were recently poached. Way back in 1906, when Ian's father, William, made his first safari to Kenya, he'd brought back this finest of horn specimens, so magnificent we'd yet to see any that compared.

While all this was going on, I managed to see the Veterinary Officer in his official department and have our old black Schipperke dog, Cricket, examined. He was suffering terribly from lung congestion, possibly caused from all the dust on the convoy journey. An examination revealed nothing could be done to alleviate Cricket's severe condition as it was more than a dust problem. The Vet advised he be put to sleep. With deep sadness we all agreed and this service was performed, very kindly free of charge.

Thankfully, our passports were eventually handed back to us as it was ascertained that the kudu horns were indeed years old. We only wanted to get away and on the long haul to Windhoek.

At Grootfontein, we unwittingly consumed some really poor-quality food in a grim little café in the late afternoon. Mostly, we needed boiling water in our thermos flasks. The café owner informed us there was no free of charge camping ground available and that it was prohibited to camp along the roadside, however, we could go to the big refugee camp which was already overflowing with Portuguese. We felt we couldn't face all that once more and were reaching the end of our tether, tired, worried, and Debbie had started vomiting and diarrhoea again. Although none of us spoke of this, we knew that soon we'd have to face the reality of no roof over our heads and zero income. With Debbie being so sick, we simply had to overcome the challenges.

Sometime during all of this, an odd-looking character walked into the café, heard what was going on and walked over to us. We exchanged introductions learning his name was John Lewis. He said our distress was clear and he couldn't just stand by without helping in some way. John listened to our story and we added that our daughter, Beryl, worked at the Kalahari Sands Hotel in Windhoek. With a few words he guaranteed us a safe place to sleep with space to keep the vehicles nearby then without further ado in an authoritative voice instructed, "Follow me!"

John was about 50, olive-skinned, of average height, brown-eyed and unshaven with locks of greasy hair. He wore no shoes, had dirty finger and toe nails and was scruffily unkempt in his attire, his clothes in need of laundering. Despite his somewhat dubious physical appearance he projected a strong, positive and delightfully optimistic, open and very friendly demeanour. Ian took to him immediately, trusting his character and integrity. John was so insistent and self-assured of his capability in assisting us, lifting our flagging spirits, that when he simply ordered us to accompany him, striding off confidently towards his car, Ian and Keith instantly followed his footsteps like lambs! He had an old hand-painted, bright yellow VW Kombi with an odd little trailer. Off we went close behind him stopping, to our surprise, at the entrance to the Police Station. Keith and Ian went in with John while we womenfolk stayed in the vehicles within hearing distance. Holding a thermos in his hand, he was met at the door by a white Policeman who casually said, "Hello, John. You've come for the night?" as if it were something he was used to our new friend doing.

"Yes," John responded affirmatively, adding with a big smile, "and I've brought 5 friends with me!"

The Policeman didn't appear the least taken aback gesturing for the men to follow him. Later, Ian and Keith told us they'd been escorted to the cells where John seemed to know the ropes then organised where the vehicles should be parked. We gathered our bedding and went inside. There was a long row of adjoining prison cells. Each was about

16 feet square at a rough guess and could house 5 inmates (who we saw), and was divided in 2 sections. One half was a roofed, windowless (with air-bricks) secure building structure with an automatically flushing toilet, this area being locked at night so the inmates had no access during hours of darkness to the other half of the cell which was the same size, but an open-air steel mesh cage (rather like a top and sides steel mesh enclosed verandah). During daylight hours the prisoners were able to go between the two.

We couldn't bear to sleep in the one enclosed unoccupied cell because it felt so claustrophobic even though it was spotlessly clean, so opted for the open-air steel mesh cage section and sandwiched our mattresses together, once more having the stars above us for the night. There was even a blanket and mattress provided so John pulled it into the cage part and joined our sleeping arrangements. It was late evening now. Over chit-chat, sitting on our mattresses, we shared our thermoses of coffee while the dogs ran in and out our open cage-gate, barking at our next door neighbours the prison inmates who were laughing, very jolly, watching us with amusement, particularly John, until they were confined to their windowless sleeping quarters. Ian and John rounded off our bedtime by telling incredibly funny 'Van der Merwe' jokes (Afrikaans jokes focusing on the character of Van der Merwe, told by many in South Africa and South West Africa) which had us in fits of laughter till we happily drifted off to sleep. We were woken from our contented slumbers about every 20 minutes or so when the cell toilet flushed automatically with a loud swishing gurgle!

Early next morning, the same kind Policeman came to see how we were and asked concernedly, "Did you have a good night?" We assured him we had, thanking him profusely for the Police hospitality.

John, as he usually did, so he told us, then visited the prisoners joking with them as he dished out cigarettes. It was gratifying to witness this genuine empathy for one's fellow-man in a less fortunate position. Then the guards came to wash out and disinfect the cells and the prisoners were led out. To our absolute horror, out came one inmate with shackles around his ankles! This man, John said, was an old friend of his, having visited him many times; he was a naturally agile, light-skinned and wrinkly-faced Bushman, perhaps 30, wearing prison garb and shorts. Because he could jump like a springbok, according to the Policeman and John, he had to be kept shackled since this was the only way to keep him imprisoned! The inmates were all a happy, jovial bunch, their cheerful relaxed attitudes towards incarceration not surprising to us – when we were in Kenya it was commonly known that prisoners considered jail to be "Kingie Georgie's Hotelie!"

We said our grateful farewells to John, expressing how much we'd enjoyed his company as he'd been a tonic for all of us, and added that if he were ever back this way again he should contact Beryl to 'phone us so he could visit wherever we'd settled.

Heading for Otavi, we spent the night in an excellent camping ground with hot water in the ablution blocks and luckily didn't have to pay for these facilities, perhaps because we arrived late and were up again at dawn. Windhoek was another full day's journey. Even though we left very early in the morning, the South West African sun was already burning hot. It was a pleasure to drive on the well-maintained broad tarmac roads and there were lots of lay-byes with trees, refuse bins, concrete tables and benches. When we were just on the outskirts of Okahandja, about 75 kilometres from Windhoek, we saw a notice advertising a private zoo. So thankful we all were that Debbie was feeling better, we thought a visit here would be a treat and pep her up. She'd have the excitement of seeing, for the first time, some African animals at close quarters, the biggest being giraffe and kudu. The owners of the zoo were professional game catchers. We learned that some of the animals would, in time, be exported. Admittance for our group cost Rand 10. To our surprise and relief, Ian brought out a Rand 50 note (South African currency used in South West Africa at the time) that he'd had the foresight to borrow somewhere on the convoy journey from a Portuguese man who'd been a diamond dealer in Angola.

At sundown, we bypassed the tiny village of Brakwater surrounded by starkly bare mountain ranges. Just off the road was a State-run camping area, a picturesque setting beneath thorn trees with spreads of green lawns, barbeque blocks and water taps. On the perimeter was an attractive hill with the most enormous scenic rock formations. The cost of the night's camping was Rand 10. It was heavenly weather.

Early the following morning, Keith broke the idyll, bringing to our attention over coffee and breakfast, "Now the holiday time is over!"

And we truly understood what he meant. For the first time in our lives we'd no longer be self-employed, facing a totally new challenge perhaps even greater than the last, which would have to be reckoned with in a different way. To begin with, not only were we once again foreigners, but refugees possessing little, having no income and no finances at our disposal. Apart from Keith with his UK diesel and petrol technician qualifications, we had only our word as testament to our capabilities. As we turned out of the Brakwater camping grounds onto the dual carriageway, Windhoek city centre was about 15 kilometres away. At last, we'd see Beryl and Stuart again.

Behind the wheel of the Merc on the last short stretch of our marathon exodus, I thought about acts of human kindness, one person to another and how, more often than not, it seems to be repaid forward to someone else rather than returned to the original giver. We'd had no opportunity of repaying Edgar's kindness – instead I'd driven the Merc out of Angola for hand-over to a Colonel Botha, my undertaking now almost complete. Our family hadn't paid anything to the mercenaries for escorting us to the South West African border, perhaps in the future we'd find a way of 'return' by assisting someone else; as with the 2 Angolan Africans who'd tirelessly helped us through the chana and I'd been unable to donate as our cash was with Ian in the Chev. I was given baby porridge, Marie biscuits and boiled egg by exceptionally considerate folk in our time of need. They had noticed I hadn't any food for the dogs and me.

I liked to think that during our extended stay under the fig tree with our Portuguese friends at 'Point X', Katwitwi, we'd found that we could be of a little help and moral support to them in their time of extreme anxiety and sorrow, a small return gesture for the kindnesses we'd received from others. John Lewis was a total stranger and a saviour in our time of distress and near despair, who'd bestowed on us a memorable night of simplicity yet true camaraderie, and we could not forget his kind deeds. Indeed we'd had blessings, the greatest being that we'd arrived safely from a country suffering civil war to peaceful South West Africa. At 'Point X', the South African Army had been generous and caring in their assistance with food, fuel and medical attention, and the Vet had extended compassion to our very sick old dog, Cricket. At Rundu, the State Hospital had tended with medical competence to our ailing little girl. So far, South West Africa had been kind to us. Perhaps I was asking too much, but I wished, hope against hope, with the lightness of optimism and soothing laughter still left in my heart by John Lewis, that the good fortune, no matter how small, would continue as we embarked on this new chapter in our lives.

Though Ian was not religious himself, one of his favourite sayings passed on to him by his strict Presbyterian Scottish father, William, popped into my mind – "The Good Lord helps those who help themselves." Yes, without doubt, the measure of our will, determination and effort would directly affect and determine the outcome of the years ahead. Ian was 45, Keith 22, Mary nearing 23, and myself 42. Debbie's 3rd birthday was not far off, in December. Between the 5 of us we had about Rand 30 cash to our names.

Viva Windhoek! With utter relief we'd reached our journey's end. Ian and I were relatively familiar with Windhoek having put Stuart into school there. First, we found parking in a side street behind the Law Courts for the lorry where there was shade and no meters, some way from the central Windhoek Kalahari Sands shopping complex. Mary and Debbie stayed in the lorry while Keith foot-slogged a considerable distance to the industrial area to look for work. Ian in the Chev with the 3 dogs accompanied me to the South African Army Headquarters in Suiderhof. We explained to the guard on duty at the Headquarters entrance the circumstances regarding the Merc and that I'd been instructed in Serpa Pinto to hand over the vehicle personally to a Colonel Botha as there was radio equipment in the boot. He then 'phoned through to someone who gave him the message that I should simply leave the car with him, whereupon I handed him the keys. Ian and I were surprised by this. When I took responsibility for the car from Edgar, he showed us the sophisticated equipment emphasising the importance of both it and the Merc reaching Windhoek for handover specifically to the Colonel. Nevertheless, I'd done as I'd undertaken.

Thankfully, we found Stuart well when we visited him at school and had to give him Rand 10 as he'd taken a bet with a pal and lost, that his parents would never leave Angola! Then it was on to see Beryl at the Kalahari Sands Hotel. She was happy, looked pretty and had good news for us. Being anxious about our safety, she'd taken the initiative and made provisional arrangements with the man in charge of Refugee Rehabilitation in Windhoek, a Mr Van As, who had reserved for us a small house on a plot at Kapps Farm, beyond the suburb of Klein Windhoek and fairly near Windhoek Airport, a distance of about 30 kilometres from the city. Beryl had also been in touch with the Chief of the Labour Department, a Mr Snyman, telling him that any day soon her parents would be arriving from Angola and they'd be hopeful of finding a job. That was further positive news. She also bought Ian some packs of cigarettes then we went back to Mary and Debbie at the lorry, parking the Chev close by so Mary could keep an eye on the dogs while Ian and I walked to the banks.

At Barclays, the Manager informed Ian his Angolan currency was absolutely worthless, he might as well throw it away. With Stuart at school in Windhoek, I had an account with Standard Bank and withdrew the small funds, approximately Rand 350. Unable to locate the British Embassy we went back to the lorry. It was late afternoon, our feet sore from all the walking. Mary and Debbie were exhausted from hours of waiting so we headed for the house at Kapps Farm. Keith went ahead in the lorry to look for a place where he could safely offload the Kombi and we followed slowly behind.

From the city centre we took the main road going east over a hill with a spectacular panoramic view of Windhoek and down the other side into signposted Klein Windhoek, then straight on out of town on a wonderfully engineered highway gradually winding around steep hills to a higher altitude. But, it was most odd – I kept seeing papers I thought I recognised blowing about on the left-hand verge of the tarmac! When I definitely knew I'd seen my London Standard Bank cheque book, I shouted to Ian to stop, but he just continued on while I explained the situation. Exasperated from a tiring long day, he responded irritably, "Women have the most vivid and ridiculous imaginations!"

I felt really silly! Reaching a flat area, we saw Keith backing up the lorry at a road maintenance pit and stopped. Sure enough, the suitcase on the roof rack of the Kombi containing our documents and important papers had blown open! Luckily, we all carried our Passports with us. Ian and I went back to where I'd seen the papers on the road, but by now the wind had scattered them even further and deep down into the gorges. There was nothing we could do about it, so we went back to Keith then on to Kapps Farm with me driving the Kombi.

The house was tiny, unfurnished and the building not yet complete – it had no inside doors – though it mattered not a jot to us as we were so appreciative of the accommodation. Situated near a dry river bed in real kudu country, the dogs were overjoyed to run around freely at last, exploring their new surroundings in the coolness of the evening. There were a few other insignificant buildings on the plot. We unpacked our bedding and mattresses on the floor and by the light of cheap candles had a tinned meal out of our now meagre supplies. My sleep that night was different – a grateful, calm tiredness. We were all safe and well, Beryl and Stuart included, and the little house held a sense of journey's end security, signifying a coming stability.

To start our new lives separately, the next day was spent unpacking and dividing the kitchen equipment, bedding and belongings between our 2 families. Ian knew our future lay in finding some sort of agricultural or land work, and that Keith's lay in machinery. We decided we could safely leave Mary, Debbie and the dogs while the 3 of us went to Windhoek the following day. Visiting Beryl again, we heard that Mr Snyman from the Labour Department had 'phoned and wanted to see us immediately. Keith went off to see the big South African engineering company, Barlows.

Mr Snyman greeted us warmly and asked us to wait while he telephoned the General Manager of a large cattle ranching company, Nuwe Westelike Ontwikkelingsmaatskappy, who desperately needed a manager for their 3 adjoining farms in the Omitara district. We only had a 15 minute wait before a Mr Pretorius arrived, and after a half-hour chat he asked whether we would be prepared to go the following day to see the property and discuss the employment position. The 3 of us returned to Kapps Farm feeling a great deal easier about our futures and with the wonderful news that Keith had been immediately employed by Barlows, working in the Caterpillar Division. Mary had fixed up the house and made it as homely as possible. There was an ancient black cast-iron stove in poor working condition, but usable, and she'd collected enough dry wood lying around outside to get a fire going. We felt so tired and couldn't think further than the present time. It never even crossed our minds that Ian wouldn't get the farm managerial post.

The following morning, we started the day in high spirits, rising very early to be in Windhoek just before 8. Mr Kallie Pretorius was waiting for us with the company car. We set off immediately on the drive to the Ranch, passing Kapps Farm and the airport, and learning that long ago during German occupation, 'Winterhoek' was the name originally given to Windhoek. Continuing a good distance further, on absolutely straight, flat-terrain two-lane highway, after about an hour we turned off left to the sign-posted village of Omitara where the tar finished at the railway line. For the next 60 kilometres, we travelled on a wide dirt road reaching the Ranch after about one-and-three-quarter hours in total. En route, Mr Pretorius told us that a few days previously a young couple from Johannesburg had applied for the job. When they reached Omitara the wife became extremely anxious, saying she'd go no further, so they turned around and drove straight back to the airport.

Ian and I were thrilled at having seen so many kudu, starting from Kapps Farm, and once on the Ranch property, still 30 kilometres before the farm homestead, we saw lots more, and plenty of other game as well – warthogs, hartebeest, gemsbok and springbok, to mention a few.

The present manager, Louis van der Westhuizen, had already spent 8 years in the position and wanted to move on to a new prospect in the Mariental district (about 3 hours drive south of Windhoek on the main road to South Africa). A number of farmers on small-holdings were successfully producing great quantities of grapes and lucerne irrigated by the gigantic new Hardap Dam Water Scheme. Louis and his wife wished to leave at the end of September. Ian and I were welcomed and without further ado, Ian was employed on *Kambingana* as Ranch Manager. He'd officially start work in 2 weeks time so that Louis could hand over the labour, livestock, vehicles and accounts etc. In the meantime, Mr Pretorius authorised that we immediately move into the attractive farm guest cottage, about 150 yards from the main house.

Louis and Dalene very kindly said we could have their 10 black Australorp fowls (good egg-layers, a real blessing) when they left.

The cottage had every convenience except air-conditioning, and was usually used for visiting company directors and their guests, particularly during the winter hunting season months. It was a very pleasant brick and plaster building with a corrugated iron roof, surrounded by bare reddish dusty earth and 2 mature thorn trees giving welcome shade. Accommodation consisted of 2 furnished twin-bed bedrooms with sufficient linen, kitchen with gas stove, big walk-in well-stocked pantry, cold and gas-heated hot water, and a very spacious furnished lounge-cum-dining room looking onto a large front verandah. Electricity was from the diesel generator near the main house, which ran from early evening till 'lights out' time usually before 10 at night, with extra generator hours allowed on laundry days. I would be responsible for making sure the cottage was clean, prepared and the laundry done for guests – it could sleep 10 people if extra camp bedding was brought by the hunters.

There was no problem regarding us living or being employed in South West Africa as we were all British citizens. The only requirement was a handwritten residency authorisation in our passports from the Windhoek Home Affairs Department.

Mary, of all of us, had the hardest knock from the entire experience of Angola and the exodus, coming through it all bravely. Not in her wildest imagination could she have contemplated the events that unfolded for her in West Africa after leaving the UK. In her words: "We'd only been 10 months in Angola, but I was very relieved and glad to leave. I may have hated Angola then, but it taught me a lot and I don't regret having gone there with Keith. It wasn't all bad and we did have enjoyable times."

So, we left Kapps Farm, Keith, Debbie and Mary expecting her 2nd child, knowing they'd be able to make new lives for themselves and their growing family, though it wouldn't be easy for any of us. Time and the coming days, I felt sure, would help us look forward more than backwards. Ian would put his all into being an excellent manager at Kambingana. No matter where we'd lived, it was his natural character to totally dedicate his talents, abilities and experience. Together, we'd build a new life.

The school term ended, and Stuart, fired up with teenage vigour and excitement at the prospect of a bushveld adventure in South West Africa came with us to our new home on the cattle Ranch known as *The Place of the Water.*

Chapter Eighteen
The Place of the Water, South West Africa

In the Herero African language of South West Africa, the name 'Kambingana' signified 'The Place of the Water' and was given by the original nomadic Herero before white people came to the country, specifically referring to the expanse of shallow flood-plain dam water their people came to rely upon as they followed the grass and rains grazing their cattle in this vast area. Much later, the farm also came to be known as 'Kambingana'.

The 3 adjoining farms comprising the Ranch property were *Kambingana* where we would live, *Karamba* and *Boomlager*, collectively known as *Kambingana Ranch*. During earlier German occupation many Herero people lost their lives, survivors fleeing across the border into neighbouring Botswana.

The Place of the Water would become our home for over 19 years, being the longest time we would live in one place out of the 5 African countries Ian or I lived in, being Kenya, Rhodesia (Zimbabwe), Angola, South West Africa (Namibia) and South Africa.

Kambingana dam, the biggest in the entire district, was fed by large volumes of water carried down the ravines into the Swart Nossob River which also filled other dams along its course. During our years, we would see Kambingana dam full – and in flood, stretching about 7 kilometres, in some places wider than the great Zambezi River bordering South West Africa and Zambia in the north. Debbie, our granddaughter, was older by then and would ride her horse, 'Ou Seun' (Afrikaans for 'Old Son/Old Boy'), bareback through the placid Kambingana dam, the water mid-shoulder level on Ou Seun most of the way. Only twice did we see the river in full spate. Smaller rainfalls just topped up the dam level.

The spillway alone of Kambingana dam was about 100 yards wide, and with a pretty solid foundation of clay we were told the dam could hold sufficient water to last about 3 years without a drop of rain. In more recent years (before us), engineers had built the dam wall and had also dug out the big 'Gat' (Afrikaans for deep 'hole') at the deepest end of the dam, which was obviously not there during earlier Herero occupation.

Nine years of drought we would witness too. Harrowing memories – attempting to rescue the awfulness of cattle, in the quest to quench their thirst, caught in the viscous mud of the Gat – most times, gratefully, we managed to save the animal. Or tying ropes around the men who waded into the thick, sucking mess then fell about as they tried to catch all the big floundering carp fish fighting desperately for breath of life without water. Every fish was washed and packed into the big freezer and the staff had fish to eat for months. As the prayed-for rains continued to elude the parched sun-baked earth, the clay bed of the dam cracked into what resembled millions of pieces of aged marble-chocolate porcelain. The dry water-crusted froth around the edges in which tiny freshwater shrimps had lost the fight to live, shrivelled to a crisp.

Eventually, crevices in the mountains trickled water into the ravines as the drought relented, softening and restoring the clay porcelain with moisture, a good rainfall producing a steady river flow. At other times the intensity of a pounding downpour turned the Swart Nossob into torrents of flash-flooding along its course, transforming Kambingana's shallow flood-plain into a shimmering mirror-like vision of sun-glistened water, the dam lying once again plump and full.

Having farmed in Kenya with a good rainfall averaging 80 inches a year, followed by cultivating tobacco in Angola where we'd been spoilt again with regular rains often 'bucketing down' in front of you, *the seemingly never-ending canvas of hot, dry South West African landscape would amplify to us the sacredness of life-sustaining water, and we'd greatly respect and understand the significant value to the Herero people of 'The Place of the Water'.*

We arrived at Kambingana, Ian and Stuart in the Ford lorry with our 5 crates of possessions, the dogs and me in the Kombi, to find Louis out working cattle. Dalene gave us the guest cottage keys and we settled in very comfortably.

The next 2 weeks we lived in a sort of limbo, getting to grips with the new life, routine and management of the farm, the language and climate. The September days were pleasurably warm with cool evenings. Pepu, Minnie and Bidou made friends with Louis and Dalene's Alsatian dog and didn't chase the fowls wandering around the backyard.

Looking straight ahead, if one stood at the back kitchen door of Louis and Dalene's main house, more or less in line and about 5 minutes walk along a sandy path was another house, the same layout and design as the main house, where a German couple, a Mr Willy Wiehl and his wife, Gis, lived. Willy was manager of machinery and maintenance, his work carried out in an enormous brick and corrugated iron-sheeting workshop behind the guest cottage. The workshop, with its own generator also supplying electricity to Mr Wiehl's house, had a vehicle maintenance pit and was equipped with all manner of tools and spare parts relevant to the upkeep of farm vehicles and agricultural equipment. With so much space, it was also used for storage of a staggering amount of fencing wire and poles, etc.

Louis spoke English fluently, while Dalene struggled. My Afrikaans was non-existent, but Ian managed well having conversed with José in Angola. Sometimes the languages of German, Afrikaans and English were, quite amusingly, muddled up together – we'd find this throughout South West Africa, which gave a further unique charm to the country and people.

The first lesson we learned about Kambingana Ranch was that we were a long way from everything. Approximately equidistant, Windhoek was about 180 kilometres away, in the centre of South West Africa, and our other closest big town, Gobabis, was to the east, not far from Babi-Babi, the border post through to Botswana.

South West Africa (Namibia) is the 34th largest country in the world, and the 15th biggest in Africa. Kambingana Ranch was the 10th biggest ranch in South West Africa, totalling 45,000 acres (just over twice the size of our Angolan fazenda) in the District of Omitara in the Omaheke Region. Interestingly, Canadian surveyors were used to carve up the territory in the Omaheke so some farms were named 'Alaska' for example.

Boomlager, with the greatest water supply from any one borehole on the 3 farms, was the furthest away at 30 kilometres from the main house on Kambingana. Karamba (the middle farm) was about 4 kilometres from Kambingana main house and lay between several small hills. Both Boomlager and Karamba had dams, big by ordinary standards though considerably smaller than Kambingana's. Karamba's dam was considered unreliable as it didn't hold water long enough, perhaps due to not having such a solid clay foundation. All the dams attracted a variety of birdlife – storks, pelicans and many different ducks.

Ultimately, it was the boreholes that reliably kept the 3 farms in crystal clear water for livestock drinking and domestic household use. By the time of our arrival, 51 boreholes had been sunk on the entire property, only 3 producing continued good water supply; a few mediocre then petering out; and the vast majority dry. In the period of drought that would come our way, Keith divined for water on Boomlager – about 5 boreholes were drilled, only one producing a little water which not long after ran dry. Some farms in our area had drilled more than 80 boreholes, and many in South West Africa reached 700 feet or more below ground level. When pumping water for the first time from a new borehole, the golden rule was to run the initial water onto the ground for 2 or 3 days because it could be poisonous to humans or animals. It was quite normal for farmers to have their water tested. Kambingana had one borehole that had been found unfit for human and animal consumption which had been sealed.

There was an instance when a new manager on the Dordabis property (between Windhoek and Omitara, one of the 19 farms in South West Africa owned by the company, the others being in the Okahandja and Otjiwarongo districts), having been warned of the 3 day necessity of first running the water onto the ground before allowing it to fill reservoirs and troughs due to the possibility of high Cobalt toxicity, for some reason or other disregarded this valuable advice and allowed cattle to drink. By the time this disaster was discovered, 267 animals lay dead with another 17 in the throes of death.

Mr Mossie Burger, the agricultural manager, and his wife, Attie, lived on Karamba, their home above the big dam. Mossie was responsible for overseeing ploughing and planting of land on Kambingana farm which produced sufficient silage (sorghum) for 4,000 stall-fed beef steers; and tomatoes, melons, cucumbers and sweet corn were grown for sale in Windhoek. The irrigation water came from

Kambingana dam. Boomlager and Karamba were too hilly, rocky or stony with very little level terrain suitable for agriculture, whereas Kambingana had ample flat land with good soil for crop-growing. All 3 farms though were perfectly suited to livestock ranching.

We got on exceptionally well with Mossie and Attie. They both spoke Afrikaans and English. It was a pity, particularly for Attie and me that we didn't live closer to one another to be able to pop over for a quick cup of tea and a bit of woman chat to break daily routine. Mossie was often on Kambingana – otherwise we communicated messages by telephone.

Seventy kilometres of dirt road stretched across the Ranch. The cattle camps were huge, one being 4,000 acres. To drive through the property checking fence lines, water piping, reservoirs, troughs and kraal railings in every camp took most of a working day with all the gates that had to be opened and closed. A neighbour once estimated that opening and closing gates alone took 4 days of a year. On our arrival, after 3 good rainfall years, the grazing grass was almost 4 foot high and all the dams full. The cattle were sleek and fat and the wild game plentiful.

Omitara was an extremely important junction in the enormous region. The district farms were connected to a central telephone exchange at Omitara village that also had a railhead and Farmers' Co-Operative.

Farmers in the area would sometimes know about a fire only if they were informed via party-line 'phone calls. It was an unwritten rule that at the sight of smoke, everyone was to be alerted. If the fire was on a neighbouring farm, all the farmers rallied with their labour, equipment and water in 44 gallon drums as quickly as possible. Drums of water permanently stood on a trailer at Kambingana ready to be hitched onto the big Ford-250 bakkie in case of fire.

Once a week, the driver of the State Railway lorry system collected and dropped off at farm entrances the various farming supplies that had been ordered from the Farmer's Co-op, as well as the locked mail bags from Omitara Post Office. The lorry driver would collect the mail bags again on his return journey to Omitara, the Postmaster having a key to each bag as did the farmers – no-one ever interfered with the district's mail bags, nor did any mail ever go missing. The whole system ran as smoothly as clockwork.

In order to take over as Manager, Ian had to count and agree with Louis on the numbers of livestock, making sure all cattle had the Kambingana brand on the left hindquarter, with different coloured ear-tags showing dates of birth. The figures were entered correctly on stock sheets and signed by both men. At this time of plenty, there were 3,000 head of cattle on the land, and another 1,000 in stock-feeding lots. Brahman, Afrikaner and Simmenthaler cattle were the breeding stock. Cross-breeding had to be done to get a quality animal that carried weight in the hindquarters, and which could withstand the harsh climate and be able to walk the long distances to the water points. Each herd had to be rounded up by the stockmen on horses, brought to the central point at Kambingana then returned to their camps on the same day. They had to be identified and accounted for by their breeding and types, selection, ages, genders, in-calf females, calves and bulls and those steers ready for the abattoir. It was a gigantic task of 2 weeks, particularly hard on the work-horses, all of which also had to be tallied, separately listing any privately owned by the stockmen. The company kept a small flock of sheep, kraaled near the main house, to provide the farm managers (ranch, agriculture and machinery/mechanic) with 2 sheep each a month as a meat ration. Cattle licks, veterinary supplies and inoculating equipment, branding and de-horning implements, fencing wire and poles, tools, vehicles, cattle scales and any buildings to do with the ranching also underwent a stocktake and the quantity of fuel in the storage tanks had to be measured.

The game could only be estimated, but each farmer had an approximate idea of how much was on his farm. Per year for Kambingana, 300 head of hartebeest were authorised for sale, a license issued and the antelope captured in the winter June or July months by an experienced game trapper then immediately exported to South Africa. Income from the sale of the hartebeest covered the annual labour wages, uniforms, raincoats, boots and weekly food rations for each staff member (2 kg of mealie meal daily, tea, coffee, flour, salt, 500g blocks of Holsum cooking fat, tobacco, matches, body and laundry soap and toilet paper etc.). South West African farmers have always carefully preserved their game. South African buyers, who always seemed short, put in their game orders well in advance and Kambingana had regular customers.

Kallie Pretorius, as company Stock General Manager, came out to Kambingana again to collect the stocktake documents and told us our telephone calls to Windhoek would be free of charge, and that we may use the cottage for our own guest accommodation, though company use took priority. He also instructed Ian to shoot 2 hartebeest every fortnight for the labour meat rations so that all 9 employees each had 10 kilos of meat every week for their families.

Louis and Dalene left for their new home in Mariental. They'd been very kind to us. We wished them well in their new life of grape and lucerne farming, and hoped to keep in touch. Then we moved our few belongings from the cottage to the main house. Once again, we put down the mattresses and bedding on the floor and opened up our camp chairs and table.

Our new home was a simple white painted square brick and plaster design, also with corrugated iron roof sheeting. It comprised 3 fair-sized bedrooms; a small covered front porch between the lounge and one bedroom (giving little space to relax in the only shade); a separate toilet; bathroom with basin, bath and shower; a small kitchen and a good-sized L-shaped lounge-dining room. At the front was a small patch of scrubby lawn with a big thorn tree outside our bedroom window which I immediately nurtured and hung from the branches a long piece of wood as a bird feeding tray. Within hours the weaver birds started to arrive, their chatter immediately cheering the atmosphere as they pecked on maize meal and went about making their individual nests. Surrounding the entire house was the same extremely dusty bare reddish earth – with Daisy's love of gardening instilled in me, I'd do something about that. Beyond the house perimeter some ragged thorn trees were dotted around with no view other than a few small bushveld camps for the sheep and work-horses so they could easily be caught. Nearly every day the skies were a wonderful bright blue. Hardly ever did we have clouds.

The noisy diesel generator providing electrical power for ourselves and the cottage was in a small brick building with a corrugated iron roof and no door, merely a doorway, at the back of the house not far from the kitchen. Our generator maintenance and limited daily running-hours were Ian's responsibility. In time, he'd bring a cable from the engine to outside the back kitchen door, enabling one to turn off the electricity at night by simply pulling on the cable instead of having to walk in the dark by torchlight to stop the generator.

The kitchen (soon to prove unbearably hot in summer then freezing cold in winter) opened from the back door onto 2 steps then directly onto dusty bare yard. On the dining room side was a separate single garage. Everything was sufficient, but the toilet and kitchen waste emptied into a large square concrete tank cesspit covered only by 3 loose corrugated iron sheets supported by 4 cross-beams of wood just outside the bathroom – a stomach-turning abhorrence, and without surrounding fencing an extremely dicey set-up. The final straw for Ian regarding the dangerous open cesspit happened one night with one of the stock horses not long after we'd moved into the house – Ou Seun fell through the ridged iron sheeting injuring himself very badly, a 15 inch cut, the flap of skin and tissue hanging down his neck. Ian doctored the awful gaping wound and with a stitch here and there secured it in place then continued treating the nasty cut which took weeks to heal, luckily leaving only a ridge on the horse's neck. But, immediately after the accident and without permission (quite unlike him), Ian rectified the problem with materials paid for by the company and put up fencing around the house allowing ample space for the garden. Some years later when the Ranch was sold, the new owner, Mr Bonadei, put in proper septic tanks for sewage waste. We later bought Ou Seun from Simon, the head stockman, having been given permission to own horses as long as they were always available for Ranch work as well.

Kallie Pretorius of his own accord, very considerately informed us that since we had no furniture, the company would lend us Rand 1,500. They simply couldn't abide their manager and his wife sleeping on a mattress on the floor. Ian's starting monthly salary was Rand 400 out of which we had to pay Stuart's school and hostel fees, clothes, buy our groceries and pay our private car insurance etc. so it took us ages to pay off this debt. I was to earn Rand 50 per month, my duties to include recording rainfall figures, being an assistant to Ian, supervising the cottage and taking care of staff medical problems.

Running short on household supplies, Ian and I made our first trip to Omitara. After about 45 minutes drive on dusty corrugated road, we crossed the railway line onto tarmac, though for only a kilometre or so as one then turned right into the village, again on a dirt road. The railway station was on the left. Opposite on the right, was a general dealer store with a big shady tree in front, owned by an elderly German couple, Mr Reichardt and his wife, Emma. Ian introduced us saying he was the new Kambingana manager and because we had no money, was asking whether he could open an account for groceries.

Mr Reichardt, who we would learn was never one to mince words, swelled out like a pouter pigeon, gave a big humph and emphatically said, "The Smits, the Smuts and the Smiths never pay their accounts, but for you, I will give credit!"

The shop had long u-shaped counters, many shelves floor to almost ceiling height on 3 walls and an old manual cash register. The Reichardts sold everything imaginable from make-up, patent medicines, clothing, fabrics of all kinds and colours for the housewife, wools, shoes and boots, canned goods, fresh meat, vegetables and fruit, even gardening requirements – really everything a farmer and his family would need. For me, it was an interesting shopping experience of unearthing not only the norm necessities, but also finding excellent offers while browsing at leisure, all accompanied by friendly customer service from the owners. I found a large, round aluminium colander for Rand 1.00, and for a bit more an excellent quality multi-purpose bread/bone knife made in Germany (both of which I still have in 2016!).

Next door, in a separate building was the liquor store also owned by the elderly couple, then the Post Office, and lastly the Farmer's Co-Op which we would hardly use as the company sent most of the Ranch requirements by lorry from Windhoek. We met the Postmaster, Manfred Hennes, and his wife, Connie, and had an instant rapport with this gentle couple – they became very dear to us. Our first month's grocery account was Rand 60. Back home, we found word had spread like wildfire – the new manager at Kambingana was a foreigner! We became known as 'Die Engelsman' ('the Englishman' in Afrikaans).

Each end of every month when the staff received their wages either Ian or I would take them shopping at Reichardt's in Omitara. We became good friends with the elderly couple, enjoyed visiting and joking, and in particular we loved Emma, a beautiful lady. Her people had come from East Germany and had owned the fine porcelain known as 'Rosenthal' in those days. The Reichardt's home was at the back of their shop. Emma grew roses in drums as their garden was tiny. She also had Muscovy ducks. After a few months, Emma very kindly gave me a pair, a drake and a duck. Ian made a big, shallow concrete pond in the garden area outside our bedroom window and jackal-proofed the fencing so the ducks could wander around safely as they pleased and lay their eggs anywhere in that section of the garden. Due to ill health, some years after we'd been on Kambingana, the Reichardt's closed their store and we'd have to travel a considerable distance further with the staff to Gobabis supermarket, an extra 3 hours drive there and back.

Our next trip was to Windhoek to buy furniture. Luckily, I'd managed to pick up 2 tables at an almost give-away price from an old lady on one of the farms in the area who was having a sale. One table went to Mary and Keith, the other was suitable for temporary use in our small kitchen as it was oblong but left little space to move around. We found all the furniture we needed at the cheapest store, the OK Bazaars, in the same town centre as the Kalahari Sands Hotel where Beryl worked. Wooden double-bed with mattress, 2 matching side-tables and a dressing table; 2 cheap spare room single beds and mattresses; a 3-piece plain old-gold fabric lounge suite and an oblong wooden coffee table; a round pine table with 4 chairs for the dining room; and 2 pine benches, all within the Rand 1,500 loan. Everything was delivered by company transport to the farm at no cost to us. When Ian could afford a better-quality dining room table the pine one would go in the kitchen. We had no loose carpets or mats to put on the Marley tiled cement floors and Beryl kindly lent us a royal blue patterned carpet for the sitting room. Curtains I made from Hessian sacking cloth which I bought by the yard at Omitara Farmers' Co-Op and stitched by hand. Ian put up shelving in the lounge using the beautiful Angolan timber planks that he and Keith had used to roll the drums of fuel on and off the lorry when they'd hidden the diesel in the woodlands then retrieved it later prior to our joining the convoy. We had the basics, and once I'd unpacked our treasured possessions the house had the feeling of 'home'.

It would take us a few years to be able to afford a second-hand paraffin fridge, twin-tub washing machine and small new television for the kitchen. In the meantime, we used the cottage fridge and freezer, and to save constant walking back and forth along the path during the day, I kept the daily fresh milk in a bucket behind a door in the coolest part of the house. After a sundowner on the front lawn when Ian had finished the day's work, the kitchen table was mostly where he'd sit for the next 19-and-a-bit years.

Steinhausen ('Stonehouse' in German) Police Station, about 4 kilometres from our house by farm road and 12 on the main dirt road, was the law enforcement for our area. It was a cluster of natural-stone buildings (no shops), one of which was now used as the Police Station, all having been built in earlier times as an army fort during the Herero/German war. The Officer in Charge was a white man, beneath him 3 other lower-ranked African policemen. Once a month, a vehicle towing a trailer carrying a large water tank was sent from the Steinhausen Police Station to Kambingana to refill as they had no water supply either from a borehole or dam. A neighbouring farm was called 'Steinhausen' as well, and we became friendly with the German owners, a very competent farmer, Gundolf Schlosser, and his wife, Irene.

We were now well into October, called 'suicide month' by South-Westers due to being unbearably hot, but more scorching weeks were yet to come. Every day, summer or winter, rain or shine, as the years would prove, water was to be Ian's biggest and constant headache through times of plenty, others of scarcity. Dam capacities and operational water-producing boreholes, though obviously vital, were not the only major water challenges. *Getting the actual water to* livestock and farm points, every day, through piping crossing an area of 45,000 acres to fill reservoirs and cattle troughs in a camp kilometres away, or come out of a tap when turned on at the house 30 kilometres distant, was Ian's *ultimate water challenge.* At any one time, 2,840 cattle, sometimes over 1,000 more, needed water every day – 700 breeding stock, 600 calves to one year, 600 weaners to two years, 600 oxen and heifers to three years, 45 bulls, and 300 oxen and heifers to three-and-a-half years. Water pipes would burst, or freeze in winter, lime-up and clog, and occasionally even be dug up by game. Borehole pumps, generator engines and fan belts running from 7 o'clock in the morning to 5 in the afternoon would break down, and with the distances involved to travel from one point to another there was also theft of the equipment. *One way or another, water was the 'lifeblood' determining success or failure for Kambingana Ranch.*

Keith, Mary and little Debbie had visited us a month after we'd all settled into our new jobs and homes. Keith drove to work daily in Windhoek, and once a week they went shopping, mainly for tinned provisions as they didn't yet have a fridge. Keith's starting salary was Rand 440 a month, but the same as with our situation, they faced considerable financial struggle after Angola. He made arrangements with Barlows Company for an advance on his pay-cheque which helped them over the next couple of months to buy a few pieces of inexpensive furniture and other necessities. Then Keith wisely sold the Chevrolet bakkie, buying a little Fiat to save further on fuel costs.

Keith: "The first few weeks in South West Africa were a torrid time for our toddler daughter, Debbie. For me, the most difficult times were those of the first year, starting out with nothing, knowing that only hard work would enable me to keep my job with Barlows Tractor Company. I really didn't know much about Caterpillar tractors so I had a lot of catch-up work to do to get on to an even level with my co-workers. Honestly, it was no joy and put me under a good deal of pressure. If it wasn't for the fact that we could go out to Kambingana where Mum and Dad were farming, ride horses and get a little freedom from the day-to-day humdrum of mechanics I would've had a few issues with life."

As a boy, Keith had helped Ian on the farm at Westlands, Kenya and his young dream was to follow in his father's footsteps and become a farmer when he grew up. Having to flee our Angolan property due to civil unrest was naturally a double blow: it was the loss of what should have been Keith's and Stuart's, our 2 sons' rightful inheritance, our

Fazenda Esperança. They had worked tirelessly side by side with dedication and achievement for their futures, so what Africa kept tearing from them in return for their love and loyalty was a raw trauma of unfair loss. Our family were, after all, born on the continent, lived and worked here and were as African as any other native of the land. Our forefathers since 1820 had helped to pioneer, build-up and move South and East Africa forward. Ian and I struggled to find an adequate way of conveying to Keith and Stuart how much we understood their heartache and that the events that had unfolded were not of our doing.

A poem by Stuart conveys his inner turmoil and longing for Angola:

HOMEWARD BOUND

I hear the call
Of the rising sun
Of the distant horizons
And gathered thunder clouds
Of starlit nights
Of thundering waterfalls
And melodious streams
Of raging rivers
Of lake waters rippling
And dew drops dripping
Of the rustle of leaves
Of the caressing grass
On the endless plain
And the singing of the wind
Of the hoof on the beaten earth
Of the fang and claw on flesh
Of the vast country where I belong
I shall follow the setting sun in answer to the call
For I will be *Homeward Bound*

On Kambingana cattle were lost over the years, few due to snake bite though this remained a constant hazard, or calves falling down ant-bear holes and occasional deaths due to lightning strikes, but mostly from poaching. Ian was accountable to management for all livestock losses. South West Africa is relatively disease free – all cattle were inoculated for any particular disease which was prevalent. Although there were plenty of ticks, there was no need for dipping. In the extensive, diverse South West African countryside poisonous zebra snakes (even in town gardens), cobras, puff adders, mambas and many other snake species were plentiful. To Stuart, a lover of these reptiles since childhood, this of course was paradise.

One morning, Ian was working on the Lister diesel engine that ran the borehole pump at Karamba water post. It had much the same set up as our house generator outbuilding (this particular Karamba water pump was a constant battle over the years). He had a Bushman staff member standing near the open doorway waiting to assist, who suddenly started whistling softly and kept looking up at the roof. Glancing at him, the Bushman pointed to Ian's foot. Looking down, Ian saw a large puff adder curled directly behind the heel of his boot. He says he doesn't know how he did it, but in one movement Ian jumped clear through the doorway. Puff adders are common snakes in East, South and South West Africa. Well camouflaged with intricate, even beautiful colour skin patterns to blend into their surroundings they are slow and sluggish often being trodden on, but have one of the swiftest bites when provoked and can strike accurately backwards, hence being responsible for a large percentage of all snake bite cases. With long front fangs, their potentially fatal venom (that works at a slower rate than that of cobras and mambas) causes tissue destruction and death of cells, swelling, intense pain, haemorrhage and even death.

One Sunday on a weekend visit, Keith had been up since dawn and gone on horseback to see the plentiful game for which Kambingana was famous. Returning home after a satisfying outing in the bush, no sooner had we sat down to a late breakfast at the dining room table than a bakkie drove into our front yard, the driver a young Afrikaans man, introducing himself as 'Johan'. In halting English, he said he lived on the 'next but one farm' and had come to make our acquaintance. We invited Johan to join us at the table for coffee and carried on chatting and eating when it suddenly occurred to Ian that our guest seemed a bit mystified in our company, and asked him, "What's the matter?"

Johan's matter-of-fact reply was that he'd, "Never seen an 'Engelsman' (Englishman) before."

From Johan's honest response we took it to imply that we were actually quite normal and therefore acceptable! A true friendship developed between us from this time on. Johan was a tall, well-built and very powerful man, with enormous hands, a happy face, wonderful laugh and a nature to match. One could never be sad or miserable around Johan, and he had the kindest heart. Whenever he visited, he'd always sweep the women in our family up off the floor into his arms and give us great big bear hugs. Johan could never pronounce Ian's name properly, so instead simply called him 'Engelsman' or 'Jan', which was fine because 'Jan' in Afrikaans is 'John' in English and 'Ian' is Scottish for 'John' so it was apt considering Ian's father was Scottish-born, William Alexander. Ian in return often endearingly called Johan 'Boertjie' (Afrikaans for 'farmer') in jest. The 2 were very close, valued and respected one another. After a few visits from Johan, Ian made a large, round sturdy 'stool' for him out of a steel grease-drum and I put a pillow on top, which was kept handy nearby because Johan's weight broke one of the pine chairs. Luckily, he didn't hurt himself, and with his splendid sense of humour he never took exception to having to sit on the drum! Johan's farm was 'Uhland'.

We also made friends with farmers Kurt and Carola Kronsbein and their young children, not too distant from us on the Omitara dirt road. Carola was a superb artist, particularly of wildlife and also painted ostrich eggs. Sigi Dau (mother of Claus, Stuart's best mate), living on the neighbouring farm, 'Damara', became a good friend too. Claus was a delightful, handsome young German lad attending the excellent German private school in Windhoek.

Lindsay arrived in late December 1975 after a few days train trip from Rhodesia to Windhoek, having worked in Salisbury the year since January. Again, we were all together for Christmas, thankfully everyone safe and well. Our Christmas tree was novel, a true South West African version of some attractive pieces of dry 'kameeldoring' (thorn tree) standing in a big pot in a corner of the sitting room. The long thorns on the bare branches were perfect for hanging decorations on plus matchboxes covered in gold or silver paper filled with different coloured Smarties (candy-coated chocolate sweets).

The bathroom and kitchen of the house had hot water via small inside gas-water-heaters on the wall, a completely unsatisfactory situation particularly in the bathroom. For a 4th time, Ian now being a fundi at this, he installed the same excellent and reliable hot-water heating system we'd had at Uruku, Westlands and our Angola Fazenda, though in South West Africa this was known as a 'donkey' (and quite appropriately so) – a base, 2 closed sides and back, a covered top and a chimney, all made of bricks and concrete, with an open front for the wood fire that heated the water in the big drum above, and a the long pipe which allowed the steam to escape reaching high above. This 'donkey' would out-live our stay of more than 19 years on Kambingana during which time we had to replace the steel drum only twice. With stones collected from Kambingana dam, we put down attractive crazy-paving around the 'donkey' and cesspit area, made pathways to the front and back kitchen entrances and planted 2 small areas of lawn and two lemon trees in the back garden.

Munde Paulus became our gardener shortly after we moved into the main house – a tall, elderly man with an already wrinkled face and arthritis in his hands, but determined to continue working. He was reliable except when 'in his cups', usually coinciding with month-end pay time and our trip with the staff to do their shopping where they also made purchases at the liquor store. The old fellow held a privileged position as we employed another man to help with his duties. As a young Ovambo (African tribe of South West Africa) boy, Munde had been employed by our neighbouring Afrikaans farmer-friend, Johan's father, Mr Willy Dempers. While drilling a borehole one day, somehow Willy's right arm became caught in the belting and was torn off, hanging by a thread of flesh. He asked Munde to get the penknife out of his pocket and cut free his severed arm. Munde, in shock and so afraid ran away. Willy, left alone, somehow managed to get the knife out, open it with his teeth and cut loose his arm. Munde loved talking about this story, which Willy Dempers verified. We never found out Munde Paulus' real age. He came to us old and grey, around 60 I would think. Apart from the times we'd take leave or be away overnight, it would be hard to imagine a day without old Munde. As rooted in the soil as the big, years old thorn tree outside our bedroom window, so was Munde

Paulus entrenched in the life and memories of our days on The Place of the Water. He was a rich character with a uniquely serene way about him, dipping his hat in respect every morning to Ian and me and puffing on his smelly tobacco pipe year after year.

Things progressed well in the garden. The scrubby front grass was extended considerably in time to become large lush green lawn with surrounding curved flowerbeds. Some pretty, mainly pink, scented roses brightened the bed under the big lounge windows, and grey-colour saltbush planted from seedlings 'Boertjie' Johan gave us grew quickly forming a thick hedge. A number of different geraniums grown from cuttings were dotted around the garden and under our front bedroom windows. Various indigenous water-wise plants and grasses were put in. Hardy plumbago hedging with pale blue flowers that never needed watering was planted under our other bedroom window and the windows in Stuart's room. At the bottom of the front garden, we amassed a substantial number of aloes.

The shade under the thorn tree was perfect for growing violets, while in the branches above a busy social gathering of birds ensued throughout the day pecking away at the feeding tray, interspersed with taking a dip in the bird bath, preening and sunning their wings. It was amusing watching their little squabbles as they went about their daily schedule and fascinating to witness their intelligence as they flew off then returned with grass and all sorts of soft downy feathers in their beaks to commence masterful architectural dexterity in building or repairing their nests. Many other bird species came to the garden joining the weavers in the thorn tree – scimitar-billed wood hoopoe, chanting goshawks, black, red and white shrike, honey-suckers, sparrows, doves, finches, thrushes, fly-catchers and grey louries.

The driveway was taken from the front right around to the back garden gate. Grape vines were planted either side of the natural-stone pathway to the kitchen door which eventually made cooling shade up the sides and over the top of the pathway by way of a trellis. Many different trees were put in – wild olives, lots of Persian Lilacs for summer shade (which lost their leaves in winter giving us welcome sun at that time of year), gum trees, and flowering peach. A large circular aloe garden was established outside the back garden gate as a roundabout in the driveway. Many tall succulent aloes were planted with their long and pointy spiky green leaves and burnt-orange flowers atop, naturally found in the South West African countryside. They were beautiful when in bloom and a favourite of the honey-sucker birds.

Willy Dempers gave us some Queensland prickly pear cuttings and 24 peach pips. The prickly pears were planted together to make a thick hedge on the side at the far end of the front garden. They grew excellently into tall plants with not so many leaves, fewer prickles than other varieties and large delicious fruit. This small orchard was surrounded by game fencing and, as with Willy's superb prickly pears, the peach pips grew beautifully into trees and in 3 years we had our first fruit. Willy's farm was 'Toronto'.

The garden became quite an impressive sight of greenery and colour surrounding the house, and I felt sure Daisy would have been pleased. There was much work to be done over the years for old Munde and his helper as the garden matured, plants being replaced or changes made, summer seeds sown for petunias, bulbs put in for ranunculi, freesias and daffodils. There was also the constant work involved of watering, weeding, mowing, trimming lawn edges and composting the soil with matured cattle manure. Apart from keeping the dust down in the house, the garden was a tranquil and relaxing setting for morning coffee, sometimes breakfast or afternoon tea out front, particularly when we had day visitors or stay-over guests, and weekend barbeques. Whatever effort or problems were encountered in establishing and maintaining our Kambingana farm garden over the years, all were thoroughly worthwhile as it became a pleasurable and welcome retreat for Ian and me as a break from daily farm work.

The staff compound was fairly far from our house, obscured by bush, on the other side of the main farm dirt road to Steinhausen to the left, or for Omitara to the right. Having no way of communicating with the staff when they were at their compound, Ian rigged up a large solid iron bar which hung from a tree branch at the front of the house on the garage side. When banged with an iron rod it sounded 'bell-like' and summoned everyone to work. It was also perfect for emergencies when no time could be lost, for example in the case of veld fires or when cattle were caught in mud in the dams.

I'd looked for a housemaid once we'd settled in a bit. Maria, a small San Bushman woman (one of the earliest tribes of Southern Africa renowned for their unique ability to live in desert conditions) had applied. I liked her immediately and gratefully employed her. She had a sweet, heart-shaped rather wrinkly face, tiny hands and feet, a very big bottom and teeth blackened from lack of attention and constant smoking. Maria was a thoroughly nice person, reliable, very willing and so pleased to have a job. We got along well together though I didn't allow her to smoke in our house. Communicating verbally was a problem. She spoke Bushmen and Afrikaans, but by showing Maria what I wanted done she quickly picked up the work. Whatever she did or said was with the minimum of fuss, she was honest in character, dainty in her movements, very precise and determined. I bought her 2 housemaid's uniforms, one pink the other green. Each had a front button-up frock with a collar, matching apron with a front pocket and lace trim around the edges, and a headscarf. She was proud of her uniform, always neat and tidy in her appearance. I also paid for her shoes, size 2 to 3, depending on the style and make. Slowly, I picked up 'kitchen Afrikaans' from Maria and many times marvelled at the very complicated clicks of her Bushmen language, way beyond my grasp. She was a great help and also understood our family pets were special to us, treating them well with kindness and care. They in turn, liked her.

I appreciated Maria taking me on long walks through the farm bush, showing me how the Bushmen can survive on grubs and chrysalises found in the ground and on the bark of trees. Roots, which always carry enough water, when shredded with a knife can be squeezed into the mouth. Another type of root that is pulped and rubbed on the hands makes a good soap. She also unselfconsciously, in complete silence, imitated for me the various animals the Bushmen stalk and kill for food. I found them a fascinating people. Out on walks with Maria, I also came to know and learn about the interesting bush birdlife – kestrels, secretary birds, kori bustards and different species of eagles.

Each morning, old Munde and Maria would have their breakfast of porridge, sandwiches and sweet coffee whilst sitting on blocks of wood near the 'donkey' chatting and enjoying a smoke. Sometimes, Maria bought cigarette paper at Reichardt's to roll her smokes using the tobacco provided in her food rations, or she'd tear pieces from the old newspapers Reichardt's used to wrap the staff's monthly shopping. When there were plenty of eggs, Maria and old Munde would have fried eggs for breakfast too, exactly as we ourselves ate. Working with old Munde in the garden and him being in charge of the 'donkey', I learnt some Afrikaans from him as well.

Maria had 2 ways of smoking – the 1st I'd seen before, where the rolled lit cigarette (no filter) burns down to the butt in the corner of the mouth, but the first time I saw Maria's 2nd way of smoking I stopped dead to take this in and try to figure it out. Instead of putting the unlit end of the rolled cigarette between her lips, she'd put the lit end of the cigarette into her mouth and have the unlit end sticking out. How she didn't burn her tongue or inside of her cheeks was amazing. I found it most strange and at the same time rather fascinating. I think it had something to do with lack of air to the lit end of the cigarette stopping it from burning down so fast. Then when she wanted a couple of puffs, she'd turn the cigarette around, take some quick drags on her smoke then put the lit end back in her mouth. I never saw old Munde smoking a cigarette. He preferred his pipe. Maria would gather Ian's filter cigarette butts together and take them home. Again, I've no idea what for. I once had to check Maria's mouth for a gum sore. Her teeth were ground down in the gums and apart from being black also had areas of dark brown, I think due to the lit end of her cigarette being inside her mouth so often.

Many hours were spent and fuel costs run up in the quest to keep water supplied to every area of the enormous property. In time, Ian requested purchase permission from the company and received 2 Suzuki fat-cat 90cc motorbikes for the daily 70 kilometre water checks of pipelines, reservoirs and water troughs, as opposed to driving big farm vehicles heavy on diesel or petrol. Introducing old Kenya ways with responsibility specifically given to individuals, Mattheus became the Ranch 'water-man' and Ian taught him how to ride the motorbikes, one being kept as a spare in case of breakdown. Mattheus recorded water details twice daily in a book kept in our kitchen and I had to *ask his permission* to water the garden. A dishevelled, exhausted Mattheus arrived at the house one day. He'd walked a long way having had quite a spill on the bike, but thankfully, was all right. In Afrikaans, his short version of the story was very funny though. Translated, it became, "That motorbike, it bucked me off!" he said wiping his brow.

Just as well there were 2 bikes as the company had to wait for an order to be sent from Japan to fix the damaged one. Mattheus, now aware of what could so easily happen on a motorbike, became very careful and ever respectful of this machine in his charge.

We went to Windhoek once a month for shopping, stopping in at the company offices for paperwork and the like. Apart from groceries, one had to think of and remember everything – bank, pharmacy, vet, post office, hairdresser, dentist, doctor, sort any problems at school or hostel for Stuart. Occasionally, the vehicle needed attention or farm supplies had to be picked up, etc. What you forgot waited till the next trip. Up early on these busy trips, we were gone before the sun could heat the car dashboard and home often only after dark. Sometimes we'd go together, or Ian alone, or myself, mostly it was just me, a 4-hour return drive. With life being quite lonely on the farm so far from town and people, and neighbours fairly distant, I looked forward to seeing some bustle of humanity, perhaps meeting a friend, having coffee and a bit of lunch, looking in shops and seeing our children, but was always relieved to be back home with Ian and our animals.

The Kalahari Sands Hotel doorman was a proud, elderly Herero gentleman always dressed in smart black tails with many glittering, decorative tin medals pinned onto his lapel and jacket, pin-stripe trousers and top hat. We gave him a good quantity of hartebeest venison for Christmas 1975 (and this would continue over the years), so we always received a great welcome when visiting the posh hotel.

When we first started work on the Ranch, Greater Kudu were thriving, stretching from Windhoek past the airport onwards, with our Steinhausen Omitara area being the most densely populated. After the airport, the tarmac highway to Omitara turn-off is long and straight as far as the eye can see. Many roads of the country are like this with considerable distances between towns so motorists often drive at speed, numerous accidents occurring due to hours behind the wheel and the driver having fallen asleep, or kudu leaping out from the side of the road in front of the vehicle. Particularly when driving at night, it was imperative that the driver have a front seat passenger as a second pair of 'kudu lookout eyes'. Even back seat passengers would sit forward and help try to spot kudu as the problem and danger was compounded by headlights shining from both directions.

The Greater Kudu, one of the largest species of antelope, is found in East and Southern Africa. Their coat colours are reddish-brown, brown to bluish-grey, with 4 to 12 vertical white stripes along their torso and a small white chevron between their eyes. Males (much larger than females) can weigh up to 315 kg, stand as much as 160 cm tall at the shoulder, have short manes along the spine, beards from the throat down, nose markings and their horns with two-and-a-half twists have a record length of 187.64 cm. Females can weigh 210 kg, standing up to 100 cm at the shoulder, are hornless and without beard or nose markings. The Lesser Kudu, a more primitive species, is found in the forests of East Africa.

In the early years our children were all based in Windhoek and came out to the farm many weekends, often arriving Friday nights, sometimes Beryl with her boyfriend, Koos, a very likeable fellow with a 'Van der Merwe' book of jokes stored in his memory, giving us plenty of laughs. Occasionally, they'd bring friends along as well, so Saturdays and Sundays our house was usually full and busy and there were always mounds of linen and clothes to be washed. The men went off with Ian around the farm or rode the motorbikes or horses in the bush. Keith and Stuart often camped overnight in the veld (bush). It was good to see the 2 brothers up to plenty of tough man-stuff again, though Keith leaping from his horse onto moving hartebeest had me grateful no serious injury ever became either of them.

It took less than a month for Lindsay to find secretarial work in Windhoek. Keith had helped her move into a bachelor flat with her few belongings. Mary and Keith's 2nd child, a son, Andrew, was born in April 1976, the year Lindsay married in Windhoek in early June. Even though finances were tight, Ian let her have the dress of her dreams made and the evening wedding reception was held on the top floor of the Kalahari Sands Hotel where Beryl was barmaid. Debbie was flower-girl looking cute in red, a photo capturing her having a tiny sip of Keith's champagne. We'd not yet had time to make many friends living so far out on the Ranch, so apart from our immediate family, some relations, a few long-time friends and a couple of new ones, most of the wedding guests were by invitation of the groom, an Englishman who worked at one of the smart, top German stores in the city centre, Wecke & Voigts.

Over supper one night, Ian and I discussed getting some geese and on-the-point-of-lay pullets to ensure we always had enough eggs. He'd already jackal-proofed the fencing in the duck area, but the pullets would require a substantial hen-house which would take Ian time to build. The chickens Louis and Dalene had left us were housed overnight in a small pen, wandering around during the day laying their few eggs all over the place. Gis, the machinery manager's wife, liked the Muscovy ducks so Ian suggested we let her have the ducks, being fast breeders, to make way for the geese. I invited Gis over for coffee the next day and she was delighted.

"*Vot ist de* name of *de* ducks," she asked.

"Muscovy," I replied.

"Mus..."

"Mus..covy," I said, slowly.

"Mus...covy," she repeated, "*ja*, Muscovy... *gut*."

So, the drake and 5 ducks were taken over to Gis' house ('Gisela' was her full German Christian name, shortened to 'Gis,' pronounced the same way as one would say 'geese' in English).

The 20 geese were very happy with their new home, wandering around grazing on grass, dabbling about in the pond, gabbling and making a lot of noise most of the time. They were excellent 'watchdogs' too. We always knew when someone strange was around or something unusual was happening from all the racket they'd make, but they started becoming upset by the comings and goings of old Munde and took to chasing and pecking him on the legs, which had the old fellow hopping about during his gardening work. When they began flying over the perimeter garden fencing the jackals became a nuisance, sneaking up and catching them, so unfortunately, we landed up having to give them away.

In winter the company directors and their invited guests would come for hunting. The very complicated, precise operation of capturing game for export sale was done in June and July by a professional game trapper from Otjiwarongo, by the name of Koosie Steyn. Kambingana was licensed to sell 300 hartebeest annually. The Ranch, particularly around Kambingana dam, had plenty of short nutritious grass hartebeest are partial to. Kambingana had more hartebeest than greater kudu or gemsbok which other farmers sold as those were more prolific on their properties.

Hartebeest are African grassland antelope with 8 subspecies, found in various countries on the continent having savannahs, open plains and woodlands. Depending on the subspecies, the body colours, horn shapes and thicknesses can vary greatly – coats from dull light sandy-brown to red, dark-blackish to sandy yellow, with 2 horns forming an open 'O' at the top or a 'U', 'V' and 'Z'-shapes, both males and females having horns which can reach 70cm in length. Their herbivore diet consists mainly of grasses with small amounts of legumes. They graze in the early mornings and late afternoons, resting in shade during the hottest daylight hours, and can live up to 20 years in the wild or 19 years in captivity. Hartebeest are generally calm in nature, but can be ferocious when provoked and form herds numbering 20 to 300. Males can weigh up to 255kg and females up to 185kg. Adults stand just over one metre at the shoulder. Hartebeest game meat is extremely popular and proven to be good for one's health due to excellent polyunsaturated/saturated fatty acid ratios. Together with trophy hunting, habitat destruction, domestic cattle land competition and human settlement some populations are declining with the hartebeest today being extinct in Morocco, Tunisia, Somalia, Algeria, Egypt, Libya and Lesotho though they have also been introduced in Zimbabwe and Swaziland.

The Afrikaans name 'hertebeest' was given by the Boers, first recorded in South African literature in 1660 by Jan van Riebeeck, the Dutch word 'hert' being 'deer' in English and 'beest' being 'beast', commonly known now as 'hartebeest'. Kambingana had Red Hartebeest (Alcelaphus buselaphus caama) which, thankfully, have an increasing population.

In the years the Ranch captured hartebeest for relocation to areas of South Africa, Koosie's adherence to the strictest safety procedures ensured a minimal loss of only 2 animals during his contract with

Kambingana. He told me that when capturing gemsbok, for example, with their very long, straight and sharply pointed horns, pieces of PVC pipe would be slipped onto their horns during transport to prevent injury to one another. Koosie was an excellent game catcher, even being offered a job in Australia to round up and catch wild horses in Far Northern Queensland.

The hartebeest capture was arranged a year in advance, lasting about 5 days each time, less if there were no hitches, and only going ahead when all procedures and every minutest detail was in place as there was no space for errors. The 1st day was for arrival of the 2-seater helicopter, equipment, game trucks and about 20 staff, then locating with Ian the exact suitable area, always on Boomlager, for setting up of the Y-shaped game capture enclosure with trucks fuelled, ready and waiting. The next 3 days was to round up by helicopter, capture and load the hartebeest and depart immediately for South Africa. Day 5 was to pack up camp and the equipment then return to the Otjiwarongo private game trapping headquarters.

During school holidays, Stuart was chosen to fly with Koosie who was his own Bell helicopter pilot, otherwise I'd go. The Y-shaped capture enclosure was a temporary, portable fence-like structure made from spaced steel droppers that could be hammered into the ground, covered across vertically on the inside from one steel dropper to the next with brown Hessian sacking to blend into the natural background, the Hessian being secured with wire to the steel droppers.

Strapped into the seat next to Koosie and with a side handle to hold onto, the job Stuart or I had was to spot the hartebeest and do the counting while Koosie navigated flying the helicopter between big thorn trees and missing the telephone poles and wires, swooping down, rounding up and directing the hartebeest with the chopper, about 10 antelope at a time, towards and into the wide opening of the capture enclosure which would then immediately be closed off by some of the men hurriedly holding up a Hessian barrier behind the animals.

From here, the hartebeest naturally rushed forward into the narrow 'straight leg' of the Y-shaped enclosure, being a small camp where any old animals, ones too young or not perfect specimens (the South African buyers were very particular) or mothers with babies were set free immediately. The remaining hartebeest were then herded forward by Koosie's men, the animals again rushing through a 2nd narrow funnel straight into the specially designed waiting game trucks with sliding doors. Once in the truck, each animal was inoculated with an antibiotic in case of injury and a mild tranquilliser, in readiness for the at least 18 hour long journey to South Africa where the game buyers were anxiously waiting. It was imperative that experienced drivers were employed as the trucks had to be driven carefully and steadily, with no sudden braking or jolting, and had to reach their destinations without further loss of time.

I found it an awesome and exhilarating experience to be in the sky, high enough to get an all-round surveillance of the area, feel the bite of freezing air, then drop down just above the tree tops to muster the game and control it by flying this way and that. I was amazed at the manoeuvrability of the Bell helicopter, a somewhat giddying experience for me, exacerbated by there being no doors on the chopper so you could lean out and better see what was going on below with the game, though I never attempted to hang over the edge for a broader view. From above or at a side angle, the scenario of running Red Hartebeest reminded me of the many Bushmen paintings I've seen that don't show the lower legs and hooves of animals.

Ian caught a young male cheetah pulling down one of the sheep in the kraal near our house. Afflicted with rickets (a vitamin D deficiency causing softening of the bone) the cheetah was fairly easy to catch. Perhaps its mother had died and the cub had been without milk for some time. We fed it a freshly shot guinea-fowl and milk daily. Koosie soon sold the cheetah on to a Saudi sheik. We received Rand 200 and I imagine the sheik paid a considerable amount more than that. My arms still bear several scars from handling the cheetah.

Old Munde's wife, Angelina, was brought in to help Maria with the laundry. Company Directors, their guests and hunters had expensive linen in the cottage, and Angelina would occasionally help with this extra ironing. She said she was Herero, but was fine featured with paler skin, extremely tall, slender and altogether good-looking; more Nilotic (northern African). She and Simon's (the headman's) wife, Constantia, wore the traditional Herero female attire much like the fashion popular in Victorian times consisting of yards of material for the voluminous heavy skirts, tight bodices and puffed sleeves ending in a tight band around the wrists. Their ornate, rather peculiarly shaped Herero head gear, usually matching the fabric of their swirling dresses, was another feature of their traditional garments, being tight cloth first wound around the head then sculpted outwards, rather horn-like to sharp ends either side. Angelina (many years younger than Munde) and Constantia were proud women. As slender as Angelina was, Constantia was plump. Both were quiet-spoken and always moved in an unhurried manner. When they sat down cross-legged as is their custom, their dresses billowed around them much like the skirts of a porcelain doll. In the South West African heat, we often wondered how they coped swathed in metres of fabric.

Ian had made a series of long outside clothes lines on our bedroom side of the house. It was essential to iron all the washing, linen and clothing due to 'Tumbo' or 'Putsi' fly larvae – to see and watch its progress once it has entered the skin is most off-putting. This fly, Cordylobia Anthropophaga, is found throughout Africa. The female lays her eggs in sandy soil already contaminated with urine or excreta, sometimes on damp clothes or nappies hanging on washing lines or bedding left to air, and bare bottoms of babies playing in sand are also susceptible. When the larvae come into contact with the skin, human or animal, they burrow into the flesh and develop, causing swellings that look like boils. Closely examined, a tiny dark opening can be seen through which the growing maggot breathes air. When the boil-like swelling is 'ripe', being when the maggot reaches maturity, one can smear Vaseline over the now enlarged hole causing it to break out for air then gently squeeze the loathsome wriggling one centimetre long white maggot out. I've seen several of these develop on dogs and humans, and once on a baby with 9 boils on his bottom.

Word reached us after a time that the machinery manager was heard to say in Omitara that he'd soon see 'Die Engelsman' off Kambingana. His wife, Gis, was a friendly person and she and I would visit one another. We didn't realise at the time though, that he and one of the Windhoek Managers were friends and they'd thoughts of putting in our place someone of their own choice. The situation, for Ian particularly, became unpleasant in his work as he had to deal with the machinery manager on a daily basis. We really started feeling unhappy.

One Sunday morning, Keith took Mary horse-riding; her first attempt. She was on 'Kipling'. This ended in disaster, as Mary's horse at a gallop went one way and she the other connecting with a thorn tree, seriously cutting her face and fracturing her one arm. Keith rushed home to get our car and take her to the Roman Catholic Hospital in Windhoek. Being Sunday, doctors weren't easily available. Mary had deep cuts on her face going through her eyelid down to her cheek, as well as under her cheek bone, and a smaller cut below her bottom lip. She had a lot of stitches. A few years later in Windhoek, Mary had cosmetic surgery with minute stitches on her eyelid as her lashes were growing into her eye causing irritation. Today, one can hardly see the scar.

Late one evening we had a visitor, a complete stranger. Like Johan, he'd heard about 'Die Engelsman' and was curious to know what we were like. His name was van Zyl from Gobabis and he spoke no English whatsoever. Luckily, he could converse with Ian whose Afrikaans had improved further. I realised there were lots of questions being asked, but since I was quite ignored by van Zyl, I retired to bed. The gentleman departed at 2 o'clock in the morning, and Ian told me 'tongue in cheek' that Mr van Zyl seemed satisfied we were bona fide!

A visit from ex-Kenya friends, the Overdycks, had a worrisome Sunday ending. Out viewing game on the Ranch, Ian drove under a thorn tree, and Kim, their daughter (my god-daughter) standing on the back of the bakkie with the other youngsters was pricked by one of the long, thick black-tipped thorns in her eye – another hurried trip to Windhoek in search of a doctor. Luckily, the eye lens wasn't pierced so no permanent damage occurred to her sight, but it was a dreadful way to end an otherwise perfect weekend. On the positive side though, Peter and Tessa had brought us their old Defy gas stove (the cost fitting Ian's budget) as they'd bought a fancy new one for their home. The heat from the old wood-burning stove that came with the house had made the kitchen unbearable in summer apart from the daily slog with chopping wood so Ian had bought us a 3-plate gas cooker which, unfortunately, in the long term also proved inadequate for our needs. Having a proper stove with 4 plates and an oven now made a big difference to our lives, particularly mine.

Beryl 'phoned early one morning from work at the Kalahari Sands Hotel, saying a dubious looking man had asked for her and then requested our contact details. Immediately, I asked her if his name was John Lewis. She replied, "Yes." I laughed and explained that John had been our 'overnight prison cell saviour' in Grootfontein when Debbie had been so sick and that we'd told him she was probably working at the Kalahari Sands. I asked Beryl to send John on to us and tell him that there'd be a welcome bed made-up for him. When Ian came back for breakfast, he had a good chuckle about Beryl's hesitant remarks regarding John's appearance!

A few hours later, up drove the hand-painted bright yellow VW Kombi and trailer which we recognised immediately. Out stepped 'our man', exactly as he'd been in Grootfontein – unshaven, shoeless, emanating a strong body odour, scruffy and dishevelled in distinctly unlaundered clothing. The trailer had a large assortment of kudu, gemsbok and springbok horns firmly tied on the top with rope. We were pleased to see one another again and know we were all well. John explained that once a year for a month he drove around South West Africa buying up quality game horns which he cleaned and polished, making them into napkin rings, ornamental lamps, bracelets and finger rings etc. which were sold on to tourist shops. He said the year had been good for him as he'd managed to get more than the usual number of horns. I said to John we'd prepared a bed for him in the guest cottage and that after his long travels he was welcome to use the bathroom before coming over to the house for a drink and lunch.

"Oh, no," he immediately responded, "while on safari I never wash till I return to Jo'burg and my wife!"

My mind flashed back to the time when John had found us, weary and worried and probably in much the same state as we now found him. We had a very pleasant time reminiscing, shared supper and John was genuinely happy that we'd found safe refuge at Kambingana. Next morning, he was off on his travels to other farms hoping to get better horns. Though we never heard from John again, he'll always be remembered. He took us under his wing when we were at our lowest.

Kudu which are browsers came regularly to our house. Once I'd established some garden beds, they displayed a distinct taste for the geraniums growing beneath our bedroom window near the big thorn tree, yet wouldn't eat from the plumbago hedging underneath our other bedroom window. Ian's side of the bed was about 4 feet from the window with the geraniums and on a moonlit night with cloudless, starry skies, we had some of the most magical memories I'll never forget and which continued all the years we lived on Kambingana. After the generator was switched off we'd lie in bed, curtains and windows wide open, propped up on our pillows, and watch the beautiful kudu come, clearly seeing the inner soft pinkness of their big ears almost transparent in the moonlight, while they daintily nipped at the tips of the plants without making a sound. They were so sure footed that no part of the garden was ever destroyed, and particularly loved to eat the ends of succulent aloe leaves and the delicately perfumed roses beneath the front lounge windows. The 5-strand (around 4 foot 8 inches high) garden fence was no deterrent to a kudu, they easily jumped it. Eventually, we had to put up a game fence (6 foot high with wire strands about 6 inches apart, and even that I've once seen an adult kudu jump) around the peach orchard on the garage side so the kudu couldn't get their heads through to nibble on the leaves or eat the fruit from the peach trees, though the rest of the garden was still accessible to them. Gemsbok or hartebeest, though not visitors to our garden but plentiful on the farm would on the other hand, dig with their hooves a dip in the sand underneath the lowest strand of wire then squeeze under the fencing lines to move freely around the bush.

The story of the Katatura State Hospital in Windhoek 'losing' Maria's new born, sickly Bushman baby was shocking. Maria's half-Bushman husband, 'Kleinbooi', was one of the farm workmen. They had 5 children living with them though I didn't know if these were all from Maria or born to another woman with Kleinbooi as the father.

Maria must have fallen pregnant shortly after starting work with us. There was no way I could tell she was 'with child' as she said nothing about it, never appeared sickly in any way requiring additional time off, her work standard remained exceptional and she continued smoking heavily. It was some months before her belly even indicated any sign of an expected baby.

South West Africa was still under South African rule and we, employees ourselves, were still fairly new to the country and the Ranch, trying to build a relationship with the staff and understand the ways of the different tribes of the workers on Kambingana. This made us a little hesitant in meddling in their personal lives. Sometimes it was better to leave well alone, but I was a bit worried about Maria continuing to work when she confirmed she was pregnant. Ian made it clear to her that should she need any time off or prefer to stay at home until after her baby was born that would be in order. The smoking part was a difficult one. I knew this wasn't good for her baby, but she'd had children before and they were apparently well. Nevertheless, this niggled me, so one day, without a 'lecturing' tone of voice, I quietly told Maria the smoking wasn't good for her baby while I rubbed my hand on my stomach, and asked if she'd understood what I'd said. She acknowledged she had. I left it at that, hoping she'd quit or at least cut down, but it made no difference.

When the child was due Maria simply advised it was 'her time' saying she'd return after the baby's birth. Lindsay was on the farm with us. Maria came over to the house a couple of days later to show us her new baby girl. Perhaps the child's Bushman name was too complicated for us to pronounce as Maria simply said her name was 'Baba' when we asked her. Lindsay and I were amazed at how exceptionally tiny the child was, like a doll, perfect in every outward respect, delicate little face, minute fingers and toes, dressed in pink and wrapped up tight in a baby blanket, her mother very proud of her.

After about 5 days, Maria came to the house saying she was fit for work, and of her own accord wished to resume her duties, now with little Baba strapped to her back in a cloth baby carrier she'd made herself. I was not completely comfortable with this as I felt somewhat concerned about the physical aspects of her doing housework with her baby on her back, and got Ian again to explain to her this time that as and when Baba needed feeding, changing or whatever else, Maria was to attend to her child first then continue with matters of the house afterwards. Often, Maria would be sitting out at the 'donkey' with the little one and was very particular about her child being clean and changed.

When Baba was 3 weeks old, Maria arrived at work in the morning carrying the child wrapped in a blanket, saying she was, "Baie siek" ("Very sick").

On quick examination, I concluded the infant needed hospital attention and told Maria we would go to Windhoek. Quickly, I made Maria and old Munde's sandwiches and sweet coffee, prepared a hurried breakfast for Ian and me, put out some lunch for Ian and made some sandwiches for our trip, not forgetting a bottle of water, while Maria fed the dogs. Then we left in the Kombi, Maria sitting next to me.

At the Katatura State Hospital grounds, hundreds of people were lying down or sleeping on the extensive lawns, some had brought blankets and food. All were waiting for medical assistance. I filled in some paperwork and was given a Receipt with a number on it. Then we waited in the queue some time until a staff member attended to us, taking the baby and returning a while later to inform us that the child had to remain in the hospital for treatment and that due to their busy schedule they would contact us, the farm worker's employer, when the patient was ready to return home and that I should await their telephone call. It was also pointed out to me that our district hospital was Gobabis and that in future we should take our staff there. Little conversation was directed to Maria regarding her child. I found this somewhat terse and 'distant', but thankfully, Baba would receive the medical care she needed. Maria and I arrived home late in the afternoon, tired.

Every work day, Maria would ask me, "Baba?" while holding her closed fist to her ear to imitate speaking on the telephone. Each time my useless answer was the same. "Nee," ("No") I replied, shaking my head.

When 2 weeks had gone by, I thought this can't be possible, there must surely be some news of the baby, and decided to telephone the hospital in the morning while everyone was having their breakfast. Old Munde and Maria were sitting at the 'donkey'. Ian was at the kitchen table having his food, and I might need him to help me translate properly to Maria if there was news of Baba. Omitara Exchange connected me through to Katatura and I read the woman on the other end of the 'phone the Receipt number and date regarding the baby's hospital admission. She said to hold on while she checked. I could hardly believe my ears when she came back on the line and informed me there was no record of any such patient being brought to their hospital!

"That's impossible!" I argued, absolutely aghast, and explained that I'd personally driven the mother and her baby to Katatura, filled in the required documentation and a staff member had taken the child, returning to advise that the infant had to stay for treatment and the hospital would 'phone us when the child could go home, but no-one had called and we were very worried.

"Perhaps you've made a mistake," I said, "please look again."

"There's no mistake," the woman countered, "I've already checked!"

I could hear the irritation in her voice. I felt my blood boil. "Then I suggest you start looking for the baby," I replied, livid from anger and frustration, "because I'm getting in my car now with the child's mother and we'll be at your hospital in two hours! Goodbye". I rang off, turning the handle on the black handset a couple of times so Omitara Exchange would know I'd finished the call.

A long, stressful day lay ahead with shock and heartache for Maria. I explained the situation to her as gently as possible with Ian listening and said we'd immediately leave for Windhoek. Hurriedly, I once more put some sandwiches and bottled water together for the trip, and we were on our way. Again, Katatura Hospital had throngs of people awaiting medical attention. Both Maria and I entered the Reception Office. The only person who dealt with the matter was the woman at the front desk. It was business as usual. Her job was merely office work, writing receipts, answering telephones, taking money, etc. I produced the Receipt for the baby's admission and we were informed there was still no trace of the infant, they would look into the situation and continue searching for the baby. There was hardly an acknowledgement of Maria let alone an apology! It was all stated simply and matter of fact – they'd telephone me, I must await a call if the child was found, that was that. Maria remained silent. We had no option but to drive home, no wiser than when we left. My heart ached for Maria. What a traumatic experience for a mother to have to go through. I couldn't imagine how she felt. I put my arm around her shoulders and we walked back to the car.

In bed that night, I thought a lot about Maria and how to cope with this horrendous situation and concluded that I should follow her cue and let her guide me. She had such a philosophical Bushman approach, and preferred to continue working. Probably it was best she be kept busy. Also, I think she wanted to be near the telephone. Waiting patiently for news of her baby, every working day for 2 months I would shake my head at Maria, silently indicating there'd been no call from Katatura.

Then the hospital telephoned one morning. Maria was hanging up the laundry and I quickly closed the hallway doors in case she came back into the house while I was on the 'phone. They'd located 'the missing baby', she'd died and been put, unmarked, in the mortuary. I was appalled. Getting hold of Ian on the walkie-talkie, he came back to the house in case I needed his help to translate this extremely upsetting news to an already heartbroken Maria. Having arranged with Katatura to collect the baby later that day and being informed that the mother must accompany me, Maria and I left for Windhoek a 3rd time. She never uttered a word the entire long drive to the hospital.

At Katatura, we reported to the woman at the front desk again. There were no explanations apart from saying the baby had been found in the mortuary freezer without any form of identification. At no time did anybody explain anything to Maria. I was so angry and kicked up a fuss, particularly as I used to be a nurse and understood the paramount importance of ensuring all patients admitted to a hospital receive as a priority either a wrist or ankle identification 'bracelet', if not both, and that bodies of deceased patients were always to have a tag fitted around the toe immediately to avoid exactly the deplorable circumstances Maria was having to cope with. Had they no regard for the trauma caused to this child's mother?

A cardboard box was delivered into Maria's hands and she was asked to identify the dead child. I had to sign a receipt confirming return of the body of the dead infant. Maria was handed an official Death Certificate. I felt so ashamed of the 'this matter is now closed' attitude and manner in which they conducted such a highly sensitive situation. They couldn't get rid of me quickly enough.

Maria remained silent again the hour-and-three-quarters drive home. I sensed that although she was understandably in great mental and emotional pain, she was also relieved to have closure and be given her 'lost' child back. My mind kept thinking about the cardboard box and her thawing tiny dead baby in the back of the car. What a heart wrenching ordeal for any mother! And I wondered how Maria felt as a Bushman who'd put her trust in the big, fancy white man's modern hospital, how would this extremely poor example of medical care be looked upon by those of her tribe with their wise old ways?

There were plenty of helping, caring hands when we arrived at Maria's house. She gravely thanked me and I hugged her. Is there anything that can be done or said to truly ease or heal a mother's aching heart at the death of her child, particularly a mother who has had to tolerate such lack of compassion and heartless disrespect?

It being law to report human farm deaths, I telephoned the Steinhausen Police Station as soon as I got home and gave them the number and date of the Death Certificate. This was acceptable and their documentation was officially closed. By sundown, Baba had been buried in a private ceremony in the way of her people on Kambingana.

In the morning, I awoke incensed at the apathy and injustice of the treatment meted out to Maria and decided I'd be resolute in getting some form of apology for the appalling circumstances she'd endured. Quite simply, it wasn't good enough. Maria unexpectedly reported for work and I trusted her judgment on the issue. By now, I understood this was her Bushman way and how she coped. Then I asked Omitara Exchange to connect me through to Katatura and spoke to the reception woman again. She couldn't grasp what I was so upset about.

"But the baby was found," she said exasperatedly, "we searched and returned the child to the mother."

I demanded to speak to someone in high authority in the hospital and realising from my tirade that I wasn't going to 'just accept' any more and 'go away' this time, she grudgingly put me through to one of the senior doctors. I went over the details with him. He said he'd get back to me. Shortly afterwards, the Head Paediatrician returned my call with many apologies. To appease my wrath and try to give me an understanding of how such a deplorable chain of events had occurred, he invited me for the day to be a guest of Katatura and see for myself exactly how the enormous hospital coped with thousands of outpatients. I took up his offer, making arrangements for another trip to Windhoek.

At last – I called Maria and conveyed the Head Paediatrician's many apologies to her. This simple respect was well overdue to this brave little mother.

"Dankie," ("Thank you") she said quietly and nodded her head, then resumed what she'd been busy doing.

It was an eye-opener for me at how stoical the Bushmen people are. I admired Maria. Throughout it all, she'd remained calm and quiet. No matter the rough road she'd had thrown before her to tread and accept, always without questioning, Maria had conducted herself with dignity in the proud manner of her tribe.

I kept my appointment at Katatura Hospital. There were approximately 20,000 outpatients daily. In a great emergency, a million meals a day could be handled. This is a super-equipped hospital. One human error slip-up in the system had caused an absolute nightmare resulting in the suffering of indescribable anguish to a helpless mother on a remote farm. Her baby had entered the hospital alive, but sickly, then became 'missing, lost and searched for' and finally was pronounced 'confirmed dead, unidentified and frozen in the hospital mortuary' – all during a long 10-week waiting period. Despite spending a day at Katatura, I remained nervous of the hospital and was relieved we had to take our staff to Gobabis. Hopefully, they'd receive better treatment there. Only time would tell.

Ian never went back to Fazenda Esperança. Several times over the years he'd say, "I never want to own another piece of Africa again in my life," never speaking further than that regarding his thoughts, emotions or heartache about Angola.

For the first few years we struggled to get by, just living month to month to make ends meet. I remember the occasion early in our lives on Kambingana, when Ian wanted to buy a freshwater fishing rod to try his luck in the Ranch dams which would have been a pleasant and inexpensive picnic outing for us when time was available. With Rand 12 in his bank account, Ian 'phoned a friend in Windhoek to please source a rod for him in one of the tackle shops, but had to put his idea on hold as the rod cost more than the money he had available.

One day, Ian received a 'phone call from Hennie van Rensburg who'd been farming tobacco in the Angola Chitembo area with his brother, Janse. Hennie said he and his wife, Martha, plus Janse's wife, Elsie, had flown out of Angola on their private plane when the war broke out and that Janse had stayed on a bit. He wanted to let Ian know that Janse had gone to our fazenda and loaded up the baled tobacco in our barns and sold it. Hennie never offered any form of remuneration or part thereof and Ian never asked for any. If anyone was to have had benefit from our tobacco, Ian and I would have preferred that it be our fazenda staff. We never heard from the van Rensburgs again.

It would take us about 10 years to get on our feet again. Even then our funds were vastly insufficient to be able to consider buying another farm or land even if Ian had wanted to, added to which we were both a decade older, time was marching, youth and vitality not on our side any more. Financially, we never recovered from our losses in Angola. Emotionally, our animals left behind stayed in our hearts always, special memories of Humpy in my thoughts daily.

I corresponded with our Angolan friends, Gil Vieira and his wife, Antonieta, who got out of the country before the war broke out. They'd given me a forwarding address and were living in Setubal, Portugal. We exchanged news (for the next 25 years until their retirement), Christmas cards and photos of their children as they grew up. Through Gil, we learnt that Edgar's father, Senhor Carmo, had finally left Serpa Pinto on 24th August 1975, flying out in his private plane. Edgar had gone to Brazil, but not found it to his liking and returned to South Africa where apparently his sister, Isabel, had found work in the Standard Bank. I tried for some years to find a contact address for any of these members of the Carmo family, but was unable to. We never managed to locate the turkey lady, timber merchant or the man who lent Ian the Rand 50, to try to repay the money we owed them. So far, we'd heard nothing of our Angolan German friend, Franz Nachtsheim, and his farming partner, August. We could only hope they were safe and well. Peter and Barbie Gill, our Angolan farming friends from the Chitembo area, had moved to Natal, South Africa. What had become of the predikant De Jager we'd no idea as, again, we'd heard nothing.

On a business trip to Windhoek one day, we met a German gentleman who told us about a couple from their community, a husband and wife both around 50 years old, who'd been on the convoy out of Angola as well. On arrival and finding safety in Windhoek, the woman had a severe nervous breakdown. Family sent money for their air-tickets to Germany, but she never recovered and was put in a home.

Keith would go back to Angola for work-related reasons, but whether or not he would ever return to our fazenda to see what had become of it would remain to be seen as there was considerable uncertainty regarding possible landmines. Princess Diana, in her future work, would highlight to the world the ghastly injuries, deaths and physically maimed lives of many Angolan people due to exploding landmines left irresponsibly buried in the ground by the warring factions during the civil unrest.

Stuart seemed happy. He found one of the farm work horses suited him so on holidays and weekends he helped with the cattle, went fishing and swimming in the dams, rode his horse every day, still enjoyed fun on the monkey-motorbike (Keith had the other one) and accompanied his father on the compulsory shooting for the labour meat rations. He became an excellent marksman and was also adept at catching snakes from weaver birds' nests high up in the thorn trees. Stuart and his German friend, Claus, spent a lot of time together and several other school buddies came home with him too.

It was a wonderful life in the open, with all the freedom our youngest son could wish for and without a care in the world. Except for him that was – Stuart felt we'd left our 'everything' at Fazenda Esperança and his heart still hankered after those times. Perhaps it also had something to do with the fact that we'd owned our farm in Angola and carved it from virgin bush, Stuart being part of the process, whereas we were now employees on an established Ranch. I think, if he'd experienced first hand the civil war turmoil that had so many people flee and been with us on the convoy out Stuart would have better understood and coped with his feelings of loss about Fazenda Esperança. At the same time, I was grateful his young mind had been spared the anguish.

But, there was no denying it, as surely as the sun would rise high over this splendid, spectacular South West Africa that had treated us with respect, restoring our shaken dignity with a home and an income in our daily life without fear, memories of Angola's vastness, allure of mystery, adventure and rich untamed land still beat in Stuart's blood.

Chapter Nineteen
Beloved Stuart, Miss Piggy Warthog & Tootsie-Wootsie Porcupine

In December 1976, Ian and I went into Windhoek for business and Christmas shopping leaving Stuart in charge. He was to take Simon, the staff headman, and one other man to shoot the 2 hartebeest for the labour meat rations. We decided to stay overnight with Keith and Mary at Kapps Farm and 'phoned Stuart. He assured us all was well, and said they'd not found any hartebeest near enough for a good shot, but that he'd picked up a starving warthog piglet wandering in a dazed fashion on the mud flats of Karamba dam, brought it home and given it a little warm milk.

Back at Kambingana and unpacked the following morning, we turned our attention to the piglet, sleeping on one of the lounge chairs wrapped in a shawl. Apart from being thin, very tiny and weak, she was also alive with blood engorged lice. We thought maybe she'd been unable to keep up with mother warthog and the other piglets or possibly a cheetah had chased them. Our first task was to get the lounge chair outside, fumigate it and wash the shawl, then get rid of the lice on the piglet with several warm baths using Sunlight Soap, Dettol disinfectant and shampoo. After being towel dried and warmed up in the sun, we teaspoon-fed her ProNutro (boxed cereal) mixed with a little warm milk which she accepted hungrily. This routine of bath, food and sleep continued for 3 days then we let her have the run of the front lawn. Within seconds she scuttled away through the hedge out into the surrounding bush. Stuart was devastated. Three days passed. We'd just adjusted to losing the piglet and talked ourselves into believing she'd be all right, when to our amazement, she came trotting up the front garden path and behaved as if she'd never been away! Following me into the kitchen, she had her ProNutro then it was bath time again just to make sure she was free of lice.

We called her 'Miss Piggy' or 'Piggy' for short, and what a darling she turned out to be. Beautifully ugly, her face had lumpy immature wart-like projections, her skin a pale grey. There were signs of 2 little tushes (small tusks growing out of each side of the mouth) and all the hair on her face, body and tail was still baby-soft, her little trotters as dainty as a ballet dancer's feet. Her tail ended in a paddle-shape with lots of hairs sticking out at the end and always stood straight up when she was busily trotting around. Stuart and Piggy bath-time became regular routine. They had terrific fun swishing the water around and a lot went over the side of the bath onto the floor, so more bath refilling went on till I said it was time to get out. Stuart mopped up the floor each night. Sometimes Stuart's good friend, Claus, would come over then there'd be the 2 boys and Miss Piggy in the bath and even more water on the floor! This is one of the happiest sights I've ever seen in my life and changed my housewife-mother ideas regarding water messed on bathroom floors. I could never feel annoyed about this. Listening to all the joyous laughter and snorts and splashing was pure music to my ears.

Piggy knew what bed-time meant. When Stuart finally climbed between the sheets she needed no urging and would easily jump in, settle down and snuggle up alongside him, sleeping soundly till morning. The rule in the house was 'up and at breakfast by 9'. I'd go into Stuart's bedroom at about 8 in the morning, to find both him and Piggy in dreamland, heads sharing the same pillow, sheet drawn up to their chins. Often, I'd stand quietly a while to imprint this utterly precious picture in my mind, Piggy's snout poking out of the bedding, perfectly content, a few inches from Stuart's nose. Stuart would vaguely 'come to', reluctant to wake. Piggy would snort and snuffle and dig deeper under the blanket. When Stuart eventually got out of bed, she would too.

After taking Piggy onto the front lawn for ablutions, it was breakfast time for the 2. Piggy was now on maize-meal porridge, just like all of us, and eating by herself which was a messy business in the beginning till she got the hang of the plastic dish which kept moving around. She soon realised she should keep her feet out and her nose in. Quickly, she understood too that the food and the dish were hers alone, and that together with the 4 cats we'd acquired from the SPCA and the dogs, our house was her home. I was brought a further 3 baby warthogs found wandering around aimlessly in the veld, their mother having probably been killed by a cheetah. They grew up outside the house eating the same diet as Piggy though she didn't think much of them, never socialising at all. They were all much photographed by various hunters. Piggy took to napping on the sofa at any time during the day and liked to bury her head behind the loose cushions so that the light didn't bother her. Any visitor who sat on the sofa beside her and dared disturb her got short shrift with a pinch from her bottom tushes which were now growing.

I was busy making brown bread one morning around 10.30, and had just finished the first kneading of the dough when the 'phone rang. I stopped to listen to the rings – yes, it was for us. Quickly, I wiped my floury hands on my apron as I walked to the hallway then picked up the receiver.

"Hello," I said, "Heather speaking."

"*Guten Morgen, Heetha.*"

"Oh, good *morgen*, Gis," I replied cheerily.

"*Ist* you *gut*?" she asked.

"Yes, thank you, Gis. Are you well?"

"*Vel*?"

"*Gut*?" I tried, again.

"*Vel...*, you *heerd de* big news?"

"No…," I said hesitantly.

"*Nein*?" she queried.

"*Nein*," I responded in the affirmative.

"*De Mukowi* man?" She sounded a bit surprised.

"The *Mukowi* man?" I racked my brains.

"*Ja, de Mukowi* man… you know *de Mukowi* man!"

I was lost, my mind raced. "What happened?" I said, trying to gain a few moments to figure out who the *Mukowi* man was.

"He murder all *de* childrens," she said sighing.

"Murdered? What…, all his children?" Incredible! How terrible, I thought.

"*Ja*, all *de* childrens," she confirmed sadly.

I paused a few moments. Must be Russian… big news? I hadn't heard anything on the radio or seen anything about it on television. "Did he have many children?" I asked.

"Many?"

"A lot," I said, finding another way to rephrase the question.

"*Ja*, a lot… *acht*!" she replied assuredly.

"Eight!" I was appalled. How hideous!

"*Nicht gut, Heetha,*"

"Good…," I was going to say 'goodness me,' but she was too quick.

"Bad, *Heetha, nicht gut.*"

"Yes, *nicht gut,*" I agreed, trying to get back to a mutual understanding of the atrocity regarding the crime in question.

"*Vel…*, I tell you, *ja?*" she said, winding up the conversation.

"*Danke*, Gis. Have a nice day."

"V*ot? Mit dis* news?" She paused. "I go now…, *ja,* A*uf Wiedersehen, Heetha.*"

"Bye-bye, Gis," I answered, putting the receiver down slowly. My German left much to be desired. Never mind, we all got by somehow or other with snippets of the 3 languages, German, Afrikaans and English.

Mukowi? Moscow? Maybe the Russian man was from Moscow, living in Windhoek. Perhaps he was a Muscovite living in Russia – could be world news. The intrigue was killing me. Murdering his 8 children! Simply awful!

The bread needed an hour to prove. I could dash over to Gis, see it on her TV hopefully, and be back in time for the second kneading of the dough. I told Maria I was going to Mrs Wiehl's and walked at a pace along the dusty path to her house, noticing a fair amount of washing on the line. Probably their generator was running; lucky me. Out of breath, I knocked on her front door.

"Hello, Gis," I said loudly, "Gis..."

She answered the door in her apron, a big spoon in her hand, "*Hallo, Heetha*, you *kom* for *de* news?"

"Yes," I answered, "if that's all right."

"*Gut, gut… kom, kom,*" she said with a smile, ushering me inside her lounge. Neat as a pin it always was. The generator was on, but not the TV. I felt disappointed. Perhaps she'd switch on for the news just now.

"*Ve* drink *de deutschen Filterkaffee, ja*?"

"Thank you, that'll be nice," I replied. Gis always made delicious coffee, and she treated Ian and me kindly whenever we saw or spoke to one other.

"Sit, sit, *bitte*," she said invitingly, indicating one of the chairs.

"*Danke*, but I'm happy to be in the kitchen with you," I answered.

"*Gut... kom*," she smiled, so I followed her through and she put the coffee percolator on. By now, I was almost splitting with suspense about the big news, but refrained from pestering her as I didn't want to appear rude.

She must've read my mind. "*Ja, de Mukowi* man... *nicht gut... kom*," she said, walking to the back door.

I stood still a moment. But, the TV's in the lounge, I thought. Anyway, best to follow her, maybe she wants to show me something outside first. She and her husband were keen vegetable gardeners.

"*De* carrots *ist gut dieses Jahr,*" Gis advised, bending down to run her hand along the lovely green, feathery tops.

And, some size they were too, I reckoned to myself, judging from the healthy crop. I admired the vegetable garden. "It's *wundebar!*" I said honestly, "Very nice, Gis – a lot of work." Everything was so precise, each row perfectly straight, but I expected nothing less, this being a natural German characteristic.

"*Dieses Jahr* I try *de* beet… beet…"

"Root," I chipped in to help her.

"*Ja,* beetroot," Gis laughed. "I forget *de wurd. Mein Englisch*!" she said as we walked towards the small wire-mesh pen Willy had made for the ducks we'd given them.

"*Meine Deutsch*!" I added.

"*Kein Deutsch*!" she corrected.

We both laughed.

"So funny," I said.

"*Ja*, funny!" she agreed.

We'd stopped at the duck house. Her humour was gone as she sombrely said, "*Diese Mukowi* man," pointing to the Muscovy drake, "*vhy* he murder all *de* childrens?"

I was absolutely stumped. The wind knocked out of my sails completely. You may as well have hit me over the head. Deflated? I felt like a pricked balloon. Big news… headlines? Police cars, wailing sirens, flashing lights… crime investigation detectives and Muscovites…? Poof! All vanished in an instant!

"*Nicht gut, Heetha,*" Gis said seriously, rubbing her forehead in thought.

"Maybe make more big house," I said slowly. It was awful about the 8 ducklings though I felt sure that the drake needed more space what with all his duck-wives, then adding the children on top of that it was definitely too cramped.

"Big house?"

"Yes, too *klein,*" I answered, walking several paces from the duck pen. "Big house to here," I advised, pointing with my foot on the ground.

"*Gut… ja, vel*, I tell Willy," she said, nodding in my direction, seemingly satisfied with this solution.

We had our coffee then I thanked her saying I had to get home to finish making my bread, and hurried back along the path. Obviously, Willy was supposed to have told Ian 'the big news'. I decided to try it out on Ian over lunch. When I was sure I was out of earshot of Gis' house, I laughed the rest of the way into our kitchen. Kneading the dough a second time, every now and then I'd burst into a fit of the giggles. Maria gave me the odd glance. There was no point trying to explain it to her, besides my Afrikaans wasn't hugely better than my German.

Maria left for lunch as Ian walked through the back door into the kitchen. I knew if I dared face him, I'd never be able to do the 'Mukowi man' and kept my back turned, exaggeratedly busy with the lunch. He walked over to the sink and started washing his hands.

"How was your morning?" I asked casually.

"We've nearly finished doing the cattle ear tags," he replied sounding pleased, and took the hand towel off the wall hook. "And yours?"

"Very eventful," I declared, trying to keep an even voice.

"That's good. Better busy than bored," Ian said. "You've got flour in your hair." I heard him pull out his chair to sit down at the table.

"Have you heard the big news?" I questioned, reaching for the much-treasured bread board we'd been given so many years back as a wedding gift.

"Big news…? No," he said thoughtfully.

"About the *Mukowi* man?" I was careful with the pronunciation.

"*Mukowi* man..., Russian?"

I knew where that thought process was headed! "No, we're having the Russians for lunch," I answered good humouredly, and heard Ian chuckle as I put 2 sausages on each plate, struggling now to stop myself from bursting into laughter. When you live on a farm, husband and wife are best friends and everything else to one another.

"First I've heard, must be new to the area," he pondered, then added, "Can you make a note to remind me to order more ear-tags. Sorry, you were saying…?"

"On the contrary," I stated matter-of-factly, "he's lived close by for some time already."

"I'll 'phone Boertjie, he'll know," Ian replied. Yes, Johan usually knew what was going on in the area, but I didn't think so this time!

"He murdered all his children," I tried to say evenly, though I was fit to pop.

"Murdered all his children?" Ian queried. From the tone of his voice he sounded quite aghast. For sure, Willy hadn't said a word to him. I couldn't afford to turn around yet.

"Yes, every one of them," I answered.

"How many did he have?" Ian was definitely interested now.

"Eight," I said.

That was as far as I got! The 2 of us had a good laugh that lunchtime. It was sad about the ducklings, but true it is, laughter is excellent for the heart. I felt as though I'd drunk a bottle of revival tonic!

About a week later, Gis popped over unexpectedly. I was busy digging in the garden working with old Munde, planting some indigenous grasses, transplanting seedlings, doing this and that. We'd been busy a while already, more than likely I had a smear of dusty, red soil on my face. Maria put her head out the front lounge window and called me. I downed tools, wiping my hands on my trousers and hurried inside, inviting Gis to join me in a much-needed cup of coffee.

I was washing my hands at the sink, the kettle on the boil, when Gis, in her natural direct way, said, "*Heetha, Englisch* peoples dress *velly* bad!"

There was no answer for that! But, it hadn't offended me. She had a point and never had she done or said anything deliberately that had been hurtful to either Ian or myself. I smiled and took out 2 coffee cups. If I'd been looking at myself through her eyes more than likely Gis' comment would have been correct. I always wore a hat and very old clothes when gardening, specially put aside for such dusty, dirty, often muddy tasks, worn for years on end until needle and cotton could no longer mend them. I must've looked a sight that day!

We bought several horses for our children and grandchildren over the years, either from Kambingana stockmen or Herero owners passing through the farm to water their animals. Most of the hacks weren't even broken in properly.

School holidays came around once more and Stuart brought a friend, Neil, home. Both lads spent the days out on horseback and we didn't worry about them knowing they'd return by sunset. But, on this particular day, the 2 didn't come home and anxiety set in. By morning, I was frantic. A missing child or children is torture to the hearts and minds of parents. One's gut turns into a twisted knot of trepidation as the mind takes control, envisioning any number and form of possible happenings. Nothing stops this endless agony except seeing one's children return. Simple daily tasks become difficult to accomplish, even down to making a cup of coffee, as mind and body become splintered in a 'waiting helpless hell'. We informed the Police and telephoned Neil's parents in Windhoek.

Robert Foster (still living in Kenya) was holidaying with us at the time and kept saying, "Those two boys have run away."

This added to my nervous tension remembering how much Stuart hankered after Angola, and I was quietly beginning to think the same.

The next day, Ian had to go to Omitara and as usual called in at the Post Office. Manfred, the Postmaster, handed him an envelope saying, "I have a letter from Stuart, to be delivered to you by hand."

Stuart wrote he was on his way home to Angola, and Neil, of his own free will, had gone with him. He said payment for the horses and saddles could be taken from his savings account and he hoped Beryl would understand about him taking her horse, 'Call-Boy'. He asked us to please look after Pepu and Piggy, and to specially thank Mossie (our

Agricultural manager), Boertjie Johan, our German farm neighbour, Kurt, and all the others for being so good to him. Stuart said he'd send us a postal address and asked that we please not contact the Police or Army, and that they'd deliberately chosen the wet season and were reasonably well-equipped. He added that he'd lost his axe and knife, but since replaced them. Lastly, he apologised for all the trouble this would cause and hoped we'd understand about him going home, and ended with 'lots of love, Stuart'. The letter was dated 8th April 1977.

The relief of knowing something at last was immense – where the boys were headed and why. We 'phoned Neil's parents again and the Police checked all the way through the farm telephone lines to Botswana. On the last farm before crossing the border, the owner telephoned in to the Babi-Babi Border Post saying 2 lads had asked permission to water their horses and camp overnight on his farm, but they'd left well before sunlight and must be somewhere in the lonely desert stretches of Botswana. Our sincere thanks forever to this farmer – it doesn't bear thinking about what could have happened had the 2 reached Angola and gone into the 'no-go' war zone with buried landmines or hostile people. They could've been captured or worse.

With the extra help from the Botswana Police, Stuart and Neil were tracked and found, our own Steinhausen Police Station informing us accordingly. Ian, Robert and 2 farm workers immediately took the Ford-250 and drove to Babi-Babi, collected the 2 boys and returned the following day. The horses were ridden back by the 2 farm staff. During their trip, exceptionally unusual heavy rain had fallen and a lot of the low-lying flat terrain either side the road to Babi-Babi was under water. Ian and Robert witnessed an amazing sight – a few of the wandering Bushmen had simply gone to sleep in the open veld, their bodies lying in water with their heads propped up on elbows and hands to keep the wet out of their ears!

All farm telephones in South West Africa had 'party' lines. When I called Mary to keep her up-to-date on Stuart and Neil, she told me she'd heard a roaring sound that afternoon which seemed to come from the river just below their house, so ran down to see what was happening. Before her eyes, a young kudu bull, in fear, was in full flight running down the dry river bed trying to flee a wall of rushing water behind him, flash-flooding from heavy rain downpour in the surrounding granite mountains. Panicked, the kudu kept bounding straight ahead instead of leaping either side onto the bush embankment. Overcome by the mighty churning water that moved faster than he could, the kudu was hurtled around in the raging torrent and drowned. Some years later, Ian and I witnessed the frightening strength of the Omaruru River in flood.

Stuart and Neil were exceptionally disappointed at being tracked down and brought home! In Stuart's case, he simply couldn't understand why we'd abandoned our beautiful property, Fazenda Esperança, after the monumental work we'd done, lost all the money we'd invested in Angola and then actually 'accepted' the situation. He detested school, under which South African Education dictated that religion dominate one's every thought. Like his father, he loathed apartheid, and felt completely stifled by city life. For us, we were just extremely grateful nothing untoward happened to either Neil or Stuart. It wasn't till Koosie Steyn, Kambingana's experienced game catcher, offered to employ and teach Stuart to be a helicopter pilot once he'd finished school, that life started improving for him. Koosie also gave Stuart a .22 rifle as a gift.

We emphatically instructed the school that Stuart not be 'hounded' with religious fanaticism and gave permission for him to play sports on Sundays if he was not at home for the weekend. They informed us that even playing Monopoly and cards was banned on Sundays! Things started to go seriously wrong at Centaurus High School when the boarding school catering was cut down to only a piece of bread or one stale bakery cake for Sunday supper. Beryl now took food to Stuart daily. Telephoning the school didn't help, they simply brushed us off. Making an appointment, we saw the Principal and said it was our wish that if Stuart wanted to attend Bible Study or Church, the choice was entirely his. Also, Stuart had been hiding some of his meals to bring home on weekends so that we could see for ourselves what the boarders were fed.

Eventually, a Windhoek Observer newspaper journalist found out about the food situation. The outcome was that 2 men in charge of the catering money had helped themselves to a sum of about Rand 320,000 and done a bunk to Cape Town. There was some talk of the stolen funds being returned, but nothing was ever done. The newspaper indicated in their column, 'We hear but do not say', that the 2 individuals had bought themselves prize properties in South Africa. Quite suddenly, there was a change in school Principal and a new English lady caterer from the UK was employed (she became a visiting friend) and the food improved. Stuart got on well and was liked by his teachers, so he made great strides in his studies. He never overcame his shame of us leaving Fazenda Esperança, our animals, home and no doubt our giant python, but grew to love Kambingana and the new, unique life we had in South West Africa and was glad to be with his Pepu and Piggy again.

The words of Stuart's poem below, 'The Farewell', reflect, I feel, a new sense of calm and acceptance within him and a realisation that wherever he would be, his spirit and Angola would forever remain inexorably 'one'.

THE FAREWELL

Look, we who be of one blood, one spirit
To the fern hills where sweet water flows,
Where moving through tall grasses, one may be alone
Befriended by the silence
Or, look to the eagle in the sky, the friend of Heaven
Painted against the darkening cloud,
And listen to the sound of thunder and see the lightning
Snake across the sky, a darkened dome

Look then, my shadow of the past
To the twilight of the wild
And there upon the horizon see something of value
The fiercest heart of the hunter who be wise, as he art cruel
Do not preen this broken heart, for to me fair friend
You never can be old

For together, thou wind-blown thoughts
And I, shall follow the honey-bird

To the crimson of the vanishing sun,
For we be together in spirit
Forever Homeward Bound

In July 1977, Lindsay gave birth to her 1st child, a son named Brendan, in Windhoek. She'd given up work a month before her baby was due. We now had 3 grandchildren – Debbie going on 5, Andrew just over a year old, and Brendan.

One weekend, a Portuguese friend, George, came to stay and left on the Sunday late afternoon. We were so pleased to hear he had a second-hand twin-tub washing machine for us at Rand 50 which Ian would collect on his next trip to Windhoek. Come evening, we couldn't find Bidou the little fluffy white dog we'd given a home to in Angola when his Portuguese owners left the country, and searched as much as we could before night fell – we'd continue looking for him in the light of day. Quite early Monday morning, I received a telephone call and the mystery of where Bidou had got to was solved. George had taken his car in early to the garage for its pre-arranged service and on opening the boot there was Bidou! With George being Portuguese, we think he reminded Bidou of his previous owners. George asked if he could keep Bidou – we agreed and were delighted Bidou's disappearance had such a happy ending!

When Ian took the dogs in the car around the Ranch with him, Piggy went too. On Sunday mornings when we could have a lie-in, Piggy would dash in from outside, jump up on our bed and lie quietly between us while we had our second or third cup of coffee and listened to the radio. She was very affectionate and loved being caressed. When I was sitting on my telephone stool (made out of an old Caterpillar tractor oil filter, covered in a fabric frill with a cushion on top) chatting on the line, Piggy would rub against my leg and I'd gently stroke behind her ear and elbow with a ball-point pen. This was so soporific she'd fall to the floor in a deep sleep for a few seconds then get up for more pen-stroking. Telephone chat was farm-wife communication and Piggy knew exactly this was her 'attention time' too.

After 2 years, we took 10 days leave and joined our dear friend, Boertjie Johan, his wife, Amanda, their children and 2 other families on a desert holiday travelling to Torra Bay, one of South West Africa's lonely, but beautiful seaside camping resorts. Maria was reliable and very good with our animals, Piggy included, and she'd be at the house twice a day to feed them all and check everything was in order. Ian sorted the labour rations etc. before we left. While we were away, the machinery manager was in charge – when he was on holiday, we looked after his dog and kept a check on his home; that was company policy.

Ian had told Johan we'd love to go to Torra Bay, but couldn't afford it. Johan, in his usual generous, kind-hearted way said he'd pay for us and we could repay him later (which Ian did). En route, somewhere in the desert on the dirt road, we stopped for a cup of coffee. There was nothing but vast bright blue, hot skies above and desolate desert all around us. A member of the party put on a cassette tape of Viennese Waltzes. Spontaneously, we took partners and danced up and down the dusty, pale-yellowish road to The Blue Danube! It was pure magic.

Stuart had brought his monkey-motorbike along and the children had a wonderful time driving between and around the enormous, smooth grey boulders that lay scattered a little inland of the sea-board at Torra Bay. Ian took to shore-fishing and became a real expert. I tried it too, but it wasn't for me, and I had no interest in learning how to bait a hook either. He always cast for me as I wasn't strong enough to get the baited line over the waves, let alone well beyond the breakers. Finding and collecting fresh bait – lumpy orange-brown, tough leathery-skinned, ugly stuff that looked like large sized fibroids – left at high tides was a job I liked doing as it meant walking the beaches, which exercised the dogs too. This 'best of all bait', known as *rooi-aas* (red bait), when rotten smelt to kingdom-come! The beaches were always littered with mussels and sometimes dead seals, and the silver-backed jackals would come any time, day or night, searching for edible pickings.

Much the same as the request from our staff at Westlands, Kenya, to bring back some sea water when we visited Malindi, our Kambingana staff had also asked us to do the same as they believed that drinking sea water would get rid of intestinal parasites. The 10 day holiday was thoroughly enjoyed by all. For us it was a tonic to be with special friends sharing a bit of relaxing time-off, temporarily able to put one's worries and workload aside, concentrating instead on the lighter side of life. If I had to find 2 words to describe Johan they would be 'happiness' and 'laughter'.

Back at Kambingana, Ian put the finishing touches to the superb large jackal-and-lynx-proof hen-house he'd made outside the back garden gate. We bought 12 'hybrid' on the point-of-lay pullets – cross-bred egg-laying poultry producing a hen that lays an egg every day for the first 2 years. From this time on we were never short of eggs, replacing the hens with new pullets every 2 years. In the mornings, they were fed their grain, given fresh water and new straw was put down when necessary. At 3 in the afternoon, they were let out of their enclosure ensuring their eggs had been laid in the hen-house, and were then free to wander around as they pleased, scratching and pecking about for a few hours until being returned to their 'luxury hen-hotel' in the late afternoon.

As a teenager now, Piggy started coming into season once a month for about 4 days, the 'scent' of her pheromones attracting wild male warthogs to the house. Piggy, however, was deeply in love with Stuart's Keeshond, Pepu, and ignored the advances from the males of her kind in preference to Pepu, never leaving his side. He on the other hand had no such feelings for her, doing everything in his power to escape her lavish attentions! It was amusing to watch Pepu crawl with great difficulty under the low single beds in Stuart's room or the spare bedroom, his only safe place from flirty Piggy, all returning to normal again once her monthly cycle was over. Grown-up now as well, 2 of the other 3 warthogs we reared had gone back to the bush. Only a male remained, and he'd fallen in love with the machinery manager's young Alsatian bitch. She thought his attentions were just playtime. Piggy, though not interested in him when she was on heat, now turned to this male warthog as a friend and he started getting tame enough to touch, but that was the extent of handling he allowed me. He still wouldn't come into the house, preferring to hang around in the familiar area of the kitchen back garden when Piggy was inside with us.

Warthogs are members of the pig family, black, brown or grey in colour with long faces, white cheek whiskers and tusks, coarse sparse hair on their bodies, a dark mane and tail, and can live up to 15 years in the wild. Males are heavier than females. They stand 64 to 85cm tall at the shoulder, weigh 50 to 75kg and are found in lightly forested or savannah areas south of Africa's Sahara Desert. Grazers, their diet consists mainly of grasses, berries, roots and bark. They often kneel or move around on their knees while eating. The warts on their faces are more pronounced in boars, primarily as protection during fights. Although they look fierce, they are sociable animals and would rather run than engage in physical confrontation, but make worthy opponents when put to the test. Their natural predators are the cheetah, wild dog, leopard, lion and spotted hyena.

Old man Dempers (Johan's father), came on a friendly visit, his big Rottweiler and Doberman dogs on the open back of his bakkie. Meeting him outside the front garden gate, Ian said he hoped the dogs wouldn't jump off the car as Piggy would chase them.

"Your pig – chase my dogs?" he said incredulously, then added, "they'll kill anything."

While we were having a relaxed cup of tea in the kitchen, the sudden piercing sound of a dog howling made us all rush out, hearts pounding for fear of what could have happened, only to find Piggy in full fighting mode, chasing the Doberman around the bakkie, giving him no time to stop and leap onto the back. We managed, with a lot of coaxing, to get her into the house and quiet her down, and old man Dempers (a wonderful, wise fellow), got his grateful dogs safely into the cab of his vehicle. It was a good laugh for all of us. Ian would chuckle about this for ages and thoroughly enjoyed telling the story.

Piggy's hair had become coarse now and the natural warthog warts more pronounced, her tusks showing quite clearly. Never at any time had she messed in the house. In the heat of summer nights she took to sleeping outdoors. When I opened the kitchen door early in the morning she'd be waiting and dash in to say hello, full of life and exuberance.

Lightning strikes, whether with or without rain, were a real hazard all the years. In a group of cattle standing under a tree in one of the big camps 3 steers were struck dead. A bull grazing in the horse paddock near the house was killed – on another occasion, a horse. Many fires were caused on farms by lightning striking dried cowpats or dead trees. Heavy winds could lift and carry flaming cowpats from one place to another so a number of fires could start simultaneously. Three children of about 8 or 9 were playing on a farm just north of Steinhausen Police Station when suddenly the rain started and thunder and lightning was so close they dived underneath an old abandoned wagon and lay next to one another. Two of them were struck dead by lightning.

Kambingana house seemed to attract lightning especially during the short rainy season of February into March. One afternoon, having tidied up the lounge after guests, I was walking towards the hallway and was shocked to feel a piece of cigarette pack cellophane I was going to throw away, sizzle up in my right hand as simultaneously a bolt of lightning flashed through an open sitting room window. It hit the telephone handset on the shelf, burning the wiring up the wall just as Stuart and Neil came out of their bedroom towards me. It was a miracle the 2 boys escaped injury, another 2 feet or so and it would have been a different story. A new handset and wiring had to be installed by the travelling telephone repairman and a piece of ceiling board inserted and painted where the big charred patch was. On another occasion, lightning damaged the small television set we had in the kitchen, and was replaced by our insurance. I soon learnt to shut all windows and doors immediately there was any show of lightning.

Our 2 American nieces from Florida (Don and Mary Rooken-Smith's daughters), Jane and Anne, came to stay one February. Keen joggers, each morning they'd go for a run down the farm dirt road that led to the Steinhausen Police Station. On this occasion, the sky looked ominous. I warned the girls that at any sign of thunder or lightning they must return at once. They thought I was over-reacting when I emphasised the dangers of lightning on the farm. Not 10 minutes later, there was a loud roll of thunder followed shortly thereafter by the return of the girls – dishevelled, badly shaken and visibly ashen. Lightning had flung them violently to the ground, their faces, hands and knees were grazed. Realising they'd just escaped death, both were dumbfounded. I was extremely relieved not to have to contact their parents in USA with any bad news. They'd been saved by the thick rubber-soled running shoes they were wearing and because they weren't near any water.

On one of Robert Foster's several Kambingana holidays with us I was driving the Kombi with him as my passenger. As we left the Omitara tarmac onto the dirt road home, lightning hit the Kombi roof carrier, with the sound of a big clash on metal. Luckily, there was no resultant damage.

The time came when Kambingana was experiencing some water shortage problems, so rationing was temporarily put in place by Ian for all staff and their families. For 4 days we'd had virtually no water in our house except for the absolute minimal to drink, cook, wash ourselves with and for toilet ablutions – to clean one's teeth a half tea-cup of water was permitted. Minimal flushing of toilets, no bathing, showering, laundry washing or garden watering, yet the machinery manager continued sprinkling his garden for some hours every day seemingly unperturbed about the needs of the considerable number of livestock which were paramount. The Ranch water and animals being Ian's responsibility, he tried again to point out the lack of water and necessity for dire emergency controls until such time as the situation improved, but was completely ignored. Eventually, in desperation facing the possible loss of cattle or horses, Ian telephoned the company and informed them that unless someone came to the property to enforce the vital water restrictions, he would resign.

Two Windhoek office managers duly arrived on the Saturday and spent some hours grilling Ian relentlessly at the kitchen table. Stuart was home from hostel and Lindsay was visiting. With 3 doors leading into the small kitchen (one from the hallway, another from the dining room and the third being the kitchen back door), Lindsay, Stuart and me (as hostess) were often in and out of the kitchen or stood at the doorways listening to the 3 men converse. By now into late afternoon, still seated around the table, the topic of snakes came into the conversation which piqued our interest immensely. Ian told the 2 managers about Stuart's passion for the reptiles over the years.

"Probably rubber snakes!" they scoffed.

Ian was getting fed up by this stage, the mocking comment wearing his exhausted patience thin. Quietly he gave Stuart a nod, his head inclined in the direction of Stuart's bedroom – an immediate, impeccably understood silent instruction from father to son. With the 2 managers talking loudly and paying little attention, Stuart left the kitchen then returned shortly, under his arm in a figure-eight with its head in his hand and used to being handled, one of his harmless 4 foot long mole snakes. Without a word, Stuart put the figure-eight snake on the kitchen table. After a couple seconds inertness, much like a rubber snake, the reptile suddenly 'came alive' breaking formation and slithered forward across the table. Two kitchen chairs were instantly flung backwards amid loud screams of alarm as the men recoiled in fright, one manager nearly falling over next to the sink. Ian never moved. That sorted the issue out. Stuart simply picked up his mole snake and went to his room. Recovering from their initial shock, the 2 started laughing – Ian as well. After they'd gone, Ian would break into guffaws of hilarity now and then as he recalled the incident, us too, Lindsay and I wondering if there were any 'skid marks' in their underwear and Stuart was as pleased as punch with his part!

The machinery manager came to see Ian about some equipment one day. Miss Piggy warthog, ever watchful and curious, went out to greet him. As he came through the front gate, he kicked out and got her full on the snout. She howled in pain and rushed to me for comfort. Piggy never forgot or forgave him – whenever she heard his car after this, even if it was going elsewhere, which was daily, her hackles would rise, she'd make fierce, angry noises and become distraught. He never again came inside our house.

Not long after this, one of the company Directors, Mr Du Preez, came out to the farm unexpectedly one day. All we were told before he left was that the machinery manager was no longer employed on Kambingana and would be leaving at once. Ian was informed that the machinery and maintenance now fell under his responsibilities as well. Their house stood empty. Life and work for Ian improved after this.

Most sunrises were a glorious sight of pale yellows, various pinks and mauves streaking across the eastern skies, though soon the scalding sun would rise. Western sunsets were a welcome relief of cooling evening air, and due to the dry dustiness were usually a red burning sun-ball lighting up the heavens in the brightest of colours as it sank behind the horizon; the nights clear celestial brightness, and on a full moon a kind of magical, almost ethereal feeling.

The pen-fed cattle were all sold. After calculations, Ian pointed out to management that the company had lost Rand 22.50 cents on each animal. All their feed grain had been imported from the Orange Free State. This was where the high costs lay. From then on, there were no longer fattening pens and Ian heaved a sigh of relief. The sweet veld grass still proved to be the best for fattening beef cattle.

Since the company was part of the impressive Kaap Cunene trawler fishing fleet in South Africa, the tomatoes grown on Kambingana by Mossie and irrigated with Kambingana dam water were for table use as well as canning purposes – used for tinned fish in tomato sauce, a product of their factories. The table tomatoes were sold in Windhoek markets. This didn't go as well as hoped. The markets indicated that 'The housewife is so fussy and only wants tomatoes of a certain size, absolutely round, no marks on them', and so forth. Annually, Mossie cultivated 4 tons of tomatoes together with huge quantities of melons, cucumbers and sweet corn. Due to 'the housewife's attitude', thousands of pounds of tomatoes lay rotting on the ground so the company now decided to close all agriculture on the Ranch. We were sad to say goodbye to Mossie and Attie, they'd been good friends to all our family and given their best to the company. They retired to a small plot of land very far from Omitara. We never saw them again though we did chat on the telephone a couple of times.

Life on Kambingana changed again. We were now the only white employees. The owner gave Ian far more carte blanche, and he alone made rules for hunting of game and decisions about the stock. Greater and better monthly beef cattle sales were recorded, new bulls of different breeds were introduced, and we had an increase in salary.

Word of 'Miss Piggy' had spread. Several strangers drove from Windhoek to "See the warthog that speaks English!" She became quite famous in her own right, and much photographed, along with her male warthog companion.

With the whole family together again for Christmas festivities, on the Saturday evening we were sitting in the front garden around the barbeque fire waiting for the coals to die down a bit before putting on the meat to cook. Suddenly, we heard a crashing through the thick saltbush hedge. Caught unawares and too astonished to immediately say or do anything, we remained seated in our camp chairs dumbfounded as we watched this bleeding human apparition with the top of his head clearly split open, the bone showing white, stumble towards us blood all over him. Then we recognised him as Nick, a Tswana Policeman from Steinhausen Police Station. He was extremely drunk. Even with my nursing experience, I took one look at his skull injuries and nearly passed out.

Keith and Stuart took control and drove Nick to Gobabis Hospital where he remained in the Emergency Room. They arrived back home by 2 in the morning. We'd 'phoned the Police Station and on Sunday morning, 2 policemen came to the Ranch to carry out an investigation. They followed the blood trail winding in and out of thorn bush from the staff compound to our house, the one Policeman saying, "You'd have thought an ox had been slaughtered there's so much blood." The weapon used was an axe and the man responsible was arrested. On the Tuesday, I telephoned the hospital who put me back onto the Police Station. The Officer on duty told me Nick had returned to work with a stitched-up head and the fracas had merely been a drunken party. All charges were withdrawn and everyone was back to normal and 'big pals' again.

I appreciated the assistance from the Gobabis Hospital doctors over the years. My anxiety, after the ghastly incident regarding Maria's little Baba, was now completely restored to trust and faith as they were very tolerant and approachable, gave a high standard of care and were particularly understanding regarding the distances we had to travel and the odd hours we required their medical help. On numerous occasions, I telephoned Dr Nel when there was something I didn't know how to cope with and he gave me instructions. At other times, when our staff needed some form of medical treatment and the only medication we had available was veterinary, the doctor would tell me exactly how to calculate the human dosage. Over the years, several more nasty alcohol or fighting-related incidents with injuries occurred with the farm staff, some involving the women, one in particular a woman, also drunk at the time, with a huge gash on the top of her head.

There were also special Government Services which served the farming districts throughout the country, one being the mobile TB (Tuberculosis) Clinic. The disease was particularly prevalent amongst the Bushmen, and was finally eradicated during the first 10 years of our time in South West Africa.

It was during the wettest time of the year when Ian was out checking the reservoirs that he came upon 2 black mambas mating and said it was a rare sight of 'contortionist ballet'. Stopping the vehicle immediately, he told the Bushman staff member on the back of the bakkie to get into the cab, then drove right up to the mambas whereupon they bit and spat venom all over the tyre. With cattle in close proximity, Ian couldn't take any chances of fatal snake bite, a certain death to livestock if struck by mambas and, unfortunately, had to shoot the snakes. Measured and photographed back home, they were 9 foot 3 inches, and 9 foot 10 inches, the female being bigger and heavier.

Piggy was becoming increasingly protective towards us. At the same time she was also wandering off a lot, sometimes with the male warthog though quite often alone. She'd get carried away with her happy times finding puddles in the rains and would wallow for hours, coming home caked with mud. I never knew or understood how she removed it, but she never came into the house dirty nor left any trace of it. Several times she wandered too far afield then a neighbour would 'phone and I'd drive 10 miles or more, sometimes most of a day there and back, to bring her home. On 6 occasions, Piggy even visited the Steinhausen Police Station 4 miles from us on farm road, 12 by main road. A new Policeman, Hennie Goosen, became a friend of ours. He'd 'phone to let me know when Piggy was there then keep her with him till I arrived. Hennie and his wife, Estelle, used to visit us fairly often. Estelle and I would exchange books. It seemed almost everyone knew about Piggy.

It took me 3 minutes flat to teach Piggy to sit and beg. We were having roast beef on a Sunday, and I think it was the smell of the meat that brought her to the table. Undoubtedly, from then on Kambingana roast beef was Piggy's favourite food. After this lesson, she would sit on her haunches in the begging position if I told her to do so, whether or not I had something to offer. She was so intelligent that when I told her to beg then gave her a pebble or a little stick, she'd roll it around in her mouth pretending to like it, and as I deliberately turned away, she'd spit it out with an, "Ugh!" She never spat out the object till I turned away. I tested her time and again and proved she didn't want to disappoint me. She understood everything we said to her. As I stood in front of the gas stove cooking each day, Piggy would lie on my feet. It was very awkward having to shuffle from side to side, as I moved, she would too.

Ian had struggled with the staff. Although they were paid monthly, had housing, food rations, uniforms, water, etc. they never seemed to have any money. He discovered they all had credit at various liquor stores, both in Omitara and at a couple of farm shops, their money being spent on alcohol. When the supply ran out, one of the men would get on a horse and be off at full speed to buy more on account, resulting in the death of a heavily pregnant mare, Mellowood. She'd been galloped for a considerable time and distance, literally dropping dead beneath the rider. From this time on, Ian never allowed anyone to take a farm horse. Ian paid off the staff's accounts and arranged that they slowly repay the company. Once clear of debt, no-one was allowed credit again. It took some months to come right, but what a difference it made to the stockmen. At month's end, they all had their full wages for the shopping trip to either Omitara or Gobabis enabling them to buy other things instead of paying off liquor bills, though incidents of inebriation still occurred, some with awful injuries due to drunken brawls or accidents.

There was a mechanical problem with one of the 2 big Ford bakkies, stuck out at Kambingana dam. Lindsay was with us at the time and Ian asked her to go with him to help drive the vehicles back home. Once he'd fixed the problem, Lindsay, not having driven a car with gears on the steering column, opted to drive the bakkie with the normal gear lever between the seats, which unfortunately, also happened to be the bigger of the 2 cars. Following Ian, she slowly navigated her way around the big dam on narrow tracks with bumps and holes concealed by grass, which first had her nerves on edge, then came all the farm gates to be opened and closed with wild Brahman cattle in camps, and still further driving. All this took some hours. Back on the long stretch of dirt road to the house, Ian picked up speed and left her to get home at her own pace.

Relieved to be on familiar terrain and tired from the tension and hours in the heat, Lindsay relaxed with a sigh of relief when suddenly a huge male greater kudu leapt from dense bush on the right side of the road directly in front of the Ford. She hit the brakes, by some miracle avoiding the stupendous antelope which immediately leapt into thick bush on the left vanishing instantly from sight. The height of the kudu's back was above that of the bonnet, the horns massive. Shaken and unable to continue driving, Lindsay switched off the ignition and sat for about 10 minutes. From this lucky miss, she fully understood how easy it is to hit a kudu leaping in front of one's car and why, in numerous cases, this kind of accident had proved fatal, particularly on the tarmac highway between Windhoek and the Omitara turn-off. There's no warning – the kudu are unpredictable, and despite keeping a careful lookout one often can't see them in the bush alongside the road.

Keith had found better employment and the family moved to Okahandja, about 60 kilometres from Windhoek, where they had a much nicer house, close to shops and 'life'. Mary was happier. Not long after, they moved again and settled in Karibib, about 4 to 5 hours drive from us, living in the town near all amenities, where Mary had a huge house, plenty of bedrooms with lots of space, kitchen, lounge, big bathroom and enormous garden. Her life started coming together again, and she deserved it. She was a wonderful wife and mother, devoted to her children and made beautiful birthday cakes, baked biscuits and ran an efficient home. Keith was content too. They befriended an elderly lady, Tannie Lottie, and her son, Albert, who lived on a farm in the area. Tannie Lottie just loved Mary, becoming her 'other mother'.

The Company Directors and Auditors arrived from Cape Town and we were instructed to go to Windhoek to see them. It was good news. Our efforts had paid off! Ian was congratulated and told that he only, of all the managers on the 19 company farms, had sent off a steady monthly supply of beef cattle (transported to Johannesburg and Cape Town abattoirs) and brought in a regular income for the Company. Our salary was raised and we were promised a bonus on every shipment of cattle as well as on hartebeest sales. Life was beginning to look up. Ian bought us a second-hand paraffin fridge which stood in the left-hand corner of the dining room, there being no space in the small kitchen. It was marvellous not having to walk backwards and forwards so often to the cottage though we still needed to use the cottage deep freezer.

Ian's aged mother, Mater, living in East London sent me Rand 250 to buy a Singer hand-sewing machine, so I took down all the hessian sacking curtains and made new fabric drapes for every room. A further wonderful surprise awaited me. A telephone call from the Manager of a large firm of office equipment in Windhoek told me to come and collect my typewriter!

"There must be some mistake," I said, "I can't afford a typewriter."

"Well, you've been given one!" he replied.

I arranged to call in on my next trip to the city, and all was explained to me quite simply. Our dear friends from Malindi days, Klaus Drabert, and his wife, Anne, living in Germany, had arranged with someone they knew going on holiday from Germany to Windhoek, to buy me a typewriter as they were having difficulty reading my handwritten letters! It was the most splendid gift and an immeasurable help in my correspondence with friends and family in different parts of the world saving me hours of letter-writing, not to mention the convenience of being able to type Ian's farm or business correspondence.

'Things happen in threes', so the saying goes. Since taking over at Kambingana, there'd been no way of sterilising the inoculating syringes and needles, no matter how often we'd asked for equipment. So I'd used my own excellent Brazilian-made pressure cooker, bought in Serpa Pinto, and was since no longer able to use it for our cooking. You could have knocked me over at my luck when the Manager in Windhoek telephoned to say I should buy myself a new pressure cooker on the Company account!

Yet a further 2 happy incidents awaited us. The telephone rang one day and a voice said in Kenyan Swahili, "*Jambo Memsahib. Habari yako*?" ("Hello, lady. How are you?). I could hardly believe my ears! Harvey Storm, who worked for the BP Company, had been sent from South Africa to take over the Windhoek branch. In my high school days, I remembered hearing about this handsome, dashing young chap from the Prince of Wales School in Nairobi. I made a trip to Windhoek to meet Harvey, for the first time, and his wife, Jenny. He told me he'd been a salesman for the oil company when we'd been farming in Kenya and had come out to Westlands to sell Ian oil and grease for the machinery. The couple visited us on Kambingana. Ian and Harvey thoroughly enjoyed chatting about old times, schools, the Kenya Regiment and farming.

Then Beryl and her boyfriend, Koos, married in a small, delightful ceremony in Windhoek with a dinner party afterwards at one of the hotels. Stuart was best man. Koos was a great favourite with everyone, especially with us, and we were so pleased to have him in the family.

Winter was upon us again. As hot as South West Africa is in summer, with Kambingana frequently reaching temperatures in the high forties Celsius, so could cold winter nights fall on average from zero down to minus ten. On one occasion, a bitter minus sixteen was measured at Kambingana dam water pump. There was a time when, at minus fourteen Celsius all the fish in the Omitara Hotel aquarium froze to death.

On the other side of the garage where the perimeter fencing for the horse paddock was and just inside the 5-strand wire fencing, on grass, was a huge stack of wooden creosote-treated fencing poles. The male warthog, as is natural to his species, dug a hole using his snout, tusks and hooves under the pile of wood posts, and another hole next to it for Piggy, each burrow big enough for a warthog to lie in comfortably, making sleeping accommodation for the 2, with a ridge of solid earth between Piggy's 'bed' and his. I was really pleased to see the progress. Natural to warthogs too is to reverse into their burrows in case they need to defend themselves or must exit at speed in case of lurking predators. Piggy would go in backwards as well and the pigs would lie there alongside one another to nap or sleep. Warthogs have an in-built bedtime clock and like to be bunked down in their burrows before it gets dark. So I made sure I soon had a solid routine established whereby I'd walk the 2 pigs to their beds by 5.30, just before dark, see them both in bottoms first, wait a bit nearby, then be able to go back to the house once I was sure they were sound asleep.

It was winter hartebeest catching season again and we expected David Boyce as helicopter pilot this time around as Koosie had been diagnosed with throat cancer and wasn't well. David was expected to arrive the evening before the game capture preparations got underway, the landing place for the chopper inside the horse paddock about 50 yards from the pile of fencing poles and warm warthog burrows. I'd just put Piggy and her boyfriend peacefully to bed, seen them asleep with their eyes shut and long lashes so beautiful (the envy of any woman), and was just about to go back to the house when the Bell helicopter flew in late, hovered above the landing spot then touched down. All this terrifying noise completely unsettled the 2 warthogs. They were scared out of their wits at the whirring rotor blades, huge blasts of wind and intense engine screaming sound, and shot out of their burrows back to the house. Piggy immediately took refuge in the kitchen while the male hovered around outside the back door.

Ian went out to meet David who was unloading his kit. He'd be staying in the cottage and needed the keys. While we waited for David to join us for supper, I tried to put the pigs to bed again carrying with me a Dietz paraffin lamp. But, the first mistake I made was forgetting that with the dryness and now cold night temperatures, the grass became so frozen it made a cracking noise when trodden underfoot. Having settled the pigs second time around, eyes shut, long lashes still, apparently calm and asleep, as I turned to go back to the house I trod on a stick of dry brittle grass. With their keen sense of hearing, the sound of the 'snap' to the pigs was about the equivalent of a fire-bell to a human! Instantly, they were out of their beds and wouldn't leave me! With no other option, I took them back to the house and petted them a bit, then started the 'piggy-winks' process 'round three,' and told them to get into their beds. They immediately complied and closed their eyes. I stood and waited till I thought they were in dreamland. Then I crept back avoiding all grass, keeping to sandy patches only, and not wanting to make any unnecessary sound left the back garden gate open.

"So far, so good," I thought to myself with a little smile of relief. The cold outside, at least around zero by now, was getting to me. What I'd forgotten though was that when one turned the kitchen door handle it squeaked. Whether the 2 pigs had been feigning sleep and silently followed me or not I'd no idea, but on hearing and knowing that familiar 'squeak' this signalled to them total evacuation and they hurtled through the garden gate, Piggy unintentionally shoving me at the door in her wild rush to get back inside the house! I temporarily gave up the idea of trying to put the warthogs to bed and decided we'd have our supper first, giving them time to calm their frayed nerves, Piggy lying quietly in the kitchen, the male snorting and snuffling around outside. Once David had gone back to the cottage, I bundled myself up warmly and escorted the 2 back to their burrows. I was greatly relieved, as they seemed to be over being spooked by the helicopter and bunked down happily for the night. For the next couple of days or so of hartebeest capture, David returned by 5 in the afternoon, so come 'piggy-winks' bedtime I had no further problems. Koosie lost his fight against cancer not long after – devastating news for us. Kambingana continued with the game capture, the operations now conducted by David Boyce. With Koosie's meticulous training, the safety record was maintained.

'Tootsie-Wootsie' came into our lives as a newly born porcupine. It's a miracle she survived, even to being seen and picked up off the ground.

The horsemen, split into 2 groups, were mustering cattle at Boomlager, separating the cows from their year-old calves. One group herded the calves into the kraals; the other drove the cows into a 4,000 acre camp, so one can imagine the galloping about by the stockmen on horseback with the wild cattle going in different directions that went on more than half the day. At some time, the thundering hooves must have disturbed a mother porcupine from her burrow. In fright, she probably dashed out and into the bush, one of her babies still clinging to her teat. Luckily, the headman, Simon, turned back toward Ian to tell him something and noticed this little baby lying in the path of the horse's hooves. He dismounted, picked up the animal and gave it to Ian who put it into his jacket pocket and drove the 30 kilometres home. In the kitchen, he handed me this tiny, soft body, no bigger than a small mouse. Covered in sand, with the umbilical cord still wet and eyelids closed, I wondered if we could really save the little mite.

I began by just keeping Tootsie-Wootsie safe in my bra awhile, a very good place to warm up small birds and animals! When I cleaned up the little body, I saw that her quills were baby-soft and very pliable, and that she was rodent-like in appearance. An old cloth was used to wrap around her while she was fed Ideal Milk from an eye-dropper, ever so many times a day. Then with a part of the cloth dampened with warm water, her face was washed, followed by her bum-end, and right on cue, she'd do her business. Then the old cloth was washed and dried ready for the next time. When Stuart was home from school, he'd get out his sleeping bag and take Tootsie-Wootsie to bed with him. They were as warm as toast, she at the very end by his feet. On shopping trips to Windhoek, I'd have to take Tootsie-Wootsie when she was little and still on Ideal Milk. In a plastic bag was the essential old cloth. We always lunched at the Kalahari Sands Hotel and none of the staff ever noticed a porcupine in their restaurant! She was better behaved than any child.

Each day as Tootsie-Wootsie grew brought the same procedure – the old cloth, food and play-time. Piggy and the dogs joined in, only the cats didn't romp and play. Tootsie-Wootsie discovered shoes which she'd drag around rather awkwardly, the manoeuvres keeping her busy for quite some time. Her best toy was the enamel potty kept in the 'loo'. When this was trailed around by the handle it made all sorts of metallic scraping sounds and kept turning on its side, then had to be righted again before continuing – another challenge for her to overcome. First, we had to be careful about shutting doors because Tootsie-Wootsie would chew on the wood at the bottom corner. Then we discovered we had to keep doors open, allowing her easy access to wherever she wanted to go, without any chewing.

As usual, I took the family out at 5 in the afternoon for walks. Initially, as she was so small, most of the time I had to carry Tootsie-Wootsie. As the days passed, she was able to walk, eventually all the way, her padded feet making no sound whatsoever. Her 'modus operandi' was to hurry along, then suddenly reverse with the same speed for short spurts, and then continue forward again. I presume this is how adult porcupines manage to leave quills in predators when they're being chased. On all our walks, as her quills began to harden, there were never any mishaps. By the time Tootsie-Wootsie was as big as a guinea-pig, she was very independent, still on Ideal Milk, but now eating other foods like carrots, cabbage stalks, dog biscuits and maize-meal porridge cooked to a very stiff consistency and anything edible which took her fancy, but never meat.

My elderly sister, Marge, and sister-in-law, Vi, came to stay with us for a week or so. Since we'd been on the Ranch in South West Africa, we'd had regular correspondence with Marge and Vi. Harold had died in August 1974, and Rob had left Angola in December that year to help Marge run their Rhodesian farm. Lex had passed away in 1975, all sad news for us and particularly for Ian as Harold and Lex were his 2 favourite (half-) brothers. Marge had since moved from Rhodesia and was now living in Natal near her family. Vi was still resident in Kenya, but holidaying with Marge. There was a lot to talk about. It was good to see them both again. Each afternoon, we went for a stroll with the dogs, Pepu, Minnie and Simba (Pepu and Minnie's pup about 2 years old now), Piggy warthog and Tootsie-Wootsie porcupine. Piggy's boyfriend didn't socialise with the dogs and Tootsie-Wootsie so he did his own thing while we were gone. We didn't walk the usual distance on these outings as I didn't want to tire Marge and Vi, but it didn't matter to the dogs, Piggy or Tootsie-Wootsie, they were happy just to have their daily 'out and about' time.

Porcupines' bodies are protected by unique long, pliable spines up to 50cm in length, flattened bristly hairs, and stiff sharp quills (rather like a large 'pin-cushion') which are a very successful form of self-defence when raised. Any predator which attacks or runs into them will be seriously injured in the face, paws or body. A porcupine quill in a lion's foot or muzzle, as an example, may break off and the wound can turn septic. Sometimes, the quills are so deeply embedded in the predator that they cannot be pulled out, which can result in the death of the animal. When calm and relaxed, the quills lie long and flat on the porcupine's back. The hair and quills are white with black annulations declining in length towards the base, the thick quills up to 30cm long. Adult females weigh around 18.5kg; males about 17kg, though some have reached 24kg. They gnaw on bark of trees as well as bones to combat a phosphorus deficiency, and their natural diet includes fallen wild fruits, bulbs, tubers and roots which they dig up, and farmers' crops such as potatoes, carrots, onions, beetroot, pumpkin, groundnuts, beans and peas. Porcupines are solitary animals, the largest rodents in the more southerly parts of Africa, but have been seen in pairs or a female with her young. They are nocturnal and prefer rocky hills and outcrops, caves and abandoned aardvark holes to rest up in during the day, but have been seen sunbathing close to their shelters.

Ian started converting our Ford lorry into a camping vehicle as we'd made plans to travel to Lüderitz in December on the west coast of South West Africa, and from there right across to the east coast of South Africa where we were to meet up with 60 other Kenyans, all on a camping and deep-sea fishing holiday at Sodwana Bay on the Natal north coast. This had been arranged by Piet Van Dyk, a great and very successful deep-sea fisherman, whose parents had been friends with my mother, Daisy, since childhood.

One morning, an Afrikaans farmer who also spoke English, Mr Human, had just had a car smash with a kudu on the main Omitara dirt road which ran through Kambingana, and called in for help. The kudu, standing in the road had jumped, landed on the bonnet and smashed the windscreen. He'd come to ask Ian to take his gun and shoot the wounded animal.

Seeing Mr Human again and with Piggy grown-up now, reminded me of the 1st time he'd called at the farm. Ian was out, so I'd offered him tea. At the time, Piggy was little. As I was without a fridge, I kept the fresh milk in a bucket behind the hallway door, being the coolest part of the house. On this particular day, old Munde had only just brought the milk to the kitchen and the bucket was still standing on the floor. Busying myself with making the tea while chatting to Mr Human, next thing I heard a gurgling sound and immediately realised the situation. Trying to get to the milk, Piggy had fallen into the bucket head first. Quickly, I picked her up, wiped her off and put her down again then scooped some milk into a jug from the bucket. Mr Human was too polite to refuse the tea, but told me now on this 2nd visit that it took all his nerve to drink it, adding that he knew English people to be 'different' and he didn't want to appear rude!

With Mr Human needing Ian's help now with the injured kudu, I'd quite forgotten to tell him about the new member of our family, Tootsie-Wootsie porcupine. We were sitting in the lounge having tea when from the toilet came the noise of the enamel potty being trailed around by Tootsie-Wootsie with a lot of clanking and clattering through the hallway into the sitting room. I merely took the potty from her, returned it to its place then picked her up. Mr Human was gobsmacked to now see a porcupine sharing the chair with me. The look of amazement on his face further endorsed that he thought English people to be quite mad. I've smiled about this amusing scene often!

Like Miss Piggy, Tootsie-Wootsie turned into a guard animal. She was wary of strangers and unknown cars, and ever watchful. She'd make grunting noises and shuffle about, all her quills standing up with a rattling sound when she was alarmed.

The telephone rang early one Tuesday morning. It was Stuart calling from Centaurus hostel.

"Hello, Mum. How are you?" he asked.

"Hello, my boy," I answered. "I'm fine. Is something wrong?" It was unusual for him to 'phone at this time of day.

"I can't talk long, just a quick call," he said. "I forgot my snakes in my clothes cupboard on Sunday. Sorry, Mum, can you take them out for me please?"

"Yes, of course, I'll get Dad to help me," I assured him.

"Thanks. I have to go now. Love to you and Dad. Bye."

"Love to you, too. Bye," I said replacing the receiver.

The weekend had ended in a rush, just one of those Sundays when time flies and you seem to get behind with most everything you're busily doing. I'd had to get Stuart back to boarding school in Windhoek before 5 o'clock. He'd never forgotten his snakes in his cupboard before. I told Ian when he came back for breakfast at 9. Immediately and bluntly, he told me I could go ahead, he wouldn't be attempting to catch the snakes! So, I said, "Okay, I'll do it." After all, someone had to do the job. I was extremely nervous. However, full of bravado I put on my gardening gloves and opened Stuart's cupboard doors to look at the shelves which had casual clothing, all neatly packed and stacked in rows. No snakes were visible. Ian nonchalantly sat on Stuart's bed, smoking a cigarette, to watch my brave performance. There appeared to be no movement anywhere, so I cautiously lifted a pile of shirts to look underneath and immediately a hissing snake head rose up and thrust out at me! I dropped the shirts – the ready snake sent me shrieking! I leapt onto the other single bed while Ian rolled around laughing on Stuart's bed! There was no way I could handle those 4 foot long snakes. So it was left to Ian. He carefully surveyed the scene now knowing where to look, and without much further ado he caught one and then the other just behind the head, and took them to their cage outside. Mole snakes are found in great variations of colours and are widespread. They're non-poisonous with small heads and muscled bodies covered in smooth scales, live on small mammals, and usually are non-aggressive. I'd never been able to handle any snake, so why I thought I could catch those 2, I don't know! Then again, perhaps Ian had figured if he could get me to do the ground work and 'flush them out', so to speak, his task would be much easier!

Piggy's death and the little we truly knew about it was a blow to our very being. I shall never forget her – our darling, always in our hearts.

The late hot days of October had arrived and Piggy, with all her freedom, had gone on her daily solitary walk-about. I expected either a telephone call from someone to fetch her or she'd return to the house. There'd been an outbreak of rabies starting in 1977, a year before, some first cases being reported in the Okahandja area which then spread, particularly affecting kudu.

As we later understood it, Piggy had wandered far on this occasion, about 20 kilometres from our home and in the late evening, seeing a farmhouse, she'd approached the garden gate and sat down waiting for someone to let her in. Christa, the German farmer's wife, on seeing Piggy sitting at their gate thought her to be a rabid warthog, fetched their shotgun and killed her. These very few details were given to us by another farmer's wife, a mutual friend of ours and Christa's. We never spoke to Christa about Piggy's death and they never mentioned the subject when they once visited us, but did show us greater friendship after this tragic accident. I couldn't bear a grudge because farmers had to kill rabid animals, though we were utterly devastated as everyone in the Omitara area apparently knew about our wonderful Piggy. People even came from Windhoek to see and photograph her. Sadly for us, though understandably, her not so tame boyfriend returned to the bush not long after and the 2 warthog burrows, side by side, remained a lonely, empty reminder.

December 1978 holidays began and Stuart had only one more school year to get through in Windhoek. He planned on being a helicopter pilot. With the money his grandmother, Mater, sent him, Stuart bought a lovely smart, upmarket Honda CB 550K 4-cylinder motorbike. It had been his dream for some time to own such a bike. He called in at Lindsay's home in Windhoek to proudly show her his shiny new wheels and say goodbye before he left to join us on holiday.

I took Tootsie-Wootsie to Carola Kronsbein our German farmer-artist friend who'd kindly take care of her while we were away. Tootsie-Wootsie would be kept in a wire enclosure about 16 feet square for her safety.

Ian had finished the changes to the Ford lorry turning it into a wonderful camping vehicle. The top and sides were covered in tarpaulin and in the back was ample space for all our camping equipment, the stove, fishing tackle, stores of dry foods, water containers, diesel, etc., so we packed up and left on the long drive to Sodwana via Lüderitz. Ian decided to take 'Spyker' (his name the Afrikaans word for 'nail'), a skinny Bushman youngster as our camp-man. Spyker had no parents and Simon found him uncooperative – he would listen only to Ian. Spyker was paid his salary and fed by us, had his own tent and bedding and would be up by 6 in the morning to get the camp fire going and rekindle it again in the evening. Being Bushman, he always knew where east and west were, helped with packing or unpacking and various odd jobs, though his main responsibility was to keep watch over our possessions which gave him plenty of time to chat to other holiday makers.

Stuart, having bought all his necessary biking gear, would leave the farm after us and first visit his long-time school pal from Treverton College, Jonathan, who lived in Howick, Natal. Then he'd go on to Cape Town to be with his girlfriend after which he'd make his way to us at Sodwana.

First stop, Lüderitz – a quaint, attractive town on a bay discovered by Bartholomew Diaz in 1487, on one of the least hospitable coasts of Africa, the gardens walled to protect plants and homes from the winds, the buildings in the style of old Germany. Kolmanskop, a ghost town just outside Lüderitz, used to be a bustling diamond mining settlement now abandoned. It is a constant battle with the windblown shifting sand dunes of the Namib Desert piling up against or filtering into and taking over buildings. Situated in a harsh environment between ocean and desert, Lüderitz inhabitants are well aware of this natural sea-wind-sand-desert phenomenon and are always prepared for the 'big' gales – anything glass gets sandblasted including car windscreens and headlights so at these times everything closes down, windows are shuttered, doors closed, vehicles put under cover. Lüderitz, a popular tourist destination is also known for its museum, seals, penguins and flamingos. We were glad to have made the trip to see it. Now it was time to set off on the long journey to the Natal north coast.

Stuart joined us before Christmas at Sodwana Bay. He'd had no problems on his extensive travels, was meticulous about the care of his Honda bike, always wore his helmet and drove with the headlights on.

We had a fantastic holiday, joined in an International Billfish Competition, caught a fair number of blue marlin and spent time with old friends. The enormous camping site accommodating about 6,000 people was set amongst forest trees above a sandy beach into which a river opened. At high tide the river mouth was flooded with sea water; at low tide people drove their 4x4 vehicles down to the edge of the beach to launch ski-boats leaving their cars, only to return to find sea water up to the bonnets. I witnessed this on several occasions. Piet van Dyk (known to the fishing community as 'Oom Piet'), an expert marlin fisherman with years of experience on the Kenya, Sodwana and Mozambican coasts, had arranged with the Parks Board that the 60 ex-Kenyans would have the privilege of camping at Sodwana before the festive season influx of Transvaalers and Freestaters, and most generously paid all the fees!

Monkeys were a nuisance at Sodwana. They'd enter camp sites and wreak havoc in the tents, particularly of food stores, tearing open bags of flour and sugar and scattering the contents around, take lids off pots and generally make a huge mess. One of Spyker's jobs was to chase off the monkeys. One day, they got into the back of the lorry and pulled the pans out of the stove, luckily with little damage other than to eat the leftover beef I'd roasted the night before. On 3 occasions, I baked the tried and trusted Kenya sandwich cakes for friends having birthdays.

Just after New Year, we left and where the Sodwana National Park road joins the main national highway we stopped and got out of the lorry to hug and say goodbye to Stuart. He was on his way down the coast to Mossel Bay to spend time with Ian's brother, Ron, his wife, Joan, and their son, Michael. Then he'd travel back to South West Africa in time for school term beginning after mid-January 1979, his last year at Centaurus.

Back home, I immediately 'phoned Carola to find out when it would be convenient to fetch Tootsie-Wootsie and thank her. The news wasn't what I'd expected. Tootsie-Wootsie had escaped from her enclosure by digging deep down, tunnelling out to freedom and into the bush. We thought she'd finally become feral and would be quite all right in her natural environment, hoping she'd find her own kind sooner or later. Still, I would miss so much her tricks and noises about the house.

I then collected Lindsay, her little son, Brendan, and Debbie to stay a few days with us on the farm. Four days after we'd arrived home, just before midnight, Ron telephoned from Mossel Bay to say he'd been trying for hours to get through, but Omitara Exchange wasn't answering. Both Ian and I spoke to Ron. Stuart had been in an accident on his motorbike and was in hospital with a compound fracture of the left lower leg (tibia) requiring surgery. His leg was in plaster from the knee down to his ankle, but Ron was visiting Stuart regularly and he was all right. Telephoning the hospital immediately, we spoke with Stuart. He said he was fine. We then telephoned a hunting guest (a friend of the Kambingana Company Directors), who was the big boss of South African Airways. He booked us on the early morning flight from Windhoek to Cape Town. He'd very kindly pay our airfares and we could reimburse him on our return. Lindsay would remain with the 2 children on the Ranch to keep an eye on things while we were gone and would let Keith, Mary and Beryl know first thing in the morning about Stuart's accident.

Ian then went to our bedroom and started packing his suitcase, taking out his dark suit which he never wore, and I asked him what he needed it for, we wouldn't be going out to dinner? In hindsight, I think Ian and probably Ron too, decided to keep from me the real situation until we could get to Stuart. Ron met us at Cape Town airport for the 4-hour or so drive to Mossel Bay.

By the time we arrived, Stuart was in a coma. I was completely unprepared for this and utterly shocked at his condition. Ian and I remained at his bedside. Stuart had an embolism which had travelled from his leg and lodged in his lung. The doctor is not one I care to remember. He showed little empathy, saying only the week before a young woman had died from a blood clot and there wasn't much hope.

The following day, 8th January 1979, our beloved son, Stuart, just turned 18 years old on 3rd December 1978, briefly looked at me in recognition and I was able to tell him, "We love you, we love you," then within seconds, he gently closed his eyes and silently faded from our lives forever.

Afterwards, Ian and I lay together some time on a single bed at Ron's house and just held each other until I could find some way forward in coping with the shock and overwhelming grief at our youngest child's death. My whole being was so flooded with mental, emotional and physical pain at losing Stuart, the only decision I could finally come to at this point in time was that my heart wanted a plain blue satin pall over Stuart's coffin with a white satin cross that I'd hand-stitch myself. Ron was a great help in taking us to buy the material.

I remember very little of the service, but do remember Ron stopping the preacher who was in 'full loud religious rant' to such extent that I completely broke down and began screaming. After leaving Mossel Bay to get our return flight from Cape Town to Windhoek, en route in Somerset West (about 35 minutes drive from the airport) our Aggett cousins gave us a private family gathering. Then we flew back taking Stuart's ashes with us to The Place of the Water, Kambingana.

We'd been gone a week. Death affects us all in different ways. Lindsay was particularly distressed by the wooden casket with Stuart's ashes. Even though she was grown and understood cremation, she couldn't comprehend that her not quite 6 foot tall younger brother could fit in such a small casket. She said she'd felt afraid alone at night on the farm and that the 2 children had slept in our big bed with her, Stuart's dog, Pepu, on the carpet next to her keeping guard, never leaving the bedside, and that he'd constantly growled throughout the nights, just this continuous low growl in his throat.

Keith, Mary, Beryl and Koos were grief stricken and still in shock. Beryl and Stuart had been very close ever since childhood. It brought home how suddenly the life of a loved one can pass, one never knows when it can happen, and how one grapples with the inner turmoil of emotions as one tries to come to terms with the pain of loss and move forward to some acceptance of a future without one so dear. What had happened was that Stuart had been on the National N2 highway where it meets the entrance to the Mossel Bay main road, on the start of his way back home to us after spending a few days with Ron and family. A bakkie with Transvaal (northern South Africa) number plates, and towing a caravan, driven by a drunk man, his wife with him, suddenly drove through a stop sign at a T-junction – Stuart, with no time to react and no other way of avoiding a collision, went through the caravan on his motorbike. Mossel Bay is a very popular east coast holiday resort on the South African Garden Route, particularly during the end of year festive season and Easter, and the town literally becomes swamped with holidaymakers.

According to witnesses, Stuart was able to speak immediately after the crash. Although there was a compound fracture in his leg, the operation was considered to be a success. However, paramedics had not administered an anti-coagulant injection to Stuart at the site of the accident, and it was doubtful that he'd been given one on admission to the hospital either. What wasn't thought of was the blood clot that broke away from the injury site in Stuart's leg and travelled silently, and fatally, into his lung. Later, independent doctors told Ian and me that it was gross negligence in not giving anti-coagulants.

The Police, after Stuart's death, asked if we wished to make a civil case against the drunk driver. We declined. There could never be any way we could bring our son back. The Police, themselves, then laid a charge. Although we received 2 letters from witnesses, we never heard from the drunk driver or his wife.

After an investigation as to why the Omitara Telephone Operator had not answered the signals, we learnt that he 'was out, canoodling under a bush' with a girl. Since there'd been many complaints about the operator, he was relieved of his post. The Insurance Company would not pay out for Stuart's motorbike because we'd not laid a charge against the drunken driver. This was a further painful and harrowing time. Finally, they agreed on a settlement amount if we could prove that Stuart had not been at fault. This entailed getting the Courts in Port Elizabeth to put all the data on micro-tapes. Once these were scrutinised, the Insurance paid us.

Pepu dog grieved inconsolably. He'd creep under Stuart's bed and if anyone approached he'd growl and want to bite if we so much as put out a hand, totally unlike his usual gentle character. He refused to leave Stuart's bedroom except to go out for ablutions and to eat or drink. Eventually, even his eating diminished to an alarming degree. We'd consulted our vet, and since there was no improvement after 3 months and with Pepu being old already, we very sadly put him to sleep. He'd been a wonderful dog, a most loyal and faithful companion to Stuart, as well as to all of us, experiencing the tough times in Angola and the trip out on the convoy. This is the first time I've witnessed a dog dying of heartache, and being Stuart's Pepu it was a double sadness in our family.

I kept Stuart's ashes on my dressing table for 6 months, unable to bring myself to part with them and understood now how Maria must have felt when Baba died. None of the staff approached Ian or me directly about Stuart's death, but their demeanour became quiet and sombre, very polite and respectful, and especially responsible in their work, carrying out Ian's instruction to the word. I think they didn't know how to cope with the awful situation, added to which there was no funeral for them to attend, no closure as such, or way to pay their respects and say goodbye. Cremation was quite 'alien' to them.

Our children, Lindsay, Keith, Mary, Beryl and Koos carried us through our time of deep sorrow and anguish. There are no adequate words that truly describe the inner pain at the loss of one's child.

One day, our dear friend, Boertjie Johan, with his kind heart, took Ian quietly aside and gently said we couldn't keep holding Stuart's ashes forever, the time had come for us to say goodbye to him. We returned to Mossel Bay by car, taking our grandson, Andrew, with us. From a boat, way out at sea, Ian broke open Stuart's casket. I just held Andrew, a lovely little boy, close to me and did not watch.

In December 2015, Stuart would have turned 55. The years have passed with some days better than others as I've held him quietly with me, always. After a long while, one begins to remember the good, happy and funny times, but always there is something to remind one of our dearest gone before us. Just the smallest thing can bring the heartache flooding back.

Pepu's real name was *Upepo* meaning *wind* in Swahili, and as penned in Stuart's fitting words below, I like to think that our youngest son's spirit – *a true child of Africa* – rests in peace free on the wind, his shadow Pepu beside him, amongst the beautiful wild orchids and flowers of our fazenda in Angola.

AS I SIT

Beneath the spreading boughs
Of this mighty tree
As old as the rock
Upon which I rest
Scarred by time
Time immemorial
I gaze across the valley
To the distant tree-line
Beyond swift water
Over which I watch
The flight of the falcon
I have heard its cry
Now gone with the wind
Of the seventeenth summer
And feel the lonely hands
Of my heart
For the heart is a lonely hunter

Daisy's Daughter
Our Lives for Africa

When I gaze across
And see the red sky at morning
When rain clouds gather
I feel the fearless adventurer
Living the way of danger
But I remember mama
Who was like
The lilies of the field
Arising in the sun
And now, I cry the beloved country

Alexander Stuart Rooken-Smith
3.12.1960 – 8.01.1979

Chapter Twenty
!Xai & the Christmas Cake

Eighteen days after Stuart's death was Lindsay's 21st birthday. None of us felt in a celebratory mood, but Stuart wouldn't have wanted this important milestone of hers to go unmarked in some way, so we all drove to Keith and Mary in Karibib for the weekend and went out for a quiet drink. A few months later, Ian bought Lindsay a little Austin motor car in excellent condition for Rand 1,000 as her birthday gift. She was thrilled.

Beryl gave birth to a baby boy on 9th April 1979, named Stuart after our son. We hoped with this baby that the sadness of her 1st child adopted in Angola would diminish and she'd find new joy in motherhood. She and Koos were now living in Okahandja.

Robert Slingsby, our Stuart's boyhood friend from Malindi days where the 2 of them spent so much time together, particularly swimming till their hair was tinged green, grew up and joined the forces fighting the border war in Rhodesia. News reached us of Robert's death on 11th April 1979. He was killed in action, dying from gunshot wounds at the age of 20. This was exceptionally heart-breaking for us to hear. I found it uncanny that the 2 had been best pals in their youth, almost inseparable, then after not seeing one another for years they both died young, 3 months apart. Robert (James) Slingsby (born 22.6.1958) was a Corporal in the Special Air Service, C Squadron, and is buried in Harare (Warren Hills) Cemetery, Harare (previously Salisbury), Zimbabwe (Rhodesia).

Returning home from shopping in Windhoek one late afternoon, as usual I stopped en route at Hidas in Klein Windhoek to get a roasted chicken à la Portuguese. At the petrol station next door, I saw an extraordinary and angry situation going on. A German farmer was on the rampage, shouting and gesticulating. Out of curiosity, I went over to speak to him. He had collected his VW Kombi from having a service and had told the VW service manager in the morning that the door over the engine at the back was giving trouble as it was loose and not shutting properly and that he never wanted to see that door open again. It must have happened that the service manager literally said to one of the workmen that they should fix the door so that it never opens again. The German farmer probably collected his car at the last moment and didn't think about checking the engine door. When he stopped at the garage, he only then noticed that it had been spot welded so that it could never open again! Absolutely furious now, he charged into the petrol station office to call the workshop who didn't answer as they were now closed. He then wanted to telephone VW in Germany! The petrol station staff were flummoxed not understanding what the trouble was or how to handle the situation since it was petrol they were putting into the car which had nothing to do with the back engine door. Having heard the story from the German farmer who was apoplectic and about to explode with fury with no let-up, I took off, wondering what the outcome would be. He certainly had my sympathy. I can still see the farmer's livid face!

Mary and Keith's 3rd child, a son, Shaun, was born on 5th September 1979. We now had 5 grandchildren.

With permission, Ian built a large back verandah onto the house which made such a difference in the heat or rainy weather and gave a lot of extra space. It ran across the entire length of the kitchen and dining room and was walled to waist height. He then constructed a carport along the far side garage wall under which 4 vehicles could be parked – again, a far more satisfactory set-up with the cars under shade and cover from the elements.

January 1980 brought us an ecstatically happy reunion with our Angola German farming friend, Franz Nachtsheim, when he visited us on the Ranch bringing a friend from his schooldays in Germany. Franz had pursued inquiries about people from his Angola days and eventually managed to get our contact details. We were all so relieved to see one another safe and well and had a lot to catch up on, though missing from this reunion was Stuart – Franz was shocked to hear of his death. Franz was now living on a plot in the southern suburb of Kibler Park, Johannesburg, running a business from the property selling spices and ingredients to the meat industry. We were most keen to hear what happened in Angola with Franz and August. Franz relates for us their experience:

"When the civil war broke out in the Serpa Pinto area at the beginning of August 1975, my farming partner, Johann August Ginkel, and I were on our way to Sá Da Bandeira to find a buyer for our first maize crop we'd harvested that year. There was a new Mill in Matala and the owners were interested in buying our entire harvest. I would be 36 years old in November that year, and August was 35. We'd withdrawn a large sum of money from our bank in Serpa Pinto 2 days before. Unable to return to our farm, Fazenda Luassivi, in Cuando Cubango Province due to the war in Serpa Pinto, we stayed on in Sá Da Bandeira, but decided to leave for South West Africa (now Namibia) after a few days as we could feel the tension. In January 1976, when the South African Army had occupied great areas of Angola, we managed to get back to our fazenda to find only a few walls of the house and parts of heavy machinery left. Everything else had been destroyed or stolen. Returning to Sá Da Bandeira, we stayed at the home of Portuguese friends who'd left the country already. Their house was fully furnished and well stocked up with all sorts of supplies as well as a huge veggie garden, chickens and ducks.

When the South African Army moved south and the MPLA took over control of Sá Da Bandeira, I did not see any chance to carry on with a normal life. Fazenda Luassivi was in a UNITA controlled area and farming not possible. August thought that things would improve and stayed on. The day after MPLA took over I left southwards. On the roads outside, there were 3 roadblocks from MPLA, but they let me pass without hassle. There was no sight of UNITA in the area. From Cahama to the South West African border, the South African Army was in control of things. I stayed in Oshakati for a couple of days and when things did not improve, I decided to return back to Alberton.

About 6 months later, August was arrested for no reason, jailed for a month in Sá Da Bandeira (now Lubango) never having been charged with any transgression then transferred to a Luanda jail for a further 10 months before being deported back to Germany. The only explanation August can give, in his opinion, for his incarceration is that the Head of Police was interested in the house and belongings where August was staying. He was not the only one arrested at the time. Hundreds of white Portuguese people shared the same fate, most of them released after a few days, but many didn't survive. It was said that as many as 88 people were pushed down the cliffs of Tunda-Vala, a gorge cut out of the Chela escarpment, dropping down 1,000m, looking towards the town of Bibala in the north. August has not spoken much about this time, but you get the distinct feeling that it was a terrible experience. I feel sad to have lost everything we'd achieved in Angola, but I've never had the feeling that I shouldn't have done the move there."

Listening to Franz and August's story made us realise the kind of consequences that could have been in store for us had we stayed on. Angola had gained Independence from Portugal on 11th November 1975, the crippling civil war taking a huge toll on the people and the country. In our opinion, we'd made it out just in time. Many of the towns and places had been renamed. Franz felt he would sometime return to see what had happened to their fazenda though the possibility of landmines was a worrying factor, but August, understandably, had so far not returned to Africa, even declining invitations to visit Franz in Johannesburg. They'd started their Angolan farming operation at the same time as ourselves and Franz relates how they'd landed up farming in this West-African country:

"I was born in Plaidt, Germany, and my introduction to Africa came about in December 1964, when I left my home country and travelled down the African continent with 2 friends from Alexandria, Egypt to Cape Town, South Africa. I'd always been interested in farming and had seen a lot of potential to do so in Africa. Arriving in Johannesburg in November 1965, I stayed on and August joined me from Germany in 1966. We were living on a farm in Alberton close to Johannesburg, renting the property from our boss, the owner of Piel's Cold Storage. Through friends, we learned of the possibility of owning land in Angola when they moved to Sá Da Bandeira in 1970, and I joined them to help move machinery and trucks to Angola, at the same time making enquiries to obtain farm land. In August 1973, I returned to Angola and worked on a farm where the owner allowed me to make use of already cultivated land to plant maize at my own cost. August joined me in Angola at the end of 1973. My land application seemed to have been forgotten about at the relevant Offices, though August's application was successful and we were granted 5,000 hectares of virgin land in Cuando

and he telephoned his parents. When they saw him they knew he needed hospitalisation. His mother 'phoned all over the world for information to help her son. The answer was always, "There is no hope. Nothing can be done." Jorg was sent by plane to the Military Hospital in Johannesburg, where he died. I attended his funeral on his parents' farm. Only a year after the trauma of our Stuart, the death of Jorg hit me hard. I couldn't stop crying for 3 days. It really knocked me to realise again how fragile life is.

Another tragedy in the vast Omitara district, of which there were several during the time we lived there, I remember clearly. A young, 6 month pregnant woman and her husband went out for target practice against the earth wall of a big dam. The young husband handed his wife the pistol while he went to the target on the dam wall to check where his shots had landed. The wife, waiting patiently for his return, must have wanted to scratch the back of her head, and did so with the barrel of the gun – her finger must have still been on the trigger. Her husband heard the shot and dashed back to find his wife had died instantly. Police ruled out foul play. The Omitara community was shattered.

Ian hadn't yet saved any money since leaving Fazenda Esperança, preferring to put the little extra he had into necessities for the house and investing in recreational pleasures as we'd lost so much in Angola and lived a secluded farm life on Kambingana. The second-hand paraffin fridge gave endless trouble so he replaced it with an electric one, and bought a Whirlpool washing machine for me as the twin-tub had packed in (the Whirlpool would last until 2013!). Ian hadn't taken all his leave since starting work on the Ranch, opting instead to work and get the extra pay, but the company now brought in a ruling that all leave due had to be taken, though they were quite agreeable to us having 5 days off at a time. We could get to the coast in a day, or to any of the resort dams, so to begin with, Ian bought us a large canoe which we named *Samaki* (fish in Swahili) for Rand 400 and later, a second-hand Hobi Catamaran we named *Falusi* (also known as Feruzi, a type of fish). Great fun was had with family and friends picnicking, canoeing and learning to sail on the Kambingana dams. I remember a weekend when there were 17 of us! We took boating and fishing trips to Von Bach Dam in the Okahandja District and Hardap Dam near Mariental, venturing as far as Walvis Bay and Mile 104 on the Skeleton Coast as well. To enable us to keep the fish we caught, Ian bought a small electric freezer that went on one of the vehicles to freeze the fish we caught, to take back to the farm.

Jeremiah, a reliable, very respectful, single middle-aged Tswana Ranch worker agreed to be our camp help, proving excellent. He was very pleased to be our holiday helper giving him a break from farm work. Ian and I, the rest of the family and friends along on outings with us, all liked Jeremiah very much. He was always given a beer with his supper, sat around the campfire with us, ate whatever we did and had his own tent and bedding. Ian taught Jeremiah how to fish which he thoroughly enjoyed, often the 3 of us or just the 2 of them, fishing together. He learnt to appreciate and carefully look after all the boating, fishing and camping equipment as Ian was particular about everything and was taught how to gut, scale and pack the catch of the day into the freezer, his own fish included. One of the reasons Ian chose Jeremiah as our camp man was that he had been a loner since starting work on the Ranch. He was quiet in character with a sense of humour, though never swam or joined us boating as he was afraid of the water.

Louis had told us about the enormous Hardap Dam on a Nature Reserve, with cottages and a magnificent circular restaurant built to over-hang the solid-rock cliffs, giving spectacular views of the dam and surrounding hills. We soon learnt to catch the best eating fish which Ian named 'Royal Kurper' using miserably thin, mostly torn apart earthworms costing Rand 1.00 per Coca-Cola tin, so Ian decided he'd breed earthworms. We took a tin-full home and let the earthworms loose in our good garden soil then bought a booklet on earthworm breeding – the procedure seemed simple. Gather a large amount of fresh horse or cattle manure (horse manure was the best), wash till absolutely free of urine then dry out. Cut a large 44 gallon drum in half lengthways. Fill the 2 halves of the drum with clean manure and a quantity of bran mixed together with soil and sand. Keep the mixture slightly damp and spread old newspapers lightly on top. The drums, which we called our 'Worm Hotels', rested on wooden supports, the legs of which were stood in tins of old engine oil and stopped any ants climbing up and eating the worms. It didn't take long for the few re-captured earthworms from the garden to breed, providing excellent freshwater fishing bait.

On one of the Von Bach Dam camp outings, Ian needed a blanket late in the night. Unknown to him, it had caught onto one of his fishing lures which had 2 sets of medium-size triple hooks. When he climbed into bed and heaved the blanket over him the fishing lure stuck firmly into his calf muscle. A good friend camping overnight with us, Peter Overdyck, using only a torch for light and a pair of pliers, cut free the hooks and extracted the shanks. Ian insisted he was all right. At dawn, we could see the wound and I sponged it often with a solution of Epsom Salts to halt infection, which worked. Luckily, he didn't need a doctor. I was amazed at Ian making no sound while having the fishing lure removed. Then again, perhaps I shouldn't have been, as he used to pull his own teeth, going into the bathroom with a pair of pliers and returning with the tooth in a mug. Although his eyes watered, he'd offer no explanation and I never asked any questions. There was a time when he had an abscess on his thumb and lanced it himself.

To add to the farm hens, we now invested in a pair of peafowl, 6 pairs of exotic bantams, 3 Araucana chickens and a pair of fantail pigeons.

Male peafowl are called peacocks; females are peahens. The male has a crested head, bright alert eyes, a sharp curved yellow beak, royal blue feathers on the body and a very splendid fan-tail with royal blue, emerald green and golden-green 'eye-like' large spots on it about which there is much superstition. When in full plumage and strutting to impress the peahen or simply just 'parading' to pass the time, peacocks are exotic and magnificent in their beauty. Peafowl are vociferous and call to each other throughout the day as they wander around looking for grasshoppers and the like. They are excellent 'watch dogs' too, noticing everything around them. Should anything unusual occur, they fly to the highest place of safety making a screeching, unmistakable distress call, soon joined by the others. As they are not strong fliers, they only make short sorties.

The peahen, in beauty and character, is in direct contrast to the peacock. She is a dull grey with a few speckles on the wings, is timid and quiet, and a very bad mother. The eggs are large (like a turkey egg), whitish in colour with brown speckles. When the chicks hatch, the peahen will unintentionally 'walk them to death' with her constant meandering about, so as soon as possible mother and babies must be caught and penned until the chicks are strong enough to follow her – usually only the strongest offspring survive. Both Ian and I loved the peafowl. The highest male in the 'pecking order' was so tame and would come onto the front lawn and verandah to show off, quite unfazed at our presence within touching distance, the glorious fan of his outspread tail almost 5 feet high. They roamed freely and laid eggs in hidden places. In time, there were 17 adult peafowl. They were intelligent enough to know to roost on the house roof-ridging, safely out of reach of predators.

One Easter for the grandchildren's holidays, I dyed the white exotic Silkie bantam chickens pink, blue, green and yellow. It was quite simple to do. Just mix each dye with boiling water in a bucket; when cool, dip in each Silkie. These are small, black-skinned chickens, slightly bigger than a true bantam, with white very fluffy feathers down to their feet. It was rather cute to have these different colour fowls walking around the garden and the dye colours lasted a few weeks. The grandkids were enthralled with this novelty!

"Oh, Granny, your chickens are so pretty!" they exclaimed with delight.

From a breeder in Germany, we bought an Araucana cock and 2 hens. These chickens originate in Chile from the Araucana Indians. They have no tail, come in various dull colours and are quite tall. The hens lay pale green to pale blue eggs. Our 3 chickens arrived in South Africa where they were quarantined for 6 weeks at Irene Veterinary Station before being sent on to us in South West Africa. We named the cock, 'Beady Eyes', because he became quite vicious and would attack anyone coming too near to his little harem of hens. Again, the grandchildren were always wide-eyed at the beauty of the Araucana eggs and couldn't eat enough blue or green boiled eggs for breakfast or supper! Combined with the dyed Silkie bantams, Easter now held a new dimension of fun for the grandkids. They'd first draw or paint on the coloured eggs before cracking the tops open with a teaspoon, then peel away the bit of shell to dunk their 'toast fingers' into the soft-boiled egg yolks.

Ian also bought me 2 pairs of pure white fantail pigeons from a breeder in Mossel Bay. They gave me much pleasure as pets, their big house divided in half, high off the ground on the front lawn. They didn't fly and were so docile and tame we could handle and stroke them. Their main pastime was to walk around their cote and gently coo to each other, a very comforting sound. Soon we had another pair, after which we took away any eggs so the females didn't go broody again.

Simon and Constantia's son, Benjamin, began to come to the house at her request at the age of 10 or 11, initially as a playmate for the grandchildren whenever they came to stay. He was just one of the kids, 'horsing around' on the lawn, playing ball, up to this and that, collecting the hen's eggs with the others, a happy task all the kids loved to do. Benjamin had lunch, tea, biscuits, sweets and cool drinks with the other youngsters.

Between visits from the children, I kept Benjamin on for collecting the eggs and taught him his numbers and alphabet in English sitting at a table on the back verandah, using school books I'd bought in Windhoek. He spoke fluent Herero and Afrikaans and was a bright youngster, but could read, write and draw only upside down. Whether he drew numbers or letters or horses and other animals, they were all upside down. This intrigued me since he was the 3rd African I'd personally met with this peculiarity – Asha in Kenya at Westlands reading magazines upside down; the gentleman at Namanga border post in Tanzania who read with serious concentration the entire one-page letter upside down from the Moshi Hotel confirming the accommodation booking for Julia and me for our climb of Kilimanjaro; and now Benjamin in South West Africa. My research into the matter would define it as a rare genetic fault known as 'spatial orientation phenomenon' whereby one's brain cannot correctly process images of what it sees yet this does not necessarily impact the quality of the person's eyesight. They can have perfect vision, but see things the wrong way up, for example reading a book holding it upside down (the eyes see the images, but the brain changes them), and not much is known as to why this happens.

Ian had bought us a big colour television for the lounge and I allowed Benjamin to watch programmes in the evenings from the back verandah looking through the big dining room window. It didn't take long before a bunch of the farm staff arrived as soon as the TV went on until our supper time around 8, when I'd tell them it was 'home time'. Their absolutely favourite programme was 'The Incredible Hulk' which sent their imaginations wild, and they loved cowboy movies and boxing.

In a scruffy backyard in Klein Windhoek, Ian had seen an old grey, decrepit-looking Land Rover Forward Control 101. After locating the owner, a blind piano player who no longer needed the vehicle, Ian bought it for Rand 250 and we towed it precariously to Kambingana, into the now empty huge workshop. It had belonged to the South African Army and had originally been used as a mobile operating theatre during the earlier years of the border war with Angola (which commenced in 1966 and would end in 1989). Ian wanted to turn it into a camper with all facilities for our fishing trips. When he had enough money saved, he contacted a friend in the UK who sent a manual to us. Ian then ordered the clutch spares from England. Whenever he had a few hours off, Ian began dismantling the interior and working on this new project.

Winter 1981 set in, once more with bitterly cold, low Kambingana night temperatures. The water in the concrete pond froze solid, but had thawed by 11 o'clock in the morning, the sun welcome and delightfully warm.

One very chilly, frosty morning, old Munde came to light the donkey-fire, dipped his hat in his usual respectful and unhurried greeting, then came rushing back to the kitchen door.

"*Kom kyk, kom nou*!" ("Come look, come now!"), he exclaimed excitedly, hat in one hand, waving and pointing outside, urging me to hurry up and accompany him. I wondered what on earth could have caused the old fellow to move this fast on his old legs on such a cold morning.

What a surprise I got and how ecstatic I was! There was Tootsie-Wootsie with her own 2 guinea-pig size babies! I could hardly believe my eyes. I'd thought she was gone forever. The babies were on their haunches with their tummies flat-up against the warm inside walls of the donkey, while Tootsie-Wootsie lay close by inside in a hunched up position. During the night, the logs in the donkey would eventually become embers then only ash remained, but the walls stayed warm all night. By 8 in the morning the logs were lit again.

It was truly a miracle. For a year after Stuart died I'd find myself often in tears. Piggy was gone too, and Pepu, then Tootsie-Wootsie went off into the bush. Now I felt elated, a sudden glow of happy warmth washed over me. I could have jumped up and down with joy and shouted for the world to hear, "Tootsie-Wootsie's back!" though of course I did neither, not wanting to scare her or the porcupine babies. From our home to Kurt and Carola's house via the main dirt road was about 30 kilometres. If one cut across through the bush it was perhaps 15 – Kambingana and Apex (their farm) shared one boundary line. It was an amazing feat, and incredibly intelligent too that Tootsie-Wootsie accomplished, finding her way back home to us, babies in tow now, after escaping from the wire enclosure at Apex a year-and-a-half earlier.

Toostie-Wootsie and her 2 babies devoured everything in our vegetable garden – all the winter carrots, beetroot, spinach, radishes, turnips, cauliflower and lettuce. They meandered around the premises coming and going through the cattle fences, digging holes under the garden wire netting, disappearing into the bush then returning when it pleased them. Although I never handled Tootsie-Wootsie again – now she wouldn't allow petting or touching and also wouldn't let anyone touch her babies – they were all quite unafraid and the dogs left them alone. Every night they slept at the donkey for warmth, a truly dear picture imprinted in my mind.

I could see in his eyes how very pleased old Munde was at the time to show me Tootsie-Wootsie had returned. I think he knew how much this would pep me up after all the sadness, but he simply couldn't understand how I allowed this little family of porcupines to eat from the vegetable garden every day and on several occasions showed his annoyance at working to grow and tend the veggies only to have them demolished by the Tootsie-Wootsie trio. I used to give old Munde vegetables, but he indicated the staff far preferred meat, gravy and mealie meal (which was part of their weekly food rations). Ian loved

Tootsie-Wootsie and didn't mind in the least that between the 3 of them they devoured the veggie patch.

Ian sold the 7-ton Ford lorry we'd brought out of Angola and bought me a pale blue Ford Cortina 'out the box' for Rand 4,580 which added definite excitement, comfort and speed to my Windhoek shopping trips and reduced the unpleasant feel of the ridges that would accumulate in the dirt roads on the Omitara stretch when the grader hadn't been around. Lindsay, on a visit, was itching to drive my new car, but on the trip home I had to tell her to pull over after some time on the dirt road as she was crawling along giving us a really bumpy ride!

As I told her, "The slower you drive on ungraded dirt roads the worse it feels. You've got to 'put foot' a bit." Out the corner of my eye, I caught her applying imaginary brakes! She told me everyone could see me on my way home, they just looked for the clouds of dust! I have to admit getting a lot of pleasure out of my nifty Cortina.

Having taken some days leave again, on our return home we found Tootsie-Wootsie and her family had disappeared. Questioning old Munde to ascertain if he knew what had happened he answered everything I asked, though without any definite explanation, and said that African people considered porcupine to be a delicacy. I was horrified when Angelina later came down to the house holding an enamel plate and offered me a taste of a piece of meat she said had been dry cooked (meaning over the coals) saying it was porcupine.

Discussing the matter with Ian, he said it best to leave it alone as without definite proof of who had killed Tootsie-Wootsie and her babies I couldn't accuse anyone. Neither could I prove that the porcupine meat Angelina offered me was definitely from our Tootsie-Wootsie trio – the porcupines had disappeared without any trace. Apart from their other rations, the staff each received 10 kilograms of meat a week, enough to feed a family, as well as thin dried 'biltong' meat strips (also known as 'jerky'). Ian never took leave without first making sure everyone had their food stocks so it wasn't for lack of meat that our Tootsie-Wootsie porcupine family, we presumed, had been killed and eaten. Nevertheless, inside me, I teetered between seething anger one moment and heartbroken emptiness the next, the only thing left to me of Tootsie-Wootsie and her babies being some quills that had naturally fallen on the ground in their travels around the garden, perfect for testing baked cakes when one needed to prick the centre to see if the mixture was cooked enough. Perhaps the reasoning behind whoever was the culprit of our 3 porcupines having met such a ghastly, sad ending – if there was indeed a culprit – was that seeing as I could no longer touch or pet them and they came and went as they pleased in and out of the bush into the garden, they were as such considered 'wild' and therefore anyone's 'game for the pot'.

Keith and family came for a weekend and he decided to ride on horseback across one of the expansive Kambingana vleis (a large low-lying area of veld that turned into a wetland in summer rains then became dry, hard barren ground in winter) looking at game. In the centre of the vlei he found an old well, approximately 15 feet deep, with a low circular wall around it. Looking inside he saw at the bottom several skeletons of hartebeest distinguished by the horns, their bones clean and bleached white, and what appeared to be the skeleton of a Brahman bull, only hard leathery skin covering the intact carcass, some small dried branches and twigs and a huge cobra swaying back and forth. When he arrived back home Keith said, "Mum and Dad, I've now seen what hell looks like," and told us of his find.

We jumped into the Ford, Ian taking his rifle and a fishing rod. A wild Brahman bull had gone missing some time back, and it would help with stock figures if he could now account to the company for the animal. I've not forgotten the scene inside the well. It was bizarre, weird and scary all at the same time and reminds me of the 'Hades' ('Hell') paintings by old masters.

All other cattle figures tallied, and Ian felt sure on looking into the well that the mystery of the missing bull had now been solved. Despite informing the company that we'd be in Windhoek on a certain day, they'd nevertheless delivered cattle to the farm in Ian's absence. Simon advised Ian on our return that during unloading of the animals one of the new prize Brahman bulls had run off and couldn't be found (Brahman cattle are notoriously wild and can jump ordinary fences quite easily when on the run). Ian contacted the office and they took responsibility. Then he requested neighbours to be on the lookout for the missing animal. He sent out the stockmen but they'd reported back with no sighting of the bull. All further efforts over the next few months trying to locate the animal proved futile. This missing bull had really niggled Ian. He was relieved the matter was now resolved.

We studied the cobra which appeared pale in colour – its skin dull without natural shine – swaying feebly back and forth, its head raised only a little, seemingly in a bewildered daze with no evidence of alertness or fluid body movement natural to a healthy snake. No doubt it was suffering a slow death from dehydration and starvation. Who knows how long it had been at the bottom of the well with no way out? Ian put the snake out of its misery with one shot then fished it out of the well with the rod. It was just over 6 foot long. The following day, Ian went out with one of the men and covered the well opening with wire mesh.

Mr du Preez, our favourite Company Director, visited us each time he came from Cape Town, and on this occasion complimented me on my lunch table saying it was the best. Praise indeed as nearly everyone on the 19 company farms provided meals for the directors' visits. He really appreciated Ian's expertise as a beef cattle manager and adviser, and began to comprehend what Ian was doing nurturing the game. From this visit onwards, a new and special relationship was born and Ian made all the decisions regarding the 3 Kambingana properties. Shortly afterwards, the company sent us a new Toyota Land Cruiser for the Ranch. Not one of my favourite vehicles, it was cumbersome in handling and manoeuvrability and felt like driving an army tank. With the exhaust pipe running under the passenger floor, I had to sit with my feet up against the dashboard on long trips to Windhoek with Ian just to get some relief from the heat emanating from the floor!

In February 1982, Marge telephoned with devastating news in the Aggett side of our family. Aubrey and Joy Aggett's youngest child, their 2nd son, Neil Hudson aged 28, was found hanging in his prison cell in Johannesburg, South Africa on 5th February 1982. Aubrey and Joy, living in Somerset West in the Cape, had been so good to us when our Stuart died in 1979. We'd stayed some days with them before returning home to Kambingana after Stuart's funeral in Mossel Bay.

Aubrey and Joy's 3 children, Mike, Jill and Neil were born and bred on a farm in Nanyuki, Kenya, where daily they beheld the magnificence of Mount Kenya. In 1964, this branch of our Aggett family moved to South Africa where both Michael and Neil studied medicine at the University of Cape Town. Neil graduated in 1976, completing his internship in the Transkei at Umtata General Hospital in 1977, followed by practicing at Tembisa Hospital in Olifantsfontein, Johannesburg, also learning the Zulu language. Whilst working at the renowned Baragwanath Hospital in Soweto (the biggest hospital in the southern hemisphere and 3rd largest in the world), Neil became increasingly concerned with the hardships endured by black South Africans under the Apartheid regime. Abandoning his promising medical career, he became involved in the black trade union movement, especially the Transvaal branch of the Food and Canning Workers' Union, supporting himself by working night shifts in the casualty ward at Baragwanath Hospital.

On 27th November 1981, Neil was detained by the Security Police of the South African apartheid regime for more than 70 days without trial, being interrogated continuously for more than 60 hours by security policeman Lieutenant Steven Whitehead and Major Arthur Cronwright. A fellow detainee, Frank Chikane, recalled how badly injured Neil was. Neil made an affidavit 14 hours before his, what is termed 'induced suicide', saying he had been assaulted, blindfolded and given electric shocks – this torture was responsible for his mental and physical condition which led him to take his own life by hanging in his cell at John Vorster Square. Tragically, the date of Neil's death coincided with his parents' 38th wedding anniversary. Dr Neil Hudson Aggett, born 6th October 1953, anti-apartheid activist and unpaid trade union organiser, was the 1st white person since 1963 to die under such circumstances and the 51st person to die in detention. His biography, written by Beverley Naidoo, is titled 'Death of an Idealist: In Search of Neil Aggett'. Kingswood College, Grahamstown, in the Eastern Cape where Neil completed his schooling with a first class matric pass, commemorates his life and selfless efforts to improve the lives of others with a stained glass window in their Kingswood College Chapel and an annual memorial service in his name. Aubrey and Joy never did learn the complete truth of the events surrounding Neil's death, compounding the immeasurable heartache and grief their family suffered.

Lindsay divorced Brendan's father in 1979, later remarried and gave birth to her 2nd child, a daughter named Kathryn Alexandra, in Walvis Bay, in March 1982. Ian kindly gave her husband our VW Kombi that had come out of Angola with us on the back of our Ford lorry.

Beryl and Koos moved from Okahandja to Johannesburg and then divorced (though Koos remained a wonderful son to us and still is in 2016 to me). Beryl was having a difficult time initially as a single mother, and their son, Stuart, came to spend some months with us. It took a little while for Ian to adjust to having a small child in the house again, particularly a busy and inquisitive 3 year old, very intelligent with lots of questions, into everything, and with endless energy. I noticed Stuart had a peculiar, offensive smell about him and was always clearing his throat. Beryl had taken him to a specialist, so he came with all the necessary antibiotics. I became more alarmed as the medication definitely wasn't helping. Finally, I 'phoned a lady paediatrician in Windhoek. The only appointment available was 7.30 in the morning, which meant we had to leave the farm very early at 5.30, getting up an hour earlier. The doctor did all the examinations, leaving to last to look up Stuart's nose. There was something very far up! With forceps, she gently withdrew a large foam rubber swab, which was foul in looks and smell. Stuart was asked, "Who put this in your nose?" He told the doctor a monster had done so. I asked that the swab be put in a phial, and when Stuart went back to Beryl I sent it with him for his mother to take to her specialist who'd been treating the child for a month!

Politically, things were 'stirring', and the Company directors decided to sell some of their properties. Kambingana was sold lock, stock and barrel to Mr Sky Bonadei and we agreed to remain in charge. The cattle muster and stock count took place again. The auditors came by air from Johannesburg. This time they were all dressed as cowboys! None of them could agree on the numbers of cattle passing through the races. After a lot of frustration, shouting and clouds of dust in the unbearable heat, one man turned to Ian and said, "How do you do it?"

Ian replied, "You count the legs and divide the number by four." After that, the auditors let well alone and never again came out to the Ranch to count stock. Ian's figures from that time on were accepted as correct. From the difficult Afrikaans pronunciation of the company name, 'Nuwe Westelike Ontwikkelingsmaatskappy', we now became part of a German tongue-twister, 'Farmverwaltung Gochaganas'.

Sky Bonadei, a carpenter by trade, had returned to South West Africa after WWII with practically nothing but a hammer and saw. He started with Government tender work in the lonely northern areas of Ovamboland, soon making a great deal of money and a very respectable name. Mr Bonadei was nicknamed 'Sky' because he used to fly to and from Ovamboland so often in his aeroplane. His pilot was his workshop manager. Quite the opposite to our previous employers, Sky Bonadei refused to give or sign any employment contract with us, saying he saw no point as 'contracts can be broken at any time'. This new work relationship began based on trust and continued as such all the years and became an excellent employment 'package' with mutual respect, utmost faith, zero financial problems and valued friendship.

'Gochaganas' was Mr Bonadei's prize dairy farm, just south of Windhoek, where he owned and operated another very successful company, Bonmilk, manufacturing yoghurt, fruit juices, cream, maas (sour milk), buttermilk, milk and long-life milk for sale and delivery to all parts of South West Africa.

It soon became obvious that Sky Bonadei had a totally different outlook regarding his employees. Ian made a number of suggestions for home improvements to the stockmen's living quarters and our new boss was happy to comply. Builders were sent to the farm. All staff living quarters had an extra room and small front stoep (verandah) added, a central cooking place was erected, separate male and female ablution blocks with tiled walls, showers, basins and toilets were soon in use. The stockmen's wives took it in turns monthly to be full-time cleaners of the ablution block, for which the lady in charge alone held the keys and was paid a salary. Children were not allowed in the ablution facilities on their own – in this way, no damage was done to the interior.

Mr Bonadei decided that Simon and his wife, Constantia, as well as old Munde and his common-law wife, Angelina, and their families would now live in the farm machinery manager's home which had been standing empty. Usually, about 10 people lived in the house. The sitting and dining room were used as extra bedrooms, and everyone seemed happy together. A wood fire was kept burning in the backyard for

Simon's family, and one in the front for Angelina's, where their individual cooking was done. The women were used to preparing their food this way, sitting with all their paraphernalia close to hand, grilling their meat over the coals and cooking their mealie meal in large, heavy 3-legged cast-iron black pots with lids. A big kettle was placed by each fire ensuring there was always boiling water for making tea or coffee. This way of living meant there was plenty of room for everyone, and the children could run around and play. What had been the original kitchen was used as a storeroom. Dry thorn tree was collected by tractor and trailer once a month for all the labour force and for our 'donkey' so no-one ever went short of firewood.

It wasn't long before the toilet in their house became blocked and overflowed. Ian was instructed by Windhoek office to lock the toilet door and keep the key. Next, the children smashed 27 of the 29 window panes, leaving only the big lounge and main bedroom window glass intact, and the bathroom mirrors soon followed. Then the fly-proof door that none of them bothered to close with the latch, fell off its hinges from hanging open all the time. All the fruit trees in the garden were cut down and every last piece of lawn grass removed leaving only dusty earth surrounding the house, which was a duplicate of our home, but had better drainage systems than we had, and included metal cupboard units in the kitchen, a sink and wood-burning stove. Rains flooded into the house through the broken windows, the violent windy season blew, and the freezing cold winter weather pervaded every room. Large pieces of corrugated iron sheeting were now propped up against the glassless windows. The carpeting in the lounge and the Marley tiling throughout the rest of the house had been ripped up, the bare concrete floors now adding further to the winter chill. Lindsay remembers an open fire in the middle of the lounge floor, probably for winter warmth and cooking.

Mr Bonadei's well-intentioned, generous idea had proven utterly disastrous. It was sad to see a good home destroyed in such a short time. When I entered the house to examine Constantia who was on the verge of giving birth to yet another baby, the air was decidedly stale. Still fully dressed in her long, full-skirted Herero frock of yards of material, she was lying on a mattress on the floor sweating profusely, attended by women who'd tied a heavy cotton cloth around her stomach. With every labour contraction they all pulled to tighten 'the girdle'. I decided Constantia must go immediately to Gobabis Hospital instead, and took her, where she'd be delivered safely and in hygienic surroundings. She now had 6 children. After this, the farm women started believing in my medical judgments and I began a regular morning sick-parade, the company granting me funds to stock a full medicine cabinet.

For the first time in years, we really enjoyed being employed. Mr Bonadei gave permission for me to run the generator whenever and for as long as I wished. A very big, new 'Minus 40' freezer was bought for the meat rations.

Ian advised Mr Bonadei to remove the sheep. They were being stolen by people passing through the farm, and secondly, he didn't like sheep on a cattle ranch for various reasons, one being worm infestations. Mr Bonadei decided to send 2 of his Friesian cows from his Gochaganas farm dairy herd to Kambingana as insufficient milk was produced for us by the stock cattle that were being used, and they were also too wild to hand-milk properly everyday. What should have been an easy, organised short milking routine was turned into a daily circus of cow-catching and kicking and tying up one back leg to a fence pole – crazy and unacceptable – the milk always arriving with some form of dirt in it. The 2 new cows produced quantity and quality hygienic, fresh milk twice a day so everyone had plenty. We were now also generously instructed to slaughter a 2 year old heifer once a year for ourselves, as well as 2 kudu or gemsbok. Ian, an excellent shot, would go out with the men and choose the heifer. Lindsay remembers one such occasion, going with her father. With one rifle shot the heifer, still grazing, dropped dead instantly. Loaded onto the bakkie, it was hung high overnight outside the big workshop, skinned the following day then made into special cuts using Ian's new electric Meatmaster with circular saws.

Mattheus became an expert butcher under Ian's tutorship, and when the staff meat was slaughtered they copied the way we packed the meat into plastic bags and stored it in the big chest freezer, Simon in charge, noting everything in an exercise book to avoid quarrels. Once a year, Mr Bonadei gave the labour a big, fat bullock which they were allowed to choose, shot by Ian. Between our poultry, fishing trips and our own meat ration, we were never short of top quality beef, venison, freshly frozen fish and farm chickens. The staff had so much meat they regularly made biltong.

Mary, in Karibib, also benefited from Mr Bonadei's takeover. She became the area representative for Bonmilk products and her life improved even further. It was good and fitting to see Mary happy, enjoying life and earning an income while still being able to spend time on her home and family. Keith bought a new Mazda car.

Various much-loved members of the family and friends from different countries visited us. One was my excellent long-time-ago Kenya English school teacher, Arthur Brindley. He came with our cousin, Sheila, and they spent a week with us. It was a special time and also a relief for me as I could eventually, after so many years of keeping this pent up for fear of no-one believing me, speak openly to Arthur about the hateful Headmaster at Nakuru Junior School who'd regularly and distastefully 'touched' girls, including me, at boarding school and got away with it for some time. I was about 12 in my last year of junior school, not yet wearing a bra though my breasts were forming. He'd forced many girls to pull down the top of their bathing costumes to their waists so he could grope their breasts, very cleverly sending a girl off alone to do something else so he could be alone with her, his chosen victim, then threatening each of us with expulsion from school if we so much as breathed a word about it. The Headmaster always chose only the girls with budding breasts. Twice he did this to me when I was wearing my new red bathing swimsuit. When he'd finished, he'd pull up my costume and put the straps straight then he'd dismiss me with the command, "Off you go now, off you go!"

I was so afraid and repulsed by this vile Headmaster with his lecherous, sordid secret but couldn't bring myself to tell my mother in case she thought I was making up stories. I did tell one of my school girlfriends though and she immediately accused me of 'telling big fat fibs'. The Headmaster also brought in a new rule that we had to wake at 6.30 in the morning, rush to the bathroom with our towels and stand in a line taking our turn to have a cold bath in the cubicles (previously we'd taken only hot baths in the evenings). Then he'd conveniently appear with the excuse that he was checking up on things which was only so he could look at us wet, cold, squealing and jumping about. One day, the Headmaster did his sordid breast groping on one of the day-girls who told her mother as soon as she arrived home. By that evening, the Headmaster had been removed from the Education Department. Arthur said he knew about the Headmaster and the French teacher having an affair (they later married), but said he'd not known the Headmaster was doing this to the girls, and was utterly shocked. Years later, when I was married to Ian and we were living in Malindi, we went for dinner at the Sindbad Hotel. I saw the ex-Headmaster sitting at the bar when we walked in and immediately told Ian we must leave. I explained the situation to him on the way home. He understood perfectly that I couldn't bring myself to be in the company of that disgusting man.

I also asked Arthur why we seemed to have no dyslexic children in those days. His answer was, yes there were, but teachers overcame this by pupils having to learn absolutely by heart, 10 words at a time, this being increased to 20 words as they grew older. Also, no class had more than 20 children.

One morning, Angelina rushed over to the house to tell me a Bushman baby girl had been born without an anus. She asked that I please get the child to the hospital so the doctors could, "Cut a hole where the baby needed one."

I sent for the infant. Her mother was a 14 year old alcoholic and smoker. On examining the baby and seeing this dire physical abnormality, I 'phoned and spoke to a doctor at Gobabis Hospital whose advice was to leave the situation alone, the child would die. Unable to bring myself to follow the doctor's advice and with the family so distressed insisting the doctors could, "Just make a hole for the baby," I took the parents and child to Gobabis for an examination. She had to be left there, and was later taken by ambulance to Windhoek State Hospital then flown, with a nursing sister in attendance, to Tygerberg in Cape Town where she underwent successful surgery. The specialists performed a complicated procedure whereby her excrement was now expelled through her vagina. On the baby's return, I had to supervise her feeding and the formula was provided. At 6 months old, she was again flown to Cape Town for follow-up treatment which we were told would require further surgery when she was 18 months old. She progressed well, was a fat, happy child, saying lots of words and had been walking for several months.

Erwin Bechtle, an elderly sport fishing client and dear friend of ours from Malindi days arrived for his holiday, bringing his younger brother, Geges who was a doctor, with him. Erwin always spent his annual month-long vacations with us on Kambingana, usually during the winter hunting season, and joined us on fishing trips. Sometimes he brought his wife, Madie, and on other occasions, family or friends. Erwin owned a pasta factory back home in Germany. Every month we received a parcel with an assortment of delicious noodles. Geges (his real name was 'Eugene') had been a Russian prisoner-of-war during WWII, and had never been to Africa. Erwin was giving him this trip as a present. Geges was also a collector of tortoise shells. One evening during dinner, I told Geges about the Bushman baby girl. Naturally, he was very interested in her medical condition. The following day I sent for the mother and child and Geges examined her on the dining room table. He was impressed at the surgical procedure and recovery of the baby. I said I'd keep Erwin updated on the child's progress once they returned to Germany so he could pass on the information to Geges as the little girl's next Tygerberg Hospital treatment at 18 months old was almost due.

The staff always thoroughly enjoyed Erwin coming to stay as he tipped them generously, particularly old Munde who did extra special shoe and boot polishing while sitting at the 'donkey'. Erwin would compliment the elderly Ovambo, saying his footwear had never been so well cleaned nor shone so much! Old Munde, proud and delighted, would dip his hat in thankful respect, pipe in the corner of his mouth.

Into the 'African holiday mood' swing of things, Erwin was keen to show Geges the wildlife of South West Africa. Ian and one of the farm workmen, Elias, carefully made a large hide in the veld, well camouflaged in the thick bush amongst the thorn trees and bushes, so the 2 elderly Germans could comfortably and quietly survey any movement of game through a 'peephole' without disturbing the animals. Ian had deliberately made the hide not far from a large natural salt-lick which the Ranch bought from Omitara Co-op (mined in huge chunks ranging in colour from dull to dirty white/grey, and weighing heavily). The salt-lick was a necessity for the cattle out in the veld, and the game, particularly the kudu, all loved to lick the rock salt, their tongues moving this way and that, over and over again, forming indentations like facets as big as a man's hand on the hard surface. Due to the weight and size, nothing else could be loaded onto the farm vehicle when Ian collected these salt-licks from Omitara, which could last a year or longer, before replacement.

The morning of the 'big game-watch' arrived. At 11 o'clock, Ian dropped the 2 old Germans off at the hide, who were warmly dressed and loaded up with camp chairs, blankets, bush hats, dark glasses, cameras and binoculars, notebooks and pencils, thermoses of coffee and plenty of sandwiches for lunch. Ian left Elias with Erwin and Geges, instructing him to take good care of the elderly gentlemen, both in their 70s, and do what they wanted, saying he'd be back to fetch the 3 of them at 5 in the afternoon. They had ample food and drink for them all. More than likely, they'd have spotted a fair amount of game by late afternoon when the winter chill came up. When Ian returned to fetch them, he found Erwin in a temper and Geges silent and crestfallen. Apparently, what had happened was that as the winter sun lowered in the sky, the rays fell on the chunk of rock salt. Geges, spying through the peep hole, thought he'd seen a gigantic tortoise. Before Erwin or Elias could stop him, he ran to the salt-lick and started trying to lift it. Elias, having been instructed to help the 2 elderly men, now followed suit to help Geges. The 2 of them tried every which way to move the salt-lick, leaving Erwin infuriated in the hide, shouting for Geges to come back, knowing their chances were zero of seeing any kudu at all with their cover 'blown'. Back home, Ian asked Elias what he thought he was doing trying to move the salt-lick as there were many rock salt chunks specifically placed in the veld for the cattle.

Elias replied that he'd thought, "That the old man had thought he'd seen a diamond and wanted to take it."

Indeed, with the correct angle of the sun's rays, the salt-licks' deep facets did glisten silvery-blue like a huge diamond. Erwin continued to harangue his brother throughout the evening. He couldn't accept that Geges could have mistaken the salt-lick for a tortoise!

"I cannot support this mistake!" Erwin kept repeating highly annoyed. However, there had been one wildlife encounter for Erwin that day. On going for a pee, a large cobra had slithered out from under the bush, but even relating this incident did little to ease Erwin's extreme irritation or offer Geges any form of reprieve. Erwin remained fixated on Geges' ridiculous notion of having seen a gigantic African tortoise. Ian and I quietly thought the story amusing and could see how Geges, never having been to Africa – we'd heard many weird or funny stories over the years – could've made the unintentional 'tortoise mix-up'. Personally, as Erwin's berating continued, I thought Geges would have been glad to get back to Germany! Perhaps Erwin was embarrassed by his brother's lack of knowledge of what he considered to be such a simple matter, considering that he was a doctor. Or maybe Erwin felt bad about Ian and Elias having taken the time to build the hide specifically for them only to have Geges ruin the day and the opportunity of seeing wild game. All turned out well the following day though on a 2nd hide outing when Erwin and Geges saw an exceptional number of kudu, hartebeest and warthogs.

The medical condition of the Bushman baby girl did not have a positive outcome despite her remarkable treatment and amazing recovery so I was unable to report a happy ending to Erwin in Germany. Shortly before her 18 month check-up was due in Cape Town, Simon reported to Ian that after a noisy weekend at the staff housing, the baby's father had rowed with his neighbour. In a huff, he'd suddenly packed the family and their belongings onto a donkey-cart and disappeared. This was a real disaster as it was vital that the child get back to Tygerberg Hospital. As her treatment was being paid for by the State, we had to report it to the Steinhausen Police. They managed to locate the family some 60 kilometres beyond Omitara, but overnight they once again upped and moved on, during which time the little girl sadly died. When the Police eventually located the family again, they questioned the father. His reply was that the baby had been healthy and as such hadn't needed to go back to hospital.

Around about the same time, on neighbouring farms, 2 other teenage alcoholic, heavy smoker mothers also gave birth to babies with abnormalities. One without an oesophagus, yet another with no anus –

both died. Old Munde's wife, Angelina, had a tiny, sickly baby girl who lived only a few weeks, her tongue unmovable, being cloven to the bottom of her mouth and gums. Angelina screamed and cried for a week after the child's death, then suddenly just stopped. When we asked Simon why there was all the screaming, he said it was their Herero custom with bereavement. Angelina and old Munde would get inebriated every weekend. Constantia never drank alcohol.

Edda Bohn, a lovely young German girl from a neighbouring farm, drove over to visit me one day. We'd just had one of our huge thunder and rain storms and the dry Swart Nossob River was running strongly, the dams overflowing and the roads awash with enormous stretches of water. Edda noticed a tiny fish floundering in a shallow puddle on the road just a few kilometres from our house. She stopped her car, jumped out, took her khaki safari hat off, filled it with water and put in the inch-long fingerling. As soon as she arrived, we put the fish, which we thought might be a carp, into the huge circular reservoir near the house. This water tank was borehole fed from Boomlager and filled the water troughs for the horses and 2 Friesian milk cows. I forgot about the fingerling.

Out fishing at Kambingana dam one day, I caught a young catfish which I took home and put into the same big water tank hoping it would keep the cement bottom clean. Occasionally, I'd throw in a few cooked marble-sized maize meal balls just in case the natural food supply of insects dropping into the reservoir was insufficient. I noticed, strangely, that each time I climbed the ladder up to the edge of the tank, a bigger fish than the catfish was coming to meet me. Quite soon, I recognised it as a carp and knew it was the grown-up fingerling Edda had picked up and brought to me. I named her 'Jawsie'. Every time I walked to the reservoir, I started calling her name, "Jawsie, Jawsie," a while before I reached the water tank on my way through the side garden and bit of low bush grass. She was remarkable. No sooner had I stood at the rim of the reservoir, up Jawsie would come ready to take the maize meal balls gently from my hand. Eventually, she even allowed me to stroke her, only once, on the top of her back along her dorsal fin. Then she started waiting for me. When I'd climbed the steps, she'd be swimming around deliberately in great circles of excitement finally coming to the edge of the reservoir, her head emerging from the water right under my hand. I saw the catfish now and then, but it wasn't tame and being a bottom feeder liked to live in the depths of the water tank.

Jawsie grew big and fat so quickly I thought she must be a hen-fish. At one time, Ian estimated her weight to be 17 or 18 pounds – he knew all about fish and their weights. To test Jawsie, I also started deliberately not calling her name while I walked to the tank. I'd just climb up quietly and wait at the edge to see what happened, my hand over the water. How she knew I was there I'll never figure out, but in a few minutes ripples would appear on the water and there she was again, right under my hand at the side of the reservoir her mouth open. It truly was amazing. I never knew a fish could be this clever. Although the water was beautifully clean, there was no way one could see down into the black depths of the reservoir, but all of a sudden with a swish, there was Jawsie. It was riveting. We loved her, this incredible and unusual pet carp hen-fish of ours. The grandchildren would feed her religiously every day when they visited, absolutely fascinated by her gentleness, holding the maize meal balls or pieces of bread for her to take from their hands, her great body so agile and beautifully gleaming with gold, cream and light green colours.

You'd hear their young voices calling, "Jawsie, Jawsie," as they waited, peering into the water. Jawsie was also filmed by a friend, Jenny Storm (now living in Australia).

Ian had bought himself some expensive, imported woodworking machinery and kept all his tools and hobby equipment in the workshop, everything laid out exceptionally neatly. He knew at a moment's notice where to find any item. This mirrored Ian's life. He looked after everything he bought or owned, and instilled in his children, "If you're going to do something, then you may as well do it properly." I've never picked up an item of clothing off the floor left by my husband. His cupboards and office were absolutely orderly, his paperwork done and filed efficiently. Ian's hands were always busy and he detested laziness, his motto 'an idle man can start getting into trouble'.

In his spare time, Ian made chests of drawers, double bunks for the grandchildren, wooden stools, tea trolleys and various other items of quality woodwork. He had done a superb job of transforming the decrepit old Land Rover Forward Control 101 into a 'home away from home' luxury camper-van. Re-sprayed in a dark green, on the outside of the vehicle we had an enclosed private shower, pull-out double kitchen sinks with hot and cold water, a generator and winch. Inside was a TV, comfortable bunk beds and storage spaces, the drinking glasses each held securely in a separate wooden hole, a bar fridge, several pieces of furniture, radio and safe-cabled electric lighting for the campsite. A tent fitted onto the side of the camper was the verandah. There was nothing we lacked in luxury or convenience whenever we took a few days leave, and the small chest freezer on the bakkie was kept filled with the fish catch of the day. The vehicles formed the perimeter of our campsite along with the other tents, the stone fireplace in the middle being the hub of camp-life. A mug of steaming coffee with condensed milk and a rusk – a popular traditional South African fairly sweet, thick finger-long biscuit made from light dough, baked slowly then dried out to a crispness in the oven overnight – was perfect for dunking in coffee or tea on an early morning sitting around the warm fire. Many nights we were late to bed chatting after our braai (barbeque), delicious smells wafting on the air, enjoying the peace and quiet of the outdoors, the great sky of twinkling stars above.

Ian then bought a 20 foot 'Kwagga' sailing yacht built in Cape Town. We called her *Johari* (jewel in Swahili). We'd had a lot of fun with the canoe and sailing the Hobi-cat, but Johari was the most versatile of the boats and became the family favourite. Built of fibreglass she was relatively light, easy to launch or load onto the trailer, had a retractable keel, we could sail her (quite complicated rigging for the sails until we got the hang of it) or use the 8 horsepower outboard motor on the transom. There was space enough for about 5 people and the dogs comfortably on the single hull, and a small cabin for shelter, rest and storage of life-jackets, fishing gear and picnic goods.

Sailing Johari at Von Bach Dam one cold, misty and overcast day, while I was adjusting the jib I slipped on the wet cabin roof and fell overboard. It took me a seemingly long time to get to the surface as I was wearing a woollen tracksuit and takkies. Ian had to tack and turnabout, sail Johari toward me and then timeously drop the mainsail before getting to me so that he could lean over the gunwale to catch my outstretched arm while the boat was still in motion. Coming alongside me, I then had a very difficult time trying to get my leg up and over the high starboard gunwale as my wet woollen clothing was so heavy, weighing me down. With Ian using his knees to bolster himself against the side of the boat, after I'd been dragged through the water for a time, he managed to lean over the side and catch hold of one arm and one ankle and pull me out of the water over the gunwale and onto the deck. Jeremiah had watched from shore where he was fishing. I was soaked to the skin and very cold so Ian decided to call it a day. Jeremiah was waiting for us when Ian docked Johari on the shoreline lorry tyre and threw the rope to him to tie to the concrete block.

"Jeremiah, did you see how I tried to drown the old lady?" Ian said jokingly in Afrikaans.

"Aw, mister… Aw, mister," was Jeremiah's reply with a grin from ear to ear.

I made a beeline back to camp to get into dry clothing again! From that time on, Ian was extremely strict about anyone aboard any of our boats wearing life-jackets. As the grandchildren grew, we spent many contented holiday hours fishing and sailing, often going around Von Bach and Hardap dams, stopping off for picnics at pretty spots along the shoreline. Ian taught his grandsons boating safety and to take care of the fishing tackle.

Ian and I also took a separate overseas holiday each in 1982. Invited by our German friends, Erwin and Madie, Ian flew to Munich in August for a couple of weeks, the first and only time he ever left African soil, sporting his new-look 'walrus' moustache. Having previously always been clean shaven, this new fad required a fair amount of maintenance and attention with the necessary waxing and curling of the moustache ends. Our German neighbour's children screamed and thought Ian was the devil when they saw the moustache, and our grandchildren were a little wary too of this unfamiliar and somewhat scary-looking 'Gan-Gan' (their term of endearment for Ian). They were relieved when one day, after his overseas holiday, Ian got fed up with the laborious moustache ritual and ended it with a good lather of shaving soap and sharp strokes of his razor!

I flew to Australia for 6 weeks to visit family and friends in October. Lindsay spent about 10 days on the farm with Ian keeping him company, making sure he had his usual breakfast and a good supper after a long day's work before she returned home. I first went to Sydney and was treated to the wonders of that beautiful city by Tony Case (Vi and Bertie's son) and his wife, Sue. I took a bus tour around New South Wales before going to Queensland where I spent time with my cousins, Sid and Barbara Dyer, then Henry Hauschild and June from Ol'Kalou days, followed by Pixie Luggett and her family from my Nakuru school days. Finally, I stayed with Peter and Leila Overdyck who'd recently arrived in Australia. They all gave me exciting and wonderful tours. June Hauschild took me to the children's zoo where I played with and fondled kangaroos, koalas and their babies – a memorable experience.

Speaking to Ian on the 'phone one night after a month away, I was shocked by the sound of his voice – he said he wasn't well and asked me to cut short my holiday and return home. I'd noticed a change in his voice for some time before leaving, but adamant, Ian wasn't one for going to the doctor. Back home, I immediately made an appointment with an Ear, Nose and Throat Specialist in Windhoek. Years of excessive tobacco, stress and dust had taken their toll on Ian. Smoking since 14, starting his life's work over again 3 times, dealing with testy labour on the Ranch, working constantly in extremely dusty conditions mustering, inoculating, loading and unloading cattle, conducting game capture drives in swirls of dust, plus the thick powdery air Ian breathed in for so long in the cab of the Chev while being towed behind the lorry out of Angola, had all finally added up. He was diagnosed with a leukoplakia lesion (cancer) on the larynx which would have to be surgically removed. The specialist was extremely careful and absolutely firm – Ian was not to speak a single word for 6 weeks after the surgery to ensure success of the procedure.

With Ian out of hospital, we packed up and went camping at Von Bach Dam, taking Jeremiah with us, returning to the Ranch overnight once a week to check on things and be present while Simon, the headman, verbally issued Ian's written orders to the staff for the week. Then we drove back to Jeremiah, also a heavy smoker, waiting at the dam, who was unable to understand from my poor Afrikaans, why Ian, who usually chatted to him so much on these trips, couldn't speak. So Jeremiah busied himself fishing from the dam shores, lit the camp fire morning and evening, cleaned the barbeque grate, gutted and washed the fish, packed them in the freezer, and generally kept the camp tidy, enjoying some hours of rest. Ian and I communicated with one another by him writing messages in an exercise book, keeping strictly to his mute 6 weeks. He'd given up smoking since his operation and mainly slept. I went to and fro to Okahandja for shopping at the new supermarket.

Returning home, Ian underwent a course of chemotherapy injections provided by the Specialist and which I administered, followed by a course of tablets. The side-effects of this latter medication so adversely affected Ian's character that he vehemently instructed me to 'burn the lot in the donkey'. With a more holistic approach from a Harley Street homeopath in England who I'd written to, I made some changes to Ian's diet of what he should and should not eat. He refused any further conventional medical treatment. Feeling better, but now back with the stresses of the Ranch, Ian started smoking again.

A camping trip to Jakkalspitz on the South West African coast one April was not an enjoyable getaway. The weather was starting to turn towards winter, mostly cold and miserable, drizzly rain and the wind blew. I probably remember this holiday more because of the tent and the jackals ('jakkals' in Afrikaans). On arrival, intentions were good as the grandkids, filled with enthusiasm, agreed to be helpful and assist their grandfather, Gan-Gan, in putting up the big tent, which was first laid out flat on the ground with all the relevant poles, guy ropes and pegs. Each child was appointed one area and all were issued instructions. The other adults watched. It soon turned into a hilarious spectacle with children pulling in different directions and landing up under the tent canvas like moles in a maze, poles falling down and around, general confusion and a lot of noise, shouts and laughter from the youngsters – to them, the more the disaster, the greater the fun and the less their concentration. Gan-Gan managed to remain focused and tolerant for a while then his patience ran out. He sent the grandchildren packing, asked for coffee and the adults helped put up the tent. Then he headed straight for the beach with his fishing rod for some peace and quiet! That first night camping, all our meat supply was taken by jackals. Ian had put it on top of the trailer. In the morning, we could see the jackal footprints and all the ripped-up plastic packets, yet we'd not heard a sound during the night, perhaps due to the wind.

The time came when Benjamin considered himself no longer a child to play with the grandkids or collect the hen eggs, so Ian took him on, initially with odd jobs for a time to prove himself capable and get him used to working full-time. Then he was employed to work with the cattle. At the age of 18, Benjamin would be circumcised according to his Herero tradition, after which he'd be considered a man. However, Maria had a little son of 7 named !Xai – pronounced 'Kai' as in the English way, but with the Bushmen click of the tongue before the 'K', which I was unable to accomplish though Maria found my version acceptable. He loved coming to the house as a playmate for the grandchildren, staying the whole day and eating with the youngsters, and Andrew and Shaun loved having !Xai come to play. There'd be a lot of running around outside, climbing this and that, jumping up and down, yelling, chasing about and general noise of kids having a good time, though being Bushman, !Xai was considerably smaller in stature with tiny hands and feet, and very agile. Come evening, they were all exhausted, having worked off a lot of energy in a healthy outdoor environment and were ready for bed.

Maria begged me to find something for !Xai to do when the grandchildren weren't with us. So I kept him on for collecting the eggs as I'd done with Benjamin, and started teaching him his English numbers twice a day by counting out loud with him the eggs, one at a time, that he brought back in the basket. !Xai didn't have the enthusiasm for learning that Benjamin had. We only got as far as counting up to 10.

Our family, since my childhood, part of which had been during the days of WWII, had always celebrated Easter, keeping alive children's beliefs in the Easter Bunny, hunting for Easter Eggs and eating painted boiled eggs for breakfast or supper. We put particular emphasis on Christmas with all its magic as a special time for children. Ian and I followed these traditions as parents, and now as grandparents I was determined to keep the wonderment of Christmas alive for our grandchildren. Inspiring my efforts every year were my own memories of young wishes and dreams about Father Christmas, presents and stockings and the Kenya 50 cent piece in the Christmas pudding. I remembered well the build-up of excitement resulting in my struggling to sleep in anticipation of Christmas morning.

Grown-up as I now am, I still have that unique feeling of joy that only Christmas brings. I have always put time and effort into Christmas and birthday cakes (another important celebration in our family) teaching myself to do delicate cake icing, and became adept at creating flowers and leaves – roses, lilies, pansies, daisies and fern, vine and rose leaves, from a wonderful book written by Gladiola Botha – all of which were edible. On one occasion, I made a donkey, donkey cart and Father Christmas with a bag of presents on top of the cake – that took some doing! Sometimes the decorations were done in hard Royal icing, other times softer fondant icing or marzipan, in a variety of colours. Using an icing gun with different nozzles, I learnt to pipe stars etc., fine lines and writing. In our Malindi days, instead of almond marzipan under the white icing on the Christmas cake, I made my own paste out of cashew nuts, which was scrumptious.

Farm life might sound like constant excitement, busy it most certainly always is, but it can also be quite lonely at times. Christmas and birthday cakes were some of the things I enjoyed making, found challenging and creatively satisfying. Apart from our animals which I could never have lived without, my other interests were embroidery, knitting, sewing and the garden.

The baking of the Christmas cake I always planned well in advance around the end of September, making sure all my chores were up-to-date for the particular day allotted as it was essential there be no interruptions. I always made a round 9 inch Christmas cake for Maria and her family as well, with raisins, sultanas and currants, so she became accustomed to seeing my annual, lengthy baking process. All the staff children received a Christmas gift of sweets from Ian and me – I'd buy an assortment of sweets and make a prettily wrapped parcel for each child. Maria was given a plucked fresh chicken from us as well, and the company slaughtered an ox for the staff festive celebrations and all employees received an extra month's payment.

There was a lot to do in creating my perfect Christmas cake every year. As a start, I had to cut to size and grease 6 pieces of brown paper then 2 layers of greaseproof paper, all to fit exactly the large heavy oval 16 inch (from one end to the other) and 4 inches high enamelled cast-iron roasting pan that had been in my family since Daisy's days. Next was weighing out the various ingredients, always with plenty of walnuts and whole plump cherries, my trusted recipes coming from the Kenya Cookery Book, followed by mixing everything together then slow baking the heavy fruit mixture a couple of hours in a low heat oven. To check if the cake was sufficiently cooked, a porcupine quill was most handy for pricking the centre. Finally, the big cake was turned out onto a wire rack. Once cooled, it was important to keep the fruitcake moist by drizzling it with brandy and sherry daily for about a month, before carefully starting on the icing stages.

Each year I tried to push my icing abilities further, giving much thought to achieving memorable different decorations. I stuck to the task at hand until I felt satisfied and proud of what I'd made, the Christmas cake, after all, being the centre showpiece of the big day. It took time, practice and a steady hand to accomplish piped icing to a standard I felt happy with. Of course there were plenty of occasions when I had to redo flowers because they just didn't look right or weren't the exact colour I wanted them to be. The petals were extremely delicate and needed to be handled carefully then stuck together. This part of the Christmas cake making I found most therapeutic as time and the creativity of my hands and mind became one as the minutes just ticked away into hours of quiet relaxation. I think Daisy's excellent cook and baker, Mwangi, would have been pleased had he known that one day I'd become quite masterful in the kitchen having started off as a young, new bride unable to fry Ian's breakfast eggs to his liking! Mwangi's pancake recipe remains one of my favourites.

Ian made me a lovely wooden tea trolley and a big wooden cake board which I covered with tinfoil. Having put aside a day for working the marzipan layer, I first covered the Christmas cake with heated apricot jam so that the almond paste stuck firmly. The final step was the absolutely smooth white fondant icing layer over the marzipan then came the decorations. This particular year, I decided to pipe in fine white icing all the names of our family around the sides of the Christmas cake with small white stars along the bottom and top edges, and make a posy of different size and colour roses on top out of marzipan.

One can't forget the Christmas pudding either – the Plum Pudding always had a lucky silver South African 50 cent piece (in place of the English sixpence) dropped in then stirred thoroughly. If the grandchildren were around then they'd each get a turn to stir the pudding 3 times and make a wish before it was steamed, the mixing bowl usually scraped clean as a whistle afterwards with spoons and much licking of lips and fingers. Come the first of December the countdown started to the big day, measured by the grandchildren in 'numbers of sleeps' left to the 25th.

Finally, all was done. The massive decorated Christmas cake was placed on the top of the tea-trolley under the see-through plastic dome lid of the food-and-plate warmer in the dining room, next to the big window that faced onto the back verandah. I stood back and surveyed my work, well-pleased with the result, the striking posy of roses in deep red, pink and yellow pretty as a picture on the white fondant icing background. Up went the thorn-tree branch Christmas tree decorated with brightly coloured baubles and plenty of fine, silver Lametta streamers to await our annual festivities of merriment with present-opening, tea with Christmas cake, and traditional English Christmas dinner with Plum Pudding and brandy sauce, hats and crackers.

Ian and I never left Kambingana between Christmas and New Year. This December, we'd made arrangements for a 5 day fishing trip to Hardap Dam to return on the evening of 23rd December. Janey and Alec Medlycott (Alec we'd met in Angola) would join us. We gave Maria the house keys. She was reliable and most capable of feeding the animals twice a day and checking all was well generally at the house. The glass window of the dining room was always left open for ventilation, leaving the gauze insect-proof shutter in place. Our instructions to Maria were that !Xai should still collect the eggs to be put in the egg-basket in the kitchen, and that she should clean the house of dust the day before we were due back. On our return, Maria was waiting for us, neat as a pin in her pretty pink uniform with white lace around the apron, but her usual happy face and cheery demeanour appeared pensive. With a long face she described to me some tale of woe regarding !Xai. Due to my limited kitchen Afrikaans, I was unable to understand the full gist of Maria's hurried anxious story and called Ian. A few Bushmen clicks inadvertently slipped into her worried explanation as she frustratingly gesticulated with her hands in the natural Bushmen manner explaining now to Ian what the problem was.

"Maria says !Xai's eaten 'the thing you made', meaning the Christmas cake," Ian elaborated, "and she only noticed yesterday when she was doing the dusting."

"Eaten the Christmas cake?" I replied, perplexed.

Clearly Maria was upset and wanted the matter dealt with so we traipsed into the dining room.

"Looks all right to me," Ian observed as we approached the tea-trolley.

"I don't notice anything wrong either," I said lifting the see-through dome lid. Maria stood silently to the side as Ian and I carefully inspected the cake. Moving the tea-trolley forward we got a closer look at the back of my creation, and yes, there it was, a 'mouse-hole' through the icing!

Fretfully, Maria instructed that we, "*Kyk binne*," ('look inside') so I fetched the cake-lifter and carefully removed it from the board, holding the heavy cake up a bit for Ian to bend down and inspect underneath, whereupon he broke into laughter.

"He's eaten about a third of it!" he exclaimed.

"Good grief! Let me have a look," I said incredulously.

Ian took over holding the cake up so I could get a look at the bottom then I also started laughing. Maria was astounded at our jovial reaction to what she considered a serious matter. When we could contain ourselves, she instructed Ian that !Xai receive some form of admonishment from him and that she'd bring !Xai to the house the next afternoon. Going to bed that night, we were still chuckling about the 'mouse-hole' in the cake.

"How do you think he managed to get his little fist out through the hole in the icing if his hand was full of cake?" I asked.

"Beats me," Ian replied, "he's not Bushman for nothing. They're experts at finding food and getting the yolk and white out of a tiny hole in an ostrich egg, equivalent to 24 hen eggs."

"Mmm...," I replied thoughtfully, "he must've put his arm through the tear in the bottom of the fly-screen, lifted the lid and first had a tiny taste of the icing, which turned into more tastes until his little arm was well inside the cake." I pondered a moment then added, "It's Christmas though... should he be punished?"

"You know how proud and particular Maria is regarding discipline of her kids. Besides, if it was one of the grandchildren they wouldn't get away with it, would they? And, we can't over-rule her authority as his mother."

"No, you're right," I answered, pulling the sheet over me as I marvelled at !Xai's ingenuity.

"Clever little fellow," Ian chortled as he turned over to go to sleep, "got to give him 10 out of 10 for that!"

"I'll just patch up the hole with a bit of icing and remember not to cut that part of the cake... looks rather like a hollow tortoise shell inside," I said, settling down for the night.

The family arrived the following day, the 24th, and in the late afternoon Maria brought !Xai over to the house. Per her request, and in front of the grandchildren, Ian gave !Xai 3 whacks with a small bush twig. It had little effect on him, he merely stalked off. But, the grandkids were thunderstruck and made sure to be absolutely polite and on their best behaviour, especially since Father Christmas was due the next day.

Some years previously, we'd had a very successful Christmas at Kambingana where we'd invited neighbours and their children. Our Koos played Santa in the red suit I'd had sewn. I had made the same arrangements again this Christmas except that a tall, young German farmer would take the role of Father Christmas. He'd have a pillow tucked into his trousers for his big tummy, long cotton-wool beard, a hessian sack over his shoulder filled with presents – one per child, all with names on, secretly bought earlier by their parents – and he had a little time to chat to the mothers and fathers before getting dressed in his Santa outfit. Christmas morning our grandchildren eager to unwrap their presents, always had us up early, unable to contain their excitement. As soon as the adults had a cup of tea or coffee in hand we made our way to the lounge, Ian sitting contentedly in his rocker watching his family, particularly the youngsters, shred paper and laugh with joy. This gave Ian more pleasure than the presents he received. Then we had breakfast and awaited our guests and Father Christmas who'd be arriving by donkey cart.

The youngsters rushed out the garden gate wide-eyed the moment they saw the cart slowly wending its way on the dusty road up to the house. The donkey was led by Benjamin with Simon holding the reins as 'driver' sitting next to Father Christmas. With great excitement, the children escorted Father Christmas in his Wellington boots, jingling his cap-bell, sack of presents over his shoulder as he kept pushing up his pillow-tummy, straightening his beard and doing a regular and overly exuberant, "Ho- Ho," to his seat under the big thorn tree in the front garden.

It didn't take long to notice the children starting to feel afraid of this Santa. A hush descended over the circle gathered around his feet. Keith had to whisper in his ear to tone down his booming, authoritarian voice and instead inflect a gentle, jolly tone befitting the occasion. Having gleaned snippets of information earlier from parents, German Santa's apparently uncanny ability to pinpoint to certain children's 'poor behaviours, homework or chores not done, had they helped their mother or not' had some of the youngsters almost scared out of their wits! Initially, some of the children sat on his lap, though as Father Christmas' questioning continued other children refused to do so despite his numerous requests. At one stage, some youngsters had to be escorted by a parent to get their present! Eventually, the sack of gifts was empty and Father Christmas left again on the donkey cart to a suitable distance where he could take off his suit and rejoin us all for tea, sandwiches and festive eats. Some kids became a bit wide-eyed again as they thought they recognised his voice, but the adults managed to convince them Santa really had left on the donkey cart to deliver presents to other children.

It was a memorable Christmas one way or another!

Chapter Twenty-One
Telescopium Beryl Marjorie

"Have you let that wily little Bushman out of the hen-house yet?" Ian asked as he came through the kitchen door at twenty-past-one, a bit later than usual for his midday meal. He'd had a hot and frustrating morning out fixing the borehole pump, yet again, at Karamba water-post.

"Yes, I have," I answered laughing, "Maria let him out when she went home for lunch."

Ian put his hat down then crossed to the kitchen sink to wash his hands. "What's the full story? After he tunnelled into the Christmas cake, I said Bushmen are experts at getting raw egg out of a shell."

For the previous 3 days the usual 10 hen eggs !Xai brought back to the kitchen had become 6. I'd mentioned this to Ian saying I'd check it out, perhaps it was time to replace some of the hens though I thought it a bit odd and too soon to get new pullets.

"Well, !Xai came over at 10 as usual, I gave him his breakfast, then he went to collect the eggs, clean the water bowls and feed the fowls," I elaborated. "I thought he was taking too long to come back with the eggs, so I sneaked out the back gate up to the chicken-house, and there he was squatted down deliciously sucking on an egg; oblivious to the world around him."

"Bet he got a shock, getting caught in the act," Ian responded, pulling out his chair to sit down at the table.

I busied myself frying the bubble-and-squeak. "Yes, he was so intent on the egg he only turned around when he heard me bolt the door on him, then he quickly threw the shell down on the straw."

"Did he kick up a fuss realising he couldn't get out?" Ian asked, fiddling with his placemat.

"Oh yes, yelled his head off, pulling at the door and wire mesh," I affirmed, putting Ian's lunch plate in front of him. "Maria heard the racket and came running outside. I told her I'd found !Xai eating a chicken's egg."

I dished some bully beef, one of Ian's favourites, onto his plate along with some slices of fried tomato and potato chip wedges.

"What did Maria say about it?" Ian responded, reaching for the Tabasco sauce.

"She gave him a right telling-off," I said, sitting down at the table, "in Bushman, not Afrikaans, so I couldn't understand a word, but with all the clicks and tone of her voice she sounded pretty fed-up with !Xai."

"Does he get eggs for breakfast sometimes too, like Munde and Maria?" Ian queried, cutting some small pieces of bully beef to put aside on his plate for the dogs, something he did all the years at mealtimes, each dog getting their treat when we'd finished eating.

"Of course, though not this week because we've been short," I assured him, buttering a slice of bread.

"Well, he's had his fair share the last few days," Ian replied, putting his napkin on his lap, then added, "but, now he's been caught red-handed, I don't think !Xai will try this trick again, best to keep an eye on him though."

The following day the hen eggs were back to 10 again. !Xai seemed to have learned his lesson! Shortly after this, Maria had some very distressing problems with her husband, Kleinbooi, the indignity of which was too much for her. She took her children, sadly said goodbye to us and returned to her San Bushmen family.

I missed Maria a lot, as did the grandchildren little !Xai. News via the 'bush telegraph' reached us that Maria had gone back to Tsumkwe, a San rural town in the Kalahari – since the dawn of time, home to the San and Khoisan indigenous hunter-gatherer people, the oldest inhabitants of southern Africa. The area is vast, dry and extremely hot, with stunning hills and scenery, and gigantic rock formations in colours ranging from all shades of the browns to pinks and purples. It truly is an artist's paradise and has many wonderful paintings in the caves, some not easily accessible, but worth the effort in climbing just to see them. One of the main features of the women is their extraordinarily big protruding bottoms, and it doesn't take much time for these naturally small-built people to become extremely wrinkled from exposure to the elements. The children are tiny in every aspect, and all grow up knowing how to survive in the harshness of this dry land and Kalahari Desert. Their language is difficult, has few words, and is articulated with complicated clicks of the tongue, something few Europeans can achieve.

Over the years, many a time we had a good chuckle remembering the endearing tale of clever little !Xai devouring Granny's 'hours in the making' Christmas creation, wondering how his tiny tummy must have felt laden with all that rich and heavy baked fruitcake! After Maria left, I was back to collecting the eggs.

A scruffy Bushman woman, Theresa, worked in the house after Maria's departure. Three weeks later, I had to let her go. The previous Christmas, old man Dempers had given us a bottle of 'Witblits' – an Afrikaner clear liquid homebrew with a high alcohol content made from grapes and also known as 'white lightning' or 'firewater' – he said a mouthful was enough!, that stood on top of the fridge in the corner of the dining room. One morning, when Theresa was supposedly dusting the dining room, I happened to quietly pop my head around the corner to find her taking some hearty swigs from the Witblits bottle. Staff had informed us prior to this that Theresa had a penchant for alcohol, which in itself was not uncommon amongst the Ranch labour, but drinking at work would pose difficulties.

A Nama woman, Francisca, who was also a Catholic, took over in a permanent position of employment with me after Maria. She was light-skinned, slightly built, pretty, clothes conscious and always had her hair done stylishly. Francisca was an absolute boon to me. She learnt everything quickly, had pride in all she did, was happy and comfortable with us both and loved our animals. I was lucky to have her, trusting her implicitly. She had 2 children, but no husband and was talented in home crafts, especially crocheting blankets and would buy many different coloured balls of wool on month-end shopping trips. Francisca was brought up in the Catholic religion and spoke Afrikaans, but picked up English easily. The Catholic Father who regularly visited Kambingana always gave Francisca communion. He seemed to know her from some time past. To me, she appeared to be a devout Catholic.

Mr Bonadei sent a bunch of workmen from his Gochaganas, Windhoek farm to rebuild some of the drinking troughs on Kambingana. After years of being trampled against by cattle they'd started to deteriorate and were losing precious water. The builders slept at the staff compound for 4 nights while working on the Ranch for 5 days. While they were rebuilding the cattle troughs, Ian and I had to go to Windhoek on business and, unfortunately, had to stay overnight. Before we left, Ian made sure all the staff and workmen, particularly because they were away from their homes and families, had a generous meat supply plus their other food rations. I made sure to cook up ample maize meal marble-sized balls for old Munde to feed Jawsie – he knew the procedure well.

The following day in Windhoek we still had business to conduct and do the shopping so arrived home, tired, only around 9 in the evening. I fed the dogs then made a salad to go with the roast chicken I'd bought on the way home in Klein Windhoek at Hidas. After supper, Ian and I fell into bed exhausted. First thing in the morning, I went to check on Jawsie and found her severed head lying on the base step of the reservoir. Old Munde arrived at 8 and told me the story of how he'd gone to the reservoir to give Jawsie her breakfast and was shocked to find the workmen had caught and eaten her, leaving her head where she'd been slaughtered. He'd left everything as he'd found it, to show me. Deeply sorrowed by the death of our amazing carp hen-fish that we'd had for years living in the reservoir and appalled by the callous act of the perpetrators – Jawsie was so beautiful, tame and trusting – I felt enraged. Again, there was nothing I could do about it.

Ian's mother, Mater, still living in a ground-floor flat alone for years in East London in the Cape was now struggling in her old age. I flew to East London where she agreed I assist in permanently admitting her to the geriatric section of the Mater Dei Hospital as she knew the doctors and some of the staff there and felt she'd be happy in that environment. I was gone for 3 weeks packing up Mater's flat and settling her in.

While speaking to Ian one night on the 'phone, he said that when out driving in the bush one of the front wheels of the Land Cruiser went into a grass-hidden ant-bear hole, the steering wheel spinning out of control and when trying to stop it his right hand had got caught and the bones (phalanges) were broken. He said I shouldn't worry as our friends, Lulu and Hendrick de Bruin, had taken care of him. They'd driven him to the Windhoek Catholic Hospital where his hand had been set in plaster and he was coping fine.

On my return to Kambingana, I could smell there was a problem with Ian's hand. Gangrene had set in. I took him back to the Catholic Hospital where the bones were re-set and he had to wait out another 6 weeks with his hand in plaster of Paris. This time there was satisfactory healing of the hand bones, but Ian's little finger was permanently bent inwards towards the palm and he couldn't straighten it, resulting in it getting in the way of everything he tried to do. Finding this such an impediment, he decided to have the little finger amputated. His surgery was at 9 in the morning and after he'd come around from the general anaesthetic we came home, Ian's hand stitched and bandaged, requiring regular disinfecting and fresh dressings. Within days the healing had taken place. I became accustomed to Ian's lack of a little finger though others noticed when shaking hands with him. Apart from not being able to hold water in his right hand if he cupped it, he managed perfectly well in all other respects and was relieved to be rid of his crooked finger. I had to go out in the Land Cruiser one day some time later on and also drove into a hole, the steering spinning wildly. Lucky for me, I'd learnt my lesson from Ian's unfortunate experience and let go of the steering wheel, suffering only a few sore fingers on both hands.

The day old Munde set himself on fire was frightening. He'd been sitting outside with Francisca at the 'donkey' while the 2 had their breakfast of porridge, bread and jam, and very sweet coffee. After this, he'd usually puff on his old pipe while polishing Ian's boots, Francisca's shoes, mine and his own to a splendid shine.

On this particular day, I was indoors doing some embroidery with my fancy, new sewing machine when I heard screams outside and Francisca ran in to tell me Munde was on fire outside by the 'donkey'. Dogs at our heels, we both rushed out to find the old man screaming and writhing on the grass with his chest area on fire and flames beginning to lick all over his legs. Francisca quickly fitted the garden hosepipe to the tap and I sprayed water over Munde thoroughly drenching him, then we removed his clothes and found he was severely burnt over his entire chest. Francisca laid the old chap gently on the lawn while I hurried indoors to get ice cubes and water, and with instructions from me, Francisca dealt with the first aid. Meanwhile, I got the bakkie ready, drove it to the back gate and with difficulty we managed to get Munde in the back lying on an old safari mattress with blankets over him. While I drove the 180 kilometres as fast as I could to Gobabis Hospital, Francisca sat with Munde applying the ice and water. If she'd not been there to help, I believe the old man may well have died from the shock and severity of the burns.

After some days, the hospital 'phoned to say Munde was ready to come home. I collected him together with all the necessary medications, and once he was back in his own house, I examined his chest and continued to dress the dreadful burns which were still very red, soft and wet, but scar tissue was forming and stretched both up and down the front of his body. Part of my treatment was for him to lie under the lemon tree on the lawn near the 'donkey' and get some sunshine to dry out the scar tissue with the help of mercurochrome. It worked.

I now learned the story of what happened. It being a bitterly cold day, Munde said he thought he'd first warm up a bit before starting the boot and shoe polishing by (ironically) lying in the sun on the lawn under the lemon tree for a while, having a quiet smoke on his pipe. But, when he flicked the lighter and moved the flame towards his pipe his woollen winter clothing caught alight.

The pieces of the puzzle now fell into place. Munde usually filled his metal cigarette lighter from the petrol depot tank at the workshop, as did all the other farm men, at the same time as the 3 farm vehicles were being refuelled. Ian had warned them on numerous occasions about being very careful not to get fuel on themselves when filling their lighters and to wash their hands afterwards. It may well be that old Munde's eyesight was not as good as it used to be or that his hands were not quite as steady and some drops of fuel must have fallen onto his woollen clothing. So when he flicked the lighter for his pipe whilst lying under the lemon tree, the flame ignited the spilt petrol on his jersey and with his arthritic fingers he panicked unable to remove his clothes. It took many months of treatment before the old man was properly healed. He continued smoking his pipe, using petrol from the depot tank to fill his lighter.

Not long after Ian's operation to remove the leukoplakia lesion from his larynx, Mr Bonadei fell ill, then another friend of ours. All 3 men had the same cancer diagnosis and operation, all were smokers. It was a tough time.

Ian made a big decision to replace the Simmenthaler bulls (tall at the shoulder and very heavy animals) with 2 smaller British breeds, Hereford and Sussex, as too many pregnant heifers were dying in the vast veld from inability to give birth, their calves from the Simmenthaler bulls being too big. From this time on, bulls from the 2 new breeds were used on virgin heifers which put an end to these unnecessary deaths, apart from which Hereford and Sussex cattle produced a heavier hind quarter as a beef animal.

In 1984, Ian's mother, Mater, passed away in East London. According to the nursing Sister on duty, she'd checked on her patient at 2 in the morning and found Mater sleeping comfortably and restfully. On her next round, she found Mater had died. Indications were that she'd died peacefully in her sleep and we were grateful and relieved that at 91 Mater had slipped away without undue suffering. She was buried in East London in the family tomb with William Alexander, Ian's father.

Keith had voluntarily applied for the Army and was called up to the South West African Territorial Force in 1984, doing his basic training at the Okahandja Military School after which he was sent to the School of Armour Tempe, Bloemfontein in the Orange Free State, South Africa, attaining the rank of 2nd Lieutenant, and was then posted to Rooikop base in Walvis Bay. In 1985, he did border duty in Angola. During Keith's Military Service, Mary re-located back to Okahandja earning an income employed as a cook in the military training camp, which she thoroughly enjoyed. The 2 elder children, Debbie and Andrew, were schooled in Windhoek.

Driving through the veld one day, Ian came upon 2 little ostrich chicks wandering aimlessly. They were very small. He thought they'd probably been left behind by the mother and were now lost as there was no sign or sounds of any other ostriches in the vicinity so he brought them home. We named them Munde and Angelina in honour of old Munde. He was so pleased. The ostrich pair would wait excitedly at the back garden fence in the early mornings and again at 4 in the afternoon for old Munde to put the sprinkler on for them. Then they sat down under the shower of water and fluffed out their feathers, swishing their open wings around, craning and weaving their necks and heads this way and that to get the droplets of water all over themselves. At other times, they'd do the same in the ash pile getting their bodies all dusted up with the 'donkey' ashes old Munde took out each morning before making a new fire. The cock was black with white patches on his wing tips, far more attractive than the hen's dull grey plumage. Both had the most beautiful long eyelashes. They became very tame probably because the male had not yet reached maturity. Each morning, they bobbed about in heightened anticipation awaiting their handful of mealie pips then spent the rest of the day wandering around pecking at this and that, grazing on weeds, grasses and wild succulents in the paddock. Playing running games with one another, they'd suddenly sprint madly around then come dashing back to their favourite spot near the 'donkey', their feeding place. Life was good for these ostriches. I took several photos of old Munde posing with them, holding their necks.

The dogs took no notice whatsoever of the ostriches. They were considered part of the home scene and spent a lot of time standing at the back gate or garden fence near the 'donkey'. They liked human company and wanted to share in our daily comings and goings, and there was the added draw of possible food as old Munde and Francisca ate their meals sitting near the fire. Full of curiosity, they noticed anything unusual happening. I never took feathers from them and can't remember any worthwhile plumage being shed. We didn't allow children near them. The ostriches were comfortable with people they knew, but could be dangerous if aroused to anger or fear, and a kick from a grown ostrich or a peck from its powerful beak could cause serious harm. When the cock ostrich showed signs of sexual maturity and his legs turned a pinkish colour, we gave both birds to Pierre Blaauw, a farmer friend of ours. It was easy to catch the pair and Pierre put a sock over each of their heads to keep them docile and manageable, then led them out to the bakkie where they were loaded, still with the socks on their heads, and driven to Pierre's farm at Witvlei where he started to breed ostriches as a business. We'd so enjoyed having them around the house. Special memories of these 2 big birds in ostrich 'seventh heaven' under our Kambingana garden sprinkler always brings back a smile to me.

We never seemed free of worries with old Munde Paulus. Weekends particularly, and Christmas and New Year, always brought some sort of problems with the staff, usually to do with drink and fighting. Many times we had to drop whatever we were doing and rush to Gobabis Hospital, nearly always late or very late at night. This Christmas morning, Ian and I were alone. We'd had a leisurely breakfast and intended having a picnic lunch and doing some fishing for carp in Kambingana dam. Packed and ready, Ian went out through the kitchen back door to get the bakkie from the garage. To his utter amazement, he found old Munde lying on the lawn under the lemon tree, covered in blood, hardly able to lift his head. The old man merely raised his right arm and beckoned for Ian to see where all the blood was coming from, speaking in a whisper. Ian took one look and yelled for me. I immediately put on a tourniquet above the wrist and, once again, we loaded Munde into the back of the bakkie, flat on the safari mattress, and I drove to Gobabis Hospital Emergency Room where I waited while the African doctor in charge examined and treated the old fellow. He told me not to worry about a thing, an artery in Munde's arm had been nicked by a shard of glass and he'd used, "The thickest possible sutures." The doctor seemed greatly amused by my shocked-nurse reaction when I saw the rope-like stitches in Munde's arm!

When he was home safely in his own bed, we questioned Munde's wife, Angelina, about what had happened. She said there'd been a monumental booze-up Christmas Eve party. Sometime in the early hours as daylight approached, with everyone else collapsed in a dead sleep not hearing, seeing or being aware of anything, Munde wanted to go outside for a pee. He couldn't see the door in his 'inebriated morning after' condition so unwittingly staggered towards the light, which came from the enormous glass window. He crashed straight through the pane, relieved himself, came in through the door and went back to bed beside Angelina. She couldn't tell at what time he came back. Although she felt something wet and warm creeping into her clothing, she looked to see what it was only when the sun was well up and to her absolute horror found it was blood. Angelina became frightened and was too drunk to do anything, except tell Munde to get to our house, where he collapsed, unbeknown to us, on the back lawn. Luckily, we'd decided to go fishing late that Christmas morning, because by the time Ian discovered the old man he was already very weak. It was a frightening scene.

The best New Year we ever had was spent at Kambingana dam. Many of our neighbours celebrated the day and late into the night with us, picnicking and fooling around. We'd taken everything imaginable in the way of festive food and drinks, and the dogs were along for the fun too. The dam was at one of its lowest levels so there was a lot of mud, all over us as well! At night, the full moon and clear starry skies brilliantly lit up the water and surrounding bush, and a gentle breeze kept everything pleasantly cool. The following New Year, we tried the big Karamba dam and while I was swimming in deep water, I noticed a large cobra swimming alongside then passing me! That put an end to all my swimming in the farm dams!

One Monday morning, Simon and his wife, Constantia, came to see Ian to complain about Jeremiah. Apparently, Jeremiah had visited their house over the weekend and become very drunk. A fierce argument ensued between Jeremiah and Constantia, and Jeremiah had slogged her in the mouth and broken off one of her front teeth at gum level. I contacted the dentist in Windhoek, a Dr Marais, who came every other week to his farm not far from Kambingana, and made an appointment for Constantia to have the tooth stump removed. Constantia was seated in the dental chair and the dentist examined her briefly, or so I thought, then he turned to me and we chatted particularly about the ostrich population on his farm, and the hunting on our place. Wondering when he would pull Constantia's tooth stump out, I asked him if he could please now see to her as I had to get back to the farm. I was astounded when he said he'd removed the stump just after she had sat in the chair. Constantia had not made even a squeak! As she had now received dental treatment, we thought all the drama had ended and everything was back to normal.

About 2 weeks later, Jeremiah came to work with the other men and said to Ian that he couldn't perform his duties as his right hand was too swollen and very painful. Ian examined his hand. It was swollen up to the wrist the size of a small cabbage, had an ugly looking colour and the skin was so stretched it seemed on the point of bursting. He asked Jeremiah what he'd done to cause this injury. Jeremiah said he'd hit Constantia in the mouth. Ian told me to prepare to take Jeremiah to Gobabis Hospital soonest possible. Once again, Dr Nel came to the rescue. He explained that bites or puncture wounds even from human teeth are extremely poisonous and that had we not come for treatment gangrene would very quickly have become a real problem. He lanced Jeremiah's swollen hand and gave him an injection and we went back to the farm with a course of antibiotic capsules, salve and bandages to keep the wound clean. Once again, there were issues between Simon, his family, and Jeremiah.

Murders were still occurring, mainly of elderly widowed women living alone on large, isolated farms. There was much talk on the streets of Windhoek about South West Africa attaining Independence. Africans were deliberately speaking English after a speech by SWAPO's (South West Africa Peoples Organisation's) Sam Nujoma encouraged them to do so.

Hans and Trudl Breede, dear friends from Munich who'd also been deep-sea fishing clients from Malindi days, decided to visit us in 1986 and watch Halley's Comet in February. It had last been seen in 1910, and revolves around the sun every 75 to 76 years, with the next sighting expected in mid-2061. Radio broadcasts informed the public of the best sighting time. Beryl was now back living and working in Windhoek, still a single mother, so Stuart, our grandson came to stay. We put a mattress on the front lawn and set the alarm clock for 4 in the morning. Through binoculars, we watched the comet come its closest to Earth. It was a magnificent sight although its short, bushy tail looked very 'muddy'. That weekend, with the boats and camping equipment, Hans and Trudl met us at Von Bach Dam. We all camped together then they stayed a couple of days with us on the farm before returning to Windhoek. Once home in Germany, we received a letter from them saying, "Dear Friends, although we love you very much, we will not visit Kambingana again unless we bring our AK 47 – a gun!" They felt where we lived was very isolated and too far from the city and civilisation.

Minnie, our dear little Miniature Pinscher given to us by our Angolan dentist, suddenly developed a hard lump that grew very fast between two of her nails on her one front paw. The Windhoek Vet removed the cancerous growth. Not long after, a gaping wound appeared on Minnie's back and the Vet advised it was kindest to put her to sleep. Ian stayed with her, I waited in the car. The situation had developed quickly and we weren't really mentally prepared. Ian was deeply saddened to lose his faithful little friend.

Mr Bonadei was always anxious that we be happy out in the bush. His triple-storey beautiful home with pool and vineyards was on Luxury Hill with a magnificent view overlooking Windhoek. Many times we were invited for the midday meal on our trips to the city. Mrs Bonadei, a small built, very dear woman imbued with the passionate Italian love of life, was a superb cook of her native cuisine and we were treated to many tasty, long-time family favourite recipes. Her kitchen was enormous with every modern appliance, the serving bowls and crockery ornate coloured porcelain. It was a pleasure to lunch with their family. Our generous employer now decided to build us a beautiful new tiled kitchen with pantry, incorporating our long back verandah, onto our house at Kambingana, together with a storeroom, and a freezer and laundry room that adjoined the single garage. The small cramped kitchen was gone, replaced by a spacious L-shaped area with plenty of cupboards, room for the fridge, a wonderful long tiled worktop next to the stove, double sink and the very handy and convenient pantry. As a surprise, Ian bought me a big National convection microwave. The first thing I cooked in the microwave was baked potatoes. What a difference this entire new set-up made to our daily lives.

As a gift some months after Minnie's passing, Beryl gave me 'Tandy', a starving tan-coloured Miniature Pinscher puppy about 6 weeks old that she'd located from a breeder in Johannesburg. Tandy was flown to Windhoek airport and Beryl brought her to us at Kambingana. It turned out the pup preferred Ian to me. Where Ian went, Tandy was his shadow, including around the Ranch and to Windhoek for business or shopping, her harness on and lead attached, in winter donning her tiny jackets I'd knitted and on which I'd embroidered her name. Ian's 6 foot 2 inch frame with his tiny best friend would walk

Windhoek together and lunch in the restaurant, Tandy never a problem. Ian made it quite clear he'd not eat in an establishment that didn't allow her in as well. Tandy grew long in the leg, was clever, loved going in the car and getting brushed, joined in on walks and accompanied us on fishing and boating trips. We now had 3 dogs – Simba (Minnie & Pepu's pup, his name meaning lion in Swahili), dear little Dumbo, a black cross-Dachshund Lindsay had given us a while back and already getting on in years, and the newest edition, Tandy, all of whom got along with one another excellently.

The day came when my over-worked electric iron packed in and having just done my shopping trip to Windhoek I had to wait another month or so before I could buy a new one. In the meantime, Angelina magnanimously offered me the use of her charcoal iron. Years before, in Kenya, we'd used such cumbersome, heavy irons with burning coals being put inside the cavity then clamped safely, and air holes along the sides. The iron is swung to and fro to cause draughts, rekindling the coals to red hot. Because of their weight these irons produce wonderfully ironed bed sheets and the like. As a thank-you, I decided to give Angelina 2 extra-large metal serving spoons with floral patterns on the handles that she could use for her cooking instead of her handmade wooden ones. My friend, Connie, had given me 3 of these spoons some years earlier after buying them at a church bazaar. Angelina was delighted.

I was astonished one morning, when an extremely angry Angelina with a countenance of thunder burst through the back door into our kitchen with a string of f-word expletives as she explained the loss of her 2 metal spoons to me. Apparently, Simon's family had invited guests for the weekend and they'd stolen the spoons. And, not only that – I'd also given Angelina's daughter, Rebecca, a dolly for Christmas and the guests had left with that in their possession as well. Angelina was furious. The heavy, voluminous skirt of her traditional Herero frock swished this way and that as she gesticulated and paced the floor venting her fury. The audacity of it all – accommodating and pandering to every need of Simon's visitors and they'd repaid her kindness and hospitality with theft. After a while, Angelina calmed down then sobbed and shed tears as we had a cup of coffee together. Those 2 inexpensive metal spoons had been really precious to her.

The same use of the f-word by Angelina I'd experienced before. After her baby died, she'd come to see me privately for some time about her inability to fall pregnant again. Then when she stopped menstruating she'd again consulted me for several months, each time saying, "F…, this month I have seen f... all!" The way she expressed it in Afrikaans was amusing. I advised that perhaps she was starting menopause, a very difficult explanation for me since my Afrikaans was in no way fluent.

We had 2 incidents regarding lice – the 1st being a young couple from East London who visited us with their 2 children. At breakfast, the mother suddenly jumped up from the table to squash a louse on her daughter's head. I sent them soonest possible to Windhoek to a chemist friend for the correct treatment for lice. Together with Francisca and Angelina, we had quite a task disinfecting all the cottage linen, pillows and bedding. The 2nd instance occurred on a Sunday morning. There was knocking on the back kitchen door. On opening it, I found a young African man with posh clothes sporting a fancy Afro hairdo with a big red plastic comb stuck in it jauntily on the side. Not knowing what this could be about I called Ian.

"Good morning," he said, and asked the man what the problem was?

The friendly, polite stranger explained he had *kraps*, which he had to repeat several times as neither of us could understand what he meant (*krap* in Afrikaans means 'scratch'). Eventually, we realised the scratching was on his scalp and concluded this was probably due to lice in his large hairdo. I could only advise him to shave off all his hair and burn it then wash his head every day for a week with Sunlight soap. We think that via the 'bush telegraph' word had got around that we were able to give medical treatment, assistance or were able to take people to hospital. However, having to account to the office for every expense and reason, taking people to hospital other than staff would not have been acceptable.

In 1988, I took a trip to China stopping over in Hong Kong, then on to Singapore and Australia a 2nd time, returning home via Taiwan. Flying into Hong Kong, the scene below was a magical sight at 4 o'clock in the morning. I was amazed at the airstrip with sea on both sides. Hong Kong never 'sleeps' and I had no fear of being on the streets any time day or night seeing all the wonders and going on the ferries, and bought a camera. Taking a hovercraft to get into Guangzhou, I was kept an hour by Immigration who were dissatisfied with my British Passport issued in Cape Town. Eventually, they let me through. While in Shanghai, I saw the Dragon Boat Race on the Yangtze, and experienced the new westernised China Hotel with a philharmonic orchestra, all the musicians dressed in black suits and bow ties. In the park below I counted 54 tourist buses. I stayed only a very short time at the zoo. The Panda was on concrete, the cleaners spraying the cage with high pressure hoses not caring if stinging jets of water hit the Panda as well, the poor animal desperately trying to get out of the way. Then I saw the monkeys, all looking decidedly ill. It was too upsetting so I went shopping instead.

Travelling a bit, I saw many things. Schools, a major toy manufacturer, markets with everything one can think of alive or slaughtered on the spot and millions of ducks. I had a frightening experience when I was surrounded by Chinese peasants with their severely handicapped small children, the parents demanding money. There wasn't a policeman in sight. Luckily, I managed to make a dash to a rickety train stuffed full of passengers which I was told carried about a million people a day crossing the borders. The countryside was beautiful with lots of flowering fruit trees, but the bus was an old, dirty rattletrap, the roads in bad condition and the toilets unbelievably horrendous.

Next stop was Singapore where the airport was simply wonderful. I visited the zoo which was marvellous and had tea with 'Leila' the Orang-utan. Staying at the Air India Hotel for 5 days, I was taken around this beautiful little country and looked after expertly by a young Chinaman, a friend of one of my Australian relatives, whose wife dealt in gemstones.

Australia, again, was filled with so many exciting things to do and see. Family and friends who accommodated me were exceptionally caring and generous, treating me to everything. I only paid for gifts I bought. Unfortunately, I picked up shingles shortly after arriving, but quickly received superb medical treatment in Mt Barker which cleared the virus so my holiday was only temporarily disrupted. I travelled on the fast Tilt Train, went to the Aborigine Dreamtime Village (an unforgettable experience of gentle, remarkable people), Mt Tambourine, the Currumbin Bird Park, and snorkelled off the exquisite Great Barrier Reef at Green Island. One of my friends had a delightfully cute baby kangaroo. I saw more of Queensland, incredulous at the cattle 'trains' – huge lorries towing up to 6 trailers loaded with beef cattle going to auction – and saw the coal railway trains pulling trucks numbering over 100 per train. In Brisbane, I went to the Expo, the Royal Yacht was in the harbour and the Commonwealth Games were being held. Despite a jam-packed memorable schedule, time was found for relaxation, eating out, leisurely browsing and shopping and these 'rest-ups' were also treasured experiences.

Taiwan was only a few hours airport stopover where security even removed the batteries from my camera. Then I was headed back home to Kambingana.

With the Transitional Government in place (constituting 6 parties formed by South Africa in 1985) and so much talk of Independence on the horizon, the farm staff kept abreast of events by listening to the radio.

One day, Mattheus handed Ian a scrap of dirty paper torn out of a school exercise book, and written by hand in pencil were the words, "You are English and Bonadei is Italian, and this farm belongs to us."

The only thoughts Ian and I had on the matter were, "Here we go again, a 3rd time!"

Ian filed the paper and when next in Windhoek gave it to Mr Bonadei, who merely threw it in the bin. Undeterred, a few months later, another written message was handed to Ian. Again, Mr Bonadei discarded it. Although we didn't know for certain, we understood him to be a SWAPO member/supporter and as such he wasn't concerned about the notes. The company now had to engage the services of a Labour Lawyer costing thousands of Rands as all sorts of things had to be adhered to. Just to make sure, copies of all documents, signatures on receipts of monthly wages, rations of meat, housing, etc. were signed for and given to the Windhoek office secretary.

The staff became surly. Benjamin, who'd been promoted from collecting hen eggs some years back and had since been working with the other farm men fully employed by the company, broke the neck of a mare while training her due to handling her badly – I hand-reared her foal which I named, 'Mackerel Skies'. Then through careless and negligent handling of a yearling calf, Benjamin almost broke its neck while Ian was castrating it. Ian kept his cool and sent Benjamin home. A week later, the Labour Union was at our door demanding detailed explanations. Ian produced the evidence which had been carefully set out in the farm diary. The other workers corroborated our version of the episode and we heard no more.

We went away for 5 days fishing to Von Bach Dam, as usual leaving Francisca to look after the house and animals. On our return, we found Simba in great pain unable to walk and immediately called the Vet. Thankfully, little Dumbo was all right. Tandy had been with us. Thorough examination revealed Simba had suffered spinal injury from being hit over the back by a solid object, something like a wooden fence pole. Although the Vet tried everything to improve Simba's condition, the trauma to his spine was too severe and we had to put him to sleep.

Radio news carried all the information about Nelson Mandela having been kept as a political prisoner in South Africa. This too had an effect on the staff. Farmers were told to prepare their employees for the voting procedure, how to go about this, and were also required to provide information to staff regarding the 6 different political parties.

Beryl telephoned one sunny, week day morning from work, saying she was worried as she'd been 'spotting' blood daily for a year. She'd not been for a check-up after the birth of her son, Stuart, 9 years earlier and hadn't had a pap smear done. I was utterly shocked. Being a single mother and holding down a job as a credit controller at a leading fashion store, she said she hadn't had the time. The next day, I went to Windhoek and checked her sanitary towel. It was definitely more than 'spotting' and necessitated her having to change her pad twice daily. Even more alarmed now, I straight away 'phoned Dr Mike Roberts (an ex-Rhodesian who'd done my hysterectomy in Windhoek) who saw

Beryl immediately and told me he'd have to do an investigation under anaesthetic and to bring her in the following day to the Windhoek State Hospital.

Mike Roberts came through to the waiting room while Beryl was recovering from the anaesthesia and sat with me. He said Beryl had 18 months to live and should be taken to Cape Town without delay. This was terrifying news. I'd realised she needed medical treatment, but a terminal cancer diagnosis of this magnitude I'd not considered. It was numbing to all my senses. Our family was in for one almighty shock. Twenty minutes or so later, Beryl joined us, still not completely on even keel, somewhat wobbly on her feet. Mike told her categorically that the cancer had entered her spine and also emphasised the short life she had left unless she underwent urgent surgery in Cape Town. He made all the necessary arrangements. The reality, gravity and finality of Dr Roberts' words Beryl, understandably, did not immediately comprehend. The first step forward and of paramount importance at this time was getting her to Cape Town.

Lindsay who'd now moved to East London, told me on the 'phone that she'd witnessed Beryl's 'spotting' more than a year earlier when she'd stayed overnight with her and had told Beryl to take it seriously and see a doctor. Lindsay had also struggled as a single working mother and admits she's also put various things off in life because she felt she didn't have the time. I'm guilty of this too, like postponing dental or medical appointments, but with women's annual check-ups, and pap smears there must be no delay. Beryl was not a smoker or drinker.

I was with Beryl in Cape Town at Vincent Pallotti Hospital for her hysterectomy. Dr Els (co-incidentally the same man who'd been the anaesthetist at my hysterectomy in Windhoek) came to talk to me, waiting outside in the hospital garden. A biopsy was done during Beryl's operation and out of 4 lymph glands (nodes) 2 were malignant. He stated clearly it was too late for any cure for Beryl. She'd been taken to ICU where I later saw her. I stayed in Tygerberg Hospital hostel in a tiny room costing Rand 10 a day and bought food from the takeaway shop.

Beryl's first cancer treatment was at Tygerberg, followed by Groote Schuur then continued at Windhoek State Hospital. She'd beat the hellish odds of only another 18 months life expectancy and lived 3 years, my memories of her time left being in 2 halves – the first utterly desperate, then the strong period and downhill slide. Helpless we felt as her family. To heal her was beyond our power. Our Stuart was gone, now we were to prepare ourselves for Beryl. I had no idea how to do that. We'd always thought our 4 children would outlive us and I could find no reasonable answer to facing the death of a 2nd beloved child.

In November 1989, our little dog, Tandy, was snatched by an eagle. Although Beryl lived in Windhoek, I felt she deserved a proper explanation and wrote her a letter as she'd given Tandy to us as a gift:

'The trauma over Tandy is still with me. I wake to visions of all sorts of things that disturb me greatly. Dad says nothing, but I'm still feeling very tearful at any given moment. He asked me to accompany him to see the new bulls he was buying from a Brahman Stud about one-and-a-half hours drive from Kambingana. We left at 9 in the morning. We couldn't take Tandy with us as usual as the Brahman Stud people had 2 Rottweiler dogs, a Fox Terrier, and 2 cheetahs wandering around their fenced garden. I, personally, took Tandy and locked her in our bedroom, instructing Francisca not to let her out. When Francisca went to clean our bedroom, she let Tandy out into the house. Simultaneously, Mattheus came home on the motorbike from checking the reservoirs, tanks and drinking troughs, and parked in the garage. Francisca was beating out carpets on the front veranda and never heard Mattheus return. He opened and came through the back kitchen door to fill in the daily Water Report Book as usual. Tandy ran out into the back garden – and Mattheus had forgotten to close the garden gate.

When we arrived back home at lunchtime, we started the frantic search for Tandy. Each second, minute and hour that ticked was almost unbearable, hoping upon hope that we'd find her. We searched for 3 days. Dad was devastated and I believe he knew there was no hope. Tandy's little footprints showed clearly she'd first gone up to the workshop to find Dad; from there, down to the kraals where he usually worked on the cattle. After that, we couldn't find where she went. Dad sent out a search party. Eventually, Tandy's tracks were found again, by 3 men on horseback – she was evidently on her way to Steinhausen. Dad and I each took a car and searched the main farm roads as far as

Omitara. He also searched the camp where Tandy had been, and I took the other dogs and a police whistle, and walked the veld, calling and whistling.

Osire, one of the horsemen, then saw an eagle eating something on the mud wall of the small dam near the house. He went closer and the eagle flew off – leaving Tandy's remains. Tandy's tracks showed she was on her way back from a neighbouring farm, getting closer to home. She'd reached as far as the small dam when the Martial eagle took her. Osire brought Tandy's remains back, and laid her on the step of the back verandah. I heard a knock on the back door, and found her entire, picked-clean little skeleton, her complete head still attached, her dear dust-covered eyes open. I wrapped her in a blanket and cried and cried, waiting for Dad's return. We buried her under an ornamental peach tree. I cannot explain our feelings of loss, except to say that at least we had found her, for which I'm most grateful to Osire, and were able to lay her to rest close to us, safe in our garden.'

The irony of Tandy and the Martial eagle is that I'd been asked to do the water-fowl bird count twice a year for World of Birds in London, also taking note of the eagles, and had been keeping an eye on a female Bateleur Eagle at Boomlager. She was now broody. I'd watched her through binoculars since the only egg had been laid. To do this I'd have to stop on the main road and climb up onto the car roof to see exactly what was happening in the untidy nest, quite visible on the flat top of a tall Acacia (thorn tree). When she saw me approaching, the eagle would hunch down thinking I could no longer see her. It had taken 4 years for the egg to be laid, and by my reckoning took 54 days before the chick hatched.

In November 1989, Keith's military career came to an end. Having attained rank of Captain in September 1987, and then successfully completing his Major's course at the School of Armour in Bloemfontein he was due for his Majority, but with South West Africa's impending Independence from South Africa and voters ready to cast their ballots in November 1989, he was de-mobbed. Nevertheless, he'd enjoyed his training in the South West African Territorial Force and found that Operations particularly was to his liking as he could use his mechanical, hunting and bush-craft skills and past experiences better. The Major's course he considered to possibly be the best and most satisfying achievement of his lifetime as it tested him physically and mentally. Having only started his military career at the age of 30, Keith felt he had an advantage over his younger trainees in most areas and was often referred to as 'Dad'.

The Labour Lawyers had sorted out the problems on both Mr Bonadei's farming properties and, thankfully, all returned to the good relationship we'd previously had with our staff on Kambingana. Our labour force of 9 men and their wives and women including 2 old crones plus Francisca were eligible to vote and geared up to go to the polls. Francisca was 'very happy' about it. Many of the white community felt the same as us; positive and prepared to accept the changes which were inevitable. This was our home – South West Africa had been good to us. Yes, we'd had some testy times with our farm staff, but generally we had an excellent relationship with them. Since coming to the country, never had we experienced any really ugly or outright 'anti' behaviour by the African people towards ourselves. We'd worked with all the staff simulating being at a polling booth, making the cross then dropping the sealed ballot paper into a cardboard box. Everyone had enthusiastically joined in, full of wonder at such a great happening. The 2 old crones were absolutely over-awed and had difficulty writing the cross. Many times we practiced, as I painstakingly held the pencil in their fingers to do the pressing and move their hands to form the 'X' correctly.

Ian worked out all the arrangements for getting to the polling booths in our area and Simon, the headman, was in charge of staff transport and getting everyone to cast their vote as I had a dental appointment the same morning so Ian and I travelled in another vehicle. When they came back they were most disgruntled! We were told that a policeman stood at each booth and watched them make the cross where he said it should go! We had to explain that there was simply nothing we could do to change that situation.

Benjamin's mother, Constantia, came and had a lengthy discussion with me about his circumcision. He was 18 now, the time had come. It was custom for the young men to be circumcised, then they could take a woman and prove they could father a child. Likewise, a young woman had to fall pregnant to prove she could give birth before any marriage could take place. But, Constantia felt afraid, expressing concern about Benjamin being held down for the procedure as he'd 'kick like a donkey' and the job would be botched. She was of the opinion that I could order arrangements for the operation to be done in Gobabis Hospital because there were so many 'bad experiences with tribal ritual circumcisions'. I think she was also under the impression I had jurisdiction over Simon, Benjamin's father, regarding this procedure.

Discussing the matter together with Simon, he stated categorically that his son must return to Hereroland and join the other young men, all of them to be initiated and circumcised. Benjamin and Constantia were away 2 months. On their return, Benjamin was very weak, thin and could hardly walk – a very worrying state. There was no need for me to examine him. Straight away, I put Benjamin in the car and drove to Gobabis Hospital where he spent 2 weeks. Constantia gave me details of the ritual circumcision. The foreskin is pulled forward and cut off with a knife by the tribal 'doctor'. The wound and penis are then dressed with a salve made from scraping the fat from milk, which is kept in a calabash. As the milk sours and is poured out, it leaves a Vaseline-like unguent around the rim of the calabash, collected with a finger, and when mixed with ash forms the salve. The young men stay apart from the community for a certain time. Noticing Benjamin's deteriorating health, Constantia decided to come home to Kambingana where she knew I'd help her.

The doctor told me Benjamin was very lucky to escape the consequences of septicaemia (blood poisoning) which could have killed him. Benjamin had always been rather special in our family. He'd played with our grandchildren, gone horse-riding and fishing with them, been taught his letters and numbers and, much later, how to drive a car, though on the farm only. We'd had some trouble with Benjamin which we considered due to 'politics' in South Africa, and were proved right as his 1st child, a baby boy, was named 'Nelson' in honour of Mandela. This was the mother's 2nd child, so she and Benjamin could now marry under Herero custom. Benjamin's younger sister, Okarapo, was never circumcised (a custom in some African tribes).

Thinking about Okarapo and female circumcision (female genital mutilation/female cutting) reminded me of the time when I was a young girl in Kenya and my harsh Aunt May had a discussion with Daisy on the matter when we went to visit her on their farm, Aggetton. I listened intently. Aunt May with her nursing expertise had experienced many problems when assisting young African girls who'd had the customary circumcision procedure as they haemorrhaged or had become infected, and the adult women had numerous other complications. A number of women struggled with childbirth. My mother had to cope with a few difficult African birthing problems as well. I remember that a number of women died during childbirth. Newspapers at the time were beginning to take note and report on these tragedies. My worst memories of this conversation were Aunt May's graphic descriptions of the actual circumcision and resulting scarring – the frightful state of the stretched, healed skin tissues, terrible disfigurations left when healed and the inability to give birth without serious problems and long protracted labour.

Aunt May had asked and had been accepted by their farm workers' wives to witness the female circumcision ceremony (done separately to boys). Only females were permitted. The young teen maidens or girls chosen were separated. Big wood fires were kept burning in a specially chosen area near the river and there was much dancing and chanting (in the stony shallows of this same river, Dawn, my cousin, youngest of Aunt May's children, would take me to wallow there in the mornings when I stayed with them). The chosen girls were naked and after some time of dancing and chanting they were required to stand in the river at waist deep level till about 2 in the morning. This was to numb them. Then an old woman, experienced in performing the procedure and a recognised and revered member of the tribe (in keeping with traditions) used the same piece of sharpened hoop-iron to very quickly remove the clitoris from each girl who'd been held down by other elder women. Aunt May stressed that the hoop-iron was rusty and that the procedure was done vigorously and quickly in a swiping motion. The circumcision would eventually add value to the bride price. (Hoop-iron is iron in long, thin strips used for binding casks/large barrel-like containers).

South West Africa gained Independence and became Namibia on 21st March 1990. Ninety-five percent of the electorate had voted. SWAPO took 57.33 percent of the vote and 41 seats in the Constituent Assembly. Sam Nujoma was elected the 1st President of Namibia. A number of changes were ordered by the new Government. Farm working hours were cut down to city office hours. No work to be done on Saturdays or Sundays. In the long run, we had more leisure hours too, but it was definitely detrimental to the farming routine. Unfortunately, agricultural properties require more than office working hours with weekends off! New laws stipulated anyone in employment or who wished to remain in employment, such as ourselves, had to be a Namibian National/Citizen or had to have been born in Namibia, and dual nationality was not allowed. We already had Identity Documents. Ian and I made a trip to Windhoek to see the British High Commission – Ian to set about getting Namibian citizenship; I kept my British passport. Keith had already become a Namibian citizen; Mary kept her Irish passport.

Beryl had met a wonderful Englishman, Edward Webber, early in 1990. After a whirlwind 2 month romance, they'd married in a private registry office ceremony. Edward changed her life so much for the better in many ways. We remain grateful to him for his commitment and complete dedication to Beryl and Stuart. Though quieter in character than Beryl, Edward has a steel resolve, and a positive approach to all aspects of daily life. Being a marathon Events Organiser and participant runner, it was inherent in Edward to never give up no matter how long the road nor steep the climb in life's challenges. Enjoying the outdoors himself, Edward understood and accepted Beryl's love of animals, her dogs, parrots, lorikeets and horses and actively engaged in every part of her life, doing together the things she loved. With an executive position, Edward was also an excellent provider. They had a beautiful home, with much-needed house help for Beryl. It was so good and a great relief to us all to see this deserved happiness for them both. Beryl looked well, appeared to be physically stronger and her emotional standing had strengthened amazingly.

Just before her birthday on 23rd June, Beryl started coughing and becoming short of breath. The doctor telephoned and suggested I go to Windhoek to look at her lung X-rays. They were a mass of marble shaped cancers. Immediately, Edward put a mattress in the back of his bakkie for Beryl and headed to Cape Town, driving through the night. They stayed with his sister. Further medical investigation revealed a tumour as big as a golf ball at the junction of Beryl's bronchi. Under Dr Gouws at Karl Bremer Hospital, she was put on steroids and her radium, chemotherapy and other treatments intensified, leaving her debilitated and mentally weak, a shadow of her former self. Her beautiful long dark hair fell out leaving little tufts; her naturally small frame shed weight alarmingly. The Windhoek oncologist said there was little hope. A Durban oncologist told me on the 'phone it would be better for Beryl to have a quality of life rather than further treatment which in the end would prolong her life by only 9 months.

Dr Gouws had told her, "Don't worry, whenever you cannot breathe, come down to see me."

Edward: "Bee had also bought a magazine in which was an article titled, 'The Golden Bullet', describing the research of Dr Gold from Syracuse University in the USA, regarding a compound called Hydrazine Sulfate. I contacted my good friend, Dr Linda Eglin, who I'd first met at Lake Turkana (previously Lake Rudolf, Kenya) in the early 1980s. I gave Linda Bee's medical history and weight etc., and she in turn telephoned Dr Gold and discussed Bee's case with him. Dr Gold gave Linda a dosage based on Bee's weight and relevant medical information. I was able to buy a kilogram of Hydrazine Sulfate from Johannesburg for maybe Rand 10 or Rand 20. A Windhoek pharmacist measured out the dosages, filling capsules for us. Within days, Bee could eat again and started putting on weight. She also took very high doses of Vitamin C throughout her illness. On our next trip to Cape Town, Dr Gouws was stunned by Bee's improvement, almost disbelieving what he was seeing."

Beryl also found a diet from Holland, the 'Moolman Cancer Diet' – she was only to eat absolutely natural foods like brown rice and tea, no coffee or chocolate etc. This also improved her strength and well-being and in time she even took up cooking, following the diet sheet meticulously. She dyed her short hair blonde; it really suited her small, fine featured beautiful face.

Edward would make the long 18 hour drive with Beryl in the bakkie on the mattress, her faith in Dr Gouws implicit. I looked after Stuart taking him to school, caring for her animals and going to the stables twice a day while they were away. Dr Gouws and I had several conversations and I cannot think how it was that Beryl survived for so long her body regularly bombarded by these ghastly high dosage treatments, particularly the radium. Seeing her suffering felt agonising. It was impossible to understand how she must have felt, but her smile and optimism remained undaunted and she never indulged in self-pity. Whatever lay ahead, Beryl faced with a positive outlook, coping with the side effects, hard as they were, as they came – there were times she could hardly eat or keep food down, other times her breathing was so poor it was heartbreaking just listening to her inhale or exhale. Her pillar of strength was Edward. Ever at her side, there was nothing he wouldn't do to help his beloved wife in her fight to live. He was truly remarkable in his unending love and care for Beryl in this most trying, difficult and extremely sad time in her life.

With her strength improved, Beryl again was able to keep herself fully occupied with her horses and animals, running her home, taking care of Stuart and his schooling, and enjoyed canoeing on the Kambingana dam. Then, amazingly, she rode in the Otjivero Endurance Marathon on her horses 'Mellone' and 'Mango Pip', a distance totalling 120 kilometres, over 2 days on the weekend of 4th and 5th May 1991. Mango Pip was a lovely new horse Edward had bought her which she'd found in Gobabis. Beryl's biggest problem wasn't the ride, but getting Mango Pip into the horse box after the event, which took ages. She rode Mellone on the Saturday, the first day of the 60 kilometre endurance marathon, then Mango Pip on the Sunday, again for the 60 kilometres. The event was held under the Rules of the Endurance Ride Association of Namibia, Beryl being issued with a Certificate for her ride on Saturday, 4th May 1991, her recorded time 4 hours, 23 minutes and 25 seconds.

It took a year for Ian and me to get over the loss of little Tandy to the eagle. First, in November 1990, 'Pammy', a happy, healthy Dalmatian puppy came into our lives, closely followed by another Miniature Pinscher pup, 'Ticci', in extremely poor health, malnourished and close to death, again as a gift from Beryl to her father. Both dogs had arrived by air from breeders in Johannesburg, a 2 hour flight. Living in Windhoek, Beryl had not physically seen the Min Pin prior to departure; all was dealt with by the breeder, and a Veterinary official who'd seen the pup signed the relevant papers and passed Ticci as healthy. Throughout that first night with Ticci, I stayed up, keeping her wrapped warmly, feeding her through an eye-dropper. She pulled through, thank heavens, and Pammy took to mothering her. I took a series of photos of Ticci's appalling condition on arrival. Some years later, I produced the pics when an investigative team was gathering information for a national TV documentary regarding the very poor practices of certain dog breeders – I'm sad and ashamed to say this dog cruelty and abuse still continues.

Ian and his brother, Ron, from Mossel Bay, decided to go on a fishing trip to Terrace Bay in mid-April 1991. I stayed behind on the Ranch to look after things, besides it would be nice for the 2 brothers to have some time together. They returned 2 days earlier than planned. I was surprised. Ron stayed only a few nights then left for home.

On 1st May 1991, Ian put his cigarettes down on the kitchen table and said he'd quit. For 2 weeks he went through severe withdrawal, but never lit another cigarette again. Then he told me he'd collapsed on the beach at Terrace Bay 3 days before they were due to return, the reason why they'd come home earlier. I immediately made an appointment with our family physician, Dr Barnard, in Windhoek where Ian underwent tests. He had only 15% lung capacity left. Keeping to a sensible diet and no longer smoking he started to feel better, was enjoying his food and gained a bit of weight.

If you stood or sat near Beryl the rattling sound in her chest was easily audible, each breath shallow. Her Windhoek oncologist had put her on liquid morphine. Beryl would take sips straight from the bottle whenever she needed it. I particularly recall a stay-over visit some time earlier, when I was washing Beryl one night in the bath at their house, her tiny frame so frail and fragile. I most remember her dainty feet and toes and how lovely she was even in the extremity of advanced cancer. It was a peaceful time together.

I was soaping her back and she was enjoying sitting in the warmth of the water when she suddenly softly said, "Mum, I don't want to die."

Mothers are supposed to have answers for their children or be able to find the right words, but none adequate came to me. Instead, I let the touch of my hand and the sponging of water on Beryl's back offer my comfort and solace to our loved daughter in her lonely, frightening heartache. If only we'd had a magic wand.

Edward and Beryl headed to Cape Town again in June 1991 for another cancer treatment. Late one afternoon, Beryl collapsed and was hospitalised at Karl Bremer. When I heard the news, I telephoned Lindsay around eleven at night, who'd moved to Cape Town in 1990. Her children were in a country boarding school. She straight away went to the hospital. There she found Edward beside Beryl, asleep in a chair with his head on the bed, holding her hand. He looked utterly exhausted, but was reluctant to leave Beryl's side even for a minute. She was on oxygen and morphine, resting quietly.

In the morning, Beryl confided that her greatest wish was to go home to Windhoek. Edward and Lindsay discussed the matter with Dr Gouws and were told that her time had come, that she should go home if that was her wish, though he was concerned that her heart might not cope in her frail condition with the take-offs and landings of the flights. Edward would drive back alone to Namibia. Lindsay returned to her flat and after several hours had made Beryl's complicated flight arrangements for the following day, with the correct medical assistance, nurse and oxygen requirements on board. I was at Edward and Beryl's home in Windhoek with Stuart, as she'd asked, together with Ian and Mary. From our side, we arranged medical flight arrival assistance and home care with a Namibian hospice. Anxiously, we all hoped we'd manage to get Beryl back home in time.

Edward and Lindsay were in constant telephone contact and Lindsay received a specific message to please visit her sister that afternoon to relieve Edward a bit so he could go home, shower and change, and also to be sure to bring some chocolate and coffee for Beryl, neither of which she'd consumed since keeping to her specific diet. Lindsay 'phoned me before she left for the hospital again. She'd ring me later from the call-box in the passageway outside Beryl's ward.

A little after 7 in the evening the 'phone rang and Stuart answered saying, "Aunty Linds wants to speak to you, Granny."

The moment Lindsay said, "Hello, Mum," I immediately knew Beryl had gone. She'd died in Lindsay's arms with calm, brave grace, coherently asking that her morphine be administered and the oxygen turned up – before Edward could get back to the hospital to be at her side. Lindsay held her and told her how much we all loved her while she played with Beryl's short curls, her hair back to her natural dark colour. It was 18th June 1991, five days before her 37th birthday on the 23rd. Lindsay said she looked truly beautiful and at peace when she finally laid Beryl's head to rest on the pillow.

Edward: "The evening before Bee died, at around 9 or 10 o'clock, Dr Gouws was on his rounds with 2 nurses. Bee talked about life and her thoughts for about 20 or 30 minutes, maybe more. It was the most beautiful and moving monologue I've ever heard. Dr Gouws and the nurses were in tears as Bee's insights into life were truly stunning. Later, the nurses told me that Bee was one of the most amazing people they'd met or treated. They'd never heard anything like it from a patient and had never before seen Dr Gouws with tears in his eyes."

We think 12 year old Stuart could not take in the news of his mother's sudden death. In heartbreak there is still disbelief. When he returned to school, he read out a short speech about his mother after Assembly. His teachers and classmates were deeply moved.

Edward: "Well before our last trip to Cape Town, Bee had said to me that if anything happened to her, she didn't want churches or ceremonies. She wanted only that I spread her ashes in the hills above Elisenheim where she rode Mellone and Mango Pip. Shortly before she died, Bee had also bought a silver trophy cup for the Riding Club. They said they'd hand it out as one of their annual trophies each year."

Linda, Edward's sister, informed him that the undertakers for the hospital was the firm 'Human and Pitt'. On hearing this, Edward said Bee would have laughed at the name. Such was her sense of humour and positive approach to everything in her life right to the very end – so Edward chose the Plumstead undertakers, Goodall and Williams, instead. Edward collected Beryl's ashes from the Cape Town Crematorium then drove the long road home. He was shattered, wanted to grieve privately and said he'd walk high up in the scenic hills and wished to be alone. They'd been married a little over 14 months. As he scattered Beryl's ashes, a little Steinbok leapt out of the bush and ran off. We like to think Beryl's spirit had entered that exquisite, delicate little buck. As a baby, Beryl, and a newborn Steinbok had been reared on the same milk formula. 'Bambi', as we called her, had grown into a beautiful animal with 2 sharp little horns. She was eventually given to the Kenya Regiment at Lanet Training Camp near Nakuru, and was their mascot till she matured and wandered off to find a mate.

Edward has remained a caring son-in-law and will always be part of our family. His love for Beryl and the joy he brought into her life, we will never forget. We had a beautiful handwritten inscription for Beryl entered into the Book of Remembrance at the Cape Town Crematorium.

Every night, no matter where I am, I faithfully make the time to go outside and look in wonder above me – 'Telescopium' is a gigantic constellation made of millions of stars far away in another galaxy. I find within me a peace which comes from knowing that high above, bright in light and warmth is our precious daughter, Beryl Marjorie, etched forever dear in the heavens.

"Know ye herewith that the International Star Registry doth hereby re-designate star number *Telescopium RA18h7m30sd-48° 30'B to the name* Beryl Marjorie – Know ye further that this star will henceforth be known by this name* this name is permanently filed in our Swiss vault* and recorded in a book which will be registered in the copyright office of the* Library of Congress* in the *United States of America* In witness whereof we hereunto set our hands and affix the seal of the*International Star Registry* this 6th day of December 1982."

Chapter Twenty-Two
Our Lives for Africa

Early one Sunday morning, Ian and I were still in bed when there was loud, insistent banging on the back door.

"Did you hear that?" I asked, giving him a nudge.

"Yes," he answered, sleepily, "I'm getting up."

I glanced at my bedside clock. "It's only just gone seven!" I said, turning over to face his side, pulling the sheet up under my chin.

"No peace for the wicked," he answered, another of his favourite sayings, as he got off the bed.

"Why is it always Sundays when there's a problem?" I observed. "You'd think everyone would enjoy a lie-in." I closed my eyes and snuggled my head into the pillow, hoping for another 5 minutes. Perhaps Ian could sort out whatever it was quickly and come back to bed. Even the dogs weren't ready to be up yet.

"It's one of the men," Ian said a couple of minutes later. "He says, *hy brand* ("he's burning")."

Brand in Afrikaans can mean 'fire' or 'burn'. I took it to mean the latter.

"All right, tell him I'm coming now," I replied grudgingly, turning over and pulling back the bedclothes. I sat on the edge of the bed a few moments then reached for my dressing gown.

Ian was back at the bedroom door. "He says, *hy brand, hy brand!*"

"Put your hand to your forehead and ask if it's his *kop* (head) that *brand* and I'll bring the thermometer and some Disprin," I replied, going to the Medicine cabinet.

Ian returned again, a bit frustrated now, "I don't know what he's going on about. He's quite agitated saying, *ja* (yes) *hy brand onder*."

Onder in Afrikaans can be either 'under' or 'below'. I took it to mean the former.

"Sounds like a temperature," I concluded. "I think he means he's burning up, not under, I'll see what else we've got." I was longing for my coffee. All we had was Disprin which would have to do and was quite all right to bring fever or a temperature down. My bladder was bursting.

"Are you in the toilet?" Ian asked from outside the closed door.

"Yes, I'll be finished in a moment," I said, reaching for the loo paper.

"I'm getting fed up with this," he replied, "he's just about doing a dance out there. Now he says, *nee* (no), his forehead isn't burning, it's *onder*."

"Just ask him, *onder wat* (under what)?" I said, pulling up my knickers.

"How long are you going to be?" Ian queried.

"I'm just washing my hands," I responded. Really, all this performance so early on a Sunday morning, can't do a wee in peace, no coffee, the sun was hardly up! I heard some talking outside then the hallway door slammed loudly.

"Oh dear," I thought to myself, "Ian's really had enough now." Imagine my surprise when I opened the toilet door to find Ian almost in hysterics, wiping tears of laughter from his eyes.

"And now…?" I asked, tentatively, standing still.

"*Onder wat*?" he guffawed.

"Yes, *onder wat*?" I repeated, starting to giggle just looking at Ian. What set him off, I wondered?

"He says, *hy was onder 'n bos met 'n ander vrou* (he was under a bush with another woman), it's his *kop* below that's burning!"

I put my hand over my mouth, not wanting to make too much noise. "I'd better call Gobabis Hospital then," I laughed softly, reaching for the 'phone. "Tell him to wait a bit, but you'll have to stop laughing first, you can't go to the door like that."

The Hospital advised us to bring the patient the following day, Monday. In the meantime, I gave Ian some Disprin tablets to give to the fellow; whether it helped or not I haven't the faintest. Ian drove the worker 360 kilometres (there and back) next day and the man received a Rand 20 injection. A week later, I drove him to the Hospital again for his follow-up 'shot', another Rand 20. The man's wife was furious and came to the house to see me about the situation. It took a lot of persuading to mollify her and became a major scandal amongst the staff. Come pay day, the cost of the injections was deducted from his wages. Company policy, unfortunately, didn't cover medical expenses for infidelity resulting in sexually transmitted diseases (STDs), but would foot the fuel bill for the 720 kilometres! The situation worsened when the wife realised her husband was Rand 40 short on his pay money, and so her berating started once more. That set Ian off laughing again!

The day my Ford Cortina silently caught fire with me at the wheel then burnt to a smouldering wreck before my eyes was one of the most surreal experiences of my life. I'd left Kambingana early that morning to get to my Book Club in Windhoek. We'd had some trouble before with the Cortina when mice invaded it whilst parked with the other vehicles under the carport alongside the garage, though none of the other cars were affected. Perhaps the Cortina had a 'soft spot' the rodents could get through. I'd taken the car into Windhoek to the agents who removed all the seats and checked everywhere thoroughly. Two drums of waste litter, stuffing materials, papers and dry grass from the mice damage were found. We assumed the problem was solved, though this wasn't the first time mice had been up to their tricks. They were plentiful on the farm and kept the cats occupied and fed.

As Ian's salary and finances improved over the years, he'd also bought me a large Yamaha electric organ with its stool which stood between the dining room and lounge. A few music books came with the organ. Self-taught, I'd learnt to read sheet music and play reasonably well, later adding some books of popular tunes to my collection. I enjoyed this musical creativity enormously though limited my early attempts to while Ian was out and about on the Ranch so as not to drive him mad with repetition until I'd gained sufficient practice. Lindsay had taken music lessons as a child so when she visited she also played the organ a bit and the grandchildren loved tinkling on the keyboard as well. A day came when the organ no longer produced sound followed not long after by an unpleasant smell and investigation turned up a dead mouse and chewed electric wires. As the instrument was too big we couldn't cart it all the way to Windhoek for repairs. At the time, I never gave a thought to mice perhaps also getting into my Cortina to build their nests, let alone chew through electrical car wires!

My most vivid memory of the last tinkling of keys on the organ was the 3rd visit from our farmer friend, Mr Human, who'd previously been stupefied when young Miss Piggy fell into the milk bucket followed by Tootsie-Wootsie with the potty. He'd popped in again one morning to say hello. Ian was out working the cattle. Once more, we had tea in the lounge and I think Mr Human was somewhat disappointed to find a 'normal' household with no unusual pets or weird happenings. When he clapped eyes on the Yamaha he said he played the organ so I asked him to give me a lesson.

"It's so easy," he assured me confidently, sitting down on the stool.

What he did was just diddle-diddle all over the keys, pressing any old note up and down the keyboard, swaying back and forth exaggeratedly. I had to keep a very straight face when thanking him.

"It's a pleasure," he replied smiling.

Both of us knew he'd no idea whatsoever! That was the last time he visited us.

As an avid reader, I'd joined a Book Club in Windhoek and usually left very early in the morning giving me time to still do my shopping after lunch. Ian had filled the Cortina with fuel so I'd be able to get home on one tank. This particular morning, he was continuing drilling a borehole at Karamba. I'd done about 30 kilometres on the dirt road heading for Omitara and was just approaching Kurt and Carola Kronsbein's turn-off up to their farmhouse on Apex (about a kilometre off the main road) when I noticed flames coming from under the dashboard, almost touching my right knee. Putting my foot on the brakes I found there were none, so I cruised to a halt at the entrance to their farm. I'd time just to collect my handbag, dark glasses, take the car keys from the ignition and get out. I tried to open the boot to remove the spare tyre, but the metal was too hot to touch. By this time, I decided it was safest to get at least 100 yards away, expecting an almighty explosion. Looking at my watch I noted it was 09h35.

On the same morning (I'd later learn), Kurt had decided to paint the interior of their house. The painter made a casual comment, "There's a car burning on the road," and Kurt told him to get on with his work and stop imagining things! Ten minutes later, the painter this time adamant, told Kurt that the car was now really in flames.

Going outside to check, Kurt found there was, indeed, a car burning, exactly at the entrance to his farm. Clouds of black smoke were reaching to the sky, looking much like the scenes on television that had made headline news of the oil wells being destroyed by Saddam Hussein's invasion of Kuwait! Kurt dashed down the road, and having surveyed the situation, said it was too late to attempt saving the car. He stayed with me till 10 past 10, by which time the car was a burnt-out wreck then drove to his machinery garage and brought his tractor and a heavy trek chain to hitch up the car skeleton and pull it right off the road. One of his staff swept up the oily black ashes into a neat pile, about 18 inches wide and 6 inches deep, onto the side of the road. As a memento, I took a very decorative piece of the windscreen, which resembled a stalactite. From Kurt's house, I telephoned the Insurance Company, and Kurt also spoke to them. Then I asked him to please take me to where Ian was drilling for water. Ian was absolutely speechless when I told him what had happened. It took me months to really comprehend what I'd witnessed.

Once the insurance investigation was completed, it was determined that the cause of the fire was directly related to mice. They'd gnawed a small hole through the plastic fuel pipe, which in turn dripped petrol onto the hot manifold thereby igniting a fire. Insurance paid us out Rand 3,000 more than the car had cost. I bought a good tumble dryer and the remainder went into my banking account.

After Ian had completed the changes to the Land Rover Forward Control 101 for our fishing trips, he'd bought 2 old Mercedes Benz cars and restored them to their former glory. The cream colour Merc he'd given to Keith; the second one, for ourselves, he'd spray painted a canary yellow saying it was unlikely to be stolen being such a bright colour. It certainly was easy to spot no matter where one parked. Just as well, because since the Cortina caught fire, the Merc was our mode of comfortable, reliable travel. Ian's enjoyment at building cars also added a yellow beach buggy to the list of these achievements.

Francisca had become such a help with the morning medical parade and took to being a nurse-aide like a duck to water. She clearly and quickly understood what she had to do and became recognised and respected by the staff, loved helping me and most of all doing these things on her own. Francisca could take temperatures and pulse rates then tell me the problem. If I couldn't deal with the ailment, we'd take the patient to Gobabis Hospital.

Constantia arrived one morning in a terrible state, out of breath and quite shaken up, her naked, kicking and screaming fat little boy clinging around her neck. She'd been trying to cope with the toddler who'd had such a bad bout of diarrhoea that his rectum was now protruding out of his anus. I managed to get a quick look then sent Francisca for the jar of Vaseline. The child wouldn't let me come near him and was now biting his mother as well, so Francisca held him down while Constantia, using Vaseline on her finger, pushed his rectum back inside his anus. Instantly, the toddler was quieted, and off went Constantia to her house in great relief, her child on her back, as quiet as a mouse.

Ian's blind eye had begun worrying him, so Dr Joffe in Windhoek performed laser surgery in 1991 to replace the lens and after about 37 years of no vision in his right eye, Ian's sight was restored which was utterly amazing to both of us.

My eldest brother, Neville, died on 14th October 1991 after a short illness borne with fortitude and no self-pity, a sad end in a Cape Town hospital having only sips of water and refusing all food. Thankfully, his daughter, Fern, was with him. His last years were lived at Bainskloof, a beautiful area of mountains in the Cape with running rivers and forests, just what he most loved.

A year after Beryl's death her horse, Mellone, developed heart trouble and died. Mango Pip was kindly bought back by the Gobabis farmer. Stuart had gone to live with his father, Koos, and wife, Tilly, in Johannesburg and would spend a holiday with us on the farm.

There would be more sad news. Old man Dempers had passed on a while back and now his son, our dear, long-time friend, Boertjie Johan, died also having fought cancer bravely. Lindsay had sat with him during one of his chemotherapy sessions in Cape Town and was so pleased to see him again. He will always be remembered by our family for his kindness, generosity and true friendship. His family left to live in South Africa and I've not seen them again.

Then Mr Bonadei lost his fight to cancer and passed away in a Cape Town hospital. Ian and I attended his funeral together with some of the Kambingana men who wished to pay their respects on behalf of all the staff. His son, Mario, took over the business. Mrs Bonadei moved to Cape Town – we missed them both very much.

Constantia became very overweight and could hardly walk. She was breathless and spent a lot of time lying down so Simon asked if I would take her to the doctor. Having made an appointment, we left for Gobabis to see Dr Nel at 11 in the morning. Constantia was examined then Dr Nel asked me to come into his consulting room. He explained that her blood pressure was sky high, common amongst Herero women. The remedy was to lose weight fast and do some walking. Back home we went with sufficient medication for 2 months. I took the ration store keys and called Constantia. Together we stacked on the table the equivalent weight of 40 pounds in wrapped Holsum cooking fat (the blocks of cooking fat each staff member received with their rations). She did not understand what I was doing or for what reason, but said nothing.

I said to Constantia, "Do you see this fat?"

She answered, "Yes."

I explained to her that this is the amount of fat you are carrying and Dr Nel says you must go on a diet and lose the weight in order to get better. She could not believe her ears or eyes. By showing Constantia graphically it brought home to her exactly what she needed to understand.

"So," I continued, "from tomorrow you start a new diet and I will be making your food for the next month."

The blocks of Holsum fat were left on the table, and when Simon came to do the weekly rations distributions, I showed and explained to him what Constantia had to do. I decided Constantia would only eat soups, drink black tea and coffee and 2 litres of water a day. From 4 teaspoons of sugar in every cup, the poor woman had to drink bitter tea and coffee. I made soups every day in the huge pot I'd brought with us from Angola which could hold 10 litres of liquid when full. There was a stack of kudu and beef bones in the freezer and plenty of fatless venison. All vegetables, including the skins, green tops and stalks were boiled up and the fat from the marrow bones was skimmed off. Constantia had to walk to my house and back again 3 times a day for her extra-large mug of soup she had for each meal. She was so good at sticking to this diet that within 2 months she was back to normal weight. I admired her. It had been a tough time for Constantia and I know she was grateful. She sincerely thanked me every day.

One morning, Francisca brought me a fledgling sparrow she'd found outside the laundry room, fallen out of its nest. It was wet and bedraggled and I put it in the cleavage of my bra. It soon warmed up and some time later when I felt the little body moving about, I found it had quite recovered. Now I could get a good look at it. Still covered in fluffy growth there were signs of wing feathers forming. I guessed it was a naughty little cock sparrow, probably getting ahead of himself a bit and taking a tumble from his nest. I named him 'Cheepy', swatted a few flies, stuck them on the end of a tooth pick and fed this new little family member. That night, he slept snugly against me in my bra. Next day, he was as chirpy as could be, so I fed him mainly on minute pieces of beef mince, only when he demanded feeding. Now I made him the perfect house inside a calabash (I hollowed out the shell of a gourd, the seeds of which I'd brought from Angola) with a round hole cut out on the side and put in an old kikoi (loincloth from Malindi days). Wherever I went around the house, I took the calabash so Cheepy never felt lonely.

Going to Windhoek for a day's shopping etc. initially posed a problem, but that was solved by keeping Cheepy in my handbag. During lunch at the Kalahari Sands Hotel Restaurant, he would pop out and get some morsel from us to keep him quiet. When we went away on fishing trips, Cheepy and his calabash would accompany us. That way he felt free to fly off wherever we were, but never went far away, and we only had to call him. At home, his favourite game was to sit on the bench near the telephone in the hallway which led out onto the front verandah. I put some seed in a shoe-polish tin on the bench and water in a tomato puree tin, for easy access. Here, Cheepy would taunt the other cock sparrows till eventually they'd come nearer and nearer the seed tin. Then Cheepy would pounce and fight, holding on to his opponents tightly with his claws and clasping them with his wings, all the while the 2 sparrows rolling around in a ball of feathers with much harsh squawking and shrieking. When his opponent was really tired and let go to fly out the door back into the garden, Cheepy was so chuffed with himself as the clear winner.

Cheepy's sparrow 'chatter-talk' was a series of cheeps, and the manner in which he cheeped meant different things. At 6 in the evening, Mattheus would start the electricity generator and I'd turn on the small television in the kitchen – we'd replaced the black and white TV with a colour one. This was Cheepy's quiet time. Like clockwork, he'd fly in and perch on the back of Ian's maroon office chair at the kitchen table, where he'd stay and watch the changing colours on the television till it was his supper time. Then I'd put him to bed in his calabash house for the night. He'd settle down immediately and with a few tiny cheeps he'd go to sleep, there to stay till first light. I learnt quickly that if I covered his doorway, he'd stay put and silent until I opened up in the morning, giving us a little more time before having to rise at 6.30. Whenever I had my afternoon rest, whether outside on a stretcher in the shade or on my bed, Cheepy watched and waited for me to lie down, then he'd fly onto my chest and hop up to nestle in either one of my 'salt-cellars' (the two natural hollows) above my collarbone. There he'd snuggle down and have a nap of about 30 seconds (we timed it), then he'd be up and onto my cheek and pull my eyelashes so that I'd pay attention to him, then he'd hop back for another short nap. Only when I got up from my rest did Cheepy fly off and amuse himself! I just adored him.

In time, Cheepy began mingling with all his friends and relations then started staying out at night. He'd outgrown his calabash. Probably he found a mate, we hoped so. Occasionally, I heard him cheeping, but always from a distance. I will treasure forever the wonderful times of friendship, companionship, love and joy we had with this dear little sparrow.

Jeremiah, our excellent camp man, became ill and returned to his Tswana home. Surprisingly, we didn't hear from him, and because he was the only Tswana the other staff never heard news either. We missed him very much. He was a good horseman, and quiet in his manners. Because he wasn't with us on our camping trips any more, we adjusted our holiday routines. With Ian's health no longer what it used to be, he gave the Hobi-Cat to Keith, and Johari, our sailing boat, to Lindsay for her son, Brendan. We stopped setting up camp and tents and instead hired fully equipped bungalows when we went away fishing.

At lunchtime one day, a bakkie rumbled to a stop outside the back gate. I opened the kitchen door to find a stranger asking for the boss. Ian heard, and came out to speak to the man who explained that Jeremiah was lying in the back of the vehicle outside and wanted to say goodbye because he way dying. Ian went out to see Jeremiah who was unable to sit up. Two days later, we heard via the 'bush telegraph' that he'd died. We were all very sad, the whole episode having a sombre effect on the staff. I was shaken. It had all happened so quickly. Ian made no comments other than that he was glad Jeremiah had come to see him.

Vi and Marge came to stay again, as well as Ron, Ian's brother from Mossel Bay. We'd all been away for a few days fishing and were on our way home, us 3 women in the yellow Merc, Ian and Ron in the big Ford bakkie. Along the Omitara stretch about 15 kilometres from Kambingana, was a stationary BMW and standing in the pouring rain an African woman waving for us to stop. The road conditions were so bad I dared not pull over for fear of getting stuck in the mud, so as I drove very slowly past her I merely stuck my head out the window and shouted, "Wait, my husband is behind me," as I knew Ian and Ron would help. It was now nearly 4 in the afternoon. About half-an-hour after we arrived home in drove the Ford trailing the BMW with the lady and her 2 children. Later, Ian told me the BMW had run out of water and the engine had seized. He and Ron had a hell of a job in the mud and rain turning the immobile car around and hitching it to the bakkie with a long tow rope.

Everyone came into the kitchen. The lady's name was Ripanga and she was drenched to the skin. Marge and Vi hustled around finding every item of suitable clothing from their wardrobes while Ripanga had a hot shower. I got coffee brewing and rusks ready. Ripanga said she was the Finance Minister's wife and that she and their children had gone to visit friends. On the way back to Windhoek the car had just stopped at the place where we found them. Her husband was in Lusaka, Zambia and wouldn't be back for 4 days. Ripanga and her very well behaved children stayed in the cottage, which I quickly prepared for them. We thoroughly enjoyed their company. They settled in quite happily, and Marge taught Ripanga how to crochet coat hanger covers. The son aged about 14 watched television most of the time, while the little girl clung to her mother. They all spoke perfect English. The son attended St Paul's English Private School in Windhoek.

Meanwhile, Benjamin had been to see me at the kitchen door, saying in Afrikaans, "Do you know these people are part of our family?"

I was busy making scrambled eggs at the time. Vi, Marge and Ripanga were in the sitting room with the children where endless and happy conversations took place since they'd been staying with us. I popped into the lounge and said to Ripanga, "If you and the children would like to visit Benjamin you are most welcome to do so."

Ripanga was sitting on the floor at Marge's feet having a crochet lesson. "Thank you, but no thank you," she replied immediately shaking her head, and continued studying the movements of Marge's hands as the crochet hook caught the wool and pulled it through in loops. So, that was that, and Benjamin didn't query having no visit from 'his family'.

On the 4th day, Ripanga said her husband surely was home by now and could she telephone. Yes, he was back and immediately sent out to Kambingana a low-loader to retrieve the BMW. Then he arrived in another BMW to collect Ripanga and the children. The goodbyes were quick, and away they went, with many thanks to us. We had a lovely surprise a few weeks later when in drove a BMW with Ripanga's husband at the wheel. He unloaded a whole lot of lovely vegetables and fruit for us in grateful thanks. He also told us that Lusaka's main street was in a terrible state of disrepair – unlike Namibia. Ripanga never forgot us, and whenever she saw us in Windhoek she would chat or wave her greetings.

In July 1994, we decided to take a trip to Henties Bay on the coast for 2 weeks and rented a holiday house. After a few days, the wind started to blow becoming a full-blown sandstorm that raged for days. It made no difference if you closed the doors and windows, the sand filtered in throughout the house from the ceiling down. The effect on Ian was horrific. He became seriously ill, hardly able to breathe. We packed up and headed home to Kambingana.

The sand in his lungs sent Ian into a downward spiral and he seemed unable to recover. I gave him a haircut as I'd done all our married lives. Then in early August, I took Ian to see our Dr Barnard in Windhoek who immediately sent us to the State Hospital. Ian was admitted, during which time he saw the attending Oncologist who ordered a scan. After a very grim 4 days on TB (Tuberculosis) treatment, Ian 'phoned to say I could collect him. The Oncologist did not speak to us before we left for Kambingana, but had prescribed sufficient TB medication for 30 days with instructions to make another appointment the following month.

Back home, I looked at Ian's x-rays and read the covering letter which clearly stated he had 3 patches on his lungs. Since I'd not personally been given the opportunity of discussing Ian's condition with the Oncologist and cannot read x-rays, I immediately contacted a long-time school friend in Radiology in Tel Aviv, Israel, and forwarded her the report from our State Hospital Radiology Department. By return, Ora Leshem telegrammed to say 3 of their doctors were of the opinion it was too late for Ian to have any form of operation.

It was a Saturday morning soon after that Ian decided it was the right time to gather the staff together and tell them he was a sick man and that he didn't know how things would continue. The men were clearly bewildered and silently went back to their houses. We informed the company Ian was struggling with his condition. By the 15th day of the TB medication he was hardly able to breathe, had great difficulty in moving and was unable to lie down on his bed. At night, having had a sedative, Ian slept upright in his recliner chair which Francisca and I had taken from the lounge to our bedroom, relieving his pain and condition a little.

I then drove to Windhoek, where with the greatest difficulty, stress and searching for the Oncologist, I finally located him, who only now told me my husband had cancer and was terminal because his condition was so far advanced. I was angered that the adverse effects of the TB medication had caused even greater unnecessary suffering for Ian and straight away went back to our house doctor who took over. By now it was late evening, and I was given sufficient morphine, and the strongest pain medication and sedative capsules. Later that week, the company paid for the transport of the special phials of Pethidine sent by Dr

Barnard, to be injected when the pain became unbearable. Ian told me to throw the remaining 15 TB tablets in the 'donkey', they'd almost killed him. I was instructed by Dr Barnard to keep a strict record of all the medication I gave to Ian and the times they were administered.

Ian's health was deteriorating, so we paid for Lindsay to come from Cape Town on the bus on 18th September 1994, to spend 5 days with her father before his condition became worse. When it was time for Lindsay to leave for her return bus trip from Windhoek, Ian was sitting at the kitchen table. They'd said their farewells.

"Better get going now or you'll miss your bus, my girl," her father said.

Lindsay walked slowly to the kitchen door then stopped, stood a moment, turned and went back to her father to hug and hold him again. It's tough facing the coming of an end to the life of a loved one, especially one's father. She didn't dare look back the 2nd time as she walked to the kitchen door.

From now on, it was life one day at a time. The company sent me a driver who stayed in the cottage. Ian was now driven around, giving his instructions and watching the work from the tail-gate of the bakkie. His last physical job was to castrate a young bull calf. For years, Mattheus had been doing castrations with Ian. Now he'd be put to the test and Ian was to check whether Mattheus could do the job. Next day, on his only attempt, Mattheus botched the surgery and the calf died from loss of blood.

Keith, who was out of Namibia at the time working at the Sadiola Gold Mine in Mali, obtained compassionate leave to fly home immediately, and with Mary drove from Windhoek to see his father for the last time. Forever etched in my mind is the scene when Keith says goodbye to his father, drives off almost through the farm gate then suddenly slams on brakes, jumps out of the car and walks back to give his father one last hug. Then they were gone and we were alone – Keith back to Mali and Mary to her home now in Windhoek. Ian put his arm around me and ever so slowly we walked back into the house without speaking. There simply were no words to convey what each of us was feeling and thinking.

Ian now gave me certain instructions, things to be done on the farm and how they should be carried out and sorting out issues pertaining to our personal lives and business. As far as was humanly possible, despite being so ill, his greatest concern was for my future alone and he wanted matters to be in order for me when he died so that his Estate could be finalised with as little trouble and delay as possible. He made a simple Last Will and advised that he'd set aside sufficient cremation funds, locking this in the safe in a marked envelope. All documents of importance were put into my name and I had signing rights on his cheques. He also arranged for the sale of the Land Rover Forward Control 101 and his woodworking machinery, tools and the beach buggy, then no longer made any trips to Windhoek.

For 3 weeks, I took over Ian's job, and through me the staff carried on their duties without fault. I know that Francisca kept them fully informed as to exactly what was going on in our house regarding Ian's health.

I telephoned Dr Barnard daily, and also kept Lindsay in Cape Town fully informed so she could book a flight immediately to Windhoek when I felt her father's time was near. Three days before the end, I had to ask dear Francisca to give me a helping hand with Ian.

On the morning of 18th October 1994, Ian got up for the last time. He liked and wanted to say good morning to the staff as they came, one by one, to the back door. Then he went back to bed. They accepted now whatever I told them and what they had to do on the farm. Dr Barnard, in this morning's 'phone call, told me to prepare myself for the worst and that home and his own bed were definitely the best place for Ian to be and rejected outright any suggestion that I bring him to the Windhoek Hospital.

As soon as dawn broke on the 19th, I knew this would be *the* day and 'phoned Lindsay immediately to book her flight. Pammy, our beautiful Dalmatian dog, instinctively knew as well because she lay tightly beside Ian the entire day, never once getting off the bed.

Lindsay's flight was booked for the afternoon, no earlier connection being available. She'd manage to get to the farm before 7 in the evening, being collected from Windhoek airport by the company driver.

I administered Ian's morphine and Pethidine and lay beside him, and when he slipped into unconsciousness, the dogs and I were with him.

The minutes ticked by as we anxiously waited for Lindsay to arrive – now came even more distressing news that her flight had been delayed by 2 hours from Cape Town.

Five hours later, with Lindsay's aircraft flying over Namibian airspace ready to land in Windhoek, Ian died at 5 minutes past 7 in the evening as I held him, our dogs, Pammy, Ticci and Dumbo beside him. After he'd drawn his last breath and his chest was still, Pammy set up a primeval howl of such eeriness that it still haunts me to this day – how can I ever forget.

Arriving in the dark after 9 at the back garden gate with the driver, Lindsay was met with the devastating news that her father had died before she could get home to be with us at the end. If the plane hadn't been delayed, she'd have made it. She spent some time alone with her father and Pammy in our bedroom. The 2 of us slept in Stuart's room in the twin beds, while Pammy remained outside our closed bedroom door the entire night howling on and off in heartache as we waited for the funeral parlour staff to arrive.

Well before 7 on the morning of 20th October 1994, their vehicle arrived and parked at the front garden gate. I fetched Ian's clean pyjamas from his cupboard and asked that they dress him in these later for his cremation. Pammy went into our bedroom to say her final goodbye and once more set up her primeval howl.

It was heart-wrenching to watch Ian's lifeless body wheeled on the stretcher from our bedroom, past us in the hallway, covered with a white sheet, down the garden path and placed in the back of their van. Lindsay and I remained fixed on the clouds of dust behind the funeral van on the dirt road as we struggled to hold with us forever one last glimpse of the man we both loved so very much.

Going outside a little later, the staff due to start work at 8, we found Benjamin sitting in one of the chairs on the front verandah, sobbing his heart out. They'd all seen the funeral van arrive. Lindsay put her arms around him in comfort, then made him coffee and sat with him for some time until he stopped crying. I think the reality of the loss of a wonderful boss and friend, and an unknown future suddenly hit all the staff as they each came, in turn to the back kitchen door, to pay their respects, old Munde dipping his hat in sadness, his stubbly beard now white and his face well wrinkled with age.

They weren't alone, for the magnitude of it now hit me. I no longer had a mate. My beloved husband, whom I'd been married to for 42 years, who'd walked with me through so many days, trials, tribulations, moments of fear and uncertainty, occasions of little and others of plenty as we shared a lifetime of vivid memories, happy and sad, the births and growing of our 4 children, then the painful loss of 2, our comfort being one another.

I suddenly realised I'd no longer be cutting Ian's hair, hear him laugh at Van der Merwe jokes, see his dear smile or have his quiet, unfailing strength of character to turn to come what may, and his total reliability and responsibility in everything. I no longer had the privilege of caring for Ian and no one to care for me. Death is final. An unfamiliar feeling of being afraid settled within me. Different to fear, it was how would I face an unknown future and life alone without Ian? I'd have to sell as much as possible, go through the stress of winding up Ian's Estate and I no longer had a home. The whole outlook was bleak in the extreme. Added to all this, I suddenly developed excruciating pain in my knees.

We were left bereft, and the grieving intensified and continued as the sense of loss became more profound. Lindsay made many 'phone calls and Omitara Exchange assisted efficiently throughout – to Keith, the company, and family and friends as we set in place arrangements for Ian's Memorial Service. I will always remain grateful to the funeral parlour for arranging Ian's cremation in the afternoon of the same day they fetched his body from the farm.

I had a meeting with all the staff and told them that I too, was leaving and that a new Manager would soon be taking over. I impressed upon them that in almost 20 years of service, Ian had always been at work on time, and that the only day he missed by not turning up, was the day before he died. All his clothes and shoes were shared out amongst the men and each received a knife from Ian's selection of good carving knives. I gave Francisca our bedroom suite and each staff member a farewell gift of money.

Packing up my furniture and possessions became a priority as I was expected to be out of the house and moved to the cottage in about a week. Lindsay, Francisca and I packed morning to night, the boxes and furniture stored at the workshop with the help of the men and the company driver.

I sent for old Munde's wife, Angelina. Ian knew that as long as he was Manager on Kambingana, Munde's employment would be guaranteed until he could no longer physically work, but when the day came that a new Manager took over, Munde Paulus would be retrenched due to his advanced age. He'd been in the area 50 years and with us for almost 20. Over some years, Ian had prepared for this difficult time in the old man's life by quietly setting aside, each month from Munde's wages, funds into a Savings Account in his name at the Post Office in Omitara. There were now 2 savings books.

Angelina arrived, ever respectful in manners as her husband, Munde, and beautifully dressed in her traditional Herero frock and head-dress. She and Munde, both now unemployable, were beside themselves with anxiety. Lindsay took her into Stuart's bedroom where Angelina preferred to sit on the floor, as is their custom, her skirt billowed around her. In Afrikaans, Lindsay explained fully, several times over, about the money Ian had put into the Savings Account for old Munde, how she could withdraw the funds at the Omitara Post Office, to try to be careful with the savings to hopefully help towards their future without an income, and very importantly, to try not to let old Munde spend the money on alcohol.

Very touched and extremely relieved that Ian had thought of Munde Paulus and made this provision for them, Angelina thanked us most gratefully. My heart felt so much better too, knowing they had a better chance now as they too packed up their possessions in readiness for their trip by donkey cart to the settlement outside Omitara near the newly built dam.

In all the heartache came another trauma. Little Dumbo, her muzzle grey, sight and hearing poor in her old canine age, somehow was missed being seen going out the back garden gate amidst all the carrying of boxes and furniture to the truck to take up to the workshop. She was used to going with Ian around the farm and waited patiently for her ride with him. The company driver, not noticing her behind the back of the truck, reversed over little Dumbo. We were numbed with shock as we later stood beside the hole dug for her in the side garden, near the duck pond. It was a monumental double sadness how Ian and our little old dog, Dumbo, went to their final rest at the same time.

Ian's Memorial Service was held on 26th October 1994 at the Windhoek Chapel. It was attended by many people. Benjamin, dressed smartly in a suit and wearing one of Ian's shirts and tie, came with us representing the farm staff. Afterwards, Sheila and Heinz Wächtler, a dear Windhoek couple we'd known for some years, gave a luncheon at their home for me and a number of close friends who'd attended Ian's Service. I'd met Sheila through the Windhoek Book Club and she and Heinz had a cherished place in our hearts. Ian's ashes were scattered in the very special Rose Garden and a marble plaque was erected on the great semi-circular Wall of Remembrance. One of the Old Mutual Senior Consultants later paid tribute to Ian at a specially-called meeting in Cape Town wherein Ian was upheld as an example of how people, when faced with terminal illnesses, should conduct their financial affairs.

With the new Manager, his wife and 4 children expected to arrive the following day and Lindsay due to return to Cape Town in a couple of days, the 2 of us and the dogs now completed our move to the cottage. Francisca cleaned the house thoroughly and I took a final walk around our garden.

Memories of having arrived almost 20 years ago to barren dust and a small sorry-looking patch of grass at the front of the house had been replaced with greenery and splendid colour surrounding the entire homestead, a wonderful testament to old Munde's years of tireless care and patience even though he suffered from arthritis in his hands. He had much to be proud of in this work. Daisy always said, "A house isn't a home without a garden," and I had to agree with her. Our Namibian garden held many special memories. The thorn tree was older and bigger, the garden birds more plentiful and their happy chatter louder. I hoped the new Managers liked birds and gardening, but at the same time I realised perhaps our efforts would not be continued.

The Manager's wife wanted the chickens so I left those for her. She also asked that I leave our 4 cats as she said they'd be good for keeping snakes away – the cats hardly came to the house having the whole farm as their hunting ground and a plentiful supply of mice.

I quite accepted that I must leave the house, as the quiet time in the cottage would serve me well to mourn privately. My time on Kambingana had come to an end and I would have to move on. Pammy and Ticci were my life now and we 3 slept together each night, silent in our sorrow without Ian.

Francisca worked full-time in the house for the new Manager and I missed her daily friendship, chatter and happy smile. She'd crocheted 2 lovely bright-coloured woollen blankets for me as farewell gifts (which I still have in 2016). Angelina helped me in the cottage a couple of times a week. Sometimes, I'd find Angelina, in her time off, just sitting quietly on the cottage front verandah floor her Herero dress billowed around her. She sensed my heartache and I appreciated this caring and sensitive gesture of companionship from her.

Living at the cottage was a truly grieving time in my complete loneliness. Looking back, I know it was very necessary. My lovely German friend and neighbour, Edda Bohn, who'd brought me Jawsie as a fingerling, came over a couple of times in the late afternoon and we'd walk together with the dogs on the sandy roads which ran along the fence lines. So loving, Edda brought me sustenance in some of my worst moments. I treasured her wonderful conversations.

Keith would be home again in December from Mali. I'd stay in the cottage till then. Perhaps we'd holiday together along the coast for a bit then I could maybe spend some time at Edward's home in Windhoek. My furniture would go into storage until I needed it. Special friends in Windhoek gave me a farewell lunch.

Shortly after the new Manager and his family moved into the house, they dug out the shady established grape vine that we'd planted and nurtured for so long covering the long pergola from the kitchen door to the back gate and some of the trees we'd put in, convinced they were snake havens. I found it easier on myself to avert my eyes from that direction.

During my weeks of solitude in the cottage, and particularly when I sat having my evening sundowner now alone, I went through a kaleidoscope of jumbled memories of my life with Ian as the vast Namibian bush silence surrounded my isolated heartache. Some moments I'd be on a high and could smile or even laugh a bit at happy flashbacks, other times I was plunged into overwhelming sadness.

I remembered Ian's dedication to nurturing the game stocks on the Ranch. His favourite music – 'Paper Doll' by the Mills Brothers during our courting in the early 1950s in Kenya, Jim Reeves, Engelbert Humperdinck, Elvis Presley and Bert Kaempfert's very popular album 'A Swinging Safari' played so often during our lives in Malindi. Ian's back-breaking commitment to our Angolan Fazenda; our wonderful family holidays at Kenya's Lake Rudolf; the rightful decency and care he'd shown to our staff wherever we'd lived; how he always gave the dogs a tiny piece of Wilson's toffee after lunch sitting on the edge of our bed; his inner strength of always getting up and on with life no matter what; his enthusiasm in jumping off the train to visit me, his young sweetheart, so many years ago, his suitcase of clothes falling open on the ground all the watu laughing at the funny sight.

The night before I left the Ranch, I'd found a sense of peace to move forward, albeit somewhat fragile, and realised the need to not only mourn, but also to celebrate Ian's life. I would love and miss him always. He'd be with me wherever I was.

Sitting outside on the cottage verandah with our Dalmatian, Pammy, and little Min-Pin, Ticci, I watched the sun sink low then disappear in dusky colour over the thorn trees as daylight drew to a close, and raised my glass to toast my husband, a truly good and honourable man who'd loved and devoted his life to his family and this great continent of Africa, proudly following his father, William Alexander's, example.

As Daisy's daughter, I'd been privileged to share such an amazing journey and could say with certainty, "To Ian, Our Lives for Africa."

I sat a while in the tranquillity of Namibia's night and patted the dogs.

"Time to say goodbye to Kambingana," I said quietly, voicing my thoughts.

Pammy and Ticci immediately looked at me expectantly, sensing a ride in the car, which had my mind turn to the Bateleur Eagle I'd been keeping an eye on for some years. She'd recently laid a 2nd egg, to be seen only by standing on the roof of a vehicle though this time I wouldn't witness her chick in the nest. I hoped she'd remain safe and well.

As we made our way inside to bed for our last sleep on the Ranch, 2 tails wagged and Beryl's star twinkled in the sky – with me the light of 3 precious lives, Stuart, Beryl and Ian – as we bade farewell to *The Place of the Water*.

Chapter Twenty-Three
My Lionel Carol

After leaving the Ranch, I holidayed with Keith and Mary a few weeks along the Namibian coast then I spent a month at Edward's home in Windhoek staying in his granny flat. Keith and Mary then helped me move to a suburb of Cape Town, South Africa where I shared a house with Lindsay and her children for a time.

Here I met my second husband, Bill. We married in Natal then settled in the small town of Greyton in the Western Cape. At the time of our marriage, Bill was Britain's youngest surviving Victoria Cross holder, decorated by the Queen for bravery during the Korean War. On a week-long celebration visit to London with him, I had the great honour and pleasure of meeting the Queen Mother, Elizabeth, who hosted a tea at St James' Palace in May 1997. She'd been present when Ian won his Farmer's Weekly medal so many years ago in 1962 at the Eldoret Royal Agricultural Show – our 'Kirriemuir Winkie' was crowned Champion Dam above all other cattle breeds. The reason the Queen Mother spent so much time chatting to Ian on that occasion was that his Kirriemuir cattle originally came from the Queen Mother's cattle bloodline. I was a spectator in the stands so didn't meet her then.

At the St James' Palace tea, Bill and I spent about three-quarters of an hour in most enjoyable conversation with the Queen Mother, each in turn sitting next to her. I told her I remembered the frock she'd worn that day in Eldoret – white with little violets and green leaf motif. She was so chuffed about this. I also related to her a short story Robert Foster had told me of the time he'd visited a *mzee* ('old' in Swahili) African gentleman in his hut one day at Lake Ol'Bolossat. Hanging on the wall was a picture of King George VI, the Queen Mother's husband.

The mzee gentleman beamed with pleasure when Robert asked him about the picture. "My Kingie Georgie," he'd responded with pride. Tears came to the Queen Mother's eyes on hearing this little tale. We also shared the fact that we both had mandarin ducks in our ponds, and that we'd each broken a leg, my leg being in a plaster cast at the time as I'd had a fall at home 3 days before flying to England with Bill.

The Queen Mother showed me her tiny hands saying, "They look like this from mucking out the stables all those years." I found her to be adorable, with beautiful violet blue eyes. These are wonderful and honoured memories for me.

My chosen sedentary lifestyle was oftentimes frustratingly tame for Bill, and I struggled to adapt to life with someone else after Ian. After 16 months, Bill and I parted and divorced amicably. Nevertheless, we shared some happy times together.

After 4 years in Greyton, I moved to the town of Caledon 35 kilometres away in 2000, where my efforts saw the opening of a branch of the SPCA (Society for the Prevention of Cruelty to Animals). I adopted an ageing Chow dog, Chinky, his black tongue alarming many people despite being a loving and gentle companion. Dearest little Ticci died of heart failure after an attack of Biliary. Having a soft spot for Min-Pins, and given time, Candy, a 6 week old black and tan puppy joined our family. Beautiful Dalmatian, Pammy, and Chinky, individually, reached old age with its accompanying ailments and went to rest peacefully with the assistance of my trusted vet, though Chinky unnecessarily and cruelly suffered kidney problems brought on by melamine found in dog kibbles, the source of this being traced back to East Asia.

Whilst in Caledon, Kambingana featured in the South African YOU magazine. Unfortunately, I misplaced the article. In time, the property was bought by the Government as part of the land resettlement programme, no longer being a cattle ranch. I never closely followed news of the Ranch after I left and the little that filtered back to me initially was that 2 of the 3 bakkies were written off and the new Manager didn't stay long. Then with the land resettlement, one occupant had a few goats, another 26 chickens, and the farm later become a squatter camp. Naturally, I hold dear memories of Kambingana and prefer to remember it at its peak when Ian was managing it.

Ron Rooken-Smith, Ian's elder brother (born 15.8.1926), died in Mossel Bay on 28th January 2001, only weeks after his wife, Joan (born 14.8.1927), passed away on 13th December 2000.

Vi packed up and left Malindi, Kenya, in 2001 with her son, Tony's help and went to live in Wallacia, New South Wales, Australia, with Tony and his wife, Sue. Vi died a year later on 13th April 2002 at the age of 92. Bertie had passed on many years before in Malindi on 10th July 1987; he was also Lindsay's god-father.

I visited my brother, Ken, in Natal a few months before he died on 27th March 2003. He'd been ailing for some time with a heart condition. Ken had taken good care of me as a child and teenager. I always looked to him as a father figure.

In 2005, I bought a house on a 2,273 square metre plot in the small Klein (Little) Karoo town of Willowmore in the Eastern Cape. Days before he'd died, Ian had said to me, "I remember a small town called Willowmore. Go and have a look at that." Starting from scratch, again, I established my last and most charming of all gardens despite living in an exceptionally hot summer climate with severe winter frosts. On 2 occasions, we even had snow, photos of which Mary turned into Christmas cards for me on her computer.

I nurtured and fed the many varieties of garden birds, and put in a large, shallow pond on the front lawn giving my feathered friends hours of pleasurable bathing with much preening and sunning of their wings accompanied by plentiful bird chatter. When all was quiet with no-one else around, a pair of Scimitar-billed Wood Hoopoes frenetically dug for grubs hidden under the lawn grass. Mouse-birds were the clowns, creeping around the bushes and trees playing silly games, eating fruit and flower petals. Four species of Sunbirds frequented the 3 syrup bird-feeders I replenished every 4th day. Two kinds of sparrows, as well as weavers, starlings and 3 types of pigeons, which bathed and dipped like ducks in the shallow pond, further enhanced this leisure time of mine when I'd done with the boring necessity of household chores. Two pairs of ground thrush began their song before break of dawn, and sang again after dark to end the day. The robins sneaked into the kitchen for bread crumbs I deliberately left on the chopping board, hopping about as they pleased, and in return, left their visiting card! Sometimes, the red-backed Mannikins came. Willy-wagtails meandered around happily and unafraid at my feet on the natural-stone verandah paving, and the Paradise Flycatchers nested and reared their young in the lush green canopy of the huge tree next to my bedroom window. There were no exotic birds or butterflies till I put down lawns.

I made some precious Willowmore friends – Philip Koen (known as 'Flippie'), Jean Strijdom and Zelda van Heerden. In 2006, at the age of 72, I bought a laptop after my hip replacement operation. Flippie has been invaluable to me with his computer expertise, patience and assistance. A most interesting character with an abundance of stimulating conversation, Flippie is also an avid stargazer. I've been privileged to enjoy enthralling Karoo nights with him out studying the clear, magical and vast heavens through his telescope.

Equipped now with modern computer technology and a printer, I started writing 'Daisy's Daughter, Our Lives for Africa' and pulled out the Family History printout Marge's son, Bruce, had sent me in the early 1990s at Kambingana. At the time, I'd simply glanced at it then put it away in a cupboard.

It was a devastating shock for me to read, 61 years after my beloved father, Lionel Carol's, death at the (young) age of 48 on 20th January 1945, having served King and Country long and valiantly in both World War I and II, that: 'At the outbreak of WWII he joined the EA Forces and was posted to the EAASC with the rank of captain and served in Abyssinia, being mentioned in despatches. Daisy divorced Lionel in 1942. He was court-martialled and found guilty of purloining WD equipment and sentenced to two-and-a-half-years imprisonment in Fort Jesus, Mombasa. He was released after two years and married a Mrs Chandler, a divorcee who farmed in Londiani. He contracted pneumonia soon after and died in the Nakuru War Memorial Hospital in 1944'.

Immediately, I noticed first the error in the year of his death. 1944 was incorrect, it was 1945. Next, Daisy told me after my parents divorced that my father had married a Mrs Chandler. I went to school with her 2 children. Something appeared wrong here with the Family History timeline. Mrs Chandler's son was about 4 years older than me. I remember after school assembly one day, specifically going over to talk to him because I couldn't understand why he could have my father yet I couldn't even see my Daddy. He spoke to me nicely, though his sister seemed distant towards me. I never saw Mrs Chandler so I've no idea what she looked like and didn't know her first name or even her initials.

After my parents' divorce, the subject of my father was strictly taboo in our house, so I knew that even if I wanted to talk about him, I should not. The only person who ever spoke to me about my father was my brother, Ken, and all the years, even when I was grown-up, Ken only spoke of our father with pride and in the most affectionate terms, often reaffirming to me Lionel Carol's strength and bravery. Looking back now, I noticed how these discussions only occurred when Ken and I were alone together, never in other company.

Since my father's death when I was going on 12 years old, I'd thought he'd become sick whilst fighting in WWII and died as a result of pneumonia. My father, imprisoned for stealing War Department equipment? My mind reeled in disbelief. As children, my parents had taught us to care for our possessions, treat the property of others with respect and that stealing was absolutely unacceptable. Ian's parents believed in the same values. We passed these teachings on to our children.

Having comprehended the enormity of this dreadful information, I had only one aim in mind – to find out the truth and the reason for my father's time served in Fort Jesus. Marge, being almost 19 years older than me, and we 2 being the only survivors of our immediate family at this time, she would surely know about this. But, on 'phoning her in Natal, I was told that all she knew was what was in the Family History and Bruce said the same. Terry (my brother, Ken's, son) also said the only thing he had to go on was what was in the Family History, but he felt it didn't make sense and didn't add up about his grandfather. Both Bruce and Terry had chosen military careers and were now living in Natal.

I felt aggrieved no-one had told me and that it had been included in the Family History without, as it seemed, any documentation to verify the information. At the same time, I felt overwhelmingly frustrated as none of my family appeared to know anything. It felt like being in front of an impenetrable wall, getting nowhere. But, the British are known for being sticklers when it comes to record-keeping. I felt very strongly that someone somewhere would have relevant records. I'd just have to stick to finding out no matter how long it took. This is an exceptionally important aspect of my life. I felt it imperative to face it head on, remove the shroud of secrecy and bring to the fore again the rightful memory of my father as a good man deserving of recognition. To start with, I'd try to get in touch with the Kenya Red Cross and Daisy's lawyers in Nairobi, if they still existed, and anyone from my youth that I felt may have heard something.

Delving into the history of Fort Jesus, I found it was a British Colonial maximum security prison of notoriety at the time of my father's incarceration. Construction of the Fort at Mombasa, Kenya, began in 1593 under Portuguese occupation to secure the safety of Portuguese living on the East African Coast. The Italian Architect/Engineer, influenced by the Renaissance era, designed the structure in the shape of a man (seen from the air) hence the name 'Jesus'.

Hostilities between nations fighting for control of Kenya from 1631 saw ownership of the Fort change hands 9 times. From 1837, it was used as barracks for soldiers. On 1st July 1895, the Fort was converted into a prison when the British Protectorate was proclaimed, the huts being removed and prison cells built. Inmates suffered deplorable conditions and harsh treatment, added to which was the dampness prisoners had to endure due to the Fort being built on a coral ridge at the entrance to the harbour. There were also torture cells. For 7 years, Fort Jesus was the only prison in the East African Protectorate. It was also used for custody of lunatics, vagrants and paupers, though they were separated from convicts. Prisoners sentenced to 6 months or more in any part of the Protectorate were sent to Fort Jesus. For convictions of less than 6 months, inmates served their incarceration in the barracks or forts of the towns where they'd been convicted.

Fort Jesus was declared a Kenyan National Park in 1958, became a Museum in 1963 after Independence, and was awarded UNESCO World Heritage Status in 2011.

In 2007, Dusty and Phoebe, 2 adorable Chihuahuas – Dusty with a long-haired coat and Phoebe short-haired – became canine companions to Min-Pin Candy as we shared an unhurried, quiet life in this Little

Karoo home I'd named *Pumzika* meaning 'Rest-a-while' in Swahili. It had ample garden space for them to run freely and keep them interested. Once a week for an outing, we'd go for a drive in the car which the 3 thoroughly enjoyed. Just picking up the car keys set off great excitement and they'd eagerly follow me down the garden path to the garage. All the birds in my garden became so tame they didn't object to the dogs. I also had a Cape grey mongoose sneaking about furtively amongst the plants for some time and would see him most days, which drove Candy crazy spending hours following his scent. The 2 Chi dogs, being so low to the ground, never glimpsed the mongoose.

On 23rd June 2008, Beryl's birthday, the constellation 'Telescopium' was in the heavens above my house at approximately 11.30 at night, almost the exact hour Beryl was born. Thanks to Flippie and his powerful telescope, this was a treasured occasion of star-gazing for me.

On 1st February 2010, Bruce emailed me a copy of the supplement to the London Gazette of 8th February 1944, page 672, which carried the information that: 'Lt. L.C. Griffin No. 82842 is cashiered by sentence of a General Court Martial on 28th January 1943 (substituted for the notification in Gazette Supplement dated 10th September 1943)'.

Terry sent me the Griffin Coat of Arms and another London Gazette article signed by the Secretary of State for War stating: 'By the KING'S Order the name of Lieutenant (T/Captain) L.C. Griffin, East African Army Services Corps, was published in the London Gazette on 23 June 1942, as mentioned in a Despatch for distinguished service. I am charged to record His Majesty's high appreciation'. Bruce informed me this was something to be proud of though I should bear in mind that thousands of others were recognised during WWII in the same way. Nevertheless, I was exceedingly glad to have it and know that something of my father's 2 loyal World War contributions was recognised. Coincidentally, the date 23rd June was my Granny Marjorie Aggett's and Beryl's birthdays.

Through Marge, Bruce advised that after my parents divorced in 1942, Military Police raided the barn at our Anchorage farm and found my father guilty of theft of only the outer casing of a War Department vehicle battery stamped with the arrow symbol. At the time of the MP's raid, Marge wasn't living at Anchorage, but farming with Harold on Merrowdown in Western Kenya. Their home was also raided by the MP's, but nothing was found. Marge said the battery casing in the Anchorage barn was old and broken, had been lying in the barn for years and was apparently found under some straw, and that at the time of finding it, the MP was speaking to my mother in the house while someone else who'd accompanied him had found the broken battery in the barn.

Even after 4 years, I still grappled to come to terms with my father's incarceration. With so little information to go on thoughts would crowd my mind as I tried to look at every possible angle. I felt something was wrong, it seemed unjust.

To deal with the straw – if the old battery was found under straw, it may well have looked as though my father had hidden it, but that didn't add up to me. My mother's sole ambition on Anchorage was that we be as self-sufficient as possible. One of her farming endeavours was growing wheat so we could have our own flour and porridge, apart from selling it for an income. Once the wheat had been harvested, threshed and baled in the fields, some of the wheat straw was kept in the barn. Vi lived with Daisy for some time, using the straw for her egg-laying poultry. It was also used for Daisy's imported Dutch seed-potatoes that were kept in the potato room on the floor in separate layers of straw till the potatoes grew 'eyes' and were planted out. There was a lot of straw in and out of Anchorage barn over the years.

Regarding the old battery – during WWII, my eldest brother, Neville (ranked Major), also served in Abyssinia (now Ethiopia) with my father and then in Burma (now Myanmar). He came home on several occasions. My middle brother, Terry (14th British Army, rank Sergeant, Temp Warrant Officer), was sent to Burma and died there in 1944 of typhoid fever before he ever got a chance to come home. Ken (a Sergeant), the youngest of the 3 (also 14th British Army), was posted to Burma too, but he didn't come home till after the war ended in May 1945.

My father and brothers were all mechanically inclined. Many Kenya military men during World War II visited Anchorage when passing through the area, and a vast number of Armed Forces soldiers on compassionate or ordinary leave were sent to my mother. Due to the long distances military vehicles were required to travel to and from other countries during the war, there were occasions when minor repairs were necessary. Military men, including my father and Neville, when returning home on leave used army vehicles. When Terry died in Burma and Neville came home to tell Daisy, Neville arrived and left in a military vehicle. I found it understandable that there were several instances where a military vehicle battery could have given trouble and required replacement and/or maintenance of some kind, hence a broken military vehicle battery casing being in our barn.

In the meantime, I'd contacted the Kenya Red Cross Association in Nairobi. A gentleman by the name of Nicholas Makutsa spent several months on the case, even telephoning me twice in Willowmore all the way from Kenya. The lawyers in Nairobi who'd assisted our family during Daisy's time and the divorce between my parents were luckily, and amazingly, still in business. My hopes were up. But, neither Nicholas, despite every effort and going beyond the norms of his duties, for which I am sincerely grateful to him, nor the lawyers could give me any details whatsoever, as there were no records to be found.

Nicholas finally advised, and with a heavy heart as he'd been so determined to help me realising my personal heartache, that all documents from Fort Jesus had been sent to Shimo-La-Tewa Maximum Security Prison, Mombasa, where a fire had destroyed all the paperwork. These 2 vital contacts were sadly a dead end, but I was determined to continue the quest to try and vindicate my father's good name and wrote to then British Prime Minister, Gordon Brown. He was helpful in putting me onto the correct Department, but they advised likewise, documentation was no longer available. I even contacted the school my father had been to, Hilton College in Natal. According to them, my father had an outstanding school record, but they too knew nothing regarding his Court Martial or time served in Fort Jesus.

Getting in touch with various family and all my dearest school friends and children I'd grown up with and whose parents knew my father and mother, I asked for any blunt information they may have to help me, no matter how painful to hear. All responses were the same.

None had heard anything regarding the matter and all were highly sceptical saying that the Lionel Carol they'd known was of good character and that theft was against his standard of personal ideals. Contacting my most dear friends and family whose parents had a very close relationship with my mother – Henry Hauschild and Sid Dyer now far away in Australia, and my cousin (Angel) Mary – they had no clue whatsoever what I was talking about. All were totally shocked.

Bruce very kindly arranged, without being asked, for someone in Kenya to photograph my father's gravestone in Nakuru North Cemetery and Terry emailed the photos on to me. I am most grateful to them both. 'In Loving Memory of LIONEL CAROL GRIFFIN who died on January 20th 1945 Age 48' – I wondered who'd commissioned the headstone. Perhaps it was Mrs Chandler, his second wife. My father's birth date was not recorded on his headstone. I found this very saddening as birthdays and birth dates had always been important in our family. It being during wartime though, perhaps there wasn't enough money for a lengthier inscription. My heart was relieved and more at peace though to see the words, "In Loving Memory..." – someone had cared enough to show that my father was loved and memories of him were held dear.

In 2012, Marge eventually told me that Daisy decided in 1945 when my father died that nothing should be divulged in order to protect me from heartache. Hence it remained what I term a pact of silence all the years, which is why my mother, Vi, Marge, Neville and Ken, or anyone else who knew about it, never said a word of it to me. When the details were typed into the Family History printout, it was assumed Daisy had told me when I'd grown up about my father's time in Fort Jesus prison. Unfortunately, she hadn't.

I could feel that Marge was between a rock and a hard place, torn between her loyalty to our mother, Daisy, and her big-sisterly love and caring for me. She knew I was in anguish; she'd always been there for me. She then added some further twists to the story. Gossip, or scandal, has it that my father, during his military time in WWII, had been friends with a married Colonel who had 'another woman lined up' and asked my father to 'take his wife off his hands'. The divorce between my parents in 1942 was instituted by Daisy apparently due to this other woman (this being the same year I last saw my father when I was going on 9). However, the alleged affair couldn't have amounted to much because she remained with her Colonel husband, and my father married Mrs Chandler. What seemed odd though, considering the significance of the other woman as the reason for the divorce between my parents, is that her name was not remembered. Even the Colonel's rank appeared not definitely recalled despite his being a friend of my father's, neither were the Colonel's Christian name or surname etched to memory.

According to Marge, the reason my father never came to visit me at Nakuru Primary School was due to the farm he moved to with Mrs Chandler in Londiani being a long way from Nakuru and Anchorage, and that the reason I couldn't go to see him at their house was because Mrs Chandler wouldn't have me stay in her home. Marge also confirmed that while my father was in prison she didn't know he was in Fort Jesus, but Neville, who served with my father in Abyssinia, would have known and therefore Daisy as well. In hindsight, logically my father wouldn't have been able to visit me at school regardless of Mrs Chandler's feelings towards me or her farm being so far away as he was in prison. If only I had known. There was no indication that anyone in our family had visited him in Fort Jesus. My heart ached at the thought of his utter loneliness. Even if I hadn't been able to see him, I would have written him letters constantly. Then he died on 20th January 1945 (the year I turned 12). I so much regret now not being told, nor being allowed to see him regardless of how sick he was. I could have put my arms around his neck and hugged him and told my Daddy how very much I loved him and always would forever. I know I would have been a comfort to him after all he'd endured. I feel guilty now for not being brave enough to ask my mother questions even though I knew I shouldn't.

As for Mrs Chandler not wanting me in her house, this too didn't make sense to me. My father gladly and willingly accepted as his own Daisy's 2 oldest children, Marge and Neville, and treated and loved them as he did Terry, Ken and me. He also took into our home 3 other children from our extended family – Sid, Patsy and Lesley (Uncle Frank's children) after their mother died. So it did not seem rational to me that my father would then marry a woman who refused to have his youngest child (me) in her home.

The story continued that when my father didn't 'take the Colonel's wife off his hands', the Colonel then had a personal vendetta against him. Even though my father was apparently forewarned by someone that the Anchorage barn would be searched, he made no attempt to remove the old battery casing or get anyone else to dispose of it on his behalf. The raid of the barn was conducted when he was not present.

Marge confirmed that Lionel Carol was released from Fort Jesus prison after 18 months (not 2 years as per the Family History) due to not only pneumonia but also malaria, and that he specifically asked for Neville to fetch him. Apparently, Neville didn't at first recognise our father. From a once strong and proud military Captain, he'd been reduced to a pathetic state of severe emaciation, his health seriously impaired. Daisy went to see him in Nakuru War Memorial Hospital and decided that I should not be allowed to see him as his physical state would have been too frightening for me. At the time, I remember much whispering about 'something' amongst family members so I wouldn't hear. Not long after, I was told my father had died.

This was the sum total of information I'd been able to acquire in 6 years regarding my father's time in Fort Jesus and the reason for his sentence. The punishment didn't appear to fit the crime or vice versa. Terry agreed – it still didn't add up. He had another source for information which he'd pursue and said we needed to be patient. I was prepared to wait no matter how long.

I still feel overcome with pain in my heart that my father suffered so in Fort Jesus. Considering his long-standing navy/military service to King and Country in Britain, Ireland, France (Battle of the Somme), East Africa and Burma during World War I and II, and South West Africa, didn't the British Government provide adequate food and medical treatment for him during his incarceration? I'm not surprised he developed pneumonia given the location of Fort Jesus and it being prone to damp. As for my father contracting malaria, this has always been a huge problem in Africa. When we lived at Malindi, not far from Mombasa, all 6 of us in our family had to take anti-malaria tablets regularly and sleep under mosquito nets. Even our Dachshund dog, Dumbo, slept under a mosquito net.

Had I been told all this after my father's death, or at least by the time I married Ian 7 years later in 1952, I more than likely could have had access to records. After I finished high school in Nairobi, I nursed in Nakuru War Memorial Hospital where Lionel Carol died. Three of our 4 children, Keith, Beryl and Lindsay were born in that hospital's maternity ward. Nakuru North Cemetery is not far from the War Memorial Hospital. I can't count how many times I walked from the hospital into Nakuru town and could have easily gone to the cemetery. I look back and see all the many lost opportunities up until 1973 when we left Kenya, especially when I was still at school or nursing in Nakuru, or when we lived at Uruku, Westlands or Malindi. At least, I could have taken flowers, had my father's date of birth recorded on his headstone and spent some precious quiet time at his graveside, giving our children the chance to come to know their grandfather just that tiny bit. Daisy had time with our children, except Stuart, who was born in 1960 not long after her death.

When we were living in Malindi, Ian and I once spent a whole week in Mombasa with Bob and Shirley Brown waiting for the ship SS Uganda to dock. Many times I'd thought of going to see infamous Fort Jesus. But, from what I'd heard of the torture cells and dankness, I had more a sense of broken and forgotten human life amongst those thick walls than any inquisitive or curious tourist need and shied away from the imposing landmark structure jutting out on the coral reef. I knew how beautiful Arab woodwork, doors and carvings could be, but even that aspect didn't pull me towards viewing Fort Jesus. The place gave me a distinct feeling of foreboding. Only now, do I understand why.

I met an elderly English lady, Mrs Katherine Fannin, one morning on one of my infrequent trips to Mombasa. Although she was extremely poor, she took it upon herself to collect fish heads, tails and bits and pieces to feed the starving cats in Mombasa. She told me that she also used to visit Fort Jesus where she handed out cigarettes to the prisoners, their hard labour being to break stones for road maintenance. Had I known at the time about my father having been incarcerated in Fort Jesus, perhaps she would have been able to give me some information. I learnt later that when the British Navy ships docked in Mombasa, the personnel were instructed to contact Mrs Fannin to see that all was well with her. It turns out she was quite famous.

All the years, Lionel Carol has lain forgotten, banished in the prime of his life, banished even in death. I think of his heartache and deteriorating health as he withstood the conditions of hard labour imposed on him those many days and long nights of solitude in the dark, dank, dampness of Fort Jesus. I hope that the love my father knew I had for him, his little daughter, gave him some measure of solace.

Also in 2012, at the age of 79, I bought a more updated laptop and experienced the technological wonders of being connected to the internet 24 hours a day. I realised what a truly amazing reference guide and learning tool the internet is and have since wondered how we coped before without Google, Google maps and Wikipedia. I've joined the ranks of the millions dependent on a computer to keep us up to date with information and in contact with friends and family anywhere in the world at the touch of a button.

My Min-Pin, Candy, reached the old age of 16 in 2012. Little Chihuahua, Phoebe, developed severe stomach complications in 2013 and did not respond sufficiently to treatment. Both dear companions of mine departed our world peacefully with compassionate veterinary assistance.

Marge passed away at the age of 97 on 21st August 2013. She'd lived an interesting life in 3 African countries and brought up 4 children. Not only had she been my dear sister, but also my lifelong friend, and loyal daughter and companion to our mother, Daisy. I remember many happy hours with Marge on holidays sharing the cooking, shopping and housekeeping, and the countless times we'd sat together chatting as we knitted jerseys for our children. Marge brought me up until the age of 6 and after Daisy's death in 1960 (15 years after my father's) it was always Marge who was the central figure maintaining our closeness and value of family. She is missed by many.

Realising my Willowmore home and garden were too big for me to cope with any longer at my age and facing a 2nd hip replacement operation, I sold the property and moved on 8th March 2014 to the little farming town of Albertinia not far from Mossel Bay in the Western Cape to be near Lindsay and her husband, Brian.

On 31st March 2014, Terry emailed me my father's Court Martial documents he'd managed to obtain from the UK. I'd been right, paperwork did still exist, and Terry had never given up the search. I am forever grateful to him.

There are thirteen A4 pages, the 1st noting my father's personal information and the rest being a Review (dated 11th November 1943, which, incidentally, is my father's birthday) of the General Court Martial held at Nairobi on 30th June to 16th July 1943 with a brief Minute Sheet of less than a page, summarising the various aspects of the case in 6 paragraphs (the author being 'JAG's Office' with an indecipherable signature dated 14th September 1943) and a Petition (which failed) from my father (dated 30th July 1943) addressed to the Army Council. Also included is a telegram to the War Office received on 8th February 1944, which advises that the Prison Governor reports the character of ex Lieutenant Griffin to be 'very good' and that he 'has worked well', noting his due release on full remission to be 26th July 1944 (at this time Lionel Carol had served 6 months). The final 4th point on a separate page notes that there appears to be no grounds for remission and asks the question, 'Do you agree that no remission be granted', to which someone with the initials DPS has written, 'I agree' with the date as 18th February 1944.

The date of my father's arrest was 11th April 1943 and he was committed to HM Prison (Fort Jesus) on 28th July 1943 – EAASC (East African Army Service Corps). The sentence was to be cashiered and to be imprisoned with hard labour for 18 months.

Army Courses: Army Bombing School, Amiens 1916 – Passed; Irish Command Bombing School, Dublin, 1917 – Passed; Army PT & Bayonet Fighting School, Aldershot, 1918 – Passed.

Previous Military Service: South West Africa 1914 – 1915; Enlisted 26.08.1916 2nd Bn The Black Watch; Commissioned 18th Irish Rifles 25.9.1917; France 1916 – 1918.

Awards: British War Medal and Victory Medal; Mentioned in Despatches for gallant and distinguished service in the Middle East including East Africa.

Wounds: Slight wounds and Gas, Somme.

I found it interesting to note that from 3.10.1939 when my father enlisted in WWII at Ol'Kalou to the date of his arrest in 1943, he had only been granted 10 days leave (in 1941).

Mrs Strange, 'wife of Major Strange', gave evidence as a witness for the Prosecution (at last I would at least know the surname of the 'other woman' and her husband as well as his correct military rank).

There were 5 Charge Sheets against Lionel Carol, the charges of which he answered fully, the details making sense and not coming across as being evasive in any way. I briefly summarise the outcome of each, joining together various aspects of the case, as a lengthy review here would entail many pages.

1st Charge Sheet – Guilty on three charges of stealing one rifle automatic Beretta and one cover, rifle, automatic Beretta (this is regarding captured Italian weapons when they were defeated in Abyssinia by the British – 'it was generally accepted that enemy stores and equipment could be taken away and everyone was helping himself' – this also refers to the 4th Charge Sheet). Acquitted (the evidence here was very vague) on one charge of allegedly stealing 251 yards of khaki drill (why would my father have tried to steal this – it just does not make sense), and one charge of negligently performing his duty where two Breda LMGs and one Lewis LMG were lost.

Regarding the Charges to do with Italian weapons, I have very firm memories of knowing people in Ol'Kalou district who'd served in Abyssinia coming back with all sorts of things including weapons – this was considered 'loot' – it was common knowledge and not considered criminal.

2nd Charge Sheet – Guilty on three charges in 1942 (three separate dates in June, July and August) of stealing a total of 52 gallons (236.39 litres) of Government (Army) petrol alleged to have been used in a private car at the instigation of the accused. This is when Mrs Strange gave her evidence – she worked in the District Commissioner's Office in Nairobi, half a mile from her residence and sometimes used her car to go to work, drawing permits for 16 gallons of petrol per month (later cut to 8 gallons).

My Toyota Tazz, as a comparison, has a 60 litre full tank capacity.

The accused said Mrs Strange gave him permits, as well as acquiring a smaller amount from his wife at his farm (Mrs Chandler's farm at Londiani). Mrs Strange said she never gave the accused any of her petrol permits and that on the one trip where she'd accompanied him she didn't know the petrol used was stolen. Mrs Strange further stated that the accused's wife (being Daisy) had obtained a divorce citing Mrs Strange as co-respondent and she was expecting to marry the accused, however, when divorced the accused broke off the engagement and she considered that he'd treated her very badly. On reading this, the old saying, "Hell hath no fury like a woman scorned" comes to mind.

The baffling part of these 'guilty' charges is that the CQMS (Company Quartermaster Sergeant) in charge of petrol and oil gave evidence that records were kept on issue of petrol, the date, vehicle number, amount of petrol drawn, driver's name or number and that it would not have been possible for an Officer to obtain petrol unless accompanied by the CQMS. He also stated that there was a 24 hour guard at the petrol dump and further that there was no shortage in the stocks in June, July or August 1942 (it seems this was completely ignored), but he agreed that there was usually a surplus – the monthly 'usually a surplus' or 'average surplus' was not asked for and not given voluntarily.

From this, I deduce that despite it being proven that no shortage in the petrol stocks existed for the indicated periods and dates in question, which would have been a 'fair' indication of theft of petrol (though not necessarily on the accused's part), nevertheless Lionel Carol was found guilty – or had the usual surplus been short by 52 gallons, again this would have been a 'fair' indication of theft (though again not necessarily on the accused's part).

The Defending Officer asked that 2 witnesses be called on Lionel Carol's behalf, being 'his wife' (this is Mrs Chandler – Daisy is referred to later as 'the accused's first wife') and a Mr Saunders, both of whom would have given evidence that towards the end of 1942 and beginning of 1943, Mrs Strange had a great animosity towards the accused. The Court refused this application.

Lionel Carol's Petition on these charges states that these 2 witnesses would also have sworn that on diverse occasions Mrs Strange had threatened him that if he married his present wife his life would be wrecked and that he was gravely prejudiced by this evidence not being before the Court; that the proceedings were actuated by malice on the part of Major and Mrs Strange; the Prosecuting Officer was heard to wager large sums with bystanders outside the Court that 'he'd put Griffin inside'; and that the convictions on these charges were contrary to the weight of evidence as there was no evidence of missing petrol at the material times and no evidence of theft.

In the 3rd paragraph of the Minute Sheet the author states the opinion that the evidence of the 2 witnesses was admissible and that the Judge Advocate was wrong in law in advising the Court to reject it, but nevertheless comes to the conclusion that it is not reasonably probable that the Court would have arrived at any other decision had this evidence been admitted and, therefore, no substantial miscarriage of justice occurred.

Personally, I find a miscarriage of justice here. Surely anyone on trial is entitled to witnesses to testify on their behalf otherwise the totality of evidence before the Court is unfairly balanced, blatantly in favour of the Prosecution. How can anyone be found guilty beyond reasonable doubt when no-one has been allowed to give evidence on his behalf, resulting in an imbalance of the scales of justice?

Finally on this point, I cannot see my intelligent father being 'engaged' to another woman while still being married to my mother as he was well aware of the shame and backlash from family towards Daisy when she had Neville as an illegitimate child. Mrs Strange being referred to as 'wife of Major Strange', indicates to me that she was still married to her husband at the time of giving evidence and I must wonder how she logically considered herself to have been 'engaged' to my father whilst still being married to her husband, as in order to marry my father she would have first had to get divorced herself.

3rd Charge Sheet – Guilty of four charges in May and December 1942, and January and April 1943, of improperly using military vehicles for other than military duty without previously obtaining a permit to do so; and four charges in May and December 1942, and January and April 1945 (April 1945 is not possible as Lionel Carol died in January 1945 – this must be a typing error, should be April 1943) of stealing the petrol involved in such use.

Here we learn that my father married Mrs Chandler on 3rd or 4th April 1943 in Jinja, Uganda, where he had to go for duty (Mrs Chandler travelled by train to Tororo, Uganda), preferring to get the marriage certificate from the District Commissioner there rather than at the DC's Office in Nairobi where Mrs Strange worked as they had quarrelled and it would have been too embarrassing.

In this section we have another incorrect date where a Captain gives evidence – it reads as 1.4.45 and is not possible as the accused was deceased by then, should be 1.4.43.

Evidence was given that only two hire permits were issued to the accused for War Department vehicles in May 1942 though there was no record of any payment having been made. In his Petition, my father said that at most the Prosecution succeeded in proving a deviation of one-and-a-half miles from the route which he was authorised to use.

4th Charge Sheet – The Court made special findings in respect of the three charges and found the accused to have been in improper possession of war materials and military equipment. This part of the proceedings is more complicated and, again, I summarise briefly.

We learn in this section of the MP's raid 'of the farm belonging to the accused's first wife' (Daisy's farm, Anchorage). There is no mention of a WD vehicle battery or of anything specific found in the barn, though 'they found a large quantity of ammunition, weapons, medical stores, etc., and also a quantity of military equipment'. The accused's room at the Officers' quarters was searched on 20.4.1943 and other items found. A box sent to the accused's friend, Mr Prentice, for safe custody was also collected with further items therein.

Lionel Carol admitted leaving two (Italian) Medical Boxes 'at his wife's farm'; the .38 ammunition belonged to his own private revolver, and whilst at the farm he saw various rounds of ammunition etc., and on several occasions troops had left kit; the rifle had been inadvertently offloaded at the farm from his vehicle and he did nothing about it as he knew it would be safe; the five second-hand WD spark plugs had been given to him by a friend; he knew nothing about Pillarbox bombs, but had permission during the Abyssinian campaign to keep the Mills grenades and detonators to hand back later.

In part of his evidence here, Lionel Carol said that 'his wife' entertained troops on a fairly large scale and had given them facilities for shooting. I assume this to be Daisy as we know she received Official written acknowledgement of her war efforts in having almost 2,000 troops, recuperating in one form or another to stay at Anchorage, Italian Prisoners of War, not forgetting other regular serving troops who often stopped off at the farm.

Regarding this point, it is quite true that Daisy did allow shooting on Anchorage when troops stayed with her. One night is clearly etched in my memory. There were plenty of water-buck on the farm, particularly down at one of the dams, and around 9 o'clock my mother allowed two English (from the UK) Army Personnel to take her rifle and our old Ford pick-up to go hunting. The outcome of that left Daisy livid. Not being able to tell the difference between a water-buck and a mule, the soldiers shot dead one of our mules, the animal bewildered by the glaring car lights standing still in front of them. Other farmers also allowed Army personnel on leave to hunt game.

According to Marge and Daisy, one MP spoke to Daisy inside the house while the other searched outside. We also know that Daisy stored many items including suitcases for people during the War, some of which the owners never fetched.

I have no memories of ever seeing any Italian Medical Boxes, but have 'in my mind's eye' a clear picture, as if it were yesterday, of my mother's little green medicine cupboard with shelves and drawers kept near her bed. We had so little in the way of medical supplies, that when I had a nasty accident during the war years, Daisy had to drive me at night (luckily there was a full moon so she didn't have to use the car headlights) to the Military Hospital in Gilgil after which I had further treatment at Nakuru War Memorial Hospital.

5th Charge Sheet – The Prosecuting Officer was unable to produce the relevant permit and Lionel Carol was acquitted as the Court ruled there was no case to answer. This was regarding trying to incriminate my father as having obtained 9 bottles of alcoholic liquor from NAAFI 'in a dubious manner'. The Selling Clerk of the NAAFI stated that he never sold alcoholic liquor without production of a card or permit from some higher authority. We know from Daisy's war efforts that she (and many other women in the area) contributed in substantial ways to NAAFI as well as helping on weekends to run the tent. Daisy always bought all her cigarettes from NAAFI. By the time I read this 5th Charge, there was a pervading sense of 'desperation' on the part of the Prosecution to 'get' the accused on whatever was possible, but in this instance it backfired.

Lionel Carol concludes his Petition (in better words than I can), that the sentence was harsh and unconscionable and that undue or no regard was given to his exceptional record in WWI and WWII and to the fact that he volunteered when he was over age for service, and had three sons serving in the forces. I agree. Obviously, there were other ways the Military could have punished Lionel Carol instead of 18 months hard labour in Fort Jesus. The horrific conditions and exceptionally harsh treatment of prisoners under the British in this notorious maximum security prison are well documented.

As with the Major and his wife's surname, there appear to be definite elements of this case which are 'strange'. Whilst endeavouring to keep an unbiased attitude on the matter having now read the transcripts, I nevertheless find myself with an unsettling sense of my father having been 'stitched up good and proper' in certain aspects which could be rightly construed as 'malice' or a 'vendetta' against him. An old saying in northern England comes to mind, 'There's nowt so queer as folk'.

In 1965, after I put our children to school in South Africa, I took the opportunity of going to stay a few days with my father's sister, my Aunt Dulcie Cameron-Ford, living in Natal, as I so wanted to know all I could about my father. As a child, she would always pass on clothing to me from my girl cousins, Priscilla and Rosamund, especially school gyms, sent to my mother during the WWII years. It was very exciting for me to receive these parcels.

Aunt Dulcie was glad to see me, loving, sweet and kind, and I was happy to be with her and spend some time with my father's side of the family. She was proud of Lionel Carol and spoke glowingly of him, promising to write me all the details of his military career. Back at Westlands, I soon received a 6 page letter on the thin white air-mail writing paper of those days, handwritten in blue pen in twirly script, giving all the details. I kept her letter with my jewellery, reading it many times over the years – with the constant opening and folding of the pages it became worn and tattered, the handwriting almost indecipherable. Never did Aunt Dulcie utter a word to me about my father in a Court Martial trial. In hindsight, I wonder if she even knew.

Mr William Prentice (known to me as Uncle Bill), a gently spoken great, big strong Irishman, brought me a present after the last time I saw my father when I was nine. It was in a long, flat box and inside, in yellow china, was a little girl's tea-set in the shape of a rabbit. After that, he bought me 2 dolly's chairs. When I had a nice bedroom of my own, Uncle Bill brought me a beautiful chair with wooden arms and floral motif fabric, absolutely suitable for a girl my age. Sometimes I used to wonder why I got presents from a man who wasn't my father. When I was at Nakuru Primary School, Uncle Bill and his wife, Marie, would sometimes on a Sunday take me out for the day. Looking back now, I wonder if the presents from Uncle Bill were actually from my father, and if taking me out some Sundays was my father's way of asking Uncle Bill to keep an eye on me and make sure I was okay.

As Lionel Carol's only remaining child, I now have some closure and final thoughts and feelings regarding his incarceration in Fort Jesus.

Perhaps to the British Military my father is just a disgraced forgotten ex-soldier in some obscure grave somewhere. To me though, he will always remain a truly good and brave man, the father who taught me solid values, who loved and cared for me and his family of 5 children, who fought for his country courageously in 2 World Wars, without hesitation and whenever called upon.

It continues to astound my reasoning why in a legal military trial he was not allowed the simple right of having 2 witnesses testify on his behalf. All the years, I was under the impression that the British Government took pride in their judicial system placing great importance on the rights of every individual to a fair trial – it is evident that my father was denied this crucial fairness. Sadly, legal history the world over has proven on many occasions to have tipped the scales of justice unfairly to the detriment of the accused, resulting in innocent people being found guilty and worse still, even being put to death.

In the final analysis, the clock can't be turned back and my opinions won't and don't make any difference. It is too late for anything to be rectified in vindicating my father's good name. My nephews, Bruce and Terry, ex-military men who attained senior rank, are of the opinion that what happened to my father is a travesty of justice against a fine man and soldier.

I will forever carry honour, love and respect for my Lionel Carol, and remain steadfast in my testament to his upstanding character and hold dear, with pride, his name. It is with relief that I now know a portion of the facts. As much as I try to put this aside, sometimes the feeling of guilt resurfaces in me about my not having had the courage to ask my mother questions.

Chapter Twenty-Four
Wally's Wedding Woes

Having undergone a 2nd complete hip-replacement operation on 9th April 2014, followed by successful Trigeminal brain surgery on 3rd March 2015 and now sufficiently recovered, I realised that I'd be happiest living with Keith and Mary in Namibia. They own Caprivi River Lodge situated on the banks of the mighty Zambezi River in the extreme north-east of the country known as the Caprivi Strip (now renamed Zambezi Region) near the Botswana, Zimbabwe (previously Rhodesia) and Zambian borders and I started packing up my little flat.

Towards the end of March 2015, Mary flew to the UK to spend a month with their children and grandchildren – Debbie and her son, Kalem; Andrew and his daughter, Laila, and young son, Hayden; and Shaun and his little daughter, Abbey. Mary flew back via George Airport in the Western Cape, where Brian and I fetched her, first having taken Dusty to the Vet for his inoculations then to the State Vet to put all his papers in order to cross through the Namibian border post. Mary was a marvellous help packing up the last items in my flat and loading my Toyota Tazz for our drive up to the Caprivi.

On Saturday, 2nd May 2015, we had a family get-together at Brian and Lindsay's home in Albertinia. Lindsay's son, Brendan, and his wife, Bea, arrived the evening before with their daughter, Helena, and 2 month old baby, Isobel Margaret (named after myself and Lindsay) – Isobel and Keith share the same birthday of 6th March. Kathryn (Lindsay's daughter), and her husband, Jean, who own a farm outside Willowmore were also able to be with us. Missing from our family gathering was Beryl's son, Stuart – he is happy living in Ireland and I hope one day to see him again. I so enjoyed being with my grandchildren and great-grandchildren before leaving for Namibia. Lindsay and Mary hadn't seen one another for 20 years. After final goodbyes to the family in the early morning on Sunday, 3rd May, Mary, Dusty and I started our journey. We took it in turns with the driving, doing 200 kilometres per stretch each, and stopping every night to stay in a Bed and Breakfast or Hotel along the way. Dusty was never a moment's problem, good as gold. By the time we reached Windhoek,

Dusty was not himself and needed veterinary attention. Examination revealed he had an enlarged prostate; he was castrated on 7th May, the surgery successful, and I was to remove his stitches on the 18th. Mary and I also sorted out my Residence Permit as well as the required finger and hand-prints.

After 4 days in Windhoek, we were on our way again on the 8th May, first visiting Albert, Tannie Lottie's son, for 4 days in Karibib. Tannie Lottie, Mary's second-mother, had been attacked at the age of 89 in her farmhouse near Karibib by 3 men on 9th November 2009. She fought for her life. Her injuries were so severe that she died in hospital from internal bleeding 2 days later. Selma, the family's long-time loyal staff member, hearing her screaming, had rushed to defend Tannie Lottie and was beaten-up very badly, almost losing an eye. It was good to see Albert and Selma again. From here, Mary and I went to Omaruru to see our special friends from Kambingana days who'd moved from Windhoek, Sheila and Heinz Wächtler, from my Book Club, who'd given the luncheon after Ian's Memorial Service. They were well and happy. I so enjoyed time with them again, albeit short. Then we headed for home at the Lodge.

The road to the Caprivi is long and straight tarmac in excellent condition, stretching way into the distance. The drive seemed endless. Turning off to Caprivi River Lodge, this section of road is a fairly smooth, yellow sandy track meandering through deep bush, then over a small bridge leading on to a rough stone built-up-road (specially constructed by Keith to withstand flooding); at the end there is a rampant, brilliant carmine-coloured bougainvillea. The road goes no further, turning directly into the Caprivi River Lodge parking lot. Suddenly, one is in another world – a totally unexpected abundance of green vegetation, as if in another country – this feeling remains till you leave. The trip-meter on my Toyota Tazz dashboard read 3,482 kms since we'd left Albertinia. The date was 14th May 2015. It had been mostly a lonely road to travel traffic-wise with only occasional cars and big lorries with trailers. Not a bit of trouble from my Tazz.

After parking the car, you walk over the little concrete bridge to the Reception. The lush green lawns are like carpets interspersed with various varieties of mango trees, the scent of which is very powerful, especially in the late afternoon, almost like the heady scent of jasmine. There are 2 varieties of banana trees, paw-paws, hibiscus shrubs and a number of tall indigenous trees, almost all touching one another, making a green canopy that the sunlight dapples through. The main Lodge Reception faces the Zambezi River a stone's throw away. This great expanse of water flows gently towards the mighty Victoria Falls many miles away. The River is changeable – when the wind gets up, the water is choppy; other times the water is as placid as a junket. The Zambezi is always fascinating with the most amazing number of waterfowl, otters, hippo and the occasional croc, and fish every now and then leaping out and splashing down again into the water.

All the Lozi (ethnic people of the area) Lodge employees are gentle and friendly. Each day, I get a hug and a kiss from 3 of them, Brenda, Trendy and Barbara who call me 'Granny' in siLozi. I've started learning some words in their language. Maureen is Mary's kitchen assistant. Makandauto, a respectful and very polite gentleman, is the Lodge Security Guard.

From the open verandah at the Lodge Reception, dining and bar area, we can watch the Zambians on the other side with their cattle, the kids sometimes playing on the sandbanks in mid-river and of course the river traffic, mainly fishermen, some in boats and others in their local dug-outs known in siLozi as *mikolo* (singular is *mukolo*). The Police Patrol Boat occasionally passes by, keeping a lookout for illegal trafficking. There are 8 separate, attractive thatch-roofed, white-painted luxury chalets facing the River perhaps 18 or 20 yards from the wooden decks over the river. The chalets all have en suite bathrooms and air-cons, and are separated by lawns, tall trees and winding brick paths. Each chalet has a bird's name. If one walks down the bank to the River there is a danger of crocs, so swimming is definitely not allowed. Notices placed in strategic positions clearly advise 'Beware of Crocodiles'. Keith has his own office called 'Springbok' near the workshops and a storage area for the boat named 'Hakuna Matata', and trailer, etc. Over the years, he has made many improvements to the Lodge with further changes yet to take place. Bernard, a highly skilled and very gifted craftsman, makes all the carved wooden furniture and bed-headboards for the Lodge, his work absolutely stunning in its detail and beauty.

To eliminate danger from crocs or hippos as far as possible, Keith has built sections of wood-and-metal balustrade walkways opening onto wooden-decking with railings, all of which have easy chairs artistically crafted from reeds. The heavy wooden dining tables with chairs are for those who wish to have al fresco meals. About 15 feet below the decking is a sandy beach with some trees, the water lapping the roots. When the River floods these trees are under water, just their tops showing and the level of the Zambezi rises to the decking floor.

Mary and Keith's 'Wacky House' is built of cement bricks, has one bedroom with an en suite bathroom, a kitchenette, car park, and pretty wrought-iron work on the small front verandah. My 'Buffalo' wooden cabin with en suite bathroom, kitchenette and verandah is near Keith and Mary's house though we are quite separate from the rest of the Lodge in our own lovely, private little area of lawn set about with mango and other indigenous trees. Anna cleans my cabin and Mary and Keith's house and also does our laundry.

The entire Lodge is a little Eden, 99% green with mainly bougainvilleas and poinsettias making the splashes of colour. An open log fire burns every evening next to the Lodge verandah. After dinner, guests sit in camaraderie around the fire, chatting and adding wood whilst having their last drink before bedtime. Vervet monkeys arrive in family troops. They are offered and gently take leftover bread and fruit at the back kitchen door. Sometimes, they visit me on the verandah at my 'Buffalo' cabin and graciously take pieces of Marie biscuit. Surprisingly, their hands are as soft as velvet and cool to the touch though their nails are hard, and they leave dusty hand prints on the varnished wooden furniture. Extremely arrogant, they will not look into my eyes and when I speak to them they take no notice whatsoever! Dusty, at first, didn't catch on that the monkeys were there, for one second around then gone in a bound. I had to pick him up and show him the monkeys in the tree, then he understood and was always ready to confront them, but they are too clever.

Most nights the owls are here – there was an occasion recently when an aardwolf was in the bush behind the Lodge. Folks who take the boat river-trip come back with amazing and truly beautiful photos of birds, this being a birder's paradise with over 400 species recorded in certain areas of the Caprivi. Daniel, the skipper for 'Skimmer' the double-decker river safari boat, has the best eyesight for finding and picking out the game and identifying the birdlife. The Zambezi has good fishing and is popular with anglers particularly for Tigerfish, some of record size.

Keith is now a photographer, safari operator and conservationist and is compiling a coffee-table luxury book of exceptional elephant photography. His summation of Angola is that it was the greatest part of his life and played a big role in the person he has become. Since leaving Angola penniless in 1975, Keith has returned to the country on numerous occasions as a soldier, in exploration with Anglo American, then as Chief Engineer in diamond mining for the Angolan Government, and lastly, just visiting. He says that whatever Angola took from him in his first stay, has been repaid tenfold with interest to him by Angola, in every aspect of life, financially or just the experience the country has given him. Keith, in many ways in his small meticulous mannerisms, reminds me of my father, Lionel Carol.

Mary is to be admired for all she has achieved. Always positive and facing her many challenges without complaint, today she's confident, absolutely capable and runs Caprivi River Lodge with passion and natural flair. After 42 years on continent Africa, Mary says she cannot imagine living anywhere else.

Whilst living in Willowmore in the Eastern Cape, I spent several month-long holidays at the Lodge with Keith and Mary in the Caprivi. They've been privileged to host the President of Namibia as a guest, and I'd thoroughly enjoyed chatting to him, a friendly and very interesting gentleman, during one of my stays. Permanently residing with them now, I was recently relaxing on the Lodge verandah one Saturday afternoon which brought to mind the story I call 'Wally's Wedding Woes' that occurred during my 2010 December trip.

Out driving in the bush in October 2009 in his Land Rover, coming towards Keith on the track was a tiny warthog, weak and on his last legs. Keith stopped his vehicle, got out, crouched down and talked to the little wild pig in a gentle voice. A week to 10 days old, he went to

Keith who picked him up and took him home. He was named 'Wally', settled in happily at the Lodge and grew up pampered and dearly loved, making friends with Beagle-dog 'Kamata', the cats, staff, Lodge guests and even the guinea-fowl. Wally was spoilt rotten, had his own bed and blanket and was tickled by all. Few guests could resist him, particularly ladies and children, and he returned the attention he received with affection, gentleness, loyalty and trust. Wally even had his own facebook page which still continues in 2016.

This particular Saturday afternoon, we'd had our lunch as had Wally, fed by Keith. Kalem, Debbie's son, had buzzed off to his cabin to play computer games. Debbie was in the workshop covering the old Fordson Major logo with sticky paper so that Keith could continue spray-painting the ancient tractor. PJ, Keith's young assistant, was somewhere around doing another of the Lodge's many maintenance jobs. Mary needed to go shopping in Katima Mulilo. I was sitting on the veranda doing some embroidery, Wally with me having first pulled a loose cushion off one of the chairs onto the floor with his mouth, fluffing it up into a comfy headrest to his liking, then proceeding to lie down and drift off to sleep for his usual afternoon nap in 'warthog dreamland'. Grown-up at 14 months old, with tusks and the ugly beauty of an adult warthog, Wally now weighed 60 to 70 kilograms.

All was peaceful and quiet, the warm weather and a satisfying lunch followed by a chocolate bar dished out by Keith, lulling one's senses into a somewhat lethargic weekend mood. Now and then you'd hear the call of a Fish Eagle or bird chatter. Even the monkeys weren't around having gone off for the afternoon. Wally was 'out for the count', fast asleep, head on his pillow, not a smidgen of worry on his warthog mind. In passing, as Mary went to her car, she'd casually said to me that a wedding party would be arriving at about 3 o'clock for a photographic shoot in the front garden and that she'd cut the number of party guests down to 14.

Looking at Wally so content in his siesta, naturally reminded me of our darling Miss Piggy at Kambingana. There'd now been 2 warthog pets in our family, both of them having been found starving in the wild, each of them giving us cherished memories while in our lives. On a usual day, all Wally had to concern himself about was being served regular hearty meals to stave off hog-hunger-pangs, a healthy dessert of mango after his lunch, much-anticipated treats such as a biscuit, perhaps 2 or 3, quite possibly a bread roll, and a nice bit of tasty cake to go with his afternoon cup of tea, all from Keith.

Beauty hardly seemed important when you had such an adorable personality oozing with charm, as Wally did, enough to thaw the frostiest human character. One couldn't help feeling fondness for Wally. When it was his bedtime, a blanket was carefully put over and tucked around him at the end of his busy day having been the centre of attention with loads of praise and affection for hours on end. I've had quite a few giggles listening to Mary tell Wally to get off the couch. Stretched out in luxury he was. And, he listened and did as he was told, but as soon as Mary was out of sight and busy again, as she usually is running the Lodge, Wally would be back on the settee. The Receptionist, Brenda, has a little daughter named Happy. She and Wally were the same age – great pals the 2 of them, 'little girl and tamed beast', so to speak. All these gentle thoughts ran through my mind as I concentrated on the delicate stitches of my embroidery, Wally keeping me company on this slow-paced afternoon.

I heard the chug-chug of a houseboat on the Zambezi, coming ever closer to the shore landing below the verandah. There was nothing amiss in this. But, as the bow hit the soft sand the shrieking started, everyone on board in the wedding party having surged to one side of the boat which had now tilted to a somewhat perilous angle despite being flat-bottomed. There was more shrieking as they tried to step off onto the loose sand river shoreline, a rather precarious operation whilst adorned in flowing wedding finery, the ladies in high heeled shoes, with no-one landside to help them alight.

This was when Wally lifted his head from his pillow, unable to see anything from his vantage point, but alert to the piercing high-pitched shrieks.

The wedding party proceeded up the river-bank and came into view, the bride radiant and beautiful in her full-length, voluminous rustling snow-white taffeta gown. There were 4 bridesmaids holding cerise coloured floral bouquets, 2 flower-girls, 2 page-boys, the very smart bridegroom and 2 other immaculately outfitted men. Everyone was dressed in white. They made their way towards the swimming pool, naturally engrossed in their own noisily exuberant and animated nuptial celebrations.

Wally took one look. Then everything happened so fast. I was taken completely by surprise. Catapulted out of his peaceful slumber first by the shrieking followed now by what may have appeared to Wally to be blindingly white apparitions in the afternoon sun, Wally's tail was instantly up, straight as an arrow, in true warthog style. In a flash, he was off the verandah like a bolt of lightning, going ballistic, tearing around the grounds at great speed, up and down and around about from one end to the other, doing some high-pitched squealing of his own alternating with heavy grunting.

At the pool now, the bridal couple and their entourage were totally absorbed in their own excited gaieties, completely unaware of how the loudness of their voices carried on the still afternoon air. The result was that a normally calm, fully-grown pet warthog was now in unusual, rampant mode on the other side of the garden and 'at the ready'. At 77, I had no chance of catching Wally, didn't even think about taking pics, and could only stand with my hand over my mouth watching the pandemonium that ensued.

The bridal group had lined up along the edge of the concrete surrounding the swimming pool when suddenly Wally burst into their midst with all the might of his possessive and protective senses. His territory had been invaded by what he probably thought was akin to shrieking aliens 'rustling about' in distinctive sun-blinding white shapes, the likes of which he'd never before seen or heard. Whatever he'd conjured up in his warthog-mind, it sure had Wally in a frantic, heightened state of alarm.

As if his straight-up warthog tail was like some precision radar instrument, Wally homed in on his targeted mission, first singling out the bride. She dashed for cover behind a tree, screaming as she clutched up crumpled folds of her beautiful long dress, abandoning her high heels as she ran. That meant nothing to Wally. He just circled the tree. Every which way the bride went around the tree trunk there was Wally to meet her, warthog tusks, warts and all. The flower-girls and page-boys had instantly joined in adding to the loud chorus of screaming and the bridesmaids upped their own high-pitched shrieking by some notches. It was complete mayhem. The dashingly handsome groom in his perfectly pressed suit, like a valiant knight, raced towards the tree to rescue his bride and eventually managed to do so by hurriedly sweeping her up into his arms.

Helpless, I stood on the verandah yelling at the top of my lungs for Mary who having returned from her shopping was in the kitchen unpacking groceries. She hurtled out to see what the pandemonium was and together we just had to watch aghast and wait out developments, expecting some of the wedding party to fall into the pool at any moment. Wally was still squealing and grunting, adding some intermittent bursts of snorting as he charged 'full-throttle' back and forth, this way and that, intent on evicting whatever had invaded his peace and space.

Like a blessed miracle, PJ suddenly appeared from somewhere and whilst Wally was on one of his charges, PJ wrestled him to the ground. With great difficulty, he pinned Wally down till Keith, having been sent for urgently, arrived from the workshop. Finally, Keith managed to get Wally onto the verandah where he spent an hour calming him down by lying beside Wally whose heart was beating fit to bust. My heart rate had increased considerably as well, my embroidery given not even a thought. Someone brought Keith a cup of tea. Eventually, Wally had recovered sufficiently from his ordeal to go into a deep sleep.

I had to admire the resolve of the wedding party as they gallantly straightened their attire and posed together for the official photographer to get some group pictures, the bride once more donning her high heels. Everyone, including ourselves, was pretty well shaken up. The frightened children had been escorted away by other family or friends who'd arrived by car and had come upon the scene at the peak of the mayhem. After all the shock and wild confusion, I took 2 photos of a sedate and smiling wedding group.

With memories of my own wedding to Ian still pictured in my mind, I had sincere empathy for the lovely bride on this her very special day, being chased by an irate pet warthog on a mission of his own. Most thankfully, the wedding group had a sense of humour and managed to see the funny side of Wally's unexpected tirade. Lindsay says she received an email from me later that evening, saying that at my age, I didn't think my heart could take this kind of thing! There would be another bridal party that month, but this time all the Lodge staff were prepared.

On 23rd June 2011, Keith released Wally with great care and sensitivity back into the wild in a specially chosen area about 150 kilometres from the Lodge, after spending a week camping in the bush with Wally until he'd 'found his feet' warthog-style. Initially, Wally was reluctant to leave the security of the tent and his blanket, but was soon enjoying exploring the bush with Keith, backing in and out of burrows choosing a nice 'house', meeting up with other female warthogs and their young, and generally adjusting sufficiently to life with his own kind. Keith took a beautiful close-up photo of Wally with his head on his blanket in his warthog burrow, and made regular trips every few weeks to check on Wally's progress – he'd settled into living in the wild and was happy. Wally is Keith's specially treasured memory, a loving experience of a friend and loyal companion.

Imprinted in my mind are Keith's emotionally touching words he said to me after the wedding party had left that Saturday afternoon in 2010 and Wally had calmed down, back to taking his usual leisurely warthog recce around the Lodge gardens.

"Mum, I love that pig."

Chapter Twenty-Five
Kesho

The 5th June 2015 was Ian's birthday – always a melancholy day for me, now almost 21 years since his death. After breakfast, I went to sit on the Lodge verandah with my laptop, little Dusty beside me, alert and waiting the anticipated arrival of the monkeys that fascinated him no end.

Out of the corner of my eye, I saw a man arrive and walk onto the verandah. He looked at me then stopped. Glancing up, I started to ask him if I could help him when suddenly he strode towards me and I recognised him. It was Franz Nachtsheim, our dear long-time Angola farming friend! I just fell into his arms. A few years before Ian's death was the last time I'd seen Franz. Helma came onto the verandah 2 minutes later and she just took me and held me. So many emotions overwhelmed me with their loving embrace that I burst into tears. What an amazing gift to receive on Ian's birthday! Then they introduced Inge, Bernd and Margret Kathmann, their friends who'd accompanied them on an Africa tour with Jimmy's Safari. Keith and Mary had last been in the company of Franz and Helma on their 1989 visit from Johannesburg to stay with us at Kambingana between Christmas and New Year. Planning this Caprivi trip some time earlier, Franz had Googled Keith's name on the internet and found him at Caprivi River Lodge. He'd then spoken to Mary on the 'phone, but hadn't given any definite idea or details of when they would be able to visit, so this was a big surprise for the 3 of us.

There was a lot for us to catch up on, everyone sitting at the long verandah table. The safari cook brought out their large cooler-boxes and made sandwiches for their group. We had our Lodge lunch later.

Franz: "We went back to our Angola fazenda on 7th August 2013, to find only pieces of the house wall and some parts of heavy machinery which they could not remove. There was also a landmine planted underneath one of the machinery parts, and the guy who had shown us the way to the fazenda told us that they had removed a mine next to the entrance. We met him after we'd been looking for a road to our Fazenda Luassivi for many hours and he led us to a place where we could cross the river. The road and bridge which we'd built was overgrown and broken-down. He knew the place because he keeps his cattle there in summer. Nobody is living there anymore and the village nearby is also deserted. There was a law introduced by the Angolan Government, that you lose your land if you leave the country for more than 45 days. They are, however, encouraging people to return and take back their land if it is not occupied by anybody else. Otherwise, you can apply for new land and start from scratch."

Helma: "When Franz turned 65, we decided to sell the company. In 2006, after we sold the property as well, we decided to get away from Johannesburg and settle in Germany. We had bought a house in the countryside a number of years ago and retired there."

Time just flew. It seemed as if Franz and Helma had only just arrived when they had to be on their way again after about 2 hours, but what a fabulous day this birthday of Ian's had turned out to be!

On 21st June 2015, Keith left the Lodge and drove to Angola to try to find our fazenda using the co-ordinates Franz and Helma had kindly emailed through of Franz and August's farm, Fazenda Luassivi, in the same southern Province of Cuando Cubango, not so far from our Fazenda Esperança. Mary and I waited out the days anxiously knowing that communication would be difficult and minimal due to poor cell 'phone reception. Although Keith had returned to Angola many times over the years, I was very apprehensive as he was alone, driving into an unknown situation regarding landmines and for long and lonely distances over unfamiliar roads. I felt some relief on the couple of occasions cell contact became available. Keith returned to the Lodge on the night of 11th July and parked outside their house, embraced Mary then walked into the garage to give me a hug. He was unshaven, covered in dust and dishevelled having driven an extremely long journey that day to get back to us and keep to his schedule. So grateful I was, to see my son back home safe and well.

Franz's map co-ordinates proved invaluable in helping Keith locate our Fazenda Esperança on 5th July 2015. I sincerely appreciate Franz and Helma's thoughtful assistance. All that remains of what was once our homestead is the concrete floor slab. What used to be huge tobacco barns and outbuildings has been reduced to rubble. The dam wall has collapsed. Keith found a depression in the ground where he thought the outside long-drop lavatory may have been. The remaining part of the hot-water system is also only the concrete floor slab. Walking around, Keith found some farm equipment like ploughs, planters and harrows and an auger used for digging fence-post holes, describing the Komatsu as now being 'half a bulldozer', with trees growing up through the ploughs and bulldozer blade. Nature has quietly returned to reclaim the land we cleared. Using his drone, Keith took a stunning photo of the amazingly straight farm road to our house that Ian had made in early 1974.

The Angolan Civil War lasted for 26 years, 4 months, 3 weeks and 3 days, starting in 1975 and ending on 4th April 2002. During this time the stretch of road 'Menongue (Serpa Pinto) – Longa – Cuito Cuanavale' was called 'The Road of Death' by FAPLA (the Angolan Army), Cuban and Soviet Forces. State-of-the-art radar and missile networks were installed in 1987 by the Soviet Union and Cuba, arranged in a line from Lubango (Sá Da Bandeira), Menongue (Serpa Pinto), Luena and Cuito Cuanavale. This very brief civil war information is enough to demonstrate that the situation and circumstances in the country, particularly in southern Angola where our fazenda was, were not conducive to farming. The Angolan civil war devastated the country's economy, infrastructure and public administration. More than a million people were internally displaced and over 500,000 people lost their lives.

Over the years, as people came to hear of our Angola experience, some questioned why Ian and I weren't bitter about it. The answer is simple. Ian achieved what he set out to do farming cattle, maize and tobacco, and with particular regard to our tobacco cultivation, the success exceeded our expectations. The lives, safety and well-being of our family are far more precious than inanimate, material objects. All the years, it weighed heavily on Ian's conscience that he'd had to leave his animals to fend for themselves at the mercy of others. I cannot recall him ever bemoaning 'any loss' or using such words regarding Angola. The wisest thing we did was to heed Edgar's advice and join the convoy. There were no regrets about having gone to farm in that country. A more detailed account of Keith's Angola trip to find our fazenda can be found at Mary's (Irish Mary Rooken-Smith's) facebook page.

I find it interesting, and somewhat ironic, that maize (corn) was introduced into Africa by the Portuguese in the 16th century. In 2015, Robert Mugabe's Zimbabwe Government realised that their land reform policies have not been successful and are asking for 'strategic' white farmers to return – the country needs $300m to import food, the figure for maize alone at 700,000 tons. The majority of white people Mugabe got rid of went to Zambia – in 2016, Zambia's maize harvest is the highest recorded and the country now exports this staple food to Zimbabwe. The 1975 United Nations Food and Agriculture Year Book ranked Rhodesia 2nd in the world for yields of maize, soya beans, wheat and ground nuts, and 3rd for cotton – in the combined rankings for all these commodities, Rhodesia was ranked 1st in the world. The country was rated best in the world for yield and quality of Virginia tobacco and was the world's 2nd largest exporter of flue-cured tobacco. Agriculture was the largest employer of labour and contributed more to gross domestic product than any other industry – all a far cry from the Zimbabwe of 2016.

Ian would have been immensely proud of Keith, not only for the huge effort he made in going back to Angola and finding our fazenda, but also for his elder son's many achievements in various fields, and for the overall success Keith has made of his life. Caprivi River Lodge receives many emails from guests – the following one, in appreciation of a stay, is memorable:

'Dear Mr Keith, sorry for my terrible english. Thank you for hospitality and collaboration. You are an honest man, a man of other times: half Sir Livingstone and half Indiana Jones. I am sure we will meet again. Saluti. Fabio e David Antonelli.'

After Dusty's castration surgery in Windhoek, he'd initially seemed fine, but recently had appeared 'out of sorts'. After our Katima Mulilo Vet, Dr Frank's, visits and discussions, I decided it was time for Dusty to be released from his suffering. His bladder had stopped functioning properly causing hydronephrosis, he wasn't eating properly, was having difficulty in his hindquarters and only wanted to sleep beside me at night. In the daytime, he lay on the lawn chewing a bone. This was his greatest joy. On 15th July 2015 in the early evening, Mary called Dr Frank who came to the Lodge again. Dusty was lying on my bed. Dr Frank gave him a sedative and painkiller in one jab. In 5 minutes, Dusty was deeply asleep and 10 minutes later, Dr Frank started the euthanasia. At no time was Dusty alone. Slowly and gently and without any sign of pain, Dusty crossed the border. Dr Frank performed the euthanasia better than any of the Vets I've known. Keith arranged for his grave to be dug. I wrapped Dusty in one of the colourful blankets Francisca crocheted for me, then Keith placed him in the grave and filled it in. I'm still feeling Dusty's loss in many ways – it's particularly lonely at night, and I miss him walking beside me to and from my 'Buffalo' cabin or lying on his cushion beside my chair on the verandah when I'm working at my laptop – my loyal little friend.

I wish only to spend my remaining years in a stable, secure environment, free from fear, though I have a few concerns regarding the future of our planet.

During our years on Kambingana, the SWA/Namibian Government Mobile Health Unit, over a period of 10 years, managed to eradicate tuberculosis. TB has now resurged to affect the lives of many in the world with a new strain resistant to medication and incurable. Many of our antibiotics are not managing to fight illnesses as effectively as they used to. Medically, we face a frightening future scenario.

Due to pesticides and herbicides, the decline in bee populations around the world is alarming. Without bees for pollination, humanity will starve.

It would be unforgivable of me if I did not pay special tribute to Dr Dame Daphne Sheldrick D.B.E. M.B.S. (born *Jenkins*, 4th June 1934), my second cousin. Our family is very proud of her. Daphne was the first person to perfect the formula and husbandry vital for rearing infant milk-dependent Elephants and Rhinos. She is known and loved the world over and deserving of every respect and praise. Founding the David Sheldrick Wildlife Trust (DSWT) in 1977, in honour of her late husband, David Sheldrick, over 200 orphaned elephant calves have been saved, being integrated back into the wild by the age of 10 to live naturally free with other elephants. The DSWT is the most successful programme in the world for the rescue and rehabilitation of orphaned elephants. In 1989, Daphne was decorated with an M.B.E. by Queen Elizabeth, followed in 2006 by being awarded a Knighthood. Daphne, among her other deserved awards, was also honoured with a Moran of the Burning Spear (M.B.S.) by the Kenya Government in 2001. I would sincerely like to thank Daphne here for her invaluable work. Where would the continent's wildlife be, particularly Africa's orphaned elephants, without Dr Dame Daphne Sheldrick?

The Elephants of my Heart
Dedicated to Dr Dame Daphne Sheldrick
5th July 2014

It wasn't like the flutter
Of a delicate butterfly
With fragile weightless wing
Beating to its silent pulse
That first entered my being

But rather the sure-footed
Tread of graceful might
Bearing down a ton
With natural ease of life
That trumpeted into my heart

I have walked behind
Sometimes steps ahead
But never have I been in front
Always forever at the side
Of the elephants in my heart

I heard you wondered
Can an elephant smile?
Yes, I say, and I often in return
Rich in treasured delight
Of the elephants in my heart

And you ask, what one thing
Set you on this path?
I have no definitive finding
For what could encapsulate
The elephants of my heart

My eyes, through lens of seeing light
Captured their individual pictures
Whilst the recorder of my being
Filmed in splendid timeless colour
All the elephants within my heart

I hear you enquire
Is their touch soft and kind?
My answer is certain
None more so gentle and true
Than the elephants of my heart

They've traversed my soul
North to South, East to West
'Morn to noon and at day's rest
Held so dear through to journey's end
Each of the elephants of my heart

Have they forgotten? Can I forget?
Does the memory of sunshine
Still give warmth on a chilly day?
A fragrance fades yet it still lingers
Such are the elephants of my heart

I have touched their tears
Whilst tasting my own
Witnessed their joy, pain and sorrow
Felt my being stretch in hope
For the elephants of my heart

Daisy's Daughter
Our Lives for Africa

The cup I hold in my hands
You've shared with me
Let us pass it to our children
A wonder their right to see
The elephants of our hearts

by Lindsay Rooken-Smith Jenions 5th July 2014

In 2013 alone, over 1,000 Park rangers were killed while protecting Africa's elephants, rhino and wildlife from poaching. Some who've survived ambush suffered being shot several times. They need every bit of help and support possible. I would like to take this opportunity of acknowledging the invaluable work our trackers and rangers do and thank them sincerely for their courage and loyalty. Unless we can stop the poaching, Africa's elephants will be gone in ten years. In honour of our continent's Wildlife Trackers and Rangers, and all Wildlife Conservationists and Conservation Groups from Africa and around the world dedicated to assisting and saving our precious wildlife, below is another of Lindsay's poems:

Africa My Soul
Ode to our Heroic Wildlife Trackers & Rangers
Wherever they may be

Africa my infinite soul
Sustenance of body and mind
Through days of faithful toil
Comfort in hands of warm soil
Oh, vast enchanting free land
Sighs heavenward to your skies
Our grateful touch to your trees
We pay honour on bended knee

Some say grown men don't cry
But tears well up from deep within
Wet cheeks dampening dusty dry skin

As gaze bears witness and falls to rest
Heinous animal atrocities by poachers
Decimating so much of Africa's best
In traumatised seconds that follow
Fury consumes one's sensitive being
Rise of raged breath within each chest
Ignites a quiet cunning and stealth
Pulse slowed to a determined crest
Feet forward on loyal tracker's quest

Africa's heartbeat loses
Her natural rhythm to the drum
Without her sacred gift of wildlife
Age-old revered songs to be sung
As our people leave their once rural life
Glittering lights found in cities and towns
We call you now together stand as one
Forget not your proud traditional past
With memories the flick of a zebra's tail
Prancing delight stripes black and white
Nibbling lips a feeding gentle giraffe
Long patterned neck stretching high
Giant hippopotamus with young at play
Wallow in water glistened by sun's rays

The ancient rhino with horn made of hair
Illogical illusion of gold shot and snared
Mighty elephant with tusks of ivory dentine
One pair to a pachyderm to last for their life
Slaughtered past the unthinkable million
Our lion depleted in canned-hunting strife
Lost to the web of syndicates and poachers
Intricately spun a woven deplorable deceit
With no end or beginning to unravel the maze
We call on our people to help us in this fight
To root out the rot preserve Africa's wildlife

Daisy's Daughter
Our Lives for Africa

By the moon's timeless silvery soft steady light
Shadows flicker as owls call the glint on steel
Asia's ignorant greed seeks its prey each night
Our animals asleep or in tranquil deserved rest
Easy targets of deaths spears, guns and knife
The morning sun revealing the horrific toll
As trackers and rangers report for their patrol
With no idea whether at the end of each day
Their lives too will be thoughtlessly torn away

Ah, Africa
Our heartfelt sighs to your star-studded skies
We pay true homage to your green life of trees
Listen to hushed messages carried on the breeze
Pray protect our brave trackers and rangers
Wherever they may be
Blessed each one by us on bended knee
In their never-ending fight to keep our animals
Evermore in our forests and on savannah plains
Living naturally as Mother Earth decreed them to be
Always to run and roam exquisitely wild and free
by Lindsay Rooken-Smith Jenions 15th April 2012

August, Franz's Angola farming partner, has not returned to Africa. The 10th July 2016 was his 76th birthday. Living in Germany all the years, he married, had a daughter and now has a baby grandson. I've thought of August often since we first met him on Fazenda Esperança and have so wanted to write or chat to him, but my inability to speak German has precluded me from doing so. I wish him peace and goodwill, and have sincere empathy for him regarding his traumatic experience in a divided and broken Angola that he still had faith in even after the shelling of Serpa Pinto. My 83rd birthday approaches on 13th November 2016, with Franz's 77th birthday following a few days later on 16th November. The years have marched by, yet neither distance nor time has faded this treasured friendship I have with Franz and Helma.

Sitting on the Lodge verandah at my laptop checking emails one day, I heard a delightful little interlude between Mary and Maureen that, for me, epitomises the privilege of living on this amazing continent when Africa's people share her gifts and live in harmony with one another and the steady heartbeat of undisturbed nature.

Mary: "The monkeys have been at the bar again eating the peanuts. You'll have to wash the bowls and put out fresh nuts."

To which Maureen replied in her polite Lozi manner, "Yes, I was just going to ask them to leave."

Having a quiet chuckle to myself, I had to momentarily stop what I was doing.

Many people and animals have touched my life in different and special ways. I am honoured to have known their love, kindness and companionship. Friends and family in various parts of the world I value highly and hold dear in each, their individual characters and the joy they bring to my everyday life.

Edward now lives in Thailand, on the tiny island of Koh Samui with his lovely wife, Tuk. They were married in 1997. It pleases us that he has found love and happiness again with Tuk. Twenty-five years later, Edward still has Beryl's parrot 'Pushkin'.

Cell 'phones, Skype, the internet and email are wonderful technological advantages. I remember being amazed at the invention of the fax machine! Without a computer, I'm beginning to question if I would ever have completed, 'Daisy's Daughter, Our Lives for Africa'.

On a hot day in Albertinia in 2014, when I was still trying to get the 'hang of' Skype, I heard a call come in on my computer. I'd just finished having a shower and had dried myself off, but hadn't yet dressed. I so love communicating with all the special folk in my life, and not wanting to miss the Skype call I hurried across to my desk. It was my nephew, Don Rooken-Smith in Florida, USA. Luckily, he has a good sense of humour. I'd completely forgotten about the built-in camera on my laptop! I saw Brian and Lindsay later that day and we had a good laugh about my 'naked Skype call'.

While I tried to find a way to publish my book, I decided to put it on the internet on my own website for people from anywhere in the world to read my story free of charge. On 24th October 2015, my website went 'live' and I wondered what *kesho* (tomorrow) would bring. The response from readers was amazing – beyond any expectations I'd dared have. I often felt completely overwhelmed at the encouraging and loving emails I received that brought treasured contact again with so many people I'd known from our Kenya days, or folk our families had known way back then. It was evident that Kenya and Africa remain special memories in the lives of many.

On 15th November 2015, I received an email from a lady living in Wales, Patsy Witchell, who'd been researching the history of Africa on the internet and by chance came across my website. She immediately recognised my father's names, Lionel Carol Griffin, and read his Chapter with interest. Patsy also had the exact same black and white photograph of my father in his khaki casual wear that I had on the 'pics gallery' of my website. It turned out that 'Mrs Chandler' had been great-aunt to Patsy's husband, Roger Witchell – Mrs Chandler being the younger sister to Roger's grandmother, Marguerite (née Worrall). There were also 4 brothers in their family – Jack, Fred, George and Alec.

So began a rewarding exchange of email correspondence and information with Patsy, a genuinely thoughtful and empathetic person with a seemingly unlimited amount of patience and tolerance to my many questions, and a natural flair for internet research. Although we don't have an exact day of birth, Mrs Chandler was born Emily Brisland Worral in England in 1902, and was called 'Em' by Marguerite who spoke of her often. I found it pleasing to be able to refer to her now as 'Emily' instead of 'Mrs Chandler'. Emily married a Harold Chandler who became a farmer in Kenya after serving in the British Forces – they had 2 children, Michael and Jennifer (with whom I went to school). We think that Lionel Carol and Harold Chandler may have served together at some point during the two Great Wars, possibly during WWI in France. Of the date or year of Emily and Harold's divorce we have no information.

From my father's Trial documents, we know that he married Emily in Jinja, Uganda on either the 3rd or 4th April 1943. After Lionel Carol's death at the age of 48 on 20th January 1945, Emily ran a general dealer store/furniture shop in Nairobi called 'Hogg' (after the name of the lady she bought the business from in 1948) and was struggling alone financially. She sold the business in 1949, and at the same young age of 48, Emily died on 26th May 1950 in Nairobi – according to what Patsy was told, due to cancer. In Emily's Will, handled by attorneys in Nairobi, she had appointed as Executor a Mrs Marjorie Saunders, wife to Mr Saunders who was denied testifying on my father's behalf at his Trial. Not long before her death, in a letter dated 4th May 1950, Emily wrote to her sister, Marguerite, who luckily kept this letter, and from Emily's words we realise her great love for my father, Lionel Carol. "As the years go by, I miss Lionel more than ever…"

Patsy also sent me 2 black and white photographs of Emily, so at last I have a picture in my mind of what my father's second wife looked like. Through the info and pics Patsy shared with me, it became clear that Emily was not only beautiful, but an intelligent woman too, and not unlike Daisy in that Emily seems to have been of a strong character able to get on with life, face the trials and tribulations as they came, remaining kind and caring.

Now that I felt this 'connection' to Emily – by marriage, she was a part of my family – I regretted not having had the opportunity to meet her and realised how tough her 'road' must have been during my father's incarceration. I'm grateful to Emily for the love and support she gave Lionel Carol during the harsh and lonely time in his life in Fort Jesus and before his death. I think of her now with fondness. My father's WWII medals remained with Emily and what happened to them after her death is a mystery. Marguerite and Emily had a close and loving sister-relationship and Marguerite kept photos of Emily and her children, the one of Lionel and some of Em's letters. When Roger's father died, these were passed on to Patsy and Roger. Patsy will always be remembered by me for caring enough to write to a complete stranger and quell much of my anxiety and heartache regarding the last few years of my father's life. Thank you, Patsy.

The 26th November 2015 would bring another website message my way. Ex-Kenyans, Robin and John Channer, now living in Australia many years, emailed me. I'd been at school with John's beautiful sister, Sue, who later had the Sue Channer School of Dancing in Nakuru. Part of their news was sad for me to read – Sue had died of cancer in 2013.

Robin and John have been wonderful advocates for promoting my book in every way possible and I thank them both for all their efforts on my behalf.

In thinking of ideas for a suitable book cover, I made contact with Karen Laurence-Rowe, the elder daughter of a long time, dear friend of ours from Kenya days, Maureen Moeton, who now lives in Cyprus. Maureen's son, named Stewart, died on 31st August 1982 just before his 26th birthday, also from a motorcycle accident.

Karen is world famous for her artwork and is one of Kenya's leading wildlife artists. In May 2012, she won the Endangered Species Category in the David Shepherd Wildlife Artist of the Year Awards and was also voted overall winner on that occasion of this prestigious annual event. She has been a supporting artist to the David Shepherd Wildlife Foundation ever since. Karen is also a founder member of Artists for Conservation and won the Simon Combes Conservation Artist Award in Canada with the Artists for Conservation group in 2015, for support of conservation through her art. On 9th January 2015, Karen launched 'Artists Against Extinction', a non-profit-making venture comprising an extremely talented group of artists helping wildlife conservation through the sale of their artwork. Experts calculate a loss of 0.1% of species every year, man being almost wholly responsible. Through their work, the artists draw attention to the beauty of nature and the vast number of species of fauna and flora under threat in our world. It is a great honour and privilege for me to have the book cover for 'Daisy's Daughter, Our Lives for Africa' painted by Karen and I thank her sincerely for this extremely generous gesture inspired by loving memories and photos of 2 of our dear pet animals in my story, Wally warthog and Tootsie-Wootsie porcupine.

Through the connections that have come to me by writing 'Daisy's Daughter, Our Lives for Africa', what has stood out boldly is the innate goodness in many people, shining through with bright intensity, an unmistakeable chain of hope and love humanity so needs to share in our troubled world. Thank you to all of you for your support and kindness.

As is usual for this time of year, the heat and humidity in the Caprivi saps one's energy as the last days of January 2016 approach. Even the snakes are out and about seeking somewhere cool as creature and human wait for the expected rains to bring relief from the high summer temperatures and raise the water level of the Zambezi. The thunder storms and lightning can be quite frightening.

I have come to think of the monkeys as the 'Little People'. With a sudden deafening crash and a scampering across the tin roof of my cabin 'Buffalo', I know the troop of vervet monkeys has arrived. They leap from the tree canopy then nimbly descend the tree trunks to gently take pieces of broken Marie biscuits from my hand, now a routine visit I enjoy. Most times their manners are excellent, waiting their turn. If a piece of biscuit accidentally drops to the ground, it is picked up, scrutinised and brushed free of sand before being eaten. Bad manners occur when older monkeys want to take over and start to grab, chasing the younger ones away. There is a definite 'pecking' order. Their antics are amazing – leaping up to take a bite from dangling mangoes, cavorting and playing see-saw on supple branches, frolicking on the lawns and playfully wrestling with each other. They are a joy to watch – not a care in the world and fearless of us humans, but they can be naughty too. Occasionally, females who 'want' a baby sneakily snatch one and run off though sometimes I think they are perhaps deliberately annoying or provoking a caring mother. Shenanigans ensue until the baby is back with its mother. The tiny newborns are ugly, but ever so cute. When they're about 10 days old they 'let go' and wander a little on their own, but always in close proximity to their mothers. Not long after, they are grubbing away at fallen mulberries and other wild fruits becoming more independent each day. Soon they join up with the other youngsters in carefree play, just enormously enjoying every day – reminding me of our own children's rough and tumble games.

Hippo pods (groups) find their favourite spots to wallow in the shallower water of the deep channel along our stretch of the Namibian side of the Zambezi, known and so named the 'Great River' in the siLozi African language. Surfacing to breathe, the hippo will bellow, grunt, snort or groan, argue and yawn vigorously, and have the occasional fierce fights with their powerful tusks slashing out at rival bulls, often inflicting bloody wounds. Other times, they rest in their reed-protected secluded sunbathing beaches on the sand island in front of the Lodge where they will lie up for half a day then enter the water when they get too hot or just to return to the safety of their watery havens. When undisturbed, hippos move casually and very quietly, even when emerging from the water onto land. At night, they graze along the river-bank and often meander behind the Lodge chalets in an area called a *malapo* – the vegetation of the malapo being irresistibly tempting with lush new grass and other plants. At flood times, the malapo is like an overflow from the Zambezi and becomes a long dam for several months until the river recedes.

Many times, just as the evening darkening takes over from the burning hot day, hippos come up onto the beach below the Lodge decks making friendly noises and grunting whilst lazily chomping on anything palatable. I've also heard them at night just outside my cabin quietly cropping the lush green lawn grass, a noise something like a soft swish, or they chomp on Mary's precious plants without doing that much damage. Makandauto, the night watchman, will call me to see the hippo when they are in the malapo. With the accompanying night sounds of Africa's cicadas and crickets, I'm privileged to be able to observe a mother and baby hippo quietly wandering around. I've also witnessed them from frighteningly close quarters dashing out of the water and away, moving at incredible speed, water splashing out in all directions. Their size is awesome. Likewise when they dash into the water, these huge animals are an unforgettable sight. They have the undeniable right of way, can be very grumpy and quarrelsome, and are known to be unpredictable and dangerous. There are many tales of hippo encounters ending in tragedy.

Occasionally we see a crocodile, mostly at night when they come out of the water and lie up on the bank underneath the decking. Makandauto then calls us to have a look. With our torches shining, the croc will slither back into the water and is gone almost silently, in a split second. Twice now, I've been in Keith and Mary's private pool over at their house and my 'Buffalo' cabin, and a juvenile snake has swum towards me. Luckily, the pool net has been at hand and I've caught it – first a cobra, and the 2nd time a spitting cobra. While resting one afternoon, Keith watched a cobra slide into his boot. He waited a while for it to settle comfortably then quietly went onto the verandah and tipped the reptile out. As for myself, I struggled to get the 2 snakes into the net – they kept slithering out and swimming toward me. Usually after supper and when he's on duty, Makandauto escorts me back to my cabin. Nevertheless, I walk very warily shining my torch in a wide swathe over the lawns and along the paths, for snakes and hippos can be surprisingly near.

We've come to the end of 'Daisy's Daughter'. Before I leave you, I wish to relate 2 short stories that remain special in my heart.

After I arrived at the Lodge with Mary in mid-May 2015, I made a dear friend, Helen, who lives in Katima Mulilo. We're both 'senior citizens' and have much in common. In April 2016, she made a trip in her Nissan 1400 bakkie from Katima to South Africa to visit various friends. On her travels she would very kindly collect my last few possessions which had been whittled down to my most precious treasures only and stored in my landlord's garage in Albertinia until we could somehow get them to Caprivi River Lodge. This would bc a mammoth driving return trip for Helen of approximately 7,000 kilometres.

Around 20th April, Helen arrived at Lindsay and Brian's home. Lindsay loved Helen instantly the moment they met at the garden gate. The 3 spent a wonderful evening together with Brian as cook per usual and pudding after supper followed by watching hilariously funny video clips on YouTube sitting at Brian's computer. Lindsay says Helen has the best laugh she's ever heard. At noon the following day, Brian and Helen went up to the landlord's garage and loaded my goods. Back home, the 3 of them repacked everything around and on top of the beautifully carved, wooden Chinese Chest I'd had for years which now contained my fragile, most delicate and smaller items. The space on the back of the little bakkie was loaded almost to the roof inside the canopy. Lindsay was worried someone might break into the car so Helen covered everything with black plastic sheets. Brian buzzed off for a few minutes and returned with a computer printed A4 paper sign 'Beware – Live Snakes in Transit' which they stuck on the inside of the canopy rear window.

Big goodbyes and Helen was gone in her dusty car – first stop Tulbagh, where she was pulled over. The gentleman who presented himself at her window was an agitated Agricultural Officer who requested that Helen immediately produce her permits for the live snakes she carried in transit! He was vastly amused at her explanation and with a broad grin and good wishes for safe travels sent Helen on her way. The sign remained in place to journey's end and at the numerous refuelling stops the petrol attendants were extremely reluctant to come close enough to fill up!

I would love to be able to tell Daisy this story of how her large, heavy oval cast-iron roasting pan that I'd had all the years and which I baked our Christmas cakes in, was safely delivered from Albertinia in South Africa all the way back to her daughter, me, in Katima Mulilo, northern Namibia by a kind-hearted lady. Helen and Daisy share many of the same admirable characteristics and would be quite at ease in one another's company enjoying a sundowner and a good laugh.

One evening in late October 2016, the kitchen staff ladies said to Mary, "Look, there is a thing under the lounge coffee table." They would not go near and stood well aside. Sockies (Mary and Keith's cat) was playing with something that, at a glance, looked like a small brown snake.

Mary rescued an inert sopping wet baby squirrel which she brought to me sitting on the Lodge's verandah. "Here, Granny," she said, "this will keep you busy."

Everyone, these days, calls me Granny – their term of endearment which I like very much.

We would do our best for this baby, but didn't think it would live. The tiny bedraggled creature, as long as my index finger, just fitted into my cupped hand. After 5 days, when we felt more certain of its survival, Mary came up with the short love-name of 'Squiggy', though in full we named this dear little squirrel 'Daisykin Squiggles'.

For probably about 6 weeks, I was worn to a frazzle having little sleep. Squiggy needed feeding every 2 hours and was as good as gold, taking first a drop, then two as she grew, of warmed Ideal milk from an eye-dropper. Lindsay's vet in faraway Mossel Bay in the Cape had kindly and urgently emailed me the correct milk mixture for feeding a baby squirrel. Squiggy was potty-trained from the beginning. After every feed, I tickled her nether end with an eye-shadow brush and she did her business on cue. At night, I kept her warm in a cosy nest I made inside my cloth sun hat with hot-water bottles placed underneath and a blanket tucked all around and under the hat, on my bedroom chair, within easy reach from my bed. Daytime, I kept Squiggy in her 'hat' home.

Life progressed and Squiggy responded in every way – growing stronger and soon learned to crawl gingerly out of my hat. To begin with, I kept her under a fly-proof dish cover on my bed. This contraption I considered a suitable play-pen and she could crawl around the netting and learn to use her very long, extremely fine claws. She soon learned to hold the eye-dropper with her front feet. Before long, the limited precious sleep I could get was constantly interrupted by the dear little feet of a loving and curious baby squirrel wanting attention – in my ears, up my nose or pushed into my mouth! It would be some time before we could confirm that Squiggy was a girl.

As the days went by, Squiggy became more adventurous. I asked Samuel, the gardener, to cut a good strong stick to balance on the window sill reaching into the mango tree outside my 'Buffalo' cabin bedroom window. As she had no mother squirrel to learn from, I would play-fight with Squiggy using an old toothbrush, the eye-shadow brush and a Bic ballpoint pen, and play 'chase' with her using the ball from a deodorant bottle in the hope that she would learn to defend herself. She thoroughly enjoyed these little jousting tournaments. Eventually, and with some encouraging and coaxing from me, Squiggy was spending her days making the acquaintance of and visiting her squirrel friends and relations in the tree canopies at the Lodge. Her favourite was the mango tree outside our cabin. She also became very possessive of me and, perched on her 'stick lookout post' at the window, would give Samuel a good 'squirrel telling-off' if she thought he was too close to our cabin whilst doing his gardening work. Helen came to visit us in 'Buffalo' one day. We were having a cup of coffee and a chat, Helen sitting in the chair next to my bed and me lying down while Squiggy, as usual, dashed about the room at a pace, here, there, up and down the curtains. Next thing, Helen suddenly got a sharp nip on the bottom from

Squiggy. In seconds, this little squirrel could silently move across or around the room without being noticed. Apart from her possessiveness, I think Squiggy was jealous on this occasion of the attention Helen was giving me. Over the weeks, I took at least 3 videos of Squiggy and a collection of photographs.

Each time I came back through our private garden gate to 'Buffalo', I would start calling for Squiggy. She would answer and come dashing back and there she would be, on my bed, going round and round in circles, showing her delight at my return. Or she'd leap onto my shoulder and whizz around. We rested in the afternoons with Squiggy nestling in my 'salt-cellars' and playing around under my chin and on my shoulders, curling up and having a game with her feet, sometimes preening herself or just trying to get comfortable for her own short nap. Squiggy was very affectionate and would often give me little kisses on my chin. She knew 4 words – her name, come, look and no. I noticed, and it was very noticeable to me, that when Squiggy was in doubt about something, she would stop and have a quick scratch at her neck – then make a decision.

The potty regimen continued by placing a saucer on the shelf, and in the middle I put three 3 small knobbly stones on which Squiggy dutifully did her business. She soon discovered a route, quickly up the door curtain into the ceiling. Some days later, she arduously dragged with great dexterity a considerable number of paper tissues to make her own cosy 'nest home' in the ceiling. It was very snug and a safe place up there. Each evening, almost on the dot of 6 o'clock, Squiggy took to sleeping 'upstairs' until 8.30 the next morning (squirrels, as I learnt, being 'late risers') and would arrive just in time to join me for breakfast, hers now consisting of various fruits, especially tiny bits of banana, crust of toast, chopped walnuts and almonds. She sharpened her teeth on wild figs, but preferred the metal window latch as the best tool.

Whenever we had some rain at night, Mary and I collected white ants which had been attracted by the electric lights. Next morning, the gardeners knew without being told to collect many more white ants still to be found in heaps especially in the garage area. These were scraped up and put into empty peanut butter jars so that for a couple of days Squiggy had a good supply of this scrumptious fresh delicacy. The fatty abdomens of white ants were definitely Squiggy's favourite – she tore off their wings and left the heads, and knew exactly how to go about this operation while holding the squirming insects. She'd gobble them up voraciously till her little tummy was full. I managed to get a number of short videos of all this using my digital camera.

Squiggy's coat slowly changed from soft, fluffy toffee-coloured fur to a coarser texture, and when this too changed to browner variations matching her friends and relations, there were many times I could tell little difference. Her large, round brown eyes were beautifully bright, intelligent and ever-watchful; her two front teeth sharp and narrow like the ends of sewing needles. Squiggy's tail had become spectacular with the faintest tiger stripes and could now fluff out like a dandelion; her toenails strong, finely tapered and curved, almost translucent. She could cling and climb with no effort. I used to look at her nails, feel them and think how marvellously sculpted they were. I suppose Squiggy had now reached about 10 inches in length from nose to the end of her tail, by this stage her tail being longer than her body. She was definitely and noticeably smaller than her 'compatriots' though had the same nimble and quick climbing agility. About this time, Squiggy began to grow out of babyhood and lost interest in her 'toys' preferring more serious matters like adventuring further afield, ascending higher into the tree canopies and even venturing onto the ground.

Keith said he felt I must not worry as he hoped Squiggy would be welcomed and assimilated into her own community sooner or later.

Mary kept saying, "You are going to miss Squiggy when she goes."

We understood that Squiggy might one day decide to 'abandon' me to live with the other squirrels in the trees.

Christmas 2016, despite all the jollifications, brought some sadness. Kamata, a much-loved Beagle dog had been with Keith and Mary for 12 years. He was an affectionate, gentle and intelligent companion, petted by the guests and staff, and had also been a great playmate and friend to Wally warthog, the 2 of them inseparable enjoying life and making this a unique happy family. When Kamata started going 'downhill', Dr Justin, the Zimbabwe vet, attended to him for several weeks. The end was very gentle with Keith beside him. Kamata was buried alongside my Dusty, forever resting peacefully in Dog Heaven.

I kept likening Squiggy's age to that of a teenager because a male squirrel started visiting right into 'Buffalo' cabin. Squiggy and I were taken by surprise. She'd dash to me for some sort of protection.

My crutch handle had holes chomped out of the sponge covers and there were other things I had to lock away from Squiggy's ever-gnawing tendencies, all of which helped to keep her needle-sharp teeth in condition. When she had a chance, she occasionally latched on to my finger nail. Altogether, the rodent signs were becoming more evident. When she started gnawing on the wooden ceiling struts I had to reprimand her. She would stop immediately as she knew she was doing wrong. If I called to Squiggy while she was out and about, she would answer with a variety of excited squeaks in acknowledgement that she had heard and was coming to me.

Squiggy wanted to be with me and was content to sit on my shoulder for the majority of our 'daylight togetherness'. As she became older and particularly during our rest-time, she was quiet and mostly groomed herself then she'd curl up into a tight ball and go to sleep on my shoulder. I shall never forget the occasional gentle stroking of her tiny front foot on my cheek when she wanted me to wake up.

Then came 6th February 2017. Keith quietly came to me while I was sitting on the verandah at my laptop. He told me that a visiting cat had caught Squiggy. Keith had chased the cat and retrieved Squiggy's lifeless body – there was not a mark on her. Just like Ian had done several times in the past, Keith was very kind to me, saying, "She must have died from fright."

With so many squirrels at the Lodge, I hoped in my heart that Keith had made a mistake. But, when I went back to my 'Buffalo' cabin after lunch and opened the gate, Squiggy did not answer when I called her and she was no longer there to leap from our cabin door curtain onto my shoulder. My heart sank and my sadness was overwhelming when I saw she wasn't dancing around in circles of happy greeting on my bed. What a devastating day. Visitors to the Lodge had seen and known little Squiggy and many folk had come to know her through my emails and pics. So ended the precious companionship Squiggy squirrel had shared with me. I miss her.

My life has been blessed with marvellous animals of one kind or another. All have brought me joy and companionship and are remembered with love, affection and gratitude. No matter any situation, nor how long or short a time one has been away, one's animals are always pleased to see you.

Shika, a Border Collie, is now part of our daily life at the Lodge. Keith felt he was ready for another dog and chose her from a litter of 13 pups. She is learning quickly and knows she must live with the monkeys, squirrels, the 2 cats (Sockies and Soppies), Mr Kip Kip (the guinea-fowl), and to greet the guests. Shika's Collie dog herding qualities are being tested on the 2 Muscovy ducks, Samson and Delilah, the latest addition to the family. They spend their days and nights enjoying life to the full dabbling, dipping and swimming in our private garden ponds. We have our suspicions though that Samson might turn out to be another Delilah!

In the tranquillity of the Lodge, with its quiet nights of twinkling starry skies above and unhurried days filled with Africa's comforting sounds around me, I can picture Ian in my mind, completely content, fishing rod in hand, casting his line into the waters of the mighty Zambezi, the continent's 4th longest River, and I feel a blessed new peace within me knowing I've eventually finished telling his story after 10 years, on and off, at my laptop.

"Who will remember me, I wonder?" Ian had said to me before he died.

The End

Keith and Wally Africa Map
by Debbie Rooken-Smith

Daisy before she became ill

Bride Heather, 22.3.1952

My father, Lionel Carol

Last photo of Stuart
with Heather & Ian,
1978 December, Sodwana, SA

Mary

Beryl & Pong
Malindi, Kenya

Little Debbie with Humpy, Angola

Asha & Lindsay
Malindi, Kenya

Humpy on motorbike,
Angola

1945: Ian, Mater, Ron, William

Ian's 1962 Farmer's Weekly Medal Eldoret, Kenya

Heather & Ian, Fish Market steps, Malindi

Lindsay & marlin, Stuart & wahoo, Malindi

Daisy & Harry Eeles

Our wedding 1952
Neville, Ian, Heather, Marge & bridesmaids

Kamau & Stuart,
Westlands

Angola, baby Humpy

Kambingana, front of house

Keith comforting Wally Warthog, Namibia

Mau Mau Times, Samburu Trackers with spears, Askaris in uniform, Forest Guard in jersey, Daisy, Mr Golding, Ken in background

Piggy, Heather, Piggy's boyfriend & dogs, Kambingana

Beryl & Mellone

Heather & children, Westlands

Ian, Kambingana dining room

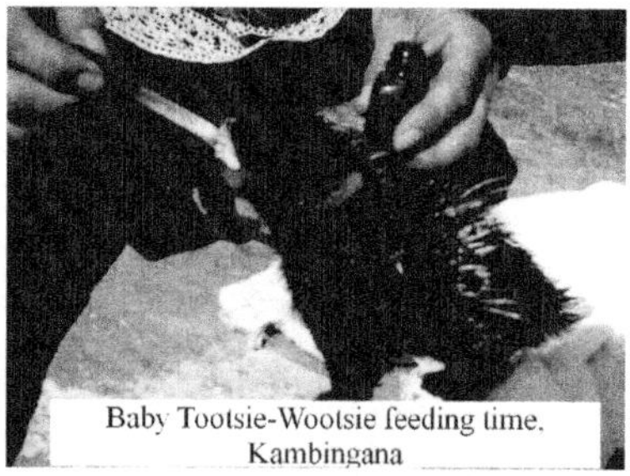

Baby Tootsie-Wootsie feeding time, Kambingana

Heather, Namibia 2015

Munde with our two tame ostriches

Kambingana, Andrew & !Xai

Angelina, Munde & children

Benjamin, donkey cart & our grandchildren

Benjamin, Simon & Mattheus

Rooken-Smith family polo team, 1955 Mugs' Mug winners
(L) Ian, Harold, Don, Bruce

Ian & Heather, Malindi

Kambingana, beef steers

Beryl's son, Stuart & Jeremiah camping & fishing, Namibia

Lake Rudolf, Lindsay standing on dead croc that bit off Turkana's leg

Keith

Hippo Neville & Daisy wallowing at Anchorage

Oxen & wagon crossing Pesi River

1962 Eldoret Royal Agricultural Show
Queen Mother & Ian (R) front

Anchorage House

Beryl, Namibia

Mary, Caprivi River Lodge, Namibia

Frank Smith (R) during Boer war

My brother, Terry

Lionel Carol,
WWI Royal Irish Rifles

Lionel Carol,
WWII Captain EAASC

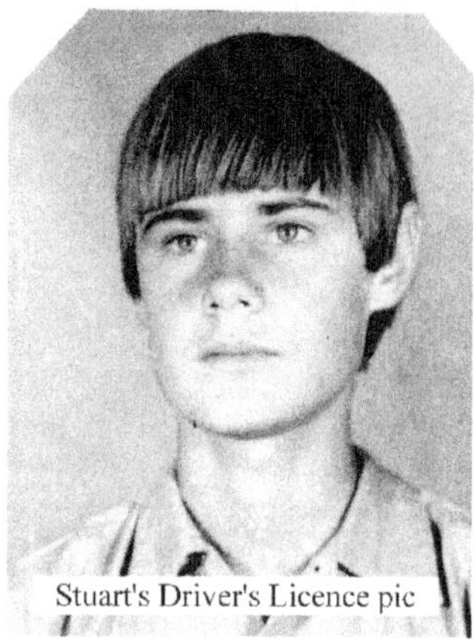

Stuart's Driver's Licence pic

Our wedding cake, 1952

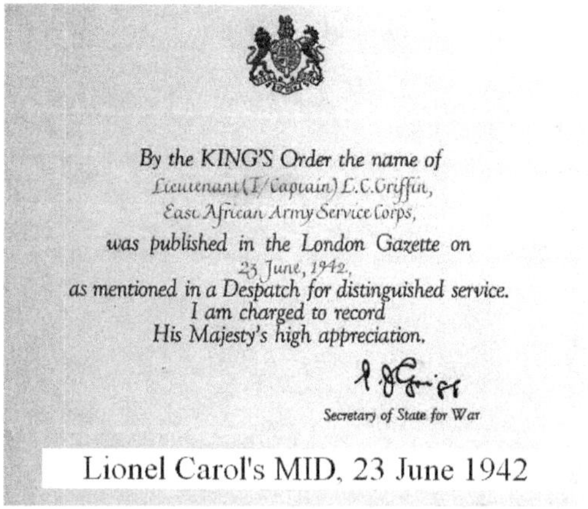

By the KING'S Order the name of
Lieutenant (T/Captain) L.C. Griffin,
East African Army Service Corps,
was published in the London Gazette on
23 June, 1942,
as mentioned in a Despatch for distinguished service.
I am charged to record
His Majesty's high appreciation.

Secretary of State for War

Lionel Carol's MID, 23 June 1942

Baby Squiggy squirrel, 2016

Ian & his 367lb black marlin, Awuni & Abdu

(L) Mohammed, Ian, Al Killeen & his black marlin, Malindi

Lionel Carol's gravestone,
Nakuru North Cemetery, Kenya

(L) Mohammed & Stuart
with his 70lb sailfish

Acknowledgements

I wish to thank the following folk for their kind contribution or assistance with completing 'Daisy's Daughter, Our Lives for Africa', and would like to acknowledge as well the support of friends and family around the world, too many to mention by name though just as much appreciated, who've had faith in my abilities and constantly encouraged me to finish writing my story. It has been a challenge of some years and a goal achieved – my love and sincere gratitude to you all.

William Alexander Rooken-Smith (posthumously)
(8.11.1854 – 18.10.1948) for his poems and riveting stories

Our beloved son, Alexander Stuart Rooken-Smith (posthumously)
(3.12.1960 – 8.1.1979) like his Grandfather, William,
also for his wonderful story & poems

Team Daisy
In acknowledgement of my fellow *Team Daisy* members
for their unwavering dedication & commitment:
Lindsay Rooken-Smith Jenions, Helen Priest,
Diane van der Westhuizen, Bruno Bernabei & Les Stephenson

Lindsay Rooken-Smith Jenions, South Africa, Managing Editor
our daughter, my thanks for her assistance, poems
& book cover design

Helen Priest, Namibia, Associate Editor

Diane van der Westhuizen, South Africa
Book cover design & typography, layout & photo formatting

Bruno Bernabei, Italy
Proofreader & contributor (San Marco Equatorial Range, Kenya)

Les Stephenson, South Africa
Consultant Editor

Daisy's Daughter
Our Lives for Africa

Karen Laurence-Rowe, Kenya
for her stunning 'Wally warthog & Tootsie-Wootsie
porcupine' book cover painting

Bruce Rooken-Smith, South Africa, my nephew
for his beautifully written Foreword

Keith & Mary Rooken-Smith, Caprivi, Namibia, our children
for standing with us through troubled Angola & tough Namibia days

Edward Webber, Thailand
for his assistance with Beryl's Chapter

Terry Griffin, South Africa, my nephew
for assistance with info regarding my father, Lionel Carol

Donald Rooken-Smith, Florida, USA, my nephew
for info regarding William Alexander Rooken-Smith

Stan Ulyate, New Zealand & Bruce Rooken-Smith, South Africa
for their exceptional work on our Family History

Patsy & Roger Witchell, UK
for info & photos regarding my father & his wife, Emily

Robin & John Channer, Australia
Les Stephenson, South Africa & John Davis, UK
for their kind words on the back cover of 'Daisy's Daughter'

Brian Jenions, South Africa
for scanning my pics & papers

Debbie Rooken-Smith, UK, our granddaughter
for her Mt Kenya Notelet + Keith & Wally Map

Kathryn van der Mescht, South Africa, our granddaughter
for her Africa Map

Franz Josef Nachtsheim & Johann August Ginkel, Germany
our Angola farming friends, for information regarding Angola

Sidney Dyer, Australia
for his grandfather, Frank Smith's, lioness story

Tony Case, Australia
Shel Arensen, Kenya
Robin Hurt, Namibia
Hieda Silva, Portugal
Philip Koen, South Africa
Nelson Benedito, South Africa
Dereck Rooken-Smith, Australia
Brien Rooken-Smith, South Africa
Grace Wairimu Mukui, Kenya/USA
Manasseh Mankuleiyo, Kenya/USA
Michael Rooken-Smith, South Africa
David Lovatt-Smith (posthumously), UK
Peter Smith (posthumously), South Africa
Stephen Spawls, Kenya Reptile Atlas, Kenya
George Edward Aggett (posthumously), Kenya
Marge Rooken-Smith (posthumously), South Africa
Nicholas Makutsa – Red Cross Association, Nairobi, Kenya

I would like to express appreciation to Wikipedia for the free internet educational tool & reference guide it provides & sincerely thank all who contribute their knowledge & expertise to its success

Though I've done my utmost best
I have not sought perfection
From the first word to the end
Rather the telling of Ian's story
Written from my heart, dear Reader friend

Index

ayah – nanny
bakshishi – tip
boma – camp/paddock
bwana – mister
chigoe – jigger
dawa – medicine
dhobi – laundry man
duka – shop
fundi – expert, skilled craftsman/craftswoman
harambee – pull/work together
johari – jewel
kanzu – similar to a kaftan
kasuku – parrot
kidogo – little/small
kikapu – basket
kikoi – loincloth
kuni – wood
kwaheri – goodbye
mbange – cannabis, marijuana, dagga, bangi, bhang
mbuni – ostrich
memsahib – Mrs/Miss
njangiri – marauder, bandit, vagrant, fugitive from justice, outcast
nugu – monkey
pikapika – piga piga/hit-hit/shoot
pombe – beer
posho – maize meal
samaki – fish
shamba – field
shenzi – rubbish
siafu – safari ants
syce – groom
taka nini? – what do you want?
toto jikoni – youngster 'run-around' assistant
tumbo – stomach
viazi – potato
watu – indigenous people

Ian & Heather's Family Index

Our Cape Settler founding fathers were:
Thomas Griffin from Finsbury, Islington (*on my father, Lionel Carol's, side*);

William Alexander Smith from Kintore, Aberdeen, Scotland *(on my husband, Ian's, side);* and

Thomas Aggett from Torquay (*on my mother, Daisy's, side*).

Thomas Griffin (born 15.05.1784 – died 24.09.1843), my great great-grandfather of Irish descent on my father's side, was the first of our founding fathers to sail to the Cape. Registered as a gunsmith, and with his heavily pregnant wife, Sarah, a midwife, they sailed with their children on the first 1820 British settler ship, the *Chapman*. Ship's records, under the 'List of Bailie's Party' reflect both parents and their children as:
Sarah 9
Thomas 8
Elizabeth 6
Harriet 4
Joseph 3
James 2
Margaret – born at sea on 9th December 1819, the day the *Chapman* finally set sail. They reached their destination, Algoa Bay, on 10th April 1820.
Thomas and Sarah had another 4 children in South Africa:
Emma (died aged 2)
Stephen William (Bill – my great-grandfather)
Charles Carter and
Henry

Charles Oliver Griffin was my grandfather.
Lionel Carol Griffin was my father.

William Alexander Smith (Ian's father) was our 2nd Cape founding father to make the crossing from Britain to South Africa. He sailed in 1859 with his parents, James and Margaret, and his younger siblings – a brother, James, and his sister, Marjorie Weir Smith. We think the Smith family made the voyage on either the ship *Aurifera* or the *New Great Britain.*

William became a farmer, and would buy several properties in the Eastern Cape area over the years, two being the farms *Bloomfield* and *Rooken.*

Thomas Aggett (born 29.03.1852), my grandfather on my mother's side, was the last of our founding fathers to brave the dangerous settler sea voyage. Together with his sisters, Emma Jane, and Elizabeth Ann, they sailed as adults from Devon to South Africa's shores, possibly a little later than 1867, and settled in the Cape Victoria East District. Apparently, the family had originally been potato farmers in England.

Daisy's parents and siblings

Thomas Aggett married Marjorie Weir Smith (William Alexander Smith's sister). They had 9 children, all born in the Cape:
Mary Ann (died at 9 months old)
Nellie (Margaret Ellen)
Ted (Thomas Edward)
Jane (Emma Jane)
Boyce (William Boyce)
May (Elizabeth May)
George (George Chick)
Daisy (Daisy Alice, my mother, born 12.07.1893) and
Ethel (Ethel Marjorie)
The name of Thomas and Marjorie's farm in the Eastern Cape was *Gwato.*
Karati was the name of their farm in Kenya.

Daisy married in Kenya and lived the rest of her life in this East African country. She had 5 children:
Marge (Marjorie) – from her 1st husband, Harry Eeles

Neville – his father was a hunter
Lionel Carol Griffin was *Daisy's* 2nd husband – they had 3 children:
Terry (Terence Oliver) – died on 07.09.1944 during WWII
Ken (Kenneth Carol) and
Heather (Heather May Isobel)

My nephew, Terry Griffin, is my brother, Ken's, son.

My Aunt May and Uncle George played a significant role in my life.
Aunt May, married to Uncle Alick Roberts, lived on the farm *Aggetton*.
Uncle George and his wife, Aunt Preto (her first name was 'Pretoria'), lived on *Mutara*.
My Uncle Ted Aggett had 2 sons – Aubrey and Hudson Boyce Aggett:
Hudson Boyce died during WWII when the Troopship SS Khedive Ismail was torpedoed.

Aubrey and his wife, Joy, would also feature a lot in my married life with Ian. Aubrey and Joy Aggett had 3 children – Michael, Jill and Neil. Both Michael and Neil became medical doctors. Neil died in a Pretoria prison in 1982 where he'd been detained for interrogation regarding fighting for human rights on behalf of the ANC.

The *Greathead* surname (originally also British Settlers) would become part of our very close, valued friends, two of whom called Daisy, 'Mum'. I was bridesmaid in the 1940s to Kay, an Irish girl, and Godfrey Greathead who lived in Ol'Kalou, Kenya.

William Alexander Smith (born 08.11.1854 – died 18.10.1948), *otherwise known as W. Rooken Smith,* married 3 times and fathered 17 children.
William's 1st wife was Emma Jane Aggett (Thomas Aggett's sister).
This union produced 8 children born *Smith* (referred to by the family as the *first litter*):
Marjorie Ann
Frank (Joseph Francis) was badly mauled by a wounded lioness
Gertrude (Gertrude Grace)
Willie (William Aggett) was killed by a German sniper in Tanganyika during WWI

Lennox Gordon
Beatrice Ellen (died in infancy and was buried on farm *Rooken)*
Donald (Donald Aggett) and
Emma Jane

William also brought up 2 other children 'like his own' though he never officially adopted them or changed their surnames – Walter (16), and his sister, Ina (8), who had 8 siblings. The two of them just turned up one morning having been 'farmed out' to other families by their father due to their mother's death.

William's 1st wife, Emma Jane, died of natural causes.

William's <u>2nd wife was Janet Peebles</u>, a governess.
They had 5 children also born *Smith* (the *second litter*):
Dorothy Ethelwyn
George (died in infancy and was buried on farm *Rooken*)
Lex (Alexander James)
Vi (Mary Violet) and
Harold (William Harold)

William's wife, Janet, died in 1918.

Lex, Vi and Harold all played a big role in my life, as well as in Ian's life as they would naturally be his 'elder half-brothers and half-sister'.

Lex later adopted the surname *Rooken-Smith.* Lex's son and only child, Brien Rooken-Smith, became Rhodesian Prime Minister, Ian Douglas Smith's Principal Private Secretary from May 1970 to October 1973.

Harold would change his surname by Deed Poll to *Rooken-Smith.* My sister, Marge, married Harold – they had 4 Rooken-Smith children: Don, Bruce, Robert (Rob) and Janet.

As a child, I grew up with Don and Bruce there being less than 5 years age difference between the 3 of us, though technically I am their aunt. Harold and Marge's two farms in Kenya were *Glenavon* and *Merrowdown*; their small-holding was *Ellegerini*. In 1965, Marge and Harold left Kenya and farmed in Rhodesia (Zimbabwe) on their property *Greenfels*.

William's 3rd wife – *Ian's mother,* known as *Mater* – was Caroline Hedwig Augusta Spangenberg (born 07.08.1893).
They had 4 children, all born with the surname *Rooken-Smith* (the *third litter*):
Janet (aged 4, died of diphtheria)
Gordon Cameron (died due to peritonitis when he was 9)
Ron (Ronald) and
Ian (my husband)

Ron Rooken-Smith had 3 children: Dereck and Ann from his 1st marriage to Daphne; and Michael from his 2nd wife, Joan.

Ian & Heather Rooken-Smith had 4 children:
Keith
Beryl (Beryl Marjorie)
Lindsay (Lindsay Margaret) and
Stuart (Alexander Stuart)
Ian's farms in Kenya were *Uruku* and *Westlands.*
Donald (Donald Aggett) Smith and his wife, Bertha Montefiore, farming on *Ol Morijo* in the Laikipia area, Kenya, would be Ian's *Uruku* farm neighbours when we married in 1952.
Fazenda Esperança was Ian's farm in Angola.

Ian & Heather's grandchildren are:
Debbie, Andrew and Shaun (Keith & Mary's daughter and 2 sons)
Stuart (Beryl's son)
Brendan and Kathryn (Lindsay's son and daughter)

Ian & Heather's great-grandchildren are:
Kalem (Debbie's son)
Laila and Hayden (Andrew's daughter and son)
Abbey (Shaun's daughter)
Helena and Isobel (Brendan's 2 daughters)

I can be contacted via my website or through our daughter, Lindsay, on tatachi@cybersmart.co.za

Printed in Great Britain
by Amazon

74665678R00363